TRIAL PRACTICE

Jury Selection

The Law, Art, and Science of Selecting a Jury
Second Edition

2003 Cumulative Supplement

James J. Gobert
Professor of Law
University of Essex

THOMSON
＊
WEST

For Customer Assistance Call 1-800-328-4880

© West, a Thomson business, 11/2003
Mat #40231658

© 2003 West, a Thomson business
All Rights Reserved

For authorization to photocopy, please contact the **Copyright Clearance Center** at 222 Rosewood Drive, Danvers, MA 01923, USA (978) 750-8400; fax (978) 646-8700 or **West's Copyright Services** at 610 Opperman Drive, Eagan, MN 55123, fax (651) 687-7551. Please outline the specific material involved, the number of copies you wish to distribute and the purpose or format of the use.

West, a Thomson business, has created this publication to provide you with accurate and authoritative information concerning the subject matter covered. However, this publication was not necessarily prepared by persons licensed to practice law in a particular jurisdiction. West is not engaged in rendering legal or other professional advice, and this publication is not a substitute for the advice of an attorney. If you require legal or other expert advice, you should seek the services of a competent attorney or other professional.

KF
8979
.J67
1990
Suppl.

Table of New and Retitled Sections

Chapter 1

The Right to a Jury Trial

§ 1:13A —Sentence enhancement *[New]*

Chapter 4

Investigation of the Venire

§ 4:3A Tax records *[New]*

Chapter 7

Challenges for Cause

§ 7:54 Jury nullifiers *[New]*

Part I

THE HISTORY, FUNCTIONS, AND FEATURES OF THE JURY

Chapter 1

The Right to a Jury Trial

> **KeyCite®:** Cases and other legal materials listed in KeyCite Scope can be researched through West's KeyCite service on Westlaw®. Use KeyCite to check citations for form, parallel references, prior and later history, and comprehensive citator information, including citations to other decisions and secondary materials.

Table of New and Retitled Sections

§ 1:13A —Sentence enhancement *[New]*

§ 1:3 American developments

n. 24.

  Add to note 24:
Altschuler & Deiss, *A Brief History of the Criminal Jury in the United States*, 61 U Chi L Rev 867 (1994).

n. 31.

  Add to note 31:

See generally Harrington, *The Law-Finding Function of the American Jury*, 1999 Wis. L. Rev. 377 (1999). Harrington notes that while permitting juries to declare the law may not have seemed out of place at a time when judges lacked legal training, there is less to be said in its favor in a more complex social and economic environment. This is not to say that jurors do not influence the development of the law. According to Harrington, legal rules can be seen as part of a cycle whereby intuitive jury notions of justice become transformed into formal legal rules.

§ 1:5 The Sixth Amendment right to a jury trial in a federal criminal case

  Add after note 40:
In Sullivan v. Louisiana, 508 U.S. 275, 113 S. Ct. 2078, 124 L. Ed. 2d 182 (1993) the United States Supreme Court indicated that at the heart of the Sixth Amendment's right to a jury trial was the right to have the jury determine

§ 1:5   JURY SELECTION: LAW, ART & SCIENCE 2D

whether a defendant's guilt had been proved beyond a reasonable doubt. For this reason a unanimous Court held that a constitutionally deficient reasonable doubt instruction required automatic reversal and was not subject to harmless error analysis. The guarantee that a jury will determine proof beyond a reasonable doubt extends to the determination of each and every element of the crime charged. In U.S. v. Gaudin, 515 U.S. 506, 115 S. Ct. 2310, 132 L. Ed. 2d 444 (1995), the defendant had been charged with violating 18 U.S.C.A. § 1001, by making false statements on Department of Housing and Urban Development loan documents. The trial judge stated that whether the false statements were material was a matter for the court to decide and charged the jury that they were "material" as a matter of law. The Ninth Circuit Court of Appeals reversed on the ground that the issue of materiality should have been decided by the jury. The United States Supreme Court granted certiorari and held that, together with the Fifth Amendment right to due process, the Sixth Amendment provides a defendant with the right to have a jury determine whether every element of the crime with which he is charged has been proved beyond a reasonable doubt. Because the materiality of the alleged false statements was an element of Section 1001, the issue should not have been decided by the judge but should have been left to the jury. The Court stated that the jury's constitutional responsibility is not limited to the determination of the facts but extends to the application of the law to those facts and the ultimate decision of guilt or innocence. See also, U.S. v. Wells, 63 F.3d 745 (8th Cir. 1995), judgment vacated on other grounds, 519 U.S. 482, 117 S. Ct. 921, 137 L. Ed. 2d 107 (1997) (issue of materiality under 18 U.S.C.A. § 1014 should have been left to jury); Harmon v. Marshall, 69 F.3d 963 (9th Cir. 1995) (complete failure to instruct jury on any element of offense required automatic reversal and was not subject to harmless error analysis).

In U.S. v. Gray, 137 F.3d 765 (4th Cir. 1998), the defendant argued that the life sentence imposed on him following his conviction by a jury impermissibly infringed on his constitutional right to jury trial. He maintained that, had he pled guilty, he would have been eligible for a downward adjustment in sentence. That adjustment, he claimed was not available after a jury trial. The court rejected the defendant's argument as factually misconceived—trial judges were permitted to make downward adjustments in sentencing after a guilty verdict if the defendant accepted responsibility for the offense.

§ 1:6 —Petty offenses

Add at end of sixth paragraph

§ 1:6

In U.S. v. Coppins, 953 F.2d 86 (4th Cir. 1991), the Court of Appeals held that for the purpose of determining whether a defendant charged with more than one petty offense was entitled to a jury trial, the maximum punishment for the offenses charged should be aggregated. If, when so aggregated, the maximum penalty exceeded six months imprisonment, the defendant was entitled to a jury trial. However, this position was rejected by the U.S. Supreme Court when it abrogated the holding in *Coppins*. Lewis v. U.S., 518 U.S. 322, 116 S. Ct. 2163, 135 L. Ed. 2d 590 (1996).

The issue of whether there is a Sixth Amendment right to a jury trial in a case where a defendant is charged with a number of offenses, none of which individually carries a sentence in excess of six months but whose aggregate term, if the defendant were to be convicted, would exceed six months, was addressed by the United States Supreme Court in Lewis v. U.S., 518 U.S. 322, 116 S. Ct. 2163, 135 L. Ed. 2d 590 (1996). The defendant was charged with two counts of obstructing the mail. Each count was subject to a maximum six-month term in prison. The defendant's request for a jury trial was rejected, but the trial judge indicated that she would not impose a sentence in excess of six months. Both the district court and the Court of Appeals affirmed the trial judge's decision. The Supreme Court granted certiorari to resolve a conflict in the Courts of Appeals (see cases cited in supp.) as to whether a defendant prosecuted in a single proceeding for multiple petty offenses, the total sentence for which could exceed six months, had a right to a jury trial.

The analytical question facing the Court was whether the right to a jury trial was determined by the maximum potential sentence facing a defendant or the nature of the offenses charged; i.e., whether they were petty or serious. The majority thought the latter. It stated that the most relevant criterion for assessing the gravity of an offense was the legislature's judgment of the offense's character, as expressed in the maximum penalty attached to its violation. In most instances an offense carrying a maximum term of less than six months in prison will be presumed to be petty. The fact that a defendant is charged with more than one such petty offense (and thus with a potential penalty of greater than six months) does not alter the fundamental character of the crimes charged. The Court concluded that the right to a jury trial was available only in respect to serious offenses, and, as the petitioner had not been charged with a serious offense, he was not entitled to a jury trial.

To reach this result the Court had to distinguish its previous decision in Codispoti v. Pennsylvania, 418 U.S. 506, 94 S. Ct. 2707, 41 L. Ed. 2d 912 (1974), where it had held that a defendant who had been convicted of several charges of criminal contempt and had been sentenced for a term in excess of six months was entitled to a jury trial. It did so on two grounds. First, as there was no statutory maximum penalty for criminal contempt, a court perforce had to use the sentence actually imposed as its measure of whether the crime was serious or petty. Second, because a contempt citation often is the product of a direct challenge to the judge's authority, and because a judge may find it difficult to remain detached under such circumstances, there is a strong argument for interposing a jury to decide the issue.

Four Justices disagreed with the majority's analysis. Justice Kennedy, with whom Justice Breyer concurred, maintained that a jury trial should be available when either the crime charged carries a penalty in excess of six months (regardless of the penalty actually imposed) or the defendant receives a sentence in excess of six months in a single trial (regardless of the potential penalty that could be imposed on each individual charge). These two Justices, however, were prepared to affirm because the offenses in question did not carry a potential penalty in excess of six months and there was and could not have been an actual penalty of over six months in light of the trial judge's statement that she would not impose such a sentence. Justices Stevens and Ginsburg agreed in principle with the two concurring Justices, but thought that the trial judge's promise of a lenient sentence was irrelevant. The critical factor for them was the maximum sentence that could be imposed by law if the defendant were to be convicted.

The decision in *Lewis* is in tension with the essential function of the jury as envisaged in the Supreme Court's seminal decision in Duncan v. State of La., 391 U.S. 145, 88 S. Ct. 1444, 20 L. Ed. 2d 491 (1968) (discussed in main text). The *Duncan* Court had described the jury as providing an "inestimable safeguard against the corrupt or overzealous prosecutor and against the compliant, biased, or eccentric judge." Duncan v Louisiana, 391 US at 155. If an "overzealous" prosecutor is prepared to charge a disfavored defendant with, say, 10 petty offenses and a "compliant, biased or eccentric" judge is prepared to impose 10 consecutive sentences of six months if the defendant is convicted on all counts, there will, after *Lewis*, be no jury to guard against the potential injustice. The problem is not hypothetical. As pointed out by Justice Kennedy, a prosecutor often has the discretion to decide whether to charge a defendant with multiple petty offenses or one serious offense. See generally Murphy, *The Narrowing of the Entitlement to Criminal Jury*, 1997 Wisconsin L. Rev. 133 (1997) (criticizing *Lewis* and the general trend to restrict the right to jury trial in criminal cases).

Right to Jury Trial § 1:7

In U.S. v. Chavez, 204 F.3d 1305, 54 Fed. R. Evid. Serv. 426 (11th Cir. 2000), the defendant, charged with violating 18 U.S.C.A. § 113(a)(4) (assault), requested a jury trial, which request was denied by the trial court. In affirming, the Court of Appeals stated that the offense was "petty", in that it carried a maximum penalty of six months imprisonment or a fine of $5,000 or both. The fact that a term of probation of five years was imposed did not change the analysis. Probation does not entail the same restriction on liberty as does a prison sentence and the probationary term is explicitly authorized in the controlling legislation. Moreover, the court found that the defendant's attempt to characterize the various conditions of probation, including restitutionary payments to the victim, as "additional penalties" was misguided, since again the conditions were authorized by statute and were reasonably related to the statutory objectives. Similarly, in U.S. v. Ballek, 170 F.3d 871 (9th Cir. 1999) it was held that a petty offense was not converted to "serious" one simply because, in addition to incarceration, the defendant was ordered to pay restitution in excess of $50,000 to victim. Restitution, explained the court, is not an additional penalty but rather constitutes a recognition of a debt already owed by the defendant.

n. 57.

Add to note 57:
See also U.S. v. LaValley, 957 F.2d 1309 (6th Cir. 1992) (potential loss of license to practice law did not convert petty offense into one that was serious); U.S. v. Paternostro, 966 F.2d 907, 22 Envtl. L. Rep. 21021 (5th Cir. 1992) (additional penalties of $5,000 fine and extended probationary period did not make failure to abide by terms of shoreline use permit a serious offense). In U.S. v. Unterburger, 97 F.3d 1413 (11th Cir. 1996), the court held that first offenders charged with the nonviolent obstruction of an abortion clinic in violation of the Freedom of Access to Clinic Entrances Act were not entitled to a jury trial because, if convicted, the maximum penalty under the Act was six months imprisonment and a $10,000 fine. Accord, U.S. v. Soderna, 82 F.3d 1370 (7th Cir. 1996); U.S. v. Balint, 201 F.3d 928 (7th Cir. 2000).

§ 1:7 —Fines only offenses

Add after fourth sentence in first paragraph:
See, e.g., U.S. v. NYNEX Corp., 781 F. Supp. 19 (D.D.C. 1991) (jury trial not required for multibillion dollar corporation facing potential fine of $1 million in contempt proceeding).

Add at end of section:
See generally Annotation, Small claims: jury trial rights in, and on appeal from, small claims court proceeding, 70 A.L.R. 4th 1119. In U.S. v. Nachtigal, 37 F.3d 1421 (9th Cir. 1994),

§ 1:7 JURY SELECTION: LAW, ART & SCIENCE 2D

the defendant was charged with operating a motor vehicle in a national park while under the influence of alcohol (DUI). Under federal law the offense was classified as a class B misdemeanor punishable by six months imprisonment and a $500 fine. As an alternative to imprisonment the court could impose a probationary term not to exceed five years. Defendant moved for a jury trial, which motion was denied. The Ninth Circuit Court of Appeals reversed, finding *Blanton* inapposite. The United States Supreme Court, however, disagreed, holding that the additional penalties proscribed for the offense were not sufficiently onerous to overcome the *Blanton* presumption that an offense carrying a maximum penalty of six months imprisonment was a petty offense. See also State v. O'Brien, 158 Vt. 275, 609 A.2d 981 (1992) (no right to jury trial in administrative driver's license proceeding). See also Clavette v. U.S., 525 U.S. 863, 119 S. Ct. 151, 142 L. Ed. 2d 123 (1998) (no right to jury trial in prosecution for killing grizzly bear in violation of Endangered Species Act where maximum sentence was six months and $25,000 fine or both, citing *Nachtigal*). Compare State v. Wiltshire, 241 Neb. 817, 491 N.W.2d 324 (1992) (overruled on other grounds by, State v. Louthan, 257 Neb. 174, 595 N.W.2d 917 (1999)) (imposition of mandatory 15-year driver's license suspension for third DWI conviction was such a significant additional penalty to entitle defendant to jury trial, even though maximum jail sentence was six months).

§ 1:8 —Contempt and quasi-criminal offenses

n. 67.
Add to note 67:
See also U.S. v. Kozel, 908 F.2d 205 (7th Cir. 1990). In *Kozel*, an attorney convicted of contempt, was ordered to do community service. The order required him to handle a limited number of pro bono cases. He argued that he was entitled to a jury trial in the contempt proceedings because the lost fees in being required to take the pro bono cases exceeded the $5,000 ceiling for petty offenses, but the Court of Appeals rejected the claim.

In U.S. v. Time, 21 F.3d 635, 40 Fed. R. Evid. Serv. 1116 (5th Cir. 1994), the court held that neither damage to reputation nor the possibility of a state bar disciplinary proceeding would be relevant in determining whether a prosecution for contempt was a "serious" offense because neither of these consequences was a penalty imposed by statute. But see U.S. v. Roach, 108 F.3d 1477 (D.C. Cir. 1997), opinion vacated in part on reconsideration, 136 F.3d 794 (D.C. Cir. 1998); and U.S. v. Rapone, 131 F.3d 188, 195–97, 72 Empl. Prac. Dec. (CCH) ¶ 45136 (D.C. Cir. 1997).

n. 68.
Add to note 68:
In Jackson v. Bailey, 221 Conn. 498, 605 A.2d 1350 (1992), however, the court held that a trial judge could impose an aggregate sentence in excess of six months for contempt without a jury trial based upon three separate

instances of contemptuous conduct, where the penalty was summarily imposed. Cases to the contrary were distinguished on the ground they involved separate postverdict trials. It is submitted, however, that the distinction is questionable, as it would allow a court through its own precipitate action to abrogate a defendant's right to a jury.

Add after note 69:
The issues arising out of criminal contempt, and the distinctions between criminal and civil contempt, were explored in some depth by the United States Supreme Court in International Union, United Mine Workers of America v. Bagwell, 512 U.S. 821, 114 S. Ct. 2552, 129 L. Ed. 2d 642, 146 L.R.R.M. (BNA) 2641, 128 Lab. Cas. (CCH) ¶ 11120 (1994). The petitioners had been fined over $52 million for violating a court injunction. The Supreme Court held that the fines were criminal in nature and that the petitioners were constitutionally entitled to a jury trial before their imposition.

The Court distinguished between criminal and civil contempt, and between direct and indirect contempt. A direct contempt occurs in the presence of the court and may be dealt with immediately and summarily. The court's interest in maintaining order is substantial, the need for extensive fact finding is not great, and there is little likelihood of an erroneous decision. An indirect contempt does not occur in the court's presence, and more in the way of procedural protection is required before punishment can be imposed.

Whether a contempt is civil or criminal turns on the character and purpose of the sanction. In the case of imprisonment, the critical issue is whether the contemnor is able to purge himself of contempt by affirmative action. A fixed sentence is punitive and indicative of criminal contempt. If, on the other hand, the contemnor is able to obtain release from jail by his own acts, if, as it were, he holds the key to his cell in his pocket, then the penalty is more likely to be deemed civil.

In the case of a fine, the contempt is civil if the aim of the fine is either to coerce a defendant into compliance with a court order or to compensate a victim for loss caused as a result of the contumacious conduct. Where the fine is not intended to be compensatory, it is civil only if the contemnor is able to purge himself of the contempt. If the fine is fixed and the contemnor is not able to avoid or reduce it through compliance, the contempt is criminal. A defendant charged with criminal contempt is entitled to the normal constitutional safeguards associated with a criminal trial, including the right to a jury.

In the case before the Court, there was no claim that the fines were compensatory. Nor were the fines related to the

§ 1:8

damage caused by the Union's actions. Nonetheless, the respondent argued that the fines should be considered civil because they could be avoided through compliance with the court's order. The petitioners claimed that the injunction primarily prohibited conduct rather than mandating affirmative acts, and thus should be deemed criminal.

The Court did not find either position to be entirely satisfactory. Rather, the Court looked at the character of the entire decree. That the contempt did not occur in the court's presence, that the court's order related to widespread, ongoing activities rather than simple, affirmative acts, and that the fines assessed ($52 million) were extremely substantial all supported the petitioners' claim to a jury trial. While recognizing that there existed a general "petty offense" exception to the right to a jury trial, including a jury trial in a criminal contempt case, the Court declined to draw a definitive line between petty and serious contempt fines. Wherever the line might ultimately be drawn, the $52 million fine imposed in the case clearly was serious. See also Harris v. City of Philadelphia, 47 F.3d 1311, 31 Fed. R. Serv. 3d 497 (3d Cir. 1995) (failure of city to submit plans for correcting prison conditions constituted contempt which could not be characterized as petty criminal offense triable without jury).

In F.J. Hanshaw Enterprises v. Emerald River Development, 244 F.3d 1128 (9th Cir. 2001), the trial court was informed of an attempt by a party to bribe the receiver. The court, having determined the truth of these allegations, ordered a $200,000 compensatory payment to be made to the opposing party and imposed a $500,000 fine against the offending party to be paid to the government. On appeal, the court held that the $500,000 sanction was criminal in nature and entitled the party to a jury trial, but the $200,000 award was civil in nature and a valid exercise of the court's inherent powers. There was accordingly no right to a jury trial in respect to it.

In U.S. v. Linney, 134 F.3d 274 (4th Cir. 1998) the court indicated in advance that it would not impose a sentence in excess of six months if the defendant was convicted. Thus the offense was appropriately treated as petty, even though it carried no specific penalty.

It can be argued that contempt proceedings are distinguishable for other "petty offences" because of the unique concerns regarding the impartiality of the sentencing judge and considerations of separation of powers. See Note, *Why Contempt is Different: Agency Costs and "Petty Crime" in Summary Contempt Proceedings*, 112 Yale L.J. 1223 (2003) (concluding that summary adjudication of contempt cases should be limited in favor of greater use of jury trials). See also Zimmerman, *Civil Contemnors, Due Process, and the Right to a Jury Trial*, 2003 Wyoming L. Rev. 205 (2003) (arguing civil contemnor should be entitled to jury trial where incarceration exceeds 18 months).

n. 70.

Add to note 70:

McCullough v. Singletary, 967 F.2d 530 (11th Cir. 1992). Compare Bradford v. Longmont Mun. Court of City of Longmont, 830 P.2d 1135 (Colo. Ct. App. 1992) (juvenile entitled to jury trial where elements of crime charged paralleled state theft statute even though juvenile would not be subject to imprisonment). The case for juries in juvenile trials is examined in the context of a state statute in Comment, *The Right to a Juvenile Jury Trial in Wisconsin: Rebalancing the Balanced Approach*, 1999 Wisconsin L. Rev. 571 (1999).

n. 71.

Add to note 71:

In respect to whether a litigant is entitled to jury trial in civil court determinations affecting the parent-child relationship, see Annotation, Right to Jury Trial in Child Neglect, Child Abuse, or Termination of Parental Rights Proceedings, 102 A.L.R. 5th 227 (collecting cases which show that whether jury trial is available usually turns on the interpretation of the state constitution or whether there is a specific state statute on point; e.g., In re Adoption of A.F.M., 15 P.3d 258, 102 A.L.R.5th 701 (Alaska 2001) (no right to jury trial under Alaska statute providing for termination of biological father's rights in adoption proceeding by another man, at least where child's conception resulted from a sexual assault)).

n. 72.

Add to note 72:

The author of Note, *Massachusetts's Sexually Dangerous Persons Law: Can Juries Make a Bad Law Better?*, 35 Harv. C.R.-C.L. L. Rev 509 (2000) argues the affirmative of the question posed in the title of the article, advocating greater use of juries in cases involving the civil commitment of sexually dangerous persons.

See also Buckley v. Barlow, 997 F.2d 494 (8th Cir. 1993) (no right to jury trial in prison disciplinary setting).

Whether a defendant has a constitutional right to a jury in a forfeiture proceeding is a matter of dispute. Compare U.S. v. Robinson, 8 F.3d 418 (7th Cir. 1993) (no constitutional right to a jury determination of forfeiture issues) with U.S. v. Garrett, 727 F.2d 1003, 15 Fed. R. Evid. Serv. 262 (11th Cir. 1984), judgment aff'd, 471 U.S. 773, 105 S. Ct. 2407, 85 L. Ed. 2d 764 (1985) (Sixth Amendment provides for right to jury trial in forfeiture proceedings). See also U.S. v. Premises Known as RR No. 1 Box 224, Dalton, Scott Tp. and North Abington Tp., Lackawanna County, Pa., 14 F.3d 864 (3d Cir. 1994). In U.S. v. Libretti, 38 F.3d 523 (10th Cir. 1994), judgment aff'd, 516 U.S. 29, 116 S. Ct. 356, 133 L. Ed. 2d 271 (1995), the Court of Appeals did not reach the issue, holding that whether or not a defendant had a right to a jury trial in a forfeiture proceeding, the defendant had waived that right by entering into a plea bargain. When the case reached the Supreme Court, the Court stated that the right to a jury determination of forfeiture was not part of the Sixth Amendment's constitutional guarantee. Libretti v. U.S., 516 U.S. 29, 116 S. Ct. 356, 133

§ 1:8

L. Ed. 2d 271 (1995). The Court viewed forfeiture as part of sentencing, where there is no right to jury trial [See McMillan v. Pennsylvania, 477 U.S. 79, 106 S. Ct. 2411, 91 L. Ed. 2d 67 (1986)]. The Court added that a trial judge could (and in some instances probably should) advise a defendant when a guilty plea will result in the loss of a statutory right to jury trial on the issue of forfeiture, and of course counsel should bring any such consequence of pleading guilty to the defendant's attention, but the Constitution did not go so far as to require either the judge or counsel to do so. In another case forfeiture case, Lopez Cantu v. U.S., 528 U.S. 818, 120 S. Ct. 58, 145 L. Ed. 2d 50 (1999) a juror had been properly excused for cause during the deliberations phase of a drug conspiracy trial, with the result that the verdict was delivered by a jury of 11. The jury then had to decide the issue of forfeiture. The defendant's argument that a new 12 person jury was required for that issue was rejected by the Fifth Circuit Court of Appeals.

In U.S. v. Colt, 126 F.3d 981 (7th Cir. 1997) the court held that a convicted offender is not entitled to a jury trial when a previously imposed sentence is subsequently modified. Similarly, in U.S. v. Pelensky, 129 F.3d 63 (2d Cir. 1997), the court held that there was no right to a jury trial in a proceeding to revoke supervised release.

§ 1:9 The Fourteenth Amendment right to a jury trial in a state criminal case

§ 1:13A —Sentence enhancement *[New]*

Absent a statutory provision to the contrary, jurors will not usually play a role in sentencing. Traditionally, sentencing decisions have been the province of the court. However, an issue that has arisen is whether a court can impose a sentence that exceeds the statutory maximum that has been prescribed for the offense of which the jury convicted the defendant.

The issue arose in Apprendi v. New Jersey, 530 U.S. 466, 120 S. Ct. 2348, 147 L. Ed. 2d 435 (2000), where the defendant had pleaded guilty to possession of a firearm for an unlawful purpose and unlawful possession of a prohibited weapon. One of the crimes carried a penalty of 5 to 10 years. However, the trial judge imposed a sentence of 12 years for that offense because, as also permitted by state statute, the judge determined that the crime was a "hate crime." The judge found by a preponderance of the evidence (the standard specified in the statute) that the defendant had committed the offense for the purpose of intimidating a person or group because of their race. The issue on appeal was whether the judge's decision violated due process because the factual determination which had resulted in the enhanced sentence had not been made by a jury.

The United State Supreme Court found that there had been a violation of due process. The Court held that any fact that increased the sentence beyond the prescribed maximum for the offense had to be submitted to a jury and proved beyond a reasonable doubt. If this were not the case, the defendant's rights both to a jury trial and due process would be violated. While the state argued that what was at issue was not an element of the crime but a "sentencing factor", the Supreme Court held that the label was not dispositive of the issue; what mattered was the fact that the defendant had been exposed to a greater punishment than that authorized by the facts as found by the jury's verdict. As the Court stated, "the relevant inquiry is one not of form, but of effect." Apprendi v. New Jersey, 530 U.S. 466, 120 S. Ct. 2348, 2365, 147 L. Ed. 2d 435 (2000). As a result of the Court's holding, any fact, other than that of the defendant's prior convictions, that increases the penalty beyond the maximum punishment prescribed by law has to be submitted to the jury for its consideration and established by proof beyond a reasonable doubt.

It may be ventured that the Court's decision in *Apprendi* does little more than provide a lesson in statutory drafting. If the penalty for a crime is five to 10 years, as it was in *Apprendi*, but another statute allows the judge to increase the penalty to 20 years upon the finding of an aggravating factor, then the Supreme Court's decision applies and the jury must be allowed to determine the presence of the aggravating factor. On the other hand, it would appear that the legislature apparently could achieve the same result by setting a sentence range of five to 20 years in the first place, in which case a judge could impose a 20 year sentence based on a finding of the same aggravating factor, but without the jury's involvement, because the sentence would not exceed the statutory maximum. If this were to occur, however, trial judges would be left with greater discretion in sentencing, contrary to the modern trend to directed discretion under sentencing guidelines. Apprendi v. New Jersey, 530 U.S. 466, 120 S. Ct. 2348, 147 L. Ed. 2d 435 (2000), had held that facts, other than that of a prior conviction, that served to increase a sentence beyond the prescribed statutory maximum needed to be decided by a jury. In Harris v. U.S., 536 U.S. 545, 122 S. Ct. 2406, 153 L. Ed. 2d 524 (2002) (disapproved of by, People v. Hayden, 2002 WL 31105409 (Cal. App. 3d Dist. 2002)), the Supreme Court considered whether *Apprendi* should apply to factors that increased the mandatory minimum sentence.

The defendant in *Harris* had pled guilty to one count of distributing marijuana. Under 18 U.S.C.A. § 924(c)(1)(A)(ii) a person who, in relation to a drug trafficking offense, brandishes a firearm shall be sentenced to not less than seven years imprisonment. The district court found that, while engaged in the selling of drugs, the defendant had brandished a semiautomatic pistol. Consequently, the district court sentenced him to the mandatory minimum term of seven years imprisonment. The Supreme Court affirmed.

The question that the Court had to resolve was whether "brandishing" a firearm was an element of a separate offense for which the defendant had not been indicted, tried, or convicted; or was simply a factor to be considered in sentencing. The plurality found that the structure of the federal prohibition suggested that "brandishing" was a sentencing factor and not an element of a separate offense. This view was reinforced by past Congressional practice and federal tradition. Framing the constitutional issue in terms of whether the authors of the Bill of Rights would have considered the elements of a sentence to be elements of a separate crime, Justice Kennedy observed that mandatory minimum sentences had not become prevalent until the latter part of the twentieth century and thus presumably would not have been in the contemplation of the authors of the Bill of Rights. Further, Justice Kennedy noted that, while sentences that exceeded the permissible maximum expanded a judge's power, mandatory minimum sentence provisions did not, as the defendant would not be subjected to an unexpectedly severe punishment. "The Constitution ensures that a defendant 'will never get more punishment than he bargained for when he did the crime'", but it does not "promise that he will receive 'anything less' than that." Harris v. U.S., 536 U.S. 545, 122 S. Ct. 2406, 2419, 153 L. Ed. 2d 524 (2002) (quoting from Apprendi v. New Jersey, 530 U.S. 466, 498, 120 S. Ct. 2348, 147 L. Ed. 2d 435 (2000)). Further, Justice Kennedy pointed out that doubt would be cast on many legislative-enacted sentencing mandatory minimum schemes if *Apprendi* were held to be apply. The conclusion of the Court was that a legislature could specify conditions for a mandatory minimum sentence without making these conditions elements of the offense, a conclusion that the Court had previously reached in McMillan v. Pennsylvania, 477 U.S. 79, 106 S. Ct. 2411, 91 L. Ed. 2d 67 (1986) and which it now reaffirmed.

Iontcheva argues that the *Apprendi* line of cases should lead to the reintroduction of jury sentencing. See Iontcheva, *Jury Sentencing as Democratic Practice*, 89 Va. L. Rev. 311 (2003) (presenting the history and merits of jury sentencing, a task for which the author maintains that the jury is well-suited).

The issue in U.S. v. Leachman, 309 F.3d 377, 2002 FED App. 0353P (6th Cir. 2002), cert. denied, 123 S. Ct. 1769, 155 L. Ed. 2d 527 (U.S. 2003) was whether a plea of guilty, which indisputably waives the right to a jury trial on the question of guilt, also waives the right to a jury trial in instances where, under *Apprendi*, a defendant is entitled to jury trial before a sentence exceeding the statutory maximum can be imposed. The Court of Appeals held that *Apprendi* only extended a defendant's due process and Sixth Amendment rights to factors that enhanced a sentence beyond the statutory maximum, and that these constitutional rights were subject to the ordinary rules of waiver. See also U.S. v. Sykes, 292 F.3d 495, 2002 FED App. 0199P (6th Cir. 2002), cert. denied, 537 U.S. 965, 123 S. Ct. 400, 154 L. Ed. 2d 322 (2002).

Arguably the key issue that needs to be addressed in respect to waiver is whether the trial judge has to specifically inform a defendant that rights under *Apprendi* are being waived in order for the waiver to be deemed knowing and voluntary. In U.S. v. Minore, 292 F.3d 1109 (9th Cir. 2002), cert. denied, 537 U.S. 1146, 123 S. Ct. 948, 154 L. Ed. 2d 848 (2003), the Court of Appeals held, as a matter of first impression, that the trial court must advise the defendant of the government's obligation under *Apprendi* to prove to a jury drug quantity by proof beyond a reasonable doubt before accepting a guilty plea. When drug quantity exposes the defendant to a higher statutory maximum sentence than he would otherwise receive, it becomes the functional equivalent of a "critical element" of the offense. Under F.R. Crim. P. 11(c)(1) governing acceptance of guilty pleas, as well as under principles of due process, the trial court must advise the defendant on each "critical element" of the offense. Accordingly, the trial court must advise defendant that, if the case went to trial, the government would have to prove drug quantity by proof beyond a reasonable doubt. But compare U.S. v. Hurlich, 293 F.3d 1223 (10th Cir. 2002) where the Court of Appeals, in a somewhat analogous situation, held that a defendant's waiver of jury trial was valid despite the failure of the trial court to inform the defendant of the possibility that his federal sentence could run consecutive to his state sentence. The Court of Appeals in *Hurlich*, however, did encourage district courts to inform defendants of all consequences of waiver, including the possibility of a consecutive sentence.

The Supreme Court applied *Apprendi* to a capital sentencing scheme in Ring v. Arizona, 536 U.S. 584, 122 S. Ct. 2428, 153 L. Ed. 2d 556 (2002) (disapproved of by, People v. Hayden, 2002 WL 31105409 (Cal. App. 3d Dist. 2002)). Under the state statute in question, after a jury had found the defendant guilty of first-degree murder, the trial judge could impose the death penalty if the judge found to be present at least one aggravating and no mitigating circumstance. The determination of aggravating factors thus served as the functional equivalent to an element of a greater offense. Although the Arizona penalty scheme had previously been held to be constitutional in Walton v. Arizona, 497 U.S. 639, 110 S. Ct. 3047, 111 L. Ed. 2d 511 (1990) (overruled by, Ring v. Arizona, 536 U.S. 584, 122 S. Ct. 2428, 153 L. Ed. 2d 556 (2002)), *Walton* had been decided prior to *Apprendi*, and the question now raised was whether the two holdings were reconcilable. In a dissent in *Apprendi*, Justice O'Connor had expressed the view that they were not, and in *Ring* the Arizona Supreme Court had agreed with her. Recognizing that the Arizona Supreme Court's construction of Arizona state law was authoritative, the United States Supreme Court overruled Walton to the extent that it allowed a sentencing judge to find an aggravating circumstance that allowed imposition of the death penalty. While the state attempted to distinguish the case from *Apprendi* on the ground the jury's return of a guilty verdict for first degree murder had already exposed the defendant to a sentence of life imprisonment or death, and thus the trial judge's finding did not "enhance" the sentence, the Supreme Court disagreed. Without the additional finding of an aggravating factor, the sentence would have been set at life imprisonment. Thus, the judge's finding, like that in *Apprendi*, had "the effect" of exposing the defendant to a greater punishment than was authorized by the verdict and therefore the relevant facts had to be found by the jury by proof beyond a reasonable doubt.

As predicted by Justice O'Connor in her dissent in *Apprendi*, the Supreme Court's decision in that case spawned an extremely large number of challenges to sentences that had already been imposed in reliance on pre-*Apprendi* law. Justice O'Connor conducted a Westlaw(tm) search covering the less than two years between *Apprendi* and *Ring* and discovered that approximately 1,802 criminal appeals had been lodged during that period in which sentences were challenged under the authority of *Apprendi* (See Ring, p. 2449, Justice O'Connor, dissenting). While most of these appeals have not succeeded, they have significantly increased the workload of an arguably already overburdened judiciary. However, the decision in *Ring* is not likely to have as great an effect because, of the 38 states which allow for the imposition of the death sentence upon a finding of aggravating factors, 29 already commit the decision to the jury. As for the remaining nine states and any others that may wish to instate the death penalty into their law of homicide, they will presumably either have to entrust to the jury the separate determination of the factors warranting imposition of a death sentence or, as suggested by Justice Scalia, concurring in *Ring*, incorporate the aggravating factors into its definition of the capital offense.

§ 1:14 The Seventh Amendment right to a jury trial in a federal civil case

n. 89.

Add to note 89:

Once a civil jury has reached its verdict, it would be a violation of the Seventh Amendment for the court to enter a judgment as a matter of law (JMOL) in contravention of that verdict. Duro-Last, Inc. v. Custom Seal, Inc., 321 F.3d 1098, 66 U.S.P.Q.2d (BNA) 1025, 55 Fed. R. Serv. 3d 60 (Fed. Cir. 2003). Sometimes, however, the issue arises in more subtle guise. For example, in Bangert Bros. Const. Co., Inc. v. Kiewit Western Co., 310 F.3d 1278 (10th Cir. 2002) the district court entered judgment in favor of a rock and sand supplier on its quantum meruit counterclaim against a general contractor notwithstanding a jury verdict in favor of the contractor on its counterclaim under a state statute. The Court of Appeals held that the court's entry of judgment was inconsistent with the jury verdict as the jury necessarily had found that the supplier had been paid in full while the quantum meruit judgment required a finding that the contractor had received benefit at the supplier's expense. In order not to undermine the jury's verdict in violation of the Seventh Amendment, the Court of Appeals held that the quantum meruit judgment had to be set aside. The jury's verdict was binding under collateral estoppel or issue preclusion principles. See also Smith v. Diffee Ford-Lincoln-Mercury, Inc., 298 F.3d 955, 13 A.D. Cas. (BNA) 588, 7 Wage & Hour Cas. 2d (BNA) 1802, 83 Empl. Prac. Dec. (CCH) ¶ 41159, 146 Lab. Cas. (CCH) ¶ 34556 (10th Cir. 2002) (district court violated plaintiff's right to jury trial in denying her front pay based on finding that she would have been terminated by employer within a few months, even if she had not been absent for medical reasons, when jury implicitly found employee would have been retained at least until date of trial).

In Carr v. Wal-Mart Stores, Inc., 312 F.3d 667 (5th Cir. 2002), the jury answered two interrogatories when, according to the court's instructions, it was supposed to answer only the first interrogatory and not the second if it decided the first in the way that it did. The judge had to attempt to reconcile the answers so as not to infringe on the Seventh Amendment right to jury trial. In fact, the judge answered the interrogatory that the jury should not have answered on the basis of his own assessment, which, according to the Court of Appeals, was tantamount to a bench trial and in violation of the Seventh Amendment. Accordingly, the Court of Appeals found that the trial court had abused its discretion and reversed the court's ruling. See also Figg v. Schroeder, 312 F.3d 625, 54 Fed. R. Serv. 3d 799 (4th Cir. 2002) (court is obliged to harmonize inconsistencies in a jury's responses on a special verdict form if it is at all possible; if not, and if viewed in the most generous light, the answers are inconsistent with each other, a new trial is ordinarily required); White v. Ford Motor Co., 312 F.3d 998, Prod. Liab. Rep. (CCH) ¶ 16463, 60 Fed. R. Evid. Serv. 933 (9th Cir. 2002), opinion amended on denial of reh'g, 335 F.3d 833 (9th Cir. 2003) (court is obliged to harmonize inconsistencies in a jury's responses on a special verdict form if it is at all possible; if not, and if viewed in the most generous light, the answers are inconsistent with each other, a new trial is ordinarily required).

The Seventh Amendment does not preclude a judge from reducing an excessive punitive damages verdict awarded by a jury. Ross v. Kansas City Power & Light Co., 293 F.3d 1041, 88 Fair Empl. Prac. Cas. (BNA) 1796, 83 Empl. Prac. Dec. (CCH) ¶ 41190 (8th Cir. 2002). The traditional remedy of remittitur, on the other hand, does require the plaintiff's consent

§ 1:14

in order to comply with the Seventh Amendment. See Thorne v. Welk Inv., Inc., 197 F.3d 1205, 82 Fair Empl. Prac. Cas. (BNA) 367 (8th Cir. 1999).

Although the Seventh Amendment is often viewed as preserving jury trial at the expense of judicial decisionmaking, Woolhandler and Collins argue that the drafters of the Seventh Amendment envisaged judicial control of juries as part and parcel of the scope of the Amendment. Woolhandler & Collins, *The Article III Jury*, 87 Va. L. Rev. 587 (2001).

Schaffner contends that in recent times the Supreme Court has shown a marked ambivalence to the Seventh Amendment. On the one had, the Court continues to extol the importance of jury trial in civil cases, on the other, it has increasingly removed particular issues from the jury's remit by holding that they are "incidental" to the basic right and has also upheld judicial review of jury verdicts, reduction of damages, and grants of new trials, all of which reduce the "integrity of the jury." Schaffner, *The Seventh Amendment Right to a Civil Jury Trial: The Supreme Court Giveth and the Supreme Court Taketh Away*, 31 U. Baltimore L. Rev. 225 (2002).

n. 92.

Add to note 92:

Personal injury tort actions for monetary damages are a prototype example of an action at law to which the Seventh Amendment applies, and the fact that the case is a class action or involves diversity jurisdiction does not affect the right to jury trial. Cimino v. Raymark Industries, Inc., 151 F.3d 297 (5th Cir. 1998). See also Coleman v. General Motors Acceptance Corp., 296 F.3d 443, 53 Fed. R. Serv. 3d 75, 2002 FED App. 0244P (6th Cir. 2002) (class treatment of claims for money damages implicates Seventh Amendment and due process right of individual class members).

For an in-depth and critical look at juries in civil cases, See *Developments in the Law—The Civil Jury*, 160 Harv. L. Rev. 1408 (1997). See also *Symposium: The American Jury: Illusion and Reality*, 48 DePaul L. Rev. 197 et seq. (1998).

Add at end of fourth paragraph:

The availability of a jury trial in federal court is a matter of federal law, even when state law claims are being tried. See, e.g., E.E.O.C. v. HBE Corp., 135 F.3d 543, 76 Fair Empl. Prac. Cas. (BNA) 495, 72 Empl. Prac. Dec. (CCH) ¶ 45241, 48 Fed. R. Evid. Serv. 866 (8th Cir. 1998). Thus, even though a claim for damages may be based on state law, whether there is a right to a jury trial in a diversity action is an issue to be decided under Seventh Amendment principles. In Kampa v. White Consol. Industries, Inc., 115 F.3d 585, 73 Fair Empl. Prac. Cas. (BNA) 1697, 70 Empl. Prac. Dec. (CCH) ¶ 44757 (8th Cir. 1997), for example, the plaintiff brought a gender discrimination suit under the state Human Rights Act but in federal court. The issue was whether she was entitled to a jury trial. Because this was a question of federal law, the fact that the state legislation provided that the case could be heard by a judge without a jury was not dispositive of the issue. The court held that the plaintiff was entitled to a jury trial because she was seeking a legal remedy (money damages). See also Gutierrez de Martinez v. Drug Enforcement Admin., 111 F.3d 1148 (4th Cir. 1997) (no Seventh Amendment right to jury trial on the issue of scope of employment in Westfall Act litigation, even though relevant state law would have provided a jury trial, because federal district court is entitled to resolve the issue and the Seventh Amendment is inapplicable); Klinger v. State Farm Mut. Auto. Ins. Co., 115 F.3d 230 (3d Cir. 1997) (claim for punitive damages under state bad faith statute triggered federal right to a jury trial under the Seventh Amendment); Todd v. Ortho Biotech, Inc., 138 F.3d 733, 76 Fair Empl. Prac. Cas. (BNA) 341, 72 Empl. Prac. Dec. (CCH) ¶ 45239 (8th Cir. 1998), cert. granted, judgment vacated on other grounds, 525 U.S. 802, 119 S. Ct. 33, 142 L. Ed. 2d 25, 79 Fair Empl. Prac. Cas. (BNA) 1015 (1998); (claims under Minnesota Human Rights Act should be tried to a jury in federal court, and jury findings on issues common to both Title VII and MHRA are conclusive); U.S. v. Ciurinskas, 148 F.3d 729 (7th Cir. 1998) (no right to jury trial in denaturalization suit, which is action in equity).

A jury trial is not available in an action seeking solely injunctive relief, or when the remedy sought is a disgorgement of illicit profits. S.E.C. v. Rind, 991 F.2d 1486, Fed. Sec. L. Rep. (CCH) ¶ 97421 (9th Cir. 1993). Nor is a party entitled to a jury trial under the Seventh Amendment when there are no factual issues for a jury to resolve. Koski v. Standex Intern. Corp., 307 F.3d 672, 89 Fair Empl. Prac. Cas. (BNA) 1865, 84 Empl. Prac. Dec. (CCH) ¶ 41358 (7th Cir. 2002). See also Duncan v. Department of Labor, 313 F.3d 445 (8th Cir. 2002) (after claim for workers' compensation wages was properly dismissed, there was no issue for jury trial); Singh v. Blue Cross/Blue Shield of Massachusetts, Inc., 308 F.3d 25 (1st Cir. 2002) (summary judgment ruling for defendants on issue of immunity under Healthcare Quality Improvement Act did not deprive plaintiff of his Seventh Amendment right to jury trial). Accord Securities and Exchange Commission v. Commonwealth Chemical Securities, Inc., 574 F.2d 90, Fed. Sec. L. Rep. (CCH) ¶ 96351 (2d Cir. 1978). See also Austin v. Shalala, 994 F.2d 1170, 41 Soc. Sec. Rep. Serv. 281, Unempl. Ins. Rep. (CCH) ¶ 17452A (5th Cir. 1993) (no right to jury trial in action to recover overpayment of Social Security benefits); Bogosian v. Woloohojian Realty Corp., 323 F.3d 55, 55 Fed. R. Serv. 3d 36 (1st Cir. 2003) (no right to jury trial in action for breach of fiduciary duty). Although there may be a Seventh Amendment right to a jury trial in a patent infringement case, the Court of Appeals in Markman v. Westview Instruments, Inc., 52 F.3d 967, 34 U.S.P.Q.2d (BNA) 1321 (Fed. Cir. 1995), aff'd, 517 U.S. 370, 116 S. Ct. 1384,

§ 1:14 Jury Selection: Law, Art & Science 2d

134 L. Ed. 2d 577, 38 U.S.P.Q.2d (BNA) 1461 (1996) held that the construction and determination of the scope of the patent was a legal question for the court to decide. *Markman* was reversed on appeal by the United States Supreme Court. Markman v. Westview Instruments, Inc., 517 U.S. 370, 116 S. Ct. 1384, 134 L. Ed. 2d 577, 38 U.S.P.Q.2d (BNA) 1461 (1996). The Court held that, as patent infringement cases had been tried at law in the 18th century, the parties in such a suit were entitled to a jury trial. If only injunctive relief is sought, on the other hand, as in Tegal Corp. v. Tokyo Electron America, Inc., 257 F.3d 1331, 59 U.S.P.Q.2d (BNA) 1385 (Fed. Cir. 2001), cert. denied, 535 U.S. 927, 122 S. Ct. 1297, 152 L. Ed. 2d 209 (2002) and cert. denied, 535 U.S. 927, 122 S. Ct. 1297, 152 L. Ed. 2d 209 (2002), there is no right to a jury trial in a patent infringement case. In *Tegal* the Court of Appeals held that where the plaintiff sought only injunctive relief and the defendant asserted only affirmative defenses and no counterclaims that neither party had a right to a jury trial. The court in Cass County Music Co. v. C.H.L.R., Inc., 88 F.3d 635, 39 U.S.P.Q.2d (BNA) 1429 (8th Cir. 1996) reached a similar conclusion in respect to copyright infringement actions, while reserving the right to a jury trial for the determination of any statutory damages. Taking issue with the appropriateness of impaneling a jury to determine statutory damages, but otherwise holding that there is no right to a jury trial in a copyright infringement action is Feltner v. Columbia Pictures Television, Inc., 523 U.S. 340, 118 S. Ct. 1279, 140 L. Ed. 2d 438, 26 Media L. Rep. (BNA) 1513, 46 U.S.P.Q.2d (BNA) 1161, 163 A.L.R. Fed. 721 (1998). Compare Segrets, Inc. v. Gillman Knitwear Co., Inc., 207 F.3d 56, 54 U.S.P.Q.2d (BNA) 1158 (1st Cir. 2000) (competitor in copyright infringement action entitled to jury trial on issue of statutory damages).

The question of whether there is a right to a jury trial in respect to damage awards in a copyright action was addressed by the United Sates Supreme Court in Feltner v. Columbia Pictures Television, Inc., 523 U.S. 340, 118 S. Ct. 1279, 140 L. Ed. 2d 438, 26 Media L. Rep. (BNA) 1513, 46 U.S.P.Q.2d (BNA) 1161, 163 A.L.R. Fed. 721 (1998). After Columbia had terminated its license agreement with various televisions stations because of delinquent royalty payments, the stations continued to broadcast the relevant programs. Columbia then proceeded to bring suit for copyright infringement under § 504(c) of the Copyright Act of 1976. The district court entered partial summary judgment for the broadcasting company and awarded statutory damages. The station owner's request for a jury trial in respect to damages was denied.

On writ of certiorari, the United States Supreme Court reversed. The Court began by examining the relevant statutory provision but concluded that it did not establish a right to a jury trial on the issue of damages. The statute made no mention of juries and consistently referred to damages being assessed by "the court", which the Court interpreted (over the dissent of Justice Scalia on this issue) to refer to the judge, not a jury. However, this did not dispose of the issue for the Court now had to determine whether there was a constitutional right to a jury trial under the Seventh Amendment.

The Court concluded that there was a right to a jury trial under the Seventh Amendment on the question of damages. The Court's historical inquiry indicated that at common law analogous actions by writers to prevent the unauthorized publication of their manuscripts were tried in courts of law, and thus before juries. The juries were also responsible for awarding damages. Moreover, there was no evidence that this practice had not been changed in America by the various copyright statutes.

Columbia did not contest this analysis so much as argue that, despite its historical lineage, statutory damages in copyright actions were equitable in nature. The Court disagreed, noting that, as a general proposition, monetary relief was legal. Columbia also relied on Tull v. U.S., 481 U.S. 412, 107 S. Ct. 1831, 95 L. Ed. 2d 365, 25 Env't. Rep. Cas. (BNA) 1857, 7 Fed. R. Serv. 3d 673, 17 Envtl. L. Rep. 20667 (1987) (discussed in main text), in which the Court had held that while the Seventh Amendment may grant a right to a jury trial on substantive issues, Congress could nonetheless authorize the trial judge to assess the appropriate amount of the civil penalty to be assessed upon a finding of liability. The Court distinguished *Tull* because there was no comparable evidence that damages in the type of litigation there involved had been decided by juries at common law. Furthermore, in *Tull* the monetary issue related to the amount of civil penalties to be paid to the government, which was analogous to a sentence in a criminal proceeding, while in the instant case the issue was the monetary damages to be awarded to a private party. In Columbia Pictures Television, Inc. v. Krypton Broadcasting of Birmingham, Inc., 259 F.3d 1186, 57 Fed. R. Evid. Serv. 559 (9th Cir. 2001), cert. denied, 534 U.S. 1127, 122 S. Ct. 1063, 151 L. Ed. 2d 967 (2002) the appellant argued that the Supreme Court's decision in *Feltner* rendered the statutory damages provision of the Copyright Act constitutionally unenforceable. The Court of Appeals disagreed, finding that the Supreme Court's decision only held the Act unconstitutional to the extent that Section 504(c) failed to provide for the jury trial guaranteed by the

§ 1:14   JURY SELECTION: LAW, ART & SCIENCE 2D

Seventh Amendment, which in no way implied that copyright plaintiffs were no longer able to seek statutory damages under the Copyright Act.

There was no common law right to a jury trial in admiralty cases, and thus the Seventh Amendment does not apply to admiralty cases. Craig v. Atlantic Richfield Co., 19 F.3d 472, 1994 A.M.C. 1354, 28 Fed. R. Serv. 3d 1044 (9th Cir. 1994). In Concordia Co., Inc. v. Panek, 115 F.3d 67, 1997 A.M.C. 2357, 37 Fed. R. Serv. 3d 1079 (1st Cir. 1997), the court stated that while there was no general right to a jury trial in an admiralty case (save for statutory exceptions), where a claim sounded in both admiralty and common law, the right to a jury trial could be obtained if the prescribed statutory procedures under 28 U.S.C.A. § 1333(1) were invoked. In the instant case, however, the defendant was deemed to have waived the right to a jury trial by designating his counterclaim as "in admiralty" with no accompanying demand for a jury. The waiver was not negated by plaintiff's subsequent demand for a jury in response to the counterclaim. See generally Sacks & Settergren, *Juries Should not be Trusted to Decide Admiralty Cases*, 34 J. of Maritime Law and Commerce 163 (2003); Koelzer, *Should We Trust Juries with Admiralty Cases?*, 34 J. of Maritime Law and Commerce 159 (2003).

The Jones Act, however, created a statutory right to a jury trial on behalf of "any seaman who shall suffer personal injury in the course of his employment." 46 U.S.C.A. § 688. The Court of Appeals in *Craig* noted that the jury trial right in § 688 was on behalf of a plaintiff but not a defendant. Thus, the right could not be invoked by the defendant in the case. Nor could the assertion of the right to a jury by the plaintiff in the case or plaintiffs in related litigation stemming from the same incident provide a basis on which the defendant could assert a right to a jury trial. Craig v. Atlantic Richfield Co., 19 F.3d 472, 1994 A.M.C. 1354, 28 Fed. R. Serv. 3d 1044 (9th Cir. 1994).

In South Port Marine, LLC v. Gulf Oil Ltd. Partnership, 234 F.3d 58, 51 Env't. Rep. Cas. (BNA) 1749, 2001 A.M.C. 609, 31 Envtl. L. Rep. 20344 (1st Cir. 2000) the court held that the plaintiff was entitled to a jury trial in an action under the Oil Pollution Act, rejecting the argument that the OPA claim was comparable to a claim in admiralty. See also Linton v. Great Lakes Dredge & Dock Co., 964 F.2d 1480, 1992 A.M.C. 2789 (5th Cir. 1992); Rachal v. Ingram Corp., 795 F.2d 1210, 5 Fed. R. Serv. 3d 1006 (5th Cir. 1986). In Ghotra by Ghotra v. Bandila Shipping, Inc., 113 F.3d 1050, 1997 A.M.C. 1936, 37 Fed. R. Serv. 3d 1001 (9th Cir. 1997), a suit brought under the Longshore and Harbor Workers

Compensation Acts (LHWCA), the court held that the plaintiff was entitled to a jury trial in respect to both in personam maritime claims based on diversity jurisdiction and in rem claims joined to the in personam claims.

In Aetna Cas. Sur. Co. v. P & B Autobody, 43 F.3d 1546 (1st Cir. 1994), the court held that there was no right to a jury trial on the issue of damages in a RICO action where a jury verdict had been returned on liability and the court could determine damages as a matter of law.

There is no general right to a jury trial in a civil action against the federal government. See Lehman v. Nakshian, 453 U.S. 156, 101 S. Ct. 2698, 69 L. Ed. 2d 548, 26 Fair Empl. Prac. Cas. (BNA) 65, 26 Empl. Prac. Dec. (CCH) ¶ 31900, 31 Fed. R. Serv. 2d 1373 (1981). When Congress waives the government's immunity by statute, it does not necessarily accord a right to a jury trial by virtue of that waiver. Only when Congress chooses to grant this right does it accrue. Lehman v. Nakshian, 453 U.S. 156, 101 S. Ct. 2698, 69 L. Ed. 2d 548, 26 Fair Empl. Prac. Cas. (BNA) 65, 26 Empl. Prac. Dec. (CCH) ¶ 31900, 31 Fed. R. Serv. 2d 1373 (1981). See also In re Young, 869 F.2d 158, 159, 130 L.R.R.M. (BNA) 2908 (2d Cir. 1989); Burzynski v. Cohen, 264 F.3d 611, 86 Fair Empl. Prac. Cas. (BNA) 1112, 81 Empl. Prac. Dec. (CCH) ¶ 40761, 2001 FED App. 0279P (6th Cir. 2001). More commonly, however, Congress will condition its consent to be sued on a plaintiff's relinquishment of the claim to a jury trial. Lehman, at 161; KLK, Inc. v. U.S. Dept. of Interior, 35 F.3d 454, 30 Fed. R. Serv. 3d 789, 129 O.G.R. 441 (9th Cir. 1994) (inverse condemnation action under the Mining in the Parks Act, 16 U.S.C.A. § 1910). Cf also U.S. v. 4.0 Acres of Land, 175 F.3d 1133, 51 Fed. R. Evid. Serv. 1586 (9th Cir. 1999) (no Seventh Amendment right to jury trial in condemnation action); Simpson v. Office of Thrift Supervision, 29 F.3d 1418 (9th Cir. 1994) (no right to a jury trial in action brought pursuant to congressional statute enacted to empower Office of Thrift Supervision to enforce public rights of an equitable nature). Whether a defendant is to be deemed a part of the federal government first must be determined. See Marcella v. Brandywine Hosp., 47 F.3d 618, 31 Fed. R. Serv. 3d 557 (3d Cir. 1995) (American Red Cross not agency of federal government for purposes of negligence action arising from plaintiff's becoming infected with HIV as a result of contaminated blood collected in volunteer donor program administered by Red Cross).

Since actions against foreign states were unknown at common law, the nonjury trial provision of the Foreign Sovereign Immunities Act has been held not to be in violation of the Seventh Amendment. Universal Consol. Companies, Inc. v.

§ 1:14   JURY SELECTION: LAW, ART & SCIENCE 2D

Bank of China, 35 F.3d 243, 1994 FED App. 0311P (6th Cir. 1994). The provision for a nonjury trial may not be taken advantage of, however, by a domestic subsidiary of a foreign company named as codefendant in a suit against the parent company. See, e.g., Gould v. Aerospatiale Helicopter Corp., 40 F.3d 1033 (9th Cir. 1994). See also In re Air Crash Disaster Near Roselawn, Ind. on Oct. 31, 1994, 96 F.3d 932 (7th Cir. 1996) (as suit under Foreign Sovereign Immunities Act is against foreign sovereign, and as foreign sovereign was not a possible defendant at common law in 1791, Seventh Amendment right to jury trial does not apply).

Even where there is no constitutional right to a jury trial under the Seventh Amendment, a court may have the authority to empanel an advisory jury. The use of such advisory juries was endorsed by the Seventh Circuit Court of Appeals in Alexander v. Gerhardt Enterprises, Inc., 40 F.3d 187, 68 Fair Empl. Prac. Cas. (BNA) 595, 65 Empl. Prac. Dec. (CCH) ¶ 43389 (7th Cir. 1994). See also U.S. v. Premises Known as RR No. 1 Box 224, Dalton, Scott Tp. and North Abington Tp., Lackawanna County, Pa., 14 F.3d 864 (3d Cir. 1994). See also Allison v. Citgo Petroleum Corp., 151 F.3d 402, 81 Fair Empl. Prac. Cas. (BNA) 501, 73 Empl. Prac. Dec. (CCH) ¶ 45426 (5th Cir. 1998). Advisory juries are to be employed in cases where jury trials are not available as a matter of right, however, and a court should not convene an advisory jury when a proper request for a jury trial has been made. See Indiana Lumbermens Mut. Ins. Co. v. Timberland Pallet and Lumber Co., Inc., 195 F.3d 368, 45 Fed. R. Serv. 3d 1241 (8th Cir. 1999) (finding the error in invoking an advisory jury harmless).

In Palace Exploration Co. v. Petroleum Development Co., 316 F.3d 1110, 1120, 54 Fed. R. Serv. 3d 924 (10th Cir. 2003), the Court of Appeals observed that an "advisory jury is not the equivalent of a Seventh Amendment jury". See also, Zabel, *Advisory Juries and their Use and Misuse in Federal Tort Claims Act Cases*, 2003 Brigham Young University L. Rev. 185 (2003) (arguing that advisory juries in FTCA cases violate both the letter and spirit of the FTCA's prohibition on jury trials).

In Doctor's Associates, Inc. v. Distajo, 107 F.3d 126 (2d Cir. 1997), the Second Circuit Court of Appeals, citing its earlier decision in Doctor's Associates, Inc. v. Stuart, 85 F.3d 975 (2d Cir. 1996), held that in cases involving arbitration, the party resisting arbitration bears the burden of showing that it is entitled to a jury trial. See also American Heritage Life Ins. Co. v. Orr, 294 F.3d 702 (5th Cir. 2002), cert. denied, 537 U.S. 1106, 123 S. Ct. 871, 154 L. Ed. 2d 775 (2003). While parties may agree to arbitration and waiver of a jury trial, whether such an agreement has been entered into is a matter of contract law, and itself subject to jury trial. See Avedon Engineering, Inc. v. Seatex, 126 F.3d 1279, 33 U.C.C. Rep. Serv. 2d 1039 (10th Cir. 1997).

Declaratory relief is, in theory, neither legal nor equitable. In order to determine whether a party seeking declaratory relief is entitled to a jury trial, it is necessary to ask whether a jury trial would have been available had declaratory relief not been sought. Northgate Homes, Inc. v. City of Dayton, 126 F.3d 1095 (8th Cir. 1997). In *Northgate Homes*, the plaintiff's objective was to enjoin the city from enforcing its zoning ordinances, and the court held that the action was equitable in nature and that there therefore was no right to a jury trial. See also Manning v. U.S., 146 F.3d 808, 40 Fed. R. Serv. 3d 1370, 28 Envtl. L. Rep. 21431 (10th Cir. 1998), (fact party was seeking only equitable relief in the form of a declaratory judgement and injunction rendered action basically equitable in nature and justified denial of jury trial).

In Marseilles Hydro Power, LLC v. Marseilles Land and Water Co., 299 F.3d 643, 53 Fed. R. Serv. 3d 218 (7th Cir. 2002) the Court of Appeals stated that the nature of the underlying suit determines the availability of jury trial, and that casting one's claim in the form of a suit for declaratory judgment, or adding a claim for declaratory judgment to one's other claims, will not create a right to jury trial that did not otherwise exist. If this were not so, anyone seeking an injunction could obtain a jury trial simply by adding a claim for declaratory relief. While rejecting the plaintiff's right to a jury trial on the basis of its complaint, the Court of Appeals nonetheless found that the right to jury trial arose when the defendant counterclaimed for damages based on a breach of contract. As there were common issues in the claim and counterclaim, a jury would be needed to resolve the facts because a judge's determination of the facts would infringe upon the Seventh Amendment's right to jury trial.

In Kobs v. Arrow Service Bureau, Inc., 134 F.3d 893 (7th Cir. 1998), an action against a debt collection agency under the Fair Debt Collection Practices Act (FDCPA), the court stated that because legal rights, sounding in tort, were at stake, there was a right to jury trial. In Ideal Electronic Sec. Co., Inc. v. International Fidelity Ins. Co., 129 F.3d 143, 42 Cont. Cas. Fed. (CCH) ¶ 77224, 39 Fed. R. Serv. 3d 477 (D.C. Cir. 1997), it was held that the matter of what constitutes reasonable attorney's fees is matter for the court and not an issue for jury trial. In Dardovitch v. Haltzman, 190 F.3d 125 (3d Cir. 1999) the court ruled that a beneficiary seeking a trust accounting was not entitled to a jury trial.

Add after the second excerpt:

In Chauffeurs, Teamsters and Helpers, Local No. 391 v. Terry, 494 U.S. 558, 110 S. Ct. 1339, 108 L. Ed. 2d 519, 133 L.R.R.M. (BNA) 2793, 114 Lab. Cas. (CCH) ¶ 11930 (1990), the respondents' members of the petitioner union brought suit against both their employer and the union. They alleged that the employer had breached the collective bargaining agreement which existed between employer and union, and that the union had violated its duty of fair representation in failing to press respondents' claims in a grievance proceeding. Injunctive relief and compensatory damages were sought, but after the employer filed for bankruptcy, the claims for injunctive relief were dismissed. The union then moved to strike respondents' demand for a jury on the ground that there was no Seventh Amendment right to a jury trial in a suit for breach of the duty of fair representation. The district court denied the motion. In an interlocutory appeal, the Fourth Circuit Court of Appeals affirmed. The United States Supreme Court also affirmed.

A plurality of the Supreme Court applied the traditional two-prong test for determining whether a party had a Seventh Amendment right to a jury trial:

1. Was the nature of the issues to be tried more analogous to those in an 18th century action in law (triable by a jury) or in equity (triable by the court)?
2. Was the relief sought legal or equitable in nature?

The plurality stated that, of these two prongs, the second was the more important given the "abstruse historical" inquiry called for by the first. (Justice Brennan, in a concurring opinion, would have gone further and held that the Seventh Amendment question should be governed solely by the answer to the second question. Justices Kennedy, O'Connor, and Scalia, dissenting, would have placed the emphasis on the first question.).

The plurality did not see that there was a clear answer to the first question. In 18th century England, no suits could arise from a union's failure to fairly represent its members (hardly surprising since collective bargaining agreements were illegal at the time). The Court therefore looked for analogous actions. The fair representation suit bore considerable resemblance to an action by a beneficiary of a trust against a trustee for breach of duty, which was equitable in nature. However, it also raised issues analogous to those found in an action in law for breach of contract. Thus, the answer to the first question was inconclusive.

Turning its attention to the second and more important prong, the plurality stated that the remedy sought, compensatory damages, was generally deemed to be legal in nature subject to a few carefully defined exceptions not here present. Damages can be deemed to be equitable when they are restitutionary, but here the damages claimed were wages and benefits to which the respondents would have been entitled had the union properly processed their grievances. Damages can also be deemed to be equitable when they are incidental to or intertwined with injunctive relief, but after the injunctive relief claims against the employer were dismissed following its filing for bankruptcy, only compensatory damages were at issue. The four-Justice plurality (along with concurring Justices Brennan and Stevens) concluded that the respondents were entitled to a jury trial under the Seventh Amendment.

Terry was applied in Wooddell v. International Broth. of Elec. Workers, Local 71, 502 U.S. 93, 112 S. Ct. 494, 116 L. Ed. 2d 419, 138 L.R.R.M. (BNA) 2881, 120 Lab. Cas. (CCH) ¶ 11010 (1991). The petitioner had brought an action against the local union and its officers, alleging that they had acted in violation of the Labor Management Relations Act (LMRA) and the Labor-Management Reporting and Disclosure Act (LMRDA) by discriminating against him in respect to job referrals. The Supreme Court held that the petitioner was entitled to a jury trial on his LMRDA claim, notwithstanding that he sought injunctive relief. The Court found that the injunctive relief was incidental to the damages claimed. It also agreed with the petitioner that the claim for lost wages should not be treated as one for restitution and incident to the claim for reinstatement, as the lost wages constituted damages for jobs for which he had not been referred.

In Spinelli v. Gaughan, 12 F.3d 853, 17 Employee Benefits Cas. (BNA) 2006, 9 I.E.R. Cas. (BNA) 214 (9th Cir. 1993), the Ninth Circuit Court of Appeals applied the Supreme Court's decisions in *Terry*, *Granfinanciera* and *Tull* to a claim that a litigant was entitled to a jury trial in a suit alleging that she was discharged in retaliation for exercising rights under ERISA. The court concluded that the statute created a right that was essentially equitable in nature and that, therefore, the petitioner was not entitled to a jury trial. Similar conclusions in respect to the unavailability of a jury in respect to ERISA claims have been reached. See Mathews v. Sears Pension Plan, 144 F.3d 461, 22 Employee Benefits Cas. (BNA) 1193 (7th Cir. 1998); Tischmann v. ITT/Sheraton Corp., 145 F.3d 561 (2d Cir. 1998); Borst v. Chevron Corp., 36 F.3d 1308, 18 Employee Benefits Cas. (BNA) 2217 (5th Cir. 1994); Houghton v. SIPCO, Inc., 38 F.3d 953, 18 Employee Benefits Cas. (BNA) 2195, 66 Fair Empl. Prac. Cas. (BNA) 97 (8th Cir. 1994); DeFelice v. American Intern. Life Assur. Co. of New York, 112 F.3d 61, 28 Employee Benefits

§ 1:14

Cas. (BNA) 1133 (2d Cir. 1997); Bittinger v. Tecumseh Products Co., 123 F.3d 877, 21 Employee Benefits Cas. (BNA) 1873, 38 Fed. R. Serv. 3d 685, 1997 FED App. 0242P (6th Cir. 1997). The basic rule that there is no entitlement to jury trial in ERISA cases is not necessarily altered by the fact that a plaintiff stands to recover money by virtue of a favorable judgment. See Adams v. Cyprus Amax Minerals Co., 149 F.3d 1156, 22 Employee Benefits Cas. (BNA) 1493 (10th Cir. 1998). The court in *Adams* distinguished equitable/restitutionary relief from legal/compensatory damages, and noted that any sums due under the former head were dependent upon an initial finding that the plaintiffs were eligible beneficiaries. As this determination was an equitable one, there was no right to a jury trial under the Seventh Amendment. See also Wilkins v. Baptist Healthcare System, Inc., 150 F.3d 609, 28 Employee Benefits Cas. (BNA) 1218, 1998 FED App. 0236P (6th Cir. 1998). See also Bowdry v. United Airlines, Inc., 58 F.3d 1483, 149 L.R.R.M. (BNA) 2714, 130 Lab. Cas. (CCH) ¶ 11356 (10th Cir. 1995) (no right to jury in action alleging a violation of the Airline Deregulation Act). However, it has been held that a litigant has a constitutional right to a jury trial in a suit under § 504 of the Rehabilitation Act. Pandazides v. Virginia Bd. of Educ., 13 F.3d 823, 4 A.D.D. 111, 2 A.D. Cas. (BNA) 1711, 88 Ed. Law Rep. 963, 63 Empl. Prac. Dec. (CCH) ¶ 42782 (4th Cir. 1994); Waldrop v. Southern Co. Services, Inc., 24 F.3d 152, 5 A.D.D. 910, 3 A.D. Cas. (BNA) 595 (11th Cir. 1994). The court in *Waldrop* cautioned, however, that a jury trial might not be available were the claimant only seeking equitable relief.

In Brown v. Sandimo Materials, 250 F.3d 120, 26 Employee Benefits Cas. (BNA) 1391, 167 L.R.R.M. (BNA) 2176 (2d Cir. 2001) the trustees of union pension and welfare funds brought suit under both LMRA and ERISA. The Court of Appeals held that the trial judge had committed error in refusing to grant the employers' demand for a jury trial on the breach of contract issue (whether the employers had breached the contract by not making payments to union pension and welfare trusts) arising under the LMRA claim, and that the error was not harmless. Having determined that the defendants were entitled to jury trial under the LMRA claim, the court did not have to address and did not address whether there was also a right to jury trial in respect to the ERISA claim.

The court in Frizzell v. Southwest Motor Freight, 154 F.3d 641, 77 Fair Empl. Prac. Cas. (BNA) 1580, 4 Wage & Hour Cas. 2d (BNA) 1505, 74 Empl. Prac. Dec. (CCH) ¶ 45504, 136 Lab. Cas. (CCH) ¶ 33725, 1998 FED App. 0285P (6th Cir. 1998) held that there is a right to jury trial under the Fam-

Right to Jury Trial § 1:14

ily and Medical Leave Act, 29 U.S.C.A. §§ 2601–1654. This conclusion was based not on the express wording of the statute, which was silent on the issue, but by reference to the relevant legislative history and the structure of the remedial provisions of the Act.

n. 100.

Add to note 100:

The mere fact that a tort claim would have been tried by a jury at common law does not preclude Congress from enacting a law that allows the claim to be tried without a jury. In such instances there is no Seventh Amendment violation. Martin v. Telectronics Pacing Systems, Inc., 70 F.3d 39, Prod. Liab. Rep. (CCH) ¶ 14411, 28 U.C.C. Rep. Serv. 2d 531, 1995 FED App. 0335P (6th Cir. 1995), cert. granted, judgment vacated on other grounds, 518 U.S. 1030, 116 S. Ct. 2576, 135 L. Ed. 2d 1091 (1996).

In Salmon v. Schwarz, 948 F.2d 1131 (10th Cir. 1991), the court stated that a litigant pursuing a claim under the Federal Torts Claims Act (FTCA) was not entitled to a jury trial and this did not violate the Seventh Amendment. In Engle v. Mecke, 24 F.3d 133 (10th Cir. 1994), where a litigant brought parallel actions under the FTCA and on constitutional grounds, the court held that because the FTCA claim was tried by the court, the Seventh Amendment did not require the court to adopt the jury damages awarded in the constitutional claim. In U.S. v. Dubose, 146 F.3d 1141 (9th Cir. 1998), as amended on denial of reh'g, (Aug. 31, 1998), the Ninth Circuit Court of Appeals held that the provisions of the Mandatory Victims Compensation Act (MVRA), which authorized civil enforcement of a lien for restitution awarded a victim under the Act, did not transform restitution into a suit subject to the Seventh Amendment's guarantee of a jury trial. See also U.S. v. Rostoff, 164 F.3d 63 (1st Cir. 1999). The court in Merex A.G. v. Fairchild Weston Systems, Inc., 29 F.3d 821, 29 Fed. R. Serv. 3d 560 (2d Cir. 1994) held that a party did not have right to a jury trial on a promissory estoppel claim.

n. 101.

Add to note 101:

In Hatco Corp. v. W.R. Grace & Co. Conn., 59 F.3d 400, 41 Env't. Rep. Cas. (BNA) 1338, 25 Envtl. L. Rep. 21238 (3d Cir. 1995) the Court of Appeals stated that an action for contribution under the Comprehensive Environmental Response, Compensation and Liability Act of 1980 (CERCLA) was not one that entitled a litigant to a jury trial. The claims involved were, according to the court, primarily equitable in nature, and ones that would have been tried by a court in equity prior to 1791.

n. 102.

Add to note 102:

See also LeBlanc-Sternberg v. Fletcher, 67 F.3d 412 (2d Cir. 1995) (jury available in action brought by government under Fair Housing Act [Title VIII of the Civil Rights Act of 1968], and fact that claim for damages is joined with equitable claim does not affect right to jury trial).

Add after note 102:

Under Fed. R. Civ. Proc. 42(b) a court may order separate trials to promote judicial economy or where a single trial would prejudice a party. However, if there are to be two jury trials, the court must be careful that the two juries are not

§ 1:14   Jury Selection: Law, Art & Science 2d

called upon to decide the same issue lest the Seventh Amendment's prescription that "no fact tried by a jury shall be otherwise reexamined" be violated. In Houseman v. U.S. Aviation Underwriters, 171 F.3d 1117, 43 Fed. R. Serv. 3d 523 (7th Cir. 1999), where the plaintiff argued that bifurcation violated his Seventh Amendment right to jury trial, the Court found that, while the two juries may have considered overlapping evidence, this was not the same as deciding the same factual issue. See also Mullen v. Treasure Chest Casino, LLC, 186 F.3d 620, 2000 A.M.C. 1519, 44 Fed. R. Serv. 3d 885 (5th Cir. 1999). A Seventh Amendment violation was found in Blyden v. Mancusi, 186 F.3d 252 (2d Cir. 1999), where the bifurcation order allowed the damages jury to reexamine issues decided by the liability jury.

In Palace Exploration Co. v. Petroleum Development Co., 316 F.3d 1110, 54 Fed. R. Serv. 3d 924 (10th Cir. 2003), the Court of Appeals held that the bifurcation of an investor's rescission claim from its breach of contract for gross negligence claim deprived the investor if the right to a jury trial under the Seventh Amendment.

Add at end of section:

In Langenkamp v. Culp, 498 U.S. 42, 111 S. Ct. 330, 112 L. Ed. 2d 343, 20 Bankr. Ct. Dec. (CRR) 1953, 23 Collier Bankr. Cas. 2d (MB) 973, Bankr. L. Rep. (CCH) ¶ 73668, 18 Fed. R. Serv. 3d 586 (1990), creditors who had submitted claims against a bankruptcy estate were in turn sued by the trustee in bankruptcy to recover, as avoidable preferences, payments which had been made to them. In the action by the trustee, the creditors asserted a Seventh Amendment right to a jury trial, which was refused. The bankruptcy court then heard the case and found against the creditors, and the creditors appealed. The Tenth Circuit Court of Appeals held that the creditors who had filed claims against the bankruptcy estate were entitled to a jury trial.

In a per curiam opinion, the United States Supreme Court reversed. The Court drew a critical distinction between those creditors who had filed claims against the bankruptcy estate and those who had not. The filing of a claim triggered the process of "allowance and disallowance of claims," and subjected the claimant to the equity powers of the bankruptcy court (citing Granfinanciera, S.A. v. Nordberg, 492 U.S. 33, 109 S. Ct. 2782, 106 L. Ed. 2d 26, 19 Bankr. Ct. Dec. (CRR) 493, 20 Collier Bankr. Cas. 2d (MB) 1216, Bankr. L. Rep. (CCH) ¶ 72855, 18 Fed. R. Serv. 3d 435 (1989)). When that claim was countered by a preference action by the trustee, the latter suit was integrated into the claims-allowance process and became triable in equity. On the other hand, if the potential claimant had not submitted a claim against the bankruptcy estate, the trustee in bankruptcy could only have recouped alleged preferential payments by bringing a legal action to recover a monetary transfer. In that case, the defendants would have been entitled to a jury trial under the Seventh Amendment.

Thus, a creditor's right to a jury trial in an action brought by a trustee in bankruptcy for alleged preferential monetary transfers turns on whether the creditor has filed a claim against the bankruptcy estate. Since the claimants in *Langenkamp* had filed such a claim, they had subjected themselves to the equity jurisdiction of the bankruptcy court and were not entitled to a jury trial on the subsequent preference action by the trustee in bankruptcy. See also SNA Nut Co. v. Haagen-Dazs Company, Inc., 302 F.3d 725 (7th Cir. 2002); Matter of Peachtree Lane Associates, Ltd., 150 F.3d 788, 32 Bankr. Ct. Dec. (CRR) 1235, Bankr. L. Rep. (CCH) ¶ 77747 (7th Cir. 1998); In re Jensen, 946 F.2d 369, 25 Collier Bankr. Cas. 2d (MB) 1351, Bankr. L. Rep. (CCH) ¶ 74339, 21 Fed. R. Serv. 3d 447 (5th Cir. 1991) (debtors did not lose the right to jury trial on prepetition claims by third parties by filing petition in bankruptcy); In re Friedberg, 131 B.R. 6 (S.D. N.Y. 1991) (prospective purchaser of property from debtor did not submit to equitable jurisdiction of bankruptcy court by requesting court approval of proposed transaction; thus no waiver of right to jury); Landscape Properties, Inc. v. Vogel, 46 F.3d 1416, 26 Bankr. Ct. Dec. (CRR) 808, Bankr. L. Rep. (CCH) ¶ 76383 (8th Cir. 1995) (claim for damages for collusion at bankruptcy sale involved legal rather than equitable claim entitling parties to a jury trial). But compare In re Marshland Development, Inc., 129 B.R. 626, 21 Bankr. Ct. Dec. (CRR) 1482, 25 Collier Bankr. Cas. 2d (MB) 360, Bankr. L. Rep. (CCH) ¶ 74110 (Bankr. N.D. Cal. 1991) (removed state court complaint seeking to recover environmental damages from Ch 11 debtors was tantamount to filing proof of claim in bankruptcy court; debtors' answer was tantamount to objection to claim and thus the proceeding was transmuted into one for claims resolution for which there was no right to jury trial); Matter of Maurice, 21 F.3d 767, 30 Collier Bankr. Cas. 2d (MB) 1809, Bankr. L. Rep. (CCH) ¶ 75825, 28 Fed. R. Serv. 3d 799 (7th Cir. 1994) (no constitutional right to jury trial in dischargeability cases heard in bankruptcy court); In re Clay, 35 F.3d 190, 26 Bankr. Ct. Dec. (CRR) 127, 31 Collier Bankr. Cas. 2d (MB) 1732, Bankr. L. Rep. (CCH) ¶ 76122 (5th Cir. 1994) (bankruptcy judge lacks both constitutional and statutory authority to conduct jury trial without consent of parties); In re Pasquariello, 16 F.3d 525, 25 Bankr. Ct. Dec. (CRR) 404, 30 Collier Bankr. Cas. 2d (MB) 1006, Bankr. L. Rep. (CCH) ¶ 75723 (3d Cir. 1994) (claimants who bring themselves

§ 1:14   JURY SELECTION: LAW, ART & SCIENCE 2D

within equitable jurisdiction of bankruptcy court not entitled to jury trial on fraudulent conveyance claim); Billing v. Ravin, Greenberg & Zackin, P.A., 22 F.3d 1242, 25 Bankr. Ct. Dec. (CRR) 904, 30 Collier Bankr. Cas. 2d (MB) 1844, Bankr. L. Rep. (CCH) ¶ 75822 (3d Cir. 1994) (debtors had no right to jury trial where legal malpractice raised as a defense to claim for fees in bankruptcy court). But compare In re Stansbury Poplar Place, Inc., 13 F.3d 122, 25 Bankr. Ct. Dec. (CRR) 95, 30 Collier Bankr. Cas. 2d (MB) 493, Bankr. L. Rep. (CCH) ¶ 75636 (4th Cir. 1993) (although bankruptcy court could not conduct jury trial, neither request for equitable accounting in connection with fraudulent conveyance proceedings nor listing of defendants as creditors precluded jury trial for monetary damages in district court); Smith v. Dowden, 47 F.3d 940, 26 Bankr. Ct. Dec. (CRR) 820, Bankr. L. Rep. (CCH) ¶ 76386, 30 Fed. R. Serv. 3d 1184 (8th Cir. 1995) (successfully withdrawn bankruptcy claim leaves parties free to seek jury trial in fraudulent transfer action). Matter of Texas General Petroleum Corp., 52 F.3d 1330, 27 Bankr. Ct. Dec. (CRR) 399, Bankr. L. Rep. (CCH) ¶ 76512 (5th Cir. 1995) (no right to a jury trial on issue of whether a liquidating trustee has standing to assert a fraudulent conveyance action).

§ 1:15 —Mixed law and equity actions

Add at end of section:

Mixed law and equity actions continue to cause problems for the courts. In Lytle v. Household Mfg., Inc., 494 U.S. 545, 110 S. Ct. 1331, 108 L. Ed. 2d 504, 52 Fair Empl. Prac. Cas. (BNA) 423, 52 Empl. Prac. Dec. (CCH) ¶ 39733, 16 Fed. R. Serv. 3d 1 (1990), the plaintiff, who was black, alleged that the respondent had discharged him because of his race and had provided inadequate references to prospective employers because he had filed charges with the Equal Employment Opportunity Commission. He brought suit under both Title VII of the Civil Rights Act of 1964 and 42 U.S.C.A. § 1981. The district court ruled that plaintiff's exclusive remedies lay under Title VII and dismissed the § 1981 claims. The district court also denied plaintiff's request for a jury trial, which would have been available had the § 1981 claims not been dismissed. At the bench trial, the district court dismissed the discriminatory discharge claim upon completion of plaintiff's case-in-chief pursuant to a motion under Fed. R. Civ. P. 41(b). After both parties had presented their evidence, the court also entered judgment for the defendant on the retaliation claim.

The Fourth Circuit Court of Appeals affirmed, even though it agreed with the petitioner that the § 1981 claims had been erroneously dismissed. Nevertheless, it upheld the lower court judgment on the theory that the district court's findings in respect to the Title VII claim were entitled to collateral estoppel effect and precluded the petitioner from relitigating his § 1981 claims. The court rejected petitioner's Seventh Amendment argument that he had the right to submit the § 1981 claims to a jury and that therefore it was inappropriate to give collateral estoppel to the district court's findings. It stated that the judicial interest in economy of resources outweighed the petitioner's interest in relitigating the § 1981 claims before a jury.

The United States Supreme Court vacated the judgment. The Court noted that it had yet to decide whether a plaintiff had a right to a jury trial in a Title VII action, but stated that it would assume for purposes of the present action that there was no such right. The Court also acknowledged that under its decision in Parklane Hosiery Co., Inc. v. Shore, 439 U.S. 322, 99 S. Ct. 645, 58 L. Ed. 2d 552, Fed. Sec. L. Rep. (CCH) ¶ 96713, 26 Fed. R. Serv. 2d 669 (1979), a Court's determination of issues in an equitable action could collaterally estop a party from relitigating those same issues in a legal action, and that in such a case the party would not have been denied his constitutional right to a jury trial. The present case differed from *Parklane Hosiery Co*, however, in two key respects: first, here both the legal and equitable claims had been brought in the same action, and, second, the district court had erroneously dismissed the legal action. Under these circumstances, the Court held that collateral estoppel did not preclude relitigation of the legal issues before a jury.

The Supreme Court reasoned that the petitioner would have been entitled to a jury trial if his § 1981 claim had not been dismissed. This was so because when legal and equitable claims are joined, a party is entitled to a jury trial in regard to the legal claim. Indeed, under the Supreme Court's holdings in Beacon Theatres, Inc. v. Westover, 359 U.S. 500, 79 S. Ct. 948, 3 L. Ed. 2d 988, 2 Fed. R. Serv. 2d 650 (1959); and Dairy Queen, Inc. v. Wood, 369 U.S. 469, 82 S. Ct. 894, 8 L. Ed. 2d 44, 133 U.S.P.Q. (BNA) 294, 5 Fed. R. Serv. 2d 632 (1962), the jury would decide the legal claims before the judge could consider the equitable claims. As a result of the district court's incorrect ruling on the § 1981 claim, the plaintiff was denied the jury trial to which he was constitutionally entitled. The Court declined to extend *Parklane Hosiery Co* to accord collateral estoppel effect to the district court's determination of equitable issues which it decided first only because it had erroneously dismissed petitioner's legal claims. To rule otherwise, stated the Court, would be anomalous: It would mean that while a district court could not deprive a litigant of his Seventh Amendment right to a jury trial by resolving an equitable claim before the jury decided the legal claim brought in the same action, it could achieve the same result by improperly dismissing the legal claim.

Nor was the Supreme Court persuaded by the Fourth Circuit's argument of judicial economy. Petitioner had properly joined his two actions in a single suit. He was constitutionally entitled to a jury trial on his legal claim, and a new trial was therefore required in any event to vindicate this Seventh Amendment right. No other remedy would suffice. Considerations of judicial economy were not a sufficient counterweight to justify a different result.

The respondent also argued that the lower Court's judgment should be affirmed because the district court would have entered a directed verdict for the respondent on the § 1981 claims had they been raised in a jury trial, drawing this inference from the fact that the district court had dismissed the wrongful discharge claim under Fed. R. Civ. P. 41(b). The Supreme Court, however, answered that there was a significant distinction between a dismissal pursuant to Rule 41(b) and a directed verdict pursuant to Rule 50(a). Under Rule 41(b), the district court weighs the evidence as a trier of fact; under Rule 50(a), the district court does not weigh the evidence, but draws all factual inferences in favor of the nonmoving party. While a court in a bench trial may decide to grant a dismissal, it may in a jury trial reason that the jury might properly find for the nonmoving party and refuse to grant a directed verdict. Thus, the wrongful discharge claim had to be remanded for a jury trial. The case for remanding the retaliation claim was even stronger as the district court had declined to grant a dismissal in regard to it.

The Civil Rights Act of 1991, which came into force on November 21, 1991, allowed for a jury trial in Title VII cases. Whether this provision should be given retroactive effect was a matter of much dispute among federal circuits. Compare U.S. v. Department of Mental Health, 785 F. Supp. 846, 58 Fair Empl. Prac. Cas. (BNA) 727, 58 Empl. Prac. Dec. (CCH) ¶ 41314, 132 A.L.R. Fed. 671 (E.D. Cal. 1992); King v. Shelby Medical Center, 779 F. Supp. 157, 58 Fair Empl. Prac. Cas. (BNA) 435, 58 Empl. Prac. Dec. (CCH) ¶ 41317 (N.D. Ala. 1991) (holding jury trial provision retroactive) with Percell v. International Business Machines, Inc., 785 F. Supp. 1229, 61 Fair Empl. Prac. Cas. (BNA) 1060, 58 Empl. Prac. Dec. (CCH) ¶ 41323 (E.D. N.C. 1992); Doe v. Board of County Com'rs, Palm Beach County, Fla., 783 F. Supp. 1379, 58 Fair Empl. Prac. Cas. (BNA) 809, 58

Empl. Prac. Dec. (CCH) ¶ 41471 (S.D. Fla. 1992); Van Meter v. Barr, 778 F. Supp. 83, 57 Fair Empl. Prac. Cas. (BNA) 769, 57 Empl. Prac. Dec. (CCH) ¶ 41209 (D.D.C. 1991) (rejecting retroactive application of jury trial provision). In Landgraf v. USI Film Products, 511 U.S. 244, 114 S. Ct. 1483, 128 L. Ed. 2d 229 (1994), the dispute was resolved by the United States Supreme Court. The Court held that the jury trial provisions of the 1991 Act were not to be applied retroactively. The Court indicated that generally the right to a jury trial was the sort of procedural change that would be given retroactive effect, and applied to trials where the underlying conduct occurred before the passage of the act but the trial after the passage of the Act. However, it distinguished the 1991 Act on the ground that the jury trial provision contained in it was inextricably linked to the creation of the right to compensatory and punitive damages. Since the Court held that this right was not to apply retroactively, it followed that the jury provision attached to it would not apply retroactively either.

In Madison v. IBP, Inc., 257 F.3d 780, 86 Fair Empl. Prac. Cas. (BNA) 77, 80 Empl. Prac. Dec. (CCH) ¶ 40628 (8th Cir. 2001), cert. granted, judgment vacated on other grounds, 536 U.S. 919, 122 S. Ct. 2583, 153 L. Ed. 2d 773, 88 Fair Empl. Prac. Cas. (BNA) 1887 (2002) the Court of Appeals held that the damages limitation provision in Title VII did not violate the Seventh Amendment. In Allison v. Citgo Petroleum Corp., 151 F.3d 402, 81 Fair Empl. Prac. Cas. (BNA) 501, 73 Empl. Prac. Dec. (CCH) ¶ 45426 (5th Cir. 1998) the court stated that once a right to jury trial attached to a claim, it extended to all aspects of that claim. In *Allison*, a Title VII action, the statutory right to jury trial applied only to the plaintiffs' pattern or practice claim, and not their disparate impact claim. Nonetheless, the court held that the right to jury trial extended to the factual issues necessary to determine liability on the pattern or practice claim and the recovery of compensatory and punitive damages. In Cooper Industries, Inc. v. Leatherman Tool Group, Inc., 532 U.S. 424, 121 S. Ct. 1678, 149 L. Ed. 2d 674, 58 U.S.P.Q.2d (BNA) 1641 (2001), the United States Supreme Court stated that a jury's award of punitive damages was not a finding of fact, and therefore appellate review of a district court's determination that the award was consistent with due process did not impair the prevailing party's right to jury trial. See also In re Exxon Valdez, 270 F.3d 1215, 2002 A.M.C. 1, 32 Envtl. L. Rep. 20320, 154 O.G.R. 1 (9th Cir. 2001). The implications of the Court's decision are examined in Litwiller, *Has the Supreme Court Sounded the Death Knell for Jury Assessment of Punitive Damages?*, 36 U. San Fran. L. Rev. 411 (2002).

In Ag Services of America, Inc. v. Nielsen, 231 F.3d 726 (10th Cir. 2000), cert. denied, 532 U.S. 1021, 121 S. Ct. 1961, 149 L. Ed. 2d 757 (2001), a jury had found for the plaintiff on the basis of its legal theory of the case. The trial judge, however, suspected that the verdict was either erroneous or a compromise, and entered judgment for the defendant on equitable grounds. The Court of Appeals held that the judge's action was in violation of the plaintiff's Seventh Amendment right to jury trial. If the trial court believed that the verdict was against the evidence and unsupportable, the proper course would have been for the court to set the verdict aside pursuant to Fed. R. Civ. P. 59(a). The decision in *Ag Services of America v. Nielsen* can be compared with that in Ed Peters Jewelry Co., Inc. v. C & J Jewelry Co., Inc., 215 F.3d 182, 46 Fed. R. Serv. 3d 1130 (1st Cir. 2000), where the district court had ruled, sua sponte, and without prior notice to the parties, that three of the counts in the case sounded in equity and therefore would not be submitted to the jury. This ruling was upheld on appeal. The critical distinction between this case and *Ag Services* relates to whether the court decides that issues are equitable before or after there has been a jury verdict. If before, the court may decide the issues for itself. If after, the court is bound by the jury's verdict. The Court of Appeals in *Ed Peters Jewelry*, however, was not approving of the approach of the trial court, suggesting that the court should have given the parties advance notice of how it intended to address the issues.

In re Friedberg, 131 B.R. 6 (S.D. N.Y. 1991), involved a number of claims arising from the complex financial dealings between the parties, and raised the issue of whether the plaintiff was entitled to a jury trial. The court first had to determine whether the action brought by the plaintiff was one for contract or tort. Looking to state law, the court found that plaintiff's suit was one in tort for rescission of a contract plus incidental damages. Rescission being an equitable remedy, the court concluded that the plaintiff was not entitled to a jury trial. The plaintiff had brought an additional action, however, alleging a statutory violation relating to unfair trade practices. This the court found to be legal in nature, in part because the plaintiff was not seeking equitable relief. It therefore held that the plaintiff was entitled to a jury trial, and that the jury could decide any factual issues common to all the claims. Finally the court held that the plaintiff did not submit to the equitable jurisdiction of the bankruptcy court, and thereby waive his right to a jury trial, by requesting court approval of a proposed transaction.

Whether a contract action is legal or equitable may turn on the remedy sought. The court in Fischer Imaging Corp. v.

General Elec. Co., 187 F.3d 1165, 39 U.C.C. Rep. Serv. 2d 324 (10th Cir. 1999) explained: whereas breach of contract actions seeking monetary damages were historically tried to a jury, actions seeking reformation of a contract or specific performance were tried to a judge. In the case, brought by the seller, the court held that the action was properly characterized as one at law, entitling the seller to a jury trial. The remedy for the erroneous denial of a jury trial was held to be a new trial before a jury. In Enserch Corp. v. Shand Morahan & Co., Inc., 952 F.2d 1485 (5th Cir. 1992), as clarified on denial of reh'g, (Mar. 9, 1992), the equitable nature of the remedy sought, contract reformation, led the court to find that the parties were not entitled to a jury trial even where there was conflicting evidence of historical facts. In contrast, in Borgh v. Gentry, 953 F.2d 1309, 22 Fed. R. Serv. 3d 114 (11th Cir. 1992), a breach of contract action was held to be legal in nature and one to which there was no right to a jury trial. See also F.D.I.C. v. Marine Midland Realty Credit Corp., 17 F.3d 715 (4th Cir. 1994) (receiver of failed financial institution entitled to jury trial in action for both compensatory damages and equitable relief). The availability of jury trial in cases wherein provisions of the U.C.C. are at issue is explored in Moses, *The Jury-Trial Right in the U.C.C.: On a Slippery Slope*, 54 S.M.U. L. Rev. 561 (2001).

In Del Monte Dunes at Monterey, Ltd. v. City of Monterey, 95 F.3d 1422, 27 Envtl. L. Rep. 20139 (9th Cir. 1996), aff'd, 526 U.S. 687, 119 S. Ct. 1624, 143 L. Ed. 2d 882, 48 Env't. Rep. Cas. (BNA) 1513, 29 Envtl. L. Rep. 21133 (1999), it was held that an inverse condemnation claim under 42 U.S.C.A. § 1983 was an action at law which entitled the property owner to a jury trial. Eminent domain proceedings, in which there is no right to a jury trial, were distinguished because of the fact that the government is a party to the suit. The Supreme Court affirmed in City of Monterey v. Del Monte Dunes at Monterey, Ltd., 526 U.S. 687, 119 S. Ct. 1624, 143 L. Ed. 2d 882, 48 Env't. Rep. Cas. (BNA) 1513, 29 Envtl. L. Rep. 21133 (1999). The Court accepted that Section 1983 did not itself confer a right to jury trial, nor did the fact that the Section referred to 'an action at law' necessarily imply a right to jury trial. Thus the Court was required to address the question of whether the Seventh Amendment conferred a right to jury trial. Although there was no action equivalent to Section 1983 at the time that the Seventh Amendment was adopted, claims brought pursuant to Section 1983 were analogous to common law tort actions, for which jury trial was available. The Court reasoned that a Section 1983 suit seeking damages for a constitutional violation was seeking legal relief and therefore should be considered an action at law within the meaning of the Seventh Amendment. The Court rejected the City's argument that there should be an exception to the general Seventh Amendment rule governing Section 1983 actions in cases alleging violations of the Takings Clause of the Fifth Amendment. Although there may be no constitutional right to jury trial in a formal condemnation proceeding (See U.S. v. Reynolds, 397 U.S. 14, 18, 90 S. Ct. 803, 25 L. Ed. 2d 12 (1970)), that was held to be an inapposite analogy, for there were fundamental differences between a condemnation proceeding (where the state conceded the right to just compensation) and a Section 1983 action to redress an uncompensated taking (where the state was resisting the payment of any compensation). The Court stated that the more appropriate analogy was to tort actions at common law to recover damages for interference with property interests.

In Mile High Industries v. Cohen, 222 F.3d 845, 47 Fed. R. Serv. 3d 778 (10th Cir. 2000), the plaintiff argued that the defendant's affirmative defenses of laches and estoppel by acquiescence presented new issues requiring a jury trial. The trial court, however, ruled that these defenses related directly to the equitable foreclosure action and that the basic issues that had to be resolved had not changed. The Court of Appeals agreed, stating that in the context of the case, the defenses were equitable in nature and triable by the court.

Del Monte Dunes was distinguished in Buckles v. King County, 191 F.3d 1127 (9th Cir. 1999). The plaintiffs argued that the zoning of their property for residential use amounted to a "taking" and that this entitled them to a jury trial under the Seventh Amendment. Unlike in *Del Monte Dunes*, however, the facts were uncontested, leaving the trial court in a position to decide the case on summary judgment as a matter of law. New Port Largo, Inc. v. Monroe County, 95 F.3d 1084, 27 Envtl. L. Rep. 20170 (11th Cir. 1996) involved a rezoning determination, and the court held that there was no right to a jury trial, although there might be "subsidiary fact" questions that would warrant the impaneling of a jury. See also U.S. v. Keller, 142 F.3d 718, 40 Fed. R. Serv. 3d 643, 28 Envtl. L. Rep. 21193, 164 A.L.R. Fed. 759 (4th Cir. 1998) (no constitutional right to jury trial in federal condemnation proceedings).

Newfound Management Corp. v. Lewis, 131 F.3d 108, 39 Fed. R. Serv. 3d 14 (3d Cir. 1997) involved an action for both quiet title (traditionally lying in equity) and trespass (traditionally legal). The consolidation of the two actions did not prevent the trial court from first resolving the issue of the proper boundaries in the quiet title suit before submitting the trespass claims to the jury.

§ 1:16 —Complex litigation

n. 109.

Add to note 109:
See also Lilly, *The Decline of the American Jury*, 72 U. Colo. L. Rev. 53 (2001) (examining the long-term viability of civil juries, particularly in complex litigation, in light of modern jury selection processes); Note, *The Constitutionality of a Complexity Exception to the Seventh Amendment*, 73 Chicago-Kent L. Rev. 865 (1998) (maintaining that a complexity exception existed at common law, and drawing further support for nonjury trial in complex cases from the Supreme Court's reference in *Markman v. Westview Instruments* (supp) to the relevance of 'functional considerations' in determining whether jury trial was required).

Add after sixth sentence in section:
Professor Vidmar examined the numerous studies of the jury's ability to deal with complex medical evidence and concluded that the case against the jury's competency had yet to be made. Vidmar, *Are Juries Competent to Decide Liability in Tort Cases involving Scientific/Medical Issues? Some Data from Medical Malpractice*, 43 Emory LJ 885 (1994). More generally, See Vidmar, *The Performance of the American Civil Jury: An Empirical Perspective*, 40 Arizona Law Rev. 849 (1998) (research does not support claims juries are moved by sympathy for plaintiffs or against deep pocket defendants, and generally reach same result as would a judge).

n. 112.

Add to note 112 after "United States Fin Sec Litig":
; Green Const. Co. v. Kansas Power & Light Co., 1 F.3d 1005, 26 Fed. R. Serv. 3d 1459 (10th Cir. 1993) (complexity of dispute did not warrant denial of request for jury trial).

Add at end of section:
One possible compromise would be to retain juries in complex litigation, but to seek jurors with the requisite knowledge and expertise to understand the issues raised by the case. See Schwarzer, *Reforming Jury Trials*, 132 FRD 575, 580 (1990); Strier, *The Educated Jury: A Proposal for Complex Litigation*, 47 DePaul L. Rev. 49 (1997) (proposing that ½ of the jurors in complex cases should be college graduates).

§ 1:17 —Written demand

Add after first sentence in section:
A failure to comply with a local rule of procedure will not in federal court invalidate a jury demand which meets the applicable federal rules of civil procedure. Partee v. Buch, 28 F.3d 636, 65 Fair Empl. Prac. Cas. (BNA) 590, 29 Fed. R. Serv. 3d 421 (7th Cir. 1994). But compare Bruns v. Amana,

131 F.3d 761, 39 Fed. R. Serv. 3d 772 (8th Cir. 1997) (failure to comply with a local rule relating to the timing of demand for a jury trial can be deemed a waiver of the right) Where a demand for a jury trial has been properly made in state court, and the case is subsequently removed to federal court, the demand for jury trial is preserved under Fed. R. Civ. Pro. 81. See, e.g., Winter v. Minnesota Mut. Life Ins. Co., 199 F.3d 399 (7th Cir. 1999).

Whether an inadvertent failure to demand a jury trial is excusable has divided the appellate courts. Compare Hoffmann v. Alside, Inc., 596 F.2d 822, 19 Fair Empl. Prac. Cas. (BNA) 825, 19 Empl. Prac. Dec. (CCH) ¶ 9187 (8th Cir. 1979) (judge may permit voluntary dismissal and refiling in order to preserve jury trial right) with Russ v. Standard Ins. Co., 120 F.3d 988, 38 Fed. R. Serv. 3d 211 (9th Cir. 1997). A particularly pertinent factor, it is submitted, should be the stage at which jury trial is sought. The further the case has proceeded without a jury, and certainly after a verdict has been returned, the less sympathetically is a court likely to look on the failure to request a jury trial. Conversely, given the central role accorded juries in the American legal system, it is submitted that courts should be receptive to allowing refiling (the approach of the court in *Hoffman v Alside, Inc.*) where there has been a technical failure to comply with statutory requirements but where correction of the oversight will not significantly disrupt the trial process.

n. 114.

Add to note 114:

What constitutes a timely demand is obviously a critical issue. Section 38(d) requires that the demand be served no later than 10 days after the Service of the last pleading. This provision shifts the focus to what constitutes a pleading. Federal Rule of Civil Procedure 7(a) states that "there shall be a complaint and an answer; a reply to a counterclaim denominated as such; an answer to a cross-claim . . .; a third-party complaint . . .; and a third-party answer. . . . No other pleading shall be allowed. . . ." Burns v. Lawther, 53 F.3d 1237 (11th Cir. 1995), the Court of Appeals held that in light of this federal rule, the special reports filed by the defendants in the case at the direction of the magistrate did not qualify as pleadings and that therefore a motion for a jury trial filed nine months after the special reports but within 10 days of the defendant's answer was not untimely. See also Frost v. Agnos, 152 F.3d 1124, 41 Fed. R. Serv. 3d 538 (9th Cir. 1998) (as the demand for jury trial was made prior to the filing of an answer by one of the defendants, the right to jury trial was not waived even though the demand was made longer than 10 days after the answer of the other defendants).

What constitutes a "demand" for a jury trial was at issue in U.S. v. Rapone, 131 F.3d 188, 72 Empl. Prac. Dec. (CCH) ¶ 45136 (D.C. Cir. 1997). The court stated that no specific form of words was required. In the case the "demand" was couched in language that appeared to appeal to the trial court's discretion, but the Court of Appeals understood the petitioners to be seeking a jury trial and this was held to be sufficient compliance with the statutory requirement. The additional factor that the petitioners had not cited the relevant statute was also deemed not to defeat their demand for a jury trial.

n. 116.
Add to note 116:
see, e.g., Kletzelman v. Capistrano Unified School Dist., 91 F.3d 68, 17 A.D.D. 1417, 35 Fed. R. Serv. 3d 942 (9th Cir. 1996) (while a court has the discretion to allow a jury trial despite an untimely demand, this discretion is narrow and inapplicable when the failure to make a timely demand is the result of oversight or inadvertence); Pacific Fisheries Corp. v. HIH Cas. & General Ins., Ltd., 239 F.3d 1000, 2001 A.M.C. 952, 49 Fed. R. Serv. 3d 278 (9th Cir. 2001), cert. denied, 534 U.S. 944, 122 S. Ct. 324, 151 L. Ed. 2d 242 (2001) (same); Zivkovic v. Southern California Edison Co., 302 F.3d 1080, 13 A.D. Cas. (BNA) 882, 53 Fed. R. Serv. 3d 1179 (9th Cir. 2002) (same); Dill v. City of Edmond, Okl., 155 F.3d 1193, 14 I.E.R. Cas. (BNA) 498 (10th Cir. 1998) (district court does not abuse its discretion in denying Rule 39(b) motion when failure to make a timely jury demand is due to inadvertence or oversight); BCCI Holdings (Luxembourg), S.A. v. Khalil, 214 F.3d 168, R.I.C.O. Bus. Disp. Guide (CCH) ¶ 9886 (D.C. Cir. 2000) (same).

A court may exercise its discretion, however, and grant a jury trial despite lack of a timely demand, particularly when there will not be prejudice to the opposing party. See, e.g., Moody v. Pepsi-Cola Metropolitan Bottling Co., Inc., 915 F.2d 201, 56 Fair Empl. Prac. Cas. (BNA) 1491, 54 Empl. Prac. Dec. (CCH) ¶ 40228, 117 Lab. Cas. (CCH) ¶ 56441, 17 Fed. R. Serv. 3d 1393 (6th Cir. 1990). See also Federal Deposit Ins. Corp. v. Cafritz, 770 F. Supp. 28 (D.D.C. 1991); Waldermeyer v. ITT Consumer Financial Corp., 767 F. Supp. 989, 55 Fair Empl. Prac. Cas. (BNA) 1598, 6 I.E.R. Cas. (BNA) 1241, 57 Empl. Prac. Dec. (CCH) ¶ 40974, 118 Lab. Cas. (CCH) ¶ 35490 (E.D. Mo. 1991); Green Const. Co. v. Kansas Power & Light Co., 1 F.3d 1005, 26 Fed. R. Serv. 3d 1459 (10th Cir. 1993) (jury trial should be granted absent "strong and compelling reasons to the contrary" even if not requested within the 10-day time limit).

In U.S. S.E.C. v. Infinity Group Co., 212 F.3d 180, Fed. Sec. L. Rep. (CCH) ¶ 90966, 55 Fed. R. Evid. Serv. 185, 46 Fed. R. Serv. 3d 625 (3d Cir. 2000), cert. denied, 532 U.S. 905, 121 S. Ct. 1228, 149 L. Ed. 2d 138 (2001) the court identified the relevant factors which needed to be considered in determining whether to grant an untimely demand for a jury trial (whether the issues were suitable for a jury trial; whether granting the motion would disrupt the schedule of the court or the adverse party; whether any prejudice would result to the adverse party; how long the party delayed in bringing the motion; and the reasons for the failure to file a timely demand) concluded that the fact that the party had changed counsel two months prior to making their jury demand (two weeks before trial) was not enough to offset the material prejudice to the government that would have resulted from granting the motion. Nor were the issues in the case particularly suitable for jury trial. The Court of Appeals concluded that under the circumstances the district court had not abused its discretion in denying the delayed demand for a jury. See also Huff v. Dobbins, Fraker, Tennant, Joy & Perlstein, 243 F.3d 1086, 49 Fed. R. Serv. 3d 228 (7th Cir. 2001) (plaintiff's request for jury trial, filed after second amended complaint and approximately two years after defendant's answer to initial complaint was untimely).

n. 117.
Add to note 117:

§ 1:17

Richards v. Procter & Gamble Mfg. Co., 753 F. Supp. 71, 19 Fed. R. Serv. 3d 185 (E.D. N.Y. 1991) (counsel's inadvertence and ignorance of federal rules not an excuse warranting a court to exercise its discretion and grant an untimely demand for a jury trial). U.S. v. Keller, 142 F.3d 718, 40 Fed. R. Serv. 3d 643, 28 Envtl. L. Rep. 21193, 164 A.L.R. Fed. 759 (4th Cir. 1998) (neither the absence of counsel, nor the failure of the government to inform landowners that they needed to demand jury trial, nor the fact that the government initially demanded a jury trial, was sufficient to excuse an untimely demand in a federal condemnation proceeding).

n. 118.

Add to note 118:

In Fuller v. City of Oakland, Cal., 47 F.3d 1522, 67 Fair Empl. Prac. Cas. (BNA) 153, 67 Fair Empl. Prac. Cas. (BNA) 992, 65 Empl. Prac. Dec. (CCH) ¶ 43431, 31 Fed. R. Serv. 3d 617 (9th Cir. 1995), as amended, (Apr. 24, 1995), the Court of Appeals held that once a trial had begun, a party could not unilaterally withdraw its demand for a jury. The other parties to the litigation were entitled to rely on the party's initial request regardless of whether they had waived their own rights to a jury trial. Withdrawal may be effected only through compliance with the appropriate federal rules of civil procedure. Where there is no entitlement to a jury trial, but one is held with the consent of both parties, the verdict of the jury has the same effect as if trial by jury had been as a matter of right. Gloria v. Valley Grain Products, Inc., 72 F.3d 497, 69 Fair Empl. Prac. Cas. (BNA) 1163 (5th Cir. 1996).

Add after second paragraph:

If a party does not make a demand for a jury trial, the case will be tried by the court. The Federal Rules, however, provide that "notwithstanding the failure of a party to demand a jury in an action in which such a demand might have been made of right, the court in its discretion upon motion may order a trial by a jury of any and all issues." Fed. R. Civ. P. 39(b). In Parrott v. Wilson, 707 F.2d 1262, 1267, 13 Fed. R. Evid. Serv. 1149 (11th Cir. 1983), the Eleventh Circuit Court of Appeals identified five factors relevant to the Court's discretion:

(1) Whether the case involved issues best tried by a jury;
(2) Whether granting the motion would disrupt the Court's or the adverse party's schedule;
(3) How greatly the adverse party would be prejudiced;
(4) How long the moving party had delayed in bringing the motion; and
(5) Why the movant had failed to file a timely demand for jury trial.

Citing these factors, the district court in Lee v. Boyle-Midway Household Products, Inc., 785 F. Supp. 533 (W.D. Pa. 1992), declined to exercise its discretion to grant a jury trial under 39(b) where the failure to demand the jury trial was the result of counsel's inadvertence or oversight. See also Annotation, Right to jury trial in action under state civil rights law, 12 A.L.R. 5th 508.

Also citing the factors identified in the Federal Rules, the Court of Appeals in U.S. S.E.C. v. Infinity Group Co., 212 F.3d 180, Fed. Sec. L. Rep. (CCH) ¶ 90966, 55 Fed. R. Evid. Serv. 185, 46 Fed. R. Serv. 3d 625 (3d Cir. 2000), cert. denied, 532 U.S. 905, 121 S. Ct. 1228, 149 L. Ed. 2d 138 (2001) found that that the explanation for the delayed motion for a jury trial, a change of counsel two months prior to the delayed demand and two weeks before trial, was not enough to offset the material prejudice to the government that would have resulted from the granting of the late motion. Nor were the issues in the case particularly suitable for jury trial. The Court of Appeals concluded that under the circumstances the district court had not abused its discretion in denying the delayed demand for a jury. See also Huff v. Dobbins, Fraker, Tennant, Joy & Perlstein, 243 F.3d 1086, 49 Fed. R. Serv. 3d 228 (7th Cir. 2001) (plaintiff's request for jury trial, filed after second amended complaint and approximately two years after defendant's answer to initial complaint was untimely).

§ 1:18 —State civil trials
n. 119.
Add to note 119:
Although the Seventh Amendment does not apply in state courts, it does apply when a federal court is called upon to determine rights arising out of state law, the *Erie* doctrine notwithstanding. Byrd v. Blue Ridge Rural Elec. Co-op., Inc., 356 U.S. 525, 537–38, 78 S. Ct. 893, 2 L. Ed. 2d 953 (1958); Hattaway v. McMillian, 903 F.2d 1440, 16 Fed. R. Serv. 3d 1177 (11th Cir. 1990). See also Pickens v. Soo Line Railroad Co., 264 F.3d 773, 12 A.D. Cas. (BNA) 333 (8th Cir. 2001), cert. denied, 535 U.S. 1057, 122 S. Ct. 1917, 152 L. Ed. 2d 826, 13 A.D. Cas. (BNA) 96 (2002) (right to jury trial in federal court is a question of federal law, even when federal court is enforcing state-created rights and obligations and even when a state statute or state constitution would preclude jury trial in state court).

Add after fourth sentence:
The cost of a jury trial may permissibly be shifted to the parties. In Butler v. Supreme Judicial Court, 611 A.2d 987 (Me. 1992), the court held that a $300 fee payable to the state upon demand of a jury trial did not unreasonably restrict the right to a civil jury trial. See also Wade v. Oglesby, 74 Ohio App. 3d 560, 599 N.E.2d 748 (6th Dist. Huron County 1991).

Add after last sentence in paragraph:
For a compendium of cases from small claims court raising the issue of a right to a jury, See Annotation, Constitutional

§ 1:18   JURY SELECTION: LAW, ART & SCIENCE 2D

right to jury trial in cause of action under state unfair or deceptive trade practices law, 54 A.L.R. 5th 631. In respect to whether a litigant is entitled to a jury trial in a state court action involving unfair or deceptive trade practices, See Annotation, Constitutional Right to Jury Trial in Cause of Action under State Unfair or Deceptive Trade Practices Law, 54 A.L.R. 5th 631 (right to jury trial will usually turn on whether the cause of action is deemed legal, in which case a jury is available, or equitable, in which case there is no right to a jury, with the majority of state courts taking the position that there is no right to a jury trial on the ground that there was no such action at common law).

In respect to whether a litigant is entitled to jury trial in civil court determinations affecting the parent-child relationship, see Annotation, Right to Jury Trial in Child Neglect, Child Abuse, or Termination of Parental Rights Proceedings, 102 A.L.R. 5th 227 (collecting cases which show that whether jury trial is available usually turns on the interpretation of the state constitution or whether there is a specific state statute on point; e.g., In re Adoption of A.F.M., 15 P.3d 258, 102 A.L.R.5th 701 (Alaska 2001) (no right to jury trial under Alaska statute providing for termination of biological father's rights in adoption proceeding by another man, at least where child's conception resulted from a sexual assault)).

§ 1:20 Waiver of the right to a jury

n. 126.

Add to note 126:

But see People v. Kirby, 440 Mich. 485, 487 N.W.2d 404 (1992) (no constitutional right to waive a jury).

Add at end of section:

In Haynes v. W.C. Caye & Co., Inc., 52 F.3d 928, 67 Fair Empl. Prac. Cas. (BNA) 1537, 67 Fair Empl. Prac. Cas. (BNA) 1755, 66 Empl. Prac. Dec. (CCH) ¶ 43559, 32 Fed. R. Serv. 3d 268 (11th Cir. 1995), the court found that where both sides had signed an order contemplating trial before a magistrate judge, and the plaintiff did not object to the nonjury trial until after the magistrate judge had issued a report and recommendation, the plaintiff had waived her right to a jury trial.

A party does not waive a previously made request for a jury trial by moving for summary judgment or by not objecting to an opponent's motion for summary judgment. Winter v. Minnesota Mut. Life Ins. Co., 199 F.3d 399 (7th Cir. 1999).

§ 1:21 —Indirect waiver of jury by waiver of trial

Add after first sentence in first paragraph:

See, e.g., Briley v. Carlin, 172 F.3d 567, 79 Fair Empl. Prac. Cas. (BNA) 1630, 76 Empl. Prac. Dec. (CCH) ¶ 46068 (8th Cir. 1999) (nothing in 1991 Civil Rights Act prevents government agency from waiving its right to a jury trial in regard to compensatory damages—whether by settlement or otherwise). Participation in a bench trial without objection also constitutes a waiver of one's right to a jury trial. Preferred RX, Inc. v. American Prescription Plan, Inc., 46 F.3d 535, 1995 FED App. 0046P (6th Cir. 1995). Likewise, the failure to make a timely objection to a court order establishing a bench trial constitutes a waiver of one's right to a jury trial. Transmatic, Inc. v. Gulton Industries, Inc., 53 F.3d 1270, 35 U.S.P.Q.2d (BNA) 1035 (Fed. Cir. 1995). See also Wilcher v. City of Wilmington, 139 F.3d 366, 13 I.E.R. Cas. (BNA) 1345, 40 Fed. R. Serv. 3d 934 (3d Cir. 1998) (plaintiffs waived right to jury trial when they acquiesced in district court's dismissal of jury).

In Flemming ex rel. Estate of Flemming v. Air Sunshine, Inc., 311 F.3d 282 (3d Cir. 2002), the surviving spouse of a passenger who had drowned following an airplane crash brought a wrongful death action, individually and as the personal representative of the passenger's estate, against the insured airline and the pilot. A partial settlement was reached under which the insured paid the spouse $500,000 in exchange for release of all claims. Certain issues, however, were reserved for the district court. The district court ruled that the spouse could not recover beyond the settlement amount and the plaintiff appealed. One of the issues in the appeal was whether the spouse had waived her Seventh Amendment right to a jury trial as a result of the partial settlement. The Court of Appeals concluded that the plaintiff had waived this right by entering into the partial settlement agreement and by subsequently acquiescing in allowing the district court to resolve remaining issues.

Add after second sentence in first paragraph:
Where an arbitration agreement is in force, a party may nonetheless be able to obtain a jury trial by showing that under prevailing law he would be relieved of the contractual obligation to arbitrate if his allegations proved to be true. See, Dillard v. Merrill Lynch, Pierce, Fenner & Smith, Inc., 961 F.2d 1148, Fed. Sec. L. Rep. (CCH) ¶ 96817 (5th Cir. 1992).

Add after third sentence in first paragraph:
In Sydnor v. Conseco Financial Servicing Corp., 252 F.3d 302 (4th Cir. 2001) the court stated that while federal policy broadly favors arbitration, a trial court must first determine whether or not there was in fact an agreement to arbitrate

§ 1:21   JURY SELECTION: LAW, ART & SCIENCE 2D

between the parties. Where there is a valid agreement, the parties waive their right to jury trial. See also Burden v. Check into Cash of Kentucky, LLC, 267 F.3d 483, R.I.C.O. Bus. Disp. Guide (CCH) ¶ 10181, 2001 FED App. 0349P (6th Cir. 2001), cert. denied, 535 U.S. 970, 122 S. Ct. 1436, 152 L. Ed. 2d 380 (2002).

A contractual agreement to waive a jury trial is legally enforceable. See, e.g., Smyly v. Hyundai Motor America, 762 F. Supp. 428 (D. Mass. 1991). See also, Medical Air Technology Corp. v. Marwan Inv., Inc., 303 F.3d 11 (1st Cir. 2002), cert. denied, 537 U.S. 1111, 123 S. Ct. 893, 154 L. Ed. 2d 783 (2003) (contractual waiver binds only parties who signed contract and courts will look to the plain language of the waiver provision to determine whether it unambiguously covers the claims asserted); Okura & Co. (America), Inc. v. Careau Group, 783 F. Supp. 482 (C.D. Cal. 1991) (jury waiver contained in loan documents, promissory notes, and guaranty did not violate public policy). If the contract provision waiving jury trial is secured by fraud or overreaching, on the other hand, the provision may be set aside. See Chase Commercial Corp. v. Owen, 32 Mass. App. Ct. 248, 588 N.E.2d 705 (1992) (accepting general principle, but finding valid jury waiver where contract negotiated between experienced business parties at arm's length, even though result was contract of adhesion). Compare Hulsey v. West, 966 F.2d 579 (10th Cir. 1992) (guarantor not bound by jury waiver provision where guarantor did not sign in individual capacity, and loan agreement containing jury waiver was executed four years after guarantor executed personal guaranty); Fairfield Leasing Corp. v. Techni-Graphics, Inc., 256 N.J. Super. 538, 607 A.2d 703, 18 U.C.C. Rep. Serv. 2d 713 (Law Div. 1992) (non-negotiated jury waiver clause that appeared inconspicuously in a standardized form contract entered into without assistance of counsel held nonenforceable). Paracor Finance, Inc. v. General Elec. Capital Corp., 96 F.3d 1151, Blue Sky L. Rep. (CCH) ¶ 74088, Fed. Sec. L. Rep. (CCH) ¶ 99315 (9th Cir. 1996) (waiver of jury trial in contract creates contractual right which generally cannot be invoked by one who is not a party to the contract). See generally Annotation, Contractual jury trial waivers in state civil cases, 42 A.L.R. 5th 53. While parties may agree to arbitration and waiver of a jury trial, whether such an agreement has been entered into is a matter of contract law, and subject to jury trial. See Avedon Engineering, Inc. v. Seatex, 126 F.3d 1279, 33 U.C.C. Rep. Serv. 2d 1039 (10th Cir. 1997).

In Middle Tennessee News Co., Inc. v. Charnel of Cincinnati, Inc., 250 F.3d 1077, 50 Fed. R. Serv. 3d 200, 186 A.L.R. Fed. 621 (7th Cir. 2001), a breach of contract action, the Court of Appeals held that Charnel had not waived its

Right to Jury Trial § 1:21

right to jury trial when the district court entered an order submitting the issues in the case to an independent accountant for resolution. Charnel had objected to the order and had filed two motions and accompanying memoranda seeking to correct the order. It did not participate in the independent accountant proceedings to avoid any inference that it consented to the waiver of a jury. Under the circumstances there was not the "clear, unequivocal evidence" of waiver of jury trial that is required and the trial court erred in entering judgment based on the independent accountant's report.

Add after fifth sentence in first paragraph:
See Herman Miller, Inc. v. Thom Rock Realty Co., L.P., 46 F.3d 183 (2d Cir. 1995) (upholding jury waiver provision in lease).

Add after last sentence in first paragraph:
See generally Syverud, *ADR and the Decline of the American Civil Jury*, 44 UCLA L. Rev. 1935 (1997).

Add after fourth sentence in second paragraph:
In U.S. v. Libretti, 38 F.3d 523 (10th Cir. 1994), judgment aff'd, 516 U.S. 29, 116 S. Ct. 356, 133 L. Ed. 2d 271 (1995), the Court of Appeals held, without deciding whether a defendant had a right to a jury trial in a forfeiture proceeding, that by agreeing to a guilty plea which included a forfeiture provision, the defendant waived any right that he might have had to a jury trial to determine which property was subject to forfeiture. The case went to the U.S. Supreme Court, and the Court stated that the right to a jury determination of forfeiture did not fall within the Sixth Amendment's constitutional ambit. Libretti v. U.S., 516 U.S. 29, 116 S. Ct. 356, 133 L. Ed. 2d 271 (1995). The Court viewed forfeiture as part of sentencing, where there is no right to jury trial See McMillan v. Pennsylvania, 477 U.S. 79, 106 S. Ct. 2411, 91 L. Ed. 2d 67 (1986). The Court added that a trial court could (and in some instances probably should) advise a defendant when a guilty plea will result in the loss of a statutory right to a jury determination of forfeitability, and of course counsel should bring this consequence of pleading guilty to the defendant's attention, but the Constitution did not go so far as to require either the judge or counsel to do so.

n. 129.
Add to note 129:
A waiver of jury trial will occur in respect to an element of an offense where the defendant admits to the element. U.S. v. Wittgenstein, 163 F.3d 1164 (10th Cir. 1998).

The issue in U.S. v. Leachman, 309 F.3d 377, 2002 FED App. 0353P

(6th Cir. 2002), cert. denied, 123 S. Ct. 1769, 155 L. Ed. 2d 527 (U.S. 2003), was whether a plea of guilty, which indisputably waives the right to a jury trial on the question of guilt, also waives the right to a jury trial in instances where, under *Apprendi* (see § 1:13A) a defendant is entitled to a jury trial before a sentence exceeding the statutory maximum can be imposed. The Court of Appeals held that *Apprendi* only extended a defendant's due process and Sixth Amendment rights to factors that enhanced a sentence beyond the statutory maximum, and that these constitutional rights were subject to the ordinary rules of waiver. In the future the critical question in cases such as *Leachman* will be whether a trial judge has to inform the defendant specifically that his rights under *Apprendi* are being waived in order that the defendant's waiver will be deemed knowing and voluntary.

Arguably the key issue that needs to be addressed in respect to waiver is whether the trial judge has to specifically inform a defendant that rights under *Apprendi* are being waived in order for the waiver to be deemed knowing and voluntary. In U.S. v. Minore, 292 F.3d 1109 (9th Cir. 2002), cert. denied, 537 U.S. 1146, 123 S. Ct. 948, 154 L. Ed. 2d 848 (2003), the Court of Appeals held, as a matter of first impression, that the trial court must advise the defendant of the government's obligation under *Apprendi* to prove to a jury drug quantity by proof beyond a reasonable doubt before accepting a guilty plea. When drug quantity exposes the defendant to a higher statutory maximum sentence than he would otherwise receive, it becomes the functional equivalent of a "critical element" of the offense. Under F.R. Crim. P. 11(c)(1) governing acceptance of guilty pleas, as well as under principles of due process, the trial court must advise the defendant on each "critical element" of the offense. Accordingly, the trial court must advise defendant that, if the case went to trial, the government would have to prove drug quantity by proof beyond a reasonable doubt. But compare U.S. v. Hurlich, 293 F.3d 1223 (10th Cir. 2002) where the Court of Appeals, in a somewhat analogous situation, held that a defendant's waiver of jury trial was valid despite the failure of the trial court to inform the defendant of the possibility that his federal sentence could run consecutive to his state sentence. The Court of Appeals in *Hurlich*, however, did encourage district courts to inform defendants of all consequences of waiver, including the possibility of a consecutive sentence.

§ 1:22 —Direct waiver of jury: The legal standard

n. 135.

Add to note 135:
The Court of Appeals in Fitzgerald v. Withrow, 292 F.3d 500, 2002 FED App. 0198P (6th Cir. 2002), cert. denied, 537 U.S. 1009, 123 S. Ct. 501, 154 L. Ed. 2d 409 (2002) held that a written waiver of a defendant's right to jury trial is sufficient to permit a bench trial by any judge on the court. A criminal defendant has no right to demand a bench trial with a particular judge. The fact that defendant may have thought otherwise did not invalidate his unambiguous written waiver made in open court and after defendant had had the opportunity to consult with counsel.

Add after second sentence in fourth paragraph:
Waiver applies only to issues raised by the pleadings at the time of the waiver; if Amendments to the pleadings raise new issues, the defendant may reassert his right to a jury trial. LaMarca v. Turner, 995 F.2d 1526 (11th Cir. 1993).

See also In re Financial Federated Title & Trust, Inc., 309 F.3d 1325, 40 Bankr. Ct. Dec. (CRR) 99, Bankr. L. Rep. (CCH) ¶ 78735 (11th Cir. 2002). A defendant may opt for a jury trial regarding guilt or innocence, but waive the right to jury trial on sentencing. See, e.g., Whitehead v. Cowan, 263 F.3d 708 (7th Cir. 2001), cert. denied, 534 U.S. 1116, 122 S. Ct. 927, 151 L. Ed. 2d 890 (2002); Todd v. Schomig, 283 F.3d 842 (7th Cir. 2002), cert. denied, 537 U.S. 846, 123 S. Ct. 184, 154 L. Ed. 2d 72 (2002). In *Whitehead*, the petitioner's claim that his waiver of a jury in respect to sentencing was invalid because the judge had failed to advise him that a jury would have had to be unanimous in order to impose the death penalty was rejected. According to the Court of Appeals, a trial judge did not have to explain the ramifications of a waiver in terms of the number of votes required for a verdict or a particular sentence in order for the waiver to be knowing or intelligent. Nor in the circumstances of the case did the advice defendant received from counsel regarding waiver rise, in the Court's opinion, to the level which would warrant a finding of ineffective assistance of counsel.

n. 136.
Add to note 136:
Whether a waiver is knowing and intelligent is a factual issue, subject to review for clear error. U.S. v. Rosa, 946 F.2d 505 (7th Cir. 1991). If a defendant does not understand English, the waiver may not be knowing and intelligent, a point recognized in *Rosa*. However, the appellate court found that other colloquies between the judge and defendant indicated that the latter did have a sufficient understanding of the language to make a knowing and intelligent waiver. That the judge at one point in the trial allowed for an interpreter was deemed not to support the defendant's argument but, rather, to illustrate the trial court's general sensitivity to the defendant's situation. See also U.S. v. Duarte-Higareda, 113 F.3d 1000 (9th Cir. 1997) (court must conduct colloquy with non-English speaking defendant to satisfy itself that waiver was knowing, voluntary and intelligent).

In Lott v. Coyle, 261 F.3d 594, 2001 FED App. 0274P (6th Cir. 2001), cert. denied, 534 U.S. 1147, 122 S. Ct. 1106, 151 L. Ed. 2d 1001 (2002), the Court of Appeals held that, for a waiver to be valid, it is not required that the defendant have a detailed, technical knowledge of the role of a jury but only a general awareness that a jury is composed of 12 members of the community in whose selection he was entitled to participate. The defendant also has to have the mental capacity to understand the implications of a waiver, which will be satisfied if the defendant understands that the jury's verdict has to be unanimous and that the judge alone will decide guilt or innocence if the defendant waives jury trial. The Court of Appeals found that there had in fact been a knowing and intelligent waiver, and furthermore, that the waiver of jury trial with respect to one charge conferred jurisdiction on a three-judge panel to hear the entire case.

In Jennings v. McCormick, 154 F.3d 542, 41 Fed. R. Serv. 3d 1474 (5th Cir. 1998), a prisoner, proceeding pro se and without the advice of counsel, signed a consent form agreeing to be tried by a magistrate judge. It was not made clear to the prisoner that he had the right to a jury trial

§ 1:22   JURY SELECTION: LAW, ART & SCIENCE 2D

or that by signing the form he would be waiving that right. Subsequently, and within the relevant time period, the prisoner did demand a jury trial, but, for reasons that were not entirely clear, his demand was not addressed. At the trial the magistrate judge made no mention of the petitioner's demand for, or right to, a jury trial. The Court of Appeals held that, despite the signing of the consent form, there had not been a knowing and voluntary relinquishment of the right to jury trial. It added that jury trial was so important that a court should indulge every reasonable presumption against waiver.

In State v. Smith, 623 So. 2d 682 (La. Ct. App. 4th Cir. 1993), writ denied, 629 So. 2d 398 (La. 1993), the court found that the fact that the defendant had initially indicated that he wished to be tried by a jury but had changed his mind after consultation with counsel was not enough to support his claim that he was coerced by counsel into waiving his right to a jury trial. There is no due process violation where a defendant waives his constitutional right to jury trial in response to a pledge by the state not to seek the death penalty. Parrish v. Fulcomer, 150 F.3d 326 (3d Cir. 1998).

Where there is reason to suspect that a defendant suffers from mental or emotional instability, the court must take particular care in determining that the waiver is voluntary, knowing, and intelligent. U.S. v. Christensen, 18 F.3d 822 (9th Cir. 1994). The Court of Appeals in *Christensen* stated that an in-depth colloquy with the defendant would generally be required.

In Hensley v. Crist, 67 F.3d 181 (9th Cir. 1995), defendant's waiver was held to have been knowingly made, even though defendant may not have known all of the appellate ramifications.

The defendant in U.S. v. Mendez, 102 F.3d 126 (5th Cir. 1996) had recently arrived from Columbia. He was young, poorly educated, and did not speak or understand English. The government had not obtained a written waiver of his decision to forego a jury trial and sought to squeeze within the limited exception to Fed. R. Crim. P. 23(a). The court held that the defendant's silence and failure to object notwithstanding, he had not made an express and intelligent waiver of his right to a jury trial.

n. 137.

Add to note 137:

In Brown v. Burns, 996 F.2d 219 (9th Cir. 1993), the court, addressing a Nevada waiver requirement analogous to that contained in Fed. R. Crim. P. 23(a), held that a written waiver was not a constitutional requirement. Rather, the requirement of a writing was intended as a means of providing the best evidence of a defendant's consent to the waiver of a jury trial. The court held that as long as the waiver was in fact voluntary, knowing and intelligent, it was valid whether or not it was in writing.

In Spytma v. Howes, 313 F.3d 363, 2002 FED App. 0415P (6th Cir. 2002) the defendant was a 15-year-old boy charged with murder. The defendant had signed a jury waiver form in open court. However, there had been no on-the-record colloquy between the judge and the defendant and the defendant subsequently maintained that he did not understand the nature of the right to jury trial and had signed the waiver only on advice of counsel. A conflict thus existed between the written document that the defendant had voluntarily signed and the defendant's testimony. In resolving this conflict, the Court of Appeals held that presumptive force should be given to the written document and that there was no evidence that the defendant was so unaware of the rudimentary elements of jury trial that

Right to Jury Trial § 1:22

his waiver could not stand. The court added that an on-the-record colloquy between a trial judge and a defendant who is about to waive the right to jury trial is not required. See also, U.S. v. Bishop, 291 F.3d 1100, 2002-2 U.S. Tax Cas. (CCH) ¶ 50488, 59 Fed. R. Evid. Serv. 150, 89 A.F.T.R.2d 2002-2745 (9th Cir. 2002), cert. denied, 123 S. Ct. 1002, 154 L. Ed. 2d 920 (U.S. 2003) (while a trial court should conduct a thorough and searching colloquy with a defendant before accepting a jury trial waiver, the failure to do so is not unconstitutional or in violation of the Federal Rules of Criminal Procedure; as the judge was not required to conduct a colloquy, any alleged shortcomings in a colloquy were irrelevant, particularly in the case at hand where the defendant was a sophisticated business proprietor and had lawyers at his side at all times).

n. 140.

Add to note 140:

Singer was applied in U.S. v. Van Metre, 150 F.3d 339, 49 Fed. R. Evid. Serv. 1156 (4th Cir. 1998). The case involved a particularly gruesome murder, and the defendant argued that a jury could be expected to be influenced by 'passion and prejudice' rather than the evidence. The Fourth Circuit Court of Appeals upheld the trial judge's decision not to allow the defendant to waive jury trial. It stated that the judge, through extensive voir dire and cautionary instructions, had effected the necessary safeguards to ensure a fair trial. See also DeLisle v. Rivers, 161 F.3d 370, 1998 FED App. 0350P (6th Cir. 1998) (trial court's denial of defendant's attempted waiver of jury trial was not a denial of due process where defendant's right to impartial jury was adequately safeguarded); U.S. v. Jackson, 278 F.3d 769 (8th Cir. 2002).

In U.S. v. Gabriel, 125 F.3d 89, 47 Fed. R. Evid. Serv. 1307 (2d Cir. 1997), the government refused to consent to the defendants' request for a bench trial. While accepting that there could be situations where such refusal would violate a defendant's right to a fair trial, the Court of Appeals found that the instant case was not one of them. The argument of the defendants, executives of airline companies, was that some jurors might have a fear of flying that could prejudice those jurors against them. The court responded that the defendants could challenge such jurors if they wished. The additional argument that one defendant might be prejudiced by the use of evidence introduced against another defendant was no better received, the court stating that the defendants could file a motion for severance if this was a cause for concern.

Add after second sentence in seventh paragraph:
In a capital case, a waiver of a jury at the trial phase may, under the applicable state law, constitute a waiver for the penalty phase as well. See, e.g., Hatch v. State of Okl., 58 F.3d 1447 (10th Cir. 1995).

n. 141.

Add to note 141:

See generally Annotation, Contractual jury trial waivers in federal civil cases, 92 A.L.R. Fed. 688.

n. 142.

Add to note 142:

Where the jury is to return a special verdict, Rule 49(a) of the Federal Rules of Civil Procedure provides that a party waives the right to a trial by jury in respect to any issue which the party has not asked to be submitted to the jury prior to the time it retires. See Kavanaugh v. Greenlee Tool Co., 944 F.2d 7, 21 Fed. R. Serv. 3d 616 (1st Cir. 1991). In Burns v. Lawther, 44 F.3d 960, 31 Fed. R. Serv. 3d 347 (11th Cir. 1995), opinion withdrawn and superseded on reh'g, 53 F.3d 1237 (11th Cir. 1995), the court held that the special reports which the court ordered physician assistants to file in response to the petitioner's complaint were not pleadings which triggered the demand for a jury trial under Fed. R. Civ. P. 38(b)(1) (requiring a written demand for a jury trial not later than 10 days after service of the last pleading directed to the issue). The court in U.S. v. Kim, 111 F.3d 1351, Unempl. Ins. Rep. (CCH) ¶ 15712B, 97-1 U.S. Tax Cas. (CCH) ¶ 50370, 46 Fed. R. Evid. Serv. 1476, 79 A.F.T.R.2d 97-2238 (7th Cir. 1997) held that the burden of requesting a jury trial rested on the plaintiff seeking to challenge a violation of the laws relating to tax withholding, and the failure to request a jury trial at the time that the taxpayer became aware that the corporate defendant had not withheld the relevant amounts constituted a waiver.

n. 143.

Add to note 143:

Rule 38(b) states that a demand for a jury trial must be made within 10 days of the last pleading directed to a jury triable issue. In U.S. v. California Mobile Home Park Management Co., 107 F.3d 1374, 20 A.D.D. 658, 36 Fed. R. Serv. 3d 1176 (9th Cir. 1997), the court held that it was the answer to a complaint filed by an intervenor, rather than the answer to the original complaint filed by the government, that was the "last pleading" directed to a triable issue for the purpose of determining whether the right to a jury trial had been waived. In Shelton v. Consumer Products Safety Com'n, 277 F.3d 998, 58 Fed. R. Evid. Serv. 96, 51 Fed. R. Serv. 3d 1131 (8th Cir. 2002), cert. denied, 537 U.S. 1000, 123 S. Ct. 514, 154 L. Ed. 2d 395 (2002), the issue again was what constituted the "last pleading." The court held that where an amended pleading presented no new issues giving rise to a trial by a jury, it was not the proper point of calculation in determining whether there had been a timely demand.

Participation in a bench trial without objection was deemed to constitute a waiver of the right to jury trial in White v. McGinnis, 903 F.2d 699, 16 Fed. R. Serv. 3d 369 (9th Cir. 1990). Accord, U.S. ex rel. Schumer v. Hughes Aircraft Co., 63 F.3d 1512, 12 I.E.R. Cas. (BNA) 1040, 40 Cont. Cas. Fed. (CCH) ¶ 76828, 136 Lab. Cas. (CCH) ¶ 10308, 33 Fed. R. Serv. 3d 543 (9th Cir. 1995), judgment vacated on other grounds, 520 U.S. 939, 117 S. Ct. 1871, 138 L. Ed. 2d 135, 12 I.E.R. Cas. (BNA) 1569, 41 Cont. Cas. Fed. (CCH) ¶ 77105, 133 Lab. Cas. (CCH) ¶ 11812 (1997). See also Preferred RX, Inc. v. American Prescription Plan, Inc., 46 F.3d 535, 1995 FED App. 0046P (6th Cir. 1995). The filing of a motion for summary judgment which is denied, however, does not constitute a waiver of a demand for a jury trial previously made. Clarin Corp. v. Massachusetts General Life Ins. Co., 44 F.3d 471 (7th Cir. 1994). In McAfee v. Martin, 63 F.3d 436, 32 Fed. R. Serv. 3d 1065 (5th Cir. 1995), the Court of Appeals held that participation in a magistrate judge's hearing without objection did not constitute a waiver of an earlier demand for a jury trial. The court stated that every reasonable presumption against waiver should be entertained. See also Thompson v. Mahre, 110 F.3d 716 (9th Cir. 1997) (by participating in and in not objecting to bench trial on the issue of whether he was entitled to qualified immunity, police officer waived his right to jury trial on issues of fact relating to qualified immunity).

In In re City of Philadelphia Litigation, 158 F.3d 723, 41 Fed. R. Serv. 3d 421 (3d Cir. 1998), despite defendant's timely demand for a jury trial, the district court had ordered a bench trial. Although the defendant had never expressly consented, either orally or in writing, to the bench trial, the Court of Appeals held that by not objecting to the Court's order, the defendant had waived her right to jury trial. In support of its decision the court cited two policy considerations: first, the inappropriateness of an appellate Court's considering issues not presented to the trial court; and second, the undesirability of encouraging the tactic of silently acquiescing in a nonjury trial by failing to make a timely objection and later demanding a new trial only after the nonobjector has lost on the merits. The Court of Appeals held that a party must make a specific objection to a nonjury trial in order to preserve any Seventh Amendment jury trial right that the party might have. In Goya Foods, Inc. v. Unanue, 233 F.3d 38 (1st Cir. 2000), cert. denied, 532 U.S. 1022, 121 S. Ct. 1964, 149 L. Ed. 2d 758 (2001) and cert. denied, 532 U.S. 1022, 121 S. Ct. 1964, 149 L. Ed. 2d 758 (2001) the court held that once a litigant had withdrawn a request for a jury trial, it could not be reinstated without the party making a formal request to that effect. See also Clark v. Runyon, 218 F.3d 915, 84 Fair Empl. Prac. Cas. (BNA) 133, 78 Empl. Prac. Dec. (CCH) ¶ 40176, 48 Fed. R. Serv. 3d 842 (8th Cir. 2000) (party, having withdrawn demand for jury trial both orally and in writing, and never having sought to reinstate it, had waived whatever right to jury trial may have existed).

A court may exercise its discretion, however, and grant a jury trial despite lack of a timely demand, particularly when there will not be prejudice to the opposing party. See, e.g., Moody v. Pepsi-Cola Metropolitan Bottling Co., Inc., 915 F.2d 201, 56 Fair Empl. Prac. Cas. (BNA) 1491, 54 Empl. Prac. Dec. (CCH) ¶ 40228, 117 Lab. Cas. (CCH) ¶ 56441, 17 Fed. R. Serv. 3d 1393 (6th Cir. 1990). See also Federal Deposit Ins. Corp. v. Cafritz, 770 F. Supp. 28 (D.D.C. 1991); Waldermeyer v. ITT Consumer Financial Corp., 767 F. Supp. 989, 55 Fair Empl. Prac. Cas. (BNA) 1598, 6 I.E.R. Cas. (BNA) 1241, 57 Empl. Prac. Dec. (CCH) ¶ 40974, 118 Lab. Cas. (CCH) ¶ 35490 (E.D. Mo. 1991); Green Const. Co. v. Kansas Power & Light Co., 1 F.3d 1005, 26 Fed. R. Serv. 3d 1459 (10th Cir. 1993) (jury trial should be granted absent "strong and compelling reasons to the contrary" even if not requested within the 10-day time limit).

The Federal Rules provide that "notwithstanding the failure of a party to demand a jury in an action in which such a demand might have been made of right, the court in its discretion upon motion may order a trial by a jury of any and all issues." Fed. R. Civ. P. 39(b). In Parrott v. Wilson, 707 F.2d 1262, 1267, 13 Fed. R. Evid. Serv. 1149 (11th Cir. 1983), the Eleventh Circuit Court of Appeals identified five factors relevant to the Court's discretion:

(1) Whether the case involved issues best tried by a jury;
(2) Whether granting the motion would disrupt the Court's or the adverse party's schedule;
(3) How greatly the adverse party would be prejudiced;
(4) How long the moving party had delayed in bringing the motion; and
(5) Why the movant had failed to file a timely demand for jury trial.

Citing these factors, the district court in Lee v. Boyle-Midway Household Products, Inc., 785 F. Supp. 533 (W.D. Pa. 1992), declined to exercise its discretion to grant a jury trial under 39(b) where the failure to demand the jury trial was the result of counsel's inadvertence or oversight. See also Annotation, Right to jury trial in action under state civil rights law, 12 A.L.R. 5th 508.

§ 1:22   JURY SELECTION: LAW, ART & SCIENCE 2D

Also citing the factors identified in the Federal Rules, the Court of Appeals in U.S. S.E.C. v. Infinity Group Co., 212 F.3d 180, Fed. Sec. L. Rep. (CCH) ¶ 90966, 55 Fed. R. Evid. Serv. 185, 46 Fed. R. Serv. 3d 625 (3d Cir. 2000), cert. denied, 532 U.S. 905, 121 S. Ct. 1228, 149 L. Ed. 2d 138 (2001) found that that the reason for the late request for a jury trial, the fact that the party had changed counsel two months prior to the late jury demand, was not enough to offset the material prejudice to the government that would have resulted from the granting of the motion. Nor were the issues in the case particularly suitable for jury trial. The Court of Appeals concluded that under the circumstances the district court had not abused its discretion in denying the delayed demand. See also Huff v. Dobbins, Fraker, Tennant, Joy & Perlstein, 243 F.3d 1086, 49 Fed. R. Serv. 3d 228 (7th Cir. 2001) (plaintiff's request for jury trial, filed after second amended complaint and approximately two years after defendant's answer to initial complaint was untimely).

Even though a defendant may have waived the right to jury trial, the ability to demand a jury may be revived if an amended complaint is filed. In In re Financial Federated Title & Trust, Inc., 309 F.3d 1325, 40 Bankr. Ct. Dec. (CRR) 99, Bankr. L. Rep. (CCH) ¶ 78735 (11th Cir. 2002), the trustee originally sought to avoid a transfer of $10,000, which was the only sum in issue. In respect to this claim, the defendant admittedly waived the right to jury trial. Thereafter, the trustee brought a new claim for over $1 million, contending that allegedly voidable sums passed through a conduit corporation, which was added as a new defendant. The Court of Appeals recognized that that the amended complaint presented an entirely different case, with dramatically greater sums of money at stake, and new issues to contend with. In these circumstances, the court held that the defendant's right to a jury trial revived. See also LaMarca v. Turner, 995 F.2d 1526 (11th Cir. 1993).

Add after note 144:

In Members v. Paige, 140 F.3d 699 (7th Cir. 1998), petitioner's demand for a jury trial was not made until 46 days after the filing of defendants' answer. However, the petitioner, a prisoner, was proceeding pro se and did not have the benefit of advice of counsel. Nonetheless, the district judge declined to excuse the delay, but apparently on the rationale that such requests by pro se litigants had to be disallowed absent authority that pro se litigants were exempt from the federal rules altogether. The Seventh Circuit Court of Appeals rejected this all-or-nothing approach, and stated that each case had to be considered on its individual merits. Because the district judge had applied a mechanical approach rather than taking into account all relevant factors, the case was remanded for further consideration.

The court in Raymond v. International Business Machines Corp., 148 F.3d 63, 40 Fed. R. Serv. 3d 1177 (2d Cir. 1998) drew a potentially far-reaching distinction between excusing the failure to make a timely demand for a jury trial under Fed. R. Civ. P. 39(b) and under Fed. R. Civ. P. 6(b)(2). In this case there was no showing that anything other than inadvertence accounted for the failure to make a timely demand for a jury trial. The defendants accordingly argued that the trial court abused its discretion in allowing a jury trial. The Second Circuit Court of Appeals agreed that the district court had erred under Rule 39(b) but found no abuse of the Court's discretion in granting leave to serve the jury demand out of time under Rule 6(b)(2). The latter provision is applicable to any time requirement under the federal rules unless expressly excepted. See Pioneer Inv. Services Co. v. Brunswick Associates Ltd. Partnership, 507 U.S. 380, 113 S. Ct. 1489, 123 L. Ed. 2d 74, 24 Bankr. Ct. Dec. (CRR) 63, 28 Collier Bankr. Cas. 2d (MB) 267, Bankr. L. Rep. (CCH) ¶ 75157A, 25 Fed. R. Serv. 3d 401 (1993). Applying Rule 6(b)(2)'s equitable criteria, the *Raymond* court found that there had been no showing of bad faith and that IBM would suffer little prejudice as a result of the delay. It concluded that the district court had acted within its discretion under Rule 6(b)(2) in granting leave to serve a jury demand out of time.

In U.S. v. Robertson, 45 F.3d 1423 (10th Cir. 1995) the defendant argued that the alleged waiver of her right to a jury trial was invalid because it was not in writing as required by Fed. R. Civ. P. 23(a). The Court of Appeals noted that there was a conflict in the circuits as to how strictly Rule 23(a) should be interpreted. Compare U.S. v. Saadya, 750 F.2d 1419 (9th Cir. 1985) (oral waiver in open court will suffice) with U.S. v. Garrett, 727 F.2d 1003, 15 Fed. R. Evid. Serv. 262 (11th Cir. 1984), judgment aff'd, 471 U.S. 773, 105 S. Ct. 2407, 85 L. Ed. 2d 764 (1985) (waiver must be in writing). The Court of Appeals in *Robertson* held that a written waiver would not be required if the record clearly indicated that the waiver was voluntary, knowing and intelligent. This had not been established in the case at bar, however, and so the court vacated the petitioner's conviction and remanded to the district court with instructions to allow her a jury trial.

The failure to raise on direct appeal a claim of involuntary waiver of one's right to a jury trial may procedurally bar subsequent consideration of such a claim. Marone v. U.S., 10 F.3d 65 (2d Cir. 1993).

In McDonald v. Steward, 132 F.3d 225 (5th Cir. 1998), the court stated that a trial judge should be reluctant to find a waiver of jury trial based on mere acquiescence to a hearing before the judge. In this case the defendant had requested a jury trial initially but subsequently agreed to allow the United States magistrate enter final judgment. The Court of Appeals said that waiver should not lightly be inferred from conduct and that the defendant's "consent" was more likely to the magistrate's presiding over a jury trial than to a trial before the magistrate. That the defendant did not articulate this position with the utmost clarity was not sufficient for

§ 1:22

the court to find a waiver of the previously made request for a jury trial. This ruling makes particularly good sense in the context of the case because the defendant was not represented by legal counsel.

§ 1:23 —Waiver of jury: Strategic considerations

Add at end of first paragraph:

One issue that needs to be considered, by plaintiffs' lawyers in civil cases is whether their clients will receive greater damages if their case is heard by a judge or jury. The issue is examined in Wissler, Hart & Saks, Decisionmaking about General Damages: A Comparison of Jurors, Judges, and Lawyers, 98 Mich. L. Rev. 751 (1999).

Add at end of eighth paragraph:

An interesting waiver issue was raised in Chateloin v. Singletary, 89 F.3d 749 (11th Cir. 1996). Under Florida law, a defendant on trial in a capital case is entitled to a 12 person jury. However, if the state waives its right to seek the death penalty, the case can be heard by a jury of six. The court in Chateloin held that the defendant's waiver, made orally in court in his presence and unobjected to by him, was effective. The facts of the case raise intriguing constitutional questions which the court did not address. If there are advantages in being tried by a 12 person jury (see main text § 2:16), is it proper for the state to induce a defendant to waive his right to a 12 person jury by offering to forego seeking the death penalty? Can a waiver under such circumstances be said to be truly voluntary?

Chapter 2

Characteristics and Features of the Jury

> **KeyCite®:** Cases and other legal materials listed in KeyCite Scope can be researched through West's KeyCite service on Westlaw®. Use KeyCite to check citations for form, parallel references, prior and later history, and comprehensive citator information, including citations to other decisions and secondary materials.

§ 2:1 Introduction

Add after fifth paragraph:

The administrative, structural, and procedural jury reforms of the past three decades are explored in Munsterman & Hannaford, *Reshaping the Bedrock of Democracy: American Jury Reform during the Last 30 Years,* 36 Judges Journal 5 (1997). The authors observe that jury reform can have ancillary, and sometimes unintended, effects in terms of costs to the state, the representativeness of the jury, and the dynamics of jury decisionmaking.

§ 2:2 Venue and vicinage

n. 7.

Add to note 7:

The statutory requirements relating to vicinage were interpreted to allow some degree of flexibility in U.S. v. Gluzman, 154 F.3d 49 (2d Cir. 1998), where the court held that jurors did not have to be drawn only from geographically adjacent counties to that in which the trial was to be held.

The boundaries comprising the vicinage can be a matter of dispute. In People v. Danielson, 3 Cal. 4th 691, 13 Cal. Rptr. 2d 1, 838 P.2d 729 (1992), as modified on denial of reh'g, (Dec. 30, 1992) and (overruled on other grounds by, Price v. Superior Court, 25 Cal. 4th 1046, 108 Cal. Rptr. 2d 409, 25 P.3d 618 (2001)), the court held that the trial judge's policy of excusing on hardship grounds all prospective jurors who lived more that one and one-half hours from the courthouse did not violate either the defendant's state or federal right to a jury of the vicinage.

n. 11.

Add to note 11:

The right to jurors from the vicinage may be waived. See, e.g., People v. Hill, 3 Cal. 4th 959, 13 Cal. Rptr. 2d 475, 839 P.2d 984 (1992) (overruled on other grounds by, Price v. Superior Court, 25 Cal. 4th 1046,

108 Cal. Rptr. 2d 409, 25 P.3d 618 (2001)). See also U.S. v. Durham, 139 F.3d 1325 (10th Cir. 1998). In *Durham*, the court rejected defendants' argument that the same standard as applied to waiver of jury trial (that the waiver be 'knowing, intelligent and voluntary') should be applicable to the waiver of vicinage. The court found the analogy unpersuasive because the defendants were not being deprived of their right to a jury trial, the waiver affecting at most the composition of the jury.

Add after first sentence in seventh paragraph:
The tension between the requirements of venue and vicinage, on the one hand, and the right to a jury representing a fair cross section of the community, on the other, is examined in Note, *Vicinage, Venue, and Community Cross-Section: Obstacles to a State Defendant's Right to a Trial by a Representative Jury*, 19 Hastings LQ 261 (1991). Although *Batson v Kentucky* (see main text Ch 8) applies only to peremptory challenges of members of the trial jury, Professor Gaines argues the case for extending the holding to jury pool discrimination when a change in venue is used to gain an unfair advantage that discriminates against the vicinage requirement, as arguably occurred in the Rodney King trial (where venue was transferred from the predominantly black urban district where the offense occurred to a virtually all-white suburban district). *Gaines, Race, Venue and the Rodney King Case:* Can *Batson* Save the Vicinage Community, 73 U Det Mercy L Rev (1996). See also Engel, *The Public's Vicinage Requirement*, 75 N.Y.U. L. Rev. 1658 (2000) ("local" jurors are needed to represent the common knowledge and values of the community, to legitimate processes and outcomes, and to permit the trial to heal the social ruptures caused by the crime).

In U.S. v. Etsitty, 130 F.3d 420, 48 Fed. R. Evid. Serv. 265 (9th Cir. 1997), opinion amended on denial of reh'g, 140 F.3d 1274 (9th Cir. 1998), the court considered, but did not decide, whether the fact that a change of venue would result in a lesser percentage of Indians in the jury pool would violate the requirement of cross section representation. The issue left open in Etsitty was resolved in U.S. v. Footracer, 189 F.3d 1058 (9th Cir. 1999), opinion withdrawn, 252 F.3d 1059 (9th Cir. 2001), where the trial of the defendant, a Native American, was transferred from the district in which his crimes were committed to a district that contained a smaller percentage of Native Americans. The defendant argued that the transfer denied him a jury pool reflecting a fair cross section of the community. The Court of Appeals held that the residents of the division where the crime was committed were not a distinctive group for purposes of Sixth Amendment analysis and, furthermore, that there was no showing of systematic exclusion of Native Americans from the jury venire.

Add after second sentence in seventh paragraph:
Ironically, in Williams v. Chrans, 957 F.2d 487 (7th Cir. 1992), residence near the scene of the crime was allowed as a proper justification for a peremptory challenge in the face of a claim that the challenge had impermissibly been based on race.

§ 2:3 —Motions for a change in venue or venire

n. 12.
Add to note 12:
A right to a change in venue may be waived if not timely made. In U.S. v. Delgado-Nunez, 295 F.3d 494 (5th Cir. 2002), cert. denied, 123 S. Ct. 994, 154 L. Ed. 2d 916 (U.S. 2003), the defendant's objection to venue was not raised before or during the trial but only after the close of trial. The Court of Appeals held that this was not an appropriate way of preserving the issue for appeal unless the impropriety of venue only becomes apparent at the close of the government's case. This was not the situation in this case, where the facts underlying defendant's motion were known at the outset of the trial. For it to hold otherwise, pointed out the court, would encourage defendants to test the merits of the government's case, holding in reserve their motion for a change in venue until they saw how well the government's case was proceeding. But compare U.S. v. Ruelas-Arreguin, 219 F.3d 1056 (9th Cir. 2000) (where defect in venue is not apparent on the face of the indictment, objection to venue at close of government's case was permissible).

§ 2:4 —Legal standards

n. 22.
Add at beginning of note 22:
See generally Levenson, *Change of Venue and the Role of the Criminal Jury*, 66 S Cal L Rev 1533 (1993); Brown, *The Role of Race in Jury Impartiality and Venue Transfers*, 53 Md L Rev 107 (1994).

n. 26.
Add to note 26:
A motion for a change in venue was denied in U.S. v. Strissel, 920 F.2d 1162, 30 Fed. R. Evid. Serv. 1079 (4th Cir. 1990). The appellate court found that what publicity had occurred was reported in relatively less well-read newspapers, was not completely adverse to the defendant and did not primarily focus on the issues at trial. The court also said that to the extent that the publicity was critical of the defendant, it did not concern issues at trial. The latter point is questionable, for unfavorable publicity which prejudices jurors against a defendant is likely to have some effect even where a defendant is charged with an unrelated offense.

In U.S. v. Washington, 836 F. Supp. 192 (D. Vt. 1993), aff'd, 48 F.3d 73 (2d Cir. 1995), the defendant was tried on a federal weapons charge, after having been convicted of murder in a state trial. Although some of the jurors were apparently aware of the state case, the court was not convinced that the pretrial publicity had adversely affected the ability of prospective jurors to be impartial to such a degree to warrant a change in venue. See also Pruett v. Norris, 153 F.3d 579 (8th Cir. 1998) (record did not justify finding that prejudice from publicity would prevent fair trial or warrant a change in venue); Spivey v. Head, 207 F.3d 1263 (11th Cir.

§ 2:4

2000) (publicity was neither sufficiently inflammatory, widespread or prejudicial to warrant change in venue).

In U.S. v. Blom, 242 F.3d 799 (8th Cir. 2001), cert. denied, 534 U.S. 880, 122 S. Ct. 184, 151 L. Ed. 2d 128 (2001) the Court of Appeals found that although there had been extensive media coverage of the case, the coverage had been neither sufficiently inflammatory or accusatory to give rise to a presumption of inherent prejudice. Moreover, the court was impressed with the various steps taken by the trial judge to defuse any possible prejudice, including moving the trial from Duluth to Minneapolis, assembling a jury pool three times the normal size and drawn from an expanded area, sending out a pretrial questionnaire to all prospective jurors asking about their exposure to the media coverage, and increasing the number of peremptory challenges. Further, there had been three days of individualized voir dire, which led to the selection of 14 jurors who said that they could put aside whatever knowledge they had of the case and be impartial. The court concluded that under the circumstances there had been no abuse of discretion in the denial of the motion for a change in venue.

n. 29.

Add at beginning of note 29:

In U.S. v. Dischner, 960 F.2d 870, 35 Fed. R. Evid. Serv. 485 (9th Cir. 1992), opinion amended and superseded on denial of reh'g, 974 F.2d 1502 (9th Cir. 1992), a research poll indicated that 69% of the people in the district were familiar with the corruption investigation which gave rise to the prosecution, and 64% of these believed that "serious dishonesty" was involved. The poll, however, did not refer to the defendants by name. The court held that this was insufficient to show that the jury pool was impermissibly tainted, noting that the reporting tended to be factual in nature, and not inflammatory. The court also found no actual prejudice on the part of the jurors.

n. 30.

Add to note 30:

See also U.S. v. Bakker, 925 F.2d 728, 32 Fed. R. Evid. Serv. 303 (4th Cir. 1991) (only in extreme circumstances will a change of venue be granted prior to voir dire; usually voir dire will be needed to determine whether an impartial jury can be impaneled). Citing *Bakker*, the Court of Appeals in U.S. v. Bailey, 112 F.3d 758 (4th Cir. 1997) held that the trial court had not abused its discretion in refusing a change of venue or individual voir dire in a case where the pretrial publicity did not give rise to a presumption of prejudice.

In State v. Bible, 175 Ariz. 549, 858 P.2d 1152 (1993), the court stated that the burden to show that pretrial publicity is presumptively prejudicial rests with the defendant and is extremely heavy on a motion for a change in venue. The court declined to presume prejudice even though the pretrial publicity had included reports that the defendant had "flunked" a lie detector test and was a convicted "child molester" who had committed "child rape," as well as containing references to other inadmissible evidence. In order to raise a presumption of prejudice the publicity, in the Court's opinion, had to be so unfair, so prejudicial, and so pervasive that the trial judge could not give any credibility to jurors' answers to voir dire questions. The less demanding test for actual prejudice required a showing that the publicity would probably result in the defendant being deprived of a fair trial. The court noted that the news items in question had appeared months apart and several months prior to the trial, and

JURY CHARACTERISTICS & FEATURES § 2:5

held that neither a finding of presumptive nor actual prejudice was warranted. See also Devier v. Zant, 3 F.3d 1445 (11th Cir. 1993) (defendant's showing that the community was familiar with the case was insufficient to sustain a claim of presumptive prejudice).

Add after first sentence in fifth paragraph:
In Ritchie v. Rogers, 313 F.3d 948, 2002 FED App. 0426P (6th Cir. 2002), extensive pretrial publicity surrounded the defendant's murder trial. The Court of Appeals, after reviewing the Supreme Court's decisions on "presumed prejudice," found that the trial court's denial of a change of venue on this ground was not contrary to, or an unreasonable application of, clearly established law. In the absence of presumed prejudice, the issue became whether the voir dire was sufficiently searching to detect "actual prejudice." The defendant argued that the use of group rather than individual voir dire constituted a denial of due process, but the Court of Appeals found that the trial judge had not committed error, either in allowing the group voir dire or in denying petitioner's motion for a change in venue.

Add after second sentence in fifth paragraph:
U.S. v. Bakker, 925 F.2d 728, 32 Fed. R. Evid. Serv. 303 (4th Cir. 1991), is instructive in that the sheer volume of publicity by itself does not require a change in venue, particularly where defendant's pretrial acts and statements contributed significantly to the publicity. The mere fact of extensive publicity does not establish that the publicity was hostile or that an irrepressibly hostile attitude pervaded the community. Stafford v. Saffle, 34 F.3d 1557 (10th Cir. 1994); U.S. v. Brandon, 17 F.3d 409 (1st Cir. 1994); Brecheen v. Reynolds, 41 F.3d 1343 (10th Cir. 1994).

§ 2:5 —Strategic considerations

Add after second sentence in first paragraph:
In Batson v. Kentucky, 476 U.S. 79, 106 S. Ct. 1712, 90 L. Ed. 2d 69 (1986) (holding modified by, Powers v. Ohio, 499 U.S. 400, 111 S. Ct. 1364, 113 L. Ed. 2d 411 (1991)) (see Ch 8), the United States Supreme Court held that the equal protection clause forbids the discriminatory use of peremptory challenges to exclude venirepersons of a particular race solely on account of their race or on the assumption that members of that race will be unable to impartially consider the state's case against the defendant. It has been suggested that the principle of *Batson* may extend to prevent motions for a change in venue where the motion is based on strategic considerations relating to the racial composition of the district wherein the trial is scheduled to take place. See Kaine, *Race, Trial Strategy, and Legal Ethics*, 24 U Rich L Rev 361 (1990).

© West, a Thomson business, 11/2003

§ 2:5

Add at end of first paragraph:

The idea that forum shopping is a form of jury selection is developed by McElhaney in McElhaney, *Picking a Jury: Who are You Talking to?*, 67 Tenn. L. Rev. 517 (2000).

Strategic maneuvering in order to secure a favorable venue is not restricted to the defense. In U.S. v. Cannon, 88 F.3d 1495 (8th Cir. 1996), African-American defendants alleged that the government had lured them into committing a drug-sale in North Dakota, in order to arrest them there and have the case tried in a jurisdiction where the jury pool would have contained few African-Americans. Most of the defendants' drug sales had taken place in Minnesota, which had a higher black population. The defendants argued that *Batson* had been violated. While expressing doubts as to whether *Batson* was even applicable, the court ruled that the defendants had failed to show either a *Batson* violation or that they would not receive a fair trial in North Dakota. The defendants' stale census statistics showed only that 2.17% of the Minnesota population was black compared to 0.6% of that of North Dakota. The court also held that the defendants had failed to meet the high threshold for establishing that the government had acted in so outrageous a fashion as to violate their due process rights. In U.S. v. Etsitty, 130 F.3d 420, 48 Fed. R. Evid. Serv. 265 (9th Cir. 1997), opinion amended on denial of reh'g, 140 F.3d 1274 (9th Cir. 1998), the court held that the fact that a change of venue would result in a lesser percentage of Indians in the jury pool did not establish systematic jury discrimination.

Add after fifth paragraph:

While a change in venue may be necessary to avoid racial discrimination against a defendant, as in Joan Little's case, it may also have undesirable discriminatory effects. This point was brought home in the Los Angeles riots of 1992. Four white police officers were on trial for beating a black motorist. An amateur photographer had captured the incident on videotape which had been shown on national television. The trial judge granted a change in venue from Los Angeles to Simi Valley, a predominantly white (1.5% black population), conservative Los Angeles suburb. The all-white jury which ultimately heard the case exonerated the defendants, precipitating a variety of reactions among public officials and the general public. Severe rioting broke out in the city in response to the verdict.

One proposal which could prevent the dilemma Los Angeles encountered would be to grant changes in venue to counties having the same ethnic and demographic profile of the county in which the crime occurred. Of course, if the reason for the request for a change of venue is the danger of racial prejudice against the defendant in the community because of, for example, the defendant's association with an extremist organization which advocated the expulsion from the country of all persons of the particular race which is predominant in that district, it would accomplish little to order a change in venue to a district with a similar racial composition.

In Mallett v. Bowersox, 528 U.S. 853, 120 S. Ct. 317, 145 L. Ed. 2d 113 (1999), the court rejected the argument of the defendant, who was black, that he was denied due process when a change in venue was ordered to a county with only a small number of black residents.

Add after sixth paragraph:

Counsel must also be sensitive to the implications of failing to move for a change in venue. In U.S. v. Orlando-Figueroa, 229 F.3d 33, 55 Fed. R. Evid. Serv. 1097 (1st Cir. 2000), a case where the defendants claimed that they had been prejudiced by adverse pretrial publicity, the court stated that the defendants' failure to move for a change in venue placed on them a significantly heavier burden to show that widespread pretrial publicity had rendered their trial presumptively unfair. See also U.S. v. Moreno Morales, 815 F.2d 725, 22 Fed. R. Evid. Serv. 1063 (1st Cir. 1987).

§ 2:7 A jury of one's peers

n. 54.

Add to note 54:

Ramirez, *A Brief Historical Overview of the Use of the Mixed Jury*, 31 Am Crim L Rev 1213 (1994). Ramirez, *The Mixed Jury and the Ancient Custom of Trial by Jury de Mediatate Linguae: A History and a Proposal for Change*, 74 BU L Rev 777 (1994); Van Ness, Preserving Community Voice: *The Case for Half-and-Half Juries in Racially-Charged Criminal Cases*, 28 J Marshall L Rev 1 (1994).

Add after first sentence in fourth paragraph:

If the right to a jury of one's peers were to be taken more seriously, the question would arise as to how best to secure this right. For one answer, See Note, *Voter Registration: A Remedy for Securing a Jury of One's Peers*, 34 Howard LJ 383 (1991).

n. 63.

Add to note 63:

In Campbell v. Louisiana, 523 U.S. 392, 118 S. Ct. 1419, 140 L. Ed. 2d 551, 172 A.L.R. Fed. 597 (1998), the United States Supreme Court addressed the question of whether a white defendant had standing to challenge alleged discrimination in the selection of the foreperson of the grand jury that had indicted him. Under state law the trial judge selected the foreperson of the grand jury from the grand jury venire, after which the remaining members were selected at random. It was undisputed that no

§ 2:7   JURY SELECTION: LAW, ART & SCIENCE 2D

black person had served as a grand jury foreperson in the parish for the previous 17 years. Citing its prior decision in Powers v. Ohio, 499 U.S. 400, 111 S. Ct. 1364, 113 L. Ed. 2d 411 (1991), in which the Court had held that a white defendant had standing to challenge the discriminatory peremptory challenges of black petit jurors (discussed in supp Ch 8), the Court held that Campbell too had standing to raise the equal protection and due process claims of black jurors who had been discriminated against. The Court's reasoning tracked that in *Powers* the defendant had suffered significant injury since the discriminatory selection process undermined the integrity of the indictment process. The accused shared a common interest with the excluded jurors in eradicating discrimination from the grand jury selection process, and therefore could be counted on to be an effective advocate for the excluded jurors. The accused also had an interest in asserting the excluded jurors' rights because a finding that there had been a constitutional violation might lead to the reversal of his conviction. Finally, the Court noted that the defendant's own due process rights may well have been violated by the selection procedure. Hobby v. U.S., 468 U.S. 339, 104 S. Ct. 3093, 82 L. Ed. 2d 260 (1984), in which the Court had held that no relief could be granted to a white defendant even if there had been a violation of due process in the selection of the foreperson of a federal grand jury, was distinguished. In *Hobby* the foreperson has already been selected to serve on the grand jury prior to his or her purely ministerial appointment to the role of foreperson, while in *Campbell* the judge's appointment of the foreperson shaped the composition of the grand jury. This difference had the practical effect of converting the case into one alleging discriminatory selection of grand juror members. Having determined the standing issue, the court in *Campbell* did not reach the substantive merits of the petitioner's claim but rather remanded for further proceedings. The *Campbell* decision is reviewed in Note, *Campbell v. Louisiana*: Rethinking Access and Remedy for Claims of Discrimination in Jury Selection, 77 NC L. Rev. 1557 (1999).

§ 2:8   —The concept of peers as it relates to jury selection

Add after note 68:

An argument to this effect was advanced, unsuccessfully, in U.S. v. Nururdin, 8 F.3d 1187, 39 Fed. R. Evid. Serv. 1143 (7th Cir. 1993). The defendant was tried by an all white jury produced by random selection, no black juror having been chosen to serve. The defendant, who was black and a resident of an inner city neighborhood, contended that white persons who lived in the city or suburbs could not understand the nature of the relationship between white Chicago police and black citizens, or the nature of life and behavior in the black inner city. The court found the argument untenable in light of Supreme Court statements that a defendant does not have the right to have persons of his or her race included on the jury.

§ 2:9 Impartiality

Add after first sentence in third paragraph:
It has been held that the concept of impartiality does not

include a requirement of impartiality in respect to the underlying crime. U.S. v. Johnson, 990 F.2d 1129 (9th Cir. 1993).

Add after first sentence in fifth paragraph:
See generally Howe, *Juror Neutrality or an Impartial Array: A Structural Theory of the Impartial Jury Mandate,* 70 Notre Dame L Rev 1173 (1995).

§ 2:11 —Supreme Court development

Add after second sentence in first paragraph:
In Holland v. Illinois, 493 U.S. 474, 110 S. Ct. 803, 107 L. Ed. 2d 905 (1990), the United States Supreme Court said that the "Sixth Amendment requirement of a fair cross section on the venire is a means of assuring not a representative jury (which the Constitution does not demand) but an impartial one (which it does)." Holland v. Illinois, 493 U.S. 474, 110 S. Ct. 803, 807, 107 L. Ed. 2d 905 (1990).

n. 81.
Add to note 81:
On appeal (See § 7:11) the burden is heaver still. In Mu'Min v. Virginia, 500 U.S. 415, 111 S. Ct. 1899, 114 L. Ed. 2d 493 (1991), the Supreme Court stated that a trial judge's determination of impartiality was not to be overturned unless there was "manifest error" (quoting Patton v. Yount, 467 U.S. 1025, 1031, 104 S. Ct. 2885, 81 L. Ed. 2d 847 (1984); Irvin v. Dowd, 366 U.S. 717, 723, 81 S. Ct. 1639, 6 L. Ed. 2d 751, 1 Media L. Rep. (BNA) 1178 (1961)). See generally Whitebread & Contreras, Free Press v. Fair Trial: *Protecting the Criminal Defendant's Rights in a Highly Publicized Trial by Applying the Sheppard-Mu'Min Remedy,* 69 S. Cal. L. Rev. 1587 (1996) (arguing that voir dire, sequestration, change of venue and postponement are inadequate means for preserving the proper balance between freedom of the press and the defendant's right to a fair trial).

n. 88.
Add to note 88:
In Whitehead v. Cowan, 263 F.3d 708 (7th Cir. 2001), cert. denied, 534 U.S. 1116, 122 S. Ct. 927, 151 L. Ed. 2d 890 (2002) the Court of Appeals analogized to *Murphy* in finding that there had not been the type of extreme media presence or circuslike atmosphere that would have warranted a presumption of prejudice.

Add after note 88:
A somewhat analogous situation to *Rideau* arose in DeLisle v. Rivers, 161 F.3d 370, 1998 FED App. 0350P (6th Cir. 1998), where the defendant's inculpatory statements had received considerable publicity in the media. Prior to trial it was determined that the defendant's statements should be suppressed. At trial the defense moved to strike for cause all prospective jurors with knowledge of the suppressed statements on the ground that such persons should

§ 2:11   JURY SELECTION: LAW, ART & SCIENCE 2D

be presumed incapable of deciding the case fairly and impartially. The Sixth Circuit Court of Appeals rejected the argument, noting that the category of cases where prejudice was presumed was extremely limited. It distinguished *DeLisle's* situation from previous 'presumed prejudice' cases: unlike in the prior cases, there had been a cessation of publicity between the time of the media coverage and the trial; furthermore, the media reports in the present case were not 'virulent' in nature. Indeed, the court observed that the defendant's so-called confession would have been somewhat confusing to many of those who read it and was not without ambiguity.

In Hale v. Gibson, 227 F.3d 1298 (10th Cir. 2000), cert. denied, 533 U.S. 957, 121 S. Ct. 2608, 150 L. Ed. 2d 764 (2001), the defendant claimed that he had been denied a fair trial when his motion for a change in venue, based on extensive media coverage of the case, was rejected. During voir dire, of 37 jurors, all but three had admitted prior knowledge of the case, and 12 stated that they held an opinion about defendant's guilt. Of the latter 12 jurors, six were ultimately seated on the jury. One even told the court that that she had discussed the case with a key witness but maintained that she could nonetheless be impartial. Despite these facts, the Court of Appeals was not prepared to presume prejudice, as the facts of the case did not rise to the level of egregiousness in Rideau, Sheppard, or Estes. Nor did the Court of Appeals find actual prejudice, as there was no indication from the jurors' responses of hostility to the defendant. The Court of Appeals concluded that the trial court had not abused its discretion in denying the motion for a change in venue.

The nature and extent of the voir dire which must be conducted in a case where there has been extensive and potentially prejudicial pretrial publicity was explored by the United States Supreme Court in Mu'Min v. Virginia, 500 U.S. 415, 111 S. Ct. 1899, 114 L. Ed. 2d 493 (1991). See Ch 7.

n. 89.

Add to note 89:

See also Minnow & Cate, *Who Is an Impartial Juror in an Age of Mass Media?*, 40 Am. U. L. Rev. 631 (1991) (cautioning against the equating of unaware and ignorant jurors with impartial jurors).

n. 93.

Add to note 93:

See also McQueen v. Scroggy, 99 F.3d 1302, 35 Fed. R. Serv. 3d 1211, 1996 FED App. 0349P (6th Cir. 1996) (no per se rule excluding jurors exposed to media reports unless it engenders a predisposition or bias that cannot be set aside).

§ 2:13 Size of the jury—Criminal trials

n. 116.
Add to note 116:
There is no right to a jury of more than 12. See Hakeem v. Beyer, 774 F. Supp. 276 (D.N.J. 1991), order vacated on other grounds, 990 F.2d 750 (3d Cir. 1993) (no constitutional right to jury of 14).

Add after first sentence in fifth paragraph:
In Cabberiza v. Moore, 217 F.3d 1329 (11th Cir. 2000), cert. denied, 531 U.S. 1170, 121 S. Ct. 1137, 148 L. Ed. 2d 1001 (2001) the Court of Appeals considered a Florida law that entitled a defendant to a 12 person jury in a murder trial unless he waived that right and agreed to be tried by a jury of six, as the defendant had done in the case. Attempting to get around what was basically a state issue of waiver, the defendant argued in federal court that the judge's acceptance of his waiver denied him due process of law and that his lawyer's consent to the six-person jury constituted ineffective assistance of counsel. The Court of Appeals rejected both claims. First, it found that defendant's waiver was valid and the trial court had not acted unconstitutionally in accepting it. Next, it found that defendant had not received ineffective assistance of counsel. Even conceding that a 12 person jury was more likely to hang, this was but one factor which an attorney had to take into account. To adopt a per se rule that a defendant was always disadvantaged by a six-person jury, which in effect was what the court would have had to have found in order to provide relief, would foreclose intelligent choices by trial lawyers in cases where a six-person jury might be to a defendant's advantage.

n. 125.
Add to note 125:
Under Federal Rule of Criminal Procedure 23(b), a court may dismiss a juror during deliberations for "just cause." The effect may be that the jury which returns its verdict will be composed of only 11 members. In U.S. v. Frazier, 274 F.3d 1185, 58 Fed. R. Evid. Serv. 138 (8th Cir. 2001), opinion superseded on reh'g, 280 F.3d 835 (8th Cir. 2002), cert. denied, 535 U.S. 1107, 122 S. Ct. 2317, 152 L. Ed. 2d 1070 (2002) and cert. denied, 536 U.S. 931, 122 S. Ct. 2606, 153 L. Ed. 2d 793 (2002) and cert. denied, 537 U.S. 911, 123 S. Ct. 255, 154 L. Ed. 2d 191 (2002) and reh'g granted and opinion vacated, (Feb. 12, 2002) the Court of Appeals rejected the argument that Rule 23(b) is unconstitutional because it violates a defendant's right to a unanimous verdict by a 12-member jury. The right to a 12-member jury may also be waived. See, e.g., U.S. v. Fisher, 912 F.2d 728 (4th Cir. 1990) (defendant's oral consent to jury of 11 constituted waiver of his right to jury of 12). See also U.S. v. Levenite, 277 F.3d 454 (4th Cir. 2002), cert. denied, 535 U.S. 1105, 122 S. Ct. 2312, 152 L. Ed. 2d 1066 (2002) (allowing 11-member jury to complete deliberations and return a verdict was not an abuse of discretion). See generally Annotation, Constitutionality and application of Federal Rule of Criminal Procedure 23(b), allowing 11-person jury to return verdict absent stipulation to that

effect by parties when one juror has been excused after start of deliberations, 107 A.L.R. Fed. 508.

Add after first sentence in seventh paragraph:
The Court's reliance on social science research was not only ironic but highly exceptional. After an exhaustive analysis of Supreme Court decisions over the period from 1970 to 1988, Professor Tanford concluded that the general practice of the Court was to ignore, distort, or display hostility to pertinent empirical findings of social science research on the jury. The Court preferred to place its trust in its own intuitions. See Tanford, *The Limits of a Scientific Jurisprudence: The Supreme Court and Psychology*, 66 Ind LJ 137 (1990).

The advantages and disadvantages of six as opposed to 12-member juries is considered in Chud & Berman, *Six-Member Juries: Does Size Really Matter?*, 67 Tenn. L. Rev. 743 (2000). The authors note that both sized juries have their advantages, and that it may be shortsighted to reject six-person juries out of hand simply because they may be less representative. For one thing, minority members of a six-person jury may be more likely to participate in deliberations, and less likely to feel intimidated, than they would be on a 12 person jury.

Add to end of section:
In Cabral v. Sullivan, 961 F.2d 998 (1st Cir. 1992), as amended, (May 1, 1992), the court held that where the relevant procedural rule provided that the jury "shall" consist of six persons and that alternates "shall" be discharged once the jury retired to deliberate, the district court had no discretion to allow alternates to deliberate with the regular jurors, absent express written agreement of the parties or a stipulation to that effect on the record.

§ 2:14 —Civil trials

Add after second sentence in third paragraph:
In federal court, the Federal Rules of Civil Procedure take priority over state rules in respect to the size of the jury, even though the case may only be in federal court pursuant to diversity jurisdiction. See Krumwiede v. Mercer County Ambulance Service, Inc., 116 F.3d 361, 74 Fair Empl. Prac. Cas. (BNA) 188, 71 Empl. Prac. Dec. (CCH) ¶ 44817, 38 Fed. R. Serv. 3d 142 (8th Cir. 1997).

Add to end of section:
There is evidence that state judges are also not bothered by six-person juries in civil cases. See Sentell, *A six-member Civil Jury in Georgia? The Trial Judges Weigh In*, 54 Mercer L. Rev. 67 (2002). In a poll of Georgia state court judges, the

author discovered that the judges, by a sizeable majority, favored reducing civil juries to six persons. Interestingly, there were strong opinions on both sides of the question with few judges feeling ambivalent on the issue.

The Advisory Committee of the Judicial Conference of the United States, noting the trend among federal district courts to utilize six-person juries, has recommended an approach that allows more flexibility than that currently in use. Under the Committee's proposal, trial courts would have the discretion to empanel a jury of not less than six nor more than 12 members. Fed R Civ Proc 48. Seven is the suggested norm for a one-day trial, with larger juries for longer trials. In exceptional circumstances, and with the agreement of the parties, a jury of fewer than six may be permissible. Notes of Advisory Committee on Rules, Fed R Civ Proc 48. The Committee also proposed the abandonment of the use of alternate jurors. Fed R Civ Proc 47.

§ 2:16 —Jury selection as a function of jury size: Strategic considerations

Add at end of section:

Under Florida law, a defendant on trial in a capital case is entitled to a 12 person jury. However, if the state waives its right to seek the death penalty, a jury of six may be utilized See Chateloin v. Singletary, 89 F.3d 749 (11th Cir. 1996). This presents a defendant with a dilemma. A jury of 12 may represent the best chance for an acquittal (see main text § 2:16), but by refusing to acquiesce in a jury of six, the defendant exposes himself to a possible death penalty.

§ 2:17 Verdict unanimity—Criminal trials

Add after third sentence in eleventh paragraph:

The right to a unanimous jury verdict in federal court cannot be waived. U.S. v. Gomez-Lepe, 207 F.3d 623 (9th Cir. 2000).

Add to the end of twelfth paragraph:

But see Flanning v. State, 597 So. 2d 864 (Fla. Dist. Ct. App. 3d Dist. 1992), holding that the defendant, with the consent of the state, could waive his right to a unanimous six-person jury verdict and accept a 5-1 majority verdict. The court set out four conditions precedent to a valid waiver:

(1) The waiver was initiated by the defendant (as opposed to the trial judge or prosecutor);
(2) The jury had informed the court that, despite having had a reasonable time to deliberate, it was unable to reach a verdict;

(3) The trial judge explained to the defendant consequences of waiver of that right; and
(4) The trial judge, having directly questioned the defendant, determined that the waiver was knowing and voluntary.

In Cabberiza v. Moore, 217 F.3d 1329 (11th Cir. 2000), cert. denied, 531 U.S. 1170, 121 S. Ct. 1137, 148 L. Ed. 2d 1001 (2001) the defendant was convicted of murder by a six-person jury, to which he had agreed and which was allowed under state law. He argued, however, that the jury had not been unanimous. The basis of this argument was the fact that the clerk had appeared to have polled only five of the six jurors to ascertain if each agreed with the verdict. The Court of Appeals, after reviewing the transcript, concluded that the verdict had in fact been unanimous and that the clerk had simply made an administrative error in not recording the poll of the sixth juror.

Add at end of section:
Although rare, there can on occasion arise the question as to the subject regarding which there needs to be unanimity. In U.S. v. Russell, 134 F.3d 171 (3d Cir. 1998), the court held that the defendant's right to a unanimous verdict had been violated by an erroneous instruction indicating that the jurors had to agree unanimously that the defendant had participated in three or more violations of federal narcotic laws. In fact the jury had to be unanimous as to the identity of the three violations. The actual instruction allowed different jurors to convict based on different beliefs as to which acts constituted the three violations.

The issue of what exactly it is that jurors must be unanimous about is explored in Morris, *Something upon which We Can All Agree: Requiring a Unanimous Jury Verdict in Criminal Cases*, 62 Montana L. Rev. 1 (2001). The author favors a "specific unanimity" instruction in certain cases that would inform the jurors as to which material facts they have to agree (as opposed to the more standard "general unanimity" direction which only tells the jury to that they must unanimously agree on guilt or innocence).

In U.S. v. Hursh, 217 F.3d 761, 54 Fed. R. Evid. Serv. 1412 (9th Cir. 2000), one of the jurors arrived several minutes late for deliberations. While waiting for the juror, the others reviewed their notes and examined the exhibits. The defendant argued that this constituted "deliberations" and that, because only 11 jurors had been present at the deliberations, the resulting verdict was not unanimous. The Court of Appeals disagreed, holding that the jurors had not engaged in deliberations simply by silently reading their notes and examining the exhibits.

Although most commentators have been critical of the decision to permit non-unanimous jury verdicts, there are some exceptions. See, e.g., Morehead, *A 'Modest' Proposal for Jury Reform: The Elimination of Required Unanimous Jury Verdicts*, 46 Kansas L. Rev. 933 (1998); Comment, *Letting the Supermajority Rule: Nonunanimous Jury Verdicts in Criminal Trials*, 24 Florida St. L. Rev. 659 (1997) (both maintaining that elimination of the requirement of unanimity would help restore public confidence in the jury system). Professor Taylor-Thompson argues that unanimous verdicts are needed in order to give voice to the views of those persons historically subordinated in American society, such as woman and people of color. See Taylor-Thompson, *Empty Votes in Jury Deliberations*, 113 Harv. L. Rev. 1261 (2000).

§ 2:18 —Civil trials

Add to end of section:
Federal Rule of Civil Procedure 48 states that "[u]nless the parties otherwise stipulate, . . . the verdict shall be unanimous." See also Murray v. Laborers Union Local No. 324, 55 F.3d 1445, 149 L.R.R.M. (BNA) 2457, 149 L.R.R.M. (BNA) 2858, 130 Lab. Cas. (CCH) ¶ 11345, 130 Lab. Cas. (CCH) ¶ 11367, 31 Fed. R. Serv. 3d 1222 (9th Cir. 1995), as amended on denial of reh'g, (July 14, 1995).

§ 2:20 Jury nullification

Add after "criminal case" in first sentence of first paragraph
This is not to say that nullification does not occur in civil cases. Commonly civil juries will find for plaintiffs whom they consider to be deserving when the suit is against an insurance company or large corporation, even if the law, strictly applied to the facts, should logically lead to a verdict for the defendant. The differences between nullification in a civil case and nullification in a criminal case are pointed out in Noah, *Civil Jury Nullification*, 86 Iowa L. Rev. 1601 (2001). Most significantly, the author argues that the danger of oppressive government action is less in lawsuits between private persons.

Juries have also been known to return verdicts that exceed proper statutory limits on damages. As a countermeasure some trial judge courts simply fail to inform the jury of the statutory limit and then reduce any verdict that exceeds it. This practice is criticized in Comment, *Jury Nullification and Tort Reform in California: Eviscerating the Power of the Civil Jury by Keeping Citizens Ignorant of the Law*, 27 Southwestern L. Rev. 99 (1997) (arguing that by not mentioning statutory ceilings on damages, and then reduc-

§ 2:20

ing awards that exceed the statutory limit, courts frustrate a jury's conscious decision to nullify).

n. 168.

Add to note 168:

An analysis of the decision in *Bushell's Case*, and, in particular, the role that "personal knowledge" plays and should play in jury nullification is presented in Note, *Between Local Knowledge and National Politics: Debating Rationales for Jury Nullification after Bushell's Case*, 111 Yale L. J. 1815 (2002).

Add after note 176:

Some confusion on this point may have set in as a result of the decision of the United States Supreme Court in Old Chief v. U.S., 519 U.S. 172, 117 S. Ct. 644, 136 L. Ed. 2d 574, 45 Fed. R. Evid. Serv. 835 (1997), where the Court upheld the admission of evidence that tended to show a guilty verdict would be morally reasonable. Pettys argues that if such evidence is admitted in favor of the government, the defendant should be allowed to introduce evidence for the purpose of demonstrating that a guilty verdict would be morally unreasonable. Pettys, *Evidentiary Relevance, Morally Reasonable Verdicts, and Jury Nullification*, 86 Iowa L. Rev. 467 (2001).

Add after note 179:

The danger in allowing nullification is that it will be exercised on an improper basis, such as race. Some, however, would not see this as necessarily a bad development, at least when exercised in favor of a minority defendant. Compare Butler, *Racially Based Jury Nullification: Black Power in the Criminal Justice System*, 105 Yale LJ 677 (1995) (proposing that black jurors should approach their task cognizant of its political nature and with an eye to exercising their powers as jurors in the best interests of the black community) with Leopold, *The Dangers of Race-Based Jury Nullification: A Response to Professor Butler*, 44 UCLA L Rev 143 (1996). The debate between Professors Butler and Leipold (who, not Leopold, was the author of *The Dangers of Race-Based Jury Nullification: A Response to Professor Butler*, 44 UCLA L Rev 143 (1996)) as to whether black jurors should be encouraged to engage in nullification in cases in which black defendants are charged with victimless crimes is continued, with contributions from the Hon. Charles Kocoran, in Symposium, The Role of Race-Based Jury Nullification in American Criminal Justice, 30 John Marshall L. Rev. 907 (1997). See also Magliocca, *The Philosopher's Stone: Dualist Democracy and the Jury*, 69 U. Col. L. Rev. 175 (1998). The author of Comment, *Jury Nullification and Race-Conscious Reasonable Doubt: Overlapping Reifications of Commonsense Justice and the Potential Voir Dire Mistake*,

47 U.C.L.A. L. Rev. 1843 (2000) makes the point that Prof. Butler's interventions may prove counterproductive if they sensitize trial judges to the dangers (imaginary or real) of nullification by minority jurors, and if this in turn leads to a removal of black jurors suspected of being potential nullifiers. This would be an unfortunate development, according to the author, for it would remove those jurors with legitimate conceptions of "reasonable doubt" infused by their of the racism which exists within the criminal justice system.

Whether or not nullification has been exercised on an improper basis is extremely difficult to determine in practice, as few jurors will be so unsophisticated to admit that they voted one way or another because of a defendant's race, ethnicity or gender. As a consequence, false claims of nullification may be suspected when a jury is predominantly of the same race, ethnic background or gender as the defendant. The way to combat such claims is to strive for more diverse juries. See Marder, *The Interplay of Race and False Claims of Jury Nullification*, 32 U. Mich. J. of Law Reform, 285 (1999).

Add after "legislature causes discomfort." in eighth paragraph:

See Note, License to Nullify: The Democratic and Constitutional Deficiencies of Authorized Jury Lawmaking, 106 Yale L J 2563 (1997) (jury nullification is inconsistent with both democratic theory and constitutional norms) Crispo, Slansky, & Yriarte, *Jury Nullification: Law Versus Anarchy*, 31 Loyola of Los Angeles L. Rev. 1 (1997) (legal and legislative remedies, and not jury nullification, should be used to correct unfair laws and harsh penalties). The contrary position is advanced in J. Gobert, Justice, Democracy and the Jury (Dartmouth 1997). Gobert points out that jury deliberations constitute one of the prime remaining examples of participatory democracy (as opposed to representative democracy) in modern society. Jury independence, including the power to nullify when justice requires, is an essential component of democratic decision-making. And See Brown, Jury Nullification within the Rule of Law, 81 Minn. L. Rev. 1149 (1997) (nullification tends to occur within the context of the rule of law, with juries simply rejecting an overly literal application of a statute, and thereby rectifying oversights by other institutional branches of the system). Finkel, Commonsense Justice; Jurors' Notions of the Law (Harv. U. Press 1995) views nullification as the jury's attempt to perfect an imperfect law. Reviewing Finkel's book, Bandekis, *Perfection by Nullification*, 105 Yale L. J. 2285 (1996) criticizes Finkel for not paying sufficient attention to cases of vengeful convictions.

§ 2:20

The case that jury nullification is largely unnecessary because the necessity defense already provides a corrective device in cases involving crimes of conscience is made in Schopp, *Verdicts of Conscience: Nullification and Necessity as Jury Responses to Crimes of Conscience*, 69 S. Cal. L. Rev. 2039 (1996). The author favors resort to the necessity defense rather than nullification both because the former operates within the context of existing legal doctrine and because it requires a balancing of the harm caused against the harm avoided, something that nullification does not. Schopp believes that nullification may trivialize crimes of conscience and may have no legitimate place in the criminal justice system. One might respond, however, that, given the technical restrictions that hedge the defense of necessity in many jurisdictions, Schopp's thesis may be less powerful in reality than in theory.

Weinstein, drawing on his long experience as a federal trial judge, observes that the extreme disaffection that encouraged nullification during the Vietnam and Watergate eras appears less prevalent in the late 1990s, with a corresponding reduction in cases of nullification. Weinstein, *The Many Dimensions of Jury Nullification*, 81 Judicature n. 4, p. 168 (1998). Judge Weinstein divides nullification into cases involving unfair laws and/or penalties, fair laws but unfair applications of the law, distrust of police and state authority, and willful disagreement or intransigence on the part of a juror. Some instances of the latter may be inevitable. Instances of the other three categories, on the other hand, should serve as an alarm clock alerting the government to faults in the legal system.

Add at end of the eighth paragraph:
Horowitz, Kerr and Niedermeier stress the need for behavioral and empirical studies to test the psychological assumptions that underlie arguments both for and against nullification. Horowitz, Kerr & Niedermeier, *Jury Nullification: Legal and Psychological Perspectives*, 66 Brooklyn L. Rev. (2001).

n. 180.
Add to note 180:
See generally Scheflin & Van Dyke, *Merciful Juries: The Resilience of Jury Nullification*, 48 Wash & Lee L Rev 165 (1991) (advocating judicial instructions to jury on its nullification power); Galiber, Latzer, Dwyer, Litman, Uviller, & McDonald, *Law, Justice, and Jury Nullification: A Debate*, 29 Crim L Bull 40 (1993); Weinstein, *Considering Jury "Nullification": When May and Should a Jury Reject the Law to Do Justice*, 30 Am Crim L Rev 239 (1993); Korroch & Davidson, *Jury Nullification: A Call for Justice or an Invitation to Anarchy*, 139 Mil L Rev 131 (1993). Note, *Jury Nullification and Jury-Control Procedures*, 65 NYU L Rev 825 (1990); Note, *Jury Nullification: Assessing Recent Legislative Developments*, 43 Case W

Res L Rev 1101 (1993); Iijima, *Fictions, Fault and Forgiveness: Jury Nullification in a New Context*, 28 U Mich L Ref 861 (1995); Brody, *Sparf and Dougherty Revisited: Why the Court should Instruct the Jury on Its Nullification Right*, 33 Am Crim L Rev 89 (1995); Comment, *Jury Nullification Should be Made a Routine Part of the Criminal Justice System, but it Won't Be*, 29 Arizona State L. J. 1127 (1997) (nullification is opposed by legal establishment).

In *Dougherty*, one of the arguments made to support the case against informing jurors of their power to nullify was that jurors were already aware of it anyway. Empirical studies, however, suggest that most individuals do not have an accurate knowledge of this authority. See Brody & Rivera, *Examining the Dougherty "All-Knowing" Assumption: Do Jurors Know their Jury Nullification Power?*, 33 Crim. L. Bull 151 (1997); Farnham, Jury Nullification: History Proves it's not a Bad Idea, 11 Criminal Justice n. 4, p. 4 (1997) (arguing that nullifiers are usually morally conscientious individuals inclined to follow the instructions of the court if at all possible). See also Comment, *Penn, Zenger and OJ: Jury Nullification—Justice or the "Wacko Fringe's" Attempt to Further its Anti-Government Agenda*, 34 Duquesne L Rev 1125 (1996) (arguing in favor of jury nullification); Note, *Opposing Jury Nullification: Law, Policy and Prosecutorial Strategy*, 85 Georgetown LJ (1996) (arguing against informing jurors of their right to nullify).

In U.S. v. Marcucci, 299 F.3d 1156 (9th Cir. 2002), cert. denied, 123 S. Ct. 1600, 155 L. Ed. 2d 334 (U.S. 2003), a case of first impression, the question arose of whether grand jurors should be told that they could refuse to indict even if they found probable cause. The language of the standard grand jury charge, as noted by the court, does not state that the grand jury "shall" or "must" indict, but simply says that it "should" indict when probable cause is present. The defendants argued that the charge should do more and should affirmatively inform the grand jury that it has no obligation to indict even if it finds probable cause. The Court of Appeals rejected this argument, stating that the grand jury clause of the Fifth Amendment contained no language requiring the grand jury to be told that it can refuse to indict if probable cause is found. In the opinion of the court, any other formulation, besides potentially rendering unconstitutional all indictments returned under the standard charge, would sow confusion among the grand jurors, who would not have any guidelines as to when they should not indict despite the presence of probable cause to indict. The Court of Appeals was further of the opinion that the standard charge, by telling the grand jury that it "should" indict, left room (albeit limited room) for it to refuse to indict, despite the presence of probable cause, when the government's case was based on passion, prejudice or injustice.

n. 181.
Add to note 181:
The history of the jury's power to decide issues of law is examined in Harrington, *The Law-Finding Function of the American Jury*, 1999 Wisconsin L. Rev. 3777 (1999). Harrington notes that while permitting juries to declare the law may not have seemed out of place at a time when judges lacked legal training, there is less to be said in its favor in a more complex social and economic environment. This is not to say that jurors do not influence the development of the law. According to Harrington, legal rules can be seen as part of a cycle whereby intuitive jury notions of justice become transformed into formal legal rules.

Add at end of section:

§ 2:20

As much as lawyers might prefer judges to tell jurors that they possess the power to nullify, what they would not want is an explicit judicial instruction to the effect that jurors have no right to nullify. Such an instruction was given by the trial court in the California case of People v. Sanchez and upheld on appeal. People v. Sanchez, 58 Cal. App. 4th 1435, 69 Cal. Rptr. 2d 16 (2d Dist. 1997). The California appeals court held that the trial court acted within its authority when it told jurors that it would remove any who indicated that he or she would be prepared to engage in nullification. The Court's decision is examined in Note and Comment, *A Community with No Conscience: The Further Reduction of a Jury's Right to Nullify in* People v. Sanchez, 21 Whittier L. Rev. 285 (1999).

§ 2:21 —Jury selection as a function of the nullification power: Strategic considerations

Add after second sentence in first paragraph:
Whether a lawyer may question jurors on voir dire regarding their openness to consider nullifying is highly debatable. Few judges would allow questions that appear to encourage jurors to violate the law. In Jones v. Wellham, 104 F.3d 620 (4th Cir. 1997), the defendant sought to ask prospective jurors whether they would follow their conscience rather than the law if they disagreed with the law. The trial judge refused to permit this question and the court of appeal held that there had been no abuse of discretion, particularly given the defendant's inability to provide authority in support of this line of questioning.

In People v. Merced, 94 Cal. App. 4th 1024, 114 Cal. Rptr. 2d 781 (1st Dist. 2001), review denied, (Mar. 13, 2002) a prospective alternate juror was removed for cause after he indicated in writing on the juror questionnaire that he recognized and believed in jury nullification. When questioned by the judge, the prospective juror stated that it was reasonable for the judge to assume that he, the juror, would not follow the law if it went against his conscience. On appeal the removal for cause was upheld. The appellate court added that the trial judge was not required to undertake an inquiry into whether the particular details of the case to be tried presented a likelihood that the juror would actually engage in nullification, as such an inquiry would itself encourage improper prejudgment of the case.

n. 183.
Add to note 183:
The Fully Informed Jury Association (FIJA), most notably, has advocated legislation which would require courts to inform jurors that they have the right to return a verdict which accords with their conscience

even though it may not accord with the strict requirements of the law. Black, *Monkeywrenching the Justice System*, 66 UMKC L. Rev. 11 (1997) evaluates such proposals and notes that the envisaged instruction would have the salutary effect of stimulating jurors to think seriously about the goals and values inherent in the criminal justice system. Professor Leipold also supports placing nullification on a statutory footing, arguing that, as it currently functions, nullification extracts too high a price in terms of procedural rules (such as the rules against special verdicts, judgements as a matter of law, and appeals by the prosecution). Leipold, *Rethinking Jury Nullification*, 82 Va. L. Rev. 253 (1996).

Part II

LAYING THE GROUNDWORK

Chapter 3

Community Analysis: Goals and Methodologies

> **KeyCite®:** Cases and other legal materials listed in KeyCite Scope can be researched through West's KeyCite service on Westlaw®. Use KeyCite to check citations for form, parallel references, prior and later history, and comprehensive citator information, including citations to other decisions and secondary materials.

§ 3:1 Introduction

Add after third sentence in second paragraph:
See Weiner & Stolle, *Trial Consulting: Jurors and Attorneys' Perceptions of Murder* 34 Cal Western L. Rev 225 (1997) (concluding that surveys presenting the facts and law of an active case to a representative sample of eligible jurors can help attorneys to select the criteria most likely to discriminate between hostile and sympathetic jurors better than simple reliance on the attorney's beliefs about juror behavior).

§ 3:2 Questionnaires, surveys, and interviews

Add at end of section:
While the value of questionnaires, surveys, and interviews is undoubted, a court in the exercise of its supervisory power may regulate or even bar their use. In U.S. v. Lehder-Rivas, 669 F. Supp. 1563 (M.D. Fla. 1987), the court held that the threat to the fair administration of justice posed by the use of pretrial surveys outweighed the free speech and fair trial interests of the party seeking to conduct the surveys. The court thought that even if a jury profile would have enhanced defendant's preparation for voir dire (and defendant had not shown that he could not have conducted voir dire adequately without a jury profile), the contact between defendant's representatives and potential jurors in what was admittedly

a highly publicized case would adversely affect the ability to select an impartial jury.

Several limiting factors in regard to the court's ruling, however, are worth noting. First, the planned surveys were to be conducted less than three weeks prior to the start of trial, and the potential publicity effect of the survey at this critical point in time troubled the court more than it might have at some earlier stage of the proceedings. Second, the defense had already questioned more than 2,000 residents of the district in a pre-voir dire survey, the results of which it was not prohibited from using. Third, the court's order extended only to potential jurors in the community in which the trial was to be held; the defendant remained free to conduct polls and surveys in other districts. Finally, several of defendant's proposed questions were, in the court's estimation, irrelevant or highly prejudicial.

In U.S. v. Collins, 972 F.2d 1385 (5th Cir. 1992), a pretrial telephone survey was commissioned by the prosecution. Among other questions, the survey asked whether the respondents agreed with the proposition that people accused of a crime ought to have to prove they are innocent. Almost two-thirds of the respondents indicated that they "somewhat" or "strongly" agreed. The respondents were then presented with a recitation of the prosecution's version of the evidence and asked whether they thought the defendants were definitely guilty, probably guilty, probably not guilty, or definitely not guilty. A large majority of those who responded thought the defendants were definitely or probably guilty. The defendants discovered the survey and informed the district court, which ordered a halt to the polling but found that the integrity of jury selection had not been compromised and the poll had not given the prosecution an unfair advantage in selecting a jury. The appellate court agreed, reasoning that the prosecution had derived no advantage from the poll because it had not uncovered the demographic and background information about the respondents that would have allowed it to make use of the raw data at jury selection.

§ 3:11 Posttrial interviews of jurors

§ 3:12 —Posttrial interviews as a basis for impeaching the verdict

n. 36.

Add to note 36:
Dall v. Coffin, 970 F.2d 964 (1st Cir. 1992).

n. 40.

Add to note 40:

In U.S. v. Gotti, 784 F. Supp. 1013 (E.D. N.Y. 1992), however, the court refused to allow the defendants, who were charged with jury tampering, to conduct inquiries of the jurors in the prior case. The court cited its concern with preventing the needless harassment of jurors, and the defendants' failure to show any basis upon which information necessary to the preparation of their defense could be obtained by such an inquiry. In Fullwood v. Lee, 290 F.3d 663, 59 Fed. R. Evid. Serv. 115 (4th Cir. 2002), cert. denied, 537 U.S. 1120, 123 S. Ct. 890, 154 L. Ed. 2d 799 (2003) where the defendant was convicted of murder, it was alleged that a juror may have been pressured by her husband, who had a particularly strong philosophical and ideological leaning in favor of the death penalty. The record in the case was, however, sparse, and the Court of Appeals remanded for an evidentiary hearing to determine whether the contact between the juror and her husband deprived the defendant of a fair trial and had a "substantial and injurious effect" on the verdict. At this hearing the district court was also directed to examine the defendant's allegations that the jury had become aware from outside sources that the defendant had been sentenced to death by another jury and, if so, to determine whether the information received was "extraneous" or "prejudicial", and whether it "had a substantial and injurious effect or influence in determining the jury's verdict."

Add after note 40:

Whether a jury has been exposed to improper extrinsic information during its deliberations, and whether, as a result, a defendant has been substantially prejudiced, is a mixed question of law and fact. Vigil v. Zavaras, 298 F.3d 935 (10th Cir. 2002). In *Vigil*, the Court of Appeals laid down a number of relevant factors for a court to consider on this issue:

(1) the degree to which the jury discussed and considered the extrinsic information;

(2) the extent to which the jury had difficulty reaching its verdict prior to receipt of the impermissible information;

(3) the degree to which the information related to a material fact in the case;

(4) the time at which the jury received the extrinsic information;

(5) the strength of the legitimate evidence; and

(6) whether the extrinsic evidence merely duplicated evidence properly before the jury.

In *Vigil*, the key issue at trial was the accuracy of the victim's identification of the defendant as her assailant. The extraneous evidence received by the jury related to whether the defendant had sufficient time to go from the locus of his alibi defense to the scene of the crime, an issue on which evidence pro and con had been presented at trial. The Court of Appeals concluded that the defendant had not been prejudiced by the extrinsic evidence sufficient to warrant the granting of habeas relief.

§ 3:12   JURY SELECTION: LAW, ART & SCIENCE 2D

In Mancuso v. Olivarez, 292 F.3d 939, 58 Fed. R. Evid. Serv. 1150 (9th Cir. 2002) the jury foreman, during deliberations, impermissibly injected extrinsic evidence regarding his belief that the defendants had previous felony convictions. The foreman's information was gained by removing tape from the bottom of photographs of the defendants that were trial exhibits and requested by the jury, and comparing the booking numbers on the photographs with booking numbers in county jail records. In doing so, the foreman drew on his prior employment as a youth counsellor with the department of corrections. The Court of Appeals held that a juror's personal knowledge of specific information regarding a defendant or the defendant's crime constituted impermissible extrinsic evidence. To determine whether the introduction of such evidence constituted reversible error, the court considered a number of factors:

(1) whether the extrinsic material was actually received, and if so, how;
(2) the length of time it was available to the jury;
(3) the extent to which the jury discussed and considered it;
(4) whether the extrinsic material was introduced before a verdict was reached, and, if so, at what point in the deliberations it was introduced; and
(5) any other matters which may bear on the issue of . . . whether the introduction [substantially and injuriously] affected the verdict.

In the case, the extrinsic material was introduced before the verdict was entered, but was not discussed at great length. Further, the jurors were only told of the foreman's belief that the defendants had a criminal record. In any event, the jurors were not exposed to the prejudicial details of the defendant's criminal history. The Court of Appeals concluded that, in the circumstances, the extraneous information did not have a substantial and injurious influence on the verdict.

In Crawford v. Head, 311 F.3d 1288 (11th Cir. 2002), a juror who was a nursing student stated in an affidavit that she had answered questions from other jurors relating to the meaning of various hair and blood sample tests and results. In another affidavit, a juror told of a nurse on the jury who had explained to another juror, who was opposed to imposing the death sentence on the ground that the hair and blood samples introduced into evidence could have come from anyone, that scientific tests could establish whether blood and hair samples came from a particular individual. The Court of Appeals found on the basis of this evidence that no juror misconduct which was in violation of the defendant's due process rights had occurred. The information in the affidavits did not indicate that any juror had introduced extrinsic evidence into the deliberations or had improperly influenced the other jurors. What had occurred was simply that the jurors had brought to bear their personal experiences in analyzing the evidence in the case, which was proper.

In an Internet age, obtaining knowledge about a case on which one is sitting as a juror can be achieved from the comfort of one's home, even if there is a newspaper blackout on reporting of the trial. Indeed, a juror could log on to the Court's own website, type in a defendant's name in a criminal case, and learn much about the defendant (such as his prior convictions) that was not disclosed in the trial. Trial judges find themselves in a dilemma, as an instruction to the jury not to search the Internet for information about the trial may serve only to suggest to jurors that there is something "out there" worth learning about, while ignoring the issue may cause jurors to believe that an Internet search is not improper. The issue has arisen primarily in respect to jurors who consulted the Internet during deliberations.

In Real v. Wal Mart Stores, Inc., 2002 WL 80664 (Cal. App. 2d Dist. 2002), unpublished/noncitable, (Jan. 22, 2002) and review denied, (May 15, 2002), a juror, during deliberations, had searched the Internet in an attempt to learn more about the meaning of "negligence." However, the juror did not reveal the results of this search to the other members of the jury because the foreman instructed him not to do so, and the juror did not discuss his findings with the other jurors. Under the circumstances the California Court of Appeal found that there was neither prejudice not a reasonable probability of harm. Also in the case another juror had contacted a friend who was a lawyer through the Internet to discuss the "conflicts that the jury was having during the deliberations." However, as the juror did not reveal the facts of the case to the lawyer or the specifics of the deliberation, and as the lawyer's response was generally anodyne, the court again found that there had not been any prejudice to the parties. See also Buford v. Group Health Cooperative of Puget Sound, 98 Wash. App. 1063, 2000 WL 44123 (Div. 1 2000).

In contrast, the court in People v. Wadle, 2003 WL 193687 (Colo. Ct. App. 2003), a criminal child abuse prosecution, found misconduct where a juror had obtained information from the Internet about the antidepressant drug Paxil, which the defendant had been taking at the time of the offense. Here, unlike in *Real*, the juror had shared the results of his

§ 3:12

search with the other members of the jury. The court found that there had been juror misconduct and that the introduction of this extraneous evidence may well have influenced the verdict. The court remanded for a new trial. It also advised that, given the problems and dangers associated with the unsupervised use of the Internet, trial judges should emphasize to jurors that they should not consult the Internet either during the trial or during deliberations. As noted, however, such a direction may only serve to inspire a search that would not otherwise have occurred to jurors and inhibit candor when the jurors are questioned about it. It may make more sense to inquire of prospective jurors during voir dire regarding the extent of their use of the Internet.

n. 41.
   Add to note 41:
   In Jones v. Cooper, 311 F.3d 306 (4th Cir. 2002), cert. denied, 123 S. Ct. 2613 (U.S. 2003), the defendant had been convicted of murder and sentenced to death. An investigator subsequently employed by the defendant interviewed one of the jurors, who made several statements that indicated that the juror may not have answered certain questions on the jury questionnaire and on voir dire honestly and may in fact have been biased. On the questionnaire, the juror had answered "no" in response to questions asking whether any friends, family or acquaintances had ever been arrested or subjected to a trial. The investigator established that this was false and the Court of Appeals agreed, but stated that under state law it would not have afforded a basis for a challenge for cause. As to the other alleged misstatements, the court was of the opinion that they were more properly characterized as "inconsistencies" than "lies". For example, while the juror stated that she "never went" to the store that was the scene of the crime, she admitted to the investigator that she had. However, on voir dire she had stated that she lived in the area and had noticed that the store was boarded up after the crime. The court thought that the discrepancy could be attributed to juror's colloquial way of indicating that she rarely patronized the store in question. Two other discrepancies, however, were arguably of greater significance. First, the juror had stated on voir dire that she only had a vague knowledge of case. However, she told the investigator that she was aware of the defendant's previous trial and death sentence. The Court of Appeals explained this away by noting that the questions on voir dire had focused only on the juror's knowledge of the robbery and murder, and not on her knowledge of the defendant's previous trial or death sentence. Secondly, the investigator's affidavit recounted the juror's statement to him "that the Bible mandates imposition of the death penalty in every case of first degree murder" and that she "could not imagine any first degree murder case in which the death penalty would not be appropriate, other than if the defendant grew up in a jungle with no contact with humanity." The Court of Appeals, somewhat incredulously it is submitted, found no inconsistency between these statements regarding the death penalty and the juror's voir dire response where she declared her support for the death penalty "when appropriate" and stated she could fairly balance aggravating and mitigating circumstances. While admitting to being "troubled" by the various misstatements by the juror, the Court of Appeals found that there had not been a violation of McDonough Power Equipment, Inc. v. Greenwood, 464 U.S. 548, 104 S.

Ct. 845, 78 L. Ed. 2d 663 (1984), and that the investigator's evidence did not demonstrate that the juror was actually or impliedly biased.

Add at end of section:
An argument for the liberalization of the present approach is made in Note, *Limitations on Attorney Postverdict Contact with Jurors: Protecting the Criminal Jury and its Verdict at the Expense of the Defendant*, 94 Colum L Rev 1950 (1994).

§ 3:14 —Court-imposed restrictions on posttrial interviews

n. 45.
Add to note 45:
U.S. v. Hooshmand, 931 F.2d 725, 32 Fed. R. Evid. Serv. 1281 (11th Cir. 1991); McElroy by McElroy v. Firestone Tire & Rubber Co., 894 F.2d 1504, Prod. Liab. Rep. (CCH) ¶ 12396 (11th Cir. 1990).

In U.S. v. Brown, 250 F.3d 907, 29 Media L. Rep. (BNA) 1779 (5th Cir. 2001), the Court of Appeals upheld the trial court's order denying the media's request for postverdict access to juror identifying information, including names and addresses, and juror questionnaires. The trial court in the case had impaneled an anonymous jury and the Court's power to protect the jurors' privacy and freedom from harassment did not end when the case ended.

Add at end of section:
In U.S. v. Antar, 38 F.3d 1348, 40, 22 Media L. Rep. (BNA) 2417, Fed. Sec. L. Rep. (CCH) ¶ 98436, 40 Fed. R. Evid. Serv. 1006 (3d Cir. 1994), the Court of Appeals discussed the matter of posttrial interviews. The court took a cautious but balanced approach. It said that a trial judge should emphasize to the jurors the importance of confidentiality and the reasons why it is necessary. The jurors should also be told that they are not required to grant a posttrial interview, and that the court will protect them from unwanted harassment. On the other hand, the Court of Appeals indicated that prohibitions on posttrial interviews are not called for absent evidence of actual or threatened harassing or intrusive interviews. It is not enough that the trial judge has general misgivings about the wisdom of such interviews. See generally Goldstein, *Jury Secrecy and the Media: The Problem of Postverdict Interviews*, 1993 Ill L Rev 295. The constitutional and ethical dilemmas facing a lawyer conducting a posttrial interview are explored in Casenote, *When Can an Attorney Ask: "What Were You Thinking?"— Regulation of Attorney Posttrial Communication with Jurors after Commission for* Lawyer Discipline v. Benton, 40 S. Tex. L. Rev. 1069 (1999).

The court in U.S. v. Cleveland, 128 F.3d 267, 25 Media L. Rep. (BNA) 2500 (5th Cir. 1997) held that a narrowly drawn postverdict order that jurors could not be interviewed regard-

§ 3:14   Jury Selection: Law, Art & Science 2d

ing their deliberations did not violate the First Amendment rights of publishers or reporters, and was not unconstitutionally vague.

§ 3:15   Financing pretrial, trial, and posttrial jury analyses

§ 3:16   —Court-appointed experts: Constitutional analysis

Add at end of the sixth paragraph:

An argument, based on *Ake*, in favor of providing a defendant who could not afford jury selection experts with such experts was rejected in Moore v. Johnson, 225 F.3d 495 (5th Cir. 2000), cert. denied, 532 U.S. 949, 121 S. Ct. 1420, 149 L. Ed. 2d 360 (2001). The court stated that, in its opinion, jury selection was not a "mysterious process" to be undertaken by lawyers only with the assistance of outside professionals. Rather, jury selection in the Court's opinion was a process that all competent lawyers should have the natural "raw materials" to be able to undertake. The court further stated that the fact that a wealthy defendant might elect to hire jury consultants did not require the state to expend its resources on consultants for indigent defendants. In any event, the court did not see that the lack of a jury consultant had in any way impacted on the defendant's ability to present his claims. One could, of course, quibble with the latter point, as a consultant who understands the psyche of the jurors would be able to advise counsel how most effectively to present the defendant's claims.

n. 58.

Add to note 58:

See also Pierce, *Selecting the Perfect Jury: Use of Jury Consultants in Voir Dire*, 14 Law & Psychology Rev 167 (1990).

Chapter 4

Investigation of the Venire

> **KeyCite®:** Cases and other legal materials listed in KeyCite Scope can be researched through West's KeyCite service on Westlaw®. Use KeyCite to check citations for form, parallel references, prior and later history, and comprehensive citator information, including citations to other decisions and secondary materials.

Table of New and Retitled Sections

§ 4:3A   Tax records *[New]*

§ 4:3A   Tax records *[New]*

In tax cases, both the government and the defendant may obtain information from the IRS regarding prospective jurors under 26 U.S.C.A. § 6103(h)(5):

> In connection with any judicial proceeding described in paragraph (4) to which the United States is a party, the Secretary shall respond to a written inquiry from an attorney of the Department of Justice (including a United States Attorney) involved in such proceeding or any person (or his representative) who is a party of such proceeding as to whether an individual who is a prospective juror in such proceeding has or has not been the subject of any audit or other tax investigation by the Internal Revenue Service. The Secretary shall limit such response to an affirmative or negative reply to such inquiry.

26 U.S.C.A. § 6103(h)(5). This section has been interpreted differently within the federal circuits. In U.S. v. Sinigaglio, 925 F.2d 339, 91-1 U.S. Tax Cas. (CCH) ¶ 50082, 68 A.F.T.R.2d 91-5189 (9th Cir. 1991), opinion amended and superseded, 942 F.2d 581 (9th Cir. 1991), as amended on denial of reh'g, (Oct. 20, 1991) and (overruled by, U.S. v. Morales, 108 F.3d 1031, 46 Fed. R. Evid. Serv. 1145 (9th Cir. 1997)), the Ninth Circuit Court of Appeals construed § 6103(h)(5) to give a defendant an "absolute right" not to proceed to trial without IRS audit record information about prospective jurors. U.S. v. Sinigaglio, 925 F.2d 339, 91-1 U.S. Tax Cas. (CCH) ¶ 50082, 68 A.F.T.R.2d 91-5189 (9th Cir. 1991), opinion amended and superseded, 942 F.2d 581 (9th Cir. 1991), as amended on denial of reh'g, (Oct. 20,

1991) and (overruled by, U.S. v. Morales, 108 F.3d 1031, 46 Fed. R. Evid. Serv. 1145 (9th Cir. 1997)). See also, U.S. v. Hashimoto, 878 F.2d 1126, 89-2 U.S. Tax Cas. (CCH) ¶ 9432, 66 A.F.T.R.2d 90-5574 (9th Cir. 1989). But in U.S. v. Huguenin, 950 F.2d 23, 91-2 U.S. Tax Cas. (CCH) ¶ 50571, 68 A.F.T.R.2d 91-5902 (1st Cir. 1991), the First Circuit gave the statutory section a less restrictive interpretation. The court said that there was nothing in the statute or its legislative history which suggested that Congress intended to disturb a district court's traditional "authority to control its docket and its public duty to offer prompt and efficient administration of justice." U.S. v. Huguenin, 950 F.2d 23, 91-2 U.S. Tax Cas. (CCH) ¶ 50571, 68 A.F.T.R.2d 91-5902 (1st Cir. 1991). Accord U.S. v. Spine, 945 F.2d 143, 147–48, 91-2 U.S. Tax Cas. (CCH) ¶ 50464, 34 Fed. R. Evid. Serv. 351, 68 A.F.T.R.2d 91-5636 (6th Cir. 1991). U.S. v. Copple, 24 F.3d 535, 94-1 U.S. Tax Cas. (CCH) ¶ 50237, 39 Fed. R. Evid. Serv. 941, 74 A.F.T.R.2d 94-6133 (3d Cir. 1994) (investigation of tax records of prospective jurors need only meet a reasonableness standard and may be time limited). The district court in *Hequenin* had denied the defendant's motion under § 6103(h)(5) for the names of prospective jurors in advance of trial. At trial, the district court had allowed voir dire questioning in respect to tax audits and investigations and had directed the prosecutor to seek verification of the information from the IRS. Although some minor discrepancies subsequently emerged, the appellate court found no reversible error. As for the procedure employed by the district court, the appellate court found that it was reasonable to assume that jurors would tell the truth on voir dire. The court also noted that even if a juror did lie (or, more likely, forget), there was little risk of prejudice against the defendant, for if anything the juror would likely be biased against the government.

It is submitted that the Ninth Circuit's interpretation of § 6103(h)(5) is more compelling than that of the First Circuit. The latter in effect renders the statutory right nugatory. It also has practical consequences. If voir dire is conducted by defense counsel, questioning as to a juror's past audits by the IRS may be resented by the juror. Such offense may not need to be risked if, as the statute contemplates, the necessary information can be obtained before trial. As a matter of trial strategy, the information may tip the balance in favor of the peremptory challenge of one juror rather than another. The First Circuit's holding converts what should be a question of trial strategy to an issue of law to be decided on appeal, an appeal that is most unlikely to succeed in that circuit.

Any delay in trial resulting from a defendant's inquiry

under § 6103(h)(5) will not count towards a claim of a violation of the Speedy Trial Act, 18 U.S.C.A. § 3161(h)(8)(A). See U.S. v. Pottorf, 769 F. Supp. 1176 (D. Kan. 1991).

§ 4:5 Juror privacy

Add after second sentence in first paragraph:

In Whitehead v. Cowan, 263 F.3d 708 (7th Cir. 2001), cert. denied, 534 U.S. 1116, 122 S. Ct. 927, 151 L. Ed. 2d 890 (2002) the Court of Appeals stated that, while the publication of juror names and addresses could impair a fair trial, it did not inevitably do so and therefore did not automatically give rise to a finding of presumed prejudice. The court found that, in the circumstances of the case, there was no reasonable possibility that the publication could have affected the jury's verdict and that a hearing to determine whether the publication had such an effect was not necessary. The defendant, according to the court, had failed to show that he had suffered any prejudice.

See generally Annotation, Propriety of, and procedure for, ordering names and identities of jurors to be withheld from accused in federal criminal trial—"anonymous juries", 93 A.L.R. Fed. 135.

Add after first paragraph:

Anonymous juries were again at issue in U.S. v. Paccione, 949 F.2d 1183, 34 Fed. R. Evid. Serv. 621 (2d Cir. 1991). The Court of Appeals stated that a trial judge should not order the impaneling of an anonymous jury without:

1. Concluding that there was a strong reason to believe that the jury needed protection; and
2. Taking reasonable precautions to minimize any prejudice to the defendants.

The government had argued in its motion that the serious nature of the charges, the potential for long prison sentences, the murder of one of the defendants in suspicious circumstances, the reputed connection of the defendants with organized crime, and the threats already received by a witness made an anonymous jury appropriate. Both the trial court and the appellate court agreed.

The trial court satisfied the second prong of the appellate Court's test by instructing the jury at the outset that the special precautions were being taken to protect them from contacts by the media. Thus, the trial court provided a plausible explanation for the anonymity and, thereby, protected the defendants from the prejudice that might have resulted had the true reasons been revealed.

In another Second Circuit case, U.S. v. Vario, 943 F.2d

236, 119 Lab. Cas. (CCH) ¶ 10907 (2d Cir. 1991), the Court of Appeals upheld the use of an anonymous jury in a trial for violations of the Racketeer Influenced and Corrupt Organizations Act (RICO) and the Taft-Hartley Act. The government had cited in support of its motion for the anonymous jury the defendant's ties with an organized crime family, grand jury tampering by one of the defendant's coconspirators, and the expected publicity surrounding the case. The Court of Appeals found the latter two reasons persuasive but was not influenced by the defendant's alleged connections with organized crime. The court was apparently concerned lest the mere invocation of the terms mob, Mafia, or organized crime be thought sufficient to justify an anonymous jury. The court wanted concrete evidence that jurors would have cause to fear for their safety. The reasoning of the court seems somewhat unrealistic; surely jurors are more afraid of and have more to fear from a defendant's possible organized crime connections than from pretrial publicity. Every effort should be made, compatible with safeguarding the defendant's rights, to allay those fears and ensure juror safety.

Other anonymous jury cases from the same circuit include U.S. v. Aulicino, 44 F.3d 1102 (2d Cir. 1995); U.S. v. Wong, 40 F.3d 1347 (2d Cir. 1994); U.S. v. Amuso, 21 F.3d 1251, 39 Fed. R. Evid. Serv. 569 (2d Cir. 1994); U.S. v. Thai, 29 F.3d 785, 40 Fed. R. Evid. Serv. 1387 (2d Cir. 1994); U.S. v. Tutino, 883 F.2d 1125, 28 Fed. R. Evid. Serv. 466 (2d Cir. 1989); U.S. v. Persico, 832 F.2d 705, 24 Fed. R. Evid. Serv. 137, 89 A.L.R. Fed. 857 (2d Cir. 1987); U.S. v. Thomas, 757 F.2d 1359 (2d Cir. 1985); U.S. v. Gotti, 777 F. Supp. 224 (E.D. N.Y. 1991). Whether an evidentiary hearing on the need for an anonymous jury is required lies in the Court's discretion. U.S. v. Aulicino, 44 F.3d 1102 (2d Cir. 1995).

In U.S. v. Collazo-Aponte, 216 F.3d 163, 54 Fed. R. Evid. Serv. 1311 (1st Cir. 2000), cert. granted in part, judgment vacated on other grounds, 532 U.S. 1036, 121 S. Ct. 1996, 149 L. Ed. 2d 1000 (2001), the defendants were charged with murder and membership in a violent, sprawling drug conspiracy. One defendant was also charged with intimidation and murder of a government witness. The Court of Appeals had no difficulty concluding that an anonymous jury was warranted. The court also approved of the precautionary measures taken by the trial judge in not mentioning the threat to juror safety, but instead justifying the anonymity by concerns relating to publicity.

In U.S. v. Eufrasio, 935 F.2d 553, 32 Fed. R. Evid. Serv. 1262 (3d Cir. 1991), the Third Circuit Court of Appeals held that a trial court may permit an anonymous jury without holding an evidentiary hearing if the court is of the opinion there is the potential for juror apprehension. See also U.S. v. Thornton, 1 F.3d 149 (3d Cir. 1993). Nor is there any inconsistency between a refusal to grant a change in venue and a decision to impanel an anonymous jury. See, e.g., U.S. v. Childress, 746 F. Supp. 1122 (D.D.C. 1990), aff'd, 58 F.3d 693 (D.C. Cir. 1995).

In U.S. v. Crockett, 979 F.2d 1204, 37 Fed. R. Evid. Serv. 217 (7th Cir. 1992), the Seventh Circuit Court of Appeals held that the trial court did not abuse its discretion in impaneling an anonymous jury. See also U.S. v. Pasciuti, 803 F. Supp. 499 (D.N.H. 1992) (upholding anonymous jury in multi-count drug prosecution against members of notorious motorcycle gang with reputation for violence, organized criminal activity and history of intimidating witnesses; also some evidence of attempt to intimidate and threaten government witnesses in case at bar); See also U.S. v. Talley, 164 F.3d 989, 51 Fed. R. Evid. Serv. 181, 1999 FED App. 0013P (6th Cir. 1999) (defendant's attempt to kill FBI agent, as well as other attempts to manipulate criminal justice system, justified impaneling of anonymous jury); U.S. v. Dakota, 197 F.3d 821, 1999, 84 A.F.T.R.2d 99-7427, 1999 FED App. 0419A (6th Cir. 1999) (trial court did not abuse its discretion in impaneling partially anonymous jury in order to minimize prejudicial effects of pretrial publicity and to avoid an emotional, political atmosphere that created a risk of jury intimidation and improper influence); U.S. v. Boyd, 792 F. Supp. 1083 (N.D. Ill. 1992).

In U.S. v. Ross, 33 F.3d 1507, 41 Fed. R. Evid. Serv. 303 (11th Cir. 1994), the Eleventh Circuit joined those circuits which had previously held that anonymous juries were permissible. The court noted that the empanelment of such a jury was a drastic measure because it might suggest to the jurors that the defendant was a dangerous person from whom the jurors needed to be protected. Such a suggestion had implications for the accused's right to be presumed innocent. The Court of Appeals cited a number of factors which might properly be taken into account:

1. The defendant's involvement in organized crime;
2. The defendant's participation in a group with the capacity to harm jurors;
3. The defendant's past attempts to interfere with the judicial process;
4. The potential that, if convicted, the defendant will suffer a lengthy incarceration and substantial monetary penalties;
5. Extensive publicity that could enhance the possibility that jurors' names would become public and expose them to intimidation or harassment.

U.S. v. Ross, 33 F.3d 1507, 1520, 41 Fed. R. Evid. Serv. 303 (11th Cir. 1994). The trial judge had found that virtually all of the above factors were present in the case and the Court of Appeals held that this was not an abuse of discretion. The Court of Appeals also approved of the trial judge's neutral explanation to the jurors that it wanted to insulate them from improper communications from either side and that its decision was no reflection on the defense.

Accord, U.S. v. Bowman, 302 F.3d 1228, 59 Fed. R. Evid. Serv. 1018 (11th Cir. 2002), cert. denied, 123 S. Ct. 1923, 155 L. Ed. 2d 829 (U.S. 2003) (district court did not abuse its discretion in sua sponte decision to empanel anonymous jury in murder and racketeering trial of motorcycle club's international president, where club had history of violent conduct and had on previous occasions sought to intimidate witnesses into not testifying, where defendant was accused of kidnapping and murdering club members to punish them for communicating with law enforcement authorities, where president was facing life sentence, and where president's capture and trial had attracted significant publicity; failure to give *Ross* instruction was not error, as defendant had not requested such an instruction).

In U.S. v. Darden, 70 F.3d 1507, 43 Fed. R. Evid. Serv. 321 (8th Cir. 1995), the Eighth Circuit Court of Appeals upheld the use of an anonymous jury. The defendants were involved in an extremely violent organized criminal enterprise, the enterprise had a history of intimidating as well as murdering witnesses and many of its members remained at large, the defendants faced possible sentences of life imprisonment, and the case had been highly publicized. There thus was, in the opinion of the court, "ample reason" for impaneling an anonymous jury. The Court of Appeals also approved of the trial court's tactic, used in other jurisdictions, of telling the jurors that they were being identified by number rather than name so that the media would not ask them questions. Accord, U.S. v. Peoples, 250 F.3d 630, 56 Fed. R. Evid. Serv. 331 (8th Cir. 2001). See also U.S. v. DeLuca, 137 F.3d 24 (1st Cir. 1998) (upholding impaneling of anonymous jury and approving judge's explanation that the jurors' identities were being kept secret in order to ensure against any extrajudicial information being conveyed to them); U.S. v. Collazo-Aponte, 216 F.3d 163, 54 Fed. R. Evid. Serv. 1311 (1st Cir. 2000), cert. granted in part, judgment vacated on other grounds, 532 U.S. 1036, 121 S. Ct. 1996, 149 L. Ed. 2d 1000 (2001) (same).

In U.S. v. Edmond, 52 F.3d 1080, 42 Fed. R. Evid. Serv. 119 (D.C. Cir. 1995), the District of Columbia Court of Appeals held that the district court had not abused its discretion in impaneling an anonymous jury. The defendants were key members of a large-scale drug conspiracy that was known to be willing to resort to violent acts to achieve its goals. They faced penalties that were among the most severe the law could impose, and the father of one of the defendants had reputedly said that he would "take care of witnesses." The trial court minimized the potentially prejudicial impact of an anonymous jury by conducting an extensive voir dire and by explaining to the jurors that the decision to keep their names confidential was not uncommon. The Court of Appeals noted that the defendants' proposed alternative of sequestration, while perhaps sufficient to ensure jury safety during the trial, would not have protected the jurors against subsequent retaliation.

In U.S. v. Krout, 66 F.3d 1420, 43 Fed. R. Evid. Serv. 129 (5th Cir. 1995), the Fifth Circuit Court of Appeals upheld the use of anonymous juries. The defendants in the case were alleged members of the Texas Mexican Mafia. This organization had been linked to numerous murders and admitted a willingness both to interfere with potential witnesses and to corrupt law enforcement authorities. Furthermore, the penalties faced by the defendants were substantial, and the case had been the subject of considerable publicity. See also, U.S. v. Riggio, 70 F.3d 336, 43 Fed. R. Evid. Serv. 856 (5th Cir. 1995) (decision to impanel anonymous jury based on defendant's organized crime connections and previous involvement in jury fraud was not abuse of trial court's discretion). U.S. v. Sanchez, 74 F.3d 562, 43 Fed. R. Evid. Serv. 1069 (5th Cir. 1996), also from the Fifth Circuit, is a rare but instructive example of a case where a Court of Appeals found that the trial court had abused its discretion in impaneling an anonymous jury. The defendant, a police officer, had been charged with various civil rights violations. The trial court, fearing that jurors might be afraid of retaliation from rogue officers or might be tampered with during an unavoidable week's delay between jury selection and trial, impaneled an anonymous jury. The Court of Appeals held that this was an abuse of discretion. Citing *Krout*, the court identified the types of factors that had proved persuasive in other cases cited in this note: the defendant's involvement in organized crime or with a group with the capacity to harm jurors; past evidence of interference with the judicial process or witnesses; the potential that, if convicted, the defendant would incur a substantial penalty; and the danger that extensive publicity could expose jurors to intimidation and harassment. Virtually none of these factors was present in Sanchez's case, however. He was not involved in organized crime nor was he a member of a group that was likely to attempt to harm jurors. There was also no evidence of previ-

§ 4:5

ous interference with either the judicial process or witnesses, and the case was not of the type that would engender the extensive publicity that might bring about intimidation or harassment of jurors. The court concluded that the defendant's right to be tried before a panel of identified jurors had been violated. Although it was argued that this error was harmless, the Court of Appeals disagreed. It placed significant value in having jurors who could be held responsible for the verdict: "The defendant has a right to a jury of known individuals not just because information such as was redacted here yields valuable clues for purposes of jury selection, but also because the verdict is both personalized and personified when rendered by 12 known fellow citizens." U.S. v. Sanchez, 74 F.3d 562, 565, 43 Fed. R. Evid. Serv. 1069 (5th Cir. 1996). This rhetoric notwithstanding, it is submitted that a court should be solicitous of the not unreasonable concerns of jurors, who should not have to incur a threat or even a perceived threat to their safety by virtue of performing a public service.

In U.S. v. Mansoori, 304 F.3d 635, 59 Fed. R. Evid. Serv. 1109 (7th Cir. 2002), as amended on denial of reh'g, (Oct. 16, 2002) and cert. denied, 123 S. Ct. 1761, 155 L. Ed. 2d 522 (U.S. 2003), the defendants were charged with a conspiracy that was alleged to have embraced a large-scale, gang-related operation with ready access to firearms and involving elements of organized crime. Although the district court did not make any specific finding that witnesses were at risk of intimidation or that justice was in danger of being obstructed, it ordered an anonymous jury to be empanelled. The Court of Appeals held that, although the defendants had the ability and incentive to threaten jurors, without additional evidence indicating that they were likely to act on that ability and incentive, there was not sufficient evidence to justify the unusual step of juror anonymity. Nonetheless the Court of Appeals held that the decision to empanel an anonymous jury was harmless in light of the judge's careful and conscientious voir dire and the overwhelming evidence of the defendants' guilt. See generally, King, *Nameless Justice: The Case for the Routine Use of Anonymous Juries in Criminal Cases*, 49 Vanderbilt L Rev 123 (1996). The case for greater protection of juror privacy is presented in Weinstein, *Protecting a Juror's Right of Privacy: Constitutional Constraints and Policy Options*, 70 Temple L. Rev. 1 (1997). Weinstein argues that jurors deserve protection against invasive, personal questioning and probing investigations into their private life, as well as against threats to their safety. He does not maintain that these juror interests should trump all others, but rather asserts that they need to be and can be taken into account in ways that do not infringe on a defendant's constitutional right to a fair trial. Possible safeguards include anonymous juries, the elimination of peremptory challenges (as has occurred in England), and the curbing of intrusive pretrial investigations by denying parties access to the jury list prior to trial.

U.S. v. Branch, 91 F.3d 699, 45 Fed. R. Evid. Serv. 676 (5th Cir. 1996) is one of the few cases where an anonymous jury was impaneled even though the case did not involve organized crime or violent defendants. The prosecution arose out of a gun battle between the Branch Davidians (the defendants in the case) and federal agents. The jurors' names were withheld but not their occupations, employers, and other information. Thus the jury was only partially or semianonymous. The judge's reasoning was that the worldwide attention that had been given the case by the media had created an emotionally charged atmosphere in which the jurors might be subjected to harassment and intimidation. The court of appeal upheld the judge's order and in addition found that the defendants had not suffered any prejudice as a result of the judge's decision. State court decisions that have dealt with the issue of anonymous juries are collected in Annotation, Propriety of using anonymous juries in state criminal cases, 60 A.L.R. 5th 39.

In U.S. v. Edwards, 303 F.3d 606, 59 Fed. R. Evid. Serv. 1042 (5th Cir. 2002), cert. denied, 123 S. Ct. 1272, 154 L. Ed. 2d 1025 (U.S. 2003) and cert. denied, 123 S. Ct. 1294, 154 L. Ed. 2d 1025 (U.S. 2003) and cert. denied, 123 S. Ct. 1286, 154 L. Ed. 2d 1025 (U.S. 2003) and cert. denied, 123 S. Ct. 1369, 155 L. Ed. 2d 209 (U.S. 2003), the defendants in a prosecution for RICO violations, extortion, mail fraud, money laundering and related crimes included a former four-term governor of the state. The trial court empanelled an anonymous jury. While acknowledging that most anonymous jury trial cases involved organized crime, the Court of Appeals, citing U.S. v. Branch, 91 F.3d 699, 45 Fed. R. Evid. Serv. 676 (5th Cir. 1996), stated that an anonymous jury might be appropriate in other cases that attracted unusually intense media interest, evoked highly-charged emotional and political fervor, and aroused deep passions in the community. The ex-governor was a polarizing figure in state politics and many of the witnesses were of comparably high profile. The defendants all faced long prison terms if convicted. Examples of attempts to interfere with the judicial process and intimidate witnesses by some of the defendants, as well as by persons who were not parties in the case, were recounted. The trial court was also concerned that jurors might be harassed by members of the media. In these circumstances, the Court of Appeals held that the decision to empanel an anonymous jury was warranted. The Court of Appeals pointed out that the degree of anonymity was limited, as the defendants had access to the jurors' zip codes and parishes, as well as extensive information contained in the long jury questionnaires. The defendants had not shown that they were prejudiced by the trial court's decision and the Court of Appeals noted that the possibility of prejudice was minimized by the judge's explanatory instruction that justified the anonymity on the basis of protecting the jurors' privacy from the media and indicated that the jurors had no reason to fear for their safety from the defendants. Accord, U.S. v. Brown, 303 F.3d 582, 59 Fed. R. Evid. Serv. 1032 (5th Cir. 2002), cert. denied, 123 S. Ct. 1003, 154 L. Ed. 2d 915 (U.S. 2003), decided on the same day.

The impaneling of an anonymous jury may have implications for other constitutional interests. In U.S. v. Brown, 250 F.3d 907, 29 Media L. Rep. (BNA) 1779 (5th Cir. 2001), various members of the news media covering a highly publicized trial challenged aspects of a judge's order for an anonymous jury. The Court of Appeals held that precluding members of the news media from interfering with or circumventing the anonymous jury order violated the petitioners' First Amendment rights. The press was entitled to report information about the jury based on facts that it had obtained from sources other than confidential court records, court personnel, or trial participants, but not information that it had illegally gleaned from confidential court files.

n. 29.

Add to note 29:

See generally Annotation, Exclusion of public and media from voir dire examination of prospective jurors in state criminal case, 16 A.L.R. 5th 152.

Add after eighth paragraph:

For an evaluation of the continuing viability of *Press-Enterprise Co* in the light of modern social science research, See Jones, *The Latest Empirical Studies on Pretrial Publicity, Jury Bias, and Judicial Remedies—Not Enough to Overcome the First Amendment Right of Access to Pretrial Hearings*, 40 Am UL Rev 841 (1991).

In U.S. v. Antar, 38 F.3d 1348, 22 Media L. Rep. (BNA) 2417, Fed. Sec. L. Rep. (CCH) ¶ 98436, 40 Fed. R. Evid. Serv. 1006 (3d Cir. 1994) the Court of Appeals held that the district court had erred in sealing the transcript of voir dire without making a particularized finding to justify the restriction on First Amendment rights.

n. 30.

Add to note 30:

In Note, *Invaluable Tool vs. Unfair Use of Private Information:*

Examining Prosecutors' Use of Jurors' Criminal History Records in Voir Dire, 56 Wash. & Lee L. Rev. 1079 (1999), the author argues that jurors have no legitimate expectation of privacy in their personal criminal records, but that, if the prosecutor makes use of these records, they should be disclosed to the defense to prevent unfairness.

n. 37.

Add to note 37:

Test was applied in U.S. v. Royal, 100 F.3d 1019 (1st Cir. 1996). The defendant, who was seeking to establish a violation of the fair cross section requirement, moved to examine the master jury wheel. The district court judge ruled that the defendant would first have to make out a prima facie case of a constitutional violation. This in effect created a Catch-22 situation, for the defendant needed access to the records in question in order to establish a prima facie case. On appeal, the first circuit reversed, holding that a federal district court could not condition the grant of a motion to inspect jury selection records upon a showing of the merits of a challenge. A defendant has an unqualified right of access to jury selection records, and only need allege that he is preparing a motion to challenge the jury selection process. However, as the Court of Appeals added, a trial judge is permitted to establish reasonable procedures as to where and when the inspection may take place under 28 U.S.C.A. § 1867(f) (parties . . . shall be allowed to inspect, reproduce, and copy such records or papers at all reasonable times during the preparation and pendency of a motion to challenge compliance with the jury selection statute). In U.S. v. Orlando-Figueroa, 229 F.3d 33, 55 Fed. R. Evid. Serv. 1097 (1st Cir. 2000) the court stated that sec. 1867(a)'s seven-day filing requirement, which applies to challenges to the jury selection process, does not apply to a motion simply to inspect jury selection records under Sec. 1867(f). Furthermore, a party seeking to inspect jury selection records is not required to submit a sworn statement of facts which, if true, would constitute a substantial failure to comply with the section. See also U.S. v. Paradies, 98 F.3d 1266, 46 Fed. R. Evid. Serv. 656 (11th Cir. 1996), as amended, (Nov. 6, 1996) (court not required to grant stay of proceedings to allow inspection of jury records); U.S. v. Schneider, 111 F.3d 197, 46 Fed. R. Evid. Serv. 1426 (1st Cir. 1997) (petitioner must show prejudice in order to obtain new trial because of nondisclosure of information contained in jury questionnaire).

Add to end of section:

In Kotler v. American Tobacco Co., 926 F.2d 1217, Prod. Liab. Rep. (CCH) ¶ 12674 (1st Cir. 1990), cert. granted, judgment vacated on other grounds, 505 U.S. 1215, 112 S. Ct. 3019, 120 L. Ed. 2d 891 (1992), the trial judge released the jury list to both sides on the Friday before the Monday when jury selection was to take place. On Monday, the plaintiff objected to the release of the list, arguing that only the defendant had the means to make effective use of this information. The appellate court described the contention as frivolous, noting that imbalances in resources were inevitable and that this fact did not render the trial unfair.

§ 4:7 Discovery of the results of juror investigations and analyses

§ 4:10 —Constitutional arguments in favor of discovery

n. 66.

Add to note 66:

In U.S. v. Collins, 972 F.2d 1385 (5th Cir. 1992), where a pretrial telephone survey had been commissioned by the prosecution but terminated by court order, the court refused to allow the poll results to be discovered by the defendants.

Add at end of sixth paragraph:

In Note, *Invaluable Tool vs. Unfair Use of Private Information: Examining Prosecutors' Use of Jurors' Criminal History Records in Voir Dire*, 56 Wash. & Lee L. Rev. 1079 (1999), the author argues that jurors have no legitimate expectation of privacy in their personal criminal records, but that, if the prosecutor makes use of these records, they should be disclosed to the defense to prevent unfairness.

Chapter 5

Mock and Shadow Juries

> **KeyCite®:** Cases and other legal materials listed in KeyCite Scope can be researched through West's KeyCite service on Westlaw®. Use KeyCite to check citations for form, parallel references, prior and later history, and comprehensive citator information, including citations to other decisions and secondary materials.

§ 5:2 Mock trials—Selecting the jurors

§ 5:4 —Observing the deliberations of the mock jury

Add at end of section:

Cases holding that a court abused its discretion in conducting voir dire are few and far between, but U.S. v. Rowe, 106 F.3d 1226 (5th Cir. 1997) indicates that it is possible and that there are limits to a judge's discretion. In this case the trial judge was found to have intimidated two prospective jurors, and, indirectly, the panel One juror, after indicating that she doubted that she could be fair because her brother was an undercover narcotics agent and her father a policeman, was told by the judge that she would be called back "again, and again, and again" until she could figure out how to put aside her personal opinions and do her duty. This exchange was overheard by the entire panel. A second juror who also admitted that she might have difficulty being impartial was subjected to similar threats. The court implied that both jurors were trying to shirk their civil obligation of jury service. When it was suggested by counsel that the judge's conduct might have the effect of inhibiting the remaining jurors' from answering voir dire questions candidly, the court specifically asked if any of the jurors had been intimidated by these exchanges. Not surprisingly, no juror indicated that they had been intimidated, but the appellate court said that it was not prepared to assume that the jurors were fools. It was clearly apparent that any juror who crossed the judge faced, at a minimum, a bawling out and, at worst, an extended tour of jury duty. The Court of Appeals held that the judge's conduct was likely to have inhibited jurors from being honest about their potential biases, thereby rebutting the presumption that jurors give truthful answers to voir dire questions. *Rowe* was distinguished in

U.S. v. Vega, 221 F.3d 789, 54 Fed. R. Evid. Serv. 1502 (5th Cir. 2000), cert. denied, 531 U.S. 1155, 121 S. Ct. 1105, 148 L. Ed. 2d 975 (2001) where, in response to a prospective juror's indication that she might not be able to be impartial, the trial judge had stated that it was his impression that the juror did not want to serve. He added that the court was not impressed with her excuse. The defendant argued that this statement sent a message to the other jurors that honest answers would be met with reprimands or reprisals from the court. The Court of Appeals stated that, unlike in *Rowe*, there had been no express or implied threat actually to punish jurors who claimed to be unable to serve, and no juror in *Vega* in fact suggested that he or she had been intimidated by the judge's comments. The court concluded that the defendant's right to a fair and impartial jury had not been violated.

§ 5:6 —The pros and cons of mock trials

Add after first sentence in first paragraph:
See also Bennett & Hirschhorn, *Voir Dire in Criminal Cases: Choosing Jurors to Judge Your Client*, 28 Trial 68 (1992) (the mock trial "forces lawyers to prepare and simplify every aspect of a case from both defense and prosecution perspectives . . . gives lawyers substantial feedback on themes, evidence, and witnesses . . . reveals case weaknesses and strengths and . . . develops the most important areas for voir dire").

n. 16.
Add to note 16:
Computer technology may also offer a way of avoiding the expenses of a mock trial. Several companies are prepared to create a "virtual" online jury to assess a lawyer's case. This will save the lawyer the complications and expense of bringing jurors together in one place, renting a courtroom, hiring a mock judge and videotaping the proceedings, all of which may be important in a case where the amount of money at stake does not justify the cost of a "live" mock jury. An attorney can place on a website, for the "virtual" jurors to read, a summary of the lawyer's position, the attorney's opening and closing statements, and the arguments most likely to be made by the opposing side. The lawyer can then solicit feedback from the "virtual" jurors on the strength of the client's case, the arguments advanced, and the lawyer's overall strategy. "Virtual" jurors can be recruited from the district in which the trial will take place, and can be screened for specific characteristics. The jurors may provide feedback either individually or in a "chat room" where they can interact and argue with each other. There are several advantages of online juries besides the savings in costs, including the unlimited number of jurors who can be recruited, and the fact that the lawyer can masquerade as a juror in the "chat room" to assess the discussion and interject thoughts and questions as the lawyer sees fit to do so. On the other hand, there are disadvantages in that the lawyer will not be able to observe the body language and facial

expressions of the online jurors, and, conversely, the jurors are not exposed to the presence and "personality" of the lawyer. The online "pool" is also limited to persons who have access to computers and who are willing to participate. See generally Hoescher, *Online mock juries offer cheap and fast opinions*, 87 ABA Journal 26 (June 2001).

Part III

THE LAW RELATING TO CHALLENGES

Chapter 6

Challenges to the Array

> Note: Cases and other legal materials listed in KeyCite Scope can be researched through West's KeyCite service on Westlaw. Use KeyCite to check citations for form, parallel references, prior and later history, and comprehensive view of case information, including citations to other decisions and secondary materials.

601 Introduction

One obvious problem that can lead to unrepresentative juries is of minority jurors fail to appear for service. One means of handling the problem is to hold the no-shows in contempt of court and punish them accordingly. A New Mexico engagement was upheld in *In re Mauldin*, 242 Ga. App. 350, 530 S.E.2d 653, 20 A.L.R.5th 355 (2000) in the case of a professional musician who was playing at an important engagement at the time and who failed to appear for jury duty and was held in contempt. See generally, *Annotation, Holding the Jurors in Contempt Under State Law*, 93 A.L.R. 5th 493.

Part III

THE LAW RELATING TO CHALLENGES

Chapter 6

Challenges to the Array

> **KeyCite®:** Cases and other legal materials listed in KeyCite Scope can be researched through West's KeyCite service on Westlaw®. Use KeyCite to check citations for form, parallel references, prior and later history, and comprehensive citator information, including citations to other decisions and secondary materials.

§ 6:1 Introduction

Add after first sentence in seventh paragraph:

One obvious problem that can lead to unrepresentative juries is if summoned jurors fail to appear for service. One means of tackling the problem is to hold the no-shows in contempt of court and punish them accordingly. A short term of imprisonment was upheld in In re Mauldin, 242 Ga. App. 350, 529 S.E.2d 653, 93 A.L.R.5th 755 (2000) in the case of a professional musician (who was playing at an out of town engagement at the time) who failed to appear for jury duty and was held in contempt. See generally, Annotation, Holding Jurors in Contempt Under State Law, 93 A.L.R. 5th 493.

n. 6.

Add to beginning of note 6:

Domitrovich, *Jury Source Lists and the Community's Need to Achieve Racial Balance on the Jury*, 33 Duq L Rev 39 (1994). See, e.g., Ramseur v. Beyer, 983 F.2d 1215 (3d Cir. 1992) (combination of voter registration and motor vehicle licensed driver lists). But see Note, *Jury Source Lists: Does Supplementation Really Work?*, 82 Cornell L Rev. 390 (1997), maintaining that multiple source lists have failed to remedy the problem of minority underrepresentation, while simply adding to the cost of jury selection. The author favors using stratified sampling techniques to identify groups overrepresented in the jury pool, with members of such groups then being randomly removed, as well as a redesigned jury questionnaire whose completion would be mandatory.

In U.S. v. Ovalle, 136 F.3d 1092, 1998 FED App. 0060P (6th Cir. 1998), the court reviewed the Jury Selection Plan for the Eastern District of

Michigan. In an attempt to ensure a proper balance of the different cognizable groups in the community, the Plan provided for the removal of one in five non-African Americans from the jury pool. This was held to be a violation of the equal protection rights of the non-black prospective jurors excluded under the Plan. The court then proceeded to examine whether, notwithstanding this effect, the Plan might be justified by a compelling governmental interest, utilizing means that were narrowly tailored to achievement of that interest. The court was prepared to accept that the government had a compelling interest in ensuring that jury pools represented a fair cross section of the community, but held that the Plan was not sufficiently narrowly tailored to achieve this objective. The Plan not only discriminated against the one-in-five white jurors who were automatically excluded from the pool but also, because its sole focus was on the exclusion of African-Americans, made no effort to ensure that Hispanics or other minorities were included in the jury pool. Thus it was not narrowly tailored to create a representative pool. The court suggested that, rather than removing qualified jurors on account of their race, it would have been preferable to expand the jury pool by diversifying the basis on which the pool was constructed. The decision and the implications are examined in Cohn & Sherwood, The Rise and Fall of Affirmative Action in Jury Selection, 32 U. Mich. J. of Law Reform 323 (1999).

Add after ninth paragraph:

One practical problem facing prospective jurors is the risk that they will lose their jobs or otherwise be disadvantaged because of the time away from work while on jury duty. The Jury Systems Improvement Act, 28 U.S.C.A. § 1875, attempts to protect jurors against intimidation, discharge, and coercion because of jury service. Still, retaliation can often take subtle forms, such as making one's working conditions so difficult and unpleasant that a reasonable person would have no hesitancy in resigning from the job. See, e.g., Hill v. Winn-Dixie Stores, Inc., 934 F.2d 1518, 6 I.E.R. Cas. (BNA) 1068, 7 I.E.R. Cas. (BNA) 1671, 119 Lab. Cas. (CCH) ¶ 10839 (11th Cir. 1991) (evidence supported finding that employer coerced or intimidated employee in violation of Act). Ironically, one of the issues on appeal in *Hill* was whether the plaintiff was entitled to a jury trial. The Court of Appeals ruled that she was.

n. 9.

Add to note 9:

Ramseur v. Beyer, 983 F.2d 1215 (3d Cir. 1992).

In Campbell v. Louisiana, 523 U.S. 392, 118 S. Ct. 1419, 140 L. Ed. 2d 551, 172 A.L.R. Fed. 597 (1998), the United States Supreme Court addressed the question of whether a white defendant had standing to challenge alleged discrimination in the selection of the foreperson of the grand jury that had indicted him. Under state law the trial judge selected the foreperson of the grand jury from the grand jury venire, with the remaining members then being chosen at random. It was undisputed that no black person had served as a grand jury foreperson in the parish for the previous 17 years. Citing its prior decision in Powers v. Ohio, 499 U.S. 400, 111 S. Ct. 1364, 113 L. Ed. 2d 411 (1991), in which the Court had held that a white defendant had standing to challenge the discriminatory peremptory challenges of black petit jurors (discussed in supp § 8:6), the Court held that Campbell too had standing to raise the equal protection and due process claims of black jurors who had been discriminated against. The Court's reasoning tracked that in *Powers*. The defendant had suffered significant injury since the discriminatory selection process undermined the integrity of the indictment process. The accused shared a common interest with the excluded jurors in eradicating discrimination from the grand jury selection process, and therefore could be counted on to be an effective advocate for the interests of the excluded jurors. The accused also had a selfish interest in asserting the excluded jurors' rights because a finding that there had been a constitutional violation might lead to the reversal of his conviction. Finally, the Court noted that the defendant's own due process rights may well have been violated by the selection procedure. Hobby v. U.S., 468 U.S. 339, 104 S. Ct. 3093, 82 L. Ed. 2d 260 (1984), in which the Court had held that no relief could be granted to a white defendant even if there had been a violation of due process in the selection of the foreperson of a federal grand jury, was distinguished. In *Hobby* the foreperson had already been selected to serve on the grand jury prior to his or her purely ministerial appointment to the role of foreperson; in contrast, in *Campbell* the judge's appointment of the foreperson shaped the composition of the grand jury. This difference in effect converted the case into one alleging discriminatory selection of grand juror members. Having determined the standing issue, the court in *Campbell* did not reach the substantive merits of the petitioner's claim but rather remanded for further proceedings.

Add at end of section:

Once a jury has been selected in a case, it may not be summarily disbanded by the judge. In *United States v Hanno*, a jury was chosen to hear the defendant's case. The start of the case was delayed for a week. During this period the trial judge dismissed six of the selected (but not yet sworn) jurors in order to free them to serve on another case. The Court of Appeals held that the trial court erred in dismissing the jurors without notice to and in the absence of the defendant and his attorney. They had been potentially disadvantaged by being denied the opportunity to participate in the decision as to whether any jurors should be released, and if so, which ones and by what methods. The trial judge also erred in failing to make a record of the proceedings in which the jurors were removed.

§ 6:2 The Federal Jury Selection and Service Act of 1968—Goals and policies

§ 6:3 —Jury plans under the Federal Act

n. 26.

Add to note 26:

In In re Jury Plan of Eastern Dist. of New York, 27 F.3d 9 (2d Cir. Jud. Council 1994), the Judicial Council of the Second Circuit declined to rule on a jury plan for the Eastern District of New York, key features of which it had previously approved. Although there were some controversial issues which had since been brought to the Judicial Council's attention in respect to the plan, the Council decided that the prudent course would be to await a formal legal challenge. In In re Jury Plan of Eastern Dist. of New York, 61 F.3d 119 (2d Cir. Jud. Council 1995), the Judicial Council of the Second Circuit gave conditional approval to a jury plan which selected jurors from five counties. However, the Council expressed a number of reservations. A great amount of travel would be required of some jurors, which could lead to early departures and late arrivals. Those with automobiles were likely to be in a better position to incur these burdens. Those without might claim hardship exemptions. The jury plan could therefore have an unacceptable discriminatory effect. The Council reserved to itself the authority to disapprove the plan at a subsequent date and requested a report after the plan had been in operation for a year.

n. 29.

Add to note 29:

Absent proof of gerrymandering, there is no basis for objecting to a jury plan that allows a jury to be drawn from one division of a district rather than from the entire district even if the larger area might have resulted in greater minority representation. U.S. v. Cannady, 54 F.3d 544 (9th Cir. 1995). Accord, U.S. v. Bahna, 68 F.3d 19 (2d Cir. 1995). The opposite argument was made in U.S. v. Ashley, 54 F.3d 311 (7th Cir. 1995)—that a narrower geographic base for selecting jurors was necessary in order to ensure adequate minority representation—but with an equal lack of success. See also U.S. v. Grisham, 63 F.3d 1074 (11th Cir. 1995) (no statutory or constitutional violation occurs when jurors are selected from district at large rather than from division of district in which crime occurred).

In U.S. v. Raszkiewicz, 169 F.3d 459 (7th Cir. 1999), the jury plan for the eastern district of Wisconsin divided the district into the Milwaukee division in the south and the Green Bay division in the north. All six Indian reservations fell within the Green Bay division, but there had not been a jury trial in the Green Bay Division since 1992. As a result, reservation Indians were not included in the venire from which defendant's jury was selected. This, the defendant argued, violated his Sixth Amendment to a jury drawn from a fair cross section of the community. The Court of Appeals held that reservation Indians were not a sufficiently distinctive group for purposes of the Sixth Amendment. There were still urban Indians eligible to serve as jurors, and reservation and urban Indians were not sufficiently culturally different as to constitute independent groups. The social scientific evidence on the point was somewhat inconclusive, however, and the court supported its position with the observation that the main purpose of the fair cross section requirement was the seating of an impartial jury and the defendant had not shown that he had been denied an impartial jury. See also U.S. v. Bushyhead, 270 F.3d 905 (9th Cir. 2001), cert. denied, 535 U.S. 1008, 122 S. Ct. 1586, 152 L. Ed. 2d 504 (2002) (failure of jury selection plan to draw juror from tribal voting lists violated neither Jury Selection and Service Act nor Sixth Amendment).

Add after subsection (4):

In U.S. v. Barnes, 158 F.3d 662 (2d Cir. 1998), the defendant sought a stay in the trial in order to benefit from a new Qualified Jury Wheel which was based on updated motor vehicle and voter registration records. The court rejected defendant's argument that the failure to order the stay denied him the opportunity for a representative jury venire. Accord, U.S. v. Diaz, 176 F.3d 52, 52 Fed. R. Evid. Serv. 380 (2d Cir. 1999).

The provision in Sec. (b)4 that the master jury wheel should be refilled at "specified times, the interval for which shall not exceed four years" was at issue in U.S. v. Shea, 211 F.3d 658, 53 Fed. R. Evid. Serv. 1353 (1st Cir. 2000), cert. denied, 531 U.S. 1154, 121 S. Ct. 1101, 148 L. Ed. 2d 973 (2001) and cert. denied, 531 U.S. 1154, 121 S. Ct. 1101, 148 L. Ed. 2d 973 (2001) and cert. denied, 531 U.S. 1154, 121 S. Ct. 1101, 148 L. Ed. 2d 973 (2001) and cert. denied, 531 U.S. 1154, 121 S. Ct. 1101, 148 L. Ed. 2d 973 (2001) and cert. denied, 531 U.S. 1154, 121 S. Ct. 1102, 148 L. Ed. 2d 973 (2001). Under the New Hampshire jury selection plan, new names were collected every four years, but it took an additional nine months before they could be integrated into the master jury wheel. The Court of Appeals stated that the purpose of the statutory time limit was to ensure that the data was reasonably fresh, and that this purpose was not defeated by the delay. The court held that the statute did not preclude a reasonable delay between the collection of data and its insertion into the wheel. Nor did the delay defeat the "random" selection requirement of the statute because it had the potential to reduce the number of young people in the wheel, as well as those who had recently relocated in New Hampshire. The court answered by stating that neither young persons nor recent immigrants to the state were the kind of distinctive groups that gave rise to either a violation of the statute or the Sixth Amendment.

§ 6:4 —Disqualifications under the Federal Act

Add after note 34:

In U.S. v. Cantu, 229 F.3d 544, 2000 FED App. 0365P (6th Cir. 2000), the defendant was charged with being a felon in possession of a firearm. After the jury had been sworn, one juror informed the judge that, many years previously, he had pled guilty to a crime that might have been a felony (the juror did not know this for a fact and the court was unsure) and that he hunted with a gun. Thus, the juror realized that he might have committed the same offense as the defendant was charged with committing. Although there was no finding that the juror was not impartial, the court decided to replace him with an alternate. On appeal it was argued that it was error to replace a juror who had not been shown to be biased. The Court of Appeals rejected this argument, pointing out that the defendant had not shown that he had been prejudiced by the substitution, and further that a judge was permitted to take steps to obviate the risk of a subsequent reversal.

Add after first sentence in fifth paragraph:
Although the "English" requirement may result in fewer members from certain ethnic backgrounds being in the jury pool, the requirement has been upheld against constitutional

§ 6:4   Jury Selection: Law, Art & Science 2d

challenge. U.S. v. Escobar-de Jesus, 187 F.3d 148, 52 Fed. R. Evid. Serv. 1039 (1st Cir. 1999); U.S. v. Flores-Rivera, 56 F.3d 319, 42 Fed. R. Evid. Serv. 499 (1st Cir. 1995) (English-only requirement did not violate either fifth or Sixth Amendment rights of defendants on ground that it effectively excluded two-thirds of population of Puerto Rico); U.S. v. Dubon-Otero, 292 F.3d 1 (1st Cir. 2002), cert. denied, 123 S. Ct. 993, 154 L. Ed. 2d 912 (U.S. 2003) and cert. denied, 123 S. Ct. 993, 154 L. Ed. 2d 912 (U.S. 2003) (requirement that jurors be proficient in English is an independent requirement and not dependent on the availability of suitable alternatives, such as simultaneous translation, that would allow jurors to be able to serve). See also U.S. v. Rioux, 97 F.3d 648, 45 Fed. R. Evid. Serv. 998 (2d Cir. 1996) (requirement that jurors speak English is reasonable and does not establish intent to discriminate against minorities); U.S. v. Candelaria-Silva, 166 F.3d 19, 51 Fed. R. Evid. Serv. 210 (1st Cir. 1999) (upholding dismissal of six prospective jurors for lack of proficiency in English). Whether a juror has the requisite ability to understand English is properly left to the discretion of the trial judge, who is in the best position to assess the juror's language competency. U.S. v. Gonzalez-Soberal, 109 F.3d 64, 46 Fed. R. Evid. Serv. 868 (1st Cir. 1997). See also U.S. v. Orlando-Figueroa, 229 F.3d 33, 55 Fed. R. Evid. Serv. 1097 (1st Cir. 2000) (trial court did not abuse its discretion in refusing to submit to prospective jurors questions which addressed their proficiency in English or in not asking jurors in Spanish if they would have any problems understanding proceedings in English. The defendants had not pointed to any evidence that any juror's ability to understand English was deficient.

Add after note 45:
In U.S. v. Speer, 30 F.3d 605 (5th Cir. 1994), the defendant's inability to communicate effectively in English, as evidenced by her failure to get across to the judge and the lawyers in the case the reason for a pending appointment, was held to justify the juror's replacement.

Add after "hearing the evidence." in the seventh paragraph:
But see U.S. v. Dempsey, 830 F.2d 1084, 24 Fed. R. Evid. Serv. 524 (10th Cir. 1987) (permitting use of interpreter to assist deaf juror).

n. 49.
   Add to note 49:
U.S. v. Greene, 995 F.2d 793, 37 Fed. R. Evid. Serv. 574 (8th Cir. 1993); U.S. v. Arce, 997 F.2d 1123, 39 Fed. R. Evid. Serv. 450 (5th Cir. 1993). But see U.S. v. Boney, 977 F.2d 624, 36 Fed. R. Evid. Serv. 1358 (D.C. Cir. 1992) (no absolute bar on jury service by felons, and therefore

failure of juror to disclose his felon status did not require automatic reversal). Similarly in Coughlin v. Tailhook Ass'n, 112 F.3d 1052 (9th Cir. 1997), where one of the jurors who heard the case had been convicted previously of marijuana possession and consequently disqualified from serving as a juror under 28 U.S.C.A. § 1865(b)(5), the Court of Appeals held that in order for the petitioner to obtain a new trial, there had to be a showing of actual bias. Accord, U.S. v. Bishop, 264 F.3d 535, 2001-2 U.S. Tax Cas. (CCH) ¶ 50762, 57 Fed. R. Evid. Serv. 1087, 88 A.F.T.R.2d 2001-5991 (5th Cir. 2001), cert. denied, 535 U.S. 1016, 122 S. Ct. 1605, 152 L. Ed. 2d 620 (2002).

The Court of Appeals in U.S. v. Barry, 71 F.3d 1269 (7th Cir. 1995) held that the exclusion of persons charged with felonies from the jury pool was not in violation of either the equal protection clause or the fair cross section requirement, even though it might have had the effect of excluding a disproportionate percentage of blacks. The court stated that the government's interest in jury probity outweighed any interest that the defendant might have in having potential felons on his jury. U.S. v. Estrella, 104 F.3d 3 (1st Cir. 1997). See also Coleman v. Calderon, 150 F.3d 1105 (9th Cir. 1998), cert. granted, judgment rev'd on other grounds, 525 U.S. 141, 119 S. Ct. 500, 142 L. Ed. 2d 521 (1998) (upholding California law precluding felons from serving on juries).

In Anderson v. Com., 107 S.W.3d 193 (Ky. 2003) the court held that a governor's order restoring a convicted felon's civil rights did not restore the felon's "right" to serve on a jury, where the governor's order specifically limited the restoration to the felon's right to vote and hold office. As a result, the court ordered a new trial in the case of a defendant who had been convicted by a jury which included the ex-felon as a member.

§ 6:5 —Exemptions under the Federal Act

Add after fourth sentence in fourth paragraph:

Another problem with allowing lawyers to serve on a jury relates to the type of questions that they may encounter on voir dire. In U.S. v. Steele, 298 F.3d 906 (9th Cir. 2002), cert. denied, 537 U.S. 1096, 123 S. Ct. 710, 154 L. Ed. 2d 646 (2002) one of the prospective jurors was employed as a public defender. The prosecutor asked the juror: "In the course of trying [felony robbery] cases, did you ever make a decision that your client was guilty and you've just got to do whatever you have got to do because that's your job." The juror answered: "I guess so, yeah. You know, it gets—the facts might show one way or the other, and you have to pursue the case if the client wants to or not, it's their decision." Defense counsel objected, arguing that the questioning tainted the jury by creating the erroneous impression that a defense attorney may have to proceed to trial even though the attorney believes the client is guilty. The prosecutor disputed this characterization, but indicated that she would discontinue the voir dire of the juror if the defense would agree to stipulate to excuse the juror for cause. The defense agreed to this stipulation, but also moved for a mistrial, which was denied. In addition, defense counsel

§ 6:5   JURY SELECTION: LAW, ART & SCIENCE 2D

refused the offer from the judge for a curative instruction because he believed that such an instruction would only serve to exacerbate the misconceptions already created. On appeal, the Court of Appeals found no abuse of the trial judge's discretion. The Court of Appeals noted that the prosecutor's question did not improperly comment on the defendant's counsel or compare defense counsel's experience with that of the juror; that the voir dire of the juror had stopped after the single question and was never referred to again; and that there was no indication that the prosecutor had intentionally sought to create the impression that all defense attorneys would lie or distort the facts to confuse a jury as to their client's guilt. The questioning also was held not to have tainted the jury pool. The juror's answer could not reasonably be viewed as an expert opinion to the effect that all defense counsel defended obviously guilty clients, and reflected only upon the experience of the particular juror. Further, the fact that the juror was dismissed for cause presumably lessened any potential prejudicial effect on the other jurors. Finally, the Court of Appeals noted that defense counsel had refused a curative instruction that could have obviated any potential prejudice.

n. 54.

Add to note 54:

A representative list of exemptions created by one district court can be found in Hittner & Nichols, *Jury Selection in Federal Civil Litigation: General Procedures, New Rules, and the Arrival of Batson*, 23 Tex Tech L Rev 407, 414 (1992).

Add after note 54:

In U.S. v. Terry, 60 F.3d 1541 (11th Cir. 1995) the Court of Appeals upheld the exemption of police from jury service under Section 1863(b). The defendant, a police officer himself, had argued that the police were a distinctive group within the community and that the failure to include them on juries deprived him of his Sixth Amendment right to a jury drawn from a fair cross section of the community. The court responded that the exemption was reasonable in light of the vital service provided by the police and the public policy consideration of not interrupting their work.

§ 6:6 —Excuses under the Federal Act

Add after third sentence of second full paragraph:
In U.S. v. DeFries, 129 F.3d 1293, 156 L.R.R.M. (BNA) 2999 (D.C. Cir. 1997), the defendants argued that whites were systematically underrepresented in the jury pool because the judge was more prone to grant them hardship deferrals. However, the claim was based only on hearsay evidence, and

the court ruled that such evidence was insufficient to establish a statutory violation. The court added that if such a practice were to be established, it would be cause for concern.

In U.S. v. Candelaria-Silva, 166 F.3d 19, 51 Fed. R. Evid. Serv. 210 (1st Cir. 1999), the First Circuit Court of Appeals ruled that the district court's excusal of four jurors on hardship grounds was not justified. The excusals had been granted ex parte, and the Court of Appeals advised that it was generally unwise to excuse jurors in the absence of counsel. The court held, however, that the errors were not a 'substantial failing' under the Jury Selection and Service Act. The number of errors was not great, and they did not frustrate the underlying principles of the Act. In particular, there had been no showing of discrimination, or that the district court's actions had prevented the jury from consisting of a fair cross section of the community. A similar procedure, wherein the trial judge screened the jurors for hardship excuses outside the presence of both the parties and counsel was upheld in U.S. v. Collazo-Aponte, 216 F.3d 163, 54 Fed. R. Evid. Serv. 1311 (1st Cir. 2000), cert. granted in part, judgment vacated on other grounds, 532 U.S. 1036, 121 S. Ct. 1996, 149 L. Ed. 2d 1000 (2001) on the authority of *Candelaria-Silva*.

The *Candelaria-Silva* case highlights a general tension that exists in respect to hardship excusals. If jury service is a right of citizenship, then a prospective juror should be able to waive that 'right' and excuse himself or herself from serving. But if parties to a legal action have the 'right' to a jury that is representative of the community, then courts should look critically on purported claims of hardship that will upset the representativeness of the jury. Furthermore, even if jury service is a right of citizenship, it may at the same time be a duty of citizenship, which consideration also cuts in favor of critically examining attempts by jurors to avoid serving. Perhaps excuses should be looked at more critically if the effect will be to remove all jurors of a cognizable group. Apparently the trial court did not take this consideration into account in McGinnis v. Johnson, 181 F.3d 686 (5th Cir. 1999). Included in the 30 venirepersons who asked to be excused were the only three blacks in the venire. One claimed a conflict with an out-of-town vacation; the second claimed high blood pressure and vision problems, as well as a need to support herself; and the third claimed a history of seizures and other medical problems. Despite the fact that the effect would be to leave a jury pool containing no African-Americans, the court granted all three excuses. The Court of Appeals found no Sixth Amendment violation because there had not been a showing of systematic exclusion. The court observed that a one-time example of under representation of a distinctive group in a jury venire was not sufficient to establish systematic exclusion. Nor was the Court of Appeals prepared to find a violation of equal protection, as the basis of the excusals was race-neutral.

Add to fifth full paragraph:
In U.S. v. Calabrese, 942 F.2d 218 (3d Cir. 1991), the trial judge sent a form letter and questionnaire to approximately 300 prospective jurors. One of the questions was whether the juror knew any of the defendants, whose names and addresses were listed. Only a yes/no answer was called for and no explanations were sought. All jurors who answered 'yes' were excused from jury service by the judge. The defendants challenged the propriety of the exclusion and the appellate court held that it violated the Jury Selection and Service Act. The court further found that the violation was a substantial one under the terms of the Act; the defendants were entitled to relief regardless of actual prejudice. Thus, the court vacated the defendants' convictions and ordered a new trial.

Particularly in lengthy trials, jury service can have significant and adverse economic consequences. Formal payments to jurors is often quite low, and may be well below the minimum wage. Some employers, either voluntarily or because they are required by law, will continue to pay a juror's salary. But what of jurors who are unemployed? In this connection the case of Brouwer v. Metropolitan Dade County, 139 F.3d 817, 4 Wage & Hour Cas. 2d (BNA) 940, 135 Lab. Cas. (CCH) ¶ 33684 (11th Cir. 1998) held immense potential significance. A former juror, who had received no compensation for her jury service, sued the county on behalf of herself and others similarly situated, claiming that the failure to pay jurors for jury service violated the Fair Labor Standards Act (FLSA). The defendant's motion to dismiss was granted and the plaintiff appealed. The Eleventh Circuit Court of Appeals held that although the county was indisputably an employer within the meaning of the FLSA, there was no employment relationship between the county and its jurors. Jury service, the court observed, was a duty of citizenship, and one that could not be shirked because it might cause financial hardship. Unlike ordinary employees, jurors did not apply for their position but were selected at random. Also, unlike ordinary employees, jurors were not subjected to an interview or any of the other processes normally used in connection with job applications. Furthermore, jurors were not eligible for employment benefits, health insurance, vacations, sick leave or any of the other accoutrements associated with employment. Nor could the state 'fire' jurors for poor performance; it was compelled to accept their verdict.

In sum, the relationship between juror and county had none of the hallmarks of an employment relationship.

The decision in *Brouwer* is no doubt a correct interpretation of the FLSA, and is supported by the pragmatic consideration that, had the plaintiff succeeded, the financial ramifications to the state could have been enormous. Nonetheless, the decision is disappointing. The economic hardship resulting from jury service can lead many otherwise civic-minded individuals to seek to avoid service. Few courts are in a position to investigate the bona fides of prospective jurors who request to be excused, and most such claims are routinely granted. The absence from the jury of persons who are excused on hardship grounds will likely skew the democratic composition and decisionmaking processes of the jury. A related argument was advanced and rejected in U.S. v. Hemmingson, 157 F.3d 347 (5th Cir. 1998). The petitioner argued that the granting of hardship excuses resulted in the underrepresentation of minorities in the jury venire. The court had granted the hardship excuses on the basis of requests made in a written questionnaire. The defendant argued that the court should have summoned the jurors to appear in the courtroom in order to ascertain their race. The Court of Appeals found no abuse of discretion in the trial judge's decision not to do so in the absence of a showing that the decision to accept the hardship claims would have been different if the jurors had appeared before the court.

Add after note 64:
In U.S. v. Petrie, 302 F.3d 1280, 59 Fed. R. Evid. Serv. 1563 (11th Cir. 2002), cert. denied, 123 S. Ct. 1775, 155 L. Ed. 2d 530 (U.S. 2003), the petitioner argued that notice informing prospective jurors of the potential length of trial and advising them how to request excusals "targeted" a less sophisticated jury pool and would prompt higher income earners to seek an excusal. As the petitioner offered no factual basis for this argument, the court found no violation of the Jury Selection and Service Act.

Add after first sentence of seventh paragraph:
Hardship excuses and occupational exemptions demonstrate the Court's empathy with the difficulties caused by jury service, but from an institutional perspective they can lead to a skewing of the cross sectional representativeness of the jury. (There is disagreement in both the courts and the literature as to whether the upper or the lower classes, and whether blue or white collar workers, are more likely to be excused on hardship grounds, with probably much depending on the views of the judge in the case as to what constitutes legitimate hardship). One possible way of accommodating the in-

§ 6:6   JURY SELECTION: LAW, ART & SCIENCE 2D

convenience that juror service entails would be for the court to allow breaks during the day (extended lunch hours or an early close to the day's proceedings), or hold some court sessions in the evening, so that jurors could attend to their affairs. See J. Gobert, Justice, Democracy and the Jury 127–29 (Dartmouth 1997). This might also address one of the main complaints of jurors, which is that they are often left to sit idly in the jury room while the court attends to its judicial business.

Add at end of section:

The case against liberal grants of hardship excuses and occupational exemptions is made in Note, *Hardship Excuses and Occupational Exemptions: The Impairment of the "Fair Cross-Section of the Community,"* 69 S Cal L Rev 155 (1995). In Sweet v. Delo, 125 F.3d 1144 (8th Cir. 1997), a capital case, the trial court on its own motion transferred a juror to the bottom of the jury list because the judge perceived, correctly, that the juror would experience personal hardship in serving on the case. The juror also happened to hold reservations regarding the death penalty, and the defendant argued that *Witherspoon* had been violated. The Court of Appeals rejected this argument, stating not only that the judge's actions had not been pretextual, but that they constituted a "neutral and humanitarian" way of addressing a common problem.

§ 6:7 Random selection of jurors

n. 67.

Add to note 67:

The court in U.S. v. Rioux, 97 F.3d 648, 45 Fed. R. Evid. Serv. 998 (2d Cir. 1996), in dismissing evidence of "Statistical Decision Theory" (SDT), which measures the likelihood that under representation is attributable to chance, stated that such evidence is not determinative as the federal Act never contemplated producing a pure random sample.

Add after second paragraph:

In U.S. v. Ovalle, 136 F.3d 1092, 1998 FED App. 0060P (6th Cir. 1998), a challenge was raised to the Jury Selection Plan for the Eastern District of Michigan. In order to achieve a proper balance of the different cognizable groups in the community, the Plan provided for the removal of one in five non-African Americans from the jury pool. The court found that the Plan substantially violated § 1862 of the JSSA, as well as the Equal Protection Clause. The decision and the implications are examined in Cohn & Sherwood, The Rise and Fall of Affirmative Action in Jury Selection, 32 U. Mich. J. of Law Reform 323 (1999).

Section(b)4 of the Act requires that the master jury wheel

should be refilled at "specified times, the interval for which shall not exceed four years". This section was at issue in U.S. v. Shea, 211 F.3d 658, 53 Fed. R. Evid. Serv. 1353 (1st Cir. 2000), cert. denied, 531 U.S. 1154, 121 S. Ct. 1101, 148 L. Ed. 2d 973 (2001) and cert. denied, 531 U.S. 1154, 121 S. Ct. 1101, 148 L. Ed. 2d 973 (2001) and cert. denied, 531 U.S. 1154, 121 S. Ct. 1101, 148 L. Ed. 2d 973 (2001) and cert. denied, 531 U.S. 1154, 121 S. Ct. 1101, 148 L. Ed. 2d 973 (2001) and cert. denied, 531 U.S. 1154, 121 S. Ct. 1102, 148 L. Ed. 2d 973 (2001). Under the New Hampshire jury selection plan, new names were collected every four years, but it took an additional nine months before they could be integrated into the master jury wheel. The Court of Appeals stated that the purpose of the statutory time limit was to ensure that the data was reasonably fresh, and that this purpose was not defeated by the delay. The court held that the statute did not preclude a reasonable delay between the collection of data and its insertion into the wheel. Nor did the delay defeat the "random" selection requirement of the statute because it reduced the number of young people in the wheel, as well as those who had recently relocated in New Hampshire. The court answered by stating that neither young persons nor recent immigrants were the kind of distinctive groups that gave rise to either a violation of the statute or the Sixth Amendment.

n. 80.

Add to note 80:

In U.S. v. Rioux, 97 F.3d 648, 45 Fed. R. Evid. Serv. 998 (2d Cir. 1996), computers were used in the jury selection process, and the court stated that their employment served to rebut a claim of discrimination based on a statistical showing of underrepresentation.

n. 82.

Add to note 82:

But compare Walker v. Goldsmith, 902 F.2d 16 (9th Cir. 1990), where persons whose surnames which began with the letters 'W' through 'Z' were not included in the venire from which defendant's jury was selected. The court found no violation of either equal protection or the fair cross section requirement on the ground that those with surnames beginning with these letters did not form a cognizable group for constitutional purposes. The court did not address whether there might have been a violation of the requirement of random selection. The random selection argument, however, was rejected in U.S. v. Eyster, 948 F.2d 1196, 34 Fed. R. Evid. Serv. 688 (11th Cir. 1991). The court reasoned that the federal act did not require "true or absolute statistical randomness." It was sufficient that the system adopted afforded no room for impermissible discrimination. U.S. v. Eyster, 948 F.2d 1196, 1213, 34 Fed. R. Evid. Serv. 688 (11th Cir. 1991). The court was not persuaded that the creation of a venire composed of jurors with surnames beginning with the letters 'A' through 'J' would result in the overrepresentation of some ethnic groups and the underrepresentation of others. See also U.S. v. McKinley, 995 F.2d 1020 (11th Cir. 1993) (no fair cross section violation where venire composed of jurors whose surnames began with B, D, F, and M).

§ 6:7

Add at end of section:

In Boston v. Bowersox, 202 F.3d 1001 (8th Cir. 1999) the Court of Appeals stated that the jury supervisor's decision to designate for jury selection the first 45 members of the qualified jury list to arrive at the courthouse was not a violation of the randomness requirement. The decision was a numerical one which did not implicate race or gender. In U.S. v. Clark, 184 F.3d 858, 52 Fed. R. Evid. Serv. 126 (D.C. Cir. 1999) the D.C. Court of Appeals held that the trial court's decision to seat even-numbered jurors before odd-numbered jurors, while unusual, did not violate the requirement of randomness absent a showing that there were relevant differences between the even and odd numbered jurors. Nor was there any basis for attributing a discriminatory motive or effect to the method of selection.

In U.S. v. Sogomonian, 247 F.3d 348 (2d Cir. 2001), the trial judge had selected the alternate jurors by lottery at the conclusion of the trial. While disapproving of the practice and advising strict adherence to Rule 24, the Court of Appeals found the judge's action not be plain error. See also U.S. v. Brewer, 199 F.3d 1283 (11th Cir. 2000).

In U.S. v. Allen, 160 F.3d 1096, 1998 FED App. 0341P (6th Cir. 1998), the jury pool for the defendants' trial was augmented by jurors who had been struck from another panel. The defendants' argued that this procedure violated the principle of random selection, but the court found no violation of the Jury Selection and Service Act. The court noted that the jurors had already been randomly selected three times: first, when their names were pulled from the voter registration list; second, when their names were selected from the master jury wheel; and finally, when they were assigned to the particular venire. The court noted that the JSSA permits reassignment of jurors for jury duty, and that the instant case was exceptional only in that the jurors were reassigned on the same day rather than at some future date.

In Hardin v. City of Gadsden, 837 F. Supp. 1113 (N.D. Ala. 1993), district-wide jury wheels were used in civil cases. The effect of the wheels was to limit the opportunity of blacks to serve on juries, as the black population was concentrated in a small geographical section of a large district, was disproportionately poor, and lacked vehicular transportation. The court held that under the circumstances both the Federal Jury Selection and Service Act of 1968 and the due process requirements of the fifth amendment were violated. The use of voter lists as a source of names for the jury wheel was not enough to remedy the defect.

§ 6:8 Selection of a jury pool—Voter registration

n. 83.
Add to note 83:
In U.S. v. Douglas, 795 F. Supp. 909 (N.D. Iowa 1991), the court held that, because the federal Act provides that either a voter registration list or the list of actual voters may be used as the source of names, the use of the latter even though contrary to the local plan, did not render the selection process unconstitutional. The fact that the voter registration rolls may not be completely current is not fatal. U.S. v. Rioux, 97 F.3d 648, 45 Fed. R. Evid. Serv. 998 (2d Cir. 1996) (registration rolls two and one-half years out of date). In U.S. v. Lara, 181 F.3d 183, 51 Fed. R. Evid. Serv. 1302 (1st Cir. 1999) the defendants established a technical failure of the state to comply with the National Voter Registration Act, from which it derived its jury wheels. However, the defendants failed to prove systematic exclusion of Hispanic jurors and thus the Court of Appeals found no violation of the fair cross section requirement. See also U.S. v. Smith, 223 F.3d 554, 54 Fed. R. Evid. Serv. 970 (7th Cir. 2000), cert. denied, 536 U.S. 957, 122 S. Ct. 2658, 153 L. Ed. 2d 834 (2002).

Add after second sentence in first paragraph:
The analogy of jury service to the electoral franchise is developed in Amar, *Jury Service as Political Participation Akin to Voting*, 80 Cornell L. Rev. 203 (1995) (arguing that decisions regarding the jury should be located in the broader context of political participation generally and protected by those Amendments directed at preventing discrimination in voting). See Note, *Voter Registration: A Remedy for Securing a Jury of One's Peers*, 34 How LJ 383 (1991) (arguing in favor of a massive voter registration drive in order to secure juries representing a fair cross section of the community).

Add after fourth sentence in first paragraph:
But see Floyd v. Garrison, 996 F.2d 947 (8th Cir. 1993) (mere fact that one identifiable group of individuals votes in lower proportion than the rest of the population does not serve to render invalid a method of jury selection based on voter registration).

n. 85.
Add to note 85:
See generally Note, *Jury Source Representativeness and the Use of Voter Registration Lists*, 65 N.Y.U. L. Rev. 590 (1990).

n. 86.
Add to note 86:
In Cunningham v. Zant, 928 F.2d 1006 (11th Cir. 1991), jury pools were selected by picking every fifth name from the voter rolls. The court found no violation of either equal protection or the fair cross section requirement.

Add after third sentence in third paragraph:
Arguably those who choose to register to vote will be better educated than those who decline to exercise their franchise.

§ 6:8 JURY SELECTION: LAW, ART & SCIENCE 2D

In U.S. v. Burgess, 836 F. Supp. 336 (D.S.C. 1993), the defendant objected that the higher educational level of the jurors yielded a jury that was not representative of the community. The court held that less educated persons were not a cognizable or distinctive group, and that, even if they were, the defendant had failed to prove that the education level of the venire was not a fair and reasonable representation of the education level of the community. Defendant's proof consisted of statistics comparing the educational level of persons over 18 in South Carolina with that of members of the venire. The educational level of the venire was somewhat higher, but not sufficiently so, in the Court's opinion, to support a Sixth Amendment claim. Defendant's claim, in any event, had to fail because he made no showing of systematic exclusion. The state had chosen its jurors at random from voter registration lists.

Add at the end of the fourth paragraph:
See also Jade, *Voter Registration Status as a Jury Service Employment Test:* Oregon's Retracted Endorsement Following Buckley v. American Constitutional Law Foundation, Inc., 39 Willamette L. Rev. 557 (2003). The author examines Oregon's brief experiment requiring that jurors be registered voters, and concludes that voter registration bears no relationship to either juror competency or juror probity.

Add after note 91:
What purported to be a sophisticated and exhaustive mathematical analysis of the number of African-Americans and Hispanics in the population compared to their presence in the master wheels used for jury selection was the basis of the claimed statutory and Sixth Amendment violations in U.S. v. Weaver, 267 F.3d 231 (3d Cir. 2001), cert. denied, 534 U.S. 1152, 122 S. Ct. 1118, 151 L. Ed. 2d 1011 (2002). The expert in demography who prepared the reports asserted that the likelihood that the under representation was the result of random chance was one in 6,603,384 for the African-Americans and one in 130,337,015 for the Hispanics. Despite these seemingly impressive statistics, the Court of Appeals found a fundamental weakness in the analysis of the expert because he failed to account for the jury questionnaire forms that were mailed but not completed and returned. Although the court noted the weaknesses in both the comparative disparity and absolute disparity tests, it found that the absolute disparity test, which seemed to be the preferred test of the federal circuits, did not support the petitioner's claim that the use of voter registration lists violated either his Sixth Amendment rights or the Jury Selection and Service Act of 1968. The court also found no evidence of persis-

tent "systematic exclusion" of African-Americans or Hispanics.

Add at the end of the fifth paragraph:
In U.S. v. Douglas, 837 F. Supp. 817 (N.D. Tex. 1993), defendant argued that blacks were typically distrustful and fearful of the judicial system, and more likely than members of other races to ignore summons for jury service. The court opined that, in an equal protection context at least, this evidence rebutted rather than supported defendant's claim of purposeful discrimination, as this distrust of the system rather than any action of the state accounted for the underrepresentation.

n. 98.
Add to note 98:
But see U.S. v. Tranakos, 690 F. Supp. 971 (D. Wyo. 1988) (Shoshone and Arapaho Indian tribes are cognizable groups for purposes of the fair cross section requirement).

n. 102.
Add to note 102:
In U.S. v. Garcia, 991 F.2d 489 (8th Cir. 1993) the court found the absence of a showing of systematic exclusion fatal to the defendant's claim that the use of voter registration lists resulted in a systematic exclusion of Hispanics from jury service. See also Floyd v. Garrison, 996 F.2d 947 (8th Cir. 1993). U.S. v. Ireland, 62 F.3d 227 (8th Cir. 1995); U.S. v. Allen, 160 F.3d 1096, 1998 FED App. 0341P (6th Cir. 1998); U.S. v. Einfeldt, 138 F.3d 373, 48 Fed. R. Evid. Serv. 1386 (8th Cir. 1998); Truesdale v. Moore, 142 F.3d 749 (4th Cir. 1998) (to substitute a showing of substantial underrepresentation for evidence of systematic exclusion would exalt racial proportionality over neutral jury selection procedures).

n. 103.
Add to note 103:
In U.S. v. Miller, 116 F.3d 641, 46 Fed. R. Evid. Serv. 1174 (2d Cir. 1997), the court found that there had not been a "substantial" violation of the Act where voter registration lists had been supplemented with motor vehicle records to create the jury pool, and there had been no showing that any ethnic group had been discriminated in respect to either of these. The plaintiffs had also failed to show any statistical underrepresentation or systemic exclusion, and therefore the court found no violation of the equal protection or cross section representation guarantees. The fact that residents of one county had been included in the master jury wheel of another county also was held not to be in violation of the Sixth Amendment, for both counties were in the same district.

Add at end of section:
The argument that the use of voter registration lists to select jurors infringes upon one's right to vote or serve as a juror was turned around in Bershatsky v. Levin, 99 F.3d 555 (2d Cir. 1996). The petitioner in this case sought a declaratory judgment and injunctive relief on the basis that the use

§ 6:8   Jury Selection: Law, Art & Science 2d

of voter registrations lists to select jurors infringed upon her constitutional right to vote. She argued that serving as a juror would be economically disadvantageous to her and that she should not have to do so in order to exercise her right to vote. The court rejected the argument and stated that a summons for jury duty was not "coercion or intimidation" within the meaning of 42 U.S.C.A. § 1973i(b) (prohibiting the placing of burdens on the right to vote). The court observed that although alternative methods of obtaining juror names could be envisaged, they had their own drawbacks: for example, using drivers licenses or tax returns would exclude citizens who either did not drive or were not required (or did not) file a tax return. Voter registration lists had the inherent advantage that they were restricted to citizens, and only citizens could serve on a jury.

    One way of tackling the problem of jurors who fail to respond to a summons for jury duty is to hold the no-shows in contempt. A short term of imprisonment was upheld in In re Mauldin, 242 Ga. App. 350, 529 S.E.2d 653, 93 A.L.R.5th 755 (2000) in the case of a professional musician (who was playing at an out of town engagement at the time) who failed to appear for jury duty and was held in contempt. See generally, Annotation, Holding Jurors in Contempt Under State Law, 93 A.L.R. 5th 493.

§ 6:9 —"Key man" systems
n. 117.
   Add to note 117:
    See also O'Neal v. Delo, 44 F.3d 655 (8th Cir. 1995), rejecting the claimed fair cross section violation. There was no proof of purposeful discrimination or systematic exclusion although one of several methods used by the sheriff in selecting the grand jury was personal references.

§ 6:11   Procedural issues relating to a statutory challenge to the array
n. 138.
   Add to note 138:
    In Campbell v. Louisiana, 523 U.S. 392, 118 S. Ct. 1419, 140 L. Ed. 2d 551, 172 A.L.R. Fed. 597 (1998), the United States Supreme Court addressed the question of whether a white defendant had standing to challenge alleged discrimination in the selection of a grand jury foreperson. The accused had been indicted by a grand jury under a state law pursuant to which the trial judge selected the foreperson of the grand jury from the grand jury venire, with the remaining members then being selected at random. It was undisputed that no black person had served as grand jury foreperson in the parish for the previous 17 years. Citing its prior decision in Powers v. Ohio, 499 U.S. 400, 111 S. Ct. 1364, 113 L. Ed. 2d 411 (1991), in which the Court had held that a white defendant had standing to challenge the discriminatory peremptory challenges of black petit jurors (discussed in supp Ch 8), the Court held that Campbell too had standing

to raise the equal protection and due process claims of black jurors who had been discriminated against. The Court's reasoning tracked that in Powers. The defendant had suffered significant injury since the discriminatory selection process undermined the integrity of the indictment process. The accused shared a common interest with the excluded jurors in eradicating discrimination from the grand jury selection process, and therefore could be counted on to be an effective advocate for the excluded jurors. The accused also had an interest in asserting the excluded jurors' rights because a finding that there had been a constitutional violation might lead to the reversal of his conviction. Finally, the Court noted that the defendant's own due process rights may well have been violated by the selection procedure. Hobby v. U.S., 468 U.S. 339, 104 S. Ct. 3093, 82 L. Ed. 2d 260 (1984), in which the Court had held that no relief could be granted to a white defendant even if there had been a violation of due process in the selection of the foreperson of a federal grand jury, was distinguished. In *Hobby* the foreperson has already been selected to serve on the grand jury prior to his or her purely ministerial appointment to the role of foreperson; in *Campbell* the judge's appointment of the foreperson shaped the composition of the grand jury. This difference in effect converted the case into one alleging discriminatory selection of grand juror members. Having determined the standing issue, the court in *Campbell* did not reach the substantive merits of the petitioner's claim but rather remanded for further proceedings.

n. 146.

Add to note 146:

U.S. v. Paradies, 98 F.3d 1266, 46 Fed. R. Evid. Serv. 656 (11th Cir. 1996), as amended, (Nov. 6, 1996) (rejecting motion because not accompanied by sworn statement of facts as required by statute); U.S. v. Contreras, 108 F.3d 1255 (10th Cir. 1997) (same). The Third Circuit appears to be the only one which does not strictly construe the requirement of a sworn statement. See U.S. v. Calabrese, 942 F.2d 218 (3d Cir. 1991).

In U.S. v. Calabrese, 942 F.2d 218 (3d Cir. 1991), the defendants challenged the propriety of the judge granting unrequested excusals from jury service to prospective jurors who indicated in response to a form letter and questionnaire that they knew one or more of the defendants. The defendants claimed a violation of the Jury Selection and Service Act. The defendants' objection was timely but they did not file the sworn statement required under 28 U.S.C.A. § 1867(d). They relied instead on the undisputed sworn testimony of the clerk who granted the exclusions. The court held that this constituted sufficient compliance with the procedural requirements of the act.

n. 147.

Add to note 147:
Dawson v. Wal-Mart Stores, Inc., 978 F.2d 205 (5th Cir. 1992).

n. 149.

Add to note 149:
See also U.S. v. Young, 38 F.3d 338 (7th Cir. 1994).

n. 159.

Add to note 159:

U.S. v. Spriggs, 102 F.3d 1245, 46 Fed. R. Evid. Serv. 181 (D.C. Cir. 1996); U.S. v. Paradies, 98 F.3d 1266, 46 Fed. R. Evid. Serv. 656 (11th Cir. 1996).

§ 6:11   JURY SELECTION: LAW, ART & SCIENCE 2D

n. 160.

Add to note 160 after US v Savides:
U.S. v. Paradies, 98 F.3d 1266, 46 Fed. R. Evid. Serv. 656 (11th Cir. 1996) (district court's sua sponte dismissal of jurors was not substantial violation of Act when based on hardship and perceived prejudice as opposed to race, ethnicity or national origin).

Add to note 160:

In U.S. v. Bailey, 76 F.3d 320 (10th Cir. 1996), the clerk had erred in calculating the number of registered voters for several counties. However, the error had only a minuscule effect on the pool from which the defendant's grand and petit jurors were chosen. The defendant had made no showing that there had been an impact on the racial composition of the grand jury pool, and the deviation in the petit jury pool was less than 1%. The Court of Appeals held that there had not been a substantial failure to comply with the provisions of the Jury Selection and Service Act. See also U.S. v. Royal, 174 F.3d 1 (1st Cir. 1999) (use of residential lists not a substantial failure to comply with Act).

In U.S. v. Erickson, 75 F.3d 470, 43 Fed. R. Evid. Serv. 944 (9th Cir. 1996), when the potential for a shortage of jurors arose, the trial court ordered that additional venirepersons be summoned from a 25-mile radius rather than from the entire district. The reason for the limitation was the Court's desire to expedite the proceedings, which might have had to be delayed if jurors had to be brought from a greater distance. However, the effect of the ruling was to exclude four Indian reservations which were outside the 25-mile radius. The Court of Appeals found that any violation of the Jury Selection and Service Act was insubstantial. There had been no showing that the representation of Indians in the venire was not fair and reasonable in relation to the number of Indians in the community, nor that there was a systematic pattern of exclusion.

In U.S. v. Fike, 82 F.3d 1315, 44 Fed. R. Evid. Serv. 479 (5th Cir. 1996) (overruled on other grounds by, U.S. v. Brown, 161 F.3d 256 (5th Cir. 1998)) and (abrogated by, U.S. v. Cantu, 230 F.3d 148 (5th Cir. 2000)) the Court of Appeals held that neither the practice of telephoning previously selected but nonappearing jurors nor the use of jurors whose service had been postponed introduced a significant element of nonrandomization into the jury selection process. To the extent that there was a violation of the Act, it was not a substantial violation. See also U.S. v. Royal, 174 F.3d 1 (1st Cir. 1999) (failure to follow up on qualification forms not completed and returned was not a substantial violation of Act).

n. 161.

Add to note 161:

In U.S. v. Ovalle, 136 F.3d 1092, 1998 FED App. 0060P (6th Cir. 1998), a challenge was raised to the Jury Selection Plan of the Eastern District of Michigan. In order to achieve a balance of the different cognizable groups in the community, the Plan provided for the removal of one in five non-African Americans from the jury pool. The court found this to be a substantial violation of § 1862 of the JSSA because it was contrary to a central purpose of the Act, namely the elimination of discrimination in the juror selection process. The decision and the implications are examined in Cohn & Sherwood, The Rise and Fall of Affirmative Action in Jury Selection, 32 U. Mich. J. of Law Reform 323 (1999).

n. 162.

Add to note 162:

CHALLENGES TO THE ARRAY § 6:12

In U.S. v. Candelaria-Silva, 166 F.3d 19, 51 Fed. R. Evid. Serv. 210 (1st Cir. 1999), the First Circuit Court of Appeals ruled that the district court's excusal of four jurors on hardship grounds was not justified. The excusals had been granted ex parte, and the Court of Appeals advised that it was generally unwise to excuse jurors in the absence of counsel. The court held, however, that the errors were not a 'substantial failing' under the JSSA. In reaching this conclusion, the court weighed the violations against the underlying principles of the Act—to preserve random selection and to base disqualifications, excuses, exemptions and exclusions on objective criteria. There had been no showing of discrimination in the case, or that the district court's actions had prevented the jury from consisting of a fair cross section of the community. Also, the number of errors (four) was small.

n. 164.
Add to note 164:
These principles were applied in U.S. v. Calabrese, 942 F.2d 218 (3d Cir. 1991), where the trial judge excused from jury service those prospective jurors who indicated that they had knowledge of one of the parties. The Court of Appeals held that the excusals, without further probing of the nature of the juror's knowledge of, or relation with, the defendants violated the Jury Selection and Service Act, that the violation was a "substantial" one, and that the defendants were entitled to relief regardless of actual prejudice. The court did not rest its decision on the lack of any disqualifying relationship between a particular juror and a defendant but, rather, on the procedure followed by the trial judge:

> Where the excusal or exclusion of a significant number of jurors is not based on one of the Act's enumerated grounds, and where the district court has not provided any basis for the excusals or exclusions, we believe that this lack of inquiry itself constitutes a substantial violation of the Act.

U.S. v. Calabrese, 942 F.2d 218, 229, (3d Cir. 1991).

Add at the end of the fifteenth paragraph:
In U.S. v. Douglas, 837 F. Supp. 817 (N.D. Tex. 1993), the judges in the division had instructed the jury clerk to telephone persons who failed to appear for jury service. The court found that although this may have constituted a technical violation of the Act, it was not a substantial failure in that it did not directly affect the random nature or objectivity of the selection process.

§ 6:12 Challenges to the array based on equal protection

n. 180.
Add to note 180:
In Hardin v. City of Gadsden, 837 F. Supp. 1113 (N.D. Ala. 1993), district-wide jury wheels were used in civil cases. The effect of the wheels was to limit the opportunity of blacks to serve on juries, as the black population was concentrated in a small geographical section of a large district, was disproportionately poor, and was likely to lack vehicular transportation. The court held that under the circumstances both the Federal Jury Selection and Service Act of 1968 and the due process requirements of the fifth amendment were violated. The use of voter lists as a source of names for the jury wheel was not enough to remedy the defect.

§ 6:12

n. 185.

Add to note 185:

In U.S. v. McKinney, 53 F.3d 664 (5th Cir. 1995), there were no Afro-Americans on the 73-member venire panel from which the appellant's jury was selected, although Afro-Americans comprised 2.28% of the community. There was also a showing of the opportunity to discriminate. The Court of Appeals, however, stated that the underrepresentation could have been the product of chance and that the opportunity to discriminate, without more, is not enough to shift the burden of proof to the government on an equal protection claim.

§ 6:13 Challenges to the array based on the fair cross section requirement

n. 193.

Add to note 193:

There is, however, no right to a jury drawn from the entirety of the judicial district or division in which the crime occurred. U.S. v. Baker, 98 F.3d 330, 45 Fed. R. Evid. Serv. 806 (8th Cir. 1996)). Accord U.S. v. Balistrieri, 778 F.2d 1226 (7th Cir. 1985)

Add after fourth paragraph:

In Holland v. Illinois, 493 U.S. 474, 110 S. Ct. 803, 107 L. Ed. 2d 905 (1990) (See Ch 8), the United States Supreme Court explained the function of the fair cross section requirement in terms of the Sixth Amendment's guarantee of an impartial jury. The Court stated that the fair cross section requirement should be understood as a means of assuring an impartial jury, not necessarily a representative one. It did so by preventing the state from constructing jury lists which eliminated cognizable groups which might be opposed to the state's case. If the state could eliminate such opposition groups from the venire, it would in effect have a considerable, and altogether invisible, power of peremptory challenge. The fair cross section requirement helped guard against such a threat.

Add after sixth paragraph:

There are critical differences, however, between an equal protection analysis and one based on the Sixth Amendment's requirement of fair cross section representation. Most notably, in order to establish a violation of equal protection, one must prove intentional discrimination. In order to establish a Sixth Amendment violation, one need only prove systematic exclusion. The systematic exclusion need not be intentional. This distinction proved critical in Ricketts v. City of Hartford, 74 F.3d 1397, 43 Fed. R. Evid. Serv. 903 (2d Cir. 1996), as amended on reh'g in part, (Feb. 14, 1996). The jury here had been drawn from the same venire as had been found to have been in violation of the Sixth Amendment's cross section requirement in U.S. v. Jackman, 46

F.3d 1240 (2d Cir. 1995). However, unlike *Jackman, Ricketts* was a civil action under 42 U.S.C.A. § 1983. A claim that the jury venire failed to satisfy the fair cross section demands of the Sixth Amendment was unavailable, since the Sixth Amendment is restricted to criminal prosecutions. The appellant argued that the jury selection procedure denied him equal protection. However, there was no evidence that the jury administrator had intentionally excluded any potential juror on account of race or ethnic background. The computer error which had led to the exclusions was inadvertent. Thus, the same jury venire that had been found unconstitutional in *Jackman* was found to pass constitutional muster in *Ricketts*. *See also* U.S. v. Esquivel, 75 F.3d 545 (9th Cir. 1996), opinion withdrawn and superseded on denial of reh'g, 88 F.3d 722, 44 Fed. R. Evid. Serv. 1390 (9th Cir. 1996).

In Richards, *The Discreet Charm of the Mixed Jury: The Epistemology of Jury Selection and the Perils of Post-Modernism*, 26 Seattle L. Rev. 445 (2003), the author identifies two models of jury selection, one that presumes that jurors have an open mind and approach cases impartially, writing on a clean slate; and the other that they are ciphers representing various political constituencies. The Supreme Court has, according to the author, attempted to steer its way between these two models, presuming impartiality but at the same time giving legal recognition to a limited class of perspectives that only jurors with a particular background will have (blacks, women, etc.). The author concludes that adjusting the jury system in this way cannot ultimately repair the damage wrought by racial, ethnic and other divisions within society.

Add after third sentence in seventh paragraph:
In U.S. v. Nururdin, 8 F.3d 1187, 39 Fed. R. Evid. Serv. 1143 (7th Cir. 1993), the defendant was tried by an all white jury produced by random selection, no black juror having been chosen to serve. The defendant, who was black and a resident of an inner city neighborhood, contended that white persons who lived in the city or suburbs could not understand the nature of the relationship between white Chicago police and black citizens, or the nature of life and behavior in the black inner city. The court found the argument untenable in light of Supreme Court statements that a defendant does not have the right to have persons of his or her race included on the jury. A similar argument was rejected in Leibengood v. State, 866 S.W.2d 732 (Tex. App. Houston 14th Dist. 1993), petition for discretionary review refused, (Apr. 20, 1994). The defendant was a dwarf. He argued that the absence of "little people" on the jury both violated the fair cross section requirement and denied him equal protection. The Court

§ 6:13

stated that even assuming that people under five feet tall were a "distinctive" group, the defendant had failed to prove their systematic exclusion from the jury. Nor had the defendant established discrimination. Indeed in the Court's view the defendant's argument amounted to a complaint that "little people are not treated differently. He would have little people sought out and purposefully inserted into jury venires unlike any other segment of society." Leibengood v. State, 866 S.W.2d 732, 735, (Tex. App. Houston 14th Dist. 1993), petition for discretionary review refused, (Apr. 20, 1994) (emphasis in original). The court held that a defendant has no such right. The possible use of racial quotas in respect to the jury pool is examined in Altschuler, *Racial Quotas and the Jury*, 44 Duke LJ 704 (1995).

n. 207.

Add to note 207:
It has also been argued that the requirements of venue and vicinage may work at cross-purposes with the effort to impanel a jury representative of a fair cross section of the community. See Note, *Vicinage, Venue, and Community Cross Section: Obstacles to a State Defendant's Right to a Trial by a Representative Jury*, 19 Hastings LQ 261 (1991).

n. 208.

Add to note 208:
Whether the principle of nondiscrimination and the principle of cross section representation are complementary or in conflict is explored in Leipold, *Constitutionalizing Jury Selection in Criminal Cases: A Critical Evaluation*, 86 Georgetown L.S. 945 (1998). See also J. Gobert, Justice, Democracy and the Jury (Dartmouth 1997). Gobert observes that the principles of equal protection and cross section representation trace their roots to different political/philosophical traditions. Equal protection is based on the philosophical principle that similarly situated individuals should be treated similarly, while cross section representation is based on the political principle which espouses democratic decision-making. A jury which represents the community is a democracy in microcosm. In constitutional terms, the right to a jury which is a fair cross section of the community can be conceived of as a right of the defendant, while the right not to be discriminated against in jury selection is a right of the individual juror, although, perforce, it will often have to be vindicated by a party to the lawsuit. See also Saunders, *Race and Representation in Jury Service Selection*, 36 Duquesne L. Rev. 49 (1997) (linking community acceptance of jury verdicts with community's perception of the jury's representativeness, and proposing legislative reforms for achieving representativeness in Pennsylvania juries).

n. 211.

Add to note 211:
Blue ribbon juries may make particular sense in cases involving complex litigation. See 132 Federal Rules Decisions p 575.

Add to the end of tenth paragraph:
As a practical matter, a party can to some extent affect the intellectual quality of the jury through the exercise of pe-

remptory challenges against venirepersons with limited education. See, e.g., U.S. v. Hinojosa, 958 F.2d 624 (5th Cir. 1992).

n. 213.

Add to note 213:

An unusual cross section argument was made in U.S. v. Edwards, 188 F.3d 230 (4th Cir. 1999) in that it was based on the dismissal of single juror, albeit the only black member of the jury, during the jury's deliberations. The juror had informed the trial court that he had received a telephone call stating that the defendants "need your help". The court dismissed the juror pursuant to Fed. R. Crim. P. 23(b) and the Court of Appeals held that this was not error.

§ 6:14 Establishing a prima facie case of a constitutional violation

n. 214.

Add to note 214:

Whether a party in fact suffers prejudice, and, if so, how much, from the exclusion of a cognizable or distinct group from the jury is a question which is difficult to answer. Social science experiments have attempted to shed some light on the inquiry. The issue is examined in King, *Postconviction Review of Jury Discrimination: Measuring the Effects of Juror Race on Jury Decisions*, 92 Mich L Rev 63 (1993).

§ 6:15 —Standing

Add after note 223:

In Campbell v. Louisiana, 523 U.S. 392, 118 S. Ct. 1419, 140 L. Ed. 2d 551, 172 A.L.R. Fed. 597 (1998), the United States Supreme Court addressed the question of whether a white defendant had standing to challenge alleged discrimination in the selection of the foreperson of the grand jury that had indicted him. Under state law the trial judge selected the foreperson of the grand jury from the grand jury venire, with the remaining members then being selected at random. It was undisputed that no black person had served as a grand jury foreperson in the parish for the previous 17 years. Citing its prior decision in Powers v. Ohio, 499 U.S. 400, 111 S. Ct. 1364, 113 L. Ed. 2d 411 (1991), in which the Court had held that a white defendant had standing to challenge the discriminatory peremptory challenges of black petit jurors (discussed in supp Ch 8), the Court held that Campbell too had standing to raise the equal protection and due process claims of black jurors who had been discriminated against. The Court's reasoning tracked that in *Powers*. The defendant had suffered significant injury since the discriminatory selection process undermined the integrity of the indictment process. The accused shared a common interest with the excluded jurors in eradicating discrimination from the grand jury selection process, and therefore could be

§ 6:15

counted on to be an effective advocate for the excluded jurors. The accused also had an interest in asserting the excluded jurors' rights because a finding that there had been a constitutional violation might lead to the reversal of his conviction. Finally, the Court noted that the defendant's own due process rights may well have been violated by the selection procedure. Hobby v. U.S., 468 U.S. 339, 104 S. Ct. 3093, 82 L. Ed. 2d 260 (1984), in which the Court had held that no relief could be granted to a white defendant even if there had been a violation of due process in the selection of the foreperson of a federal grand jury, was distinguished. In *Hobby* the foreperson has already been selected to serve on the grand jury prior to his or her purely ministerial appointment to the role of foreperson, while in *Campbell* the judge's appointment of the foreperson shaped the composition of the grand jury. This difference in effect converted the case into one alleging discriminatory selection of grand juror members. Having determined the standing issue, the court in *Campbell* did not reach the substantive merits of the petitioner's claim but rather remanded for further proceedings.

In U.S. v. Ovalle, 136 F.3d 1092, 1998 FED App. 0060P (6th Cir. 1998), where the Jury Selection Plan for the Eastern District of Michigan attempted to achieve a balance of the different cognizable groups in the community by providing for the removal of one in five non-African Americans from the jury pool, a preliminary issue was whether the defendants should be allowed third-party standing in order to raise an equal protection challenge to the Plan. Utilizing the test in *Powers*, the court stated that where the jury selection plan discriminated against an identifiable group, both the defendant and members of the group who were excluded suffered injury: the defendants' injury consisted of being denied the 'neutral jury selection procedures' to which they were entitled and the excluded citizen's injury was being denied the opportunity to serve on a jury. Furthermore, there was a commonality of interest between the defendants and the excluded jurors in that both wished to eliminate racial discrimination from the jury selection process. A further consideration in favor of allowing third party standing was that it would be extremely unlikely for the excluded jurors to bring an equal protection claim in their own right. The decision and the implications are examined in Cohn & Sherwood, The Rise and Fall of Affirmative Action in Jury Selection, 32 U. Mich. J. of Law Reform 323 (1999).

n. 225.

Add to note 225:

An argument that women approach decisional tasks differently than men—they are less concerned with the strict application of rules and think

Challenges to the Array § 6:16

beyond simple binary, win-loss solutions—is developed in Dooley, *Sounds of Silence on the Civil Jury*, 26 Valparaiso L Rev 405 (1991); Benlevy, *Venus and Mars in the Jury Deliberation Room: Exploring the Differences that Exist among Male and Female Jurors during the Deliberation Process*, 9 S. Cal. Rev. L. & Women's Stud. 445 (2000). Interestingly, Klein and Klastorin discovered little statistical relationship between gender diversity on a jury and whether the jury would reach a verdict. Klein and Klastorin, *Do Diverse Juries Aid or Impede Justice?*, 1999 Wis. L. Rev. 553 (1999).

Professor Marder supports the view that gender diversity makes a difference to the quality of deliberations. She argues, in particular, that the tone and thoroughness of deliberations, and the extent of juror satisfaction is higher on gender diverse jurors. Marder, *Juries, Justice, and Multiculturalism*, 75 S. Cal. L. Rev. 659 (2002). Her conclusion is that gender, and, indeed, cultural diversity should be prized on juries and that judges should do all they can to encourage such diversity.

Add after third sentence in seventh paragraph:

In Mata v. Johnson, 99 F.3d 1261 (5th Cir. 1996), vacated in part on reh'g, 105 F.3d 209 (5th Cir. 1997), defense counsel had entered into an agreement with the prosecutor to exclude all black members of the venire from the jury. The trial judge had implicitly approved by allowing the challenge of the jurors without requiring a statement of reasons. The court of appeal stated in no uncertain terms that this practice was a clear violation of equal protection principles and impermissible. The decisions of the Supreme Court were intended to protect not only the rights of the accused, but also the rights of the jurors.

§ 6:16 —Cognizability

n. 233.

Add to note 233:

The mere fact that jurors have served in previous cases tried by the same prosecutor does not render the jurors 'distinctive' or justify a finding that a subsequent jury composed of these individuals does not constitute a fair cross section of the community. U.S. v. Hill, 146 F.3d 337 (6th Cir. 1998).

A number of federal circuits have adopted the test of cognizability enunciated in Willis v. Zant, 720 F.2d 1212 (11th Cir. 1983). Under this test a defendant must show:

(1) That the group is defined and limited by some factor (i.e., that the group has a definite composition such as race or sex);

(2) That a common thread or basic similarity in attitude, ideas, or experience runs through the group; and

(3) That there is a community of interests among members of the group such that the group's interest cannot be adequately represented if the group is excluded from the jury selection process. Willis v. Zant, 720 F.2d 1212, 1216 (11th Cir. 1983).

The *Willis* test has been adopted in the Ninth Circuit (U.S. v. Fletcher, 965 F.2d 781 (9th Cir. 1992)), the Eighth Circuit (U.S. v. Canfield, 879

§ 6:16   Jury Selection: Law, Art & Science 2d

F.2d 446 (8th Cir. 1989)), the Sixth Circuit (Ford v. Seabold, 841 F.2d 677 (6th Cir. 1988)); and the First Circuit (Barber v. Ponte, 772 F.2d 982, 19 Fed. R. Evid. Serv. 215 (1st Cir. 1985)).

n. 241.

Add to note 241:

See also U.S. v. Gelb, 881 F.2d 1155 (2d Cir. 1989) (recognizing Jews as a distinctive group in the community but finding that the case that they were underrepresented on the venire had not been made).

n. 242.

Add to note 242:

In U.S. v. Burgess, 836 F. Supp. 336 (D.S.C. 1993), the defendant objected that the high educational level of the jurors was not representative of the community. The court held that less educated persons were not a cognizable or distinctive group, and that, even if they were, the defendant had failed to prove that the education level of the venire was not a fair and reasonable representation of the education level of the community. Defendant's proof consisted of statistics comparing the educational level of persons over 18 in South Carolina with that of members of the venire. The educational level of the venire was somewhat higher, but not sufficiently so, in the Court's opinion, to support a Sixth Amendment claim. There was, in any event, no showing of systematic exclusion.

n. 243.

Add to note 243:

Willis v. Kemp, 838 F.2d 1510 (11th Cir. 1988). See also Ford v. Seabold, 841 F.2d 677 (6th Cir. 1988) (same). McQueen v. Scroggy, 99 F.3d 1302, 35 Fed. R. Serv. 3d 1211, 1996 FED App. 0349P (6th Cir. 1996) (no per se rule excluding jurors exposed to media reports unless it engenders a predisposition or bias that cannot be set aside).

Section (b)4 of the Federal Jury Selection and Service Act requires that the master jury wheel should be refilled at "specified times, the interval for which shall not exceed four years". This section was at issue in U.S. v. Shea, 211 F.3d 658, 53 Fed. R. Evid. Serv. 1353 (1st Cir. 2000), cert. denied, 531 U.S. 1154, 121 S. Ct. 1101, 148 L. Ed. 2d 973 (2001) and cert. denied, 531 U.S. 1154, 121 S. Ct. 1102, 148 L. Ed. 2d 973 (2001). Under the New Hampshire jury selection plan, new names were collected every four years, but it took an additional nine months before they could be integrated into the master jury wheel. The Court of Appeals stated that the purpose of the statutory time limit was to ensure that the data was reasonably fresh, and that this purpose was not defeated by the delay. The court held that the statute did not preclude a reasonable delay between the collection of data and its insertion into the wheel. Nor did the delay defeat the "random" selection requirement of the statute because it reduced the number of young people in the wheel, as well as those who had recently relocated in New Hampshire. The court answered by stating that neither young persons nor recent immigrants to the state were the kind of distinctive groups that gave rise to either a violation of the statute or the Sixth Amendment.

n. 244.

Add to note 244:

; Brewer v. Nix, 963 F.2d 1111 (8th Cir. 1992); Silagy v. Peters, 905 F.2d 986, 30 Fed. R. Evid. Serv. 395, 30 Fed. R. Evid. Serv. 399 (7th Cir. 1990).

n. 245.

Add to note 245:

CHALLENGES TO THE ARRAY § 6:16

In Leibengood v. State, 866 S.W.2d 732 (Tex. App. Houston 14th Dist. 1993), petition for discretionary review refused, (Apr. 20, 1994), the defendant, a dwarf, argued that the absence of "little people" on the jury violated both the fair cross section requirement and the requirements of equal protection. The court stated that even assuming that people under five feet tall were a "distinctive" group, the defendant had failed to prove their systematic exclusion from the jury. Nor had the defendant established discrimination. Indeed in the Court's view the defendant's argument amounted to a complaint that "little people are not treated differently. He would have little people sought out and purposefully inserted into jury venires unlike any other segment of society." Leibengood v. State, 866 S.W.2d 732, 735, (Tex. App. Houston 14th Dist. 1993), petition for discretionary review refused, (Apr. 20, 1994) (emphasis in original). The court held that a defendant has no such right.

Section(b)4 of the Federal Jury Selection and Service Act requires that the master jury wheel should be refilled at "specified times, the interval for which shall not exceed four years". This section was at issue in U.S. v. Shea, 211 F.3d 658, 53 Fed. R. Evid. Serv. 1353 (1st Cir. 2000), cert. denied, 531 U.S. 1154, 121 S. Ct. 1101, 148 L. Ed. 2d 973 (2001) and cert. denied, 531 U.S. 1154, 121 S. Ct. 1102, 148 L. Ed. 2d 973 (2001). Under the New Hampshire jury selection plan, new names were collected every four years, but it took an additional nine months before they could be integrated into the master jury wheel. The Court of Appeals stated that the purpose of the statutory time limit was to ensure that the data was reasonably fresh, and that this purpose was not defeated by the delay. The court held that the statute did not preclude a reasonable delay between the collection of data and its insertion into the wheel. Nor did the delay defeat the "random" selection requirement of the statute because it reduced the number of young people in the wheel, as well as those who had recently relocated in New Hampshire. The court answered by stating that neither young persons nor recent immigrants to the state were the kind of distinctive groups that gave rise to either a violation of the statute or the Sixth Amendment.

Add before last sentence of last paragraph:
In U.S. v. Tranakos, 690 F. Supp. 971 (D. Wyo. 1988), it was held that Shoshone and Arapaho Indian tribes were cognizable groups for purposes of the fair cross section requirement.

In contrast, in U.S. v. Raszkiewicz, 169 F.3d 459 (7th Cir. 1999), the Court of Appeals declined to draw a distinction between reservation and urban Indians. The jury plan for the eastern district of Wisconsin divided the district into the Milwaukee division in the south and the Green Bay division in the north. The Green Bay division included all six Indian reservations. There had not, however, been a jury trial in the Green Bay Division since 1992, which meant that reservation Indians were not included in the venire from which defendant's jury was selected. This, the defendant argued, violated his Sixth Amendment to a jury drawn from a fair cross section of the community. The Court of Appeals held that reservation Indians were not a sufficiently distinctive group for purposes of jury representativeness. There were still urban Indians eligible to serve as jurors, and

§ 6:16   JURY SELECTION: LAW, ART & SCIENCE 2D

reservation and urban Indians were not sufficiently culturally different to constitute independent groups. The social scientific evidence was inconclusive in the Court's opinion, but it found support for its decision in the fact that the main purpose of the fair cross section requirement was the securing of an impartial jury, which the defendant had not claimed he had been denied. See also U.S. v. Bushyhead, 270 F.3d 905 (9th Cir. 2001), cert. denied, 535 U.S. 1008, 122 S. Ct. 1586, 152 L. Ed. 2d 504 (2002) (failure of jury selection plan to draw juror from tribal voting lists violated neither Jury Selection and Service Act nor Sixth Amendment).

n. 246.
Add to note 246:
Compare State v. Atwood, 171 Ariz. 576, 832 P.2d 593 (1992), opinion modified on denial of reconsideration, (July 10, 1992) and (disapproved of by, State v. Nordstrom, 200 Ariz. 229, 25 P.3d 717 (2001)) (persons not employed by businesses having policy of compensating employees during jury duty not distinctive group for fair cross section purposes); State v. Tillman, 220 Conn. 487, 600 A.2d 738 (1991) (practice of clerk of excluding prospective jurors whose employers would not pay them the difference between their daily wages and their jurors' wages did not create a "distinctive" group).

n. 247.
Add to note 247:
In State v. Tillman, 220 Conn. 487, 600 A.2d 738 (1991), the court held that the practice of the clerk of excluding prospective jurors whose employers would not pay them the difference between their daily wages and their jurors' wages did not create a "distinctive" group.

Add to note 247:
In U.S. v. Hirschberg, 988 F.2d 1509, 38 Fed. R. Evid. Serv. 542 (7th Cir. 1993), the court declined to find the wealthy to be a suspect class. In U.S. v. Spriggs, 102 F.3d 1245, 46 Fed. R. Evid. Serv. 181 (D.C. Cir. 1996) the court made the point that because the fair cross section requirement applies to the pool of jurors before any jurors are excused, hardship excusals that might be argued to skew the composition of the jury cannot give rise to a fair cross section claim.

In U.S. v. Footracer, 189 F.3d 1058 (9th Cir. 1999), opinion withdrawn, 252 F.3d 1059 (9th Cir. 2001) the trial of the defendant, a Native American, was transferred from the district in which his crimes were committed to a district that contained a smaller percentage of Native Americans. The defendant argued that the transfer denied him a jury reflecting a fair cross section of the community. The Court of Appeals held that the residents of the division where the crime was committed were not a distinctive group for purposes of Sixth Amendment analysis and, furthermore, that there was no showing of systematic exclusion of Native Americans from the jury venire.

Add at end of section:
The author of Comment, Rethinking the Fair Cross-Section Requirement, 84 Cal L Rev 101 (1996) advocates a functional approach to defining "distinctiveness". The court

should weigh whether affording the group protection would help to guard against the arbitrary exercise of prosecutorial authority, would preserve public confidence in the fairness of the proceedings, and would promote the shared civic responsibility for the administration of justice. If it would, then the group should be deemed distinctive for cross section analysis purposes.

§ 6:17 —Disparity

n. 249.

Add to note 249:

In State v. Neely, 112 N.M. 702, 819 P.2d 249 (1991), the court stated that analysis of Hispanic surnames was not in itself an adequate indicator of whether an individual was of Hispanic descent [the individual could be married to an Hispanic], and such data could not be used to show underrepresentation of Hispanics. This same problem has arisen in respect to *Batson* violations (See U.S. v. Esparsen, 930 F.2d 1461, 32 Fed. R. Evid. Serv. 1191 (10th Cir. 1991) (discussed in § 8:6)), but arguably the difficulties in the present context are more acute. *Batson* claims arise at trial. The jurors are present, their racial identity is often obvious, and they can be questioned appropriately. When attempting to establish underrepresentation of a distinctive group in the community, on the other hand, the party asserting the claim needs to be able to determine what percentage of that community the group in question constitutes. To conduct a demographic census is expensive and time-consuming. Government statistics may be out of date and often undercount minorities. Using surnames would seem a practical, relatively cheap, and reasonably accurate alternative. However, in U.S. v. Lopez, 147 F.3d 1 (1st Cir. 1998), the court stated that defense counsel's visual inspection of the venire and the examination of jurors' names was not a sufficient foundation on which to base a fair cross section challenge to the composition of the jury.

n. 250.

Add to note 250:

In Rideau v. Whitley, 237 F.3d 472 (5th Cir. 2000), cert. denied, 533 U.S. 924, 121 S. Ct. 2539, 150 L. Ed. 2d 708 (2001), the court held that the state's grand jury selection procedures were unconstitutional. For its conclusion the court relied on the mathematical disparity between the percentage of blacks in the community (16+%) and that on defendant's grand jury (5%), the non-neutrality of the selection process, the failure of jury commissioners to identify and seek out black grand jurors, and the fact that the underrepresentation had continued over a significant period of time.

The mere fact that a venire contains no black member is itself insufficient to establish even a prima facie case. U.S. v. Hill, 197 F.3d 436 (10th Cir. 1999); U.S. v. Brown, 91 F.3d 1109 (8th Cir. 1996). See also Trice v. Ward, 196 F.3d 1151 (10th Cir. 1999) (where registered voter lists used for jury pools, evidence of racial composition of community will not suffice to establish underrepresentation or systematic exclusion); U.S. v. Cooke, 110 F.3d 1288 (7th Cir. 1997). In Ramseur v. Beyer, 983 F.2d 1215 (3d Cir. 1992), the court stated that the limited size of the defendant's survey and the fact that it covered only a two-year period was insufficient to satisfy *Castenada*'s requirement of a showing of substantial underrepresentation over a significant period of time. Where computers are

§ 6:17   JURY SELECTION: LAW, ART & SCIENCE 2D

used in the jury selection process, it is more difficult to sustain a claim of discrimination based on a statistical showing of underrepresentation. U.S. v. Rioux, 97 F.3d 648, 45 Fed. R. Evid. Serv. 998 (2d Cir. 1996).

Add after first paragraph:

The problem of establishing the percentage of a given ethnic or religious group on the venire was highlighted in U.S. v. Gelb, 881 F.2d 1155 (2d Cir. 1989). The defendant argued that the Court's practice of granting postponement of jury service to Jewish venirepersons during the period of their religious festivals had the effect of denying him a jury representative of a fair cross section of the community. The Court of Appeals recognized that Jews were a distinctive group in the community but found that the claim that they were underrepresented on the venire had not been established. The court declined to credit the defendant's argument that the jurors' surnames indicated that virtually none of them were Jewish, stating that "stereotypical ethnic or religious characterizations of surnames are unreliable and only tenuous indicia of the jury's makeup." U.S. v. Gelb, 881 F.2d 1155, 1162, (2d Cir. 1989). One could presumably establish religious identity by asking prospective jurors their religious preference or affiliation. The difficulty with that approach is that it might embarrass some jurors, introduce an undesirable religious element into a case where religion was not an issue, and allow those who were of a mind to discriminate against the group in question to do so. See U.S. v. Alarape, 969 F.2d 349 (7th Cir. 1992) (trial judge served the interest of justice by declining to ask jurors questions about religion where it was not an issue in the case). The problem of proving underrepresentation on the venire is not so acute with respect to claims of race or gender because the relevant information, if not contained on the juror form, is easily ascertained by the simple expedient of observing the jurors. For an analysis of the conclusion that the court in *Gelb* reached the right result for the wrong reason, See Note, *United States v Gelb*: *The Second Circuit's Disappointing Treatment of the Fair Cross-Section Guarantee*, 57 Brook L Rev 341 (1991). U.S. v. Gallegos, 108 F.3d 1272 (10th Cir. 1997); U.S. v. Contreras, 108 F.3d 1255 (10th Cir. 1997); U.S. v. Aguirre, 108 F.3d 1284 (10th Cir. 1997); U.S. v. Rodriguez-Aguirre, 108 F.3d 1228, 46 Fed. R. Evid. Serv. 813 (10th Cir. 1997); and U.S. v. Morales, 108 F.3d 1213 (10th Cir. 1997) involved similar appeals by codefendants convicted of drug-related offenses. One of their arguments was that Hispanics were underrepresented in the jury pool. However, they failed to present evidence regarding the racial composition of the district, despite the Court's indication that it was prepared to allow supplementation of the record.

In the absence of this information, the Court of Appeals ruled that the defendants had failed to satisfy the second prong of the *Duren* test.

What purported to be a sophisticated and exhaustive mathematical analysis of the number of African-Americans and Hispanics in the population compared to their presence in the master wheels used for jury selection was the basis of the claimed statutory and Sixth Amendment violations in U.S. v. Weaver, 267 F.3d 231 (3d Cir. 2001), cert. denied, 534 U.S. 1152, 122 S. Ct. 1118, 151 L. Ed. 2d 1011 (2002). The expert in demography who prepared the reports asserted that the likelihood that the under representation was the result of random chance was one in 6,603,384 for the African-Americans and one in 130,337,015 for the Hispanics. Despite these seemingly impressive statistics, the Court of Appeals found a fundamental weakness in the analysis of the expert because he failed to account for the jury questionnaire forms that were mailed but not completed and returned. Although the court noted the weaknesses in both the comparative disparity and absolute disparity tests, it found that the absolute disparity test, which seemed to be the preferred test of the federal circuits, did not support the petitioner's claim that the use of voter registration lists violated either his Sixth Amendment rights or the Jury Selection and Service Act of 1968. The court also found no evidence of persistent "systematic exclusion" of African-Americans or Hispanics.

Add after fourth sentence in fourth paragraph:
The situation envisaged in the text in fact arose in U.S. v. Horne, 4 F.3d 579 (8th Cir. 1993), where there were no blacks on the panel from which defendant's jury was chosen, although 2.9% of the district was black. The court stated, somewhat incredibly: "Appellants have failed to present adequate evidence that the representation in the venire was not fair and reasonable in relation to the admittedly small number of Afro-Americans in the District of Minnesota's Fourth Division." See also Thomas v. Borg, 159 F.3d 1147 (9th Cir. 1998) (under absolute disparity test the fact that there were no blacks on a jury panel in a county with an approximate 5% black population was not sufficient to establish a Sixth Amendment violation).

Add at end of fourth paragraph:
Similarly absurd results were achieved in U.S. v. Nururdin, 794 F. Supp. 277 (N.D. Ill. 1992), aff'd, 8 F.3d 1187, 39 Fed. R. Evid. Serv. 1143 (7th Cir. 1993), where the court subtracted the 5% African-American representation on the jury panel from the 14.9% African-American representation in

§ 6:17

the community and concluded that the 9.9% difference failed to meet the minimum 10% differential required by *Swain*. Likewise, in U.S. v. Douglas, 837 F. Supp. 817 (N.D. Tex. 1993), the court found that the percentage of Afro-Americans in the relevant district was 10.413%, while the percentage on the venire over a 13 month period was 7.66%. Subtracting the latter figure from the former, the court concluded that the absolute disparity of 2.34% was insufficient to support a finding of a Sixth Amendment violation.

What are the appropriate statistics to which to apply an absolute disparity test? In U.S. v. Esquivel, 75 F.3d 545 (9th Cir. 1996), opinion withdrawn and superseded on denial of reh'g, 88 F.3d 722, 44 Fed. R. Evid. Serv. 1390 (9th Cir. 1996), the defendant argued that there was an absolute disparity of 14.5% between the percentage of Hispanics in the population and the percentage of Hispanics in the jury pool. However, defendant's statistical analysis was based on census data which, in the opinion of the Court of Appeals, gave a misleading impression. Not all Hispanics were eligible to vote, and those who were ineligible would not be eligible for jury duty either. According to the court, the true absolute disparity after the necessary adjustments was only 4.9%, which was insufficient to support a claim of a constitutional violation. See also U.S. v. Nelson, 137 F.3d 1094, 48 Fed. R. Evid. Serv. 1184 (9th Cir. 1998) (underrepresentation of Hispanics insufficient to establish violation of fair cross section requirement under absolute disparity test). Similarly, in U.S. v. Fike, 82 F.3d 1315, 44 Fed. R. Evid. Serv. 479 (5th Cir. 1996) (overruled on other grounds by, U.S. v. Brown, 161 F.3d 256 (5th Cir. 1998)) and (abrogated by, U.S. v. Cantu, 230 F.3d 148 (5th Cir. 2000)), the court stated that the pertinent point was not the percentage of Afro-Americans in the population but the percentage of Afro-Americans who were eligible for jury duty. This yielded an absolute disparity of 2.34%, which the court held insufficient to establish a constitutional violation.

Similarly, the Tenth Circuit Court of Appeals in U.S. v. Shinault, 147 F.3d 1266 (10th Cir. 1998), stated that the proper comparison to determine whether a distinctive group was underrepresented in the jury pool was not between the percentage of the group in the population and the percentage of the group in the jury pool, but rather between the percentage of the group that was eligible for jury service and that which was in the jury pool. The difficulty with using the group's percentage in the population as a point of comparison was that members of the group in question might be ineligible for jury service at a higher rate than the general population. For instance, Asians, one of the groups alleged to be underrepresented, were less likely to be citizens, according to the court. Asians might also be less likely to speak English. Nonetheless, as the appropriate statistics were not available, the court agreed to accept the defendant's census data. The court then found that even using the defendant's data, there was not a sufficiently large disparity under the absolute disparity test used in the jurisdiction to make out a constitutional violation. The court recognized that the small numbers of the relevant groups to some extent distorted an absolute disparity test, but observed that distortion would also occur under a comparative disparity test when the group in question was small. See also U.S. v. Rioux, 97 F.3d 648, 45 Fed. R. Evid. Serv. 998 (2d Cir. 1996).

n. 256.
Add to note 256:
   In U.S. v. Horne, 4 F.3d 579 (8th Cir. 1993), there were no blacks on the panel from which defendant's jury was chosen, although 2.9% of the district was black. The court found that the appellants had failed to present adequate evidence that the representation in the venire was not fair and reasonable in relation to the "admittedly small number" of Afro-Americans in the district. Given the complete absence of blacks on the panel, it is difficult to see what more the defendants could have shown in this regard. The Court's point that there had been no proof of systematic exclusion was more well taken. A similar case on the facts was U.S. v. Pion, 25 F.3d 18 (1st Cir. 1994). The 1990 census on which the defendant relied showed that 4.2% of the district consisted of Hispanics, but that only 0.99% of those who responded to the juror questionnaire were Hispanic. The court noted that under the absolute disparity standard, the difference of 3.4% was insufficient to make out a constitutional claim. As in *Horne*, the court appeared to be on more solid ground in stating that there had been no showing of systematic exclusion in the jury selection process. Indeed the court characterized the district as using the "broadest data available—resident lists," a fact which the defendant did not dispute. U.S. v. Pion, 25 F.3d 18, 23 (1st Cir. 1994). Citing to its opinion in *Pion*, the court in U.S. v. Rodriguez, 162 F.3d 135, 50 Fed. R. Evid. Serv. 1030 (1st Cir. 1998) rejected a similar systematic exclusion claim that appeared to track the dissent in *Pion*. See also U.S. v. Lopez, 147 F.3d 1 (1st Cir. 1998); U.S. v. Royal, 174 F.3d 1 (1st Cir. 1999); U.S. v. Benjamin, 252 F.3d 1 (1st Cir. 2001).
   In U.S. v. McKinney, 53 F.3d 664 (5th Cir. 1995), there were no Afro-Americans on the 73-member venire, although they made up 2.28% of the community. The court reasoned that statistically one would expect 1.66 Afro-Americans to be on a randomly drawn 73-member panel. However, normal statistical deviations meant that on some panels Afro-Americans would be overrepresented (two or more) and on others underrepresented (one or zero). The court concluded that the underrepresentation in the present case was not a violation of the Jury Selection and Service Act, particularly in light of the fact that there was no evidence of either systematic exclusion or discrimination. For these reasons the court also found no violation of the Sixth or Fourteenth Amendments. See also U.S. v. Steen, 55 F.3d 1022 (5th Cir. 1995); U.S. v. Ashley, 54 F.3d 311 (7th Cir. 1995).

n. 257.
Add to note 257:

§ 6:17   Jury Selection: Law, Art & Science 2d

While recognizing the potentially misleading nature of both the absolute and comparative disparity standards, the Court of Appeals in U.S. v. Rogers, 73 F.3d 774 (8th Cir. 1996) opined that the comparative disparity test probably provided a more meaningful measure of disparity, particularly in a state such as Iowa where the black population was under 2% of the total. The court further indicated that the probability that any underrepresentation was due to chance was another factor to be considered. The court, however, reluctantly concluded that it was bound by a previous decision in U.S. v. Garcia, 991 F.2d 489, 491 (8th Cir. 1993), which had held that the Iowa jury selection plan in question was not unconstitutional. It accordingly limited itself to urging reconsideration of *Garcia* in order to promote public confidence in the criminal justice system. The author of the opinion observed that nearly 22% of all convicted defendants in the state were black but that it was rare for an African-American to serve on a jury, and suggested that the Iowa federal district court might consider modifying its jury selection plan to increase the likelihood of minority participation.

In U.S. v. Chanthadara, 230 F.3d 1237 (10th Cir. 2000), cert. denied, 534 U.S. 992, 122 S. Ct. 457, 151 L. Ed. 2d 376 (2001) the Court of Appeals recognized the limitations of both an absolute disparity test and a comparative disparity test. Neither works particularly well when the numbers in question are small. Nonetheless, the court proceeded to apply each test separately. It concluded that neither test established a prima facie violation of the constitutional requirement. The court was requested also to consider standard deviations but summarily stated that such calculations would represent merely a manipulation of the same numbers that it had just held were insufficient to establish a Sixth Amendment violation.

Add after eighth paragraph:

The Ninth Circuit Court of Appeals has held that absolute disparities of less than 7.7% are insubstantial and constitutionally permissible. See, e.g., U.S. v. Sanchez-Lopez, 879 F.2d 541 (9th Cir. 1989). See also U.S. v. Irurita-Ramirez, 838 F. Supp. 1385 (C.D. Cal. 1993) (absolute disparity level ranging from .1 to 4.7% for blacks, Hispanics, and Asians not unconstitutional). The court in Johnson v. McCaughtry, 92 F.3d 585 (7th Cir. 1996) held that even conceding that persons aged 18–25 were a distinctive group, an actual disparity of 9% and a comparative disparity of 33% between their incidence in the population and their presence in the jury pool was insufficient to make out a constitutional violation of the fair cross section requirement. See also U.S. v. Gault, 141 F.3d 1399 (10th Cir. 1998). In U.S. v. Esquivel, 88 F.3d 722, 44 Fed. R. Evid. Serv. 1390 (9th Cir. 1996), a 4.9% absolute disparity was held insufficient to establish a violation of the fair cross section requirement. Although the first time that the government presented the relevant census data was on appeal, the court did not find any waiver.

n. 262.

Add to note 262:

Citing *Casteneda*, the Missouri Supreme Court, sitting en banc in

State v. Shurn, 866 S.W.2d 447 (Mo. 1993), as modified on denial of reh'g, (Dec. 21, 1993), found no constitutional violation in respect to a grand jury composed of 9.17% blacks where blacks accounted for 11.26% of the population.

§ 6:18 —Discriminatory intent and systematic exclusion

n. 267.

Add to note 267:

Proof of under representation of a distinctive group in the community without a showing of systematic exclusion will not suffice to make out a violation of the fair cross section requirement. U.S. v. Phillips, 239 F.3d 829 (7th Cir. 2001), cert. denied, 534 U.S. 884, 122 S. Ct. 191, 151 L. Ed. 2d 134 (2001) and cert. denied, 534 U.S. 967, 122 S. Ct. 379, 151 L. Ed. 2d 289 (2001); U.S. v. Warren, 16 F.3d 247 (8th Cir. 1994). Phea v. Benson, 95 F.3d 660 (8th Cir. 1996) (no showing of systematic exclusion) See also U.S. v. Pion, 25 F.3d 18 (1st Cir. 1994). U.S. v. Rodriguez, 162 F.3d 135, 50 Fed. R. Evid. Serv. 1030 (1st Cir. 1998) (reaffirming *Pion*). Nor will systematic exclusion be inferred from mere proof of underrepresentation. U.S. v. Hardwell, 80 F.3d 1471, 44 Fed. R. Evid. Serv. 571 (10th Cir. 1996), on reh'g in part, 88 F.3d 897 (10th Cir. 1996); U.S. v. McKinney, 53 F.3d 664 (5th Cir. 1995); U.S. v. Edwards, 69 F.3d 419, 43 Fed. R. Evid. Serv. 225 (10th Cir. 1995). U.S. v. Sotelo, 97 F.3d 782, 45 Fed. R. Evid. Serv. 1054 (5th Cir. 1996) (mere fact that there is only one Hispanic among 50 venirepersons does not establish a prima facie case of a fair cross section violation); U.S. v. Alix, 86 F.3d 429 (5th Cir. 1996) (fair cross section violation cannot be established simply by looking at the composition of the jury panel at defendant's trial); U.S. v. Anderson, 139 F.3d 291 (1st Cir. 1998) (fact that there was only one African-American in defendant's jury pool did not establish a constitutional violation absent a showing of systematic exclusion of African-Americans); U.S. v. Smallwood, 188 F.3d 905 (7th Cir. 1999) (despite fact that only 5% of those reporting for jury duty were black, compared to an alleged 25% of the community, defendant's claim of a violation of the fair cross section requirement failed because he produced no evidence of systematic exclusion); Matima v. Celli, 228 F.3d 68, 83 Fair Empl. Prac. Cas. (BNA) 1660, 79 Empl. Prac. Dec. (CCH) ¶ 40306 (2d Cir. 2000), case considered closed by U.S. supreme court, (Mar. 5, 2002); U.S. v. Buchanan, 213 F.3d 302, 54 Fed. R. Evid. Serv. 265, 2000 FED App. 0060P (6th Cir. 2000), as corrected on denial of reh'g, (May 22, 2000) and cert. denied, 531 U.S. 1202, 121 S. Ct. 1212, 149 L. Ed. 2d 125 (2001) and cert. denied, 532 U.S. 1000, 121 S. Ct. 1666, 149 L. Ed. 2d 646 (2001); Roberson v. Hayti Police Dept., 241 F.3d 992, 49 Fed. R. Serv. 3d 327 (8th Cir. 2001). See also Trice v. Ward, 196 F.3d 1151 (10th Cir. 1999) (where registered voter lists used for jury pools, evidence of racial composition of community will not suffice to establish under representation or systematic exclusion); U.S. v. Joyner, 201 F.3d 61 (2d Cir. 2000), decision clarified on denial of reh'g, 313 F.3d 40 (2d Cir. 2002) (where district court used voter registration and motor vehicle bureau lists to select venire, mere fact that venire contained only one black out of 500 prospective jurors did not establish systematic exclusion). In U.S. v. Lara, 181 F.3d 183, 51 Fed. R. Evid. Serv. 1302 (1st Cir. 1999) the defendants established a technical failure of the state to comply with the National Voter Registration Act, from which it derived its jury wheels. However, the defendants failed to prove systematic exclusion of Hispanic jurors and the Court of Appeals found no violation of the fair cross section

§ 6:18

requirement. See also U.S. v. Olaniyi-Oke, 199 F.3d 767 (5th Cir. 1999) (court did not abuse its discretion in denying motion for continuance to investigate jury containing an alleged unrepresentative number of minorities).

What purported to be a sophisticated and exhaustive mathematical analysis of the number of African-Americans and Hispanics in the population compared to their presence in the master wheels used for jury selection was the basis of the claimed statutory and Sixth Amendment violations in U.S. v. Weaver, 267 F.3d 231 (3d Cir. 2001), cert. denied, 534 U.S. 1152, 122 S. Ct. 1118, 151 L. Ed. 2d 1011 (2002). The expert in demography who prepared the reports asserted that the likelihood that the under representation was the result of random chance was one in 6,603,384 for the African-Americans and one in 130,337,015 for the Hispanics. Despite these seemingly impressive statistics, the Court of Appeals found a fundamental weakness in the analysis of the expert because he failed to account for the jury questionnaire forms that were mailed but not completed and returned. Although the court noted the weaknesses in both the comparative disparity and absolute disparity tests, it found that the absolute disparity test, which seemed to be the preferred test of the federal circuits, did not support the petitioner's claim that the use of voter registration lists violated either his Sixth Amendment rights or the Jury Selection and Service Act of 1968. The court also found no evidence of persistent "systematic exclusion" of African-Americans or Hispanics.

In U.S. v. Footracer, 189 F.3d 1058 (9th Cir. 1999), opinion withdrawn, 252 F.3d 1059 (9th Cir. 2001) the trial of the defendant, a Native American, was transferred from the district in which his crimes were allegedly committed to a district that contained a smaller percentage of Native Americans. The defendant argued that the transfer denied him a jury pool reflecting a fair cross section of the community. The Court of Appeals held that the residents of the division where the crime was committed were not a distinctive group for purposes of Sixth Amendment analysis and, furthermore, that there was no showing of systematic exclusion of Native Americans from the jury venire.

In U.S. v. Erickson, 75 F.3d 470, 43 Fed. R. Evid. Serv. 944 (9th Cir. 1996) a potential shortage of jurors was threatened. The trial court ordered that additional venirepersons be summoned from a 25-mile radius rather than from the entire district. The reason for the limitation was the Court's desire to expedite the proceedings, which might have had to be delayed if jurors had to be brought from a greater distance. However, the effect of the ruling was to exclude four Indian reservations which were outside the 25-mile radius. The Court of Appeals found the defendants had failed to establish a prima facie case of discrimination under the *Duren* test. The court stated that even assuming that the defendants could prove that the representation of Indians in the venire was not fair and reasonable in relation to the number of Indians in the community, there had been no showing of a systematic pattern of exclusion. See also U.S. v. Tapia, 59 F.3d 1137 (11th Cir. 1995) (no showing of underrepresentation or systematic exclusion); U.S. v. Esquivel, 75 F.3d 545 (9th Cir. 1996), opinion withdrawn and superseded on denial of reh'g, 88 F.3d 722, 44 Fed. R. Evid. Serv. 1390 (9th Cir. 1996); U.S. v. Fike, 82 F.3d 1315, 44 Fed. R. Evid. Serv. 479 (5th Cir. 1996) (overruled on other grounds by, U.S. v. Brown, 161 F.3d 256 (5th Cir. 1998)) and (abrogated by, U.S. v. Cantu, 230 F.3d 148 (5th Cir. 2000)). U.S. v. Gallegos, 108 F.3d 1272 (10th Cir. 1997); U.S. v. Contreras, 108 F.3d 1255 (10th Cir. 1997); U.S. v. Aguirre, 108 F.3d 1284 (10th Cir. 1997), U.S. v. Rodriguez-Aguirre, 108 F.3d 1228, 46 Fed. R. Evid. Serv. 813 (10th Cir. 1997), and U.S. v. Morales, 108 F.3d

1213 (10th Cir. 1997) involved similar appeals by codefendants convicted of drug-related offenses. One of their arguments was that Hispanics had been systematically discriminated against by the trial judge when he had made a number of pre-voir dire excusals based on the answers to jury questionnaires. The judge, however, indicated that he did not look at the surnames of the jurors in making the excusals and the questionnaires themselves did not ask the jurors to indicate their ethnicity. Under the circumstances the Court of Appeals held that there had been no equal protection violation.

n. 268.

Add to note 268:

Systematic exclusion cannot be established by evidence of a single venire. Wharton-El v. Nix, 38 F.3d 372 (8th Cir. 1994); See also U.S. v. Phillips, 239 F.3d 829 (7th Cir. 2001), cert. denied, 534 U.S. 884, 122 S. Ct. 191, 151 L. Ed. 2d 134 (2001) and cert. denied, 534 U.S. 967, 122 S. Ct. 379, 151 L. Ed. 2d 289 (2001) (makeup of any given venire is not significant, provided all rules for jury selection have been observed); U.S. v. Williams, 264 F.3d 561, 57 Fed. R. Evid. Serv. 1124 (5th Cir. 2001) (showing of under representation can not be based on a single venire, and defendant's failure to introduce evidence of the percentage of blacks in the community and the composition of other venires failed to provide court with a baseline against which it could compare composition of defendant's venire); U.S. v. Alanis, 265 F.3d 576 (7th Cir. 2001), cert. denied, 535 U.S. 1095, 122 S. Ct. 2289, 152 L. Ed. 2d 1049 (2002) (statistical evidence drawn from one county out of 11 included in jury venire failed to provide trial court with basis for determining whether alleged under representation was constitutionally deficient).

Measuring the extent to which a group is underrepresented poses a practical problem. The issue is explored in Note, *A Proposal for Measuring Under representation in the Composition of the Jury Wheel*, 103 Yale LJ 1913 (1994).

In State v. Whitfield, 837 S.W.2d 503 (Mo. 1992), the court stated that although the decision not to provide child care for potential jurors may have prevented some women from jury service it was not sufficient in itself to establish a violation of the equal protection clause absent a showing of intentional discrimination.

In Leibengood v. State, 866 S.W.2d 732 (Tex. App. Houston 14th Dist. 1993), petition for discretionary review refused, (Apr. 20, 1994) the defendant, a dwarf, argued that the absence of "little people" on the jury violated the fair cross section requirement and denied him equal protection. The court stated that even assuming that people under five feet tall were a "distinctive" group, the defendant had failed to prove their systematic exclusion from the jury. Nor had the defendant established discrimination. Indeed in the Court's view the defendant's argument amounted to a complaint that "little people are not treated differently. He would have little people sought out and purposefully inserted into jury venires unlike any other segment of society." Leibengood v. State, 866 S.W.2d 732, 735 (Tex. App. Houston 14th Dist. 1993), petition for discretionary review refused, (Apr. 20, 1994) (emphasis in original).

n. 269.

Add to note 269:

In Rideau v. Whitley, 237 F.3d 472 (5th Cir. 2000), cert. denied, 533 U.S. 924, 121 S. Ct. 2539, 150 L. Ed. 2d 708 (2001), the court found the state's grand jury selection procedures were unconstitutional. The court

§ 6:18   JURY SELECTION: LAW, ART & SCIENCE 2D

cited the mathematical disparity between the percentage of blacks in the community (16+%) and that on defendant's grand jury (5%), the non-neutrality of the selection process, the failure of jury commissioners to identify and seek out black grand jurors, and the fact that the underrepresentation had continued over a significant period of time.

In U.S. v. Douglas, 837 F. Supp. 817 (N.D. Tex. 1993), it was shown that blacks were underrepresented on venire panels. The defendant argued that blacks were typically distrustful and fearful of the judicial system, and more likely than members of other races to ignore summons for jury service. The court held that, in an equal protection context at least, this evidence rebutted rather than supported defendant's claim of purposeful discrimination, as this distrust of the system rather than any action of the state accounted for the underrepresentation. In U.S. v. Esquivel, 88 F.3d 722, 44 Fed. R. Evid. Serv. 1390 (9th Cir. 1996), the court stated that where the defendant had made no showing that the jury selection procedure utilized was susceptible to abuse or was racially biased, it became even more critical that the defendant demonstrate discriminatory intent in order to succeed in his claim of an equal protection violation.

Add after second paragraph:

Systematic exclusion need not be deliberate. In U.S. v. Osorio, 801 F. Supp. 966 (D. Conn. 1992), the district court held that the inadvertent exclusion of residents of the New Britain and Hartford communities from the qualified jury wheel resulted in the exclusion of approximately two-thirds of the blacks and Hispanics in the division, and constituted systematic exclusion of those groups from jury selection, thereby giving rise to a prima facie case of a fair cross section violation. To remedy the exclusion identified in *Osorio*, the clerk added 22 names from the two excluded cities in compiling a venire of 100 persons. In U.S. v. Jackman, 46 F.3d 1240 (2d Cir. 1995), the Court of Appeals found that, while this remedial measure resulted in some increase in minority representation, it was insufficient to overcome the problem of underrepresentation of blacks and Hispanics. As a result defendant's right to have his jury selected from a fair cross section of the community had been violated.

In Ricketts v. City of Hartford, 74 F.3d 1397, 43 Fed. R. Evid. Serv. 903 (2d Cir. 1996), as amended on reh'g in part, (Feb. 14, 1996), the jury had been drawn from the same venire as in *Jackman* (above). However, unlike *Jackman*, *Ricketts* was a civil action under 42 U.S.C.A. § 1983. A claim that the jury venire failed to satisfy the fair cross section demands of the Sixth Amendment was therefore not available since the Sixth Amendment is restricted to criminal prosecutions. The appellant instead argued that the flaw in jury selection constituted a violation of the equal protection clause of the fourteenth amendment. However, to establish a violation of equal protection, one must prove intentional discrimination. There was no evidence that the jury administrator had

Challenges to the Array § 6:18

intentionally excluded any potential juror on account of race or ethnic background. The computer error which had led to the exclusions was inadvertent.

Another example of a case where discrimination was evident on the face of, in this instance, a Jury Plan, is U.S. v. Ovalle, 136 F.3d 1092, 1998 FED App. 0060P (6th Cir. 1998). Here the Jury Selection Plan for the Eastern District of Michigan, in its attempt to achieve a balance of the different cognizable groups in the community, provided for the removal of one in five non-African Americans from the jury pool. As there could be no doubt that the jurors' race was the reason for their exclusion from the pool, the court held that it was unnecessary to resort to the three pronged test of *Casteneda v. Partida.* In particular, the court stated that there was no need for a showing of evidence of underrepresentation. The decision and the implications are examined in Cohn & Sherwood, *The Rise and Fall of Affirmative Action in Jury Selection*, 32 U. Mich. J. of Law Reform 323 (1999).

n. 276.

Add to note 276:

Mere knowledge by the jury commissioners of the race of each member of the venire, coupled with the fact that blacks were underrepresented in criminal court venires, was held not to be sufficient to establish intentional discrimination in Ward v. Whitley, 21 F.3d 1355 (5th Cir. 1994). See also U.S. v. Williams, 264 F.3d 561, 57 Fed. R. Evid. Serv. 1124 (5th Cir. 2001) (no showing of sufficient opportunity to discriminate to warrant finding of an equal protection violation based on Court's decision to expand jury venire to district as a whole).

In U.S. v. Ovalle, 136 F.3d 1092, 1998 FED App. 0060P (6th Cir. 1998), the Jury Selection Plan of the Eastern District of Michigan, in an attempt to achieve a balance of the different cognizable groups in the community, provided for the removal of one in five non-African Americans from the jury pool. The court held that this was a violation of the equal protection rights of the prospective jurors excluded under the Plan. However, this did not end the Court's inquiry. It stated that the plan could be upheld if it served a compelling governmental interest, and if the means chosen to achieve that interest were narrowly tailored. The court accepted that the government had a compelling interest in ensuring that jury pools represented a fair cross section of the community. The Michigan Plan foundered on the second requirement, in that it was not narrowly tailored to achieve this objective. The Plan not only discriminated against the one-in-five white jurors who were automatically excluded from the pool but also, because its sole focus was on the exclusion of African-Americans, made no effort to ensure that Hispanics or other minorities were represented in the pool. Thus the Plan was not narrowly tailored to impanel a representative pool. The decision and the implications are examined in Cohn & Sherwood, The Rise and Fall of Affirmative Action in Jury Selection, 32 U. Mich. J. of Law Reform 323 (1999).

Chapter 7
Challenges for Cause

> **KeyCite®:** Cases and other legal materials listed in KeyCite Scope can be researched through West's KeyCite service on Westlaw®. Use KeyCite to check citations for form, parallel references, prior and later history, and comprehensive citator information, including citations to other decisions and secondary materials.

Table of New and Retitled Sections
§ 7:54   Jury nullifiers *[New]*

§ 7:1   Introduction

Add after first sentence in fourth paragraph:
In Morgan v. Illinois, 504 U.S. 719, 112 S. Ct. 2222, 119 L. Ed. 2d 492 (1992), the United States Supreme Court stated that "[part] of the guaranty of a defendant's right to an impartial jury is an adequate voir dire to identify unqualified jurors." Morgan v. Illinois, 504 U.S. 719, 112 S. Ct. 2222, 2230, 119 L. Ed. 2d 492 (1992). The Court was speaking in the context of a capital case.

n. 5.
   Add to note 5:
   In Morgan v. Illinois, 504 U.S. 719, 112 S. Ct. 2222, 119 L. Ed. 2d 492 (1992), the United States Supreme Court held that a trial judge in a capital case must, upon request, inquire as to whether any juror would automatically vote in favor of the death penalty if the defendant were convicted. The inquiry was mandated to assure that the defendant could exercise his challenges for cause, with those jurors who would automatically vote in favor of the death penalty being properly subject to challenge for cause.

§ 7:4   —American jurisdictions today: An overview

After first sentence in second paragraph:
In Kotler v. American Tobacco Co., 926 F.2d 1217, Prod. Liab. Rep. (CCH) ¶ 12674 (1st Cir. 1990), cert. granted, judgment vacated on other grounds, 505 U.S. 1215, 112 S. Ct. 3019, 120 L. Ed. 2d 891 (1992), a products liability suit against cigarette manufacturers, the court held that it was not error to exclude prospective jurors who asserted that their opinion of the relationship between smoking and lung cancer would not be changed by the evidence.

§ 7:4   JURY SELECTION: LAW, ART & SCIENCE 2D

Add after third paragraph:

The Court of Appeals in U.S. v. Torres, 128 F.3d 38 (2d Cir. 1997), provides a useful discussion of the differences between actual, implied, and inferred bias. Actual bias (or bias in fact) is based on an admission of nonpartiality by a juror or a finding to this effect by the trial judge. In *Torres* a juror who had structured real estate deals similarly to those entered into by defendants charged with money laundering stated that he could not be impartial in the case because he would feel that he was on trial. The court, finding actual bias, held that the juror had been properly excused. See also U.S. v. Gonzalez, 214 F.3d 1109 (9th Cir. 2000) (juror whose ex-husband had regularly bought and sold drugs, leading to their divorce, should have been dismissed for actual or implied bias, particularly where juror equivocated when asked if she could be impartial); Fields v. Woodford, 281 F.3d 963 (9th Cir. 2002), opinion amended and superseded, 315 F.3d 1062 (9th Cir. 2002).

The issue of implied bias arose in Fields v. Woodford, 309 F.3d 1095 (9th Cir. 2002), opinion amended, 315 F.3d 1062 (9th Cir. 2002), where a prospective juror disclosed on voir dire that his wife had been the victim of an assault, beating and robbery. What the juror did not reveal, however, was that she had also been kidnapped and raped. Had the juror revealed this information, the parallel between his wife's experience and the facts of the case would have been more evident, as the defendant in the case was on trial for kidnapping, robbery, and rape, as well as for murder. Apart from the issue of dishonesty and whether there had been a violation of McDonough Power Equipment, Inc. v. Greenwood, 464 U.S. 548, 104 S. Ct. 845, 78 L. Ed. 2d 663 (1984) [discussed in main text § 9:20], the Court of Appeals questioned whether the juror may have been so affected by his wife's experience to make out a case of "implied bias". This possibility was heightened by the allegation of the defense that the juror had discussed the case with his wife. As no credibility determination to which it owed deference had been made, the Court of Appeals remanded for an evidentiary hearing.

In contrast, implied bias does not arise as a result of an admission by a juror, but rather is presumed in certain situations where objective circumstances give rise to a concrete doubt that the juror in question is capable of being impartial. For instance, implied bias will arise where there is a relationship that would cause the average person in the position of the juror to be biased. An example is where the juror is a relative of one of the parties or lawyers in the case. In cases of implied bias, the juror is conclusively presumed to be biased regardless of actual bias (a relative of a party might in fact be ambivalent as to which party won the case). Therefore, the juror's assertion that he or she is capable of being impartial is irrelevant, and the judge need not ask a question such as whether the juror believes himself capable of following the Court's instructions. See U.S. v. Gonzalez, 214 F.3d 1109 (9th Cir. 2000); Dyer v. Calderon, 151 F.3d 970, 982 (9th Cir. 1998) ("Even if the putative juror swears up and down that it will not affect his judgment, we presume conclusively that he will not leave [implied bias] at the jury room door."). In U.S. v. Polichemi, 201 F.3d 858 (7th Cir. 2000), on reh'g, 219 F.3d 698, 54 Fed. R. Evid. Serv. 1407 (7th Cir. 2000), cert. denied, 531 U.S. 1168, 121 S. Ct. 1131, 148 L. Ed. 2d 997 (2001) the court found implied bias in the case of a juror who worked for the United States Attorney's Office. It ruled that the juror should have been excused for cause. In U.S. v. Gonzalez, 214 F.3d 1109 (9th Cir. 2000), a drug-related case, the court found both actual and implied bias where the ex-husband of a prospective juror had regularly bought and sold drugs, leading to their divorce, and the juror repeatedly equivocated when asked if she could be impartial. In contrast, neither actual nor implied bias was found in U.S. v. Cerrato-Reyes, 176 F.3d 1253 (10th Cir. 1999), where the defendant was charged with a drug-related offense and the suspect juror belatedly revealed that she lived in a Hispanic neighborhood and was fearful because of prior experiences with non-Hispanic drug dealers. The juror also made strong negative statements about her Hispanic neighbors. Nonetheless, the juror's repeated denials of prejudice were held sufficient to support the trial judge's ruling that the juror was not biased. See also Fields v. Woodford, 281 F.3d 963 (9th Cir. 2002), opinion amended and superseded, 315 F.3d 1062 (9th Cir. 2002).

Finally, bias may be inferred in situations where a juror discloses information that suggests a risk of partiality sufficiently significant to warrant excusing the juror but not so great as to make mandatory a presumption of bias. Inferred bias is based on facts developed during voir dire. Whether to actually draw the inference of bias is a matter that falls within the trial judge's discretion. Arguably, in a case involving possible inferred bias, the juror's statements as to his or her ability to be impartial are extremely relevant, but in *Torres* the Court of Appeals seemed to imply that they were not. Perhaps the court simply meant to express the more conventional view that the judge was not bound by a juror's professed assertions of impartiality. In U.S. v. Gaitan-Acevedo, 148 F.3d 577, 49 Fed. R. Evid. Serv. 590, 1998 FED App. 0143P (6th Cir. 1998), the court stated that presuming that a juror is not impartial is justifiable only in extreme

§ 7:4

cases. It gave as examples a juror who was a close relative of one of the participants in the trial, or a juror who was a witness or otherwise involved in the case. See also Fitzgerald v. Greene, 150 F.3d 357 (4th Cir. 1998); U.S. v. Gonzalez, 214 F.3d 1109 (9th Cir. 2000); Fields v. Woodford, 281 F.3d 963 (9th Cir. 2002), opinion amended and superseded, 315 F.3d 1062 (9th Cir. 2002). In U.S. v. Nelson, 277 F.3d 164 (2d Cir. 2002), cert. denied, 537 U.S. 835, 123 S. Ct. 145, 154 L. Ed. 2d 54 (2002) the court found actual bias where a juror during voir dire expressed his dissatisfaction with the state proceedings that had resulted in an acquittal of one of the defendants. On further questioning the juror said that, while he would like to think of himself as objective and able to give the defendants a fair trial, he honestly did not know whether he could.

§ 7:5 Procedures

Add after first sentence in first paragraph:

Because a judge has an independent responsibility to secure a constitutionally acceptable jury, the judge can commit error by not scrutinizing challenges made by the parties. A judge cannot simply defer to a challenge which is acceptable to both sides. In Mata v. Johnson, 99 F.3d 1261 (5th Cir. 1996), vacated in part on reh'g, 105 F.3d 209 (5th Cir. 1997), for example, counsel for the defense had agreed with counsel for the prosecution to exclude all black members of the venire from the jury. The judge had accepted the parties' challenges without requiring a statement of reasons. The court of appeal held that this was a clear violation of equal protection principles and impermissible.

In Alvarado v. State, 822 S.W.2d 236 (Tex. App. Houston 14th Dist. 1991), petition for discretionary review refused, (Apr. 29, 1992), the court stated that a trial judge has no authority to excuse on his own motion a prospective juror unless the juror is "absolutely disqualified" under state law. A less absolutist approach was taken in State v. Hadley, 815 S.W.2d 422 (Mo. 1991), where the court said that a trial judge is not precluded from, but is under no duty to strike a juror on its own motion. Both positions, it is submitted, are ill-conceived. It is the trial judge's responsibility to protect the state's and public's interest in a fair trial by impaneling an impartial jury. Even if both sides are willing to retain a juror who clearly is biased, the court must safeguard the integrity of the judicial proceeding. In Pierre v. State, 607 So. 2d 43 (Miss. 1992), the court stated that a trial judge has the power to remove a biased juror sua sponte, even if neither side has challenged the juror. U.S. v. Paradies, 98 F.3d 1266, 46 Fed. R. Evid. Serv. 656 (11th Cir. 1996) (upholding district court's sua sponte dismissal of jurors based on hardship and perceived prejudice). See also People v. Lopez, 3 Cal. App. 4th Supp. 11, 5 Cal. Rptr. 2d 775 (App. Dep't Super. Ct. 1991) (trial court may on its own motion raise a *Batson* objection, because of its obligation to ensure a jury drawn from a fair cross section of the community and free from racial discrimination); U.S. v. Thornton, 1 F.3d 149 (3d Cir. 1993) (trial judge acted permissibly in removing juror who exchanged in nonverbal communication with criminal defendant); Lacy v. State, 629 So. 2d 688 (Ala. Crim. App. 1993) (no error for judge, despite absence of a challenge from either party, to excuse juror regarding whose impartiality there existed doubts); U.S. v. Jensen, 41 F.3d 946 (5th Cir. 1994) (judge acted properly in dismissing prospective juror sua sponte). In State v. Bible, 175 Ariz. 549, 858 P.2d 1152 (1993), the court held that where the defendant claimed on appeal that the judge erred in failing to remove sua sponte certain jurors which the defendant had not challenged, the defendant was required to demonstrate fundamental error.

In U.S. v. Cantu, 229 F.3d 544, 2000 FED App. 0365P (6th Cir. 2000), the defendant was charged with being a felon in possession of a firearm. After the jury had been sworn, one juror informed the judge that many years previously he had pled guilty to a crime that might have been a felony (the juror did not know this for a fact and the court was unsure) and that he regularly hunted with a gun. Thus, the juror realized that he might have committed the same offense with which the defendant was charged. Although there was no finding that the juror was not impartial, the court decided to replace him with an alternate. On appeal it was argued that it was error to replace a juror who had not been shown to be biased. The Court of Appeals rejected this claim, pointing out that the defendant had not shown that he had been prejudiced by the substitution, and further that a judge was permitted to take steps to obviate the risk of a subsequent reversal.

A judge may dismiss a juror during the middle of the trial for reasonable cause. See, e.g., U.S. v. Millar, 79 F.3d 338 (2d Cir. 1996) (dismissal of juror whose father died suddenly during trial not an abuse of discretion). See also U.S. v. Neeley, 189 F.3d 670, 53 Fed. R. Evid. Serv. 35 (7th Cir. 1999) (trial judge did not err in discharging juror who, after deliberations had begun, became involved in custody hearing which focused on three grandchildren and who was awarded temporary custody, as juror would not be able to give proper attention to the deliberations); U.S. v. Edwards, 188 F.3d 230 (4th Cir. 1999) (district court did not err in dismissing, without further inquiry, juror who informed court that he had received telephone call stating that the defendants "need your help"). In contrast, in U.S. v. Vega, 285 F.3d 256, 58 Fed. R. Evid. Serv. 431 (3d Cir. 2002), a juror indicated during trial that he felt threatened by the fact that a spectator (the defendant's brother) was staring at him from the gallery. The trial judge conducted a thorough voir dire of the juror and determined that he could remain impartial and that no other jurors had been improperly influenced. On appeal these findings were held not to constitute an abuse of discretion.

A court may dismiss a juror during deliberations for "just cause" under Rule 23(b) of the Federal Rules of Criminal Procedure. Most cases involve a physical or emotional incapacity to continue with the deliberations. E.g., U.S. v. Levenite, 277 F.3d 454 (4th Cir. 2002), cert. denied, 535 U.S. 1105, 122 S. Ct. 2312, 152 L. Ed. 2d 1066 (2002); U.S. v. Frazier, 274 F.3d 1185, 58 Fed. R. Evid. Serv. 138 (8th Cir. 2001), opinion superseded on reh'g, 280 F.3d 835 (8th Cir. 2002), cert. denied, 535 U.S. 1107, 122 S. Ct. 2317, 152 L. Ed. 2d 1070 (2002) and cert. denied, 536 U.S. 931, 122 S. Ct. 2606, 153 L. Ed. 2d 793 (2002) and cert. denied, 537 U.S. 911, 123 S. Ct. 255, 154 L. Ed. 2d 191 (2002) and reh'g granted and opinion vacated, (Feb. 12, 2002) (also rejecting the claim that Rule 23(b) is unconstitutional because it violates a defendant's right to a unanimous verdict by a 12-person jury).

In U.S. v. Anderson, 303 F.3d 847, 59 Fed. R. Evid. Serv. 1514 (7th Cir. 2002), cert. denied, 123 S. Ct. 1604, 155 L. Ed. 2d 341 (U.S. 2003), a juror, on the last day of the trial, informed the judge at an in camera hearing that an employee in the juror's family business knew one of the government witnesses in the case. Further, the employee had called the juror during the trial (even though the juror had not given the employee her telephone number) and had asked questions about the trial. The juror testified that she had become paranoid and had ended the conversation with the employee. Subsequently, the juror's brother informed her that the employee wanted the juror to deny that she knew the employee. The court upheld the removal of the juror for just cause under Rule 23(b), Fed. R. Crim. P. finding that the juror's ability to serve impartially may have been compromised. The employee clearly had an interest in the case and apparently was attempting to influence the juror.

However, "just cause" does not extend to problems in the deliberations caused by a juror's contrariness because he or she disagrees with the others in respect to the merits of the case or the sufficiency of the evidence. See U.S. v. Symington, 195 F.3d 1080 (9th Cir. 1999). But compare U.S. v. Abbell, 271 F.3d 1286 (11th Cir. 2001), cert. denied, 537 U.S. 813, 123 S. Ct. 74, 154 L. Ed. 2d 16 (2002) (dismissal of juror who, during deliberations, refused to apply the law as instructed by the court was not abuse of discretion); U.S. v. Baker, 262 F.3d 124 (2d Cir. 2001) (upholding trial judge's decision to dismiss a juror who refused to participate in deliberations); U.S. v. Edwards, 303 F.3d 606, 59 Fed. R. Evid. Serv. 1042 (5th Cir. 2002), cert. denied, 123 S. Ct. 1272, 154 L. Ed. 2d 1025 (U.S. 2003) and cert. denied, 123 S. Ct. 1294, 154 L. Ed. 2d 1025 (U.S. 2003) and cert. denied, 123 S. Ct. 1286, 154 L. Ed. 2d 1025 (U.S. 2003) and cert. denied, 123 S. Ct. 1369, 155 L. Ed. 2d 209 (U.S. 2003) (just cause existed for the dismissal of juror based on the juror's lack of candor and an inability to follow instructions; holdout jurors are not immune from dismissal after commencement of deliberations based on just cause). In U.S. v. Mulder, 273 F.3d 91, 168 L.R.R.M. (BNA) 2681, 58 Fed. R. Evid. Serv. 742 (2d Cir. 2001), cert. denied, 535 U.S. 949, 122 S. Ct. 1344, 152 L. Ed. 2d 247 (2002), the court declined to excuse two jurors who complained that the extended deliberations were imposing severe financial hardship upon them. The Court of Appeals found no abuse of discretion, in part because defense counsel did not press their objections to the jurors, apparently gambling on the jurors being more likely to favor their clients' cause.

A judicial attempt to preserve the jury as constituted entering the deliberations may also give rise to constitutional objections. In Packer v. Hill, 277 F.3d 1092 (9th Cir. 2002), as amended on denial of reh'g and reh'g en banc, (Feb. 27, 2002) and opinion amended and superseded on clarification, 291 F.3d 569 (9th Cir. 2002), cert. granted, judgment rev'd, 537 U.S. 3, 123 S. Ct. 362, 154 L. Ed. 2d 263 (2002) the Court of Appeals found that the trial judge's statements and actions aimed at preserving the composition of the jury and not having to remove a juror who asked to be excused for health reasons were unduly coercive and constituted a denial of due process warranting habeas corpus relief. Compare U.S. v. Lemmerer, 277 F.3d 579 (1st Cir. 2002), cert. denied, 537 U.S. 901, 123 S. Ct. 217, 154 L. Ed. 2d 173 (2002) (Court's reminder to recalcitrant juror of sworn duty to continue deliberating in good faith constituted "eminently reasonable course").

If a request for a juror's dismissal appears to stem from the juror's views of the merits or the evidence, a judge has two options: the judge can order the jury to continue its deliberations; or the judge can declare a mistrial. U.S. v. Symington, 195 F.3d 1080 (9th Cir. 1999). See also U.S. v. Thomas, 116 F.3d 606 (2d Cir. 1997). In U.S. v. Hursh, 217 F.3d 761, 54 Fed. R. Evid. Serv. 1412 (9th Cir. 2000), a juror, after the close of evidence, sent the judge a note stating his belief that it would have been helpful if counsel had heard

§ 7:5   JURY SELECTION: LAW, ART & SCIENCE 2D

his question. On appeal the defendant argued that this note indicated the juror's bias. The Court of Appeals disagreed, stating that there was nothing in the note to suggest that the juror had already made up his mind, or would not deliberate, or would not base his verdict on the evidence.

Jurors who have been observed sleeping during the trial pose a problem for the trial judge. On the one hand, the juror in question may well have missed critical evidence, but, on the other, it is problematic for the court to dismiss a juror after a trial has begun. The tendency in these cases is to rely on the sound judgment of the trial court, which had the opportunity to observe the juror firsthand. Different results may occur depending on the egregiousness of the juror's lapses. Thus, in U.S. v. Bradley, 173 F.3d 225 (3d Cir. 1999), corrected, 188 F.3d 98 (3d Cir. 1999) the Court of Appeals held that the trial judge did not commit error in dismissing a juror who had been observed sleeping during the summation of each side. In contrast, in U.S. v. Diaz, 176 F.3d 52, 52 Fed. R. Evid. Serv. 380 (2d Cir. 1999), the Court of Appeals held that the trial court had not abused its discretion in not excusing a juror who was observed sleeping. The judge had opined that the incident appeared to be an isolated occurrence and that the juror was generally alert and attentive to the evidence. In Sallahdin v. Gibson, 275 F.3d 1211 (10th Cir. 2002) the court stated that while one of the jurors apparently had trouble staying alert at times, there was no clear indication that juror actually ever fell asleep. Thus the failure to excuse the juror did not deprive the defendant of a fair and impartial jury, and defense counsel was not ineffective in failing to raise the issue on appeal. See generally Annotation, Inattention of juror from sleepiness or other cause as ground for reversal or new trial, 59 A.L.R. 5th 1.

In U.S. v. Beckner, 69 F.3d 1290 (5th Cir. 1995), the Court of Appeals, having found that there had been sufficient pretrial publicity to raise a significant possibility of prejudice, proceeded to examine the adequacy of the trial court's voir dire on this issue. The trial court had not specifically inquired about what each juror had read or heard about the case. While the judge did ask whether any juror had been so affected by the pretrial publicity that he or she could not be completely fair and impartial, the Court of Appeals found that this was an abdication of responsibility. In effect the trial court had allowed the jurors to decide their own impartiality. In the opinion of the Court of Appeals, the trial court had an independent responsibility to determine each juror's impartiality.

Beckner can be compared with U.S. v. Bieganowski, 313 F.3d 264 (5th Cir. 2002), cert. denied, 123 S. Ct. 1956, 155 L.

Ed. 2d 851 (U.S. 2003). Here too, there had been publicity about the defendant prior to trial which gave rise to a significant possibility of prejudice. During voir dire, one prospective juror had revealed the contents of an inflammatory article in the presence of the panel. After the juror's disclosure, however, the defendant did not request the judge to conduct individual voir dire, although the Court of Appeals stated that this would have been prudent and within the court's discretion. The Court of Appeals also thought that the trial judge would have been better advised to engage in further questioning of the entire venire after the prospective juror had revealed the contents of the article in its presence. In the event, the juror who had revealed the content of the article did not ultimately serve on the jury, the defense having exercised a peremptory challenge to remove him. That, of course, did not resolve the issue of whether the jury had been tainted by the juror's revelations. Without reaching this issue, the Court of Appeals found that the defendant had not suffered such a degree of prejudice to justify a reversal of his conviction. The trial court had instructed the jury not to consider what they had read in the papers, noting that "the papers are not always correct" and, at the conclusion of voir dire, further instructed the jury that "anything you may have seen or heard outside the courtroom is not evidence and must be totally disregarded. You are to decide this case solely on the evidence presented here in court." The fact that the jury had convicted the defendant on only 10 of the 15 counts with which he had been charged indicated to the Court of Appeals that the jury had methodically assessed each of the charges against the defendant. Finally, the Court of Appeals noted that the evidence of guilt was overwhelming.

In U.S. v. Vega, 72 F.3d 507 (7th Cir. 1995), the Court of Appeals held that the trial judge had been justified in removing for cause a juror who had disobeyed the Court's instructions with respect to the handling of his notes and a marshal's instructions regarding the use of the telephone. The fact that the person in question was the sole Hispanic juror on the panel did not justify a contrary result.

Add after second sentence in first paragraph:
A secondary question is whether to excuse the entire panel after one juror has made statements that could affect the impartiality of the remaining jurors. The issue often arises in connection with prejudicial pretrial publicity, but it can come up in other contexts as well. Judges are naturally reluctant to excuse the entire panel and start anew, and will usually examine the remaining jurors to see if they have been corrupted by the improper remarks. If the judge

§ 7:5   Jury Selection: Law, Art & Science 2d

determines that the jurors can be impartial, the case will proceed. See, e.g., People v. Love, 222 Ill. App. 3d 428, 165 Ill. Dec. 10, 584 N.E.2d 189 (1st Dist. 1991). U.S. v. Moutry, 46 F.3d 598 (7th Cir. 1995) (failure of trial judge to strike entire panel after one prospective juror had made a potentially prejudicial remark in front of the other jurors held not to be plain error); U.S. v. Register, 182 F.3d 820 (11th Cir. 1999) (district court, which had opportunity to observe jurors during trial, did not abuse its discretion in not inquiring to see if jury had been tainted by comments of juror dismissed because of exposure to inappropriate outside contact). In U.S. v. Chastain, 198 F.3d 1338, 53 Fed. R. Evid. Serv. 1107 (11th Cir. 1999), cert. denied, 532 U.S. 996, 121 S. Ct. 1658, 149 L. Ed. 2d 640 (2001) one juror, whose son was a policeman, stated she might be prejudiced in favor of the government, and another offered the opinion that the criminal justice system was more solicitous of criminals than victims. Both jurors were ultimately dismissed and the trial judge asked the remaining jurors whether they could follow the Court's instructions regarding the law. On appeal, it was held that the trial judge did not commit error in not allowing defense counsel to pose additional questions to the jurors following the comments of the dismissed jurors. The Court of Appeals commented that the statements of the two jurors were "somewhat common place and relatively innocuous." In U.S. v. Shannon, 21 F.3d 77 (5th Cir. 1994), the court asked whether there was anyone on the panel who could not serve as a fair and impartial juror in the case. One juror responded by stating that he thought that any person who had been brought to trial was guilty of something. The judge then rebuked the juror in front of the other jurors and excused the juror from service. The defendant made no objection at the time, but subsequently claimed that the judge's chastisement of the juror may have had a chilling effect on the candor of the remainder of the panel in responding to voir dire questions. The Court of Appeals held that the trial court did not abuse its discretion and that the remarks did not deprive the defendant of a fair and impartial jury. The problem, of course, can be avoided by questioning the jurors individually in camera. See § 9:8.

In U.S. v. Steele, 298 F.3d 906 (9th Cir. 2002), cert. denied, 537 U.S. 1096, 123 S. Ct. 710, 154 L. Ed. 2d 646 (2002) it emerged during voir dire that one of the jurors was an attorney employed as a public defender. The prosecutor then proceeded to ask the juror: "In the course of trying [felony robbery] cases, did you ever make a decision that your client was guilty and you've just got to do whatever you have got to do because that's your job." The juror answered: "I guess so, yeah. You know, it gets—the facts might show

CHALLENGES FOR CAUSE § 7:5

one way or the other, and you have to pursue the case if the client wants to or not, it's their decision." Defense counsel objected, arguing that the questioning tainted the jury by creating the erroneous impression that a defense attorney may have to proceed to trial even though the attorney believes the client is guilty. The prosecutor disputed this characterization, but indicated that she would discontinue the voir dire of the juror if the defense would agree to stipulate to excuse the juror for cause. The defense agreed to this stipulation, but also moved for a mistrial, which was denied. In addition, defense counsel refused the offer from the judge for a curative instruction because he believed that such an instruction would only serve to exacerbate the misconceptions already created. On appeal, the Court of Appeals found no abuse of the trial judge's discretion. The Court of Appeals noted that the prosecutor's question did not improperly comment on the defendant's counsel or compare defense counsel's experience with that of the juror; that the voir dire of the juror had stopped after the single question and was never referred to again; and that there was no indication that the prosecutor had intentionally sought to create the impression that all defense attorneys would lie or distort the facts in order to confuse a jury as to their client's guilt. The questioning also was held not to have tainted the jury pool. The juror's answer could not reasonably be viewed as an expert opinion to the effect that all defense lawyers defended obviously guilty clients, and reflected only upon the experience of the particular juror. Further, the fact that the juror was dismissed for cause presumably lessened any potential prejudicial effect on the other jurors. Finally, the Court of Appeals noted that defense counsel had refused a curative instruction that could have obviated any potential prejudice.

n. 21.

Add to note 21:

McQueen v. Scroggy, 99 F.3d 1302, 35 Fed. R. Serv. 3d 1211, 1996 FED App. 0349P (6th Cir. 1996) (finding by trial judge that jurors could follow instructions of court and put aside biases is one of historical fact). In U.S. v. Evans, 272 F.3d 1069 (8th Cir. 2001), cert. denied, 535 U.S. 1029, 122 S. Ct. 1638, 152 L. Ed. 2d 642 (2002) and cert. denied, 535 U.S. 1072, 122 S. Ct. 1949, 152 L. Ed. 2d 852 (2002) and cert. denied, 535 U.S. 1087, 122 S. Ct. 1981, 152 L. Ed. 2d 1038 (2002) and cert. denied, 537 U.S. 857, 123 S. Ct. 221, 154 L. Ed. 2d 93 (2002) one of the jurors, on the fourth day of trial, overheard a conversation among other jurors concerning the lack of professionalism and lack of interest of defense counsel. Defense counsel sought to have the juror excused but the trial judge credited the juror's statement that he would be able to keep an open mind, remain impartial and reserve determination of guilt or innocence until the conclusion of the trial. On appeal it was held that the judge's decision to accept the juror's assurances were within the court's discretion.

n. 22.

Add to note 22:

§ 7:5   JURY SELECTION: LAW, ART & SCIENCE 2D

See also U.S. v. Webster, 162 F.3d 308 (5th Cir. 1998); Image Technical Services, Inc. v. Eastman Kodak Co., 125 F.3d 1195, 44 U.S.P.Q.2d (BNA) 1065 (9th Cir. 1997) (no actual bias shown, and thus no abuse of discretion, in trial judge's refusal to excuse for cause juror who had prior unsatisfactory dealing with corporate defendant, but who, when questioned on voir dire, maintained he could be fair and impartial); Owens v. U.S., 528 U.S. 894, 120 S. Ct. 224, 145 L. Ed. 2d 188 (1999) (judge did not err in refusing to excuse for cause juror who initially expressed doubt about ability to fairly consider evidence but ultimately stated she would try to do so); U.S. v. Ray, 238 F.3d 828 (7th Cir. 2001), cert. denied, 532 U.S. 1045, 121 S. Ct. 2014, 149 L. Ed. 2d 1015 (2001) (trial court did not abuse its discretion in refusing to excuse for cause juror whose answers to questions on questionnaire and in court were in conflict, where juror's situation was complex and juror provided satisfactory clarifying explanations).

In Walzer v. St. Joseph State Hosp., 231 F.3d 1108, 84 Fair Empl. Prac. Cas. (BNA) 527, 80 Empl. Prac. Dec. (CCH) ¶ 40669 (8th Cir. 2000), the Court of Appeals found that the trial court had not abused its discretion in refusing to dismiss for cause, in a Title VII action by an employee claiming gender discrimination based on her dismissal because of alleged abuse of her children, a juror who had been arrested for violating an ex parte protection order issued on behalf of his wife. The juror had also failed to raise his hand in response to a question asking whether there was any juror who did not agree with the proposition that workplaces should be free from discrimination. The juror subsequently stated that he had not heard the question but would have raised his hand if he had. There was thus no reason to believe that the juror opposed antidiscrimination laws. The violation of the ex parte order against his wife was deemed not relevant as the case was not about domestic abuse.

n. 23.

Add to note 23:

The abuse of discretion standard may not be appropriate when a challenge for cause is based on a juror's response to a pretrial questionnaire. In U.S. v. Chanthadara, 230 F.3d 1237 (10th Cir. 2000), cert. denied, 534 U.S. 992, 122 S. Ct. 457, 151 L. Ed. 2d 376 (2001) the court, although reserving the issue for another day, flagged the problem of whether a trial court had an obligation to voir dire prospective jurors before removing any for cause based on their views of the death penalty. One of the difficulties with excusing jurors based on responses to a questionnaire is that the trial judge is deprived of the opportunity to observe and assess juror credibility. This opportunity is one of the main reasons for applying an "abuse of discretion" standard when reviewing court rulings on for-cause challenges. Because the opportunity to observe the juror is lacking when the challenge is based on a questionnaire response, the court in *Chanthadara* concluded that the trial judge's decision was not entitled to any particular deference and reviewed de novo whether the questionnaire responses warranted the excusal for cause of several jurors. However, the scope of even this dicta is somewhat clouded by the fact that the responses related to the jurors' views on the death penalty.

n. 27.

Add to note 27:

Although courts generally strain to believe jurors who maintain they can be impartial, on occasion a court will disbelieve a juror's assertion of impartiality. An example occurred in U.S. v. Moore, 149 F.3d 773, 49 Fed. R. Evid. Serv. 995 (8th Cir. 1998), where the record suggested likely

CHALLENGES FOR CAUSE § 7:5

partiality but the juror asserted that he could be impartial. The district court's decision to strike the juror for cause was held to be within the Court's discretion and "virtually unassailable on appeal." U.S. v. Moore, 149 F.3d 773, 780, 49 Fed. R. Evid. Serv. 995 (8th Cir. 1998). However, In Wolfe v. Brigano, 232 F.3d 499, 2000 FED App. 0394P (6th Cir. 2000), the court found that it was error for the trial judge to reject for-cause challenges where the jurors in question gave tentative commitments to try to decide the case on the evidence presented in trial, in circumstances where there was serious doubt about the jurors' ability to be impartial.

The author of Casenote, *Friends and Foes in the Jury Box: Walls v. Kim and the Mission to Stop Improper Juror Rehabilitation*, 53 Mercer L. Rev. 929 (2002) argues that judges should not take at face value a juror's promise to be impartial when there is evidence to the contrary for the judge has a duty to ensure the selection of a fair and impartial jury. The problem is compounded when the judge's decisions are reviewed under an "abuse of discretion" standard. The Casenote examines the decision in Walls v. Kim, 250 Ga. App. 259, 549 S.E.2d 797 (2001), cert. granted, (Jan. 10, 2002) and judgment aff'd, 275 Ga. 177, 563 S.E.2d 847 (2002) in the course of which the court criticizes the leeway generally given to rehabilitating biased jurors.

Add after second paragraph:

A judge may excuse a juror sua sponte, but rarely will a judge be held to have acted improperly in not doing so. See U.S. v. Simmons, 961 F.2d 183 (11th Cir. 1992). In McQueen v. Scroggy, 99 F.3d 1302, 35 Fed. R. Serv. 3d 1211, 1996 FED App. 0349P (6th Cir. 1996), the court held that the trial judge had not acted improperly in removing a juror who had violated his oath not to communicate with others and did not report a conversation about the case with his brother-in-law. Nor was there any constitutional violation absent proof that the jury which heard the case was not impartial.

In U.S. v. Lopez, 271 F.3d 472, 58 Fed. R. Evid. Serv. 460 (3d Cir. 2001), cert. denied, 535 U.S. 908, 122 S. Ct. 1211, 152 L. Ed. 2d 148 (2002) and cert. denied, 535 U.S. 962, 122 S. Ct. 1376, 152 L. Ed. 2d 368 (2002), a juror had sent the judge a note on the fourth day of trial requesting that the defendant stop staring at her. The defendant's counsel moved that the juror be struck because of her negative feelings towards the defendant. The judge not only denied the motion to strike but also declined to question the juror to explore the issue. On appeal, it was held that neither ruling constituted an abuse of the judge's discretion.

In U.S. v. Howell, 231 F.3d 615, 55 Fed. R. Evid. Serv. 1314 (9th Cir. 2000), cert. denied, 534 U.S. 831, 122 S. Ct. 76, 151 L. Ed. 2d 40 (2001), the court held that the trial court did not have to permit the defense to question a juror whose answers to voir dire questions posed by the prosecutor revealed a basis for challenging the juror for cause. The Court's view seems to preclude any possibility of answers to defense questions that would rehabilitate the juror. Such close-

§ 7:5   JURY SELECTION: LAW, ART & SCIENCE 2D

mindedness stands in stark contrast to the common judicial practice of asking jurors whether they can be fair and impartial, despite having admitted a potential ground for their challenge for cause, and decide the case on the evidence. See also U.S. v. Breen, 243 F.3d 591 (2d Cir. 2001), cert. denied, 534 U.S. 894, 122 S. Ct. 214, 151 L. Ed. 2d 152 (2001) (juror who had admitted lying on voir dire could be dismissed without defense counsel's consent). The author of Casenote, *Friends and Foes in the Jury Box: Walls v. Kim and the Mission to Stop Improper Juror Rehabilitation,* 53 Mercer L. Rev. 929 (2002) argues that judges should not take at face value a juror's promise to be impartial when there is evidence to the contrary for the judge has a duty to ensure the selection of a fair and impartial jury. The problem is compounded when the judge's decisions are reviewed under an "abuse of discretion" standard. The Casenote examines the decision in Walls v. Kim, 250 Ga. App. 259, 549 S.E.2d 797 (2001), cert. granted, (Jan. 10, 2002) and judgment aff'd, 275 Ga. 177, 563 S.E.2d 847 (2002) in the course of which the court criticizes the leeway generally given to rehabilitating biased jurors.

n. 29.

Add to note 29:

In Note, *Articulating the Inarticulable: Relying on Nonverbal Behavioral Cues to Strike Jurors during voir dire,* 38 Ariz. L. Rev. 739 (1996), the author argues that nonverbal indices of deception should be sufficient to provide the grounds for a challenge for cause.

n. 33.

Add to end of note 33:

U.S. v. Brooks, 161 F.3d 1240, 50 Fed. R. Evid. Serv. 899 (10th Cir. 1998).

n. 34.

Add to note 34 after "Ross":

State v. Isgitt, 590 So. 2d 763 (La. Ct. App. 3d Cir. 1991);

Add to note 34 after "Mount":

; Adams v. Aiken, 965 F.2d 1306 (4th Cir. 1992), cert. granted, judgment vacated on other grounds, 511 U.S. 1001, 114 S. Ct. 1365, 128 L. Ed. 2d 42 (1994); Bright v. Coastal Lumber Co., 962 F.2d 365 (4th Cir. 1992).

Add to end of note 34:

See also U.S. v. Gillis, 942 F.2d 707 (10th Cir. 1991) (exhaustion of peremptory challenges not required where there were insufficient peremptory challenges to remove all tainted venire members).

In Thomas v. Com., 864 S.W.2d 252 (Ky. 1993) the court pointed out that *Ross* was decided on the basis of state law, the United States Supreme Court decision merely establishing that the law in question did not violate a defendant's federal constitutional rights. Other states, however, remained free to adopt different approaches, and thus the *Thomas* court held that under Kentucky law a defendant is entitled to a reversal where the defendant had been forced to exhaust his peremptory challenges against prospective jurors who should have been excused for cause.

CHALLENGES FOR CAUSE § 7:5

n. 35.
Add to note 35:

Getter v. Wal-Mart Stores, Inc., 66 F.3d 1119, 43 Fed. R. Evid. Serv. 94 (10th Cir. 1995) (erroneous denial of challenge for cause deemed harmless error where juror in question was excused by means of peremptory challenge). See also Staley v. Bridgestone/Firestone, Inc., 106 F.3d 1504, Prod. Liab. Rep. (CCH) ¶ 14871, 46 Fed. R. Evid. Serv. 526 (10th Cir. 1997).

In U.S. v. Martinez-Salazar, 146 F.3d 653 (9th Cir. 1998), the Ninth Circuit Court of Appeals held that an erroneous refusal to excuse a juror for cause violates a defendant's fifth amendment rights when it forces the use of a peremptory challenge and, furthermore, requires automatic reversal. On writ of certiorari to the U.S. Supreme Court, the decision of the Ninth Circuit was reversed. U.S. v. Martinez-Salazar, 528 U.S. 304, 120 S. Ct. 774, 145 L. Ed. 2d 792 (2000). The Supreme Court held that even though the district court may have erred in refusing to remove a prospective juror for cause, the defendant's constitutional rights were not denied or impaired by his having to exercise a peremptory challenge to remove the suspect juror. For purposes of the Sixth Amendment, the critical issue is whether the jury that tried the defendant was impartial. As long as the jury was impartial, the defendant's Sixth Amendment rights were not violated even though he had to expend a peremptory challenge to achieve that result. Nor were defendant's due process rights infringed, as he was not compelled to use a peremptory challenge to remove the juror; he could have allowed the juror to serve and subsequently claimed a denial of his Sixth Amendment right. Needless to say, this is not an attractive choice, but the Supreme Court opined that "a hard choice is not the same as no choice." The defendant had received the number of peremptory challenges to which he was entitled by law, and he was not compelled to exercise a peremptory challenge to cure the trial court's error. The Supreme Court's decision does not foreclose a successful appeal where a judge has erroneously rejected a challenge but it would appear that a defendant would have to show that:(a) he has exhausted his full complement of peremptory challenges, (b) he would have used the peremptory challenge he expended on the suspect juror to strike some other juror, (c) he requested and was denied additional peremptory challenges, and (d) the jury that heard the case was not impartial. The Supreme Court's decision does resolve a long existing controversy among the federal courts regarding whether automatic reversal should follow the erroneous denial of a challenge for cause (Compare U.S. v. Polichemi, 201 F.3d 858 (7th Cir. 2000), on reh'g, 219 F.3d 698, 54 Fed. R. Evid. Serv. 1407 (7th Cir. 2000), cert. denied, 531 U.S. 1168, 121 S. Ct. 1131, 148 L. Ed. 2d 997 (2001); U.S. v. Hall, 152 F.3d 381, 49 Fed. R. Evid. Serv. 1503 (5th Cir. 1998); U.S. v. Cambara, 902 F.2d 144 (1st Cir. 1990) (all holding that the erroneous failure to remove a juror for cause requires automatic reversal) with U.S. v. Brooks, 161 F.3d 1240, 50 Fed. R. Evid. Serv. 899 (10th Cir. 1998); U.S. v. Sithithongtham, 192 F.3d 1119 (8th Cir. 1999); U.S. v. Farmer, 923 F.2d 1557, 33 Fed. R. Evid. Serv. 188 (11th Cir. 1991); U.S. v. Morales, 185 F.3d 74 (2d Cir. 1999) (all holding that the erroneous denial of a challenge for cause constitutes reversible error only if the jury which sits is not impartial), as well as harmonizing the approach in federal courts to erroneous denials of peremptory challenges with that which the Supreme Court had previously articulated in Ross v. Oklahoma, 487 U.S. 81, 108 S. Ct. 2273, 101 L. Ed. 2d 80 (1988), a case involving state law but raising comparable constitutional issues (see main text). A related issue to that considered in *Martinez-Salazar* occurs when a trial court abuses its

§ 7:5　　　　　　　Jury Selection: Law, Art & Science 2d

discretion in striking prospective jurors for cause. In U.S. v. Brooks, 175 F.3d 605 (8th Cir. 1999) the Court of Appeals held that the defendants were not entitled to reversal absent a showing that the jurors who heard the case were not impartial. See also U.S. v. Osigbade, 195 F.3d 900 (7th Cir. 1999) (no showing that defendant was prejudiced by Court's erroneous decision to discharge juror). In *Padilla-Mendoza* the trial court had excused for cause two jurors who had expressed the opinion that marijuana should not be prohibited. On appeal this was held to be error absent an inquiry as to whether, despite their beliefs, the two could perform their duties as jurors. The Court of Appeals, however, declined to reverse because there had been no showing that the jurors who had convicted the defendant were not impartial. See generally Childs, *The Intersection of Peremptory Challenges, Challenges for Cause, and Harmless Error*, 27 Am. J. Crim. L. 49 (1999) (although written prior to the Supreme Court's decision in Martinez-Salazar, the author thoughtfully examines whether lawyers should have to use peremptory challenges to rectify judicial errors in refusing challenges for cause).

Add after second sentence in sixth paragraph:
In Bonin v. Vasquez, 794 F. Supp. 957 (C.D. Cal. 1992), aff'd, 59 F.3d 815 (9th Cir. 1995), the court invited the petitioner, who had exhausted his peremptory challenges, to renew a request for additional peremptories. The defendant failed to do so, and on appeal by the defendant the court found no constitutional violation in the trial judge's failure to award additional peremptory challenges.

n. 38.
　Add to note 38:
　　Callins v. Collins, 998 F.2d 269 (5th Cir. 1993).

n. 39.
　Add to note 39:
; Dawson v. Wal-Mart Stores, Inc., 978 F.2d 205 (5th Cir. 1992). See also U.S. v. Rowe, 144 F.3d 15 (1st Cir. 1998) (failure to raise claim of juror bias, known during trial, until after trial constitutes waiver of claim); U.S. v. Pennington, 168 F.3d 1060 (8th Cir. 1999) (defendant waived claim that district court erred in not excusing juror who was employee of witness by not challenging juror when jury was impaneled despite being aware of the basis for challenge and that the witness might be called).

n. 40.
　Add to note 40:
; State v. Bible, 175 Ariz. 549, 858 P.2d 1152 (1993) (state rule allowed for challenge for cause after trial had begun where ground for challenge not known previously). See generally Note, *Juror Bias Undiscovered during voir dire: Legal Standards for Reviewing Claims of a Denial of the Constitutional Right to an Impartial Jury*, 39 Drake L Rev 201 (1989–90).

　　In similar vein, a court, on its own motion, can excuse a juror for grounds that come to light during the trial. In U.S. v. Purdy, 144 F.3d 241 (2d Cir. 1998), the husband of a juror, on the fourth day of the trial, approached the defendants and expressed views sympathetic to the defense. Defense counsel informed the judge, who proceeded to question the juror. The juror stated that she was not aware of the incident, and had not discussed the case with her husband. Although the judge said that there was no reason to doubt the juror's answers, the judge nonetheless discharged the juror. On appeal the defendant argued that the judge should have taken less drastic precautionary measures short of discharging the juror, such as sequestering the jury or simply cautioning the jurors not to discuss the case with anybody. The defendant argued that he might well have been prejudiced by the juror's discharge because it could be expected that the juror, like her husband, held views sympathetic to the defense. The Second Circuit Court of Appeals, however, upheld the trial judge's ruling, stressing the latter's broad discretion to replace a juror if there is reasonable cause to do so. The trial court's decision was held to be reasonable, given the strong views of the juror's husband and the likelihood that he would impress those views on his wife. See also U.S. v. Bornfield, 145 F.3d 1123, 49 Fed. R. Evid. Serv. 601 (10th Cir. 1998) (trial court did not abuse its discretion in dismissing alternate juror who voiced displeasure at slow pace of trial in presence of other jurors). Compare U.S. v. Gaitan-Acevedo, 148 F.3d 577, 49 Fed. R. Evid. Serv. 590, 1998 FED App. 0143P (6th Cir. 1998) (court did not abuse its discretion in not dismissing juror who, during the trial, apprehended three of his students smoking marijuana).

§ 7:6 Preconceived opinions

Add to end of first paragraph:
Sometimes the converse situation arises, where a juror indicates bias with the aim of avoiding jury duty. In U.S. v. Chandler, 996 F.2d 1073, 39 Fed. R. Evid. Serv. 304 (11th Cir. 1993), as modified, (Sept. 30, 1993), a juror was overheard telling other jurors that "[t]he way to get off this case is to say the defendant looks guilty." The court held that this remark did not render the juror incompetent to serve, and that it was therefore not an abuse of the Court's discretion to refuse to remove the juror for cause.

Add after second sentence in second paragraph:
See, eg., U.S. v. Martinez-Salazar, 146 F.3d 653 (9th Cir. 1998), judgment rev'd, 528 U.S. 304, 120 S. Ct. 774, 145 L. Ed. 2d 792 (2000).

Add after second paragraph:
U.S. v. Hines, 943 F.2d 348 (4th Cir. 1991), is illustrative. Among the charges against the defendant were some relating to drugs. One of the jurors admitted to being familiar with the adverse effects of drugs and drug abuse as a result of her professional experience in a chemical dependency unit. The trial judge asked the juror whether she could put aside her personal feelings about drug use and decide the case on the evidence. The juror replied "I think so." This satisfied the judge, who refused to remove the juror for cause. The appellate court upheld the judge's ruling. The court indicated, however, that in some instances an ambiguous response such as "I think so" may require clarification, but the trial judge was in the best position to make that determination. The ap-

§ 7:6   Jury Selection: Law, Art & Science 2d

pellate court pointedly noted that the defendants did not exercise a peremptory challenge against the juror although they still had available challenges to do so if they had wished. See also Ray v. Gream, 860 S.W.2d 325 (Mo. 1993) (although some prospective jurors initially had indicated a bias in favor of family members in a case involving a contested will, the Court's finding, after independent questioning of the jurors, that the jurors could set aside "preconceived notions" did not constitute an abuse of discretion); State v. Bible, 175 Ariz. 549, 858 P.2d 1152 (1993) (mere knowledge of relevant scientific testing procedures is not sufficient to disqualify a juror).

In U.S. v. Parker, 133 F.3d 322, 48 Fed. R. Evid. Serv. 785 (5th Cir. 1998), the court held that there had been no abuse of discretion in the Court's dismissal of a juror who claimed, based on his brother-in-law's criminal conviction, to have a "healthy skepticism" of evidence such that he would be suspicious of any evidence even before he had seen or heard testimony on point.

Add after first sentence in third paragraph:
The failure to make a determination as to whether two jurors who had expressed the opinion that marijuana should not be prohibited could, despite their beliefs, perform their duties as jurors was held to be error in U.S. v. Mendoza, 157 F.3d 730 (9th Cir. 1998). However, the Court of Appeals declined to reverse because no showing had been made that the jurors who convicted the defendant were not impartial or were unable to perform their duties. The trial court's dismissal of the two jurors could not be said to have resulted in a biased pro-government jury.

§ 7:8 —Subject to change by proof
n. 52.
Add to note 52:

In Thompson v. Altheimer & Gray, 248 F.3d 621, 85 Fair Empl. Prac. Cas. (BNA) 897, 80 Empl. Prac. Dec. (CCH) ¶ 40636 (7th Cir. 2001) a prospective juror expressed the belief in a race discrimination case that some claims against employers were spurious. The Court of Appeals found that the comment itself did not indicate bias ("it is not bias to cling to a belief that no rational person would question") but held that the judge had erred in not determining whether the juror could suspend her belief and follow the judge's instructions. As there were no assurances in the record to indicate the juror's belief was "shakable" or that the juror could exercise a judgment unaffected by her belief, the Court of Appeals held that the verdict could not stand. The Court stated that the trial judge should have obtained unequivocal, credible assurances that the juror could follow the Court's instructions and suspend judgment until she had heard all of the evidence.

§ 7:9 —Opinion of the law
Add after first sentence in first paragraph:

In State v. Jackson, 629 So. 2d 1374 (La. Ct. App. 2d Cir. 1993), writ denied, 637 So. 2d 1046 (La. 1994), a juror stated that he thought that the law should be changed, but indicated that he would apply the existing standards and not his own ideas. The court held that there was therefore no basis for excusing the juror for cause. This case might be compared with that of People v. Merced, 94 Cal. App. 4th 1024, 114 Cal. Rptr. 2d 781 (1st Dist. 2001), review denied, (Mar. 13, 2002), where a prospective alternate juror indicated in writing on the juror questionnaire that he recognized and believed in jury nullification. When questioned by the judge, the prospective juror stated that it was reasonable for the judge to assume that he, the juror, would not follow the law if it went against his conscience. The juror was removed for cause and the decision to do so was upheld on appeal. The appellate court added that the trial judge was not required to undertake an inquiry into whether the particular details of the case to be tried presented a likelihood that the juror would actually engage in nullification, as such an inquiry would itself encourage improper pre-judgment of the case.

In Wolfe v. Brigano, 232 F.3d 499, 2000 FED App. 0394P (6th Cir. 2000), the court held in a criminal case that where a juror had an ongoing business relationship with the victim's parents and had spoken to and listened to the parents, it was an abuse of the trial judge's discretion to deny a for-cause challenge to the juror, particularly where the juror had stated that he did not think that he could be fair and impartial.

Add after second sentence in first paragraph:
See Wolfe v. Brigano, 232 F.3d 499, 2000 FED App. 0394P (6th Cir. 2000) (in absence of affirmative and believable statement that jurors could set aside their opinions and decide case on the evidence and in accordance with the law, failure to dismiss jurors for cause was unreasonable). In U.S. v. Nelson, 277 F.3d 164 (2d Cir. 2002), cert. denied, 537 U.S. 835, 123 S. Ct. 145, 154 L. Ed. 2d 54 (2002) the court found actual bias where a juror during voir dire expressed his dissatisfaction with the state proceedings that had resulted in an acquittal of one of the defendants. On further questioning the juror said that, while he would like to think of himself as objective and able to give the defendants a fair trial, he honestly did not know whether he could. In effect, according to the Court of Appeals, the juror had admitted that he could not follow the applicable law and accordingly it was an abuse of discretion to deny the defendants' challenge for cause.

In Com. v. Chambers, 528 Pa. 558, 599 A.2d 630 (1991), the court held that a juror had been properly excused for

§ 7:9　　　　　Jury Selection: Law, Art & Science 2d

cause after stating that she would not convict unless definitely, absolutely satisfied of guilt and, in case of doubt, would require that guilt be proven "to the nth degree." Similarly, in Drew v. Collins, 964 F.2d 411 (5th Cir. 1992), the court held that the prospective juror's repeated statements during voir dire in a capital case that be would apply a standard higher than reasonable doubt warranted the juror's excusal for cause. See also Beck v. State, Dept. of Transp. and Public Facilities, 837 P.2d 105 (Alaska 1992) (challenge for cause should have been granted against juror who exhibited substantial inclination to be governed by her own opinions and who stated that "maybe" she could apply Court's definition of negligence); Nelson v. State, 832 S.W.2d 762 (Tex. App. Houston 1st Dist. 1992) (juror who is biased against law applicable to case must be excused when challenged, even if juror claims to be able to set aside bias and be impartial).

In Richardson v. Bowersox, 188 F.3d 973 (8th Cir. 1999) the trial court struck three prospective jurors who stated that they would not consider imposing the death penalty on the defendant unless the state proved he was the one who pushed the victims off the bridge. However, under state law a defendant could be found guilty of first-degree murder based on a theory of accomplice liability. Thus, it was held that the trial court did not err in finding that the jurors' views would impair their performance as jurors.

In U.S. v. Geffrard, 87 F.3d 448 (11th Cir. 1996), it came to light during deliberations that one of the jurors belonged to an obscure religion, (Swedenborgianism), the effect of whose doctrines would not allow the juror to follow the judge's instructions. The judge decided to excuse the juror and accept a verdict of the remaining 11. The court of appeal held that this method of proceeding was permissible under Fed. R. Crim. P. 23(b), and that the matter fell within the judge's discretion. The court held that, under the circumstances, the judge had not abused that discretion.

n. 55.

Add to note 55:

People v. Reaud, 821 P.2d 870 (Colo. Ct. App. 1991); State v. Ramsey, 864 S.W.2d 320 (Mo. 1993), as modified on denial of reh'g, (Oct. 26, 1993). In U.S. v. Quintero-Barraza, 57 F.3d 836 (9th Cir. 1995), opinion amended and superseded on denial of reh'g, 78 F.3d 1344 (9th Cir. 1995), the appellant based his ineffective assistance of counsel claim in part on the fact that counsel had failed to challenge a prospective juror who stated his belief that a defendant was guilty until proven innocent and that it would be difficult for him to be impartial. Counsel not only did not challenge the juror, but expressed his admiration of the juror's truthfulness. The court ruled that this was a tactical decision that counsel was entitled to make, and that it would pay due respect to the oath taken by the juror. See also

CHALLENGES FOR CAUSE § 7:9

Keel v. French, 162 F.3d 263 (4th Cir. 1998) (failure to raise questionable *Batson* claim did not establish ineffective assistance of counsel);Miller v. Francis, 269 F.3d 609, 2001 FED App. 0366P (6th Cir. 2001), cert. denied, 535 U.S. 1011, 122 S. Ct. 1592, 152 L. Ed. 2d 509 (2002) (failure to challenge juror with some prior knowledge of case from having served as welfare caseworker for victim's mother did not constitute ineffective assistance of counsel)Yeatts v. Angelone, 166 F.3d 255 (4th Cir. 1999) (voir dire of jurors in death penalty case did not give rise to claim of ineffective assistance of counsel where counsel failed to inform jurors that death penalty could not be imposed unless they unanimously found presence of aggravating factor). Compare Kirk v. Raymark Industries, Inc., 61 F.3d 147, 42 Fed. R. Evid. Serv. 883, 155 A.L.R. Fed. 701 (3d Cir. 1995) (juror who indicated in jury questionnaire that he could not be fair to company that made, distributed, or installed products that contained asbestos should have been excused for cause in mesothelioma action, even though juror stated upon questioning that he could be fair).

In U.S. v. Scott, 159 F.3d 916 (5th Cir. 1998), it was held that the trial judge had not erred in rejecting defendant's challenge for cause to two prospective jurors who at first stated that they would draw negative inferences from a defendant's failure to testify, but upon subsequent questioning by the judge, indicated they could put aside such inferences and base their verdict only on the evidence in the case.

Add to end of section:

In U.S. v. Joseph, 892 F.2d 118 (D.C. Cir. 1989), it was held that the trial court did not abuse its discretion in excusing a juror who indicated that he would follow the instructions of the Lord rather than those of the judge if the juror perceived a conflict between the two.

Determining the willingness of a juror to follow the law may not be as simple as asking a question to this effect, as revealed in Morgan v. Illinois, 504 U.S. 719, 112 S. Ct. 2222, 119 L. Ed. 2d 492 (1992). The trial judge had asked the jurors, in general terms, whether they would follow the law. The judge had rejected the defendant's request for a specific question as to whether any juror would automatically vote in favor of the death penalty if the defendant were to be convicted. The state argued that the Court's general questioning was adequate to protect the defendant's rights but the United States Supreme Court disagreed. The Court thought jurors might in their own minds see no inconsistency between responding affirmatively to questions about following the law or impartiality and thinking that one convicted of a capital crime should automatically be sentenced to death. Their position might well satisfy their own personal conception of fairness and impartiality. Yet, one who believed that a death sentence should automatically follow conviction of a capital offense and was unwilling to consider mitigating circumstances as required and defined by law would not be acting in accordance with the law. Because the capital defendant was on trial for his life and constitutional concerns could easily be alleviated, the Court was strengthened in its conviction that the defendant should be permitted to probe more closely the jurors' views on this critical issue. It thus found that the trial judge's general line of questioning was not sufficient.

The case illustrates a more pervasive problem. Jurors often will assert impartiality, usually believing that they are impartial. It often takes detailed questioning to uncover deep-seated biases of which the juror may not be aware. The cursory examination typically conducted by the trial court is often inadequate for this purpose. See also U.S. v. Gillis, 942 F.2d 707 (10th Cir. 1991). In this case, the judge's general questioning regarding impartiality was inadequate to determine whether jurors might be prejudiced as a result of having been subjected to voir dire in a previous trial against the defendant on similar charges.

It might seem that lawyers in particular would hold strong opinions on the law, and for that reason, as well as for the undue influence that a lawyer might have in the deliberations, would be disqualified from serving on a jury. However, many states do not provide automatic disqualifications or exemptions from jury service to attorneys, and in U.S. v. Magana, 118 F.3d 1173, 47 Fed. R. Evid. Serv. 626 (7th Cir. 1997) the court held that there had been no prejudice from the fact that a former US attorney had served as a juror in the case. The lawyer-juror had agreed to follow the judge's instructions and refrain from giving his own opinions on the law.

§ 7:10 The problem of pretrial publicity

Add after first paragraph:
See generally *Symposium on the Selection and Function of the Modern Jury*, 40 Am U L Rev 541 (1991).

n. 58.
Add to note 58:
Flamer v. State of Del., 68 F.3d 736 (3d Cir. 1995). But compare U.S. v. Orlando-Figueroa, 229 F.3d 33, 55 Fed. R. Evid. Serv. 1097 (1st Cir. 2000) (no error in denial of motion for continuance based on pretrial publicity where publicity was not inflammatory and "ran the gamut from maligning to championing to defending to praising to simply reporting on the defendant's situation"). Although there is a theoretical gain from a continuance in that memories fade and the prejudicial publicity is forgotten, this gain may turn out to be illusory if a fresh round of news stories about the case appears at the time of trial. Judicial monitoring of the situation may be required. Even then, while a juror may have forgotten a prejudicial news story read many months previous, evidence presented in the trial may jog the juror's memory.

n. 59.
Add to note 59:

In U.S. v. Blom, 242 F.3d 799 (8th Cir. 2001), cert. denied, 534 U.S. 880, 122 S. Ct. 184, 151 L. Ed. 2d 128 (2001) the Court of Appeals found that although there had been extensive media coverage of the case, the coverage had been neither sufficiently inflammatory nor accusatory to give rise to a presumption of inherent prejudice. Moreover, the court was impressed with the various steps taken by the trial judge to defuse any prejudice, including moving the trial from Duluth to Minneapolis, assembling a jury pool three times the normal size and drawn from an expanded area, sending out a pretrial questionnaire to all prospective jurors asking about their exposure to the media coverage, and increasing the number of peremptory challenges. Further, there had been three days of individualized voir dire, which led to the selection of 14 jurors who said that they could put aside whatever knowledge they had of the case and be impartial. The court concluded that under the circumstances there had been no abuse of discretion in the denial of the motion for a change in venue.

A court is likely to be less sympathetic to a defendant's complaints about pretrial publicity where defendant's own acts and statements generated much of the publicity. See U.S. v. Bakker, 925 F.2d 728, 32 Fed. R. Evid. Serv. 303 (4th Cir. 1991). The court will likewise be less sympathetic to a claim of prejudicial publicity if the defendant fails to move for a change in venue. See, e.g., U.S. v. Orlando-Figueroa, 229 F.3d 33, 55 Fed. R. Evid. Serv. 1097 (1st Cir. 2000).

Add after second paragraph:

Empirical studies suggest that voir dire is not a particularly effective tool for discovering and combating the effects of prejudicial pretrial publicity. See, e.g., Kerr, Kramer, Carroll, & Affini, *On the Effectiveness of Voir Dire in Criminal Cases with Prejudicial Pretrial Publicity*, 40 Am U L Rev 665 (1991). The authors assert that judges tend to overvalue voir dire as a means of combating such publicity and as a consequence overlook superior alternatives such as continuances, change of venue, and change of venire.

Add at end of second paragraph in section

But see Whitebread & Contreras, *Free Press v. Fair Trial: Protecting the Criminal Defendant's Rights in a Highly Publicized Trial by Applying the Sheppard-Mu'Min Remedy*, 69 S. Cal. L. Rev. 1587 (1996) (arguing that voir dire, sequestration, change of venue and postponement are all inadequate methods for preserving the proper balance between freedom of the press and the defendant's right to a fair trial).

n. 60.

Add to note 60:

In U.S. v. Lowe, 145 F.3d 45, 49 Fed. R. Evid. Serv. 687 (1st Cir. 1998) the trial judge during voir dire asked whether any of the jurors had read or heard anything about an escape relating to the case, and proceeded to excuse for cause two jurors who stated that they could not be fair and impartial due to publicity about the escape. A third juror, who stated that he could put aside what he had heard and decide the case on the evidence, was not excused. The appellate court found no abuse of discretion in these rulings.

§ 7:10   JURY SELECTION: LAW, ART & SCIENCE 2D

In U.S. v. Orlando-Figueroa, 229 F.3d 33, 55 Fed. R. Evid. Serv. 1097 (1st Cir. 2000), a case involving substantial but not particularly inflammatory pretrial publicity, the trial judge had asked the jurors if any had read or seen anything about the case. The judge then proceeded to individually question each juror who had answered affirmatively as to the circumstances under which the juror had been exposed to the publicity and whether, despite the exposure, the juror could decide the case only on the evidence presented. Several jurors were excused by the court. On appeal, this method of proceeding was upheld, the Court of Appeals stating that there was no error in the trial court's decision not to individually voir dire each and every prospective juror.

See also U.S. v. Washington, 836 F. Supp. 192 (D. Vt. 1993), aff'd, 48 F.3d 73 (2d Cir. 1995); U.S. v. Flores, 63 F.3d 1342, 42 Fed. R. Evid. Serv. 1365 (5th Cir. 1995).

Add after note 63:
In contrast, the Court of Appeals in Thompson v. Borg, 74 F.3d 1571 (9th Cir. 1996) held that the defendant was not prejudiced by a juror's disclosure during voir dire that he had read in a newspaper that the defendant had pleaded guilty but had later withdrawn his guilty plea. The court held that even if the disclosure fell within the category of juror misconduct, the error was harmless.

Add at end of fifth paragraph:
The problem of conducting an effective voir dire in respect to pretrial publicity is compounded when an anonymous jury is impaneled. In U.S. v. Edmond, 52 F.3d 1080, 42 Fed. R. Evid. Serv. 119 (D.C. Cir. 1995), the trial court asked jurors to complete a 20-page questionnaire. The questions probed generally about the newspapers that the jurors regularly read and the television programs they regularly watched. The questionnaire did not, however, focus the jurors' attention on the particular defendants except to the extent that it listed the names of each defendant and asked whether any of the jurors knew of or were connected with any of these persons. The Court of Appeals stated that, as a general matter, such questioning was too indirect and oblique to yield an effective assessment of exposure to potentially prejudicial media coverage. The trial court was better advised to have asked the jurors what they had read or heard about the case. Other aspects of the voir dire, including the use of questions which conflated exposure to pretrial publicity with an ability to render a verdict based solely on the evidence, also came in for criticism. However, despite its finding that the voir dire was far from ideal, the Court of Appeals concluded that it satisfied constitutional requirements. The fact that the case was popularly referred to by the name of one of the defendants may also have helped to ensure that any exposure to prejudicial publicity would come to light as a result of the answers to the question about knowledge of the named defendants.

§ 7:10

n. 74.
 Add to note 74:
 In U.S. v. Lanier, 33 F.3d 639, 41 Fed. R. Evid. Serv. 219, 1994 FED App. 0305P (6th Cir. 1994), reh'g en banc granted, judgment vacated, 43 F.3d 1033 (6th Cir. 1995) and on reh'g en banc, 73 F.3d 1380 (6th Cir. 1996), vacated, 520 U.S. 259, 117 S. Ct. 1219, 137 L. Ed. 2d 432 (1997) and opinion vacated, 114 F.3d 84 (6th Cir. 1997), it was held that the mere fact that a copy of a local newspaper containing an article about the case had been left in the jury room did not establish prejudice to the defendant. See also U.S. v. Rutgard, 108 F.3d 1041 (9th Cir. 1997), opinion amended and superseded on reh'g, 116 F.3d 1270 (9th Cir. 1997) (no abuse of discretion where judge failed to probe the effect of pretrial publicity beyond making routine inquiries where the news accounts in question were sporadic and located on the inner pages of the metropolitan newspapers).

n. 76.
 Add to note 76:
 In Mu'Min v. Virginia, 500 U.S. 415, 111 S. Ct. 1899, 114 L. Ed. 2d 493 (1991) (See § 7:11), Justice Kennedy, dissenting, suggested that there were in fact two distinct lines of cases recognized in the Court's past opinions. One involved trials which took place in an atmosphere so highly charged and corrupting of the trial process that it was reasonable for the Court to presume that a fair trial could not have been held, or an impartial jury seated. In the other, less extreme situations, the issue was only whether individual jurors had been biased by exposure to pretrial publicity which was less dramatic, less corrupting. The former line of cases was characterized by decisions such as *Irvin* and *Rideau*; the latter by decisions such as *Murphy*. In Hill v. Brigano, 199 F.3d 833, 1999 FED App. 0426P (6th Cir. 1999), the Court of Appeals, accepting that Mu'Min was the governing authority, found a less substantial case of pretrial publicity than in Mu'Min. Although the jurors were aware of the publicity, they stated that they could be impartial. Under the circumstances, the Court of Appeals held that no error had been committed by the trial court in limiting defense voir dire. Likewise, in Whitehead v. Cowan, 263 F.3d 708 (7th Cir. 2001), cert. denied, 534 U.S. 1116, 122 S. Ct. 927, 151 L. Ed. 2d 890 (2002) the Court of Appeals analogized to Murphy in finding that there had not been the type of extreme media presence or circuslike atmosphere that would have warranted a presumption of prejudice.

It has been stated that the burden in respect to presumptively prejudicial publicity not only rests with the defendant, but also is extremely heavy on a motion for a change in venue. State v. Bible, 175 Ariz. 549, 858 P.2d 1152 (1993). In this case the court declined to find presumptive prejudice where the pretrial publicity had included reports that the defendant had "flunked" a lie detector test and was a convicted "child molester" who had committed "child rape," as well as containing references to other inadmissible evidence. The court observed that the items in question had appeared months apart and several months prior to the trial. The court stated that in order to be deemed presumptively prejudicial the publicity would have to be so unfair, so prejudicial, and so pervasive that the trial court could not give any credibility to jurors' answers to voir dire questions. See also Devier v. Zant, 3 F.3d 1445 (11th Cir. 1993) (defendant's showing that the community was familiar with the case was insufficient to sustain a claim of presumptive prejudice). Stafford v. Saffle, 34 F.3d 1557 (10th Cir. 1994) (mere fact of a case receiving extensive publicity does not establish that the publicity was hostile or that an ir-

§ 7:10   JURY SELECTION: LAW, ART & SCIENCE 2D

repressibly hostile attitude pervaded the community); Brecheen v. Reynolds, 41 F.3d 1343 (10th Cir. 1994) (no error where trial court made specific finding that, despite exposure to publicity, panel's statements of impartiality could be trusted). McQueen v. Scroggy, 99 F.3d 1302, 35 Fed. R. Serv. 3d 1211, 1996 FED App. 0349P (6th Cir. 1996) (no per se rule excluding jurors exposed to media reports unless it engenders a predisposition or bias that cannot be set aside); U.S. v. Sherwood, 98 F.3d 402 (9th Cir. 1996) (a defendant is not entitled to ignorant jury and fact that 96% of jurors were aware of case did not establish presumed or actual prejudice). U.S. v. Bailey, 112 F.3d 758 (4th Cir. 1997) (trial court did not abuse its discretion in refusing a change of venue or individual voir dire in case where pretrial publicity did not give rise to a presumption of prejudice); U.S. v. Rutgard, 116 F.3d 1270 (9th Cir. 1997) (where the pretrial publicity had been intermittent, not extensive, and generally confined to the inner pages of newspapers, the trial court did not abuse its discretion in not going beyond the usual inquiry as to whether jurors had read anything about the case).

Add after "impartiality less reliable." in eleventh paragraph:

A somewhat analogous situation to *Rideau* arose in DeLisle v. Rivers, 161 F.3d 370, 1998 FED App. 0350P (6th Cir. 1998), where defendant's inculpatory statements had received considerable publicity in the media. Prior to trial it was determined that these statements of the defendant should be suppressed. At trial the defendant moved to strike for cause all prospective jurors with knowledge of the suppressed statements on the ground that such persons should be presumed incapable of deciding the case fairly and impartially. The Sixth Circuit Court of Appeals rejected defendant's argument that the state trial judge's denial of this blanket challenge for cause denied him due process. The Court of Appeals noted that the category of cases where prejudice was presumed was extremely limited. It distinguished *DeLisle's* situation from previous "presumed prejudice" cases. Unlike in the prior cases, there had been a cessation of publicity between the media coverage and the trial. Also, the reporting had not been as "virulent" in nature as in the presumed prejudice cases. Indeed, the court observed that the defendant's so-called confession would have been somewhat confusing to many of those who read it and was not without ambiguity.

In Hale v. Gibson, 227 F.3d 1298 (10th Cir. 2000), cert. denied, 533 U.S. 957, 121 S. Ct. 2608, 150 L. Ed. 2d 764 (2001), the defendant claimed that he had been denied a fair trial when his motion for a change in venue, based on extensive media coverage of the case, was rejected. During voir dire, only three of 37 jurors stated that they had no prior knowledge of the case, and 12 admitted that they held an opinion about defendant's guilt. Of these 12, six were seated on the jury. One even admitted that she had discussed the case with a key witness but maintained that she could nonetheless be impartial. The Court of Appeals was not prepared to presume prejudice, as in its opinion the facts of the case did not rise to the level of egregiousness in *Rideau, Sheppard,* or *Estes.* Nor did the Court of Appeals find actual prejudice, as there was no indication from the jurors' responses of hostility to the defendant. The Court of Appeals concluded that the trial court had not abused its discretion in denying the motion for a change in venue.

n. 78.

Add to note 78:

See also Minnow & Cate, *Who Is an Impartial Juror in an Age of Mass Media?,* 40 Am. U. L. Rev. 631 (1991) (cautioning against mistaking unaware and ignorant jurors for impartial jurors).

n. 81.

Add to note 81:

See also Knapp v. Leonardo, 46 F.3d 170 (2d Cir. 1995) (in era of modern communications it is nearly impossible to find a juror who has not been exposed to some measure of information regarding a highly publicized case; it is only required that the jurors be impartial and not ignorant). See generally Whitebread & Contreras, *Free Press v. Fair Trial: Protecting the Criminal Defendant's Rights in a Highly Publicized Trial by Applying the Sheppard-Mu'Min Remedy,* 69 S. Cal. L. Rev. 1587 (1996) (rejecting the adequacy of voir dire, sequestration, change of venue and postponement as methods for preserving the proper balance between freedom of the press and the defendant's right to a fair trial).

Add before the last paragraph:

In U.S. v. Beckner, 69 F.3d 1290 (5th Cir. 1995), the Court of Appeals, having found that there had been sufficient pretrial publicity to raise a significant possibility of prejudice, proceeded to examine the adequacy of the trial court's voir dire on this issue. The trial court had not specifically inquired about what each juror had read or heard about the case. While the judge did ask whether any juror had been so affected by the pretrial publicity that he or she could not be completely fair and impartial, the Court of Appeals found that this was an abdication of responsibility. In effect the trial court had allowed the jurors to decide their own impartiality. In the opinion of the Court of Appeals, the trial court had an independent responsibility to determine each juror's impartiality.

Beckner can be compared with U.S. v. Bieganowski, 313 F.3d 264 (5th Cir. 2002), cert. denied, 123 S. Ct. 1956, 155 L. Ed. 2d 851 (U.S. 2003). Here too, there had been publicity about the defendant prior to trial which gave rise to a significant possibility of prejudice. During voir dire, one prospective juror had revealed the contents of an inflammatory article in the presence of the panel. After the juror's disclosure, however, the defendant did not request the judge to conduct individual voir dire, although the Court of Appeals stated that this would have been prudent and within the court's discretion. The Court of Appeals also thought that the trial judge would have been better advised to engage in further questioning of the entire venire after the prospective juror had revealed the contents of the article in its presence. In the event, the juror who had revealed the content of the article did not ultimately serve on the jury, the defense having exercised a peremptory challenge to remove him. That, of course, did not resolve the issue of whether the jury had been tainted by the juror's revelations. Without reaching this issue, the Court of Appeals found that the defendant had not suffered such a degree of prejudice to justify a reversal of his conviction. The trial court had instructed the jury not to consider what they had read in the papers, noting that "the papers are not always correct" and, at the conclusion of voir dire, further instructed the jury that "anything you may have seen or heard outside the courtroom is not evidence and must be totally disregarded. You are to decide this case solely on the evidence presented here in court." The fact that the jury had convicted the defendant on only 10 of the 15 counts with which he had been charged indicated to the Court of Appeals that the jury had methodically assessed each of the charges against the defendant. Finally, the Court of Appeals noted that the evidence of guilt was overwhelming.

Add at end of section:

In most cases involving pretrial publicity the publicity in question relates to the case being litigated or the parties in that case. In Waldorf v. Shuta, 3 F.3d 705 (3d Cir. 1993), on the other hand, the publicity pertained to an unrelated case in which a $30 million verdict was returned. It was not disputed that a newspaper article describing the award had been brought into the jury room by one juror, had been reviewed by at least one other juror, and had been the topic of discussion. The defendant argued that the damage award in the case described in the paper may have provided the jurors with a prejudicially impermissible yardstick to measure the damages in the case at hand, where similar injuries were alleged. The court of appeal held that the trial judge's in camera questioning of jurors to determine whether the verdict could have been affected by the publicity was insufficiently thorough to detect prejudice, and that the trial judge relied too heavily on the jurors' self-assessments of their impartiality.

Waldorf v Shuta (above) might be compared with Government of Virgin Islands v. Weatherwax, 77 F.3d 1425 (3d Cir. 1996). In *Weatherwax* a juror was observed carrying a newspaper containing an article about the trial that allegedly gave an inaccurate and unfavorable account of the defendant's testimony. The matter was brought to defense counsel's attention, but he declined to relate the incident to the trial judge or move for a mistrial. The Court of Appeals held that this was not a "fundamental decision" of the type that a defendant has the ultimate authority to make. The attorney in the case had consulted with the defendant, and had taken into account his views as well as those of his family as to the appropriate course of action, even though he ultimately decided not to follow their advice. The court held that the lawyer's judgment that he had as favorable a jury as reasonably could be expected, and did not wish to hazard a retrial before a possibly less favorable jury, was a tactical decision that the lawyer was entitled to make. Thus the appellant's claim of ineffective assistance of counsel failed. The court declined to express an opinion as to whether the lawyer had breached a duty owed to the court, but stated that even if he had done so, it would only warrant disciplinary sanctions against the lawyer and not a reversal of the defendant's conviction. The *Weatherwax* decision is critically reviewed in Note, *A Caribbean Fantasy? The Case of the Juror Who Misbehaved and the Attorney Who Let Him Get Away with It: Violation of Sixth Amendment Rights to an Impartial Jury and Effective Assistance of Counsel in Government of the Virgin Islands v. Weatherwax*, 42 Villanova L. Rev. 275 (1997).

In U.S. v. Murray, 103 F.3d 310, 46 Fed. R. Evid. Serv. 223 (3d Cir. 1997) (distinguished by, U.S. v. Ramos, 971 F. Supp. 186 (E.D. Pa. 1997), order aff'd, 151 F.3d 1027 (3d Cir. 1998)), the court found no abuse of discretion in the Court's decision not to excuse a juror who had read an article about the pending case, where the court had satisfied itself that the juror was impartial The juror was unable to remember all of the article, denied forming an opinion regarding guilt, and affirmed that she would decide the case on the evidence.

In Cox v. Norris, 525 U.S. 834, 119 S. Ct. 89, 142 L. Ed. 2d 70 (1998), there had been, prior to the defendant's trial, several newspaper articles on capital punishment. The court held that these articles did not require a continuance and that the defendant had not been denied an impartial jury where the voir dire established that the jurors had not been affected by the publicity.

A somewhat atypical case of "publicity" occurred in U.S. v. Allen, 247 F.3d 741, 56 Fed. R. Evid. Serv. 1144 (8th Cir. 2001), cert. granted, judgment vacated on other grounds, 536 U.S. 953, 122 S. Ct. 2653, 153 L. Ed. 2d 830 (2002) and cert. denied, 123 S. Ct. 2273, 156 L. Ed. 2d 132 (U.S. 2003) where, during a recess in jury selection, the sentencing decision in a related case was returned and engendered a loud emotional outburst which included screams and crying. The outburst was heard by several members of the defendant's venire panel. In response the district court took several remedial steps, including asking general voir dire questions, individual questions on the emotional outbursts, and cautionary instructions reminding the panel to avoid and disregard anything seen or heard outside the courtroom. The defendant, however, argued that the court had abused its discretion in not striking the entire panel, and, in the alternative, not striking those jurors who admitted to having heard the outburst. On appeal the court found no abuse of the judge's discretion. As most of the panel had not heard the outburst, and as those who had heard the outburst could not be certain about what it related to, there was no obvious prejudice to the defendant. The district court's individual questioning was held to be sufficient to uncover any prejudice resulting from the incident. Defense counsel had agreed to the judge's questions and had been given the opportunity to ask follow-up questions. An emotional outburst, but this time from the plaintiff and a witness, was at issue in Griffin v. City of Opa-Locka, 261 F.3d 1295, 86 Fair Empl. Prac. Cas. (BNA) 1254 (11th Cir. 2001), cert. denied, 535 U.S. 1033, 122 S. Ct. 1789, 152 L. Ed. 2d 648, 88 Fair Empl. Prac. Cas. (BNA) 1599 (2002) and cert. denied, 535 U.S. 1034, 122 S. Ct. 1789, 88 Fair Empl. Prac. Cas. (BNA) 1600 (2002). The first incident in question occurred when, before voir dire, the plaintiff, in an emotional state and crying, had walked through the lobby where the jury panel was waiting and where several of the jurors had observed her. The City moved to strike the entire panel, but the district court denied the motion. The denial was upheld on appeal, the Court of Appeals noting that the trial judge had questioned each of the prospective jurors regarding the incident and how it might affect their impartiality. All the jurors selected had indicated that they could ignore the incident and decide the case on the evidence. The second incident involved a witness who broke down and cried on the witness stand. The judge declined to grant a motion for a mistrial, and the Court of Appeals held that, as the judge was in the best position to assess the possible prejudicial effect of the outburst, the decision lay within his discretion, which had not been abused. The judge had given curative instructions and, indeed, had ultimately struck the testimony of the witness. See also Whitehead v. Cowan, 263 F.3d 708 (7th Cir. 2001), cert. denied, 534 U.S. 1116, 122 S. Ct. 927, 151 L. Ed. 2d 890 (2002) (outburst by victim's mother in presence of jury, while unfortunate, did not require a new trial).

§ 7:11 —Examination of juror

Add after first sentence in first paragraph:
The fact that one juror admits to exposure to media accounts of the issues in a case and therefore needs to be questioned about such exposure does not require the trial court to voir dire the entire jury. See U.S. v. Strissel, 920 F.2d 1162, 30 Fed. R. Evid. Serv. 1079 (4th Cir. 1990).

Add after first paragraph:
The nature and extent of the voir dire which must be conducted in a case where there has been extensive and potentially prejudicial pretrial publicity was explored by the United States Supreme Court in Mu'Min v. Virginia, 500 U.S. 415, 111 S. Ct. 1899, 114 L. Ed. 2d 493 (1991). The defendant had previously been convicted of first-degree murder. While on a work detail, he escaped from custody and committed another murder.

This second murder was the subject of considerable coverage in the local press. Included were features about the relatively innocuous circumstances which provoked the killing (reputedly an argument about the price of a carpet), details of Mu'Min's previous history of violence (including the fact that he may have escaped the death penalty for his earlier crime only because the death penalty was not in force in Virginia at that time) and the fact that he had been denied parole on numerous occasions, reports of Mu'Min's confession to the murder, and statements from public officials indicating their belief in Mu'Min's guilt.

At trial, Mu'Min moved for a change in venue and, failing that, individual voir dire of the jurors. Both motions were denied. The trial judge also denied Mu'Min's proposed voir dire questions directed at ascertaining the content of the news reports seen, heard, or read by the jurors. The judge initially questioned the jurors as a group, but after one juror admitted to having formed a belief about the defendant's guilt and was excused for cause, the judge conducted the voir dire in groups of four. When a juror indicated knowledge of the case from outside sources, the judge would ask whether the juror had formed an opinion and whether the juror could nonetheless be impartial. Eight of the members of the jury eventually impaneled had read or heard of the case, although all indicated that they could be fair and impartial.

Mu'Min was convicted and sentenced to death. On appeal, he challenged the voir dire procedures at his trial, with specific emphasis on the failure of the trial judge to question jurors about the "content" of the news items to which they had been exposed. His claim was that the procedures used

§ 7:11   JURY SELECTION: LAW, ART & SCIENCE 2D

violated his Sixth Amendment right to an impartial jury, as well as his due process right to a fair trial. The United States Supreme Court affirmed.

The majority of the Court was willing to concede that "content" questions might prove helpful to a trial judge, but held that they were not constitutionally required. (Because this was a state case, review was limited to whether a constitutional violation had occurred; had the case arose in federal court, the Court could have exercised its supervisory powers.) The Constitution only protects a defendant against a trial which is fundamentally unfair. It does not require individual voir dire or content questioning.

The majority emphasized the wide discretion accorded to the trial judge in the conducting of voir dire. It noted that such discretion made particularly good sense in relation to pretrial publicity, where the local judge was very likely to be aware of the extent and depth of that publicity. A trial judge's determination of impartiality was not to be overturned unless there was "manifest error" (quoting Patton v. Yount, 467 U.S. 1025, 1031, 104 S. Ct. 2885, 81 L. Ed. 2d 847 (1984); Irvin v. Dowd, 366 U.S. 717, 723, 81 S. Ct. 1639, 6 L. Ed. 2d 751, 1 Media L. Rep. (BNA) 1178 (1961)).

Irvin v. Dowd, 366 U.S. 717, 81 S. Ct. 1639, 6 L. Ed. 2d 751, 1 Media L. Rep. (BNA) 1178 (1961), on which Mu'Min relied, was distinguished as involving more extensive, more inflammatory, and more damaging publicity than that involved in Mu'Min's case. Over half of the 430 jurors questioned in *Irvin* were deemed to be biased, and 8 of the 12 jurors finally seated had admitted to an opinion as to guilt. In contrast, far fewer jurors in Mu'Min's case were deemed to be biased, and the eight jurors who were eventually seated who had heard or read something about the case all claimed to have no opinion about the defendant's guilt.

The majority also found misplaced Mu'Min's invocation of the American Bar Association's Standards for Criminal Justice. The ABA standards would require individual voir dire with respect to pretrial publicity when there was a substantial possibility that a juror would be ineligible to serve because of such exposure. The majority said that this standard was more demanding than that required by the Constitution, in that mere exposure to prejudicial publicity, without more, could prove disqualifying. Under the constitutional standard, a judge had further to determine whether the juror had formed such a fixed opinion about the case that he or she could not be impartial. The majority also noted that the ABA standards had not commended themselves to a majority of the courts that had considered them.

Four Justices dissented in *Mu'Min*. Justice Marshall,

joined by Justices Blackmun and Stevens, maintained that without "content" questioning, a trial judge could not realistically assess a juror's impartiality. He advanced three reasons for this position. First, content questioning was needed to determine whether the publicity to which a juror had been exposed reached the level, recognized in Supreme Court precedents, that the juror's assertion of impartiality should not be believed. Second, content questioning was necessary because a juror's own declaration of impartiality inevitably rested on the juror's understanding of the meaning of that term, while a trial judge had to apply a constitutional standard of impartiality. The answers to content questioning helped to ensure that the constitutional standard would be applied. Third, content questioning promoted both accurate fact-finding and accurate assessment of the credibility of a juror who claimed to be able to be impartial. Finally, Justice Marshall argued that the justification for appellate court deference to a trial judge's finding of impartiality, as required under the "manifest error" standard, was the assumption that the trial court had conducted a sufficiently intensive voir dire to make an informed judgment about the juror's impartiality. If the trial judge had in fact failed to probe the juror's impartiality any more than to ask the juror whether he or she could be impartial, the claim for appellate court deference was significantly weakened.

The latter point was also emphasized by Justice Kennedy in a separate dissent. He objected to a mode of proceeding whereby a juror's impartiality could be presumed from the juror's silence. This was possible under the procedure invoked by the trial judge, as jurors were questioned in a group, and attested to their impartiality by remaining silent when the relevant questions were asked of the group. Justice Kennedy pointed out that under such an approach, a judge could not make a meaningful assessment of an individual juror's credibility. He favored individual questioning once a juror admitted to having been exposed to pretrial publicity.

In U.S. v. McVeigh, 153 F.3d 1166, 50 Fed. R. Evid. Serv. 541 (10th Cir. 1998) (disapproved of by, Hooks v. Ward, 184 F.3d 1206 (10th Cir. 1999)), the defendant, charged with the Oklahoma City bombing, claimed that the refusal to allow voir dire questions designed to ascertain whether the pretrial publicity regarding the case would bias the jurors' view of the appropriate sentence for anyone convicted of the crime violated his rights under *Mu'Min*. While prepared to accept that juror impartiality was as important at the penalty phase as at the guilt phase, the Eighth Circuit Court of Appeals found no constitutional violation. The trial judge had stressed the importance of maintaining an open mind, the parties were allowed to ask questions regarding the prospective jurors' ability to set aside the effects of the publicity, and the jurors were instructed that they were to consider only the evidence presented in court and disregard anything read, seen, or heard outside of the courtroom. In addition, there had been a change of venue and a two year gap between the bombing and the trial. Finally, the court observed that the fact that the jurors unanimously had accepted seven of the 13 mitigating factors advanced by the defendant indicated their open-mindedness on the issue of mitigation.

In Britz v. Thieret, 940 F.2d 226 (7th Cir. 1991), the defendant's initial conviction was reversed. His second trial ended in the declaration of a mistrial when the jury was unable to reach a verdict. At issue was the voir dire conducted at the third trial. The judge did not specifically inquire as to juror knowledge of the previous conviction but, rather, asked whether any juror had heard of the case and in what context. The judge also asked, if any juror had heard of the case, whether the knowledge resulted in the formation of an opinion which would affect the juror's ability to decide the case on the evidence presented in court. This approach was inconsistent with the general federal practice of excusing for cause a juror who was aware of the defendant's prior criminal record. The appellate court held, however, that this departure from federal practice by a state trial court did not rise to the level of constitutional error. Mere knowledge of a previous conviction is not a basis for a challenge for cause and the voir dire conducted by the trial court was sufficient to allow the defendant to intelligently exercise his peremptory challenges. Indeed, the court found that the voir dire in the case was identical in most respects to that which the Supreme Court had upheld in *Mu'Min*. *Mu'Min* was applied in Deel v. Jago, 967 F.2d 1079 (6th Cir. 1992), where approximately 50 articles had appeared in the local papers discussing the murder with which the defendant was charged. The court reviewed the articles and concluded that they were neither so numerous nor inflammatory as to render the trial court's refusal to conduct an individualized voir dire fundamentally unfair. *Mu'Min* is analyzed in Supreme Court Review, *Sixth Amendment—The Right to an Impartial Jury: How Extensive Must Voir Dire Be?*, 82 J Crim L & Criminology 920 (1992).

Add after first sentence in third paragraph:
In Spencer v. Murray, 5 F.3d 758 (4th Cir. 1993), the court upheld the peremptory challenge of a juror who had not heard anything about the case, which had been the subject of extensive publicity, accepting as race-neutral the prosecutor's assertion that such lack of knowledge raised concerns about the literacy and educational level of the juror, and whether the juror was an informed citizen.

§ 7:11

Add after third paragraph:

In U.S. v. Bascope-Zurita, 68 F.3d 1057 (8th Cir. 1995), two Bolivians were on trial for drug offenses. During voir dire a juror recounted an incident in which he had witnessed two Bolivians displaying large sums of money in a bar. The juror recalled thinking that the Bolivians were engaged in drug dealing. However, he could not say for sure whether the two defendants were the persons whom he had seen. He also said that he could put the incident out of his mind and render a fair judgment based on the evidence, and that he did not believe that all Bolivians were drug dealers. A challenge for cause to the juror was denied. The Court of Appeals found that this was not an abuse of the trial court's discretion.

Add at end of section:

While a court understandably tends to focus on pretrial publicity involving the case before it, the effects of "generic prejudice" should not be overlooked. The term is used to refer to the negative and oftentimes inflammatory media coverage of a perceived social evil, such as drugs, drunk driving, or child abuse. The effects of this coverage can be quite insidious, even if there is no publicity about the individual case. The jury may be convinced that the social problem is so serious that "somebody ought to be punished," and begin with a strong bias against any defendant charged with the relevant crime. See the remarks of Judge Mikva in *Symposium, Selecting Impartial Juries: Must Ignorance Be a Virtue in Our Search for Justice, Panel One: What Empirical Research Tells Us, and What We Need to Know About Juries and the Quest for Impartiality, Annenberg Washington Program Conference, May 11, 1990*, 40 Am U L Rev 547, 564–65 (1991).

An example of generic prejudice can be seen in a case involving child abuse. This topic has been the subject of much media attention in recent years, and it is predictable that prospective jurors will harbor strong negative feelings against child abusers. Nonetheless, jurors have been allowed to sit where they have indicated they can give the defendant a fair trial. See, e.g., State v. Long, 590 So. 2d 694 (La. Ct. App. 3d Cir. 1991); Burnham v. State, 821 S.W.2d 1 (Tex. App. Fort Worth 1991). It is rarely wise for counsel to ignore the subject, however, and the jurors' exposure and reaction to any relevant publicity should be explored on voir dire for the potential effects of generic prejudice. At the very least the jurors can be sensitized to the fact that the general publicity is not necessarily relevant to the facts of the particular case and, indeed, there should not be an assumption that any defendant charged with child abuse is automati-

§ 7:11

cally guilty. See also U.S. v. Johnson, 990 F.2d 1129 (9th Cir. 1993) (concept of impartiality does not include a requirement of impartiality in respect to the underlying crime). Cf U.S. v. Payne, 944 F.2d 1458, 33 Fed. R. Evid. Serv. 1316 (9th Cir. 1991) (trial judge should direct specific questions as to the jurors' attitudes and feelings towards child abuse). Compare Noltie v. Peterson, 9 F.3d 802 (9th Cir. 1993) (no error in failing to excuse for cause juror who admitted she "might" have some difficulty being fair in a case involving sexual abuse of a young child, but who repeatedly stated that she hoped she would be fair and that she would try to be fair). For a study of how generic prejudice works in the context of drug prosecutions, See Doppelt, *Generic Prejudice: How Drug War Fervor Threatens the Right to a Fair Trial*, 40 Am U L Rev 821 (1991).

Generic publicity need not necessarily be negative. For example, through advertising and sponsorship, corporations strive to create a positive public image. A litigant suing such a corporation should be allowed the leeway in voir dire to explore with jurors the effect of such "image advertising."

§ 7:12 Prior personal experiences

Add after second paragraph:

In Brooks v. Zahn, 170 Ariz. 545, 826 P.2d 1171 (Ct. App. Div. 1 1991), the court held that a registered nurse was not disqualified for that reason alone from serving on a jury in a medical malpractice action. Similarly, the court in U.S. v. Marji, 158 F.3d 60, 49 Fed. R. Evid. Serv. 1522 (2d Cir. 1998) held that there had been no abuse of discretion in the district judge's decision not to dismiss for cause a juror who was a volunteer fireman even though the case involved criminal charges arising from the defendant's alleged scheme to set fire to his business in order to collect on the insurance. The judge had questioned the juror at length and was satisfied that he could serve impartially.

Add after third paragraph:

In Kotler v. American Tobacco Co., 926 F.2d 1217, Prod. Liab. Rep. (CCH) ¶ 12674 (1st Cir. 1990), cert. granted, judgment vacated on other grounds, 505 U.S. 1215, 112 S. Ct. 3019, 120 L. Ed. 2d 891 (1992), plaintiff brought an action against cigarette manufacturers for damages which resulted in her husband's death from lung cancer. The trial judge excused for cause all prospective jurors who smoked. However, one juror was seated who "smoked a couple of cigarettes per week." The trial court ruled that this casual smoking did not make the juror a "smoker" such that she should be excused for cause. On appeal, the trial court's ruling was upheld. In contrast, in Kirk v. Raymark Industries, Inc., 61 F.3d 147, 42 Fed. R. Evid. Serv. 883, 155 A.L.R. Fed. 701 (3d Cir. 1995) the court held in a mesothelioma case that the past personal exposure of a long-term union steward to asbestos, coupled with the fact that he had been the recipient of a significant amount of one-sided literature regarding asbestos and the fact that many of his friends had tested positive for asbestos, justified a challenge for cause.

Add after first sentence in fourth paragraph:
In U.S. v. Hall, 152 F.3d 381, 49 Fed. R. Evid. Serv. 1503 (5th Cir. 1998) (abrogated by, U.S. v. Martinez-Salazar, 528 U.S. 304, 120 S. Ct. 774, 145 L. Ed. 2d 792 (2000)), a capital case, a juror was asked whether she could consider the fact that the defendant had grown up in a dysfunctional, abusive family as a mitigating factor. The juror responded equivocally, noting that her own family was "not exactly perfect . . . and might to a degree be dysfunctional, but that doesn't give me the right to go out and commit violent acts." The court held that, considered in the context of the rest of the voir dire of the juror, this statement was insufficient to find an abuse of discretion in the trial judge's refusal to dismiss the juror for cause.

n. 89.
Add to note 89 after "Nailor":
People v. Powell, 224 Ill. App. 3d 127, 166 Ill. Dec. 631, 586 N.E.2d 589 (1st Dist. 1991) (victim of unsolved felony properly excused in criminal prosecution).

Add to note 89 after "Abbott":
; Amirault v. Fair, 968 F.2d 1404 (1st Cir. 1992) (fact that juror in prosecution for indecent assault, battery, and rape of child had herself been raped 40 years previous did not automatically disqualify juror for bias, where juror claimed to have blocked memory of rape); Golden v. State, 603 So. 2d 2 (Fla. Dist. Ct. App. 3d Dist. 1992) (no error in burglary trial for refusal of challenge for cause to juror who had once been robbed at gunpoint, but who responded affirmatively to question as to whether she would acquit if state failed to prove its case); State v. Nalls, 835 S.W.2d 509 (Mo. Ct. App. E.D. 1992) (no error in refusing to dismiss juror who had been victim of attempted burglary, where juror felt she had been treated fairly by criminal justice system and said she would follow Court's instructions). In Gonzales v. Thomas, 99 F.3d 978 (10th Cir. 1996), the court held that a juror who had been the victim of a "date rape" 25 years previously was not being dishonest in answering no to a voir dire question as to whether she had ever been involved in a similar incident to the one that gave rise to the prosecution for criminal sexual penetration. The juror's experience was distinguishable from the case on which she was sitting for the juror had not been subjected to violence and did not suffer trauma as a result of the incident. The court added that a rape victim is not incapable as a matter of law of being an impartial juror in a rape trial.

In U.S. v. Miguel, 111 F.3d 666 (9th Cir. 1997), the Court of Appeals

§ 7:12   Jury Selection: Law, Art & Science 2d

held that the trial court in a sexual abuse case had not abused its discretion in refusing to excuse for cause two jurors who had indicated that they themselves had been the victims of child molestation and two others who were relatives of victims of child molestation. The trial judge had questioned all four jurors individually and had concluded that they could be fair and impartial. The holding is questionable, given that the psychological trauma experienced by child sex abuse victims is often repressed and as a result may not surface in response to voir dire questioning.

Add to note 89:
See generally Annotation, State v. Shields, 709 S.W.2d 556, 65 A.L.R.4th 739 (Mo. Ct. App. E.D. 1986).

Add after note 89:
In Alexander v. U.S., 512 U.S. 1244, 114 S. Ct. 2761, 129 L. Ed. 2d 876 (1994), it was held that the court had not abused its discretion in a robbery trial in failing to excuse for cause jurors who had themselves been victims of robberies, where the jurors had indicated that they could serve impartially. Citing Ross v. Oklahoma, 487 U.S. 81, 108 S. Ct. 2273, 101 L. Ed. 2d 80 (1988) (discussed in main text) the Court of Appeals also indicated that it was necessary for the defendants to demonstrate that they had been prejudiced by the trial court's failure to honor their challenges for cause, which forced them to expend peremptory challenges to remove the jurors in question.

In U.S. v. Lowe, 145 F.3d 45, 49 Fed. R. Evid. Serv. 687 (1st Cir. 1998), a case involving charges of a sexual nature, the trial court declined to excuse for cause two prospective jurors, one of whom had been sexually molested in the past and the other of whom who had been the victim of an attempted rape 40 years previous. Both jurors maintained that they could be fair and impartial, and the trial judge, after questioning the jurors, had agreed. The Court of Appeals found no abuse of discretion.

n. 90.
Add to note 90:
However, in U.S. v. Badru, 97 F.3d 1471, 45 Fed. R. Evid. Serv. 1026 (D.C. Cir. 1996), the Court of Appeals held that the right to question jurors about their involvement in crime did not extend to questions as to whether any of the jurors' friends had ever been charged with a criminal offense.

In U.S. v. Walker, 99 F.3d 439 (D.C. Cir. 1996) the court held that a juror's failure, in response to a question as to whether he had been accused of a crime other than a traffic offense during the last 10 years, to disclose that he had been acquitted of a misdemeanor nine years and nine months previous (the actual charge had been filed 10 years and six months previous) was not sufficient to justify a new trial under McDonough (discussed in main text § 9:10) (discussed in main text sec.).

§ 7:13 —Prior experiences of family members

Add after first sentence in third paragraph:

Many of the decisions are difficult to reconcile. Compare Chapman v. State, 593 So. 2d 605 (Fla. Dist. Ct. App. 4th Dist. 1992) (trial court erred in failing to excuse for cause juror whose mother had been murdered and who indicated on voir dire that, as a result, she could be more inclined to convict where there was evidence of violence towards the victim); Wilkins v. State, 607 So. 2d 500 (Fla. Dist. Ct. App. 3d Dist. 1992) (juror's statement that he was uncertain whether he would be influenced by fact that his five-year-old niece had been sexually attacked a year earlier and the perpetrator had not been prosecuted created a reasonable doubt as to whether juror could be fair and impartial) with Mooney v. State, 817 S.W.2d 693 (Tex. Crim. App. 1991) (upholding Court's refusal to excuse juror who admitted that members of her family had been murdered in recent years and who vacillated on whether this fact would prejudice her against the defendant, but who finally concluded that she could abide by her juror's oath; Fox v. State, 602 So. 2d 484 (Ala. Crim. App. 1992) (juror whose cousin had been murdered could sit on capital murder case where juror professed impartiality); State v. Nalls, 835 S.W.2d 509 (Mo. Ct. App. E.D. 1992) (no error in refusing to dismiss juror whose uncle had been murdered where juror maintained she could be fair and impartial).

In U.S. v. Gonzalez, 214 F.3d 1109 (9th Cir. 2000), a case involving drugs, the court found implied bias where the ex-husband of a prospective juror had regularly bought and sold drugs, leading to their divorce, and the juror repeatedly equivocated when asked if she could be impartial. See also Fields v. Woodford, 281 F.3d 963 (9th Cir. 2002), opinion amended and superseded, 315 F.3d 1062 (9th Cir. 2002).

In U.S. v. Powell, 226 F.3d 1181, 55 Fed. R. Evid. Serv. 972 (10th Cir. 2000), cert. denied, 531 U.S. 1166, 121 S. Ct. 1128, 148 L. Ed. 2d 995 (2001) the Court of Appeals held that the trial court's rejection of a challenge for cause to a juror whose daughter had been raped was not clearly erroneous in a case where the defendant was charged with kidnapping for sexual gratification, contact, exploitation, and assault. The trial court had found neither actual or implied bias on the part of the juror. The holding is questionable, especially as the juror had apparently wavered before stating she would "really try" to put aside her daughter's experience and be fair. Any analysis that turns on the factual distinctions between what had happened to the juror's daughter and the facts of the case arguably will take insufficient account of the psychological processes that would inevitably affect a person in the juror's situation.

Add to end of section:

§ 7:13

See generally Annotation, State v. Shields, 709 S.W.2d 556, 65 A.L.R.4th 739 (Mo. Ct. App. E.D. 1986).

§ 7:16 Prior knowledge of facts
n. 100.
Add to note 100:

Mere knowledge of relevant scientific testing procedures is not sufficient to disqualify a juror. See State v. Bible, 175 Ariz. 549, 858 P.2d 1152 (1993).

Add after first paragraph:

Retrials following an initial trial ending in a mistrial or a reversal of a conviction on appeal raise obvious issues with respect to prospective jurors' prior knowledge of the case. Curiously, both of these scenarios occurred in Britz v. Thieret, 940 F.2d 226 (7th Cir. 1991). The defendant's initial conviction was reversed on appeal and his second trial ended in the declaration of a mistrial when the jury was unable to reach a verdict. At the third trial, the judge did not specifically inquire as to juror knowledge of the previous conviction. Instead, the judge asked whether any juror had heard of the case and in what context and, if a juror had heard of the case, whether the knowledge resulted in the formation of an opinion which would affect the juror's ability to decide the case on the evidence presented in court. This approach is inconsistent with the general federal practice of excusing for cause a juror who is aware of the defendant's prior criminal record. The appellate court held, however, that this departure from federal practice by a state trial court did not rise to the level of constitutional error. Mere knowledge of a previous conviction is not a basis for a challenge for cause and the voir dire conducted by the trial court was sufficient to allow the defendant to intelligently exercise his peremptory challenges.

Add after fourth paragraph:

Compare U.S. v. Washington, 836 F. Supp. 192 (D. Vt. 1993), aff'd, 48 F.3d 73 (2d Cir. 1995), where the defendant was tried on a federal weapons charge, after having been convicted of murder in a state trial. Although some of the jurors were apparently aware of the state case, this knowledge by itself was held not to justify a challenge for cause. The court did exclude those jurors who knew the outcome of the state case, and ensured itself that those who knew of the state trial but not the verdict could be impartial.

§ 7:17 Prior jury service—Statutes

§ 7:18 —Basis for challenge for cause
n. 110.
Add to note 110:

In U.S. v. Parmley, 108 F.3d 922 (8th Cir. 1997), 18 members of the jury panel in defendant's retrial had been summoned and subjected to voir dire in his previous trial (which ended in a mistrial when the jury was unable to agree on a verdict), but did not serve on the jury. One of the jurors on the second panel had, moreover, discussed the case with a juror on the first panel, and the latter had indicated her belief that the defendant was guilty. The defendant moved to quash the second panel, but the trial court refused and the Court of Appeals held that this was not an abuse of discretion. The mere fact of overlapping venires does not create a presumption of actual bias such as to justify the defendant's motion. As for the juror who had discussed the case with a member of the first panel, the court accepted her claim that she would not be influenced by the discussion and would judge the case on the evidence. Whether or not this was a technically correct holding, it would seem that the better practice would have been to start afresh with jurors who had not been associated with the first case in any way.

n. 112.

Add to note 112:
Johnson v. Schmidt, 83 F.3d 37 (2d Cir. 1996) (same jury may not be used for two unrelated cases brought by prisoner unless fully informed consent is obtained).

n. 113.

Add to note 113:
U.S. v. Garcia, 936 F.2d 648, 33 Fed. R. Evid. Serv. 206 (2d Cir. 1991) (government special agent).

Add after note 113:
The mere fact that jurors have served in previous cases tried by the same prosecutor is not grounds for disqualification in a subsequent case. See U.S. v. Hill, 146 F.3d 337 (6th Cir. 1998).

Add at end of section:
In U.S. v. Foster, 57 F.3d 727 (9th Cir. 1995), on reh'g en banc, 133 F.3d 704 (9th Cir. 1998) cert. granted, judgment vacated on other grounds, the trial court had questioned the jurors about prior jury service but not about prior jury service in drugs cases. The Court of Appeals held that this was not an abuse of discretion.

§ 7:19 —Criminal cases

n. 114.

Add to note 114 after "Farrar":
However, the right to be tried by a jury other than the one which convicted a codefendant can be waived, as occurred in U.S. v. Zarnes, 33 F.3d 1454 (7th Cir. 1994).

n. 116.

Add to note 116:
In U.S. v. Gillis, 942 F.2d 707 (10th Cir. 1991), it was held that it was error for the trial judge to allow jurors who had been on a panel from which a previous jury had been selected to sit on a subsequent jury

§ 7:19

considering related and similar charges against the defendant without determining whether the information to which the jurors might have been exposed as a result of the voir dire in the first trial might prejudice them in the second trial. The danger of prejudice was particularly acute because both trials involved methamphetamine distribution conspiracies, both indictments also charged the use of firearms in connection with the drug trafficking offense, and the two trials were only one month apart. Gillis was applied in Quintero v. Bell, 256 F.3d 409, 2001 FED App. 0205P (6th Cir. 2001), cert. granted, judgment vacated on other grounds, 535 U.S. 1109, 122 S. Ct. 2324, 153 L. Ed. 2d 152 (2002), where the defendant was prosecuted for escape. Seven jurors at his trial had served on a previous jury where his co-escapees were convicted. In these circumstances the court held that the defendant's Sixth Amendment right to an impartial jury was violated. The fact that the jurors claimed that they could be impartial was held under the circumstances not to overcome the presumption of bias. See also U.S. v. Real Property Known and Numbered as Rural Route 1, Box 137-B, Cutler, Ohio, 24 F.3d 845, 1994 FED App. 0166P (6th Cir. 1994) (new trial should not be automatically ordered where juror has served on a case involving the same witnesses or parties absent showing of actual bias arising from previous service). However, the mere fact that members of a jury panel have been questioned as potential jurors in another case having some similarities will not warrant the excusal of the entire panel. Solis v. Walker, 799 F. Supp. 23 (S.D. N.Y. 1992). In U.S. v. Bartelho, 71 F.3d 436, 43 Fed. R. Evid. Serv. 501 (1st Cir. 1995), the indictment in another case, involving the same model of firearm and an identical witness as involved in defendant's case, was inadvertently read to the jury during voir dire. The defendant's motion to discharge the panel on the ground that the jurors might associate him with the other defendant (who faced an unrelated trial on a more serious charge) was denied. On appeal, the court held that the defendant had failed to make a specific showing of bias or prejudice.

Add at end of first paragraph:

The reasoning has also been held not to apply to a subsequent case involving the same defendant but on different charges. See, e.g., Carver v. State, 203 Ga. App. 197, 416 S.E.2d 810 (1992).

n. 119.

Add to note 119:

See also U.S. v. Quesada-Bonilla, 952 F.2d 597 (1st Cir. 1991) (no prejudice in judge's refusal to strike for cause jurors who had served on previous case involving the same judge, the same defense counsel, and similar handwriting issues). In U.S. v. Collazo-Aponte, 216 F.3d 163, 54 Fed. R. Evid. Serv. 1311 (1st Cir. 2000), cert. granted in part, judgment vacated on other grounds, 532 U.S. 1036, 121 S. Ct. 1996, 149 L. Ed. 2d 1000 (2001), a federal drug trial, the court held that the impartiality of a juror was not tainted by the fact that the juror had previously served as a juror in an unrelated drug case involving one of the government witnesses. The judge instructed the juror to disregard his previous jury experience in considering the present case and not to discuss the previous case with the other jurors.

n. 123.

Add to note 123:

In some jurisdictions jurors are selected to hear multiple cases. While acknowledging that in some cases such a mode of proceeding might prejudice a defendant, the court in U.S. v. Walling, 974 F.2d 140 (10th Cir. 1992) upheld the general practice. While the mass voir dire of a jury which will serve on more than one trial is not per se improper, a defendant has the right to request a supplemental voir dire if there is reason to believe that interim service may have prejudiced the jurors. See U.S. v. Hartsfield, 976 F.2d 1349, 36 Fed. R. Evid. Serv. 1237 (10th Cir. 1992).

§ 7:21 Acquaintance with parties, witnesses, or attorneys

Add to first paragraph:

Occasionally, the personal relationship between jurors is an issue. If the goal is to have each juror reach an independent judgment on the evidence, it is arguably unwise to have two related jurors, one of whom is likely to have great influence over the other, on the jury. Nonetheless, it has been held that where neither juror manifests bias, there are no grounds for a challenge for cause. Moss v. Lockhart, 971 F.2d 77 (8th Cir. 1992) (no error in failing to strike for cause a venireman whose mother had already been impaneled as a juror).

§ 7:22 —Personal or social relationships generally

n. 127.

Add to note 127:

; Bailey v. Board of County Com'rs of Alachua County, Fla., 956 F.2d 1112 (11th Cir. 1992).

n. 128.

Add to note 128:

In U.S. v. Long, 301 F.3d 1095 (9th Cir. 2002), cert. denied, 123 S. Ct. 1314, 154 L. Ed. 2d 1069 (U.S. 2003), the issue was whether to excuse for cause two jurors who had accused each other of misconduct consisting of discussing the case with family members and predetermining the defendant's guilt/innocence. The district court conducted an in camera interview with one of the jurors, and subsequently informed the parties of the results. The judge also questioned both jurors in chambers with the attorneys, but not the defendant, present. Defense counsel eventually requested that both jurors remain on the jury because of concerns with the alternates. The trial judge found that the jurors could keep an open mind and could deliberate with each other. The Court of Appeals found that this was not an abuse of the judge's discretion.

n. 129.

Add to note 129:

In Andrews v. Collins, 21 F.3d 612 (5th Cir. 1994), the court held that the presence on the jury panel of the father-in-law of the homicide victim's grandson did not deprive the defendant of his right to an impartial jury. The juror's daughter's relationship with the grandson had ended prior to the trial and the grandson was deceased. Furthermore, there was nothing to indicate that the relationship had in any way affected the fairness of the proceedings. In U.S. v. McLeod, 53 F.3d 322 (11th Cir. 1995), a juror stated that she had known the family of the victim for 15 years, but the

§ 7:22   JURY SELECTION: LAW, ART & SCIENCE 2D

victim himself was only an acquaintance whom she had not seen in five years. The juror asserted that she could be fair to both sides. In light of this evidence, the district court denied a challenge for cause and the Court of Appeals held that the district court had not abused its discretion. See also U.S. v. Davis, 306 F.3d 398, 2002 FED App. 0329P (6th Cir. 2002), cert. denied, 123 S. Ct. 1290, 154 L. Ed. 2d 1054 (U.S. 2003) (fact juror knew the mother of a government witness, without more, did not rise to the level of prejudice necessary for declaring a mistrial).

In contrast, the court in Wolfe v. Brigano, 232 F.3d 499, 2000 FED App. 0394P (6th Cir. 2000), held that where a juror had admitted that she and her husband were close friends of the victim's parents, and that her husband had discussed the killing of the victim with the parents, it was an abuse of the trial judge's discretion to deny a challenge for cause to the juror, particularly where the juror had stated that it was hard for her to say whether she would be influenced by her relationship with the parents.

n. 130.

Add to note 130:

For a court to exclude a prospective juror with knowledge of one of the parties without more closely probing the nature of the relationship and whether it will affect the juror's impartiality may constitute error. In U.S. v. Calabrese, 942 F.2d 218 (3d Cir. 1991), the trial judge sent a form letter and questionnaire to approximately 300 prospective jurors. One of the questions asked whether the juror knew any of the defendants, whose names and addresses were listed. Only a yes/no answer was called for and no explanations were sought. All jurors who answered 'yes' were excused from jury service by the judge. The defendants challenged the propriety of the exclusion and the appellate court held that it violated the Jury Selection and Service Act. Exclusion based on the mere fact of knowledge of a defendant is not justified; nor, added the court in dicta, would it be an acceptable basis for a challenge for cause. The court further found that the violation was a substantial one under the terms of the act and the defendants were entitled to relief regardless of actual prejudice. Thus, the court vacated the defendants' convictions and ordered a new trial. But compare U.S. v. Shea, 211 F.3d 658, 53 Fed. R. Evid. Serv. 1353 (1st Cir. 2000), cert. denied, 531 U.S. 1154, 121 S. Ct. 1101, 148 L. Ed. 2d 973 (2001) and cert. denied, 531 U.S. 1154, 121 S. Ct. 1102, 148 L. Ed. 2d 973 (2001) (upholding dismissal of prospective jurors who were acquainted with counsel).

n. 131.

Add to note 131:

People v. Leger, 149 Ill. 2d 355, 173 Ill. Dec. 612, 597 N.E.2d 586 (1992) (no error in refusing to excuse for cause juror who maintained she could be impartial in case where juror and husband had socialized with murder victim's husband some 10 years previous and juror's daughter was acquainted with victim's daughter); Marshall v. State, 598 So. 2d 14 (Ala. Crim. App. 1991) (challenge for cause to juror employed as maid by rape victim's family who knew victim personally and to another juror who knew victim's family held properly denied where jurors indicated that they could be fair and impartial); U.S. v. Harris, 293 F.3d 970, 2002 FED App. 0207P (6th Cir. 2002), cert. denied, 537 U.S. 1073, 123 S. Ct. 672, 154 L. Ed. 2d 568 (2002) (district court did not err in not excluding for cause a juror who worked with the husband of an expert witness in the case when juror maintained he could be impartial).

Add at end of second paragraph:

CHALLENGES FOR CAUSE § 7:22

Often the court will ask whether the juror can be fair and impartial despite the relationship and decide the case on the evidence. As a practical matter, an affirmative answer will generally be forthcoming. Few jurors will want to concede that they cannot be impartial. It is questionable whether such an answer should be taken at face value. Expressing a healthy skepticism in this regard, the court in Montgomery v. Com., 819 S.W.2d 713 (Ky. 1991) stated that jurors with close personal relationships with parties, counsel, or witnesses could not be rehabilitated by some "magic question" as to whether they would be able to set aside their personal knowledge, views, sentiments, and opinions and decide the case solely on the evidence. The court in Thomas v. Com., 864 S.W.2d 252 (Ky. 1993), agreed, adding that the statement of jurors who had already indicated a disqualifying bias that they would accept the responsibility to decide the case impartially was not determinative. What mattered in ruling on the challenge for cause was the probability of prejudice. See also Casenote, *Friends and Foes in the Jury Box: Walls v. Kim and the Mission to Stop Improper Juror Rehabilitation,* 53 Mercer L. Rev. 929 (2002) where the author argues that judges should not take at face value a juror's promise to be impartial when there is evidence to the contrary for the judge has a duty to ensure the selection of a fair and impartial jury. The problem is compounded when the judge's decisions are reviewed under an "abuse of discretion" standard. The Casenote examines the decision in Walls v. Kim, 250 Ga. App. 259, 549 S.E.2d 797 (2001), cert. granted, (Jan. 10, 2002) and judgment aff'd, 275 Ga. 177, 563 S.E.2d 847 (2002) in the course of which the court criticizes the leeway generally given to rehabilitating biased jurors.

n. 132.

Add to note 132:

Williams v. Com., 14 Va. App. 208, 415 S.E.2d 856 (1992) (error to deny challenge to juror who gave eulogy at victim's funeral; juror who had worked alongside victim for three or four months; juror who, having read of "horrible" death which befell victim, had formed an impression regarding defendant's guilt; and juror so closely associated with defendant's family that it would have "bothered" him to sit on the case).

Add at end of third paragraph:

A general social relationship to members of the community was held to disqualify a juror in State v. Esposito, 223 Conn. 299, 613 A.2d 242 (1992). The juror had stated on voir dire that acquitting the defendant would put her in an awkward position in her neighborhood where the crimes would remain unsolved. The court held that this constituted a personal stake in the outcome of the case, and raised a conclusive presumption of bias. Accordingly, the trial court was held to have abused its discretion in overruling a challenge for cause to the juror.

§ 7:23 —Relationship with witness

n. 136.
Add to note 136:
See, e.g., State v. Gesch, 167 Wis. 2d 660, 482 N.W.2d 99 (1992) (juror who was brother of state's only police witness held biased as a matter of law). In an unusual case, Frost v. U.S., 525 U.S. 810, 119 S. Ct. 40, 142 L. Ed. 2d 32 (1998), a juror was placed in a position where it was alleged he might have to be a witness. The juror had overheard a remark by a witness ("You all take care of me") that the witness subsequently denied making. The argument advanced was that the juror in effect would become a witness to the witness's credibility, and that such a role might compromise the juror's impartiality. Neither the trial court nor the Court of Appeals was persuaded.

n. 138.
Add to note 138:
U.S. v. Humphrey, 34 F.3d 551 (7th Cir. 1994) (no reversible error in failing to excuse for cause juror whose husband was cousin of witness where juror stated that relationship did not affect her assessment of witness's credibility and defendant failed to demonstrate prejudice).

In U.S. v. Rhodes, 177 F.3d 963 (11th Cir. 1999), it was held that the trial court had not abused its discretion in refusing to strike for cause a juror who was a cousin of a government witness. The juror had stated that her cousin had a good memory and would remember "exactly" what had happened, that she assumed that her cousin would testify truthfully, and that she would feel awkward in the future if she did not believe her cousin. The court then questioned the juror and elicited from her the response that she could put to one side her relationship with the witness and assess her testimony fairly and impartially. The trial judge declined to excuse the juror for cause and the Court of Appeals held that this was not an abuse of discretion. The decision is highly dubious given the obvious respect that the juror had for her cousin and her professed unwillingness not to believe her.

In U.S. v. Medina, 161 F.3d 867 (5th Cir. 1998), on the last day of the trial, a juror realized that one of the witnesses testifying in the defendant's behalf, as well as the defendant, was a former high school classmate of his. The district court and defense counsel proceeded to examine the witness, who stated that when he first became aware of the relationship, he feared retaliation, but that his concerns had dissipated and would not affect his decision. The appellate court found no abuse of discretion in the district judge's decision to deny defendants' request to excuse the juror.

Add after second sentence in fourth paragraph:
In Enoch v. Gramley, 70 F.3d 1490 (7th Cir. 1995), a juror told the court after she had been sworn that she may have met one of the prosecution's witnesses several years previous, but that, even if she had, she could be fair and impartial. The defendant's challenge for cause to the juror was denied and the Court of Appeals held that this was not error.

CHALLENGES FOR CAUSE § 7:25

n. 143.

Add to note 143:

See also Morris v. Spencer, 826 S.W.2d 10 (Mo. Ct. App. W.D. 1992) (no abuse of discretion in refusal to excuse jurors who had been patients of defendant physician). Compare Dixon v. Hardey, 591 So. 2d 3 (Ala. 1991) (abrogated by, Bethea v. Springhill Memorial Hosp., 833 So. 2d 1 (Ala. 2002)) (doctor-patient relationship between juror and defendant physician constitutes prima facie evidence of prejudice).

§ 7:25 —Business or professional relationship with party

Add after first sentence in first paragraph:

Sometimes a business relationship will not come to light until after voir dire is completed. U.S. v. Herndon, 156 F.3d 629, 49 Fed. R. Evid. Serv. 1551, 1998 FED App. 0274P (6th Cir. 1998) provides an extreme example. In this case a juror remembered during deliberations that he may have had prior business dealings with the defendant. Defense counsel's request to interview the witness for possible bias was rejected by the trial court. On appeal it was held that the relationship was an "extraneous" (as opposed to an internal) influence that might have tainted the deliberations with information not subject to the procedural safeguards of the trial. The appellate court stated that under the circumstances the trial court had a duty to investigate the allegation of juror partiality and that the court had abused its discretion in denying the defendant a meaningful opportunity to prove actual bias. Allowing the defendant to "make a record" for the purpose of appeal was held not sufficient to discharge the trial court's obligation. The conviction and sentence were vacated and the case was remanded for a hearing in which the defendant would be given the opportunity to prove actual bias.

n. 156.

Add to note 156:

But compare Nathan v. Boeing Co., 116 F.3d 422, 12 I.E.R. Cas. (BNA) 1783, 47 Fed. R. Evid. Serv. 648 (9th Cir. 1997), holding that the trial court in a retaliatory discharge suit did not abuse its discretion in failing to remove two employees of the company. The court had assured itself that the jurors could decide the case fairly and without fear of retaliation. The result seems questionable, for the very possibility that there might be merit in the plaintiff's claims might not only make employees of the defendant afraid to rule against the company (lest they themselves be the object of a retaliatory discharge) but also apprehensive about giving voice to their own fears of possible retaliation (lest they be perceived as disloyal). The court suggested that the result might have been different if the employees had also owned stock in the company, but the plaintiff had failed to inquire on this point.

Add after second sentence in fourth paragraph:

§ 7:25　　　　　Jury Selection: Law, Art & Science 2d

Compare Rine By and Through Rine v. Irisari, 187 W. Va. 550, 420 S.E.2d 541 (1992) (trial judge abused discretion in medical malpractice suit in refusing to strike juror employed as nurse at defendant hospital). In Wolfe v. Brigano, 232 F.3d 499, 2000 FED App. 0394P (6th Cir. 2000), the court held in a criminal case that where a juror had an ongoing business relationship with the victim's parents and had spoken to and listened to the parents, it was an abuse of the trial judge's discretion to deny a for-cause challenge to the juror, particularly where the juror had stated that he did not think that he could be a fair and impartial juror.

n. 162.

Add to note 162:

In U.S. v. Zichettello, 208 F.3d 72 (2d Cir. 2000), cert. denied, 531 U.S. 1143, 121 S. Ct. 1077, 148 L. Ed. 2d 954 (2001), the defendants were charged with conspiring to violate the Racketeer Influenced and Corrupt Organizations Act (R.I.C.O.) and related offenses. The labor union for the city's transit police officers was implicated, but the trial court refused to excuse a juror who managed a portfolio that included the pension fund for the city's police department. On these facts, the Court of Appeals found no abuse of the trial judge's discretion. The court noted that the trial judge had made a determination that the juror could be impartial.

n. 163.

Add to note 163:
U.S. v. Tibesar, 894 F.2d 317 (8th Cir. 1990).

n. 167.

Add to note 167:
Accord U.S. v. Maseratti, 1 F.3d 330 (5th Cir. 1993).

§ 7:28　—Business or professional relationship with attorney in absence of statute

n. 190.

Add to note 190:

See also Allread v. State, 582 N.E.2d 899 (Ind. Ct. App. 2d Dist. 1991) (fact defendant's counsel was representing juror's wife did not establish prejudice of juror).

n. 198.

Add to note 198:

State v. Cox, 826 P.2d 656 (Utah Ct. App. 1992) (abuse of discretion to fail to remove for cause juror who was client of prosecuting attorney and brother-in-law of chief of police). See also Canty v. State, 597 So. 2d 927 (Fla. Dist. Ct. App. 3d Dist. 1992) (juror who had been burglarized should have been excused where defendant's attorney had represented perpetrator in burglary prosecution); U.S. v. McCarthy, 961 F.2d 972, 35 Fed. R. Evid. Serv. 478 (1st Cir. 1992) (upholding trial court's excusal for cause of juror whose brother had been prosecuted by the prosecutor in the case). In Peoples Bank of Pratt v. Integral Ins. Co., 251 Kan. 809, 840 P.2d 503 (1992), the court indicated that the lawyer or law firm involved had an affirmative obligation to disclose the fact that it was actively representing a prospective juror in civil litigation. In such circumstances,

Challenges for Cause § 7:31

continued the court, actual prejudice need not be shown. U.S. v. Barone, 114 F.3d 1284, 47 Fed. R. Evid. Serv. 211 (1st Cir. 1997) (no abuse of discretion in dismissing juror whose cousin had been represented by the defendant's attorney, even though relevant facts only came to light during deliberation and dismissal led to verdict returned by 11 jurors).

Add at end of fifth paragraph:
An extension of this approach to jurors whose relatives work for one of the lawyers in the case was made in Nichols v. Thomas, 788 F. Supp. 570 (N.D. Ga. 1992) (trial court should not have refused to dismiss for cause juror who was husband of prosecutor's volunteer investigator; work of juror's wife directly involved subject criminal prosecution and juror was thus impliedly biased).

§ 7:30 —Family relationship to attorney or witness

Add after second sentence in first paragraph:
For example, in Thomas v. Com., 864 S.W.2d 252 (Ky. 1993), the court held that a juror should have been struck for cause when it was revealed that the juror's wife was a first cousin to the prosecuting attorney. The court declined to draw a distinction between relationships by blood and relationships by affinity. In either situation the relationship raised a question about the juror's ability to be impartial.

Add at end of section:
Compare U.S. v. Baker, 10 F.3d 1374, 38 Fed. R. Evid. Serv. 638 (9th Cir. 1993), as amended, (Dec. 13, 1993) and (overruled on other grounds by, U.S. v. Nordby, 225 F.3d 1053 (9th Cir. 2000)) (no requirement of disclosure of every possible government witness).

§ 7:31 —Family relationship to interested or biased person

Add at end of section:
In Tidemann v. Nadler Golf Car Sales, Inc., 224 F.3d 719, 47 Fed. R. Serv. 3d 810 (7th Cir. 2000), a civil case, the Court of Appeals held that a juror who owned a golf car, whose manufacturer she did not know, was not sufficiently biased to warrant the trial court's excusing the juror for cause in a case where an operator of a reconditioned golf car had sued, among others, the seller and reconditioner of the car for injuries sustained when the car had allegedly lurched forward and crashed.

In Bracy v. Gramley, 81 F.3d 684 (7th Cir. 1996), judgment rev'd on other grounds, 520 U.S. 899, 117 S. Ct. 1793, 138 L. Ed. 2d 97 (1997) and cert. granted, judgment vacated on other grounds, 520 U.S. 1272, 117 S. Ct. 2450, 138 L. Ed.

2d 209 (1997), the defendant's attorney was aware that one of the jurors was the wife of a state court judge who had once sentenced the defendant for armed robbery. The attorney, however, did not challenge the juror. This arguable error in judgment was compounded when the lawyer revealed to the jury that the juror's husband (whom he identified by name) had given the defendant the most severe sentence that he had ever received. Thus, the lawyer inadvertently reminded the juror of her husband's past dealing with the defendant, a fact which she might well not have been aware of or might have forgotten. Nonetheless, the Court of Appeals held that this reasoning was too speculative to support appellant's claim of ineffective assistance of counsel.

§ 7:32 Pecuniary interest
n. 221.
  Add to note 221:
  Getter v. Wal-Mart Stores, Inc., 66 F.3d 1119, 43 Fed. R. Evid. Serv. 94 (10th Cir. 1995) (error to reject challenge for cause to juror who owned stock in defendant company and whose wife was employed by defendant).

Add after first sentence in third paragraph:
An example is provided by Vasey v. Martin Marietta Corp., 29 F.3d 1460, 65 Fair Empl. Prac. Cas. (BNA) 663, 65 Empl. Prac. Dec. (CCH) ¶ 43283, 128 Lab. Cas. (CCH) ¶ 57709, 40 Fed. R. Evid. Serv. 1333 (10th Cir. 1994). A prospective juror who was an employee of a company which did consulting work for the defendant was challenged for cause as having a pecuniary interest in the outcome of the case. The challenge was rejected and the plaintiff exercised a peremptory challenge against the juror. The Court of Appeals held that the Court's rejection of the challenge for cause was correct. The juror's financial interest was held to be too remote and indirect to warrant a presumption of bias, particularly in light of the juror's assurances to the court that he could be impartial. The Court of Appeals drew a distinction between the case at bar and those such as Gladhill v. General Motors Corp., 743 F.2d 1049, 16 Fed. R. Evid. Serv. 967 (4th Cir. 1984) (stockholder in corporation which is party to lawsuit held incompetent to serve on jury) and Francone v. Southern Pac. Co., 145 F.2d 732 (C.C.A. 5th Cir. 1944) (employee of party to lawsuit presumptively incompetent to serve on jury) where the juror had a direct financial interest in the outcome.

§ 7:33 Connection with insurance company
n. 228.
  Add to note 228:

See generally Calnan, *The Admissibility of Insurance Questions during voir dire: A Critical Survey of Federal Approaches and Proposals for Change*, 44 Rutgers L Rev 241 (1992).

n. 236.

Add to note 236:

See generally Annotation, Prospective juror's connection with defendant's insurance company as ground for challenge for cause, 9 A.L.R. 5th 102.

n. 237.

Add to note 237:

Where prospective jurors had provided information regarding their occupations, it was held improper to ask on voir dire whether any of them were employed in the insurance business. Harner v. Dougherty Funeral Home, Inc., 752 F. Supp. 690 (E.D. Pa. 1990).

§ 7:34 Insurance company advertising

Add after note 250:

In Smith v. Vicorp, Inc., 107 F.3d 816, 37 Fed. R. Serv. 3d 145 (10th Cir. 1997), it was held that there had been no abuse in the trial court's not questioning the jurors specifically about "tort reform bias" (a code phrase for a bias against awarding large damages because of the perceived detrimental effect on the availability and cost of insurance). The court had asked general questions on the subject, and the appellant had not shown that she had been in any way prejudiced by the Court's failure to ask the specific questions requested.

Add before last paragraph:

State law in Utah requires a trial court to afford a plaintiff the opportunity to probe prospective jurors as to possible "tort reform bias" (a code phrase for a bias against awarding large damages because of the perceived detrimental effect on the availability and cost of insurance). See Barrett v. Peterson, 868 P.2d 96 (Utah Ct. App. 1993). In Smith v. Vicorp, Inc., 107 F.3d 816, 37 Fed. R. Serv. 3d 145 (10th Cir. 1997), the Court of Appeals declined to adopt the state court rule.

At end of last paragraph in section:

See generally Annotation, Propriety of inquiry on voir dire as to juror's attitude toward, or acquaintance with literature dealing with, amount of damage awards, 63 A.L.R. 5th 285.

§ 7:38 Prejudice—Labor unions

§ 7:39 —Intoxicants and gambling

n. 268.

Add to note 268 after "Thiesen"

§ 7:39

U.S. v. Gonzalez-Balderas, 11 F.3d 1218 (5th Cir. 1994) (juror's past conviction for narcotics offense posed substantial potential for bias in trial of narcotics trafficker and justified dismissal for cause). But compare U.S. v. Chandler, 996 F.2d 1073, 39 Fed. R. Evid. Serv. 304 (11th Cir. 1993) (fact that juror had son-in-law in jail for conviction of marijuana offense did not establish bias in case involving drug prosecution). In Davis v. Executive Director of Dept. of Corrections, 100 F.3d 750 (10th Cir. 1996), a capital case, the court held that a juror who stated that he would deem the fact that the defendant's crime was alcohol-related to be a mitigating factor that would outweigh any aggravating factors was properly excused The court in McQueen v. Scroggy, 99 F.3d 1302, 35 Fed. R. Serv. 3d 1211, 1996 FED App. 0349P (6th Cir. 1996) avoided this problem by rejecting voir dire questions that inquired whether jurors thought that the use of drugs or alcohol could mitigate punishment in a death penalty case.

n. 269.

Add to note 269 after "State":
People v. Lanter, 230 Ill. App. 3d 72, 172 Ill. Dec. 147, 595 N.E.2d 210 (4th Dist. 1992);

n. 270.

Add to note 270:
State v. Gleason, 65 Ohio App. 3d 206, 583 N.E.2d 975 (1st Dist. Hamilton County 1989) (in trial for driving under the influence, court did not abuse its discretion in refusing to dismiss jurors who expressed the opinion that it was wrong to drink and drive, where jurors also stated that they were prepared to acquit if they believed that defendant's ability to operate his vehicle was not appreciably impaired by the alcohol he had consumed).

n. 271.

Add to note 271:
It was held in McQueen v. Scroggy, 99 F.3d 1302, 35 Fed. R. Serv. 3d 1211, 1996 FED App. 0349P (6th Cir. 1996), a death penalty case, that the trial judge had committed no error in not allowing voir dire questions as to whether jurors agreed that the use of drugs or alcohol could mitigate punishment.

Add at end of section:
A bias in favor of intoxicants may also form the basis of a proper dismissal for cause. See e.g., U.S. v. McCarthy, 961 F.2d 972, 35 Fed. R. Evid. Serv. 478 (1st Cir. 1992) (juror's statement that he favored the legalization of drugs held sufficient to justify the Court's excusal of the juror for cause).

§ 7:40 —Religion

n. 276.

Add to note 276:
In Society of Separationists, Inc. v. Herman, 939 F.2d 1207 (5th Cir. 1991), on reh'g, 959 F.2d 1283 (5th Cir. 1992), an atheist refused to both take the required oath or to affirm, the juror explaining that in her opinion an affirmation was just as religious as an oath. The judge jailed her for contempt and she subsequently brought suit under 42 U.S.C.A. § 1983, claiming a violation of her rights under the free exercise clause of the Constitution. The Court of Appeals upheld her claim and granted declara-

CHALLENGES FOR CAUSE § 7:40

tory relief. In the future, a judge faced with a similar situation will either have to allow the individual to withdraw from jury duty without penalty or somehow attempt to accommodate the juror's constitutionally protected beliefs. This might be accomplished by permitting an alternative form of avowal that both satisfies the juror's religious scruples and the requirements of the judicial system. Only if the juror refuses to make this religion-neutral avowal could the judge impose sanction. It is not the judge's role, in any event, to attempt to evaluate the merit of the religious belief, as long as it is sincerely held and not so bizarre or nonreligious in character so as not to come within the ambit of the free exercise clause.

n. 277.
Add to note 277:

See also U.S. v. Alarape, 969 F.2d 349 (7th Cir. 1992) (trial judge served the interest of justice by declining to ask jurors questions about religion where it was not an issue in the case). If, however, the juror's religious beliefs will frustrate the carrying out of the obligations of jury duty, the juror may have to be excused. In U.S. v. Joseph, 892 F.2d 118 (D.C. Cir. 1989), it was held that the trial court did not abuse its discretion in excusing a juror who indicated that he would follow the instructions of the Lord rather than those of the judge if the juror perceived a conflict between the two. Similarly, in U.S. v. Geffrard, 87 F.3d 448 (11th Cir. 1996), one of the jurors belonged to an obscure religion (Swedenborgianism), the effect of whose doctrines would not allow the juror to follow the judge's instructions. The issue came to light during deliberations and the judge decided to dismiss the juror and accept a verdict of the remaining 11. The court of appeal held that this method of proceeding was permissible under Fed. R. Crim. P. 23(b), and was within the judge's discretion. The court held that, under the circumstances, the judge had not abused that discretion because the juror's religious beliefs prevented her from being able to apply the law. See also U.S. v. Burrous, 147 F.3d 111 (2d Cir. 1998) (trial court may remove juror who indicates during deliberation that he is unable to render a verdict because of a personal religious objection).

n. 279.
Add to note 279:

See also Congregation of the Passion, Holy Cross Province v. Touche Ross & Co., 224 Ill. App. 3d 559, 166 Ill. Dec. 642, 586 N.E.2d 600 (1st Dist. 1991), judgment aff'd, 159 Ill. 2d 137, 201 Ill. Dec. 71, 636 N.E.2d 503 (1994) (denial of supplemental voir dire questions concerning jurors' religious affiliations, contributions, and attitudes was not error where court did not preclude questioning regarding membership in and employment by religious organizations and orders, and questioning regarding weight jurors would give to the testimony of religious authorities); U.S. v. Millar, 79 F.3d 338 (2d Cir. 1996) (district court's voir dire inquiry into potential religious prejudice was not inappropriate where accused was a priest).

n. 283.
Add to note 283:

In U.S. v. Salameh, 152 F.3d 88, 50 Fed. R. Evid. Serv. 602 (2d Cir. 1998), the defendant argued that he had been denied a fair trial because the trial judge had not asked sufficiently probing questions regarding the jurors' bias towards Muslims, Arabs and Islamic Fundamentalists. The judge had divided jury selection into three stages. In the first the judge had addressed jurors in groups of 50, asking general questions and excusing those jurors who expressed bias against the defendants or hesitancy about serving in the case. In the second stage, the judge had randomly divided the jurors into five groups of 12, asking each group a series of questions designed to uncover religious or ethnic prejudice. Again, jurors who expressed bias were excused. In the final stage, the judge questioned each of the remaining jurors individually, with counsel present. More specific questions about Muslims and religion were asked. Following this third stage, the parties were allowed to make, first, challenges for cause, and then, peremptory challenges. The Second Circuit Court of Appeals ruled that although the trial judge had not used the defendant's proposed questions verbatim, his inquiry was proper, thorough, and not an abuse of discretion.

§ 7:41 —Race generally

Add after first paragraph:

In State v. Varner, 643 N.W.2d 298 (Minn. 2002) racial bias was improperly introduced into the proceedings by a chance remark from one juror to other jurors during a break in a drug and firearm prosecution. The juror had observed that, in his experience, "if you were to walk down that street [in the area of the alleged crime] being a white person and if you were not either beat up or robbed, it was considered a miracle." The Minnesota Supreme Court held that the remark raised serious questions of possible prejudice to the defendant and obligated the trial judge to grant the defendant's request to question all of the jurors about their possible exposure to the comment.

A judge, when conducting voir dire, must be careful not to unwittingly inject inappropriate racial issues into the trial Tyus v. Urban Search Management, 102 F.3d 256, 45 Fed. R. Evid. Serv. 1428 (7th Cir. 1996) involved alleged racially discriminatory advertising by an apartment complex. On voir dire the trial judge asked whether any of the jurors lived in public housing, and, if so, the racial composition of that housing. The court of appeal stated that the judge's questions intimated that racial problems arose from the presence of blacks in public housing and therefore went beyond the permissible limits of voir dire. But compare U.S. v. Van Chase, 137 F.3d 579, 48 Fed. R. Evid. Serv. 1180 (8th Cir. 1998) (judge's comments designed to alert jurors to possible bias against Native Americans did not constitute plain error). In U.S. v. Cordova, 157 F.3d 587, 50 Fed. R. Evid. Serv. 263 (8th Cir. 1998) the court counseled that in making an inquiry about racial prejudice, a trial judge must take care not only to admonish against such bias, but also not to overemphasize race. In this case the defendants' proposed voir dire question on racial bias was held to have invited the judge to comment on the issue. The judge did so, acknowledging that while there might be some individuals who would

Challenges for Cause § 7:42

infer guilt in part based on race, any such inference was inappropriate and unfair to the defendants. The appellate court found that this comment was not an abuse of discretion and did not deprive the defendants of a fair trial.

§ 7:42 —Supreme Court development on race prejudice

n. 296.
Add to note 296:

See also U.S. v. Brown, 938 F.2d 1482, 33 Fed. R. Evid. Serv. 790 (1st Cir. 1991) (mere fact that defendant was black and all government's witnesses, as well as all jurors, were white did not require judge to conduct voir dire on issue of racial prejudice, even if such questioning might have been advisable).

In Goins v. Angelone, 226 F.3d 312 (4th Cir. 2000) (abrogated by, Bell v. Jarvis, 236 F.3d 149 (4th Cir. 2000)), the trial court refused to ask two race-related questions proposed by the defendant: (1) "Have you ever experienced fear of a person of another race? If so, what were the circumstances?" and (2) "Do you think that African-Americans are more likely to commit crimes than whites? If so, why? " The Court of Appeals was required to determine whether there were "special circumstances" to the case, comparable to those described in *Ristaino v. Ross*, which would mandate an inquiry into racial prejudice during voir dire. The only "special circumstance" that the defendant could point to, however, was the fact that he was a black man who was about to be tried by a predominantly white jury. This was clearly not enough, even given that the defendant was on trial for a capital crime, where the risk of an improper sentence also had to be considered under the Supreme Court's decision in *Turner v. Murray* (see main text). In the case before the court, both the defendant and his victim were of the same race, the crime was not racially motivated, and there was no racial dimension to the defense. In short, race was not an element in the case except for the different race of the defendant and the jurors.

In U.S. v. Montenegro, 231 F.3d 389 (7th Cir. 2000), the defendants sought to extend the logic of *Ristaino v. Ross* to prejudice based on foreign citizenship. The Court of Appeals noted that *Ristaino v. Ross* was triggered by a request for voir dire on race, and that no such request had been made by the defendants in the case. The judge was under no obligation to raise the issue sua sponte. The court added that the wiser course generally is to ask questions designed to identify racial prejudice when so requested by a defendant, noting that the U.S. Supreme Court had adopted this position under its supervisory authority over the federal courts. The Court of Appeals did not pursue this nonconstitutional line of analysis, however, as the trial had taken place in a state rather than a federal court.

Add after third full paragraph:

In U.S. v. Borders, 270 F.3d 1180 (8th Cir. 2001) the Court of Appeals stated that even in a case where a nonviolent, victimless crime was charged, and thus inquiry into possible racial or ethnic prejudice was not constitutionally mandated, it was better to inquire into the matter of such prejudice when the defendant had so requested in order to avoid the

§ 7:42   Jury Selection: Law, Art & Science 2d

appearance of injustice. In this nonconstitutional context, the failure to honor a request by the defendant for such an inquiry could amount to reversible error if the circumstances of the case indicated that there was a reasonable possibility that racial or ethnic prejudice might have influenced the jury. In its supervisory role, an appellate court should examine what steps a trial court that had rejected the defendant's request had taken to ensure that racial or ethnic prejudice was not present. The trial court in the case was found to have satisfied its responsibility in this regard and the mere fact that the defendant was black and the jury all-white did not warrant the finding of a constitutional violation.

Add after first clause in second sentence in fourth paragraph:
But see Com. v. Gray, 415 Pa. Super. 77, 608 A.2d 534 (1992) (defendant accused of interracial crime is entitled to have prospective jurors informed of race of victim and questioned on issue of racial bias).

n. 298.
Add to note 298:
In U.S. v. Escobar-de Jesus, 187 F.3d 148, 52 Fed. R. Evid. Serv. 1039 (1st Cir. 1999) the court held that counsel's statement that his client was African-American and that racism exists in Puerto Rico were not, standing alone, the type of special circumstances that would require a court to ask prospective jurors if racial prejudice would be a factor in their verdict.

n. 299.
Add to note 299:
Accord U.S. v. Brown, 938 F.2d 1482, 33 Fed. R. Evid. Serv. 790 (1st Cir. 1991) (while mere fact that defendant was black and all government's witnesses, as well as all jurors, were white did not require judge to conduct voir dire on issue of racial prejudice; more prudent approach would have been to allow such questioning). In U.S. v. Reddix, 106 F.3d 236, 46 Fed. R. Evid. Serv. 508 (8th Cir. 1997), it was held that the trial court did not abuse its discretion in addressing the issue of defendant's race in voir dire and inquiring as to whether it might affect the jurors' decision. The court of appeal made the point that it was appropriate that federal judges should investigate possible racial prejudice where the defendant was of a racial minority.

In U.S. v. Barber, 80 F.3d 964, 44 Fed. R. Evid. Serv. 281 (4th Cir. 1996) an interracial couple was charged with laundering the proceeds from the sale of marijuana. The trial judge refused to allow voir dire questioning regarding juror racial attitudes and the Court of Appeals affirmed. The latter reasoned that the charge had no racial overtones, and that race was not bound up with the conduct of the trial. It was not prepared to entertain the thesis that there might be some jurors who might be inclined to convict because of a bias against interracial couples. The court stated that to allow questioning on racial attitudes might prove socially divisive and inject race into a trial which had no racial dimensions. A dissenting opinion noted that there had been a 300-year taboo on interracial marriages in the state, that it was not until 1967 that state antimiscegenation laws forbidding such marriages were held unconstitu-

CHALLENGES FOR CAUSE § 7:45

tional [Loving v. Virginia, 388 U.S. 1, 87 S. Ct. 1817, 18 L. Ed. 2d 1010 (1967)], and that public opinion polls indicated that marriages between blacks and whites were still disapproved of by a majority of southerners. In light of this background, and given the fact that the defendants' marriage was undenied and its interracial character obvious, it would have seemed that the better practice, regardless of any legal strictures, would have been to allow questioning on the issue of racial prejudice.

n. 300.

Add to note 300:

The ethical propriety of using race in formulating one's peremptory challenge strategy is considered in Kaine, *Race, Trial Strategy, and Legal Ethics*, 24 U Rich L Rev 361 (1990).

§ 7:44 —Membership in racially biased organizations

Add after first sentence in first paragraph:

On the other hand, in Kinder v. Bowersox, 272 F.3d 532 (8th Cir. 2001) a prospective juror asked to speak to the judge in private and told him that he belonged to a "white organization." The juror made the statement under the mistaken impression that the "traveler's protection association" to which he belonged excluded minorities. The juror, however, asserted that he was not a racist. Nonetheless, the judge excused the juror for cause on the basis that he could not be fair to the defendant. On appeal, it was found that the Court's evaluation of the situation and excusal of the juror was not unreasonable or an abuse of discretion.

Add at end of section:

Gangs are widely perceived by many in society as antisocial and racist organizations. The very term "gang" carries negative connotations. In a case where a gang member was being prosecuted for murder on a theory of accountability, Gardner v. Barnett, 199 F.3d 915 (7th Cir. 1999), the Court of Appeals started from the premise that, although the constitution did not require voir dire into biases against street gangs, state law did (People v. Jimenez, 284 Ill. App. 3d 908, 220 Ill. Dec. 97, 672 N.E.2d 914 (1st Dist. 1996)). The Court of Appeals thought, however, that the trial court's questions designed to discover familiarity with gangs as a result of personal experience were sufficient to satisfy whatever obligation the court might have had in this regard. Moreover, the Court of Appeals expressed the opinion that Jiminez should not be followed in federal court, the better practice being to leave the issue to the sound discretion of the trial judge.

§ 7:45 —Politics

n. 312.

Add to note 312:

§ 7:45   JURY SELECTION: LAW, ART & SCIENCE 2D

In U.S. v. Goland, 959 F.2d 1449 (9th Cir. 1992), the court held that it was not improper for the trial judge to decline to ask jurors their political affiliation or which candidates they voted for in the election, even though the prosecution was for illegal contributions to a political campaign. The judge did ask whether the jurors had voted in the election, whether they were active in politics or had participated in any federal campaign, and whether they were familiar with the FEC or federal election law. Whether this was sufficient to allay the risk of possible prejudice is debatable. Arguably the better practice in the unique circumstances of the case would have been to allow the requested questions.

§ 7:46   —Certain witnesses

n. 326.

Add to beginning of note 326:

In Derden v. McNeel, 938 F.2d 605 (5th Cir. 1991), on reh'g, 978 F.2d 1453 (5th Cir. 1992), the prosecutor was permitted to obtain promises from jurors that they: (1) would neither consider the testimony of coconspirators to be inherently untruthful, nor disbelieve witnesses who had entered into plea-bargaining agreements; and (2) would weigh the coconspirators' testimony as anybody else's. On appeal, it was held that this line of voir dire was improper under state law, which required uncorroborated testimony of an accomplice to be viewed with great caution and suspicion. The trial judge's instructions to this effect at the end of the trial were not deemed sufficient to remedy the improper voir dire.

Add after fifth paragraph:

See generally Annotation, Examination and challenge of federal case jurors on basis of attitudes toward homosexuality, 85 A.L.R. Fed. 864; Annotation, Examination and challenge of state case jurors on basis of attitudes toward homosexuality, 80 A.L.R. 5th 469; Note, *The Double Bind: Unequal Treatment for Homosexuals within the American legal Framework*, 20 B.C. Third World L.J. 145 (2000).

n. 329.

Add to note 329:

State v. Kelly, 823 S.W.2d 95 (Mo. Ct. App. E.D. 1991) (trial court did not err in refusing to strike juror who initially indicated belief that police officer would not lie on stand, but who then stated she was prepared to keep an open mind).

n. 330.

Add to note 330:

U.S. v. Victoria-Peguero, 920 F.2d 77, 1993 A.M.C. 1520 (1st Cir. 1990); U.S. v. Contreras-Castro, 825 F.2d 185 (9th Cir. 1987); U.S. v. Armendariz-Mata, 949 F.2d 151, 34 Fed. R. Evid. Serv. 399 (5th Cir. 1991); U.S. v. Muldoon, 931 F.2d 282 (4th Cir. 1991); Rainey v. Conerly, 973 F.2d 321 (4th Cir. 1992); U.S. v. Evans, 917 F.2d 800 (4th Cir. 1990), overruled by, U.S. v. Lancaster, 96 F.3d 734 (4th Cir. 1996). *Contra* U.S. v. Nash, 910 F.2d 749 (11th Cir. 1990). In U.S. v. Martinez, 981 F.2d 867, 37 Fed. R. Evid. Serv. 748 (6th Cir. 1992), the court held that while the trial judge did not ask the requested questions as to whether the prospective jurors' relationships with police officers would cause them to favor the testimony of a police officer if the officer's testimony conflicted with that of a civilian,

CHALLENGES FOR CAUSE § 7:46

the court did inquire as to whether any of the jurors had a close relationship with law enforcement officials and, if so, whether the relationship would cause them to favor the prosecution or defense. The trial judge also had instructed the jury that the same standards of credibility applied to both police and non-police witnesses. Under these circumstances, the appellate court concluded that there had been no abuse of the trial judge's discretion in refusing to ask the requested questions. In U.S. v. Lancaster, 96 F.3d 734 (4th Cir. 1996), the court held that the trial judge did not commit an abuse of discretion in declining to ask jurors whether they would be biased in favor of law enforcement personnel, despite the fact that the government's case depended solely on the testimony of law enforcement agents. The court of appeal looked at the voir dire as a whole and found it satisfactory. The *Lancaster* decision is reviewed in Note, *United States v. Lancaster: The Fourth Circuit Reverses Course on Jury voir dire in "Swearing Contest" Cases*, 76 North Carolina L. Rev. 233 (1997). The author criticizes the court in *Lancaster* for limiting the amount of critical information available to parties in cases that are essentially "swearing contests" between the police and other witnesses, and argues that the limitation will infringe upon the constitutional right to an impartial jury.

Asking a question in the abstract as to whether jurors would believe a prison guard over a prison inmate was held "woefully" insufficient to justify a finding that jurors who answered affirmatively would not be impartial in U.S. v. Ricketts, 146 F.3d 492, 49 Fed. R. Evid. Serv. 931 (7th Cir. 1998). The court added that "generalized questions of the sort asked . . . [were] a slim basis upon which to base a challenge for cause." U.S. v. Ricketts, 146 F.3d 492, 496, 49 Fed. R. Evid. Serv. 931 (7th Cir. 1998).

n. 331.
Add to note 331 after "Nolan":
In U.S. v. Amerson, 938 F.2d 116 (8th Cir. 1991), the Court of Appeals found error in the trial judge's refusal to excuse for cause jurors who indicated that they would give greater credence to testimony of police officers than testimony of other witnesses. The decision in part turned on its particular facts. Witness credibility was in all probability likely to determine the result and the witnesses for the government were police officers. See also U.S. v. Jones, 193 F.3d 948 (8th Cir. 1999) (trial judge committed reversible error in not excusing for cause juror who indicated that she believed that police officers were less likely to be untruthful than other witnesses); State v. Bingham, 176 Ariz. 146, 859 P.2d 769 (Ct. App. Div. 1 1993), redesignated as opinion, (Sept. 23, 1993) (error to require defendant to use peremptory challenge to remove juror who indicated a predisposition to favor testimony of police officers over that of other witnesses; juror should have been dismissed for cause). Compare U.S. v. Payne, 944 F.2d 1458, 33 Fed. R. Evid. Serv. 1316 (9th Cir. 1991) (failure to inquire as to whether jurors would be unduly influenced by the testimony of law enforcement officers was not an abuse of discretion where the testimony of the officers was of relatively minor importance, there was corroborating evidence by non-law enforcement officers, the trial court gave an appropriate instruction regarding the weight to be given to each witness's testimony, and voir dire questions were asked relating to juror's friends and relatives in law enforcement). See also U.S. v. Lawes, 292 F.3d 123 (2d Cir. 2002) (failure to ask proposed voir dire questions regarding jurors' attitudes toward police was not reversible error). In U.S. v. Morales, 185 F.3d 74 (2d Cir. 1999) the Court of Appeals held that the trial court had not abused its discretion in not excusing for cause three

§ 7:46   JURY SELECTION: LAW, ART & SCIENCE 2D

jurors who were either themselves law-enforcement officers or closely related to law enforcement. The decision is highly questionable in light of the fact that some of the charges against the defendants related to the felony murder and attempted murders of police officers. The court was swayed by the jurors' assertions that they could be impartial).

§ 7:47   —Certain types of litigation and defenses

Add after first sentence in fifth paragraph:
See also U.S. v. Polichemi, 201 F.3d 858 (7th Cir. 2000), on reh'g, 219 F.3d 698, 54 Fed. R. Evid. Serv. 1407 (7th Cir. 2000), cert. denied, 531 U.S. 1168, 121 S. Ct. 1131, 148 L. Ed. 2d 997 (2001) (no error in refusing to excuse for cause jurors who had initially said that they would be biased in favor of law enforcement officers but subsequently stated they could decide the case based on the evidence); U.S. v. Duncan, 191 F.3d 569 (5th Cir. 1999) (trial court did not err in rejecting challenge for cause to juror who initially expressed a bias in favor of law enforcement witnesses, but upon further voir dire, affirmed that she could be fair and reject the testimony of a law enforcement officer whose testimony lacked credibility).

See, e.g., People v. Zurenko, 833 P.2d 794 (Colo. Ct. App. 1991) (juror who was member of voluntary organization found to prevent child abuse and to assist victims thereof should have been excused for cause in sexual assault prosecution).

n. 346.

Add to note 346 after "Leonard":
Compare People v. Seuffer, 144 Ill. 2d 482, 163 Ill. Dec. 805, 582 N.E.2d 71 (1991) (juror who initially had expressed disapproval of insanity defense on ground it had been abused, but who subsequently stated that he would consider expert testimony in assessing insanity claim, but without automatically or blindly adopting such testimony, was not subject to challenge for cause).

n. 347.

Add to note 347:
But compare People v. Bommersbach, 228 Ill. App. 3d 877, 170 Ill. Dec. 894, 593 N.E.2d 783 (1st Dist. 1992) (no error in trial judge's refusal to ask opinions regarding validity and value of psychiatric testimony where issue was whether defendant was a sexually dangerous person).

§ 7:50   Physical condition and intellectual functioning

n. 358.

Add to note 358:
Where the disability arises during the trial, the court may properly excuse the juror and proceed with the remaining jurors. See, e.g., U.S. v. Dischner, 960 F.2d 870, 35 Fed. R. Evid. Serv. 485 (9th Cir. 1992), opinion amended and superseded on denial of reh'g, 974 F.2d 1502 (9th Cir. 1992).

§ 7:50   CHALLENGES FOR CAUSE

See also U.S. v. Gonzalez-Soberal, 109 F.3d 64, 46 Fed. R. Evid. Serv. 868 (1st Cir. 1997) (excusal of juror whose health appeared in jeopardy was not an abuse of discretion) In federal court the authority is Federal Rule of Criminal Procedure 23(b). Prejudice will be found, however, if the juror is dismissed without factual support or for a legally irrelevant reason. U.S. v. Huntress, 956 F.2d 1309 (5th Cir. 1992). The court in *Huntress* also ruled that if a juror is excused for a valid reason after deliberations have begun, the judge should accept an 11-juror verdict rather than substitute an alternate juror. A dismissal under Rule 23(b) is an unusual procedure, and one that needs to be justified by a finding of "just cause." U.S. v. Araujo, 62 F.3d 930 (7th Cir. 1995). In *Araujo* the Court of Appeals held that the decision to dismiss a juror whose car had broken down and who was stranded was an abuse of discretion. Similarly, in U.S. v. Donato, 99 F.3d 426 (D.C. Cir. 1996), the court of appeal found that the trial court had abused its discretion in dismissing a juror after the jury had been instructed but before it had begun deliberations. The juror was dismissed because she had airplane tickets to go out of state in order to teach a course and was concerned that the deliberations would interfere with her plans. Apparently the court of appeals' concern was that the trial judge had failed to develop the record sufficiently fully and did not explain why the existing record was adequate to allow the ruling. It is instructive to compare Donato with U.S. v. Nelson, 102 F.3d 1344 (4th Cir. 1996), where it was held that the trial court had not abused its discretion in dismissing two jurors during trial because their travel plans conflicted with the jury deliberations. The court of appeal in Nelson stated that while it might have been preferable to retain the originally selected jury, there was no abuse of discretion absent a showing of prejudice. However, it is difficult to know what "prejudice" means in this context. Establishing that the jury's deliberations would have taken a different course had the jurors participated will prove difficult if not impossible in practice and will invariably be speculative.

In U.S. v. Quiroz-Cortez, 960 F.2d 418 (5th Cir. 1992), the court found that while the trial judge had improperly substituted an alternate juror after the jury had begun it deliberations, the error was harmless if the defendant suffered no prejudice from the substitution. This approach is questionable because, given the prevailing restrictions on the discovery of juror deliberations (See § 3:12), it would seem nearly impossible to establish prejudice. Nevertheless in U.S. v. Olano, 507 U.S. 725, 113 S. Ct. 1770, 123 L. Ed. 2d 508 (1993), the United States Supreme Court held that the presence of alternates in the jury room during deliberations was not plain error where the alternates had been instructed that they were not allowed to participate and there was no evidence that they had participated or "chilled" the jury's deliberations. In U.S. v. Cencer, 90 F.3d 1103, 1996 FED App. 0230P (6th Cir. 1996), it was held that the defendant had waived any prohibition against the substitution of alternate jurors during deliberations by agreeing to the substitution. While the defendant had objected to the judge's jury instructions, he had made no attempt to retract his consent to the substitution. See also Watkins v. Kassulke, 90 F.3d 138, 1996 FED App. 0218P (6th Cir. 1996) (defendant's double jeopardy rights not violated where defendant consented to additional jurors being selected after jury had been sworn); U.S. v. Isom, 88 F.3d 920 (11th Cir. 1996) (when originally selected alternate jurors were made part of the regular jury, defendants lost the ability to use peremptory challenges allocated for alternate jurors with respect to them; no de facto mistrial or violation of double jeopardy occurred when trial court conducted further jury selection to select new alternates). Although a trial

§ 7:50   Jury Selection: Law, Art & Science 2d

court can declare a mistrial when a juror is dismissed pursuant to Rule 23(b), it is not obligated to do so, and may choose to proceed with an 11-member jury. See U.S. v. Harrington, 108 F.3d 1460 (D.C. Cir. 1997). It also has the option of substituting alternate jurors, but before doing so, it may have to obtain the consent of the parties. See Fed. R. Crim. P. Rule 24(c). In U.S. v. Beard, 161 F.3d 1190 (9th Cir. 1998), where the trial court had failed to secure defendant's consent to the substitution of two alternate jurors, the Court of Appeals reversed. See also Annotation, Selection and impaneling of alternate jurors under Rule 24(c) of Federal Rules of Criminal Procedure, 119 A.L.R. Fed. 589; Annotation, Substitution, under Rule 24c of Federal Rules of Criminal Procedure, of alternate juror for regular juror before jury retires to consider verdict in federal criminal case, 115 A.L.R. Fed. 381.

In U.S. v. Patterson, 26 F.3d 1127 (D.C. Cir. 1994), the trial judge summarily dismissed a juror who experienced severe chest pains during jury deliberations and had gone to visit her physician. However, the judge did not make an express finding to the effect that it was necessary to excuse the absent juror. The D.C. Court of Appeals held that under the circumstances the defendant's right under federal Rule 23(b) to a 12-person jury had been violated. Compare U.S. v. Acker, 52 F.3d 509, 42 Fed. R. Evid. Serv. 181 (4th Cir. 1995) (no violation of Rule 23(b) where judge excused injured juror during deliberations and allowed verdict to be returned by remaining 11 jurors); Murray v. Laborers Union Local No. 324, 55 F.3d 1445, 149 L.R.R.M. (BNA) 2457, 149 L.R.R.M. (BNA) 2858, 130 Lab. Cas. (CCH) ¶ 11345, 130 Lab. Cas. (CCH) ¶ 11367, 31 Fed. R. Serv. 3d 1222 (9th Cir. 1995) (juror may be permissibly excused if scheduling conflict prevents juror's continuing participation in the deliberations but not if reason for excusal is that juror is lone holdout against required unanimous verdict); U.S. v. Chorney, 63 F.3d 78 (1st Cir. 1995) (trial court did not abuse its discretion in dismissing juror whose eldest son died during deliberations). In Claudio v. Snyder, 68 F.3d 1573 (3d Cir. 1995), the Court of Appeals stated that the trial court's decision to substitute an alternate juror after deliberations had begun was in violation of the relevant state criminal rule of procedure, but, because there was no showing of prejudice, there was no constitutional violation. The Court of Appeals added that although the trial court did not specifically direct the jury to begin its deliberations anew, its instruction to take whatever time was required to inform the replacement juror of the previous deliberations, as well as each juror's point of view, and not to proceed until the juror was thoroughly familiar with the evidence and the views of the other jurors' constituted the functional equivalent of such an instruction.

If it is proper to dismiss a juror because of illness, the fact that the juror is the sole black on the panel is arguably irrelevant. In U.S. v. McMasters, 90 F.3d 1394 (8th Cir. 1996), the court held that there had been no abuse of discretion when the trial judge dismissed the jury's only black member when she became ill. In U.S. v. Gibson, 135 F.3d 257 (2d Cir. 1998), the court held that the trial judge had not committed error in excusing an elderly juror who had been hospitalized after collapsing in the subway and in accepting a verdict of 11 rather than declaring a mistrial. See also U.S. v. Mack, 159 F.3d 208, 50 Fed. R. Evid. Serv. 281, 1998 FED App. 0311P (6th Cir. 1998).

By agreeing to proceed without an alternate juror, the potential consequence being to authorize an 11-person verdict should one of the jurors have to be excused, the defendant in effect waives whatever right he may have to a jury of 12. See U.S. v. Mahler, 141 F.3d 811 (8th Cir. 1998).

n. 362.
   Add to note 362:

CHALLENGES FOR CAUSE § 7:50

See also U.S. v. Dempsey, 830 F.2d 1084, 24 Fed. R. Evid. Serv. 524 (10th Cir. 1987) (permitting use of interpreter to assist deaf juror and denying motion to strike juror for cause). Accord People v. Coleman, 223 Ill. App. 3d 975, 166 Ill. Dec. 312, 586 N.E.2d 270 (1st Dist. 1991), decision aff'd in part, rev'd in part on other grounds, 155 Ill. 2d 507, 187 Ill. Dec. 479, 617 N.E.2d 1200 (1993).

Rush v. Smith, 45 F.3d 1197 (8th Cir. 1995), reh'g granted and opinion vacated, (Mar. 16, 1995) and on reh'g, 56 F.3d 918 (8th Cir. 1995), raised a similar issue. A juror (in fact the sole black juror on the panel) was unable to attend court because of a recent snowfall. The judge declined to authorize a marshal to transport the juror to court because the courthouse was reduced to skeletal staff. The judge also refused plaintiff's offer to send a taxi to bring the juror to court because the judge deemed the provision of transportation by a party to the suit to be problematic. The Court of Appeals found that the dismissal of the juror under the circumstances was not an abuse of the Court's discretion.

Add after fifth paragraph:
Pregnant women might be thought to constitute a special class of jurors whose physical condition prevented their being able to serve on a jury. The decisions of trial judges to excuse pregnant jurors have not been disturbed on appeal. The reported cases, however, have generally involved a complicating factor beyond mere pregnancy. In U.S. v. Helms, 897 F.2d 1293 (5th Cir. 1990), for example, it was held that it was not an abuse of discretion for the trial judge to discharge a pregnant juror who went into labor during the deliberations; and in U.S. v. Wilson, 894 F.2d 1245 (11th Cir. 1990), it was held that the trial court did not abuse its discretion in excusing a pregnant juror suffering from an abscessed tooth. In U.S. v. Shenberg, 89 F.3d 1461, 45 Fed. R. Evid. Serv. 58 (11th Cir. 1996), the jury had deliberated for a month when the judge excused a pregnant juror who went into labor. The judge was prepared to stay the deliberations to allow the juror to give birth and return to the deliberations, but the juror's physician strongly recommended against this course of action. Deeming that any additional delay would be clearly inadvisable, the judge then ordered the remaining 11 jurors to resume their deliberations. The judge's refusal to replace the juror was upheld on appeal. Given the amount of deliberation that had already taken place, there was a greater likelihood of prejudice if the juror had been replaced with an alternate than if the jury returned a verdict subscribed to by only 11 members.

Add at end of section:
A judge must tread carefully in deciding to excuse a handicapped juror, as this action may violate the handicapped person's rights under the Rehabilitation Act of 1973. 29 U.S.C.A. § 794. See DeLong v. Brumbaugh, 703 F. Supp. 399 (W.D. Pa. 1989). See also Hittner & Nichols, *Jury Selection*

in Federal Civil Litigation: General Procedures, New Rules, and the Arrival of Batson, 23 Tex Tech L Rev 407, 447 (1992).

§ 7:51 Nervous or emotional condition

n. 370.
Add to note 370:

In U.S. v. Virgen-Moreno, 265 F.3d 276 (5th Cir. 2001), cert. denied, 534 U.S. 1095, 122 S. Ct. 843, 151 L. Ed. 2d 721 (2002) and cert. denied, 535 U.S. 977, 122 S. Ct. 1452, 152 L. Ed. 2d 393 (2002), it was held that the district court had not abused its discretion in excusing a juror during deliberations who had sent the court a note indicating that she was having difficulty concentrating as a result of three deaths of family members and friends during the week. The Court of Appeals stated that the court was not required to conduct an evidentiary hearing before removing the juror on the basis of its discretion.

In Perez v. Marshall, 119 F.3d 1422 (9th Cir. 1997) it was held that there was good cause for removing a juror because of the juror's emotional instability, the judge having reached this conclusion based on extensive interviews with the juror, the juror's statements and physical appearance, and statements from other jurors. Although the reasoning appears unexceptional, it takes on a different coloration when, as was the case in *Perez v Marshall*, the juror in question is the lone holdout for an acquittal. See also U.S. v. Beard, 161 F.3d 1190 (9th Cir. 1998) (no error in excusing two jurors for just cause, one of whom was emotionally distraught because of comments made to her by the second juror).

n. 372.
Add to note 372:

Compare U.S. v. Frank, 901 F.2d 846 (10th Cir. 1990) (no error in refusing to excuse juror who indicated that she was nervous about remaining in hotel by herself for fear of becoming the victim of violence); U.S. v. Shea, 211 F.3d 658, 53 Fed. R. Evid. Serv. 1353 (1st Cir. 2000), cert. denied, 531 U.S. 1154, 121 S. Ct. 1101, 148 L. Ed. 2d 973 (2001) and cert. denied, 531 U.S. 1154, 121 S. Ct. 1102, 148 L. Ed. 2d 973 (2001) (no error in refusal to excuse juror who expressed fear of the defendants).

n. 375.
Add to note 375:

See also Clemmons v. Sowders, 34 F.3d 352, 1994 FED App. 0297P (6th Cir. 1994) (trial court decision not to excuse juror who indicated that he was under stress was not an abuse of discretion after judge questioned juror in chambers and concluded that there was no reason to believe that the juror's anxiety rendered him incompetent to understand the issues and engage in deliberations). Compare Hansen v. State, 592 So. 2d 114 (Miss. 1991) (prospective juror properly excluded on basis of statement that ability to focus might be affected by week-old marriage and residence in new house).

Add at end of section:

In State v. Jackson, 629 So. 2d 1374 (La. Ct. App. 2d Cir. 1993), writ denied, 637 So. 2d 1046 (La. 1994), the court held that the trial judge had not erred in refusing to dismiss for cause a juror required by his employer to work until midnight following the end of the day's judicial proceedings.

The defense argued that the lack of sleep may have affected the juror's impartiality but the trial judge had satisfied herself that this was not the case.

§ 7:52 Connection with law enforcement

n. 377.
Add to note 377:
See also Gilbert v. State, 593 So. 2d 597 (Fla. Dist. Ct. App. 3d Dist. 1992) (juror who indicated that friendship with police might prevent her from being impartial in trial of police officer should have been excused from jury).

n. 378.
Add to note 378:
Compare U.S. v. LaRouche, 896 F.2d 815 (4th Cir. 1990) (refusal of trial judge to dismiss for cause all employees of investigative agencies upheld on appeal).

n. 379.
Add to note 379:
State v. Roderick, 828 S.W.2d 729 (Mo. Ct. App. E.D. 1992) (no error in refusing to excuse for cause wife of police chief where juror maintained that she would not be more inclined to credit testimony of police officer); U.S. v. Nururdin, 8 F.3d 1187, 39 Fed. R. Evid. Serv. 1143 (7th Cir. 1993) (no error in refusing to strike for cause two jurors related to law enforcement personnel, a third who was a prison employee, and a fourth who was an FBI agent and had once met one of the assistant United States attorneys who prosecuted the case); U.S. v. Beasley, 48 F.3d 262 (7th Cir. 1995) (no error in refusing to excuse for cause juror whose brother was a police chief and whose son was a police officer where juror indicated she could be impartial). McQueen v. Scroggy, 99 F.3d 1302, 35 Fed. R. Serv. 3d 1211, 1996 FED App. 0349P (6th Cir. 1996) (no error in not upholding challenge for cause of juror who knew police chief and who indicated that he would be inclined to believe a police officer's word over that of a stranger, but qualified this by stating only if they were not speaking under oath). In U.S. v. Brown, 26 F.3d 1124 (D.C. Cir. 1994), a youth correction officer reported his law enforcement background on the jury questionnaire but failed to raise his hand when the panel was asked on voir dire about law enforcement background. The oversight was brought to the Court's attention by defense counsel and the court questioned the juror in chambers. The defendant challenged the juror for cause on the basis that he had lied in not raising his hand and because the in-chambers questioning may have intimidated the juror. The court rejected the challenge. The issue of actual bias of the juror was not raised at trial, and the court on appeal rejected the argument that a law enforcement officer had automatically to be excused whenever the defendant was charged with assaulting a police officer.

Who qualifies as "law enforcement personnel" may not always be clear. In U.S. v. Wright, 119 F.3d 630, 47 Fed. R. Evid. Serv. 554 (8th Cir. 1997), a juror, in response to a voir dire question regarding his relationship to law enforcement personnel, failed to disclose that he was the nephew of a tribal children's court judge. On appeal, it was held that this answer was not necessarily dishonest and did not deprive the defendant of a fair trial. To avoid such problems, counsel should be specific about the individuals being inquired about when asking questions relating to a juror's relation-

§ 7:52   JURY SELECTION: LAW, ART & SCIENCE 2D

ships with law enforcement personnel (e.g., police, prison and probation officers, judges, etc.).

In U.S. v. Dickerson, 248 F.3d 1036, 56 Fed. R. Evid. Serv. 1216 (11th Cir. 2001), cert. denied, 536 U.S. 957, 122 S. Ct. 2659, 153 L. Ed. 2d 835 (2002), the Court of Appeals found no error in the trial judge's refusal to dismiss for cause a juror who admitted that he was a friend of a judge, and who further stated "you have to meet certain criteria to get a trial, and if you do that, it will be a waste of money if you don't have enough evidence." Neither the trial judge nor the appellate court thought that the juror had indicated bias by his remark and, in any event, the district court had assured itself that the juror would be able to evaluate the evidence objectively and render a fair decision.

n. 380.

Add to note 380:

; U.S. v. Mendoza-Burciaga, 981 F.2d 192 (5th Cir. 1992) (no error in denying challenge for cause to employee of detention center where defendant was being held where juror indicated that she knew nothing about the trial, could be fair, and would follow judicial instructions); U.S. v. Munoz, 15 F.3d 395 (5th Cir. 1994).

Regardless of the standard which the court applies in respect to challenges for cause, it would seem desirable, if not necessary, to question jurors as to their connection with law enforcement personnel. Yet in Davis v. State, 333 Md. 27, 633 A.2d 867 (1993), it was held that the defendant was not entitled to ask whether any members of the venire were employed as law enforcement officers or had friends or relatives in the law enforcement field.

n. 381.

Add to note 381:

See also Depree v. Thomas, 946 F.2d 784 (11th Cir. 1991) (juror who had relatives on police force not automatically subject to challenge for cause).

n. 385.

Add to note 385 after "Williams":

Depree v. Thomas, 946 F.2d 784 (11th Cir. 1991) (ex-deputy sheriff); Smith v. State, 201 Ga. App. 82, 410 S.E.2d 202 (1991) (retired police officer); U.S. v. Bryant, 991 F.2d 171 (5th Cir. 1993) (no error in failing to excuse for cause juror whose husband had been chief of police for 21 years, or juror who had been deputy sheriff for 16 years prior to retirement); U.S. v. McIntyre, 997 F.2d 687, 38 Fed. R. Evid. Serv. 1440 (10th Cir. 1993) (no error in refusing to dismiss for cause juror who had been police officer 12 years previously).

Add to note 385 after "Clark":

State v. Gary, 822 S.W.2d 448 (Mo. Ct. App. E.D. 1991) (error for trial court to refuse defendant's challenge for cause to former police officer who worked in same department as victim, who knew state's witnesses, and who admitted a prejudice in favor of police officers).

§ 7:53 Qualification in death penalty cases

Add at beginning of section:

As the death penalty is the most severe punishment authorized by law, one would expect a court to allow greater

CHALLENGES FOR CAUSE § 7:53

leeway in voir dire regarding juror attitudes towards it. There are limits, however. In McQueen v. Scroggy, 99 F.3d 1302, 35 Fed. R. Serv. 3d 1211, 1996 FED App. 0349P (6th Cir. 1996), where the trial judge had rejected voir dire questions as to whether the jurors believed that the death penalty was a deterrent, the court of appeal held that such questions were indeed irrelevant. The court of appeal also upheld the trial judge's decision not to allow questions as to whether jurors agreed that the use of drugs or alcohol could mitigate punishment. Similarly, in Herman v. Johnson, 98 F.3d 171 (5th Cir. 1996), it was held that the state trial judge did not commit error in refusing to allow voir dire questions on the legal standards that the jurors would use in evaluating mitigating evidence in the sentencing phase of a capital case. Accord, Soria v. Johnson, 207 F.3d 232 (5th Cir. 2000). The trial judge in U.S. v. Tipton, 90 F.3d 861 (4th Cir. 1996) had asked the jurors "do you have any strong feelings in favor of the death penalty." This was held sufficient to determine pro-death penalty bias. Accordingly, the court of appeal held that the defendants were not entitled to conduct detailed questioning regarding specific mitigating factors. In Wheat v. Johnson, 238 F.3d 357 (5th Cir. 2001), cert. denied, 532 U.S. 1070, 121 S. Ct. 2226, 150 L. Ed. 2d 218 (2001), the Court of Appeals held that there was no constitutional right to question prospective jurors on their understanding of parole and parole eligibility. Accord, Collier v. Cockrell, 300 F.3d 577 (5th Cir. 2002), cert. denied, 537 U.S. 1084, 123 S. Ct. 690, 154 L. Ed. 2d 586 (2002) (capital murder defendant has no constitutional right to ask voir dire questions regarding state parole law). See also Moore v. Gibson, 195 F.3d 1152 (10th Cir. 1999) (where trial court has determined that juror should be struck for cause, it is not required to afford counsel who opposes this ruling the opportunity for further examination for purposes of rehabilitating the juror); but compare Hill v. Brigano, 199 F.3d 833, 1999 FED App. 0426P (6th Cir. 1999) (even if trial court erred in not allowing rehabilitation of two jurors dismissed because of views on capital punishment, defendant not entitled to relief unless he can show jury which convicted him was not impartial). In Mackall v. Murray, 109 F.3d 957 (4th Cir. 1997), as amended, (Apr. 2, 1997) and reh'g en banc granted, opinion vacated, (May 21, 1997) and on reh'g en banc, 131 F.3d 442 (4th Cir. 1997) the court drew a distinction between jurors' views on the death penalty and the jurors' ability to follow the law, only questions relating to the latter being required.

In *Probing "Life-Qualification" through Expanded Voir Dire*, 29 Hofstra L. Rev. 1209 (2001), Blume, Johnson and Threlkeld argues that traditional voir dire often fails to work effectively in death penalty cases. The authors argue for in-

§ 7:53

dividual, sequestered voir dire, greater allowance of attorney-conducted voir dire, greater use of questionnaires and an expanded range of topics of permissible inquiry. See also Betele & Bowers, *How Jurors Decide on Death: Guilt is Overwhelming; Aggravation Requires Death; and Mitigation is No Excuse*, 66 Brooklyn L. Rev. 1011 (2001) (arguing that jurors should not be pressed to commit to being able to impose a death sentence, and that it should be sufficient that they agree that they would consider such a sentence); Sunby, *The Capital Jury and Empathy: The Problem of Worthy and Unworthy Victims*, 88 Cornell L. Rev. 343 (2003).

In Sellers v. Ward, 135 F.3d 1333 (10th Cir. 1998), the court reiterated the general proposition that the scope of voir dire questioning lies in the discretion of the trial judge and held that the judge had not abused this discretion in not allowing questions as whether the jurors would consider the defendant's youth as a mitigating factor, where the voir dire taken as a whole was adequate to detect jurors who might not be impartial. In Gilbert v. Moore, 525 U.S. 840, 119 S. Ct. 103, 142 L. Ed. 2d 82 (1998), the court found no constitutional violation in a capital case where the trial judge had declined to excuse for cause jurors who indicated that they would not consider the defendant's lack of a criminal record as a mitigating circumstance.

Although challenges for cause based on pre-voir dire questionnaires are usually nonproblematic, greater caution may need to be exercised in death penalty cases. In U.S. v. Chanthadara, 230 F.3d 1237 (10th Cir. 2000), cert. denied, 534 U.S. 992, 122 S. Ct. 457, 151 L. Ed. 2d 376 (2001) the court, although reserving the issue for another day, flagged the problem of whether a trial court had an obligation to voir dire prospective jurors before removing any for cause based on their views of the death penalty. One of the difficulties with excusing jurors based on responses to a questionnaire is that the trial judge does not have the benefit of observing juror demeanor. This opportunity is one of the main reasons for applying an "abuse of discretion" standard when reviewing judicial dispositions of challenges for cause. Because the opportunity to observe the juror is lacking when the challenge is based on questionnaire responses, the court in *Chanthadara* concluded that the trial judge's decision was not entitled to any particular deference and reviewed de novo whether the questionnaire responses warranted the excusal for cause of several jurors under the *Witherspoon-Witt* standard. The court found that the questions on the questionnaire did not accurately state the controlling legal standard, and that in at least one instance, a juror had been excused for cause despite the fact that her responses were too ambiguous to justify her dismissal. The court held that the error was not harmless and proceeded to vacate the sentence of death and remand for resentencing

Add at end of second paragraph:

In Szuchon v. Lehman, 273 F.3d 299 (3d Cir. 2001) a prospective juror was excused after stating that he did not believe in capital punishment. The Court of Appeals found a violation of *Witherspoon*, as the correct basis for a challenge of a juror was an inability on the part of the juror to follow the law or the judge's instructions. To excuse a juror merely because of the juror's conscientious or religious objection to capital punishment constituted an impermissible expansion of *Witherspoon*. A juror who objects to the death penalty will be allowed to serve if the juror is able to set aside his personal beliefs and apply the rule of law.

In Mann v. Scott, 41 F.3d 968 (5th Cir. 1994), the prosecutor, after reminding the jurors of their oath to render a verdict according to the law and the evidence, asked prospective jurors if they would be able to impose the death penalty if they emotionally believed that the defendant did not deserve to die but intellectually knew that the evidence required the imposition of the death penalty. The prosecutor's challenge for cause to the four jurors who answered this question negatively was upheld on appeal. The Court of Appeals said that while mere emotional opposition to capital punishment alone is insufficient to justify the removal of a juror for cause, it was when it rose to the level where it interfered with the juror's ability to follow the law. The presumption of correctness to which the trial court's exclusion of the jurors was entitled had not been overcome in the case.

While it would be improper to attempt to secure a commitment from jurors that they would apply the death penalty, the court in Byrd v. Collins, 209 F.3d 486, 2000 FED App. 0121P (6th Cir. 2000), cert. denied, 531 U.S. 1082, 121 S. Ct. 786, 148 L. Ed. 2d 682 (2001) held that this was not what had happened in the case. The prosecutor had asked prospective jurors whether they could impose the death penalty if they believed that the defendant was guilty of aggravated murder beyond a reasonable doubt and aggravating circumstances outweighed mitigating factors. In effect, according to the Court of Appeals, the prosecutor had simply asked the jurors whether they could follow the law. The Court of Appeals further stated that it was permissible for the prosecutor to comment on the nature and manner of the murder at issue in voir dire in order to ascertain whether the jurors could remain fair and objective in the face of the emotional impact of a brutal crime.

For many opposed to the death penalty, the source of their

opposition lies in their religious beliefs. When this is the case, the juror's First Amendment free exercise rights are arguably implicated by a challenge for cause based on their view of the death penalty. The author of Note, *Free Exercise Rights of Capital Jurors*, 101 Columbia L. Rev. 569 (2001) argues that religious rights should be protected in capital cases even if they might incline a juror against capital punishment. The author further advocates a strict scrutiny standard of review. See also Simson & Garvey, *Knockin' on Heaven's Door: The Role of Religion in Death Penalty Cases*, 86 Cornell L. Rev. 1090 (2001). It should not automatically be assumed, however, that all religious jurors are opposed or equally opposed to the death penalty. Eisenberg, Garvey and Wells conducted a study in which they found that Southern Baptists were more inclined to impose the death penalty than members of other religions. Eisenberg, Garvey & Wells, *Forecasting Life and Death: Juror Race, Religion and Attitude Toward the Death Penalty*, 30 J. Legal Stud. 277 (2001). The authors also found that whites were more likely to vote for the death penalty than blacks.

In Sweet v. Delo, 125 F.3d 1144 (8th Cir. 1997), a capital case, the trial court on its own motion transferred a juror to the back of the panel because the juror would experience personal hardship in serving on the case. The juror also happened to hold reservations regarding the death penalty, and the defendant argued that *Witherspoon* had been violated. The Court of Appeals rejected this argument, stating not only that the judge's actions had not been pretextual, but that they constituted a "neutral and humanitarian" way of addressing a common problem.

n. 391.

Add to note 391:

In Drew v. Collins, 964 F.2d 411 (5th Cir. 1992), the court held that a prospective juror's repeated statements during voir dire in a capital case that he would apply a standard higher than reasonable doubt warranted the juror's excusal for cause. The court also held that the trial judge properly excused a juror who indicated that he would apply the death penalty only if the defendant was shown likely to murder again rather than likely to engage in future acts of violence as provided for in the relevant statute. Similarly in Johnson v. Collins, 964 F.2d 1527 (5th Cir. 1992), the appellate court stated that a prospective juror who declared that he or she would answer negatively to a special issue on the penalty phase of the capital trial, even though the state had proven it beyond a reasonable doubt, would be disqualified from serving on the jury. See also Corwin v. Johnson, 150 F.3d 467 (5th Cir. 1998) (upholding excusal for cause of juror who asserted that, in keeping with her conscience, she would apply her own higher standard of proof for imposition of death penalty); LaRette v. Delo, 44 F.3d 681 (8th Cir. 1995) (upholding excusal of juror who indicated that she would vote against the death penalty unless the victim "was extremely close to [her]"); Deputy v. Taylor, 19 F.3d 1485 (3d Cir. 1994) (ambiguous answers and demeanor of jurors in responding to

CHALLENGES FOR CAUSE § 7:53

questions about the death penalty justified Court's excusal of jurors as biased against the death penalty); Truesdale v. Moore, 142 F.3d 749 (4th Cir. 1998) (same); Webster v. U.S., 528 U.S. 829, 120 S. Ct. 83, 145 L. Ed. 2d 70 (1999) (although juror stated that she believed that capital punishment was a deterrent to crime, other statements indicated juror's equivocal attitude toward death penalty and warranted excusal for cause under *Witt*). See also U.S. v. Moore, 149 F.3d 773, 49 Fed. R. Evid. Serv. 995 (8th Cir. 1998) ("deference must be paid to trial judge who sees and hears the juror"); Fuller v. Johnson, 114 F.3d 491 (5th Cir. 1997) (removal of juror opposed to capital punishment was justified where trial judge determined juror's views would prevent or substantially impair performance of duties in accord with instructions and oath). A trial judge does not have to make explicit findings of fact or conclusions of law before excusing a juror in a death penalty case. McFadden v. Johnson, 528 U.S. 947, 120 S. Ct. 369, 145 L. Ed. 2d 287 (1999).

n. 392.
Add to note 392:
The prosecution, however, may use its peremptory challenges to excuse jurors not excludable under *Witherspoon*. Brown v. Dixon, 891 F.2d 490 (4th Cir. 1989). See also U.S. v. Barnette, 211 F.3d 803, 53 Fed. R. Evid. Serv. 1346 (4th Cir. 2000); Sallahdin v. Gibson, 275 F.3d 1211 (10th Cir. 2002).

There are degrees of objections to the death penalty. In Howard v. Moore, 525 U.S. 843, 119 S. Ct. 108, 142 L. Ed. 2d 86 (1998), the prosecutor peremptorily challenged 6/7 prospective black jurors, but only 4/35 white jurors. The court held that this made out a prima facie case of discrimination but that the prosecutor's explanation that the jurors were challenged because of their opposition to the death penalty was race neutral. Although many of the white jurors who had not been challenged had also expressed reservations regarding the death penalty, the prosecutor claimed that the objections voiced by the black jurors had been stronger. In response to a claim that the challenges had been made on a racially discriminatory basis, the court held that this explanation was sufficient to satisfy the minimal requirements of *Purkett v. Elem* (see supp). In a somewhat factually similar case, Kilgore v. Bowersox, 124 F.3d 985 (8th Cir. 1997), the prosecution used 5/9 peremptory challenges to strike all the black jurors on the panel, with the result being that the defendant was tried by an all white jury. The claim that the challenges were in violation of *Batson* (see main text) was rejected, the court accepting the prosecutor's explanation that the jurors were challenged because of their reservations regarding the death penalty and not because of their race. (See also U.S. v. Moore, 149 F.3d 773, 49 Fed. R. Evid. Serv. 995 (8th Cir. 1998)). Although several white jurors with similar reservations were not challenged, the prosecutor explained that their objections to capital punishment were relatively weaker than those of the black jurors. In contrast, in Yancey v. State, 813 So. 2d 1 (Ala. Crim. App. 2001), cert. denied, (July 6, 2001) the court found a *Batson* violation where several black prospective jurors were allegedly struck for their views on capital punishment, but a white perspective juror who held similar views was not challenged. The Court's belief that the challenges were discriminatory was no doubt reinforced by the fact that the prosecution had also struck black prospective jurors who had committed traffic and misdemeanor offenses while not challenging six white prospective jurors who had committed like offenses. See also Pitsonbarger v. Gramley, 141 F.3d 728 (7th Cir. 1998) (peremptory challenge of jurors opposed to death penalty is not unconstitutional).

§ 7:53

In U.S. v. Ortiz, 315 F.3d 873, 59 Fed. R. Evid. Serv. 1063 (8th Cir. 2002), cert. denied, 123 S. Ct. 2095, 155 L. Ed. 2d 1078 (U.S. 2003) the defendants, charged with murder, argued that the government had used several of its peremptory challenges to strike African-American jurors because of their race. The Court of Appeals found that the challenges had been exercised on a race-neutral basis. One juror was struck because he had no views on the death penalty (but the juror had also indicated that he had been treated badly by the police, and had been placed wrongfully in a line-up. The juror also seemed to pay greater attention when the defense read out its witness list than when the prosecution read its list). A second juror had been challenged because of his age and the prosecutor's opinion that older jurors seemed to have more difficulty sentencing someone to death because they were facing their own mortality. While a white juror of similar age had not been challenged, her situation was distinguished by the fact that she had indicated that accountability was important to her. A third juror was challenged because, although she indicated she could impose the death penalty if warranted, she appeared to be more strongly opposed to the death penalty than other members of the venire.

In U.S. v. Barnette, 211 F.3d 803, 53 Fed. R. Evid. Serv. 1346 (4th Cir. 2000) the Court of Appeals held that the trial court was within its discretion in excluding for cause a juror who indicated that he was unclear as to his opinion on the death penalty, stated that he would try to follow the law and would consider the death penalty, but also said that "if given the two choices, I would weigh heavily on not wanting to go the death penalty unless it was very, very, very well warranted."

After note 392:
Even if a court applies the incorrect standard on voir dire in a death penalty case, thereby forcing the defendant to use peremptory challenges to remove the jurors in question, it will not necessarily lead to reversal. The critical point under Ross v. Oklahoma, 487 U.S. 81, 108 S. Ct. 2273, 101 L. Ed. 2d 80 (1988) (discussed in main text) is whether the jury actually impaneled is impartial. Applying *Ross* in the context of a death penalty case, the Court of Appeals in Siripongs v. Calderon, 35 F.3d 1308 (9th Cir. 1994) held that this required the defendant to establish that one or more of the impaneled jurors was unduly prone to impose the death penalty. The fact that the defendant may have been required to use a peremptory challenge to excuse a juror who would have been excused for cause had the trial court adopted the correct legal standard was not by itself determinative under *Ross*. See Soria v. Johnson, 207 F.3d 232 (5th Cir. 2000). See also Murray v. Groose, 106 F.3d 812 (8th Cir. 1997) (defendant failed to show that race was pretext for peremptory challenge of black jurors who were weak on death penalty, had relatives who had been charged or convicted of crime, and where one of the jurors indicated a dislike of prosecutors).

The shoe of course can be on the other foot. In Pitsonbarger v. Gramley, 103 F.3d 1293 (7th Cir. 1996), cert.

granted, judgment vacated on other grounds, 522 U.S. 802, 118 S. Ct. 37, 139 L. Ed. 2d 6 (1997) the trial judge's failure to excuse for cause a juror with a predisposition in favor of the death penalty, which in turn forced the defendant to exercise a peremptory challenge to remove the juror, was held not to have deprived the defendant of his constitutional rights. There was no indication that the jury which heard the case was not impartial The decision thus was controlled by that of the Ross v. Oklahoma, 487 U.S. 81, 108 S. Ct. 2273, 101 L. Ed. 2d 80 (1988) (discussed infra note 392 and in main text § 8:13). See also Cox v. Norris, 525 U.S. 834, 119 S. Ct. 89, 142 L. Ed. 2d 70 (1998) (holding that as long as the jury which heard the case was impartial, the fact that the defendant had to use a peremptory challenge to achieve that result was irrelevant; also, the trial court had not abused its discretion in failing to excuse for cause a juror who favored the death penalty but claimed he could be evenhanded and did not philosophically lean towards the death penalty).

n. 393.

Add to note 393:

In Greene v. Georgia, 519 U.S. 145, 117 S. Ct. 578, 136 L. Ed. 2d 507 (1996) the United States Supreme Court held that the Witt standard, while establishing the constitutional standard to be applied in determining whether a juror should be excused for cause because of his or her views on the death penalty, and also establishing that federal courts must grant a presumption of correctness to a state court's finding of juror bias, does not control the standard of review which state appellate courts need apply when reviewing state trial courts' rulings on jury selection in capital cases.

n. 396.

Add to note 396:

Lesko v. Lehman, 925 F.2d 1527 (3d Cir. 1991), perhaps reflects the type of situation that the Supreme Court had in mind. A juror initially told the prosecutor that she would be prepared to vote for the death penalty if the case warranted it. Her answers to defense counsel, on the other hand, were more ambiguous. Finally, in response to questioning by the court, the juror indicated that her opposition to capital punishment would prevent her from voting to impose the death penalty. The trial judge then upheld a challenge for cause, which decision was affirmed on appeal. See also Kinder v. Bowersox, 272 F.3d 532 (8th Cir. 2001) (no abuse of discretion in excusing jurors who equivocated about their ability to impose death penalty) Pickens v. Lockhart, 4 F.3d 1446 (8th Cir. 1993) (juror's repeated response of "if I had to" when questioned as to whether she would consider the death penalty indicated a person who might not in fact be able to consider the death penalty and warranted her excusal for cause); Sallahdin v. Gibson, 275 F.3d 1211 (10th Cir. 2002) (jurors who indicated that they would try to follow court's instructions but the bulk of whose responses suggested that they could not impose a death sentence were properly excused); Bannister v. Armontrout, 4 F.3d 1434 (8th Cir. 1993) (ordained minister properly excused who, although stating that he

§ 7:53

would consider the death penalty, indicated that it was against his conscience and, when questioned as to whether there were any circumstances in which he would vote for the death penalty, answered: "[a]s a pastor I would feel it would ruin my entire ministry if I would say 'yes'") Castro v. Ward, 138 F.3d 810 (10th Cir. 1998) (upholding challenge for cause of juror who repeatedly stated that she did not know whether or not she could actually impose the death penalty); Spivey v. Head, 207 F.3d 1263 (11th Cir. 2000) (although juror's statements were at times contradictory, testimony taken as whole indicated juror's views would prevent or substantially impair her ability to impose death penalty and justified trial court's decision to excuse juror for cause); Cannon v. Gibson, 259 F.3d 1253 (10th Cir. 2001), cert. denied, 535 U.S. 1080, 122 S. Ct. 1966, 152 L. Ed. 2d 1026 (2002) (same).

In Davis v. Executive Director of Dept. of Corrections, 100 F.3d 750 (10th Cir. 1996), the court upheld the challenge of jurors who indicated that they did not believe in capital punishment and did not think that they could vote to impose it, but who also stated that they would follow the law. The court applied a deferential standard of review of the trial judge's finding that the jurors were not impartial. The court also upheld the excusal of a juror who stated that if the crime was alcohol-related, he would deem that a mitigating factor that would outweigh any aggravating factors. The willingness of jurors opposed to the death penalty to consider its imposition in extreme situations (such as in respect to Adolph Hitler or the killer of a young child) does not render them immune from a challenge for cause based on their reservations regarding capital punishment generally. Antwine v. Delo, 54 F.3d 1357 (8th Cir. 1995).

In U.S. v. Bernard, 299 F.3d 467 (5th Cir. 2002), cert. denied, 123 S. Ct. 2572 (U.S. 2003) and cert. denied, 123 S. Ct. 2572 (U.S. 2003) a prospective juror stated on the jury questionnaire: "I do not feel I have the right to judge whether a person lives or dies. I could not do that." When questioned on voir dire, however, the juror indicated that she had changed her mind and could return a death penalty in limited circumstances; but she also stated "she could not be sure about this." The prosecution challenged the juror for cause and the district court sustained the challenge on the basis of its impression that the prospective juror would not be able to faithfully and impartially apply the law. The Court of Appeals affirmed, finding no abuse of discretion.

No specific form of questioning is required in a capital case voir dire. In Mackall v. Angelone, 131 F.3d 442 (4th Cir. 1997), it was held that the trial court, although declining to ask prospective jurors their views on the death penalty, did ask sufficient questions from which the defendant could determine whether the jurors views would prevent or substantially impair the performance of their duties or whether jurors would automatically vote to impose the death penalty. See also Yeatts v. Angelone, 166 F.3d 255 (4th Cir. 1999) (voir dire of jurors in death penalty case did not give rise to claim of ineffective assistance of counsel where counsel failed to inform jurors that death penalty could not be imposed unless they unanimously found presence of aggravating factor). See also Neill v. Gibson, 263 F.3d 1184 (10th Cir. 2001), on reh'g, 278 F.3d 1044 (10th Cir. 2001), cert. denied, 537 U.S. 835, 123 S. Ct. 145, 154 L. Ed. 2d 54 (2002) (failure to ask three jurors if they would automatically vote to impose a death sentence did not constitute ineffective assistance of counsel in absence of a showing of prejudice, which had not been made); Stanford v. Parker, 266 F.3d 442, 2001 FED App. 0334P (6th Cir. 2001), cert. denied, 537 U.S. 831, 123 S. Ct. 136, 154 L. Ed. 2d 47 (2002) (failure to ask jurors "life-qualifying" questions during general voir dire did not amount to ineffective assistance of counsel).

CHALLENGES FOR CAUSE § 7:53

In Richardson v. Bowersox, 188 F.3d 973 (8th Cir. 1999) the trial court struck three prospective jurors who stated that they would not consider imposing the death penalty on the appellant unless the state proved he was the one who pushed the victims off the bridge. However, under state law a defendant could be found guilty of first-degree murder based on a theory of accomplice liability. Thus, it was held that the trial court did not err in finding that the jurors' views would impair their performance as jurors.

n. 406.

Add to note 406:

These developments, with particular focus on the future of social science research in the death qualification context, are discussed in Thompson, *Death Qualification after* Wainright v Witt *and* Lockhart v McCree, 13 Law & Hum Behav 185 (1989). See also Cox & Tanford, *An Alternative Method of Capital Jury Selection*, 13 Law & Hum Behav 167 (1989); Smith, *Due Process Education of the Jury: Overcoming the Bias of Death Qualified Juries*, 18 S.W.U.L. Rev. 493 (1989). A feminist perspective on the capital juror is provided in Howarth, *Deciding to Kill: Revealing the Gender in the Task Handed to Capital Jurors*, 1994 Wis L Rev 1345. See also *Symposium: Race, Crime and the Constitution*, 3 U. Pa. J. Const. L 1 (2001); Baldus, Woodworth, Zuckerman, Weiner and Broffitt, *The Use of Peremptory Challenges in Capital Murder Trials: A Legal and Empirical Analysis*, 3 U. Pa. J. Const. L. 3 (2001); Gross, Commentary: *Race, Peremptories, and Capital Jury Deliberations*, 3 U. Pa. J. Const. L. 283 (2001).

The fact that a jury has been death-qualified does not violate the rights of a noncapital defendant who is being tried jointly with a capital defendant. Buchanan v. Kentucky, 483 U.S. 402, 107 S. Ct. 2906, 97 L. Ed. 2d 336, 25 Fed. R. Evid. Serv. 120 (1987); Furman v. Wood, 190 F.3d 1002 (9th Cir. 1999).

Add at end of section:

In Morgan v. Illinois, 504 U.S. 719, 112 S. Ct. 2222, 119 L. Ed. 2d 492 (1992), the United States Supreme Court considered the problem of jurors who would automatically vote to impose the death penalty if a defendant were convicted of a capital crime. The trial judge had acceded to the state's request to ask jurors if they would automatically vote against the death penalty regardless of the facts; however, the judge had refused the defendant's request to ask if there were any jurors who would automatically vote in favor of the death penalty regardless of the facts. The United States Supreme Court reversed.

The Supreme Court addressed four issues:

1. Whether the jury at the sentencing stage of a capital trial was required to be impartial;
2. Whether a defendant may challenge for cause a juror who will automatically vote in favor of the death penalty regardless of the facts or instructions of the trial court;
3. Whether the trial court is required, upon request, to

§ 7:53   Jury Selection: Law, Art & Science 2d

      inquire into a prospective juror's views on capital punishment; and
4. Whether the voir dire in the case was constitutionally deficient.

The Court had little difficulty with its first question. Both the Sixth and Fourteenth Amendments require that the jury charged with sentencing in a capital case be impartial. But what constitutes impartiality? In Wainwright v. Witt, 469 U.S. 412, 105 S. Ct. 844, 83 L. Ed. 2d 841 (1985) (discussed in the main text) and Adams v. Texas, 448 U.S. 38, 100 S. Ct. 2521, 65 L. Ed. 2d 581 (1980), the Court had held that jurors who would automatically vote against the death penalty were not impartial and could be removed for cause. The Court applied the rationale of these decisions and held that jurors who would automatically vote for the death penalty were also not impartial and could be removed for cause. The Court stated that even if one such juror was impaneled and the jury voted for the death penalty, the state would not be entitled to execute the sentence.

The problem confronting the defendant, however, was of a more practical nature: how to identify jurors who would automatically vote in favor of the death penalty? In addressing this question, the Court proceeded from the premise that part of a defendant's guaranty to an impartial jury was the right to an adequate voir dire to identify unqualified jurors:

> Were voir dire not available to lay bare the foundation of petitioner's challenge for cause against those prospective jurors who would always impose death following conviction, his right not to be tried by such jurors would be rendered as nugatory and meaningless as the State's right, in the absence of questioning, to strike those who would never do so.

Morgan v. Illinois, 504 U.S. 719, 112 S. Ct. 2222, 2232, 119 L. Ed. 2d 492 (1992).

Voir dire was conducted in the case and the Court had, therefore, to determine its adequacy. The state maintained that the trial court's general questioning about juror willingness to be fair and follow the law was sufficient to protect the defendant's rights. The Supreme Court disagreed. The Court thought that jurors might in their own minds see no inconsistency between responding affirmatively to questions about fairness or impartiality and thinking that one convicted of a capital crime should automatically be sentenced to death. Their position would satisfy their own personal conception of fairness and impartiality. Yet, one who believed that death should automatically follow from conviction of a capital offense and was unwilling to consider mitigating circumstances as required and defined by law would not be following the law. Because the capital defendant was on trial for his life and related constitutional concerns could be alleviated, the Court was strengthened in its conviction that the defendant should be permitted to probe more closely the jurors' views on this critical issue. It thus found that the general questioning conducted by the trial judge was not sufficient.

The implications of *Morgan* are examined in Casenote, *Morgan v Illinois: The Defense Gets the Reverse-Witherspoon Question*, 44 Mercer L Rev 997 (1993); Note, *Morgan v Illinois: An Attempt to Provide Equality in the Selection of Capital Sentencing*, 38 Vill L Rev (1993); Belt, *Morgan v Illinois: The Right to Balance Capital Sentencing Juries as to Their Views on the Death Sentence Is Finally Granted to Defendants*, 24 NM L Rev 145 (1994).

In U.S. v. McVeigh, 153 F.3d 1166, 50 Fed. R. Evid. Serv. 541 (10th Cir. 1998) (disapproved of by, Hooks v. Ward, 184 F.3d 1206 (10th Cir. 1999)), the defendant was on trial for the Oklahoma City bombing. In reviewing his claims that *Morgan* had been violated, the Court of Appeals examined both "general *Morgan* questions" (those seeking to determine whether jurors would automatically impose the death penalty); and "specific *Morgan* questions" (those seeking to ascertain whether the pretrial publicity regarding the bombing would bias the jurors' view of the appropriate sentence for anyone convicted of the crime). The court found only one occasion where counsel had been denied the opportunity to ask a "general *Morgan* question", and found that this instance was not an abuse of the Court's discretion. In contrast, there had been repeated instances where the government's objection to "specific *Morgan* questions" had been sustained, and these had given rise to a continuing objection by the defendant. The questions for the most part were designed to elicit whether the jurors felt that the circumstances surrounding the bombing were so aggravating that no mitigating factor could compensate. The Court, again, however, found no abuse of the trial court's discretion, holding that *Morgan* did not require questioning about specific mitigating or aggravating factors. See also Stanford v. Parker, 266 F.3d 442, 2001 FED App. 0334P (6th Cir. 2001), cert. denied, 537 U.S. 831, 123 S. Ct. 136, 154 L. Ed. 2d 47 (2002) (Court's refusal to allow capital defendant to ask "life-qualifying" questions of prospective jurors during individual voir dire did not violate Morgan where defendant was allowed to ask such questions during general voir dire).

In Bunch v. Thompson, 949 F.2d 1354 (4th Cir. 1991), a pre-*Morgan* case, the Court of Appeals found that the trial judge did not err in declining to remove two jurors who

§ 7:53   JURY SELECTION: LAW, ART & SCIENCE 2D

initially maintained that the death penalty should be imposed in every case of murder, regardless of the facts and circumstances, but who changed their positions upon questioning.

In State v. Ross, 623 So. 2d 643 (La. 1993), a juror professed to a belief that the death penalty should always be imposed upon a defendant convicted of first degree murder. The Louisiana Supreme Court held that the juror should have been excused for cause, as the statement indicated an inability on the juror's part to follow the law given by the court. See also Thomas v. Com., 864 S.W.2d 252 (Ky. 1993) (juror's assertion that he would definitely vote to impose the death penalty if defendant was convicted indicated a bias so strong that the juror was not subject to rehabilitation). On the other hand it was held in State v. Ramsey, 864 S.W.2d 320 (Mo. 1993), that a juror's indication that the juror "leaned" toward the death penalty was not itself enough to warrant dismissing the juror for cause. Likewise, in U.S. v. Chandler, 996 F.2d 1073, 39 Fed. R. Evid. Serv. 304 (11th Cir. 1993), the court stated that it was acceptable for a juror to be a proponent of the death penalty, as long as the juror would not automatically vote to impose it. See also Murray v. Delo, 34 F.3d 1367 (8th Cir. 1994) (no error in rejection of challenge for cause to two jurors who admitted bias in favor of death penalty where jurors indicated that they could follow the court's instructions and consider alternative punishments).

In dicta (because the defendant had procedurally defaulted his claim) in Oken v. Corcoran, 220 F.3d 259 (4th Cir. 2000), cert. denied, 531 U.S. 1165, 121 S. Ct. 1126, 148 L. Ed. 2d 992 (2001), the Court of Appeals stated that Morgan would be satisfied by the following four questions:

 (1) Do you have any strong feeling, one way or the other, with regard to the death penalty?;

 (2) Do you feel that your attitude, regarding the death penalty, would prevent or substantially impair you from making a fair and impartial decision on whether the defendant is not guilty or guilty, based on the evidence presented and the court's instructions as to the law?;

 (3) Do you feel your attitude, regarding the death penalty, would prevent or substantially impair you from making a fair and impartial decision on whether the defendant was or was not criminally responsible by reason of insanity, based on the evidence presented and the court's instructions on the law?;

 (4) Do you feel that your attitude, regarding the death

penalty, would prevent or substantially impair you from sentencing the defendant, based upon the evidence presented and the court's instructions as to the law which is applicable?

A juror in a death penalty case may not refuse to consider, as a matter of law, relevant mitigating evidence, and a juror who indicates an ability to do so should be excused for cause. See Soria v. Johnson, 207 F.3d 232 (5th Cir. 2000). In the case, however, the defendant exercised a peremptory challenge against the juror in question, and thus was not denied an impartial jury.

Add after end of section:
In U.S. v. Hall, 152 F.3d 381, 49 Fed. R. Evid. Serv. 1503 (5th Cir. 1998) (abrogated by, U.S. v. Martinez-Salazar, 528 U.S. 304, 120 S. Ct. 774, 145 L. Ed. 2d 792 (2000)), the court considered the challenges to a number of jurors in a capital case. Although several had indicated that they favored the death penalty (one because it saved taxpayer moneys), the jurors also indicated that they were prepared to base their decision on the evidence and follow the instructions of the judge, and would consider mitigating as well as aggravating factors and not automatically reject a sentence of life imprisonment. In these circumstances the court found no abuse of discretion in the trial judge's decision not to allow the defendant's challenge for cause to each of the jurors.

§ 7:54 Jury nullifiers *[New]*

The topic of jury nullification has been examined previously (see §§ 2:20, 2:21 main text). The question left unexplored was whether a juror's willingness to engage in nullification could be made the basis for a challenge for cause. In U.S. v. Thomas, 116 F.3d 606 (2d Cir. 1997), the second circuit Court of Appeals addressed whether a sitting juror, suspected of being a nullifier, could be dismissed from the panel. The juror had been the subject of a complaint by other members of the jury, who had gained the impression that the juror was not prepared to decide the case in accord with the controlling law, but rather intended to vote for an acquittal on racial grounds. The trial judge proceeded to interview the juror in camera, seeking to determine whether "just cause" existed to dismiss the juror under Fed. R. Crim. Proc. 23(b) and concluded that there was. The Court of Appeals reversed, holding that, while as a general proposition a judge had the authority to dismiss a juror who intended to nullify, the juror in the instant case should not have been dismissed because he had not said anything during the in camera interview to indicate conclusively that he would not follow the law. To justify a dismissal of a juror, there would, according to the court, need to be proof beyond a reasonable doubt that the juror was going to engage in nullification. The *Thomas* decision was distinguished in U.S. v. Baker, 262 F.3d 124 (2d Cir. 2001), where the Court of Appeals upheld the trial judge's decision to dismiss a juror who refused to participate in deliberations. The key difference between this case and *Thomas* was between a nullifier who would vote without regard to the evidence and a juror who refused to carry out one of the obligations of jury duty, namely that of deliberating with the other jurors. See also U.S. v. Abbell, 271 F.3d 1286 (11th Cir. 2001), cert. denied, 537 U.S. 813, 123 S. Ct. 74, 154 L. Ed. 2d 16 (2002) (dismissal of juror who, during deliberations, refused to apply the law as instructed by the court was not abuse of discretion).

In People v. Merced, 94 Cal. App. 4th 1024, 114 Cal. Rptr. 2d 781 (1st Dist. 2001), review denied, (Mar. 13, 2002) a prospective alternate juror was removed for cause after he indicated in writing on the juror questionnaire that he recognized and believed in jury nullification. When questioned by the judge, the prospective juror stated that it was reasonable for the judge to assume that he, the juror, would not follow the law if it went against his conscience. On appeal the removal for cause was upheld. The appellate court added that the trial judge was not required to undertake an inquiry into whether the particular details of the case to be tried presented a likelihood that the juror would actually engage in nullification, as such an inquiry would itself encourage improper prejudgment of the case.

The *Thomas* decision, although involving the dismissal of a sitting juror, has obvious implications for jury selection, and in particular whether a juror's intent to nullify can be the basis for a challenge for cause. It implies that it would not be improper for a court to dismiss for cause a prospective juror who unequivocally indicated on voir dire such an intent. Constitutional considerations aside, the decision is likely to promote a lack of candor on the part of jurors being questioned on voir dire. Indeed, it is jurors who strongly believe in the principles, perhaps extra-legal, which may be at stake in a case who will be most inclined to conceal their attitudes if they perceive that it would lead to their dismissal from the jury panel. By excluding not automatic but potential nullifiers (those who would not automatically vote to nullify but who would be open to the possibility in appropriate circumstances), the likely effect will be to impanel a jury that is more prone to favor conviction than would be a panel selected at random. Comparable arguments, however, have been rejected in respect to the somewhat analogous question of whether in a capital case the exclusion of those opposed to the death penalty leads to juries which are more conviction-prone. See Lockhart v. McCree, 476 U.S. 162, 106 S. Ct. 1758, 90 L. Ed. 2d 137 (1986).

While the decision in *Thomas* is radical in suggesting that a juror's willingness to nullify may be made the basis for the juror's removal from the panel, its effect in practice is likely to be diluted considerably by the heavy burden of proof that the court imposed in order to show that a juror does intend to nullify. In a case where the evidence of nullification arises, as in *Thomas*, during deliberations, the Court's holding places the trial judge in the uncomfortable position of having to compromise the traditional sanctity of the jury room in order to make a determination of whether a juror does in fact intend to engage in nullification.

Thomas has been the subject of considerable academic comment. See, e.g., Recent Case, *Criminal law—Jury Nullification*, 111 Harvard L. Rev. 1347 (1998); Note, *United States v. Thomas: Pulling the Jury Apart*, 30 Conn. L. Rev. 731 (1998). Professor King argues that there is no constitutional bar to the exclusion of nullifiers, or to placing restrictions on those who would advocate nullification outside the courtroom [as urged, most prominently, by the Fully Informed Jury Association (FIJA)]. King, *Silencing Nullification Advocacy Inside the Jury Room and Outside the Courtroom*, 65 U. Chicago L. Rev. 433 (1998).

As much as lawyers might prefer judges to tell jurors that they possess the power to nullify, what they would not want is an explicit judicial instruction to the effect that jurors have no right to nullify. Such an instruction was given by the trial court in the California case of People v. Sanchez and upheld on appeal. People v. Sanchez, 58 Cal. App. 4th 1435, 69 Cal. Rptr. 2d 16 (2d Dist. 1997). The California appeals court held that the trial court acted within its authority when it told jurors that it would remove any who indicated that he or she would be prepared to engage in nullification. The Court's decision is examined in Note and Comment, *A Community with No Conscience: The Further Reduction of a Jury's Right to Nullify in People v. Sanchez*, 21 Whittier L. Rev. 285 (1999).

Chapter 8
Peremptory Challenges

> **KeyCite®:** Cases and other legal materials listed in KeyCite Scope can be researched through West's KeyCite service on Westlaw®. Use KeyCite to check citations for form, parallel references, prior and later history, and comprehensive citator information, including citations to other decisions and secondary materials.

§ 8:1 Introduction

n. 15.

Add to note 15:

Although not retreating from its position in *Stilson* that there is no constitutional right to peremptory challenges, the United States Supreme Court in Holland v. Illinois, 493 U.S. 474, 110 S. Ct. 803, 107 L. Ed. 2d 905 (1990), recognized the strong constitutional basis for peremptory challenges: "One could plausibly argue [although we have said to the contrary, See Stilson v. U S, 250 U.S. 583, 586, 40 S. Ct. 28, 63 L. Ed. 1154 (1919)] that the requirement of an 'impartial jury' impliedly compels peremptory challenges." Holland v. Illinois, 493 U.S. 474, 110 S. Ct. 803, 107 L. Ed. 2d 905 (1990) (emphasis in original). In contrast, the Kentucky Supreme Court in Thomas v. Com., 864 S.W.2d 252 (Ky. 1993), stated that the right to exercise peremptory challenges against qualified jurors was not an impartial jury question but one of due process.

Add after fifth paragraph:

A court's denial or impairment of a party's right to exercise its peremptory challenges is ground for reversal without a showing of prejudice. Swain v. Alabama, 380 U.S. 202, 219, 85 S. Ct. 824, 13 L. Ed. 2d 759 (1965) (overruled by, Batson v. Kentucky, 476 U.S. 79, 106 S. Ct. 1712, 90 L. Ed. 2d 69 (1986)) (overruled by, Batson v. Kentucky, 476 U.S. 79, 106 S. Ct. 1712, 90 L. Ed. 2d 69 (1986) (holding modified by, Powers v. Ohio, 499 U.S. 400, 111 S. Ct. 1364, 113 L. Ed. 2d 411 (1991)); Knox v. Collins, 928 F.2d 657 (5th Cir. 1991). In *Knox*, the trial judge promised to give a parole instruction to the jury, but later reneged on that promise. The initial promise, however, colored the defense's strategy in exercising its peremptory challenges. The Fifth Circuit Court of Appeals held that defendant's right to intelligently exercise his peremptory challenges had been unconstitutionally interfered with.

n. 18.

Add to note 18:

§ 8:1   JURY SELECTION: LAW, ART & SCIENCE 2D

The value of the peremptory challenge in eliminating extremes of partiality and thereby facilitating the impaneling of an impartial jury was emphasized by the United States Supreme Court in Holland v. Illinois, 493 U.S. 474, 110 S. Ct. 803, 107 L. Ed. 2d 905 (1990).

n. 27.

Add to note 27:

The ethical propriety of using race in formulating one's peremptory challenge strategy is considered in Kaine, *Race, Trial Strategy, and Legal Ethics*, 24 U Rich L Rev 361 (1990). The possibility of a violation of the Thirteenth Amendment in these circumstances is developed by Colbert, *Challenging the Challenge: Thirteenth Amendment as a Prohibition against the Racial Use of Peremptory Challenges*, 76 Cornell L Rev 1 (1991).

§ 8:2 Number of peremptory challenges

n. 32.

Add to note 32:

; Annotation, Number of and procedures for exercising peremptory challenges allowed in federal criminal trial for selection of regular jurors—modern cases, 110 A.L.R. Fed. 626. In Comment, *Don't Mess with Texas Voir Dire*, 39 Houston L. Rev. 201 (2002) the author argues against proposals for a reduction in the number of peremptory challenges.

n. 33.

Add to note 33:

In U.S. v. Machado, 195 F.3d 454 (9th Cir. 1999) the defendant argued that, because he was charged with two separate misdemeanor violations (and thus, if convicted on both counts, liable to a term of imprisonment comparable to that imposed for a felony conviction), he should not be limited to the three peremptory challenges normally allowed in a misdemeanor prosecution. The Court of Appeals disagreed, holding that the length of time that a defendant might wind up serving in prison if convicted was irrelevant to the number of peremptory challenges to which he was entitled. Rather, it was the maximum length of imprisonment for the most serious charge that was determinative. Where several misdemeanor charges were properly joined, that fact did not increase defendant's entitlement to peremptory challenges. Accord, U.S. v. Ming, 466 F.2d 1000, 72-1 U.S. Tax Cas. (CCH) ¶ 9449, 29 A.F.T.R.2d 72-1240 (7th Cir. 1972). Although one can understand the Court's concerns—should a defendant charged with, say, 50 misdemeanors be entitled to 150 (50 X 3) peremptory challenges?—the holding does allow an unscrupulous prosecutor, bent on limiting a defendant's peremptory challenges, to cumulate numerous misdemeanor charges rather than bring a single felony charge. Perhaps the assumption is that no prosecutor would engage in such dubious tactics, but an alternative and arguably preferable solution would have been to allow a defendant 10 challenges if the maximum penalty that the defendant faced was the same as that which would be faced by a defendant charged with a felony. Cf. also U.S. v. Hutchings, 751 F.2d 230, 17 Fed. R. Evid. Serv. 1274 (8th Cir. 1984) (in multi-count felony prosecution, defendant was not entitled to 10 peremptory challenges per charge).

n. 37.

Add to note 37:

Although there is no set number of peremptory challenges required by the Constitution, the failure to allow a defendant the number of statutory challenges provided by state law implicates a Fourteenth Amendment liberty interest. See Vansickel v. White, 166 F.3d 953 (9th Cir. 1999). In *Vansickel*, however, the petitioner had failed to make a timely objection. The Court of Appeals found that there had been no prejudicial error, as required for federal habeas review of procedurally defaulted claims.

Fahringer argues that the trend towards a reduction in the number of peremptory challenges (or their elimination altogether) is shortsighted and misguided Fahringer, *The Peremptory Challenge: An Endangered Species,* 31 Crim. L Bull 400 (1995).

n. 45.
Add to note 45 after "Williams":
U.S. v. Burger, 773 F. Supp. 1430 (D. Kan. 1991); U.S. v. Cochran, 955 F.2d 1116, 35 Fed. R. Evid. Serv. 786 (7th Cir. 1992); Turpin v. Kassulke, 26 F.3d 1392, 1994 FED App. 0224P (6th Cir. 1994); U.S. v. Whitehead, 238 F.3d 949 (8th Cir. 2001).

Add after fourth sentence in fifth paragraph:
In Lafevers v. State, 1991 OK CR 97, 819 P.2d 1362 (Okla. Crim. App. 1991), the court held that the trial judge had committed reversible error in requiring codefendants with antagonistic defenses to share the statutory complement of peremptory challenges. The decision might be compared with that in U.S. v. Gibbs, 182 F.3d 408, 1999 FED App. 0140P (6th Cir. 1999). In *Gibbs*, eight defendants were allotted 16 peremptory challenges and instructed that they were to exercise the challenges jointly. When the defendants were unable to agree on whether to challenge two particular jurors, they moved the court either to grant them additional challenges or to authorize each defendant to exercise certain challenges independently of the others. Instead, the court held a vote of the defendants, which resulted in a four-four tie. The court then proceeded with the case, with the result that the two contested jurors served on the jury. On appeal, it was held that the defendants had failed to show a denial of their right to exercise peremptory challenges. The Court of Appeals stated that, given the benefit of hindsight, it would have been better to allocate a certain number of challenges to each defendant in cases of conflict, but that the trial court had not abused its discretion.

n. 47.
Add to note 47:
In U.S. v. Magana, 118 F.3d 1173, 47 Fed. R. Evid. Serv. 626 (7th Cir. 1997), the trial judge granted defendants two additional peremptory challenges but this was less than the number sought by the defendants. On appeal the court held that in a multi-defendant case, whether to grant additional peremptory challenges, as well as the appropriate number of additional challenges to grant, rested within the discretion of the trial judge, and that there that had not been an abuse of that discretion.

In Tidemann v. Nadler Golf Car Sales, Inc., 224 F.3d 719, 47 Fed. R. Serv. 3d 810 (7th Cir. 2000), a civil case, the Court of Appeals held that

§ 8:2   Jury Selection: Law, Art & Science 2d

the trial court had acted within its discretion in allotting the two defendants three extra peremptory challenges.

Add after first sentence in sixth paragraph:
But see State v. Mayer, 589 So. 2d 1145 (La. Ct. App. 5th Cir. 1991), writ denied, 609 So. 2d 251 (La. 1992) (request for additional peremptory challenges properly denied where there was no statutory provision for allowing additional challenges). In In re Air Crash Disaster, 86 F.3d 498, 44 Fed. R. Evid. Serv. 1102, 34 Fed. R. Serv. 3d 1067, 1996 FED App. 0157P (6th Cir. 1996), the trial court had implicitly recognized its discretion to increase the number of peremptory challenges allowed by awarding each side eight peremptory challenges (rather than the three allotted by statute). There was no error in the Court's rejection of a motion by the airline for six peremptory challenges to be used in selecting the jury and another three to be used in selecting alternate jurors.

Add after second sentence in sixth paragraph:
Although typically parties will be pleased to receive additional peremptory challenges, the downside of the practice was pointed out in Rodriguez v. Riddell Sports, Inc., 242 F.3d 567, Prod. Liab. Rep. (CCH) ¶ 16004, 56 Fed. R. Evid. Serv. 708 (5th Cir. 2001). The defendant here argued that the extra challenges (seven instead of the normal three) had permitted the plaintiffs to remove that sector of the population consisting of educated, middle-class and upper middle-class persons. The challenge failed because the defendant did not prove his contention to the Court's satisfaction, but the point that additional peremptory challenges will allow a party that is so inclined greater scope for removing a distinct segment of the population is one that it is well to bear in mind.

In Bonin v. Vasquez, 794 F. Supp. 957 (C.D. Cal. 1992), aff'd, 59 F.3d 815 (9th Cir. 1995), the court invited the petitioner, who had exhausted his peremptory challenges, to renew a request for additional peremptories. The defendant failed to do so, and on appeal by the defendant the court found no constitutional violation in the trial judge's failure to award additional peremptory challenges.

Add after fourth sentence in sixth paragraph:
It also lies within a trial court's discretion to condition the grant of additional peremptory challenges to one side upon its consent to granting additional peremptory challenges to the opposing side. See U.S. v. Vaccaro, 816 F.2d 443, 22 Fed. R. Evid. Serv. 1570 (9th Cir. 1987) (abrogated on other grounds by, Huddleston v. U.S., 485 U.S. 681, 108 S. Ct. 1496, 99 L. Ed. 2d 771, 25 Fed. R. Evid. Serv. 1 (1988)).

PEREMPTORY CHALLENGES § 8:2

Add after sixth paragraph:
In Mills v. GAF Corp., 20 F.3d 678, 1994 FED App. 0104P (6th Cir. 1994), the trial court decided to try two related asbestos cases concurrently and to select the juries for each case at the same time from the same pool. A peremptory challenge exercised during the first selection did not remove the challenged juror from consideration for the second jury. To remove the same prospective juror from both panels, a party would have to exercise two of its peremptory challenges. There were, however, separate peremptory challenges allocated for each case. The Court of Appeals held that this method of selection did not unconstitutionally impair a party's exercise of its peremptory challenges. It defended the logic of the approach by observing that a juror might be struck in the first selection because the juror was judged to be less desirable than other members of the panel, but in the second selection the same juror might be retained because he or she was seen as better than the alternatives. In any event, the defense had failed to exercise all of its available peremptory challenges, and none of the jurors from the first panel were in fact seated on the second jury.

Sometimes only 11 jurors remain on the jury after all peremptory challenges have been exhausted. When the twelfth juror is then selected does either party have the right to exercise a peremptory challenge against him or her? See U.S. v. Springfield, 829 F.2d 860 (9th Cir. 1987) (allowing defendant to exchange one of the peremptory challenges previously used in order to strike the twelfth juror, but denying any additional peremptory challenge); U.S. v. Christoffel, 952 F.2d 1086 (9th Cir. 1991) (no error in not granting additional peremptory challenge to strike twelfth juror when no request made for additional challenge).

n. 51.
Add to note 51:
U.S. v. Schlei, 122 F.3d 944, 48 Fed. R. Evid. Serv. 143 (11th Cir. 1997) (defendant waived claim that he should have been granted additional peremptory challenges by not exhausting those allotted to him).

Add at end of section:
Under the Confrontation Clause, defendants are entitled to be present during all stages of their trial, including jury selection. A similar right is conferred by Federal Rule of Criminal Procedure 43(a). In U.S. v. Gibbs, 182 F.3d 408, 1999 FED App. 0140P (6th Cir. 1999) the Court of Appeals held that any alleged violation of this right to be present during jury selection was subject to both harmless error and plain error analysis. In *Gibbs*, the court held that, even conceding error, the defendants had not been prejudiced by their not being present during isolated portions of the voir dire. In

§ 8:2   JURY SELECTION: LAW, ART & SCIENCE 2D

U.S. v. Collazo-Aponte, 216 F.3d 163, 54 Fed. R. Evid. Serv. 1311 (1st Cir. 2000), cert. granted in part, judgment vacated on other grounds, 532 U.S. 1036, 121 S. Ct. 1996, 149 L. Ed. 2d 1000 (2001) the court held in a multi-defendant conspiracy trial that the defendants right to be present at all critical stages of the trial had not been violated when the trial judge had restricted participation in sidebar conferences to two defense lawyers at the most. In contrast, in Preferred Properties, Inc. v. Indian River Estates, Inc., 276 F.3d 790, 2002 FED App. 0006P (6th Cir. 2002), cert. denied, 536 U.S. 959, 122 S. Ct. 2663, 153 L. Ed. 2d 838 (2002), a civil case, the court held that the parties had the right to be present in person during the voir dire absent compelling reasons, which a district court had to place on the record so as to be reviewable on appeal.

§ 8:3   Procedures
n. 52.

Add to note 52:

See generally Annotation, Number of and procedures for exercising peremptory challenges allowed in federal criminal trial for selection of regular jurors—modern cases, 110 A.L.R. Fed. 626.

Add after note 52:

A failure to make a timely objection to the method of allocating peremptory challenges will constitute a waiver. In U.S. v. Broadus, 7 F.3d 460, 39 Fed. R. Evid. Serv. 765 (6th Cir. 1993), the parties agreed to a "use it or lose it" system, in which a peremptory challenge not exercised at the appropriate juncture would be lost forever. Defendant's objection to this approach was not made until jury selection was virtually complete. The court held that it was therefore not timely. The court gratuitously added that the "use it or lose it" system was not unfair to the defendant, even though as a result of the system the defendant wound up with only nine peremptory challenges rather than the 10 prescribed by federal law. In U.S. v. Sherwood, 98 F.3d 402 (9th Cir. 1996) the court held that the defendant had waived his right to be present when peremptory challenges were made at sidebar by giving no indication that he wished to be present.

In an extraordinary case of first impression, the Court of Appeals held in U.S. v. Harbin, 250 F.3d 532 (7th Cir. 2001) that the prosecution's midtrial use of a peremptory challenge to eliminate an impartial juror violated the defendant's due process rights. The challenge had been lodged on the sixth day of an eight-day trial, the government maintaining that it had "saved" the challenge from jury selection, despite the trial judge's earlier admonition that peremptory challenges could not be used once a potential juror had been passed.

The Court of Appeals reasoned that peremptory challenges do not survive the jury selection process, drawing support for its position not only from constitutional (due process) considerations but also from statutory (Fed. R. Crim. P. 24) considerations. The effect of the trial judge's allowance of the challenge was to grant the prosecution unilateral control over the composition of the jury during the trial stage and the lack of notice precluded the defendants' intelligent exercise of their peremptory challenges. Policy considerations further reinforced the Court's holding, as to have ruled otherwise would have encouraged parties to engage in fishing positions during trial or to refrain from pursuing certain lines of inquiry during voir dire in order to leave open the possibility of a midtrial challenge. That the challenge was based on new information was also deemed irrelevant. The Court indicated that if the new information had indicated a juror's lack of impartiality, a challenge for cause might not have been inappropriate. Finally, the Court of Appeals held that the trial court's error was fundamental and required automatic reversal.

In Hidalgo v. Fagen, 206 F.3d 1013 (10th Cir. 2000), a civil case, counsel, in peremptorily challenging a juror, had referred to his preference for male as opposed to female jurors. While this may have been in violation of the Supreme Court's holding in *JEB v. Alabama ex. rel. T.B.* (discussed in this supplement), the plaintiff did not object. The Court of Appeals held that the trial judge was not under a sua sponte obligation to raise this claim in a civil context unless the error was one which seriously affected "the fairness, integrity or public reputation of judicial proceedings" (citing Glenn v. Cessna Aircraft Co, 32 F.3d 1462 (10th Cir. 1994).

n. 53.

Add to note 53:

See also U.S. v. Miller, 946 F.2d 1344 (8th Cir. 1991) (accord); Jones v. Ryan, 987 F.2d 960 (3d Cir. 1993).

In U.S. v. Norquay, 987 F.2d 475, 38 Fed. R. Evid. Serv. 162 (8th Cir. 1993) (abrogated by, U.S. v. Thomas, 20 F.3d 817 (8th Cir. 1994)), the Court of Appeals upheld a trial judge ruling that the defense and government were to make their peremptory challenges simultaneously without knowledge of each other's choices. A similar "blind strike" method of jury selection was used by the trial court and affirmed by the Court of Appeals in U.S. v. Warren, 25 F.3d 890 (9th Cir. 1994). The Court of Appeals stated that even when both the government and the defendant struck the same juror there was no impairment of the defendant's full use of his peremptory challenges. Accord U.S. v. Harper, 33 F.3d 1143 (9th Cir. 1994).

Add after third paragraph:

In U.S. v. Anderson, 39 F.3d 331 (D.C. Cir. 1994), reh'g in banc granted, judgment vacated, (#90-3041)(Feb. 9, 1995) and on reh'g in part, 59 F.3d 1323 (D.C. Cir. 1995), the trial

§ 8:3   JURY SELECTION: LAW, ART & SCIENCE 2D

judge had granted the defense 12 peremptory challenges and the government seven (instead of 10 and six). The parties were to alternate exercise of their peremptory challenges. In subsequent rounds challenges were limited to jurors who had replaced those who had been previously removed. Because of the disparity in the number of challenges allotted to the parties, the trial court in *Anderson* had permitted the government to delay exercising its peremptory challenges for several rounds while requiring the defense to exercise its challenges at the end of each round. This provided the government with the tactical advantage of being able to view a wider range of jurors before deciding whom to challenge. Although the Court of Appeals was somewhat troubled by this approach, it did not find that the trial judge had committed reversible error. The preferable procedure and that apparently envisioned by the drafters of the federal rules, however, would have been to require each party to exercise its challenges at the end of each round. Assuming that one juror was peremptorily challenged by each side in each round, this would have left the defendants with the final five challenges.

In U.S. v. Thompson, 76 F.3d 442 (2d Cir. 1996), the trial court had employed the "jury box" system for selecting jurors. The selection process consisted of three rounds. In each round the government and defense were allotted a set number of peremptory challenges. The defendant was allotted five challenges in the first round, four in the second round (which now included substitutes for jurors challenged in the first round), and one in the third; the government was allotted three challenges in the first round, two in the second and one in the third. Challenges not exercised in the appointed round were deemed waived, a fact disclosed to the parties in advance. Defendant objected to this procedure because ultimately he found himself without any peremptory challenges even though there was one juror still to be selected whose identity he did not know. The Court of Appeals held that this method of jury selection was not an abuse of the trial court's discretion.

n. 58.

Add to note 58:

The use of a "struck" system of jury selecting was upheld in U.S. v. Broxton, 926 F.2d 1180 (D.C. Cir. 1991). In U.S. v. Patterson, 215 F.3d 776 (7th Cir. 2000), cert. granted in part, judgment vacated in part, 531 U.S. 1033, 121 S. Ct. 621, 148 L. Ed. 2d 531 (2000) the Court of Appeals held that where a "struck" system of jury selection was employed, the court was not required to prioritize the members of the panel in regard to the order of their selection. The defendants had argued that the failure to prioritize restricted their ability to exercise peremptory challenges on those prospective jurors most likely to be called to serve. The advantage to

§ 8:5 PEREMPTORY CHALLENGES

be gained was minimal, however, and, more crucially, no showing had been made that the jurors who sat on the jury were not impartial. Thus, the court found no error.

Add after sixth sentence in fourth paragraph:
Where the method for selecting jurors is prescribed by statute, an individual judge's partial use of a "struck jury" method of selection was held to be reversible error. State v. Echineque, 73 Haw. 100, 828 P.2d 276 (1992).

Add at end of fourth paragraph:
See generally Nichols, *Some Thoughts on How to Use the Struck System in Jury Voir Dire,* 46 Wash St B News 11 (1992).

n. 62.
Add to note 62:
See also Kotler v. American Tobacco Co., 926 F.2d 1217, Prod. Liab. Rep. (CCH) ¶ 12674 (1st Cir. 1990), cert. granted, judgment vacated on other grounds, 505 U.S. 1215, 112 S. Ct. 3019, 120 L. Ed. 2d 891 (1992) (trial judge permitted additional peremptory challenge to party who was allegedly unaware of Court's 'use-it-or-lose-it-rule' whereby failure to exercise a peremptory challenge at the appropriate time constituted a waiver of the challenge).

§ 8:4 Discriminatory peremptory challenges: The pre-*Batson* state of the law

n. 74.
Add to note 74:
Because of the difficulties in establishing a Swain violation, it should not be surprising that appellate counsel, as a matter of strategy, often chose to emphasize more promising grounds of appeal. Such a strategic decision has been held not to constitute ineffective assistance of counsel. See Blair v. Armontrout, 976 F.2d 1130 (8th Cir. 1992); Horne v. Trickey, 895 F.2d 497 (8th Cir. 1990). The Court of Appeals in Ford v. Norris, 67 F.3d 162 (8th Cir. 1995) found a violation in Swain.

§ 8:5 Batson v Kentucky

n. 83.
Add to note 83:
The Supreme Court's decision applies also to alternate jurors. See U.S. v. Harris, 192 F.3d 580, 1999 FED App. 0340P (6th Cir. 1999) (noting that at the time the alternate jurors were selected, the court and parties had no way of knowing whether they would ultimately serve). Nor is there an exception from *Batson* for cases involving race-related issues. U.S. v. Pospisil, 186 F.3d 1023 (8th Cir. 1999).

Although *Batson* was decided under the equal protection clause, its prohibition extends to the federal government through the due process clause of the Fifth Amendment. U.S. v. Hughes, 970 F.2d 227, 36 Fed. R. Evid. Serv. 633 (7th Cir. 1992).

n. 89.
Add to note 89:

A distinction can be drawn between challenges based on race and challenges based on a juror's opinions on racial issues. In Tolbert v. Gomez, 190 F.3d 985 (9th Cir. 1999) a black juror was challenged after approaching the bench to express strong concerns regarding racial prejudice in the judicial system. Apart from this intervention, the juror was undistinguishable from the others on the panel. On appeal the trial court's grant of the challenge was upheld, the Court of Appeals viewing it as a case where a juror was challenged because of his opinions (albeit about race) rather than because of his race.

Add to end of section:

In Allen v. Hardy, 478 U.S. 255, 106 S. Ct. 2878, 92 L. Ed. 2d 199 (1986), the Supreme Court held that *Batson* would not be applied retroactively on collateral review to convictions that had become final before the date *Batson* was decided. In Williams v. Chrans, 945 F.2d 926 (7th Cir. 1991), the court stated that the holding of *Hardie* was not affected by the fact that the defendant's conviction was for a capital crime. However, in Griffith v. Kentucky, 479 U.S. 314, 107 S. Ct. 708, 93 L. Ed. 2d 649 (1987), the Court held that *Batson* would be applied to those cases not yet final when *Batson* was decided.

A case that seemingly fell somewhere between these two stools was presented in Ford v. Georgia, 498 U.S. 411, 111 S. Ct. 850, 112 L. Ed. 2d 935 (1991). In a pre-*Batson* trial, the defendant had filed a motion in advance of voir dire seeking to prevent the prosecutor's exercise of peremptory challenges on a racial basis, which the defendant alleged had occurred in the past. The motion was denied. At trial the prosecution in fact used nine of its 10 peremptory challenges to strike black prospective jurors. Following his conviction, the defendant claimed that the prosecution had acted unconstitutionally, although the constitutional provision the defendant alleged to have been violated was the Sixth Amendment. The United States Supreme Court vacated the conviction and remanded the case for further consideration in light of *Griffith*. On remand, the Georgia Supreme Court decided that Ford had not timely raised his *Batson* claims, notwithstanding the fact that *Batson* had not been decided at the time of Ford's trial, and that under a state procedural rule, also not in force at the time of Ford's trial, his failure to make a timely *Batson* claim precluded further relief.

Relying on Ford v. Georgia, 498 U.S. 411, 111 S. Ct. 850, 112 L. Ed. 2d 935 (1991), the Court of Appeals in Allen v. Lee, 319 F.3d 645 (4th Cir. 2003), reh'g en banc granted, opinion vacated, (Mar. 24, 2003), a case where the trial took place prior to the Supreme Court's decision in *Batson* (and, accordingly, where the standards of Swain v. Alabama, 380 U.S. 202, 85 S. Ct. 824, 13 L. Ed. 2d 759 (1965) (overruled by, Batson v. Kentucky, 476 U.S. 79, 106 S. Ct. 1712, 90 L.

Ed. 2d 69 (1986)) controlled), held that defendant's unsuccessful pretrial motion based on *Swain* sufficed to preserve a subsequent *Batson* claim. The court distinguished between cases where a defendant has not made any challenge under either *Batson* or *Swain*, thus not alerting the trial court to any alleged impropriety, and the present case, where the trial court had been afforded the opportunity to address the constitutional objections. See also Cochran v. Herring, 43 F.3d 1404 (11th Cir. 1995), opinion modified on denial of reh'g, Cochran v. Herring, 61 F.3d 20 (11th Cir. 1995).

The decision was again appealed to the United States Supreme Court, which again reversed. It held that the original pretrial motion, although perhaps inartfully drawn, raised the substance of an equal protection claim. It further held that a state procedural bar could not operate retroactively to preclude consideration of a defendant's *Batson* claims. Thus, there was not an adequate and independent state procedural ground which would bar federal court review of the *Batson* claim.

The effect of the Supreme Court's retroactivity decisions relating to *Batson* is that cases may still arise which are controlled by *Swain*. One such case was Andrews v. Deland, 943 F.2d 1162 (10th Cir. 1991). At the Board of Pardons meeting in 1989, the prosecutor at the original trial, approximately 15 years previous and long before the Supreme Court's decision in *Batson*, admitted that he had removed the only black juror on the voir dire panel partly for racial reasons. This admission alone, however, was not sufficient to satisfy *Swain*'s requirement of a showing of systematic exclusion of blacks. The exception developed in some circuits covering cases where the prosecutor conceded at trial an intent to exclude an identifiable group was deemed to be inapplicable because the prosecutor's admission was not made at trial. See also Davis v. Greer, 13 F.3d 1134 (7th Cir. 1994) (failure to show a history of purposeful discrimination held to defeat claimed violation of *Swain*); Capers v. Singletary, 989 F.2d 442 (11th Cir. 1993) (defendants failed to establish prima facie case of *Swain* violation; numerous black jurors had in fact served, and failure of prosecutor to exercise available peremptory challenges to remove blacks tended to rebut any inference of intentional discrimination). In McCall v. Delo, 31 F.3d 750 (8th Cir. 1994), the prosecutor had used his peremptory challenges to strike all six blacks from the venire, with the result that the defendant was tried by an all-white jury. The Court of Appeals stated that even if the defendant would have a valid claim under *Batson*, the case arose before that decision and was governed by *Swain*. As the defendant had presented no evidence of a pattern of strikes over time, his constitutional argument had to be rejected.

§ 8:5

Even if *Batson* has only limited retroactive effect, its general philosophical tenor may affect the thinking of courts called upon to decide cases under the *Swain* standard. Arguably, this phenomenon occurred in Horton v. Zant, 941 F.2d 1449 (11th Cir. 1991). In this case, the court found that the presumption that the state's peremptory challenges had not been used in a nondiscriminatory manner was rebutted by statistical evidence. The prosecution had used its peremptory challenges over a seven-year period to remove 462 blacks but only 164 whites. Some blacks and women did serve, although it was clear from a memorandum written by the prosecutor that he sought to limit these numbers to the minimum the law allowed. In *Swain*, however, the Supreme Court found that no blacks had served on a jury in the relevant county in 15 years but this did not rebut the presumption of nondiscrimination. While the facts of *Horton* seem far less egregious than those in *Swain*, the conclusion of the court was the opposite. This is not to say the Court's decision in *Horton* was incorrect, only that the changing judicial climate in respect to racially inspired peremptory challenges provided the judges with the leeway to avoid a restrictive reading of *Swain*.

"*Swain*" evidence was also deemed relevant in the United States Supreme Court's decision in Miller-El v. Cockrell, 537 U.S. 322, 123 S. Ct. 1029, 154 L. Ed. 2d 931 (2003), where the trial had taken place prior to the Court's decision in *Batson* and the Court had the benefit of the habeas petitioner's pretrial *Swain* hearing at which he attempted to show a pattern of discrimination aimed at generally excluding African-Americans from juries. At this pretrial hearing, several district attorneys, judges and others claimed to have observed a systematic pattern of excluding black jurors (although other similarly qualified witnesses testified to the contrary). The defense also presented evidence of a formal policy of the District Attorney's Office to exclude minorities from jury service. The Supreme Court found that this historical record of discrimination was revealing of the culture of the District Attorney's Office, and cast doubt on the prosecutor's motives and claim of nondiscrimination in the petitioner's case.

§ 8:6 —Establishing a prima facie case
n. 109.
Add to note 109:
Where a prosecutor offers a race-neutral explanation for peremptory challenges alleged to be in violation of *Batson*, and the trial court rules on the ultimate issue of intentional discrimination, the question of whether a prima facie case initially existed becomes moot on appeal. See Hernandez v. New York, 500 U.S. 352, 111 S. Ct. 1859, 114 L. Ed. 2d 395 (1991). See

also Gillam v. U.S., 528 U.S. 900, 120 S. Ct. 235, 145 L. Ed. 2d 197 (1999); Matthews v. Evatt, 105 F.3d 907 (4th Cir. 1997); Johnson v. Love, 40 F.3d 658 (3d Cir. 1994); cf. Mahaffey v. Page, 151 F.3d 671 (7th Cir. 1998), opinion vacated in part on reh'g, 162 F.3d 481 (7th Cir. 1998). (where defendant's showing at the *Batson* hearing was sufficient as a matter of law to require the State to come forward with race-neutral explanations for each of the challenged strikes and the court never required the State to do so, defendant established a *Batson* violation).

In Eagle v. Linahan, 279 F.3d 926 (11th Cir. 2001) the Court of Appeals found that the existence of a prima facie case had been implicitly accepted by the trial judge when, in rejecting a *Batson* claim by the defendant, he commented that "both [the defense and the prosecution] were doing what [they] could to get the different races off."

- **n. 110.**
  Add to note 110:
  In Ford v. Georgia, 498 U.S. 411, 111 S. Ct. 850, 112 L. Ed. 2d 935 (1991), the Supreme Court declined to impose any uniform rule governing the timing of a *Batson* claim, stating that this was a matter for local authorities to decide. The Court, however, observed that a state rule which required that a *Batson* claim be raised between the time of the selection of the jurors and the administration of their oath would be sensible. The Court further observed that a state could reasonably adopt a rule that a *Batson* claim would be deemed untimely if raised for the first time on appeal, or after the jury was sworn or, conversely, before the jury's members were selected. A number of courts have formally held that a *Batson* claim must be made at the latest before the venire is dismissed and before trial commences. E.g., U.S. v. Parham, 16 F.3d 844 (8th Cir. 1994); U.S. v. Romero-Reyna, 867 F.2d 834 (5th Cir. 1989). See also Government of Virgin Islands v. Forte, 806 F.2d 73 (3d Cir. 1986) (contemporaneous objection generally required); McCrory v. Henderson, 82 F.3d 1243 (2d Cir. 1996) (*Batson* objection not made until after conclusion of jury selection is not timely); U.S. v. Franklyn, 157 F.3d 90 (2d Cir. 1998) (*Batson* challenge raised after voir dire was completed, challenged jurors had been dismissed, and court had reconvened after lunch recess, held not timely). Accord, Weeks v. New York State (Div. of Parole), 273 F.3d 76, 87 Fair Empl. Prac. Cas. (BNA) 161, 81 Empl. Prac. Dec. (CCH) ¶ 40822 (2d Cir. 2001).

In Carter v. Hopkins, 151 F.3d 872 (8th Cir. 1998), the court noted that one advantage of a timely objection is that it allows for the creation of a record for review. Lengthy delays before a *Batson* claim is raised (in this case, 11 years) are problematic because the prosecution is put in the position of having to explain challenges long after it is reasonable or practicable to expect recall of why a challenge was made (citing McCrory v. Henderson, 82 F.3d 1243, 1251 (2d Cir. 1996)). In such cases, the court held, it would be unfair to apply *Batson*'s burden-shifting framework.

The reason why courts are reluctant to entertain non-timely *Batson* challenges is explained in Morning v. Zapata Protein (USA), Inc., 128 F.3d 213 (4th Cir. 1997). If a meritorious *Batson* challenge is raised during the selection process, the strike may simply be disallowed. However, after dismissal of the venire, the only remedy may be a retrial, which will result in significant burdens and costs to the parties, the court, and the witnesses. It is for this reason that non-timely objections will usually be deemed to be waived. See also U.S. v. Parham, 16 F.3d 844 (8th Cir. 1994); U.S. v. Maseratti, 1 F.3d 330 (5th Cir. 1993); U.S. v. Humphrey, 287 F.3d 422, 2002 FED App. 0131P (6th Cir. 2002) (overruled by, U.S. v. Leachman, 309 F.3d 377, 2002 FED App. 0353P (6th Cir. 2002)).

§ 8:6   JURY SELECTION: LAW, ART & SCIENCE 2D

In Ruff v. Armontrout, 77 F.3d 265 (8th Cir. 1996) it was held that by not raising a *Batson* claim at trial or on direct appeal, the defendant had waived his claim. He was therefore barred from raising it for the first time on habeas corpus absent a showing of cause and prejudice or actual innocence. The defendant maintained that his failure was excused because *Batson* had yet to be decided at the time of his trial. The Court of Appeals agreed that a novel legal theory can constitute cause to excuse a procedural default, but held that the jury composition claim underlying *Batson* was not so novel that it could not have been anticipated by the petitioner. See also Hill v. Jones, 81 F.3d 1015 (11th Cir. 1996); Chambers v. Johnson, 197 F.3d 732 (5th Cir. 1999).

However, because the trial court arguably has an affirmative duty to ensure a jury drawn from a fair cross section of the community and free from racial discrimination, it should have the authority to raise a *Batson* objection on its own motion. See, e.g., People v. Lopez, 3 Cal. App. 4th Supp. 11, 5 Cal. Rptr. 2d 775 (App. Dep't Super. Ct. 1991). See also Lemley v. State, 599 So. 2d 64 (Ala. Crim. App. 1992) (trial judge can conduct a *Batson* hearing sua sponte, even absent an objection, if judge suspects that a party's peremptory challenges are being exercised in a racially discriminatory manner). Compare Doe v. Burnham, 6 F.3d 476 (7th Cir. 1993) (court should await an objection before intervening to set aside a peremptory challenge which might be violative of *Batson*). In U.S. v. Elliott, 89 F.3d 1360 (8th Cir. 1996) the defendant claimed for the first time on appeal that the prosecutor had exercised peremptory challenges against several black jurors because of their church-related activities but not against similarly situated religious white jurors. While acknowledging that there might be merit in the defendant's claim, the court of appeal held that it had been waived because it was not timely. Likewise, in Garcia v. Excel Corp., 102 F.3d 758 (5th Cir. 1997) it was held that a *Batson* claim was untimely when first raised on appeal, and that even if the opposing party does not raise the timeliness issue, the judge should do so sua sponte. See also U.S. v. Abou-Kassem, 78 F.3d 161, 44 Fed. R. Evid. Serv. 499 (5th Cir. 1996); U.S. v. Maseratti, 1 F.3d 330 (5th Cir. 1993). See also U.S. v. Tipton, 90 F.3d 861 (4th Cir. 1996) (claim of gender discrimination first made on appeal was untimely); McCrory v. Henderson, 82 F.3d 1243 (2d Cir. 1996) (failure to object to discriminatory use of peremptory challenges prior to conclusion of jury selection waived objection).

In U.S. v. Thomas, 303 F.3d 138 (2d Cir. 2002), the question was whether the defendants had waived their *Batson* claims after they had made a timely, unsuccessful objection during jury selection conducted before a magistrate judge, but had not sought review of the magistrate's rulings by the district judge prior to the jury being sworn. The defense argument was that their objection had been lodged immediately and at the time when relief was most readily available and that, furthermore, they lacked notice as to the proper timing of an appeal of a disputed *Batson* ruling. The Court of Appeals agreed, noting that the practice in the district was not clear nor was it clear that it would be enforced by the finding of a waiver. The need for an immediate appeal to the district judge was also not obvious, given that the latter was not present during jury selection and thus could not rely on his own observations to resolve the dispute. However, the court stated that, in the future, parties should be advised that delay in bringing a *Batson* issue promptly before a district judge may result in waiver.

n. 111.

Add to note 111:

The failure of defense counsel to make an objection of any kind during voir dire was found to constitute a waiver of the defendant's *Batson* claim in U.S. v. Cashwell, 950 F.2d 699 (11th Cir. 1992).

In Cooperwood v. Cambra, 245 F.3d 1042 (9th Cir. 2001), cert. denied, 534 U.S. 900, 122 S. Ct. 228, 151 L. Ed. 2d 164 (2001), the Court of Appeals found that *Batson* had not been violated by the prosecutor's peremptory challenge of a black juror without having asked the juror any voir dire questions. It is hard to see how a prima facie case could be established under such circumstances. The Court of Appeals seemed to have been influenced by the fact that the previous two jurors who had been excused had both been white, two black women remained on the jury, and the ultimate composition of the jury included the two black women, three Asian-Americans, and one Pacific Islander. From these arguably irrelevant facts, the court inferred that racial bias had not animated the challenged strike.

In Hopson v. Fredericksen, 961 F.2d 1374 (8th Cir. 1992), the Court of Appeals held that the appellant had failed to properly preserve a *Batson* claim for appeal. Appellant's counsel had not attempted to rebut the reasons advanced to justify the peremptory challenge in question and did not request the trial judge to articulate on the record her reasons for overruling the *Batson* objection. See also Nance v. State, 598 So. 2d 30 (Ala. Crim. App. 1992) (defendant's *Batson* claim barred on appeal where defendant failed to object prior to swearing of jury); U.S. v. Chandler, 12 F.3d 1427 (7th Cir. 1994) (only by specifically requesting the trial court to rule on a *Batson* claim does a defendant preserve the claim for appellate review).

Add after third sentence in second paragraph:

"Timeliness" issues generally arise in respect to *Batson* challenges that are made too late, but can a *Batson* claim be premature? In Overton v. Newton, 295 F.3d 270 (2d Cir. 2002) the defendant raised, and the state court denied, a *Batson* challenge before jury selection was completed and therefore before the final racial composition of the jury could be known or the prosecutor's use of its peremptory challenges could be established. In such circumstances, the trial judge does not have a full record on which to base a ruling. The trial judge in *Overton* denied the *Batson* challenge, and the Court of Appeals held that this ruling was not an unreasonable application of *Batson*. Defense counsel's error lay in not renewing his *Batson* claim after jury selection was completed or at least after a full record was established.

Add after second sentence in third paragraph:

One of the more bizarre cases on standing is that of the Fifth Circuit Court of Appeals in U.S. v. Huey, 76 F.3d 638 (5th Cir. 1996). At the trial of Huey and a codefendant Garcia for drug-related offenses, Garcia had objected to Huey's use of all of his peremptory challenges to remove Afro-American jurors. It appeared that the reason he did so (although the trial court had not required an explanation) was that the government would be introducing tapes and transcripts that

§ 8:6

contained harsh and offensive racial epithets uttered by Huey. The Court of Appeals held that Garcia had standing to challenge the peremptory challenges by his codefendant and that Huey had in fact improperly exercised his peremptory challenges on an impermissible racial basis in violation of *Batson*. This holding would not in itself have been so exceptional except for the fact that it had the effect of reversing Huey's conviction as well as Garcia's; both had been tried by an improperly constituted jury. Thus Huey, having uttered offensive racial epithets in the course of committing a crime, having violated the dictates of *Batson* by his systematic exclusion of those racial minorities whom he had insulted, yet nonetheless having been convicted, was able to obtain a reversal of his conviction and a new trial by virtue of his own impolitic and unconstitutional actions. It would seem that the Court's decision might well have the effect of encouraging abuses of the criminal justice system.

A contrary result to *Huey* was reached in U.S. v. Boyd, 86 F.3d 719 (7th Cir. 1996), where the Fifth Circuit Court of Appeals held that the black defendant in the case had failed to show that his counsel was ineffective for using a peremptory challenge to remove the only black member of the venire. Huey and Boyd are examined in Note, *The Current State of the Peremptory Challenge*, 39 William and Mary L. Rev. 961 (advocating a return to the pre-*Batson* state of the law) and in Comment, *Fulfilling the Promise of Batson: Protecting Jurors from the Use of Race-Based Peremptory Challenges by Defense Counsel*, 64 U Chicago L. Rev. 1311 (1997). The author of the Comment argues that a defendant should not be able to obtain a new trial because of the unconstitutional conduct of his or her lawyer in excluding jurors because of race, and that contrary rule would encourage unconstitutional peremptory challenges and manipulation of the system. The author notes that the problem could be significantly obviated if judges were to initiate *Batson* hearings in such circumstances sua sponte. Compare Recent Case, *Constitutional Law—Equal Protection—Seventh Circuit Denies a Criminal Defendant's Objection to His Counsel's Race-Based Peremptory Challenge*, 110 Harv. L. Rev. 1334 (1997) (Seventh Circuit should have carved out "presumed prejudice" exception to accommodate *Strickland and Batson*).

n. 116.

Add to note 116:

Empirical studies in fact provide some support for the proposition, that many would maintain was based on stereotypical reasoning, that an acquittal in a criminal case was more likely in a district containing a high percentage of black and Hispanic jurors. See, e.g., Levine, *The Impact of Racial Demography on Jury Verdicts in Routine Adjudication*, 33 Crim. L. Bull. 523 (1997).

Peremptory Challenges § 8:6

n. 117.
Add to note 117:
The logic as well at the ultimate position advanced in the main text was accepted by the United States Supreme Court in Powers v. Ohio, 499 U.S. 400, 111 S. Ct. 1364, 113 L. Ed. 2d 411 (1991). The defendant, who was white, maintained that the prosecution's exercise of peremptory challenges to remove seven black venirepersons from his jury constituted a violation of *Batson*. In order to reach the merits of defendant's argument, the Court had first to address the issue of standing: Was the defendant an appropriate party to raise this claim, given that he belonged to a race different from that of the excluded jurors? The Court answered in the affirmative.

In reaching this conclusion, the Court emphasized the harm that discriminatory challenges caused both to the integrity of the judicial process and to the dignity of the excluded jurors. The latter were denied the opportunity to participate in the democratic processes of government and were stigmatized because of the color of their skin, apart from whatever qualifications for jury service they might possess. Although one could concede the validity of these points, they did not necessarily resolve the standing issue.

The Court advanced a three-step argument in support of allowing the defendant to have third-party (jus tertii) standing to assert the rights of the blacks who were alleged to have been improperly challenged by the prosecutor. First, the defendant had suffered an "injury in fact" such as to give him a concrete interest in raising the jus tertii claim. Discrimination in jury selection cast doubt on the integrity of the jury which convicted him and on its verdict, as well as doubt about the trial court and its willingness to adhere to the requirements of the Constitution. A verdict delivered by a jury from which blacks had been wrongfully excluded was less likely to be accepted, either by the defendant or by the community. Second, both the defendant and the excluded jurors shared a common interest in eliminating racial discrimination from jury selection. Furthermore, there was no reason to doubt that the defendant would be an effective advocate for the rights of the excluded jurors, since he stood to gain the reversal of his conviction. Third, the excluded jurors were unlikely to be in a position to assert the violation of their own rights. Although they could sue on their own behalf, they had little incentive, financial or otherwise, to do so. Thus, the Court concluded that a white defendant had standing to raise an equal protection claim on behalf of blacks wrongfully excluded from jury service because of the prosecution's exercise of racially inspired peremptory challenges. The Ninth Circuit Court of Appeals in Jones v. Gomez, 66 F.3d 199 (9th Cir. 1995) held that Powers established a new rule of law which would not be applied retroactively.

In Tankleff v. Senkowski, 135 F.3d 235 (2d Cir. 1998), it was held that the trial court erred in rejecting *Batson* challenges on the basis that the defendant was not of the same race as the excluded jurors and that this was not harmless error. See also Bui v. Haley, 321 F.3d 1304 (11th Cir. 2003) (fact that defendant was Vietnamese and challenged jurors were black, and fact that defendant was tried before the Supreme Court's decision in Powers v. Ohio, 499 U.S. 400, 111 S. Ct. 1364, 113 L. Ed. 2d 411 (1991), were not relevant considerations in determination of whether peremptory challenge for which prosecutor offered no reasons was race-neutral).

On the other hand, the Court of Appeals in Keel v. French, 162 F.3d 263 (4th Cir. 1998), while not disputing the correctness of the Supreme

© West, a Thomson business, 11/2003

§ 8:6   JURY SELECTION: LAW, ART & SCIENCE 2D

Court's holding in *Powers*, may have let the issue of race identity between defendant and juror enter by the back door by stating that the fact that the defendant and the jurors were of different races "eliminates the argument that the jurors sympathize with the defendant because they share the same race." Keel v. French, 162 F.3d 263, 271 (4th Cir. 1998).

In Holland v. Illinois, 493 U.S. 474, 110 S. Ct. 803, 107 L. Ed. 2d 905 (1990) (See § 8:12), the Supreme Court had reached a similar conclusion regarding the standing of a white defendant to raise a Sixth Amendment challenge to the allegedly wrongful exclusion of blacks from his petit jury. Although the defendant in that case lost on the merits, he was accorded standing to raise the constitutional claim. In Edmonson v. Leesville Concrete Co., Inc., 500 U.S. 614, 111 S. Ct. 2077, 114 L. Ed. 2d 660 (1991) (See § 8:10), the United States Supreme Court accorded standing to a party in a civil case to assert the rights of jurors who had been subjected to discriminatory peremptory challenges. The Court's reasoning in the case indicated that standing will in all likelihood be granted to a civil petitioner who is not of the same race as the excluded jurors.

The holdings in *Holland* and *Powers* are examined in Note, Holland v Illinois *and* Powers v Ohio: *The Discriminatory Effect of the Peremptory Challenge Evaluated from the Sixth and Fourteenth Amendments*, 13 Crim Just J 335 (1992). See also Comment, Powers v Ohio: *The Death Knell for the Peremptory Challenge*, 28 Idaho 349 (1991/92).

In U.S. v. Malindez, 962 F.2d 332 (4th Cir. 1992), the Court of Appeals held that the Supreme Court's decision in *Powers* did not eliminate the prima facie case requirement of *Batson*.

The reasoning in *Powers* was extended in Campbell v. Louisiana, 523 U.S. 392, 118 S. Ct. 1419, 140 L. Ed. 2d 551, 172 A.L.R. Fed. 597 (1998). In this case, which involved neither peremptory challenges nor the composition of the petit jury, the United States Supreme Court was faced with the question of whether a white defendant had standing to challenge alleged discrimination in the selection of the foreperson of the grand jury that had indicted him. Under Louisiana state the trial judge selected the foreperson of the grand jury from the grand jury venire, after which the remaining members of the grand jury were chosen at random. It was undisputed that no black person had served as a grand jury foreperson in the parish for the previous 17 years. Citing *Powers*, the Court held that Campbell too had standing to raise the equal protection and due process claims of black jurors who had been discriminated against. The Court reasoned that, as in *Powers*, the defendant had suffered significant injury since the discriminatory selection process undermined the integrity of the indictment process. The accused shared a common interest with the excluded jurors in eradicating discrimination from the grand jury selection process, and therefore could be counted on to be an effective advocate in support of their interests. The accused also had a selfish interest in asserting the excluded jurors' rights because a finding that there had been a constitutional violation might lead to the reversal of his conviction. Finally, the Court noted that the defendant's own due process rights may well have been violated by the selection procedure. Hobby v. U.S., 468 U.S. 339, 104 S. Ct. 3093, 82 L. Ed. 2d 260 (1984), in which the Court had previously held that no relief could be granted to a white defendant even if there had been a violation of due process in the selection of the foreperson of a federal grand jury, was distinguished. In *Hobby* the foreperson has already been selected to serve on the grand jury prior to his or her purely ministerial appointment to the role of foreperson; in contrast, in *Campbell* the judge's appointment of the foreperson shaped the composition of the grand jury. This difference in effect converted the case into one alleging discriminatory selection of grand juror members. Having determined the standing issue, the court in *Campbell* did not reach the substantive merits of the petitioner's claim but rather remanded for further proceedings.

Add after first sentence in fifth paragraph:
It should be noted that where the petitioner's *Batson* challenge takes the form of a habeas corpus proceeding in federal court, the factual findings of the state courts are entitled to a presumption of correctness and may not be set aside, absent procedural error, unless they are "not fairly supported by the record." Purkett v. Elem, 514 U.S. 765, 115 S. Ct. 1769, 131 L. Ed. 2d 834 (1995) (citing Marshall v. Lonberger, 459 U.S. 422, 103 S. Ct. 843, 74 L. Ed. 2d 646 (1983) and 28 U.S.C.A. § 2254(d)(8)). See also Soria v. Johnson, 207 F.3d 232 (5th Cir. 2000); Greer v. Mitchell, 264 F.3d 663, 2001 FED App. 0304P (6th Cir. 2001), cert. denied, 535 U.S. 940, 122 S. Ct. 1323, 152 L. Ed. 2d 231 (2002).

Add after fifth sentence in fifth paragraph:
A commonsense approach to this issue, and one that no doubt accords with the day-to-day practice in many courts, can be seen in Mejia v. State, 328 Md. 522, 616 A.2d 356 (1992). The court said that when a party, based on visual observations and criteria such as surnames and language, asserts that a particular venireperson is a member of a cognizable group, and the opposing side having had the opportunity to make similar observations does not challenge the assertion, the fact of group membership will be deemed established for *Batson* purposes, and no additional evidence on the point will be required.

Add after sixth sentence in fifth paragraph:
The establishment of such a record will be complicated once the venire is dismissed. However, if the defendant does not request that the venire be preserved or recalled, there is no error. U.S. v. Collins, 972 F.2d 1385 (5th Cir. 1992). The failure to establish a record of the racial composition of the jury was held not to be fatal to a *Batson* claim in Rosa v. Peters, 36 F.3d 625 (7th Cir. 1994). However, the value of the decision as precedent may be limited, for the defendant in the case, a non-black, had attempted to object to the peremptory challenge of black jurors. The case arose prior to the Supreme Court's decision in Powers v. Ohio, 499 U.S. 400, 111 S. Ct. 1364, 113 L. Ed. 2d 411 (1991) (discussed above) that a defendant did not have to be of the same race as the challenged jurors to raise an alleged violation of *Batson*.

Absent a record, an attempt to reconstruct the racial composition of a trial jury is likely to be problematic. See

Anderson v. Cowan, 227 F.3d 893 (7th Cir. 2000) (where court was unable to discern race of jury or other excluded venire members because of a lack of a record of the racial composition of the venire pool, defendant's claim of a *Batson* violation reduced itself to the fact that two black jurors had been excused, which the court held insufficient to establish a prima facie case of discrimination). A request for further discovery in a habeas corpus proceeding is possible, but there is no automatic right to such discovery. See Deputy v. Taylor, 19 F.3d 1485 (3d Cir. 1994). In Simmons v. Beyer, 44 F.3d 1160 (3d Cir. 1995), the absence of a record, including information regarding how many black jurors had been peremptorily challenged at the petitioner's trial and the reasons for any challenges, was held not to preclude habeas relief where the petitioner had established a colorable claim of a *Batson* violation.

n. 119.
Add to note 119:
But compare U.S. v. Esparsen, 930 F.2d 1461, 32 Fed. R. Evid. Serv. 1191 (10th Cir. 1991). In *Esparsen*, the court found that the defendant had failed to establish a prima facie case in part because he had not established that the challenged jurors were in fact Hispanic, despite having Hispanic surnames. The court observed that the jurors could be married to Hispanics and not themselves be Hispanics. Arguably, however, the court missed the point. If the prosecutor thought that because of their surnames the jurors were Hispanic, and challenged them for this reason, that would be strong evidence of a violation of *Batson*, even if it subsequently were to be established that the jurors were not in fact Hispanic. Mistaken identity can also work to the prosecutor's advantage, however. In U.S. v. Guerra-Marez, 928 F.2d 665 (5th Cir. 1991), the prosecutor struck a juror other than the one whom he intended to strike. The court stated that "because the error was inadvertent, no intent [to exclude the juror on the basis of race] should be inferred." U.S. v. Guerra-Marez, 928 F.2d 665, 673 (5th Cir. 1991). Indeed, the error in all probability worked to the defendant's advantage, since the prosecutor was saddled with an unwanted juror.

Add after first sentence in seventh paragraph:
Courts have stated that the exercise of even one peremptory challenge on an improper racial basis can violate *Batson*. See, e.g.: Coulter v. Gramley, 93 F.3d 394 (7th Cir. 1996); Splunge v. Clark, 960 F.2d 705 (7th Cir. 1992). In Eagle v. Linahan, 279 F.3d 926 (11th Cir. 2001) the Court of Appeals found the trial court, in seeking to determine whether there had been a violation of *Batson*, erred in its exclusive reliance on a comparison of the proportion of blacks on the petit jury to the proportion of blacks in the venire. The court continued that the peremptory challenge of even one juror on racial grounds violates *Batson*, and therefore the presence of other blacks on the jury, while of significance, did not preclude a finding of a *Batson* violation.

In Allen v. Lee, 319 F.3d 645 (4th Cir. 2003), reh'g en banc granted, opinion vacated, (Mar. 24, 2003), the Court of Appeals found that a prima facie case of a *Batson* violation had been made out where the prosecutor had used 11 of 13 of its peremptory challenges to exclude African-American jurors when 36.3% of the venire consisted of African-Americans. The fact that the majority of the jurors actually seated in he case were African-American did not affect the Court's analysis. The Court of Appeals stated that the focus should be on the prospective jurors who were excluded and not on those who were empanelled, and that the exclusion on racial grounds of even one juror violates *Batson*. Noting that a prosecutor can control who is struck but not necessarily who is empanelled, the Court of Appeals stated that "the best and most direct evidence in a *Batson* challenge is evidence of whom the government chose to strike, because that is something over which the prosecutor has complete and undiluted control." Allen v. Lee, 319 F.3d 645, 656 (4th Cir. 2003), reh'g en banc granted, opinion vacated, (Mar. 24, 2003).

n. 120.

Add to note 120:

In U.S. v. Esparsen, 930 F.2d 1461, 32 Fed. R. Evid. Serv. 1191 (10th Cir. 1991), the court stated that the number of challenges used against members of a particular race is not itself determinative of a *Batson* violation, but needs to be considered in conjunction with other factors, such as the percentage of members of that race in the venire and the rate at which members of that race were struck in comparison with nonmembers. U.S. v. Esparsen, 930 F.2d 1461, 1467-68 32 Fed. R. Evid. Serv. 1191 (10th Cir. 1991). See also U.S. v. Dawn, 897 F.2d 1444 (8th Cir. 1990) (defendant alleging violation of *Batson* must develop a record, beyond mere numbers, to establish a violation); Luckett v. Kemna, 203 F.3d 1052 (8th Cir. 2000) (mere numbers alone insufficient to establish prima facie *Batson* violation in case where the prosecution had used eight of nine peremptory challenges to remove African-American jurors, as well as one African-American alternate juror, resulting in a jury with one African-American member and one African-American alternate); U.S. v. Day, 949 F.2d 973 (8th Cir. 1991) (numerical analyses, standing alone, do not establish a prima facie case); U.S. v. Brown, 941 F.2d 656 (8th Cir. 1991); U.S. v. Willie, 941 F.2d 1384, 91-2 U.S. Tax Cas. (CCH) ¶ 50409, 33 Fed. R. Evid. Serv. 1113, 68 A.F.T.R.2d 91-5371 (10th Cir. 1991) (mere fact that in a trial of a Native American Indian the prosecutor removed one of two Indian jurors did not establish a prima facie violation of *Batson*, particularly where the prosecutor, despite having unused challenges, did not seek to remove the other Native American from the jury). In U.S. v. Lewis, 40 F.3d 1325, 41 Fed. R. Evid. Serv. 661 (1st Cir. 1994) the prosecutor had challenged one of the three black members of the venire, the defense had challenged a second, and the third was not challenged by either side even though the prosecutor had two peremptory challenges remaining. The Court of Appeals stated that these facts cast doubt on the sufficiency of defendant's prima facie case of a *Batson* violation. The court also found that the prosecutor's explanations for the challenges were race-neutral. In any event, it is

§ 8:6   JURY SELECTION: LAW, ART & SCIENCE 2D

potentially fatal for a defendant seeking to assert a *Batson* violation to fail to provide evidence relating to the racial composition of the venire or the jury ultimately impaneled. See Chakouian v. Moran, 975 F.2d 931 (1st Cir. 1992) (absent evidence as to whether other black members of the venire were called and seated as jurors, defendant's *Batson* claim was "pure conjecture"); U.S. v. Hernandez-Herrera, 273 F.3d 1213 (9th Cir. 2001), cert. denied, 537 U.S. 868, 123 S. Ct. 272, 154 L. Ed. 2d 114 (2002) (defendant's objection to peremptory challenge of juror based on the fact that she was only juror with a "Hispanic sounding surname" was, even if accurate (which was disputed by the government which asserted that two other jurors had Hispanic sounding surnames) was alone insufficient to establish a prima facie case of a *Batson* violation).

n. 121.

Add to note 121:

But see U.S. v. Esparsen, 930 F.2d 1461, 32 Fed. R. Evid. Serv. 1191 (10th Cir. 1991) (mere presence of jurors of a certain race on the jury does not automatically negate a *Batson* violation, although it is a relevant factor to be considered in determining whether a prima facie case has been established); U.S. v. Joe, 928 F.2d 99 (4th Cir. 1991) (fact that five black jurors were seated on defendant's jury entitled to substantial consideration in regard to whether a *Batson* violation had occurred but did not itself foreclose finding of a violation).

In Lancaster v. Adams, 324 F.3d 423 (6th Cir. 2003) the trial court initially ruled that the prosecutor had violated *Batson* by using a peremptory challenge to strike an African-American juror. However, after the prosecutor subsequently did not challenge another African-American, the trial court reversed its ruling in respect to the first juror and held that *Batson* had not been violated. The Court of Appeals granted habeas relief, holding that the decision to select the second juror did nothing to cure the wrong that may have been committed in excluding the first juror on the basis of race.

In U.S. v. Smith, 324 F.3d 922 (7th Cir. 2003), the court stated, somewhat questionably it is submitted, that the fact that the government used its final peremptory challenge to strike a white juror rather than the one black juror remaining in the pool was evidence of a lack of a racially discriminatory intent. If this were the case, a prosecutor could challenge as many black jurors on improper grounds as it wished so long as it reserved its final challenge for a white juror.

In U.S. v. Jiminez, 983 F.2d 1020 (11th Cir. 1993), the court stated that the fact that seven of the impaneled jurors were African-Americans, while not precluding the possibility of a *Batson* violation, was relevant in the highly deferential review which was required. See also Central Alabama Fair Housing Center v. Lowder Realty Co, 236 F.3d 629 (11th Cir. 2000); Brown v. Kinney Shoe Corp., 237 F.3d 556, 84 Fair Empl. Prac. Cas. (BNA) 1510, 80 Empl. Prac. Dec. (CCH) ¶ 40585 (5th Cir. 2001), cert. denied, 534 U.S. 817, 122 S. Ct. 45, 151 L. Ed. 2d 17 (2001). The court in U.S. v. Steele, 178 F.3d 1230 (11th Cir. 1999) stated that the unchallenged presence of protected class members on a jury undercuts an inference of impermissible discrimination that might otherwise arise from the exercise of peremptory challenges. In U.S. v. Diaz, 176 F.3d 52, 52 Fed. R. Evid. Serv. 380 (2d Cir. 1999) the Second Circuit Court of Appeals stated that "[o]nly a rate of minority challenges significantly higher than the minority percentage of the venire would support a statistical inference of discrimination", quoting U.S. v. Alvarado, 923 F.2d 253, 255 (2d Cir. 1991). And in a case alleging sex discrimination in jury selection, U.S. v. Brisk,

171 F.3d 514, 51 Fed. R. Evid. Serv. 932 (7th Cir. 1999), the court held that the fact that the government used four of its six peremptory challenges to exclude women from the venire did not establish a prima facie case of discrimination in light of the fact that the government neither used a significant number of its total challenges to remove women, nor removed a significant number of women. In Shurn v. Delo, 177 F.3d 662 (8th Cir. 1999) the Court of Appeals held that the prosecution's stated reasons for its peremptory challenges of black jurors were race-neutral, with the court supporting this conclusion with the fact that the prosecutor peremptorily challenged five non-black jurors, left two blacks on the jury, and challenged non-black jurors exhibiting characteristics similar to those used to justify the challenge of the black jurors. In U.S. v. Bishop, 959 F.2d 820 (9th Cir. 1992), in contrast, the court held that the mere representativeness of the jury, while evidence of a nondiscriminatory motive, was not in itself sufficient to avoid a finding of a violation of *Batson*. According to the *Bishop* court, *Batson* could be violated by the challenge of one black juror for racial reasons. Accord Splunge v. Clark, 960 F.2d 705 (7th Cir. 1992).

n. 123.

Add to note 123:

In Turner v. Marshall, 63 F.3d 807 (9th Cir. 1995) (overruled by, Tolbert v. Page, 182 F.3d 677 (9th Cir. 1999)), the court was prepared to find a *Batson* violation even though four African-Americans served on defendant's jury. The objection was to the prosecutor's peremptory challenges against five African-Americans. The court stated that the fact that the prosecutor had not attempted to remove all minority jurors weighed against the defendant's *Batson* claim but in itself was not dispositive. Also relevant was the fact that the percentage of challenges against minorities was disproportionately higher than the percentage of minorities in the venire. Much of the blame for the result, however, rested with the trial court, which was apparently so satisfied with the racial mix of the jury that it failed to inquire into the reasons for the prosecution's peremptory challenges.

n. 124.

Add to note 124:

The point seems to have been lost on the court in U.S. v. Moreno, 217 F.3d 592 (8th Cir. 2000), holding that the challenge of a Hispanic-American juror who admitted to past contact with drugs did not violate Batson. The court added that the fact that another Hispanic-American served on the jury reinforced its conclusion that the challenge of the juror in question was not done for racial motives.

In Miller v. U.S., 135 F.3d 1254, 48 Fed. R. Evid. Serv. 1089 (8th Cir. 1998), the court found race-neutral the peremptory challenge of one black juror who was familiar with the area of the crime and who had friends and family who themselves had problems with law enforcement; and another black juror who had relatives with a case that was pending against the police department from which two of the witnesses belonged. The court, however, supplemented these relatively uncontroversial rulings with a statement that the fact that "the government did not use its peremptory challenges to remove the greatest number of blacks from the jury negated an allegation of purposeful discrimination." It is submitted that here the court went too far, and, indeed, if such a proposition were correct, it would significantly undermine the mandate of *Batson*.

n. 126.

Add to note 126 after "Fleming":

§ 8:6   JURY SELECTION: LAW, ART & SCIENCE 2D

Ex parte Yelder, 630 So. 2d 107 (Ala. 1992) (state's use of 24 of its 32 peremptory challenges to remove 24 of 27 black venire members raised strong inference of racial discrimination requiring clear and cogent explanation in rebuttal, which state did not provide); Cochran v. Herring, 43 F.3d 1404 (11th Cir. 1995), opinion modified on denial of reh'g, Cochran v. Herring, 61 F.3d 20 (11th Cir. 1995) (fact that prosecution struck only seven of nine prospective black jurors while having sufficient challenges to remove all blacks from the jury did not preclude a finding of a *Batson* violation).

In Eagle v. Linahan, 279 F.3d 926 (11th Cir. 2001) the Court of Appeals found the trial court, in seeking to determine whether there had been a violation of *Batson*, erred in its exclusive reliance on a comparison of the proportion of blacks on the petit jury to the proportion of blacks in the venire. The court continued that the peremptory challenge of even one juror on racial grounds violates *Batson*, and therefore the presence of other blacks on the jury, while of significance, did not preclude a finding of a *Batson* violation. But compare U.S. v. Yang, 281 F.3d 534, 61 U.S.P.Q.2d (BNA) 1789, 2002 FED App. 0062P (6th Cir. 2002), cert. denied, 123 S. Ct. 1015, 154 L. Ed. 2d 912 (U.S. 2003) (final makeup of jury is relevant to a finding of discrimination).

Add after fourth sentence in tenth paragraph:
In appropriate circumstances, statistics alone can be used to establish a prima facie case of a *Batson* violation. See Allen v. Lee, 319 F.3d 645 (4th Cir. 2003), reh'g en banc granted, opinion vacated, (Mar. 24, 2003) (prima facie case of a *Batson* violation made out where prosecutor used 11 of 13 of its peremptory challenges to exclude African American jurors when 36.3% of the venire consisted of African Americans); Henderson v. Walls, 296 F.3d 541 (7th Cir. 2002), cert. granted, judgment vacated on other grounds, 123 S. Ct. 1354, 155 L. Ed. 2d 194 (U.S. 2003) and cert. denied, 123 S. Ct. 1361, 155 L. Ed. 2d 203 (U.S. 2003) (state court's rejection of analysis comparing excluded African-American jurors with white jurors at prima facie stage of a *Batson* inquiry was unreasonable); Overton v. Newton, 295 F.3d 270 (2d Cir. 2002). See also Mahaffey v. Page, 162 F.3d 481 (7th Cir. 1998). However, as the Court of Appeals held in Williams v. Woodford, 306 F.3d 665 (9th Cir. 2002), while statistics can be useful, merely citing the number of African-Americans peremptorily challenged by the prosecution will not, in and of itself, be sufficient to raise an inference of discrimination. Further information, such as how many African-Americans were in the venire, how large was the venire, how many African-Americans served on the jury, and whether there was a statistical disparity between the number of African-Americans and the number of white jurors challenged peremptorily, was needed to support defendant's *Batson* claim.

Some courts are of the view that a showing of disparity is not even necessary. See, e.g., Weems v. State, 262 Ga. 101,

416 S.E.2d 84 (1992) (fact that percentage of blacks on jury was greater than percentage of blacks in array did not preclude a finding of a *Batson* violation). But compare Scott v. State, 599 So. 2d 1222 (Ala. Crim. App. 1992) (overruled on other grounds by, Smith v. State, 612 So. 2d 1314 (Ala. Crim. App. 1992)) and (overruled on other grounds by, Ex parte Thomas, 659 So. 2d 3 (Ala. 1994)) (no prima facie case of discrimination established where percentage of blacks on jury was greater than percentage of blacks on venire).

Add after second sentence in twelfth paragraph:
See Nickerson v. Lee, 971 F.2d 1125 (4th Cir. 1992), as amended, (Aug. 12, 1992); U.S. v. Branch, 989 F.2d 752 (5th Cir. 1993); U.S. v. Uwaezhoke, 995 F.2d 388 (3d Cir. 1993); U.S. v. Changco, 1 F.3d 837 (9th Cir. 1993). In McCain v. Gramley, 96 F.3d 288 (7th Cir. 1996) the court held that the fact that the prosecution's percentage of peremptory challenges of black jurors was higher than the percentage of its challenges of white jurors did not by itself establish a prima facie case of a *Batson* violation. The court stated that it was necessary to look at the totality of the circumstances, including the voir dire questions of the parties and the final composition of the jury. Mitchell v. Rees, 114 F.3d 571, 1997 FED App. 0168P (6th Cir. 1997) (mere fact that no blacks served on defendant's jury did not establish *Batson* violation); Brewer v. Marshall, 119 F.3d 993 (1st Cir. 1997) (prosecution's exercise of 4/9 peremptory challenges against 4/6 black jurors did not establish a prima facie violation of *Batson* in absence of any suggestion of bias or improper motive). Compare Howard v. Moore, 525 U.S. 843, 119 S. Ct. 108, 142 L. Ed. 2d 86 (1998) (peremptory challenge of 6/7 prospective black jurors by prosecutor, but only 4/35 white jurors, established prima facie case of discrimination).

In Central Alabama Fair Housing Center v. Lowder Realty Co., 236 F.3d 629 (11th Cir. 2000), the court stated that the fact that a party had used its peremptory challenges to strike two white jurors, neither of whom had made any statements during voir dire that would justify striking them, was, as a matter of law, insufficient to establish a prima facie case. The court stated that the mere fact that striking a juror or set of jurors of a particular race did not necessarily create an inference of racial discrimination, and that the number of persons of a particular race struck took on meaning only when viewed in light of other information such as the racial composition of the venire, the race of other jurors struck, and the voir dire answers of those jurors who were struck compared to the answers of those jurors who were not struck. The court concluded that a showing that a party had used its peremptory challenges against jurors of a particular race did not, standing alone, establish a prima facie case. The court advised that a party advancing a *Batson* challenge should present facts not just numbers indicating discrimination. See also Brown v. Kinney Shoe Corp., 237 F.3d 556, 84 Fair Empl. Prac. Cas. (BNA) 1510, 80 Empl. Prac. Dec. (CCH) ¶ 40585 (5th Cir. 2001), cert. denied, 534 U.S. 817, 122 S. Ct. 45, 151 L. Ed. 2d 17 (2001); U.S. v. Bergodere, 40 F.3d 512 (1st Cir. 1994).

n. 130.

Add to note 130:

In Wade v. Terhune, 202 F.3d 1190 (9th Cir. 2000) the court, citing *Batson*, stated that in order to find a prima facie case of discrimination there had to be a "reasonable inference" that a party had excluded a juror on the basis of race. The court in Terhune compared this standard to that articulated in the California state courts, specifically in People v. Wheeler, 22 Cal. 3d 258, 148 Cal. Rptr. 890, 583 P.2d 748 (1978) (holding modified by, People v. Willis, 27 Cal. 4th 811, 118 Cal. Rptr. 2d 301, 43 P.3d 130 (2002)) and (disapproved of by, Fernandez v. Roe, 286 F.3d 1073 (9th Cir. 2002)), as interpreted in People v. Bernard, 27 Cal. App. 4th 458, 32 Cal. Rptr. 2d 486 (4th Dist. 1994) (disapproved of on other grounds by, People v. Box, 23 Cal. 4th 1153, 99 Cal. Rptr. 2d 69, 5 P.3d 130 (2000)), and found that the California standard did not comport with *Batson* in that it required a showing of a "strong likelihood" of discrimination in order to establish a prima facie case. The Wade/Batson standard was applied in Fernandez v. Roe, 286 F.3d 1073 (9th Cir. 2002), cert. denied, 537 U.S. 1000, 123 S. Ct. 514, 154 L. Ed. 2d 395 (2002), the Court of Appeals holding that the prosecutor's challenges of both African-American jurors on the panel and a number of Hispanic jurors made out a prima facie case of a *Batson* violation that required an explanation from the prosecutor. That one Hispanic juror was ultimately seated was held not to be dispositive of the issue.

n. 131.

Add to note 131:

In Simmons v. Beyer, 44 F.3d 1160 (3d Cir. 1995) the Court of Appeals cited five factors relevant to determining whether a party had established a prima facie case:

(1) the number of racial group members in the panel;
(2) the nature of the crime;
(3) the race of the defendant and the victim;
(4) a pattern of strikes against racial group members; and
(5) the prosecution's questions and statements during voir dire.

See also Mitchell v. Rees, 114 F.3d 571, 1997 FED App. 0168P (6th Cir. 1997) (without knowledge of how many peremptory challenges were exercised by the state and how many were exercised against nonminority jurors, state court was not in a position to determine whether there had been a systematic pattern of strikes against minority jurors).

n. 133.

Add to note 133 after "Washington":
See also Powers v. Palacios, 813 S.W.2d 489, 490 n 1 (Tex. 1991).

Add after note 133:

§ 8:6 PEREMPTORY CHALLENGES

In U.S. v. Omoruyi, 7 F.3d 880 (9th Cir. 1993), the prosecutor conceded that the reason for the peremptory challenges of two unmarried female jurors was a concern that the jurors would be attracted to the male defendant. The court took this as an admission of a discriminatory motive and found that there had been unconstitutional discrimination on the basis of gender. The court said that a showing of a discriminatory motive displaces the need for proof of a pattern of discrimination. As a consequence the fact that the jury contained six women was deemed irrelevant. Similarly, in Johnson v. Vasquez, 3 F.3d 1327 (9th Cir. 1993), the prosecutor admitted that he had been prepared to accept the only black juror on the panel. When, however, he saw defense counsel excusing jurors of other races, he peremptorily challenged the juror. The court stated that the prosecutor's admission was strong evidence that the challenge was racially motivated.

n. 134.

Add to note 134:

But see U.S. v. Gordon, 974 F.2d 97 (8th Cir. 1992) (mere fact that excluded venireperson made no statements during voir dire provided no basis for inferring juror was excluded because of race. Accord U.S. v. Young-Bey, 893 F.2d 178 (8th Cir. 1990).

n. 135.

Add to note 135:

; Guthrie v. State, 598 So. 2d 1013 (Ala. Crim. App. 1991).

n. 136.

Add to note 136:

; Splunge v. Clark, 960 F.2d 705 (7th Cir. 1992). But compare Dunham v. Frank's Nursery & Crafts, Inc., 967 F.2d 1121 (7th Cir. 1992) (peremptory challenge of black but not white hairdresser despite counsel's general aversion to hairdressers as jurors was permissible in light of explanation that counsel preferred not to have two jurors of same occupation, and other individual nonracial characteristics of juror).

In Devose v. Norris, 53 F.3d 201 (8th Cir. 1995) the court found that the prosecution's stated justification for its striking of three black jurors—that they suffered from burnout from previous jury service—was pretextual given its failure to pursue the issue of burnout with five prospective white jurors who had comparable jury experience. Similarly in U.S. v. Stewart, 65 F.3d 918 (11th Cir. 1995), where the defendants had exercised peremptory challenges against 75% of the black prospective jurors, the Court of Appeals, in upholding the trial court's disallowance of one of the strikes, stated that the reasons that had been given by the defendant should have logically led to the challenge of similarly situated white jurors, but did not. But compare U.S. v. Kunzman, 54 F.3d 1522, 42 Fed. R. Evid. Serv. 115 (10th Cir. 1995) (no *Batson* violation although a black juror was peremptorily challenged because of lack of experience with real estate transactions and white jurors with no real estate experience were not challenged); Holder v. Welborn, 60 F.3d 383 (7th Cir. 1995) (prosecutor's decision to peremptorily challenge a black juror who was feared to harbor feelings of selective prosecution against the County because it had dropped charges against the alleged murderer of her brother while not challenging several white jurors who had had "brushes with the law" held permissible); U.S. v. Moreno, 217 F.3d 592 (8th Cir. 2000) (challenge of Hispanic-American juror because of admission of past contact with drugs was not pretextual despite failure to strike another juror who also admitted to past contact with drugs where latter juror vehemently rejected drug use).

In U.S. v. Novaton, 271 F.3d 968, 57 Fed. R. Evid. Serv. 1470 (11th Cir. 2001), cert. denied, 535 U.S. 1120, 122 S. Ct. 2345, 153 L. Ed. 2d 173 (2002) and cert. denied, 537 U.S. 850, 123 S. Ct. 193, 154 L. Ed. 2d 80 (2002) and cert. denied, 537 U.S. 858, 123 S. Ct. 228, 154 L. Ed. 2d 96 (2002) and cert. denied, 537 U.S. 1031, 123 S. Ct. 576, 154 L. Ed. 2d 447 (2002) the Court of Appeals stated that although a white juror who worked for the courts and knew the attorneys in the case had not been challenged, and a Hispanic juror with these traits had been struck, the two situations were distinguishable in that the Hispanic juror had also worked for a judge who had been prosecuted by the federal government, and this additional aspect of the Hispanic juror's background could lead a prosecutor to strike the Hispanic juror but not the white juror. Similarly, the court stated that the fact that three Department of Education employees had not been challenged while a Hispanic social worker had been challenged was not necessarily discriminatory as the positions of the respective jurors may not have been equally "liberal" despite their similar employment.

In Turner v. Marshall, 121 F.3d 1248 (9th Cir. 1997), as amended, (Sept. 22, 1997); Scarpa v. DuBois, 38 F.3d 1, 14 (1st Cir. 1994), the claimed justification for the peremptory challenge of a minority juror was the juror's reluctance to view gruesome photographs, but a nonminority juror who had displayed an even greater reluctance had not been challenged. With no other explanation having been proffered for the challenge, the court found the stated reason to be pretextual. The fact that four other minority jurors had served on the jury was held insufficient to offset the constitutional violation.

In Yancey v. State, 813 So. 2d 1 (Ala. Crim. App. 2001), cert. denied, (July 6, 2001) the court found a *Batson* violation where several black prospective jurors were allegedly struck for their views on capital punishment, but a white prospective juror who held similar views was not challenged. The Court's belief that the challenges were discriminatory was no doubt reinforced by the fact that the prosecution had also struck black prospective jurors who had committed traffic and misdemeanor offenses while not challenging six white prospective jurors who had committed like offenses.

Add after first sentence in eighteenth paragraph:
In Cochran v. Herring, 43 F.3d 1404 (11th Cir. 1995), opinion modified on denial of reh'g, Cochran v. Herring, 61 F.3d 20 (11th Cir. 1995) a former prosecutor testified that the past practice of the prosecutor's office had been to exercise peremptory challenges against blacks because of their perceived tendency to be anti-police, anti-establishment, and distrustful of police testimony. The Court of Appeals held that this testimony, inter alia, supported a finding of a *Batson* violation even though the prosecutor had not removed all blacks from the jury despite having sufficient challenges to do so.

Add after eighteenth paragraph:
Past practice worked to the prosecution's advantage in U.S. v. Seals, 987 F.2d 1102 (5th Cir. 1993), where the trial judge, in accepting the neutrality of the prosecutor's explana-

tions for his peremptory challenges, cited his personal knowledge and experience with both the prosecuting attorney and the prosecutor's office.

The Third Circuit Court of Appeals has identified five factors which a trial court should consider in assessing whether a prima facie case of a *Batson* violation has been established:

(1) How many of the cognizable racial group are in the venire panel;
(2) The nature of the crime;
(3) The race of both the defendant and victim;
(4) Whether there has been a pattern of strikes against black [or other cognizable racial group] jurors in the particular venire; and
(5) The prosecutor's questions and statements during the selection process.

Jones v. Ryan, 987 F.2d 960, 970–71 (3d Cir. 1993) (citing U.S. v. Clemons, 843 F.2d 741, 747 (3d Cir. 1988)); Deputy v. Taylor, 19 F.3d 1485 (3d Cir. 1994).

n. 144.

Add to note 144:

It is now generally agreed among the federal courts of appeals that a trial court's determination of whether a prima facie case was established will be reviewed deferentially and will only be reversed if the trial court has committed clear error. See Tolbert v. Page, 182 F.3d 677 (9th Cir. 1999); Brewer v. Marshall, 119 F.3d 993 (1st Cir. 1997); U.S. v. Stewart, 65 F.3d 918 (11th Cir. 1995); U.S. v. Bergodere, 40 F.3d 512 (1st Cir. 1994); U.S. v. Branch, 989 F.2d 752 (5th Cir. 1993); U.S. v. Casper, 956 F.2d 416 (3d Cir. 1992); U.S. v. Moore, 895 F.2d 484 (8th Cir. 1990); U.S. v. Grandison, 885 F.2d 143 (4th Cir. 1989).

§ 8:7 —Rebutting a prima facie claim

n. 145.

Add to note 145:

Until the defendant makes a prima facie case of racial discrimination, the prosecution is under no duty to proffer a race-neutral explanation for its peremptory challenges. Chakouian v. Moran, 975 F.2d 931 (1st Cir. 1992). However, if the prosecution voluntarily places on record the reasons for its peremptory challenges, the court may review these even where the defendant has not shown a systematic pattern of exclusion. Parker v. Singletary, 974 F.2d 1562 (11th Cir. 1992); Johnson v. Love, 40 F.3d 658 (3d Cir. 1994). The better practice would seem to be to have the prosecution place on record its neutral explanation contemporaneously, in order to render more difficult the manufacture of after-the-fact pretextual explanations. Nonetheless, the failure to object to a delay in placing the prosecutor's reasons on record will constitute a waiver of such a claim. U.S. v. Collins, 972 F.2d 1385 (5th Cir. 1992). U.S. v. Denman, 100 F.3d 399 (5th Cir. 1996) provides a fair example. Here the court of appeal upheld a peremptory challenge of a black juror who was from the town where the prosecutors had conducted a high profile investigation which had

§ 8:7   JURY SELECTION: LAW, ART & SCIENCE 2D

engendered bad feeling among the townspeople. In addition, the juror in question was related to an alleged unprosecuted target of the investigation. It is doubtful whether either of these explanations, alone or in tandem, would have justified a challenge for cause but they were sufficient to support a peremptory challenge.

The burden of coming forward with neutral explanations is normally that of the prosecutor who appeared in the original trial and who made the peremptory challenges which are alleged to be in violation of Batson. In Bui v. Haley, 321 F.3d 1304 (11th Cir. 2003), however, the prosecutor had since become the State Attorney General, and he declined to appear either as counsel or as a witness. In his place he sent one of his assistants from the original trial who had been seated with him during the jury selection process. The Court of Appeals ruled, however, that the assistant's explanations were entitled to no probative value for she had not discussed with the prosecutor the reasons for his challenges and her attempted reconstruction of his reasoning was mere conjecture. The explanation that the prosecutor had offered at trial that he did not strike prospective jurors on the basis of their race but on the basis of who would be prone to acquit was deemed too vague and insufficiently specific to satisfy the state's burden of establishing race-neutral explanations.

In Evans v. Smith, 220 F.3d 306 (4th Cir. 2000), cert. denied, 532 U.S. 925, 121 S. Ct. 1367, 149 L. Ed. 2d 294 (2001), a case in which the trial was held two years before *Batson* was decided, the court offered an interesting perspective on Batson's requirements. According to the court, *Batson* does not require individualized explanations for each peremptory challenge but can be complied with if a party can provide an overarching general explanation for its peremptory challenges that is race neutral. The decision is examined in Casenote, 13 Cap. Def. J. 165 (2000).

n. 146.
Add to note 146:

Explanations for peremptory challenges of minority jurors run the gamut from some which would arguably have warranted a challenge for cause to others which seem to be contrived and featherweight. Numerous examples of the latter are offered in footnote 155, infra. An example of the former is U.S. v. Wiggins, 104 F.3d 174 (8th Cir. 1997), where two black jurors were challenged peremptorily, one because the police had discovered drugs in his apartment during a raid and the other because his brother had been convicted for possessing crack cocaine, and the case to be tried was a drugs prosecution.

In Heno v. Sprint/United Management Co., 208 F.3d 847, 82 Fair Empl. Prac. Cas. (BNA) 837 (10th Cir. 2000), an employment discrimination action, the court found that a black prospective juror's support of affirmative action, coupled with his feeling that he had been discriminated against in the workplace, were race-neutral reasons for a peremptory challenge of the juror. Interestingly, but questionably, the court observed that the juror's beliefs against discrimination in the workplace were not automatically linked to race but could be held in regard to any heterogeneous group. See also U.S. v. Copeland, 321 F.3d 582, 61 Fed. R. Evid. Serv. 231, 2003 FED App. 0061A (6th Cir. 2003), upholding as race-neutral the peremptory challenge of an Hispanic juror who appeared preoccupied with his own personal injury litigation and who informed the court that he would probably be unavailable for jury duty on some of the days of the trial because he would have to attend to his own civil case.

n. 147.
Add to note 147:

In U.S. v. Payne, 962 F.2d 1228, 35 Fed. R. Evid. Serv. 686 (6th Cir. 1992), however, the court found acceptable an explanation that two black jurors had been excused not because of their race, but because of their association with black activist groups. The decision is questionable because it seems to infringe on the jurors' constitutional freedom of association. The Court's decision may to some extent have found support in the fact that not all black jurors were excluded from the jury. In U.S. v. Hinton, 94 F.3d 396 (7th Cir. 1996) the fact that a juror wore a "Malcolm X" hat and sat with his arms folded across his chest during voir dire was held to provide a race neutral explanation for the peremptory challenge of the juror. While the hat may have reflected admiration of Malcolm X, many individuals choose clothing because of its distinctiveness and provocativeness, in which case the hat may have had no political significance whatsoever. Even if it did, an expression of political opinion does not necessarily undermine a juror's ability to be impartial. Compare Randolph v. State, 203 Ga. App. 115, 416 S.E.2d 117 (1992) (membership in all-black professional or social organization not legitimate basis for exercise of peremptory challenge).

In U.S. v. McMillon, 14 F.3d 948, 38 Fed. R. Evid. Serv. 1334 (4th Cir. 1994), the court, in upholding the prosecutor's use of a peremptory challenge against a venireperson who was the same age, race and sex as the defendant, observed that it was not unusual to challenge jurors who had traits in common with an accused and might therefore sympathize with him or her. The difficulty with this analysis, as the court itself recognized, is that it would justify the peremptory challenge of a black juror in a case where the accused was also black. The court tried to draw a distinction between what it had in mind and the requirements of *Batson*:

> While *Swain* and *Batson* instruct that race cannot be a trait on which a strike is premised, the approach best expressed by the familiar phrase "There but for the grace of God go I" remains a standard and permissible justification for peremptory challenges.

U.S. v. McMillon, 14 F.3d 948, 953, 38 Fed. R. Evid. Serv. 1334 (4th Cir. 1994). This distinction is hard to reconcile with the express statement in *Batson* that the prosecutor could not rebut a prima facie case of discrimination by stating that the challenge was based on an assumption that "jurors of the defendant's race . . . would be partial to the defendant because of their shared race." Batson v. Kentucky, 476 U.S. 79, 106 S. Ct. 1712, 90 L. Ed. 2d 69 (1986) (holding modified by, Powers v. Ohio, 499 U.S. 400, 111 S. Ct. 1364, 113 L. Ed. 2d 411 (1991)).

In Rush v. Smith, 56 F.3d 918 (8th Cir. 1995), the trial judge commented to the jury on the tendency of races to "stick together." The Court of Appeals was scathing in its criticism of these remarks:

> The Court's statements . . . are beyond inappropriate: they egregiously and obnoxiously flout even minimal standards of judicial propriety and integrity, and we strongly reprimand the court for engaging in behavior that has no place in the courts of the United States.

Id. However, because the defendant had failed to object to the judge's comments, the Court of Appeals was limited to reviewing the case for plain error. It concluded that regardless of the impropriety of the judge's remarks, the overall fairness of the trial had not been destroyed.

An unusual fact situation arose in U.S. v. Lara, 181 F.3d 183, 51 Fed. R. Evid. Serv. 1302 (1st Cir. 1999) where the defendant's attorney, after informing the jurors that the testimony would include allusions to the fact that the defendant's gang did not welcome African-American members, asked a black male juror whether that knowledge might affect his ability

§ 8:7   Jury Selection: Law, Art & Science 2d

to decide the case fairly. The juror replied that he could be fair and impartial under any circumstance, at which point the defendant applauded. The trial judge reprimanded the defendant and the prosecution subsequently used a peremptory challenge to remove the juror. On appeal, the court found no violation of *Batson*. The challenge was justified on the grounds that the defendant's outburst may well have compromised the impartiality of the juror, either by intimidating him or by creating an artificial affinity. These explanations were race-neutral and the appellate court held that the judge's decision to excuse the juror was not clearly erroneous.

n. 148.
   Add to note 148:
   The strength of the burden of rebuttal placed on the prosecution may vary with the strength of the prima facie case established by the opposing party. In Ford v. State, 262 Ga. 558, 423 S.E.2d 245 (1992), where the prosecutor exercised its peremptory challenges against nine black and one white prospective jurors from a qualified venire of 10 blacks and 32 whites, the court held that the prosecution carried an especially heavy burden of rebuttal. The court said that when the racial makeup of the group excluded closely parallels the racial makeup of the venire, virtually any neutral explanation will suffice; but as the racial makeup of the group excluded deviates further and further from the racial makeup of the venire, it becomes increasingly likely that racial bias is the real reason for the disparity and correspondingly greater scrutiny must be given to the proffered explanations.

Add after fifth paragraph:
It is error for a trial court not to indicate whether it credits explanations given for peremptory challenges alleged to be in violation of *Batson*. Galarza v. Keane, 252 F.3d 630 (2d Cir. 2001).

Add after third sentence in seventh paragraph:
In U.S. v. Alcantar, 897 F.2d 436 (9th Cir. 1990), the court stated that the fact that a juror of the same race as the defendant might overly identify with him was not a neutral reason for the exercise of a peremptory challenge against the juror.

After seventh paragraph add:
See also Cavise, *The Batson Doctrine: The Supreme Court's Utter Failure to Meet the Challenge of Discrimination in Jury Selection*, 1999 Wisconsin L. Rev. 501 (1999) ("only the most overtly discriminatory or impolitic lawyer can be caught in *Batson's* toothless bite and, even then, the wound will be only superficial").

In U.S. v. Causey, 185 F.3d 407 (5th Cir. 1999) the Court of Appeals asserted that unless a discriminatory intent is inherent in a prosecutor's explanations, the reasons offered will be deemed race-neutral. This statement, standing alone, begs the question whether the race-neutral explanation bears any relationship to the juror's ability to serve. Arguably, in order to determine the latter question and to satisfy itself that the explanation is not pretextual, the trial court should ask how the race-neutral characteristic relates to the challenged individual's ability to serve as a juror in the case. An example of how this more discriminating approach works can be seen in U.S. v. Evans, 192 F.3d 698 (7th Cir. 1999), where the prosecution challenged an African-American juror who worked as an auditor for the city's aviation department. Being an auditor is certainly a race-neutral factor, but the more critical issue, it is submitted, is how the juror's job impacted on her ability to serve in the case. The prosecutor explained that the defendant was charged with abusing his expense account while a city alderman and the government planned to call city auditors to testify about the city's reimbursement rules and procedures. The prosecutor further explained that he was concerned that the challenged juror might be inclined to apply a personal standard of propriety based on her background and knowledge, as well as whatever preconceptions she might have about what should and should not be paid, and how claims should be processed. See also King v. Moore, 196 F.3d 1327 (11th Cir. 1999) (peremptory challenge of black minister was justified by fact that juror was in process of establishing prison ministry and defendant had indicated he intended to call prison ministers to testify to his good character).

n. 155.

Add to note 155:

See also U.S. v. Valley, 928 F.2d 130 (5th Cir. 1991) (race-neutral reasons advanced by prosecutor not shown to be pretextual); U.S. v. Guerra-Marez, 928 F.2d 665 (5th Cir. 1991). In U.S. v. Hendrieth, 922 F.2d 748, 32 Fed. R. Evid. Serv. 210 (11th Cir. 1991), the defendant, who was black, was tried by an all-white jury, the prosecutor having peremptorily challenged the three black prospective jurors on the panel. The prosecutor explained that one juror was challenged because she was the sister-in-law of a defense witness, the second because she admitted bias against the government, and the third because she was "inattentive and rubbing and rolling her eyes during voir dire." The trial court found these explanations acceptable and the appellate court affirmed.

In U.S. v. Feemster, 98 F.3d 1089 (8th Cir. 1996), the court held that there had been no *Batson* violation where a black juror who had taken a course in criminal law and had sat for the LSAT was challenged peremptorily while white jurors with some legal education but who had taken neither courses in criminal law or sat the LSAT were not.

See also U.S. v. Valley, 928 F.2d 130 (5th Cir. 1991) (race-neutral reasons advanced by prosecutor not shown to be pretextual); U.S. v. Guerra-Marez, 928 F.2d 665 (5th Cir. 1991). In U.S. v. Hendrieth, 922 F.2d 748, 32 Fed. R. Evid. Serv. 210 (11th Cir. 1991), the defendant, who was black, was tried by an all-white jury, the prosecutor having peremptorily challenged the three black prospective jurors on the panel. The prosecutor explained that one juror was challenged because she was the sister-in-law of a defense witness, the second because she admitted

§ 8:7   JURY SELECTION: LAW, ART & SCIENCE 2D

bias against the government, and the third because she was "inattentive and rubbing and rolling her eyes during voir dire." The trial court found these explanations acceptable and the appellate court affirmed.

In U.S. v. Feemster, 98 F.3d 1089 (8th Cir. 1996), the court held that there had been no *Batson* violation where a black juror who had taken a course in criminal law and had sat for the LSAT was challenged peremptorily while white jurors with some legal education but who had taken neither courses in criminal law or sat the LSAT were not. In Heno v. Sprint/United Management Co., 208 F.3d 847, 82 Fair Empl. Prac. Cas. (BNA) 837 (10th Cir. 2000), an employment discrimination action, the court found that a black prospective juror's support of affirmative action, coupled with his feeling that he had been discriminated against in the workplace, provided race-neutral reasons for his peremptory challenge. Interestingly, but questionably, the court observed that the juror's beliefs against discrimination in the workplace were not automatically linked to race but could be held in regard to any heterogeneous group.

In U.S. v. Day, 949 F.2d 973 (8th Cir. 1991), the government justified one of its alleged discriminatory challenges on the basis that the juror worked at a hotel whose occupants and employees had been the focus of numerous criminal investigations. It justified another challenge on the basis the juror was young, had a sporadic employment history as a teacher, and did not own property. Both reasons were found by the court to be race-neutral and not pretextual. Similarly, in U.S. v. Miller, 939 F.2d 605 (8th Cir. 1991), the court found that the prosecutor had satisfied his burden to come forward with race-neutral explanations where one juror was struck because of her associations with legal services, another because he had professional ties with the law firm that represented the defendant, a third because she was employed by a business which the prosecutor believed had ties with narcotics traffickers, and others because they were professional educators and the prosecutor believed that teachers tended to be more forgiving and sympathetic to defendants. See also U.S. v. Fuller, 942 F.2d 454 (8th Cir. 1991) (peremptory challenge of black juror who was unemployed and whose family was unemployed was permissible in prosecution of defendant who was unemployed); U.S. v. Sneed, 34 F.3d 1570 (10th Cir. 1994) (peremptory challenge of Chinese-American juror was based on juror's discomfort in discussing previous felony charge against her husband, her work in the counseling field and the fact that she lived in a liberal community, and was not in violation of *Batson*); U.S. v. Ferguson, 23 F.3d 135, 1994 FED App. 0136P (6th Cir. 1994) (peremptory challenge based on fact black juror had been wrongly beaten by police 20 years previous upheld against *Batson* challenge); U.S. v. McCoy, 23 F.3d 216 (9th Cir. 1994) (fact that juror had three children and problem with gangs was race-neutral reason for peremptory challenge); U.S. v. Perez, 35 F.3d 632 (1st Cir. 1994) (juror's employment as receptionist at public housing authority in inner city where she might have been exposed to drugs was race-neutral reason for peremptory challenge of Spanish surnamed juror in drugs trial); U.S. v. Canoy, 38 F.3d 893 (7th Cir. 1994) (peremptory challenge of Asian juror held to be race-neutral where English was not juror's first language and what defendant may have said over telephone was at issue in trial); U.S. v. Davis, 40 F.3d 1069, 40 Fed. R. Evid. Serv. 1036 (10th Cir. 1994) (peremptory challenge of black female teacher and juror who had been inattentive held race-neutral); U.S. v. Lampkins, 47 F.3d 175 (7th Cir. 1995) (peremptory challenge of female juror who had ex-boyfriend and uncle who had been convicted of drug distribution was gender-neutral); Palmer v. Lares, 42 F.3d 975, 41 Fed. R. Evid. Serv. 1209 (5th Cir. 1995) (prosecutor's perception that sole black

§ 8:7
PEREMPTORY CHALLENGES

juror was hostile and did not want to be in courtroom held race-neutral); U.S. v. Fike, 82 F.3d 1315, 44 Fed. R. Evid. Serv. 479 (5th Cir. 1996) (overruled on other grounds by, U.S. v. Brown, 161 F.3d 256 (5th Cir. 1998)) and (abrogated by, U.S. v. Cantu, 230 F.3d 148 (5th Cir. 2000)) (peremptory challenge of Afro-American because of his distrust of the United States justice system was not in violation of *Batson*); U.S. v. Diggs, 82 F.3d 195, 44 Fed. R. Evid. Serv. 345 (8th Cir. 1996) (peremptory challenge of sole black juror not in violation of *Batson* where juror failed to return to courthouse for remaining jury selection after midmorning recess, had connection with business that had been criminally prosecuted, and was observed with his head in his hand and his eyes closed); U.S. v. Jenkins, 52 F.3d 743 (8th Cir. 1995) (facial expressions, body language and other signs of disinterest justified peremptory challenge of black jurors); U.S. v. Johnson, 54 F.3d 1150, 41 Fed. R. Evid. Serv. 924 (4th Cir. 1995) (peremptory challenge of one black juror whose husband had been involved in criminal activity and another who knew two possible government witnesses was race neutral); U.S. v. Tolliver, 61 F.3d 1189 (5th Cir. 1995), cert. granted, judgment vacated on other grounds, 516 U.S. 1105, 116 S. Ct. 900, 133 L. Ed. 2d 834 (1996) and cert. granted, judgment vacated on other grounds, 519 U.S. 802, 117 S. Ct. 40, 136 L. Ed. 2d 4 (1996) (government provided race-neutral explanation of black jurors—one appeared disinterested and possibly sympathetic to young defendants because of her employment in a school cafeteria; another had potential antagonism against state stemming from a conviction 25 years previous; a third was employed by a cellular telephone company which might be dependent on drug dealers as customers; the brother of a fourth juror had been convicted of murder and the sister of a fifth had been arrested on narcotics charges; and the final struck juror appeared somewhat disinterested and lived in the area where the activity of the defendants had taken place); U.S. v. Ali, 63 F.3d 710 (8th Cir. 1995) (no racial pretext in challenge of black juror who believed that her father had been wrongfully pursued by law enforcement authorities).

See also, U.S. v. Blackman, 66 F.3d 1572, 43 Fed. R. Evid. Serv. 211 (11th Cir. 1995) (juror who maintained that "it was wrong to judge a person because judgment belongs to God" was properly subject to a peremptory challenge); U.S. v. Carr, 67 F.3d 171, 43 Fed. R. Evid. Serv. 125 (8th Cir. 1995) (peremptory strike of one black juror because she was unemployed and rented her residence and another because she had unimpressive work record held non-pretextual); U.S. v. Eubanks, 68 F.3d 272 (8th Cir. 1995) (peremptory challenge of lone black juror in federal case justified by 15 year-old nolo contendere plea, resulting in fine and probation, in state court); Sledd v. McKune, 71 F.3d 797 (10th Cir. 1995) (in case involving child abuse, state was justified in exercising peremptory challenge against black juror who strongly asserted belief that to spare the rod was to spoil the child); Troupe v. Groose, 72 F.3d 75 (8th Cir. 1995) (peremptory challenge of black juror who was disagreeable, offensive and uncommunicative held race neutral); U.S. v. Fields, 72 F.3d 1200 (5th Cir. 1996) (black juror's youth, avoidance of eye contact with prosecutor, and flirtatious looks at defendants constituted race neutral explanation for government's peremptory challenge); McKeel v. City of Pine Bluff, 73 F.3d 207, 43 Fed. R. Evid. Serv. 734 (8th Cir. 1996) (where defendant was a diagnosed paranoid schizophrenic, peremptory challenges by defense of one black juror who worked with mental health patients and another whose facial expressions and body language indicated hostility to defense held not pretextual); Keel v. French, 162 F.3d 263 (4th Cir. 1998) (upholding as race neutral challenge of nine black jurors because they

§ 8:7   JURY SELECTION: LAW, ART & SCIENCE 2D

expressed hesitation about imposing death penalty); U.S. v. Grimmond, 137 F.3d 823, 48 Fed. R. Evid. Serv. 1400 (4th Cir. 1998) (challenge to black elderly lady juror upheld because it appeared that she might have been incapable of understanding complicated issues in drug conspiracy case); Malone v. Vasquez, 138 F.3d 711 (8th Cir. 1998) (upholding as race neutral peremptory challenges of one black juror who was struck because she had been a victim of an armed robbery, another because he seemed familiar to the prosecutor and was the son of a minister, and a third because he resided in the area of the crime); Caldwell v. Maloney, 159 F.3d 639 (1st Cir. 1998) (black juror's equivocation as to how she would weigh police officer's testimony provided race neutral justification for peremptory challenge of juror); Gillam v. U.S., 528 U.S. 900, 120 S. Ct. 235, 145 L. Ed. 2d 197 (1999) (finding race neutral explanation for peremptory challenge of black juror who had been unemployed for a year where government expressed concern over juror's ability to serve conscientiously); U.S. v. Serino, 163 F.3d 91 (1st Cir. 1998) (Asian-American juror's occupation as social worker was valid race neutral explanation for peremptory challenge); U.S. v. Martinez, 168 F.3d 1043(8th Cir. 1999) (peremptory challenge of Native American juror because of her age, marital status, body language, and eye contact during voir dire not pretextual); U.S. v. Boyd, 168 F.3d 1077 (8th Cir. 1999) (fact that African-American juror had relatives in jail and appeared restless, impatient, and disinclined to participate in trial were valid race-neutral reasons for peremptory challenge); Morse v. Hanks, 172 F.3d 983 (7th Cir. 1999) (prosecutor's peremptory challenge to only black member of panel held justified by juror's youth); U.S. v. Diaz, 176 F.3d 52, 52 Fed. R. Evid. Serv. 380 (2d Cir. 1999) (concern that black clergyman's attendance at funerals might impair his concentration was race-neutral reason for challenge; concern that another black juror's favorable impression of street gang was also race-neutral); U.S. v. Morrow, 177 F.3d 272 (5th Cir. 1999) (prosecutor's explanation that black juror was challenged not because of her race but because she indicated that she never read magazines or books other than the Bible, and did not watch television, held race-neutral); U.S. v. Steele, 178 F.3d 1230 (11th Cir. 1999) (government's explanations for six peremptory challenges of women jurors, two because they were elementary school teachers of whom the prosecutor was "leery", three because they worked in the medical industry and the defendant was a pharmacist, and one because she was a hair stylist subject to hearing gossip about the case all held to be gender-neutral); U.S. v. Parsee, 178 F.3d 374, 52 Fed. R. Evid. Serv. 650 (5th Cir. 1999) (peremptory challenge of woman juror because she was a teacher of disabled persons, and worked in an area where one of the defendants was raised and where drug problems were common was sex-neutral explanation for strike).

See also, U.S. v. Cobb, 185 F.3d 1193 (11th Cir. 1999) (peremptory challenge of mother of three who had never been married and who was on welfare, causing the prosecutor to question her morality, was race-neutral); U.S. v. Smallwood, 188 F.3d 905 (7th Cir. 1999) (upholding as race-neutral peremptory challenge of black venire member who was a teacher, thought the defendant looked familiar, conveyed attitude of superiority through body language, and may have been biased against law enforcement); Stubbs v. Gomez, 189 F.3d 1099 (9th Cir. 1999) (peremptory challenge of one black juror whose desire to attend daughter's graduation was felt could possibly compromise her duties as juror and another who failed to reveal on jury questionnaire that she had been a victim of a violent crime 15 years previous, and of a third who lacked employment experience and experience outside the home, and whose demeanor and lack of

Peremptory Challenges § 8:7

eye contact conveyed disinterest in serving, were all race-neutral); Tolbert v. Gomez, 190 F.3d 985 (9th Cir. 1999) (no violation of *Batson* where black juror was challenged after approaching bench to express strong concerns regarding racial prejudice in judicial system); U.S. v. Griffin, 194 F.3d 808, 52 Fed. R. Evid. Serv. 1593 (7th Cir. 1999) (peremptory challenge of African-American juror because she was probably a social worker and did not look around courtroom, when requested to do so to see whether she recognized anybody, held race-neutral and non-pretextual); U.S. v. Jones, 195 F.3d 379 (8th Cir. 1999) (peremptory challenge of one black juror because she was a social worker and another because he nodded to defendant's brother in the hallway outside the courtroom held race-neutral).

See also, U.S. v. Bryce, 208 F.3d 346, 54 Fed. R. Evid. Serv. 184 (2d Cir. 1999), as amended on denial of reh'g, (Jan. 19, 2000) (age of juror was race-neutral explanation for challenge); U.S. v. Jones, 224 F.3d 621 (7th Cir. 2000) (finding race-neutral government's explanation for four peremptory challenges of African-American jurors: the first was struck because of inattentiveness and the fact that she was unemployed, watched soap operas, was not active outside home, and was observed sleeping while other jurors were being questioned; the second was struck because of her body language and the fact that she looked at the defendants but not at the government while answering voir dire questions; the third was struck because he had a close friend who was in the same profession as the defendant; and the last was struck because her son had been convicted of a crime that she did not believe he had committed); U.S. v. Montgomery, 210 F.3d 446 (5th Cir. 2000) (black social worker's alleged lack of intelligence constituted a race-neutral explanation for government's peremptory challenge); U.S. v. Barnette, 211 F.3d 803, 53 Fed. R. Evid. Serv. 1346 (4th Cir. 2000) (opposition to death penalty was race-neutral explanation for peremptory challenge); U.S. v. Marrowbone, 211 F.3d 452, 54 Fed. R. Evid. Serv. 541 (8th Cir. 2000) (inattentiveness and demeanor justified peremptory challenge of Native American prospective juror); U.S. v. Buchanan, 213 F.3d 302, 54 Fed. R. Evid. Serv. 265, 2000 FED App. 0060P (6th Cir. 2000), as corrected on denial of reh'g, (May 22, 2000) and cert. denied, 531 U.S. 1202, 121 S. Ct. 1212, 149 L. Ed. 2d 125 (2001) and cert. denied, 532 U.S. 1000, 121 S. Ct. 1666, 149 L. Ed. 2d 646 (2001) (juror's stated distrust of newspapers provided race-neutral explanation for challenge of only black juror on panel); U.S. v. Jones, 245 F.3d 990 (8th Cir. 2001) (juror's grooming, dress style, inattentiveness and demeanor were all race-neutral factors, as was the fact that the juror shared a common profession with the defendant); U.S. v. Cordoba-Mosquera, 212 F.3d 1194 (11th Cir. 2000), cert. denied, 531 U.S. 1131, 121 S. Ct. 893, 148 L. Ed. 2d 800 (2001) (inattentiveness, signaled by body language and mannerisms, provided race-neutral explanation for peremptory challenge); McCurdy v. Montgomery County, Ohio, 240 F.3d 512, 2001 FED App. 0044P (6th Cir. 2001) (body language indicating passivity and disinterestedness provided race-neutral explanation for challenge); U.S. v. Walton, 217 F.3d 443, 55 Fed. R. Evid. Serv. 192 (7th Cir. 2000) (inattentiveness was a valid race-neutral explanation for peremptory challenge of black juror); U.S. v. Moreno, 217 F.3d 592 (8th Cir. 2000) (Hispanic-American's admission of contact with drugs provided race-neutral explanation for peremptory challenge); Hidalgo v. Fagen, 206 F.3d 1013 (10th Cir. 2000) (challenge of Hispanic juror because of her youth was race-neutral); U.S. v. Williams, 264 F.3d 561, 57 Fed. R. Evid. Serv. 1124 (5th Cir. 2001) (peremptory challenge of two African-American jurors based on fact that one had smiled at the defendant and the other lived in defendant's voting

§ 8:7   JURY SELECTION: LAW, ART & SCIENCE 2D

district held to be race neutral); U.S. v. Alanis, 265 F.3d 576 (7th Cir. 2001), cert. denied, 535 U.S. 1095, 122 S. Ct. 2289, 152 L. Ed. 2d 1049 (2002) (lack of education and fact juror was unemployed were race-neutral criteria for exercise of peremptory challenge against only black member of venire); U.S. v. Campbell, 270 F.3d 702 (8th Cir. 2001), cert. denied, 535 U.S. 946, 122 S. Ct. 1339, 152 L. Ed. 2d 243 (2002) (peremptory challenge of juror who, as part of his job as a parole officer, argued on behalf of inmates and criminal defendants and ensured that their rights were protected held to be race-neutral); U.S. v. Yang, 281 F.3d 534, 61 U.S.P.Q.2d (BNA) 1789, 2002 FED App. 0062P (6th Cir. 2002), cert. denied, 123 S. Ct. 1015, 154 L. Ed. 2d 912 (U.S. 2003) (no *Batson* violation where three women jurors were challenged peremptorily, one because of an "attitude" problem, another because she was unemployed, and the third because she lacked the "necessary background" to be a juror); U.S. v. Humphrey, 287 F.3d 422, 2002 FED App. 0131P (6th Cir. 2002) (overruled by, U.S. v. Leachman, 309 F.3d 377, 2002 FED App. 0353P (6th Cir. 2002)) (peremptory challenge of black juror based on juror's hypertension was race-neutral).

See also U.S. v. Castorena-Jaime, 285 F.3d 916 (10th Cir. 2002) (juror's nervousness, inattentiveness and distraction provided race-neutral explanations for peremptory challenge); U.S. v. Ortiz, 315 F.3d 873, 59 Fed. R. Evid. Serv. 1063 (8th Cir. 2002), cert. denied, 123 S. Ct. 2095, 155 L. Ed. 2d 1078 (U.S. 2003) (challenge to juror who had written jury questionnaire form that she "tried not to let anything or anybody steal her joy" suggested to the government that she might be "out there somewhere" and was race-neutral); U.S. v. Bartholomew, 310 F.3d 912, 59 Fed. R. Evid. Serv. 1482, 2002 FED App. 0396P (6th Cir. 2002), cert. denied, 123 S. Ct. 1005, 154 L. Ed. 2d 923 (U.S. 2003) (peremptory challenge of black female juror because she had a loud voice, was physically large, and seemed opinionated held to be race-neutral and nondiscriminatory); U.S. v. Milan, 304 F.3d 273 (3d Cir. 2002), cert. denied, 123 S. Ct. 1956, 155 L. Ed. 2d 869 (U.S. 2003) (upholding as race-neutral the peremptory challenge of black female juror whom the prosecutor thought would not "blend" with the other jurors because she had moved from the north New Jersey to south New Jersey only three years previously); U.S. v. Campbell, 317 F.3d 597, 60 Fed. R. Evid. Serv. 1197, 2003 FED App. 0032P (6th Cir. 2003) (government offered race-neutral explanation for challenge of African-American juror based on her age, educational level, single status and the fact that she lived in the neighborhood where the relevant events had taken place); U.S. v. Humphrey, 287 F.3d 422, 2002 FED App. 0131P (6th Cir. 2002) (overruled by, U.S. v. Leachman, 309 F.3d 377, 2002 FED App. 0353P (6th Cir. 2002)) (fact that juror's hypertension would have been exacerbated had he served provided race-neutral explanation for challenge of African-American juror); U.S. v. Murillo, 288 F.3d 1126, 59 Fed. R. Evid. Serv. 23 (9th Cir. 2002), cert. denied, 537 U.S. 931, 123 S. Ct. 333, 154 L. Ed. 2d 228 (2002) (government advanced race-neutral explanation for peremptory challenge of Filipino juror having shown that juror did not read books, that "Judge Judy" was her favorite TV show, and that juror had communication difficulties); U.S. v. Brown, 289 F.3d 989 (7th Cir. 2002) (challenge of African-American juror because she was a school teacher was not improper where prosecutor proffered that he would have struck any teacher; challenge of second African-American juror because her husband had been convicted of a crime involving a firearm, albeit over 20 years previously, was also race-neutral; and challenge of third African-American juror because she testified for the defense at her mother's murder trial was a legitimate race-neutral explanation); U.S. v.

§ 8:7 PEREMPTORY CHALLENGES

Steele, 298 F.3d 906 (9th Cir. 2002), cert. denied, 537 U.S. 1096, 123 S. Ct. 710, 154 L. Ed. 2d 646 (2002) (peremptory challenge of minority juror who indicated personal belief that minorities were discriminated against in the criminal justice system was race-neutral); U.S. v. Brown, 299 F.3d 1252, 59 Fed. R. Evid. Serv. 410 (11th Cir. 2002), cert. granted, judgment vacated, 123 S. Ct. 1928, 155 L. Ed. 2d 847 (U.S. 2003) (peremptory challenge of three African-American jurors held race-neutral where one had worked in felony division of county clerk's office and might have developed relationships with felons; the second because he had friends who used cocaine, as well as a nephew who was in prison on a cocaine-related charge; and the third who had been on a prior jury panel that had been unable to reach a verdict); Hayes v. Woodford, 301 F.3d 1054 (9th Cir. 2002) (no *Batson* violation where one African-American juror was challenged because of outstanding traffic warrant and was in the middle of obtaining a divorce from a state correctional officer; another was challenged because he had been refused employment by the police department and was prone to exaggeration; and a third because a wallet found at the scene of the crime belonged to a person employed by juror's daughter); Simmons v. Luebbers, 299 F.3d 929 (8th Cir. 2002), cert. denied, 123 S. Ct. 1582, 155 L. Ed. 2d 314 (U.S. 2003) (explanation for peremptory challenge of minority juror based on juror's indecisiveness, attitude towards jury service, lack of support for death penalty, and job working for downtown post office [prosecutor claiming to have had poor results from other jurors who worked at post office], was race-neutral).

U.S. v. Ortiz, 315 F.3d 873, 59 Fed. R. Evid. Serv. 1063 (8th Cir. 2002), cert. denied, 123 S. Ct. 2095, 155 L. Ed. 2d 1078 (U.S. 2003) illustrates how *Batson* can become intertwined with challenges based on a juror's views on the death penalty. The defendants, charged with murder, argued that the government had used several of its peremptory challenges to strike African-American jurors because of their race. The Court of Appeals found that the challenges had been exercised on a race-neutral basis. One juror was struck because he had no views on the death penalty (but he had also indicated that he had been treated badly by the police, and had been placed wrongfully in a line-up; and the juror also seemed to pay greater attention when the defense read out its witness list than when the prosecution read its list). A second juror was challenged because of his age and the prosecutor's opinion that older jurors seemed to have more difficulty sentencing someone to death because they were facing their own mortality. While a white juror of similar age had not been challenged, her situation was distinguished by the fact that she had indicated that accountability was important to her. A third juror was challenged because, although she indicated she could impose the death penalty if warranted, she also appeared to be more strongly opposed to the death penalty than other members of the venire. See also Simmons v. Luebbers, 299 F.3d 929 (8th Cir. 2002), cert. denied, 123 S. Ct. 1582, 155 L. Ed. 2d 314 (U.S. 2003) (prosecutor's peremptory challenge of minority juror, based on juror's indecisiveness, attitude towards jury service, lack of support for death penalty, and job working for downtown post office [prosecutor claiming to have had poor results from other jurors who worked at post office], were based on race-neutral factors).

In U.S. v. Williams, 272 F.3d 845, 58 Fed. R. Evid. Serv. 822 (7th Cir. 2001), as amended on clarification, (Feb. 11, 2002) and cert. denied, 535 U.S. 947, 122 S. Ct. 1339, 152 L. Ed. 2d 243 (2002) the government struck all four African-American members of the jury pool. Three of the challenges were relatively uncontentious and were not argued to be in violation of *Batson*. In respect to the fourth juror, the government indicated

§ 8:7   JURY SELECTION: LAW, ART & SCIENCE 2D

that the juror in question shared the last name of a family notorious for its involvement in drugs in the area, and that therefore it questioned the juror's denial of acquaintance with witnesses in the case. However, the government also indicated that it did not have the time to engage in the requisite discovery to confirm its suspicions. The Court of Appeals found that the government's reasons were clear, specific, related to the case and racially neutral, and that the government's reasons for not conducting an investigation of the juror further were legitimate.

The problem of questionable race-neutral explanations is examined in Raphael & Ungvarsky, *Excuses, Excuses: Neutral Explanations under Batson v Kentucky*, 27 U Mich J L Ref 229 (1993).

In a civil case, Moore v. Keller Industries, Inc., 948 F.2d 199 (5th Cir. 1991), the court found that the defendants' articulated explanations for its peremptory challenges relating to age, familial relationships, appearance during questioning, and background knowledge, were sufficiently race-neutral to rebut the alleged claim of a *Batson* violation. In U.S. v. Patterson, 258 F.3d 788 (8th Cir. 2001) the peremptory challenge of an African-American woman juror was upheld against a claimed violation of *Batson*, the prosecution having established that the juror knew the defendant as well as people who associated with him and several potential witnesses in the case. While these reasons would seem clearly valid to justify the challenge, perhaps more questionable was the Court's reference to the fact that the defendant's residence was located in the same area as the juror's church.

n. 156.

Add to note 156:

After a party has rebutted a prima facie case by offering a racially-neutral explanation, the opposing party may still argue that the reasons advanced are pretextual. In U.S. v. Pospisil, 186 F.3d 1023 (8th Cir. 1999), the trial court's finding of pretext was held not to be clearly erroneous where the defendants' race-neutral explanations for their peremptory challenges, that the challenged black jurors had heard news accounts of the offense and were government employees in some capacity, was undercut by the fact that similarly situated Caucasians were not challenged and defense counsel admitted that race was a factor because African-Americans would have difficulty deciding the case and might identify with the victim. Similarly, in U.S. v. Mahan, 190 F.3d 416, 1999 FED App. 0315P (6th Cir. 1999), where the defendant was charged with an alleged hate crime with racial overtones, his allegedly race-neutral explanation, that he challenged the one African-American on the jury because she was a widowed clerical worker, was held to be pretextual. In Jones v. Jones, 938 F.2d 838 (8th Cir. 1991), the Court of Appeals held that, after the prosecutor put forward racially-neutral explanations and the defendant's attorney moved simply to quash the jury, the trial court was not required to consider the issue of pretext. In Splunge v. Clark, 960 F.2d 705 (7th Cir. 1992), pretext was found where most of the questions asked of the challenged juror were race-related and the alleged justification for the challenge was the juror's lack of understanding of the burden of proof. Pretext was also found in Jones v. Ryan, 987 F.2d 960 (3d Cir. 1993), where the prosecutor attempted to justify the peremptory challenge of a black venireperson on the ground that she had a child of the same approximate age as the defendant; two white jurors who had children of a similar age had not been challenged, however. See also Johnson v. Love, 40 F.3d 658 (3d Cir. 1994) (explanation that peremptory challenge of black female jurors was justified by fact that such jurors would not be sympathetic to cause of black defendant who allegedly had murdered white man who solicited young black boys for sexual favors held not sufficient to rebut alleged *Batson* violation). Compare Great Plains Equipment, Inc. v. Koch Gathering Systems, Inc., 45 F.3d 962 (5th Cir. 1995) (party alleging *Batson* violation did not carry burden of showing that peremptory challenge of black juror for not paying child support was pretextual or otherwise inadequate).

In ruling on whether a peremptory challenge is pretextual and based on purposeful discrimination, a trial judge should make a clear and definitive ruling. In Lewis v. Lewis, 321 F.3d 824 (9th Cir. 2003), the Court of Appeals was highly critical of the trial judge's ruling that the government's peremptory challenge of a black juror was "probably reasonable."

The decision in McClain v. Prunty, 217 F.3d 1209 (9th Cir. 2000) arguably provides an instructive model of how a court should approach the various stages of a *Batson* inquiry. The prosecutor in the case had peremptorily challenged 10 prospective jurors, including all three black jurors on the panel. The appeal focused on two of the latter jurors, referred to as SR and JH. According to the prosecution, SR was challenged because her son was incarcerated and because the juror apparently did not feel that he had been treated fairly by the system, because the prosecutor believed that the juror had lied about her occupation, and because the juror did not engage in group decision-making either at work or home. The Court of Appeals held that these explanations were all race neutral. However, the court then found that the explanations, although race-neutral, were pretextual. The first two reasons were contrary to the facts and a misrepresentation of what the juror had said, and the third was belied by the fact that a non-black juror who similarly lacked group decision-making experience had not been challenged. Likewise, in respect to JH, the court found that the prosecution's explanation for its peremptory challenge—that the juror worked part-time in a drug program as a rehabilitation counselor (and was thus likely to root for the underdog), and was overly educated, highly intellectual and unlikely to be able to get along with other jurors—was race-neutral. Again, however, the court found that the characterization of what the juror had said had been distorted and the explanation for the challenge was pretextual. The prosecutor's assertion that JH's body language, which consisted of her having her elbow on her chair, indicated hostility to the prosecution, was singled out for being patently frivolous. The Court of Appeals was also highly critical of the deference paid to the prosecution's reasons by the trial court, which had refused to "second-guess" the prosecutor. According to the Court of Appeals, such deference was contrary to clearly established federal law whereby judges were obliged under *Batson* to determine if purposeful discrimination had been established.

A similar approach was taken by the Court of Appeals in Riley v. Taylor, 277 F.3d 261 (3d Cir. 2001), where the prosecutor in a capital case had peremptorily challenged all three prospective black jurors in the pool. In finding the challenge of one of the black jurors to be pretextual, the court took note of the fact that the juror was struck because he was allegedly inattentive while a white juror who was similarly inattentive was not challenged. Another of the black jurors was challenged because of his unwillingness to return the death penalty (according to the prosecutor, signified by the juror's "significant pause" before answering the prosecutor's question) while a white juror with seemingly similar views was not challenged. The Court of Appeals discerned from these examples a pattern of suspect peremptory challenges, indicating that the whole could be greater than the sum of its parts. The absence of rebuttal data was held to further undermine the prosecutor's assertion that its challenges were race-neutral. A final damaging point was evidence indicating that peremptory challenges had been utilized to similar effect in all capital murder trials within the same year. Because the prosecutor's explanations were deemed not to be credible or plausible, the court declined to give the state court's findings of fact the traditional level of appellate court deference, and the Court of Appeals concluded that defendant's constitutional rights under *Batson* had been violated.

In Davis v. Baltimore Gas and Elec. Co., 160 F.3d 1023 (4th Cir. 1998), the Fourth Circuit Court of Appeals held that the failure to argue pretext constitutes a waiver of a *Batson* objection. See also Hopson v. Fredericksen, 961 F.2d 1374 (8th Cir. 1992); U.S. v. Rudas, 905 F.2d 38 (2d Cir. 1990). The issues are examined in Richards, *The Discreet Charm of the Mixed Jury: The Epistemology of Jury Selection and the Perils of Post-Modernism*, 26 Seattle L. Rev. 445 (2003).

Arguably a prosecutor's reasons for striking a juror should be even more closely scrutinized when the juror is the only member of the panel of the same racial or ethnic background as the defendant. Thus in Mahaffey v. Page, 162 F.3d 481 (7th Cir. 1998), the court held that a prima facie showing of a *Batson* violation had been established where the defendant was black, the state had challenged all seven black jurors on the panel, the crimes at issue were racially sensitive, and the court had failed to compare the characteristics of the struck jurors with those of white jurors who had been accepted on the jury. Accord, U.S. v. Williams, 272 F.3d 845, 58 Fed. R. Evid. Serv. 822 (7th Cir. 2001), as amended on clarification, (Feb. 11, 2002) and cert. denied, 535 U.S. 947, 122 S. Ct. 1339, 152 L. Ed. 2d 243 (2002). Other courts, however, have been less impressed by the fact that that the prosecution has used its peremptory challenges to strike all minority jurors on the panel. See, e.g., Caldwell v. Maloney, 159 F.3d 639 (1st Cir. 1998) (upholding peremptory challenges of four black jurors on panel, even though it resulted in no black jurors serving in a racially charged case); Webster v. U.S., 528 U.S. 829, 120 S. Ct. 83, 145 L. Ed. 2d 70 (1999) (upholding peremptory challenges of all four blacks and sole Asian on jury panel); (U.S. v. Maxwell, 160 F.3d 1071, 1998 FED App. 0338P (6th Cir. 1998) (upholding peremptory challenge of only remaining black member of venire); U.S. v. Serino, 163 F.3d 91 (1st Cir. 1998) (peremptory challenge of sole Asian-American juror on panel could be justified by occupation as social worker); U.S. v. Buchanan, 213 F.3d 302, 54 Fed. R. Evid. Serv. 265, 2000 FED App. 0060P (6th Cir. 2000), as corrected on denial of reh'g, (May 22, 2000) and cert. denied, 531 U.S. 1202, 121 S. Ct. 1212, 149 L. Ed. 2d 125 (2001) and cert. denied, 532 U.S. 1000, 121 S. Ct. 1666, 149 L. Ed. 2d 646 (2001) (juror's stated distrust of newspapers provided race-neutral explanation for challenge of only black juror on panel).

In U.S. v. Joe, 8 F.3d 1488, 39 Fed. R. Evid. Serv. 920 (10th Cir. 1993) the defendant was a Native American Indian and the prosecution had used one of its peremptory challenges to remove the only Native American Indian on the venire. The court accepted as race-neutral the prosecutor's explanation that the juror had been challenged because she was an artist, was only 25 years of age, and had failed to respond to a questionnaire as to whether she owned or rented a home. It is hard to understand how any of the factors cited reflected adversely on the juror's ability to serve, but the prosecution stressed its belief that artists tend not to be pro-government and that it was concerned about the juror's life experiences and maturity. And see U.S. v. Childs, 5 F.3d 1328, 37 Fed. R. Evid. Serv. 1344 (9th Cir. 1993) (upholding peremptory challenge of lone

§ 8:7

Native American Indian on panel because juror appeared hesitant and suggestible); Palmer v. Lares, 42 F.3d 975, 41 Fed. R. Evid. Serv. 1209 (5th Cir. 1995) (prosecutor's perception that sole black juror was hostile and did not want to be in courtroom held race-neutral); U.S. v. Bergodere, 40 F.3d 512 (1st Cir. 1994) (peremptory challenge of sole black juror justified by juror's statement that it would be a struggle to be impartial and that he had problem with cases involving adults and drugs); U.S. v. Vasquez-Lopez, 22 F.3d 900 (9th Cir. 1994) (peremptory challenge of sole black juror because of disinterest and inattentiveness held permissible); Jackson v. City of Little Rock, 26 F.3d 88, 65 Fair Empl. Prac. Cas. (BNA) 1 (8th Cir. 1994) (peremptory challenge of sole black juror on grounds juror had sons with drug problems and might have unduly credited testimony of drug prevention program officer upheld). In Rush v. Smith, 45 F.3d 1197 (8th Cir. 1995), reh'g granted and opinion vacated, (Mar. 16, 1995) and on reh'g, 56 F.3d 918 (8th Cir. 1995) the sole black juror on the panel was unable to attend court because of a recent snowfall. The judge declined to authorize a marshall to transport the juror to court because the courthouse was reduced to skeletal staff. The judge also refused plaintiff's offer to send a taxi to bring the juror to court because the judge deemed the provision of transportation by a party to the suit to be problematic. The Court of Appeals found that the dismissal of the juror under the circumstances was not an abuse of the court's discretion.

Miller-El v. Cockrell, 537 U.S. 322, 123 S. Ct. 1029, 154 L. Ed. 2d 931 (2003), the Supreme Court provided guidance on the types of considerations that would support a claim that peremptory challenges that, while on their face race-neutral, were in fact exercised in a discriminatory manner in violation of *Batson*. The technical issue in the case was whether a Certificate of Appealability (COA) should have been granted to review the district court's dismissal of the petitioner's habeas corpus application (28 U.S.C.A. § 2253, as amended by the Antiterrorism and Effective Death Penalty Act of 1996, 28 U.S.C.A. § 2254(e)(1) (AEDPA). In order to obtain a COA, the petitioner had to demonstrate "a substantial showing of the denial of a constitutional right." A petitioner satisfies this burden by showing that "jurists of reason could disagree with the district court's resolution of [the petitioner's] constitutional claims or that jurists could conclude the issues presented are adequate to deserve encouragement to proceed further." The petitioner does not have to show that the appeal would succeed. However, under 28 U.S.C.A. § 2254(e)(1), factual determinations by state courts are presumed to be correct absent "clear and convincing evidence" to the contrary. Applying these standards, the Supreme Court held that the COA should have been issued.

Although the COA is not the occasion for ruling on the merits of a habeas claim (indeed, if a court were to decide the merits and use this adjudication to justify the denial of a COA, it would be exceeding its jurisdiction), the Supreme Court nonetheless felt that, in order to reach a decision in the case, it was necessary to engage in an extensive, although not definitive, review of the evidence of discrimination in the exercise of the prosecution's peremptory challenges. Before the Supreme Court, the State conceded that the petitioner had satisfied step one of *Batson*'s three-step framework (demonstrating a prima facie case), while the petitioner conceded that the State had satisfied step 2 (proferring a race-neutral explanation for its challenges). The critical issue thus became whether the petitioner had established that the prosecution's race-neutral explanations were pretextual and that a discriminatory intent lay behind the challenges. The Court noted that this issue often boils down to whether the prosecutor's race-neutral explanations are credible, and offered sev-

§ 8:7

eral factors that a court might wish to consider in assessing credibility, including the prosecutor's demeanor, the reasonableness or improbability of the prosecutor's explanations, and whether the explanations had some basis in accepted trial strategy.

The first set of factors to which the Court drew attention related to the conduct of prosecutors in the case. The Court noted that prospective African-American jurors had been excluded from petitioner's jury as a result of peremptory challenges in a ratio significantly higher than that for non-blacks—while 91% of the prospective African-American jurors had been peremptorily challenged, only 13% of the non-black prospective jurors had been similarly challenged. This statistical disparity, according to the Court, raised an inference of discrimination. This inference was strengthened by the fact that three of the State's proffered race-neutral rationales for striking the African-American jurors—ambivalence about the death penalty, hesitancy to vote to execute defendants capable of being rehabilitated, and the jurors' own family history of criminality—pertained to non-black jurors who were not challenged.

Secondly, the Court noted that on voir dire the prosecution had questioned venire members regarding their views on the death penalty differently depending on their race. Before being asked whether they could sentence the defendant to death, the African-American jurors were given a graphic description of an execution. The white jurors were asked their views without this prefatory description of the execution process. Jurors were also questioned differently depending on their race regarding their willingness to impose the minimum sentence for murder. The purpose behind the different approaches taken to questioning black and non-black jurors was apparently to elicit responses that would sustain a challenge for cause to the black jurors. According to the Supreme Court, the disparate questioning based on race constituted evidence of purposeful discrimination.

Finally, the Court examined what it saw as a potentially discriminatory use of "jury shuffling". This Texas procedure allows parties to rearrange the order in which jurors are brought forward for voir dire examination. In the case, the prosecution had sought a jury shuffle when a predominate number of black jurors were scheduled to be called early-on for examination. By requesting a shuffle, the prosecutor could reduce the chances of the African-American jurors being needed for the jury, as a jury might be selected before their names could be reached. This too raised a suspicion that the State was trying to exclude as many African-Americans from the jury as possible. Testimony that the Dallas County District Attorney's Office had admitted to using this process in the past to manipulate the racial composition of the jury only served to reinforce this suspicion. This evidence of past practice, which the Supreme Court felt detracted from the prosecutor's credibility, had been ignored by the state courts.

The trial in the case had taken place prior to the Supreme Court's decision in *Batson*, so the standards of Swain v. Alabama, 380 U.S. 202, 85 S. Ct. 824, 13 L. Ed. 2d 759 (1965) (overruled by, Batson v. Kentucky, 476 U.S. 79, 106 S. Ct. 1712, 90 L. Ed. 2d 69 (1986)) would have controlled the initial hearing before the trial court. At that hearing, the petitioner had presented evidence of discrimination aimed at excluding African-Americans from juries generally, as required by *Swain*. Several district attorneys, judges and others claimed to have observed a systematic pattern of excluding black jurors (although other witnesses testified to the contrary). The defense also presented evidence of a formal policy of the

District Attorney's Office to exclude minorities from jury service. According to the Supreme Court, this historical record of discrimination not only revealed the past culture of the District Attorney's Office, but also cast doubt on the prosecutor's claim of not having any racially improper motive in the petitioner's case.

As the district court had given insufficient consideration of the above evidence and had accepted uncritically the state court's evaluation of the prosecutor's demeanor, and as the Court of Appeal had evaluated the COA application in the same non-searching manner, the Supreme Court reversed. The Court found that the lower courts had incorrectly merged the "clear and convincing" evidence standard of 28 U.S.C.A. § 2254(e)(1), which pertains to state court determinations of fact, and the unreasonableness requirement of 28 U.S.C.A. § 2254(d)(2), which relates to state court decisions and applies to the granting of habeas relief. As a result, too demanding a standard had been imposed on the petitioner. The lower courts had also been incorrect in not inquiring whether a "substantial showing of the denial of a constitutional right" had been proved as required under 28 U.S.C.A. § 2253(c)(2).

Add after note 156:
The burden of rebuttal is also eased if the prosecution is permitted to support its peremptory challenges by reference to personal knowledge or information supplied by outside sources, as was allowed in Com. v. Snodgrass, 831 S.W.2d 176 (Ky. 1992). Arguably the better practice would be to require the party to question the juror in respect to the allegedly disqualifying grounds, thus placing on record the relevant information as well as the juror's response. In Note, *True Lies: the Role of Pretext Evidence under* Batson v Kentucky *in the* Wake of St. Mary's Honor Society v Hicks, 94 Mich L Rev 488 (1996), the author explores the relationship between pretext and intentional discrimination.

The requirements of *Batson* can also pose ethical dilemmas for an attorney because the Supreme Court's decision tacitly encourages lawyers to manufacture race-neutral reasons for challenged jurors. See Anderson, *Catch Me If You Can: Resolving the Ethical Dilemmas in the Brave new World of Jury Selection,* 32 NE L Rev 343 (1998). Anderson argues that the solution lies in the expansion of jury pools, reform of voir dire, and the allowance of a certain number of affirmative juror selections by both parties. See also Ramirez, *Affirmative Jury Selection: A Proposal to Advance Both the Deliberative Ideal and Jury Diversity,* 1998 U. of Chicago Legal Forum 161; Fukurai, *A Quota Jury: Affirmative Action in Jury Selection,* 25 Journal of Criminal Justice 477 (1997).

If one were to accept that the principle of affirmative action should be applied to jury selection, the question would remain of how to go about achieving a racially mixed jury. One method would be to draw upon the ancient concept of the jury de mediatate linguae and allocate half (or some other percentage) of places on the jury to persons of the same race or ethnic background as each party. See Ramirez, *The Mixed Jury and the Ancient Custom of Trial by Jury de Mediatate Linguae: A History and a Proposal for Change*, 74 BU L Rev 777 (1994). Another possible approach would be to allow each side to affirmatively choose a number of jurors. See Anderson, *Catch Me If You Can: Resolving the Ethical Dilemmas in the Brave New World of Jury Selection*, 32 NE L Rev 343 (1998). A third model, initially adopted in Hennepin County, Minnesota, would require the seating of a jury that reflected the racial composition of the community. See Fukurai & Davies, *Affirmative Action in Jury Selection: Racially Representative Juries, Racial Quotas, and Affirmative Juries of the Hennepin Model and Jury de Mediatate Linguae*, 4 Va. J. Soc. Pol. & L 645 (1997). The Hennepin model, however, will not prove effective in seating minority jurors when the percentage of the minority within the community was small. So, for example, if 10% of a community were black, the jury would have to contain only one black member. That lone juror might find it difficult to effectively counter any discriminatory tendencies of the majority, and certainly would in a jurisdiction that allowed supermajority verdicts. Thus some social scientists have suggested that there needs to be a core of minority jurors (the number typically proposed being three) for their arguments to carry any weight. See Fukurai, *A Quota Jury: Affirmative Action in Jury Selection*, 25 Journal of Criminal Justice 477 (1997).

The application of affirmative action principles to jury selection, while no doubt well-intentioned, is not without its constitutional difficulties. In U.S. v. Nelson, 277 F.3d 164 (2d Cir. 2002), cert. denied, 537 U.S. 835, 123 S. Ct. 145, 154 L. Ed. 2d 54 (2002) the trial judge had decided that the jury, as constituted after voir dire, was insufficiently racially and religiously diverse. Accordingly when one of the impaneled jurors was excused for illness, the court sua sponte removed a second juror who was white and filled the two newly created vacancies with an African-American and a Jewish juror, the record leaving no doubt that the jurors were selected specifically because of their race and religion. The Court of Appeals held that this procedure was improper and in violation of the principle of race neutrality. That the procedure had been agreed to by the parties was deemed irrelevant. In U.S. v. Allen-Brown, 243 F.3d 1293 (11th Cir. 2001), cert. denied, 534 U.S. 1010, 122 S. Ct. 496, 151 L. Ed. 2d 407 (2001), the Court of Appeals similarly held that the desire to obtain a more diverse jury was not a valid ground for allowing a race-based challenge.

Affirmative action in jury selection is troubling also from a theoretical perspective, as the process would seem to encourage jurors to think of themselves as representatives of a particular racial or ethnic perspective rather than as objective triers of fact. If parties were to be allowed to affirmatively choose jurors, it would open the door to the conscious selection of jurors holding a racial animus, or, more generally, jurors who were simply prejudiced in favor or against one of the parties. In practice, affirmative jury selection would likely lead to more hung juries. On a philosophical, affirmative jury selection may be at odds with the concept of an impartial jury. See generally J. Abramson, We, The Jury (Basic Books 1994); J. Gobert, Justice, Democracy and the Jury (Dartmouth 1997).

In U.S. v. Ovalle, 136 F.3d 1092, 1998 FED App. 0060P (6th Cir. 1998), the Sixth Circuit Court of Appeals reviewed the Jury Selection Plan of the Eastern District of Michigan. In an attempt to ensure a proper balance of the different cognizable groups in the community, the Plan provided for the removal of one in five non-African Americans from the jury pool. This was held to be a violation of the equal protection rights of the non-black prospective jurors who were effectively excluded under the Plan. The right to an impartial jury may also be compromised by affirmative jury selection. The decision and the implications are examined in Cohn & Sherwood, The Rise and Fall of Affirmative Action in Jury Selection, 32 U. Mich. J. of Law Reform 323 (1999).

The author of Casenote, *Jurors and Litigants Beware— Savvy Attorneys are Prepared to Strike:* Has Purkett v. Elem Signalled *the Demise of the Peremptory Challenge at the Federal and State Levels*, 52 U. of Miami L. Rev. 635 (1998)) advances the concept of a quasi-cause challenge, which would have to be case-related. Also concerned with lawyer ethics, but addressing the problem from a different perspective, is Charlow, *Tolerating Deception and Discrimination after Batson,* 50 Stanford L. Rev. (1997). Charlow notes that a judicial finding of a pretextual explanation for a discriminatory peremptory challenge necessarily implicates the ethics of the lawyer making the challenge and exposes him or her to possible personal liability. However, the author argues that the costs of sanctions—possibly unwarranted punishment of the lawyer and a resulting chilling effect on the raising of contentious peremptory challenges—militate against sanctions even if that means that a certain level of lawyer disingenuousness may have to be tolerated. In practice the opposite had proved to be the case, with peremptory challenges often being found to be race-neutral where the explanation for the challenge is based on a juror's alleged demeanor or body language. See, e.g., U.S. v. Chen, 131 F.3d 375 (4th Cir. 1997) (upholding as race-neutral the peremptory challenge of black juror based on the juror's demeanor); U.S. v. James, 113 F.3d 721 (7th Cir. 1997) (body language provided race-

§ 8:7   JURY SELECTION: LAW, ART & SCIENCE 2D

neutral explanation for peremptory challenge of black juror); U.S. v. Perkins, 105 F.3d 976 (5th Cir. 1997) (prosecution's explanation that black juror shook his head and had disgusted look on his face was race-neutral); Washington v. Johnson, 90 F.3d 945 (5th Cir. 1996) (black juror's obstinate manner held race-neutral basis for peremptory challenge); Troupe v. Groose, 72 F.3d 75 (8th Cir. 1995) (upholding peremptory challenge based on perception that black juror was disagreeable, offensive and uncommunicative); U.S. v. Cure, 996 F.2d 1136 (11th Cir. 1993) (facial expressions, demeanor and inattentiveness were race-neutral explanations for peremptory challenges); U.S. v. Daly, 974 F.2d 1215, 36 Fed. R. Evid. Serv. 1100 (9th Cir. 1992) (upholding peremptory challenge of juror who sat "stone-faced" during humorous interlude); U.S. v. Todd, 963 F.2d 207 (8th Cir. 1992) (upholding peremptory challenges of black jurors who appeared inattentive, impatient, and hostile); Reynolds v. Benefield, 931 F.2d 506 (8th Cir. 1991) (hostile body language constituted race-neutral basis for peremptory challenge).

The case that nonverbal indices of deception should be sufficient not only to withstand a *Batson* challenge, but also to provide the basis for a challenge for cause is made in Note, *Articulating the Inarticulable: Relying on Nonverbal Behavioral Cues to Strike Jurors during Voir Dire,* 8 Ariz. L. Rev. 739 (1996).

But see Reynolds v. Benefield, 931 F.2d 506 (8th Cir. 1991). The hostile body language of the juror provided race-neutral explanation for the peremptory challenge. In Caldwell v. Maloney, 159 F.3d 639 (1st Cir. 1998), the First Circuit Court of Appeals, in overturning a federal district court's finding of a *Batson* violation, particularly noted that the district court had given insufficient attention to "considerations of [the juror's] body language, intonation, demeanor, pacing and the like and to the trial judge's superior ability to evaluate these considerations." Caldwell v. Maloney, 159 F.3d 639, 653 (1st Cir. 1998).

n. 159.

Add to note 159:

See also Burks v. Borg, 27 F.3d 1424, 1429 (9th Cir. 1994) (in exercising peremptory challenges, trial attorney is entitled to make credibility determinations, and "to take into account tone, demeanor, facial expression, emphasis—all those factors that make the words uttered by the prospective juror convincing or not."). In Brown v. Kelly, 973 F.2d 116 (2d Cir. 1992), the court, while affirming that impressions of the conduct and demeanor of a prospective juror during voir dire could provide the basis for a peremptory challenge, stated that because of the subjective nature of the grounds, the prosecutor was well-advised to make contemporaneous notes as to the specific behavior that rendered the juror unsuitable. See also Clark v. State, 601 So. 2d 284 (Fla. Dist. Ct. App. 3d Dist. 1992) (prosecutor's receiving "bad vibes" from black juror during voir dire was not clear and reasonably specific explanation justifying peremptory challenge). In U.S. v. Scott, 26 F.3d 1458 (8th Cir. 1994), the prosecutor attempted to justify a peremptory challenge of a black juror on the basis of his feeling that the juror did not want to be in court and did not like the process. The Court of Appeals expressed concern about such subjective judgments and advocated developing a record which included the specific behavior which had led the prosecutor to have doubts about the juror. Nonetheless it found no constitutional violation, in part because the trial judge had indicated that he had a similar impression regarding the juror. The author of Note, Articulating the Inarticulable: Relying on Nonverbal Behavioral Cues to Deception to Strike Jurors during voir dire, 38 Ariz. L Rev argues in favor of allowing nonverbal cues to form the basis of a justification to a challenge based on *Batson*.

In McClain v. Prunty, 217 F.3d 1209 (9th Cir. 2000) the prosecutor asserted that a juror's body language, which consisted of her having her elbow on her chair, indicated hostility to the prosecution. The Court of Appeals found this reasoning to be patently frivolous. In part on this basis, it concluded that the prosecution's explanation for the peremptory challenge of the juror was pretextual.

Add after ninth paragraph:

In Hernandez v. New York, 500 U.S. 352, 111 S. Ct. 1859, 114 L. Ed. 2d 395 (1991), the Supreme Court provided further guidance as to the nature of the race-neutral explanation required to be shown by the prosecutor in order to rebut a prima facie case of a *Batson* violation. The petitioner, who was Latino (Hispanic), objected to the prosecutor's use of four peremptory challenges to exclude Latino jurors at his trial. Two of the challenged jurors had brothers who had been convicted of crimes, and the petitioner did not press his objection to the challenge of these. In respect to the other two challenges, the prosecutor volunteered, before being requested to do so by the trial court, that the jurors were both bilingual and that he was concerned that they might not accept the official interpreter's translation of the testimony of the Latino witnesses who were to appear at trial. This concern was based not solely on the jurors' bilingualism, but also on the fact that the jurors had looked away from him and hesitated before responding to his question as to whether they would accept the official interpreter's translation. The prosecutor argued that he had no motive to exclude Latino jurors because the complainants as well as the state's civilian witnesses were Latinos. See also Sheridan, "Another White Race": Mexican Americans and the Paradox of Whiteness in Jury Selection, 21 Law and History Review 109 (2002) (arguing Hernandez v. State, 160 Tex. Crim. 72, 251 S.W.2d 531 (1952), judgment rev'd, 347 U.S. 475, 74 S. Ct. 667, 98 L. Ed. 866 (1954) reflects the Court's ambivalence to the status of Latinos and whether they constitute a "race," with the effect being to deny Latinos full and equal citizenship).

§ 8:7   Jury Selection: Law, Art & Science 2d

Some confusion seems to have developed regarding the relative burdens of proof required by *Batson*. The confusion is in part the product of a failure to distinguish between the burden of going forward (or presenting evidence), and the burden of persuasion. The former may shift from defense to prosecution and back again in the course of a *Batson* inquiry, but the ultimate burden of persuasion remains with the party alleging the violation of *Batson*. The point was made in the Supreme Court's opinion in *Purkett v Elem*: "[T]he burden shifts to the State to come forward with a neutral explanation [but] the ultimate burden and persuasion regarding racial motivation rests with, and never shifts from, the opponent of the strike." Purkett v. Elem, 514 U.S. 765, 115 S. Ct. 1769, 1771, 131 L. Ed. 2d 834 (1995). A number of federal courts have found this clarification to be helpful and it is now common to cite it. See, e.g., McCrory v. Henderson, 82 F.3d 1243 (2d Cir. 1996); Gibson v. Bowersox, 78 F.3d 372 (8th Cir. 1996); McKeel v. City of Pine Bluff, 73 F.3d 207, 43 Fed. R. Evid. Serv. 734 (8th Cir. 1996).

On these facts, the United States Supreme Court found that the prosecutor had satisfied the burden of rebuttal established in *Batson*. In reaching this conclusion, the Court drew a critical distinction (the dissenters did not agree that the distinction was as critical as the majority made it out to be) between discriminatory intent and discriminatory impact. It is discriminatory intent which must be proven in order to establish a violation of the equal protection clause. The mere fact that a prosecutor's peremptory challenge strategy may have a discriminatory impact will not preclude a finding that the strategy is race-neutral and thus not in violation of *Batson*. This is not to say that discriminatory impact is irrelevant—it may be evidence of discriminatory intent.

Applying these principles to the facts of *Hernandez*, it was probable, although by no means certain, that those jurors who were bilingual would also be Latino. The peremptory challenges were not, however, based on the fact that the jurors were Latino or even that they were bilingual. Rather, they were based on the prosecutor's reservations about the jurors' willingness to accept the official interpreter's translation of testimony which the jurors were capable of interpreting for themselves. It was therefore incorrect to maintain, as did the defendant, that the prosecutor used Spanish-language fluency as a proxy for ethnicity. There might well have been non-Latino prospective jurors who were bilingual and whom the prosecutor judged would also have been unwilling to accept the official interpreter's translation, who too would have been challenged. (It would obviously be to a prosecutor's advantage to make such a showing and/or to show that there were bilingual Latino jurors who were not struck.) The fact that the prosecutor's peremptory challenges may have had disproportionate impact therefore did not in and of itself preclude the court from finding that the prosecutor's explanations were race-neutral and sufficient to discharge his obligation of rebuttal under *Batson*.

Similar issues arose in U.S. v. Jordan, 223 F.3d 676 (7th Cir. 2000) where the Court of Appeals ruled that the peremptory challenge of two Latino jurors was not pretextual. One juror was excused because his wife taught Spanish at DePaul University, described as a hotbed of dissent regarding the defendants. Also relevant was the fact that one of the defendants and several of his character witnesses had also taught at DePaul. The juror in question also had unpleasant experiences with the military in Argentina. These factors were deemed to provide a race neutral explanation for the juror's challenge. While the government had also expressed concern that the juror's knowledge of Spanish might incline her not to defer to the government's translations of taped statements, the district court had not credited this explanation and neither did the Court of Appeals. Bilinguilism, as Justice Kennedy had pointed out in Hernandez, was not a race-neutral ground for striking a juror. The second juror was also fluent in Spanish but the reason for this juror's challenge was his bad relationship with two Hispanic aldermen who had spoken out against one of the government's witnesses in the case. This too was deemed to be a race-neutral explanation for the peremptory challenge of the juror.

The distinction between discriminatory intent and discriminatory impact arose again in U.S. v. Bartholomew, 310 F.3d 912, 59 Fed. R. Evid. Serv. 1482, 2002 FED App. 0396P (6th Cir. 2002), cert. denied, 123 S. Ct. 1005, 154 L. Ed. 2d 923 (U.S. 2003). In this drug conspiracy prosecution, several of the prosecutor's peremptory challenges of blacks were claimed to be in violation of *Batson*. The prosecutor explained that he had struck one of the jurors because she had shot her husband and had a son who had been convicted of a felony, and another because she had raised money to hire an attorney to represent her grandson in a criminal case. In respect to these challenges, the defendants argued that because a disproportionate number of blacks were incarcerated in the prison system, the explanations were not race-neutral. Citing Hernandez v. New York, 500 U.S. 352, 111 S. Ct. 1859, 114 L. Ed. 2d 395 (1991), the Court of Appeals held that such discriminatory impact, though not irrelevant, was not conclusive in the determination of whether peremptory challenges were race-neutral. Further, the court noted that the removal of the two jurors in question was not based simply on the fact that they had relatives in the criminal justice system: one had shot her husband and the other had raised money to hire an attorney for a criminal defendant.

In Tinner v. United Ins. Co. of America, 308 F.3d 697, 89 Fair Empl. Prac. Cas. (BNA) 1843 (7th Cir. 2002), cert. denied, 123 S. Ct. 1623, 155 L. Ed. 2d 484, 91 Fair Empl. Prac. Cas. (BNA) 608 (U.S. 2003) the attorney for the defendant in a Title VII suit alleging race discrimination asked every member of the panel whether they knew or had heard of anyone who filed a discrimination claim. The one affirmative response came from the only African-American juror on the panel, who stated that her sister had filed a discrimination lawsuit and that her experience had been an "ordeal." The defendant exercised a peremptory challenge to remove this juror. The plaintiff alleged a violation of *Batson*, claiming that the questions were surrogates for race, and thus constituted purposeful discrimination. The trial court rejected the *Batson* claim, and the Court of Appeals affirmed, finding that the challenge was race-neutral and not pretextual. Both the fact that the juror's sister had filed a discrimination lawsuit and the fact that the juror characterized the experience as an "ordeal" constituted race-neutral reasons for the challenge. Nor did the Court of Appeals accept the argument that because the question might have had a disparate impact (as members of a racial minority were more likely to face discrimination in the workplace and thus more likely to respond affirmatively to the question), it indicated purposeful discrimination.

In Devose v. Norris, 53 F.3d 201 (8th Cir. 1995) the court found that the prosecution's stated justification for its striking of three black jurors—that they suffered from burnout from previous service—was pretextual given its failure to pursue the issue of burnout with five prospective white jurors who had comparable jury experience. Similarly, in U.S. v. Stewart, 65 F.3d 918 (11th Cir. 1995), where the defendants had exercised peremptory challenges against 75% of the black prospective jurors, the Court of Appeals, in upholding the trial court's disallowance of one of the strikes, stated that the reasons that had been given by the defendant should have logically led to the challenge of similarly situated white jurors, but did not. In Riley v. Taylor, 277 F.3d 261 (3d Cir. 2001), where the prosecutor in a capital case had peremptorily challenged all three prospective black jurors in the pool, the court took specific note of the fact that the juror was struck because he was allegedly inattentive while a white juror who was similarly inattentive was not challenged. Another of the black jurors was challenged because of his unwillingness to return the death penalty (according to the prosecutor, signified by the juror's "significant pause" before answering the prosecutor's question) while a white juror with seemingly similar views was not challenged. The Court of Appeals discerned from these examples a pattern of suspect peremptory challenges, and concluded that defendant's constitutional rights under *Batson* had been violated. But compare U.S. v. Kunzman, 54 F.3d 1522, 42 Fed. R. Evid. Serv. 115 (10th Cir. 1995) (no *Batson* violation although black juror was peremptorily challenged because of lack of experience with real estate transactions and white jurors with no real estate experience were not challenged); Holder v. Welborn, 60 F.3d 383 (7th Cir. 1995) (prosecutor's decision to peremptorily challenge a black juror who was feared to harbor feelings of selective prosecution against the County because it had dropped charges against the alleged murderer of her brother while not challenging several white jurors who had had "brushes with the law" held permissible). In Yancey v. State, 813 So. 2d 1 (Ala. Crim. App. 2001), cert. denied, (July 6, 2001) the court found a *Batson* violation where several black prospective jurors were allegedly struck for their views on capital punishment, but a white prospective juror who held similar views was not challenged. The Court's belief that the challenges were discriminatory was no doubt reinforced by the fact that the prosecution had also struck black prospective jurors who had committed traffic and misdemeanor offenses while not challenging six white prospective jurors who had committed similar offenses.

Justices O'Connor and Scalia would have stopped at this point. The four justices in the plurality, however, went on to state that their decision should not be read as implying that the exclusion of bilingual speakers was wise, or even that it would be constitutional in all cases. In some communities, and for some ethnic groups, proficiency in a certain language may in fact be a proxy for race and unconstitutional under the equal protection clause. While the plurality's dicta did not affect the result in *Hernandez*, they did serve to emphasize that the Court expects trial judges to look at each case individually, and to be wary of excuses for the exercise of peremptory challenges that have a discriminatory impact.

In Pemberthy v. Beyer, 19 F.3d 857 (3d Cir. 1994), also involving the peremptory challenges of Spanish-speaking jurors, the Court of Appeals held that *Batson* applied only to classifications that were subject to "strict" scrutiny under the equal protection clause, such as race and national origin, or classifications which were subject to "heightened" scrutiny, such as gender. Classifications based on the ability to speak or understand a particular foreign language, such as Spanish, did not rise to this level. The court was not prepared to accept that language-based classifications were always a proxy for race or ethnicity. Because of the close association between language and ethnicity, however, the court advised the trial court to carefully assess the challenger's actual motivation. The Court's decision is examined in Recent Case, 108 Harv. L Rev 769 (1995). See also Comment, *Protecting Both Ethnic Minorities and the Equal Protection Clause,* 1997 BYU L. Rev. 101 (arguing in support of *Pemberthy* and, to like effect, U.S. v. Munoz, 15 F.3d 395 (5th Cir. 1994), and against finding peremptory challenges based on foreign language ability to be a proxy for ethnic discrimination).

The *Hernandez* decision is criticized in Hsieh, *Language-Qualifying Juries to Exclude Bilingual Speakers,* 66 Brooklyn L. Rev. 1181 (2001). The author argues that not only will the decision result in the elimination of knowledgeable jurors, but that it will inevitably lead to fewer Spanish-speaking persons serving on juries. In Comment, *Hispanics: Not a Cognizable Ethnic Group,* 63 U Cin L Rev 497 (1994), the author argues that it is demeaning to the diversity of Spanish speaking peoples to lump them together into a single cognizable group for jury selection purposes.

One arguably invaluable source of information in confirming or rebutting a claim of discrimination in the exercise of peremptory challenges is the notes kept by the lawyer who made the allegedly discriminatory challenges. These, however, have been held to be protected under the "work product" doctrine. See People v. Mack, 128 Ill. 2d 231, 131 Ill. Dec. 551, 538 N.E.2d 1107 (1989); Guilder v. State, 794 S.W.2d 765 (Tex. App. Dallas 1990). Compare Salazar v. State, 795 S.W.2d 187 (Tex. Crim. App. 1990) (prosecuting attorney ordered to produce notes after using them to refresh his recollection as to the reasons for his exercise of peremptory challenges).

Distinguishing *Hernandez,* the Ninth Circuit Court of Appeals held in U.S. v. Bishop, 959 F.2d 820 (9th Cir. 1992) that the prosecutor's claimed justification for challenging a black juror—that the juror lived in a predominantly low-income, black neighborhood and was likely to believe that police picked on black people—was not an adequate race-neutral explanation sufficient to satisfy the dictates of *Batson.* The court observed that, in modern society, residence can become a proxy for race. Compare Johnson v. State, 600 So. 2d 32 (Fla. Dist. Ct. App. 3d Dist. 1992) (disapproved of by, Williams v. State, 638 So. 2d 935 (Fla. 1994)) and (disapproved of by, Rock v. State, 638 So. 2d 933 (Fla. 1994)) (disapproved of by, Williams v. State, 638 So. 2d 935 (Fla. 1994)) and (disapproved of by, Rock v. State, 638 So. 2d 933 (Fla. 1994)) (fact juror resided in high crime area was invalid justification for peremptory challenge absent connection between residence and facts of case).

The implications of *Hernandez* are explored in *Perea*, Hernandez v New York: *Courts, Prosecutors, and the Fear of Spanish*, 21 Hofstra L Rev 1 (1992); Casenote, Hernandez v New York: *Allowing Bias to Continue in the Jury Selection Process*, 19 Ohio NU L Rev 151 (1992); Note, Hernandez v New York: *Applying Batson to Peremptory Strikes of Bilinguals—Should Language Ability Be a Surrogate for Race?*, 16 Nova L Rev 1567 (1992).

n. 160.
  Add to note 160:
   However, in Hurd v. Pittsburg State University, 109 F.3d 1540, 117 Ed. Law Rep. 95, 73 Fair Empl. Prac. Cas. (BNA) 1448, 70 Empl. Prac. Dec. (CCH) ¶ 44615 (10th Cir. 1997), an age discrimination suit, the defendant exercised a peremptory challenge against the sole black juror on the panel on the ground that the juror had served on a jury which had found for an employee in a railroad benefits case. Both the court and opposing counsel pointed out that the juror had not stated that the jury in that case had rendered a verdict for the employee, only that a verdict had been reached. Nonetheless, despite the fact that the justification for the defendant's peremptory challenge of the juror was thus factually inaccurate, the court held that the defendant had proffered a race neutral explanation for the challenge.

   In Hernandez v. New York, 500 U.S. 352, 111 S. Ct. 1859, 114 L. Ed. 2d 395 (1991), the Supreme Court addressed the judge's role in determining whether a *Batson* violation had been made out and, more specifically, in determining whether a prosecutor's race-neutral explanation was valid or pretextual. The Court repeated the position enunciated in *Batson* that the question of discriminatory intent was one of fact for the trial judge, and that the judge's determination should be accorded great deference on appeal. This deference was justified because the determination of whether the prosecutor's explanation was pretextual often turned on the prosecutor's credibility, which the trial judge was in the best position to evaluate. Objective evidence bearing on the issue might be minimal, and the best evidence was likely to be the demeanor of the prosecutor. Nor was this policy of deference to be displaced because the findings in question related to a constitutional issue. The findings of the trial judge on the issue of discriminatory intent are not to be overturned unless they are "clearly erroneous."

   The Court of Appeals in U.S. v. Perez, 35 F.3d 632 (1st Cir. 1994) also stressed the importance of the prosecutor's demeanor and at the same time advised that a district court should specifically state on the record whether it found the reasons for a challenged strike to be race-neutral and why it chose to believe or disbelieve the explanation proffered by the prosecutor.

   The importance of demeanor and credibility in determining whether a prosecutor's explanation for a peremptory challenge is pretextual has been repeatedly emphasized. See e.g., Miller-El v. Cockrell, 537 U.S. 322, 123 S. Ct. 1029, 154 L. Ed. 2d 931 (2003); U.S. v. Thomas, 320 F.3d 315 (2d Cir. 2003); Lewis v. Lewis, 321 F.3d 824 (9th Cir. 2003); Tinner v. United Ins. Co. of America, 308 F.3d 697, 89 Fair Empl. Prac. Cas. (BNA) 1843 (7th Cir. 2002), cert. denied, 123 S. Ct. 1623, 155 L. Ed. 2d 484, 91 Fair Empl. Prac. Cas. (BNA) 608 (U.S. 2003); U.S. v. Thomas, 303 F.3d 138 (2d Cir. 2002); Hayes v. Woodford, 301 F.3d 1054 (9th Cir. 2002).

   The Court found that the trial court's findings in *Hernandez* were not clearly erroneous. Apart from the evidence of demeanor available to the trial judge, the fact that the prosecutor had proffered an explanation for the challenges without being asked to do so by the judge was deemed significant. Moreover, the prosecutor had disclaimed knowledge of which jurors were Latinos (the group alleged to have been discriminatorily challenged), and arguably had little incentive to eliminate Latinos from the jury, as the complainants and civilian witnesses were all Latinos. Finally, only three of the jurors who were challenged were clearly Latino and, for two of these, the prosecutor had advanced verifiable and legitimate explanations for the challenges. While these explanations might not have justified a challenge for cause, the fact that they correspond to recognized bases for challenges for cause reinforced the conclusion that they were race-neutral.

The "not clearly erroneous" standard of review articulated in *Hernandez* will prove problematic for any party seeking to overturn a *Batson* ruling. U.S. v. Roberts, 163 F.3d 998 (7th Cir. 1998) illustrates the point. The defendant was charged with distributing crack cocaine in Gary, Indiana. The prosecutor's explanation for its peremptory challenge of two black jurors was that the first was an elementary school teacher and it had been the government's experience that elementary teachers "tend to find that there are no bad kids". The second challenge was justified on the ground that the juror had lived and raised her children in the city where the crime had occurred, and thus might identify with the defendant. The appellate court observed that "the proposition that elementary school teachers think that all children are angels is fantastic; no teacher today is unaware of or indifferent to antisocial activity by some pupils . . . " U.S. v. Roberts, 163 F.3d 998, 998-999 (7th Cir. 1998). In respect to the peremptory challenge based on the juror's residence, the court noted that as 81% of the population of Gary, Indiana was black, residence could easily be a proxy for race. The Court's conclusion was that "the reasons offered for these two strikes are so flimsy that the possibility of pretext is substantial." U.S. v. Roberts, 163 F.3d 998, 999 (7th Cir. 1998). Nonetheless, the court, although stating that "the judge could have drawn the inference that race was a better explanatory variable than the feeble reasons the prosecutor offered", held that the judge's rulings were "not clearly erroneous." U.S. v. Roberts, 163 F.3d 998 (7th Cir. 1998).

Add after note 160:
There is much to be said for a reviewing court examining the overall pattern of a prosecutor's peremptory challenges in addition to looking at each challenge in isolation. Thus, even though each challenge on its own may be facially race-neutral, the cumulative effect of a number of individually acceptable but somewhat suspicious explanations may suggest a discriminatory intent. Illustrative is U.S. v. Wallace, 32 F.3d 921 (5th Cir. 1994). Six black jurors were peremptorily challenged: one because he kept his hat on in court even though having been asked to remove it, which was taken as a lack of respect for authority; a second because she was employed by the police department and one of the prosecutors had in the past brought criminal charges against police officers; a third because she was retired, old and feeble, and the prosecutor feared she would not be able to hold her own in jury deliberations; a fourth because she was a social

worker, whom the prosecutor thought tended to sympathize with criminal defendants, and who had also been the victim of two car thefts, where a key government witness in the trial had twice been convicted of car theft; a fifth simply because she was a social worker; and a sixth who too was a social worker but who also had an ongoing tax dispute with the federal government and had once been represented by the defendant's counsel. Apart from the explanation regarding the juror who was in dispute with the government on a tax matter and who had been represented by the defendant's counsel, the reasons for the challenges seem somewhat flimsy, particularly when looked at as a whole. Nevertheless the Court of Appeals found that the trial court did not err in accepting that each of the explanations was race-neutral.

In Alverio v. Sam's Warehouse Club, Inc., 253 F.3d 933, 88 Fair Empl. Prac. Cas. (BNA) 233, 80 Empl. Prac. Dec. (CCH) ¶ 40627 (7th Cir. 2001), a sexual harassment case, the venire consisted of three women and 11 men. The defendant peremptorily challenged all three women and the issue was whether this constituted impermissible gender discrimination in violation of *JEB v. Alabama ex rel. TB*. The Court of Appeals found that the defendant had identified unique characteristics that pertained only to the three women jurors—unemployment, participation as a plaintiff in a lawsuit, and employment in an insurance company—as well as a general lack of work experience, which satisfied the demands of *Batson* and *JEB*. The fact that an all-male jury heard the case did not, in itself, establish that the peremptory challenges had been discriminatory. The court was not prepared to entertain the contention that sexual harassment juries had necessarily to include female jurors, which it characterized as a sexist idea.

The court in Coulter v. Gilmore, 155 F.3d 912 (7th Cir. 1998) elevated virtually to the status of a defining test an approach that required comparison of jurors of one race who are peremptorily challenged with jurors of other races having similar characteristics but who are not challenged. The court was extremely critical of judges who examined each challenge in isolation for facially neutral reasons, stating that "any procedure that omits the totality inquiry would exonerate the user of peremptories in virtually every case, unless the lawyer was foolish enough to announce her discriminatory purpose in so many words." Coulter v. Gilmore, 155 F.3d 912, 921 (7th Cir. 1998). The court stated that the "crucial and determinative" inquiry in a *Batson* claim was "whether the state has treated similarly situated venirepersons differently based on race." Coulter v. Gilmore, 155 F.3d 912 (7th Cir. 1998). This requires a trial court to consider the totality of the circumstances, and to evaluate

§ 8:7   Jury Selection: Law, Art & Science 2d

the differential approach taken by the state to similarly situated black and non-black jurors. See also Mahaffey v. Page, 162 F.3d 481 (7th Cir. 1998), where the court found a prima facie showing of a *Batson* violation where the defendant was black, the state had challenged all seven black jurors on the panel, the crimes at issue were racially sensitive, and the court had failed to compare the characteristics of the struck jurors with those of white jurors who were accepted on the jury. In Dudley v. Wal-Mart Stores, Inc., 166 F.3d 1317, 79 Fair Empl. Prac. Cas. (BNA) 136, 75 Empl. Prac. Dec. (CCH) ¶ 45753 (11th Cir. 1999), the court drew an interesting distinction between cases where an appellate court was affirming a district court's rulings on peremptory challenges and cases where it was being asked to overrule the district court. An appellate court would give "great deference" to the district court's findings before holding they were erroneous, and the fact that there was not 100% consistency in that two jurors with similar traits were not treated the same is not necessarily fatal.

It may be a strategic error to attempt to bolster what may be a valid reason for a peremptory challenge with less persuasive reasons in support of the challenge. In Lewis v. Lewis, 321 F.3d 824 (9th Cir. 2003), the Court of Appeals stated that the proffer of various questionable reasons for a peremptory challenge with one or two otherwise adequate reasons may undermine the prosecutor's credibility to the extent that the trial court should sustain a *Batson* challenge. See also U.S. v. Chinchilla, 874 F.2d 695 (9th Cir. 1989).

Add after tenth paragraph:

The Supreme Court significantly watered down the prosecutor's burden of rebuttal in Purkett v. Elem, 514 U.S. 765, 115 S. Ct. 1769, 131 L. Ed. 2d 834 (1995). The respondent had been convicted of second degree murder in a Missouri state court. During juror selection, he had objected on *Batson* grounds to the peremptory challenge of two black males. The prosecutor explained that one of the jurors had long, unkempt hair, a moustache and a goatee type beard; and that the other also had a moustache and a goatee type beard and had previously been involved in a supermarket robbery in which a sawed-off shotgun had been pointed at him (no gun had been used in the instant case and the prosecutor feared that its absence might lead the juror to believe that this was not a real robbery). The trial judge ruled that the peremptory challenges were permissible. *Purkett v Elem* was applied in U.S. v. Spriggs, 102 F.3d 1245, 46 Fed. R. Evid. Serv. 181 (D.C. Cir. 1996), as amended, (Feb. 20, 1997), where it was held that the prosecutor's explanation for her peremptory challenge of all white jurors (an all-black jury heard the case) was that she was looking for "average, typical, born-and-bred DC residents . . . people who had raised families in this city, people who have a stake in the community" satisfied Purkett's modest standards. One cannot help but wonder whether the same explanation would have been accepted if the case had involved the peremptory challenges of black jurors in a rural neighborhood in order to allow the seating of an all-white jury. The view that Purkett v Elem will allow greater scope to judgment and intuition in the exercise of peremptory challenges is taken by the author of Note, Purkett v Elem: *Resuscitating the Nondiscriminatory Hunch,* 33 Houston L Rev 1267 (1996).

The Missouri Court of Appeals affirmed, finding that the "state's explanation constituted a legitimate hunch" and failed "to raise the necessary inference of racial discrimination." State v. Elem, 747 S.W.2d 772, 775 (Mo. Ct. App. E.D. 1988). The respondent then filed a motion for habeas corpus. The federal district court reached the same conclusion as the state courts, but the Court of Appeals for the Eighth Circuit reversed. Elem v. Purkett, 25 F.3d 679 (8th Cir. 1994), cert. granted, judgment rev'd, 514 U.S. 765, 115 S. Ct. 1769, 131 L. Ed. 2d 834 (1995) It found the prosecutor's explanation inadequate because the factors cited were facially irrelevant to the question of whether the jurors were qualified to serve in the particular case. The Eighth Circuit would have required that the prosecutor articulate plausible race-neutral reasons that "would somehow affect the person's ability to perform his or her duties as a juror."

The United States Supreme Court reversed in a per curiam opinion. The Court began by reiterating the three step procedure required under *Batson*. First, the opponent of the peremptory challenges had to make out a prima facie case of racial discrimination. Then the prosecutor had to come forward with a race-neutral explanation. Finally, after a race-neutral explanation had been tendered, the trial court had to decide whether the opponent of the challenges had carried his burden of proving racial discrimination. The Court saw the instant case as raising a step two question, and described the prosecutor's obligation at this stage as follows:

> The second step of this process does not demand an explanation that is persuasive, or even plausible. "at this [second] step of the inquiry, the issue is the facial validity of the prosecutor's explanation. Unless a discriminatory intent is inherent in the prosecutor's explanation, the reason offered will be deemed race neutral."

Purkett v. Elem, 514 U.S. 765, 115 S. Ct. 1769, 131 L. Ed. 2d 834 (1995) (quoting from Hernandez v. New York, 500

U.S. 352, 360, 111 S. Ct. 1859, 114 L. Ed. 2d 395 (1991)). The Supreme Court thought that the Court of Appeals had erred in conflating *Batson's* second and third steps, and in requiring that the prosecutor's explanation be not only neutral but persuasive. Persuasiveness, according to the Court, did not enter the picture until the third stage. At that point implausible or fantastic justifications might be found to be pretextual, but the burden would rest on the opponent of the peremptory challenges to demonstrate this. Applying these teachings to the case before it, the Court found that the explanation of the prosecutor was race neutral, as long hair, moustaches, and goatee beards were not confined to members of a particular race, and satisfied the prosecutor's burden under the second step. (Although the Court did not discuss the issue, the point might have been made that challenges based on moustaches and beards discriminated against men in violation of J.E.B. v. Alabama ex rel. T.B., 511 U.S. 127, 114 S. Ct. 1419, 128 L. Ed. 2d 89, 64 Empl. Prac. Dec. (CCH) ¶ 42967 (1994) (discussed in Supp)).

The Supreme Court's holding can be criticized for its undue formality. The Court reduces the prosecutor's obligations under second step to a pro forma technicality that one could fairly confidently predict will be easy to satisfy. The Court thus drains the second step of all significance. Arguably, it facilitates evasion of *Batson's* requirements. Indeed, as noted by dissenting Justices Stevens and Breyer, the majority's quarrel with the Eighth Circuit appeared to be based on the fact that it took literally the Supreme Court's admonition in *Batson* that the prosecutor's explanations must not only be neutral but "related to the particular case to be tried." It may be too soon to tell whether the decision in *Purkett v Elem* represents a growing dissatisfaction on the Court with a perceived increasing number of meritless *Batson* claims or merely shifts appellate court attention to the third step in the *Batson* three-step analysis. In either case it seems clear that the effect of the decision will be to ease the prosecutor's burden and reduce the likelihood of a finding of a *Batson* violation.

In *Purkett* the Supreme Court stated that "the ultimate burden of persuasion regarding [discriminatory] motivation rests with, and never shifts from, the opponent of the strike." 514 U.S. at 768. The trial judge has the ultimate responsibility of determining the credibility of any race-neutral explanation offered for a peremptory strike. In Barnes v. Anderson, 202 F.3d 150 (2d Cir. 1999), the Court of Appeals held that the trial judge had committed error in declining to rule on the credibility of the race-neutral explanations offered by the attorneys for their challenges of minority jurors. In normal circumstances the court would have remanded the case for further inquiry, but, as the original trial judge had since died, it ordered a new trial. The reasoning of *Barnes v. Anderson* was followed in Jordan v. Lefevre, 206 F.3d 196 (2d Cir. 2000), where the court held that the trial court's ruling that the government's peremptory challenges had been race-neutral was insufficient to satisfy *Batson's* third step requirement of an absence of pretext. While the prosecutor had claimed that one of the black jurors challenged had been struck on the grounds that he was young and with no supervisory experience, a white juror of the same age who also had no supervisory experience and had only been in her job for eight months, was not challenged. As the principal difference between the two jurors was their race, the credibility of the prosecutor's explanation was undermined and the Court of Appeals reversed. In U.S. v. McFerron, 163 F.3d 952, 1998 FED App. 0380P (6th Cir. 1998), the defendant, a black woman, exercised seven of her 10 peremptory challenges against white males. The government objected and the court called upon the defendant to explain the basis for her challenges. The explanations were somewhat vague but basically indicated the defendant's feeling that the jurors were too conservative for her liking. The district court rejected the proffered explanations, holding that the defendant "had failed in her burden of persuasion." The defendant appealed on the ground that the court had erred in imposing upon her the "burden of persuasion." The Court of Appeals agreed, stating that under the second prong of *Purkett* the defendant had only to advance a nondiscriminatory explanation for the challenges, and that it was only at the third stage of the inquiry, when deciding whether the opponent of the strike had proved purposeful discrimination that the persuasiveness of the justification came into play. In any event, the burden of persuasion rested with the opponent of the strike. Characterizing the lower Court's error as a "structural" one (see Arizona v. Fulminante, 499 U.S. 279, 111 S. Ct. 1246, 113 L. Ed. 2d 302 (1991)) which affected the entire conduct of the trial from beginning to end, the court declined to find the error harmless. See also U.S. v. Hall, 152 F.3d 381, 408, 49 Fed. R. Evid. Serv. 1503 (5th Cir. 1998) (abrogated by, U.S. v. Martinez-Salazar, 528 U.S. 304, 120 S. Ct. 774, 145 L. Ed. 2d 792 (2000)); Tankleff v. Senkowski, 135 F.3d 235, 248 (2d Cir. 1998); U.S. v. Underwood, 122 F.3d 389, 392 (7th Cir. 1997); U.S. v. Annigoni, 96 F.3d 1132, 1143 (9th Cir. 1996). In U.S. v. Blotcher, 142 F.3d 728 (4th Cir. 1998), the court stated that the explanation of the defendant, who was black, for exercising a peremptory challenge against a white juror did not have to be rational or reasonable, but only genuine.

Although it might seem unlikely that a prosecutor could

§ 8:7   JURY SELECTION: LAW, ART & SCIENCE 2D

ever fail to satisfy the second stage of the *Purkett* test, this did occur in U.S. v. Hill, 146 F.3d 337 (6th Cir. 1998). The prosecutor advanced no reason why he had struck a particular juror, and said only that he could assure the court that it was not on the basis of race. The Court of Appeals held that a mere denial of an impermissible motive coupled with an assertion of good faith was insufficient to satisfy the government's burden. There had to be an articulated explanation. See also Bui v. Haley, 321 F.3d 1304 (11th Cir. 2003).

In Lewis v. Lewis, 321 F.3d 824 (9th Cir. 2003) the Court of Appeals made the telling observation that, while the explanation for a peremptory challenge might be race-neutral, the method of gathering the information on which this conclusion has been reached might not be race-neutral. The Court of Appeals in *Lewis* was not prepared to credit the prosecutor's explanation that a juror was a "loner" and failed to interact well with the other jurors when the prosecutor's conclusions appeared to be based only on his own observations, at least until a determination was made that the prosecutor's explanations were credible.

It is unclear whether a party may justify a peremptory challenge of a minority juror by the desire to increase the likelihood of another juror's serving. In U.S. v. Gibbs, 182 F.3d 408, 1999 FED App. 0140P (6th Cir. 1999), the Court of Appeals disapproved of this practice, noting that the reason why the prosecution might have a preference for a lower-listed juror could simply be the fact that the latter was not African-American. This decision can be compared with that in Morse v. Hanks, 172 F.3d 983 (7th Cir. 1999). Here the prosecutor explained his peremptory challenge of a black juror in part on the grounds that he wanted to increase the chances that a nurse further down in the jury pool would be seated. He explained his partiality to nurses on the grounds that the charge in the case was drug-related and nurses understood chain of custody and controlled substances better than most. The other reason proffered by the prosecutor for the strike related to the juror's youth. The Court of Appeals found no violation of *Batson*. It did not, however, comment on the appropriateness of challenging one juror to increase the chances of another juror being seated.

The author of Casenote, *Jurors and Litigants Beware— Savvy Attorneys Are Prepared to Strike:* Has Purkett v. Elem Signaled *the Demise of the Peremptory Challenge at the Federal and State Levels?*, 52 U. of Miami L. Rev. 635 (1998), argues that the Supreme Court's decision in *Purkett* has virtually returned the legal system to the pre-*Batson* state of the law, where mere hunches were allowed to justify the challenge of prospective jurors. If so, it is fair to ask how *Batson* is to be given practical effect? Some see the answer lying with ethical prosecutors and judges prepared to look critically at peremptory challenges of minority jurors. See Johnson, *Batson Ethics for Prosecutors and Trial Court Judges,* 73 Chicago-Kent L. Rev. 475 (1998); Cavise, The *Batson* Doctrine: The Supreme Court's Utter Failure to Meet the Challenge of Discrimination in Jury Selection, 1999 Wis. L. Rev. 501 (1999) (Batson has generated large amounts of litigation without much in the way of pay-off; neutral explanations under *Purkett v. Elem* should have to make sense). But compare Smith, *"Nice Work if You Can Get It": "Ethical" Jury Selection in Criminal Defense,* 67 Fordham L. Rev. 523 (1998) (arguing that a lawyer's primary obligation is to the client and therefore lawyers should not regard *Batson, J.E.B.,* and *McCollum* as establishing ethical mandates).

n. 161.

Add to note 161:
; Reynolds v. Benefield, 931 F.2d 506 (8th Cir. 1991). See also People v. Cannon, 227 Ill. App. 3d 551, 169 Ill. Dec. 681, 592 N.E.2d 168 (1st Dist. 1992) (state failed to establish race-neutral exclusion on basis of age of juror [71] where it had accepted five white jurors of retirement age); State v. Grate, 310 S.C. 240, 423 S.E.2d 119 (1992) (alleged basis for striking 22-year-old and 28-year-old black jurors, lawyer claiming to want older jurors, was belied by lawyer's failure to challenge 21-year-old white juror). People v. Manuel, 182 A.D.2d 711, 582 N.Y.S.2d 735 (2d Dep't 1992) (claim that black juror was challenged because of having relative who had been prosecuted for crime held to be pretextual when similar test not applied to non-blacks); Davidson v. Harris, 30 F.3d 963 (8th Cir. 1994) (explanation that black female had young children held to be pretextual in light of fact that white female jurors with young children of approximately the same age were not similarly challenged); Brown v. Kinney Shoe Corp., 237 F.3d 556, 84 Fair Empl. Prac. Cas. (BNA) 1510, 80 Empl. Prac. Dec. (CCH) ¶ 40585 (5th Cir. 2001), cert. denied, 534 U.S. 817, 122 S. Ct. 45, 151 L. Ed. 2d 17 (2001) (reason for peremptory challenge of black juror, that party was worried that juror's prior experiences with litigation would influence him, held to be pretextual in light of party's failure to challenge two white jurors who had also been parties to litigation).

In U.S. Xpress Enterprises, Inc. v. J.B. Hunt Transport, Inc., 320 F.3d 809, 60 Fed. R. Evid. Serv. 772, 55 Fed. R. Serv. 3d 280 (8th Cir. 2003) the Court of Appeals found that a peremptory challenge of an African-American juror on the ground of the juror's medical background was pretextual when three white jurors with comparable medical background were not challenged. This conclusion was reinforced by the fact that the African-American juror was not questioned about how his medical experience would affect his evaluation of the evidence. Indeed, the party making the peremptory challenge admitted at a bench conference that evidence on the issue on which the juror's medical background might have had a bearing would not even be introduced at the trial.

In Lewis v. Lewis, 321 F.3d 824 (9th Cir. 2003) pretext was again found following a comparative analysis of minority jurors subject to peremptory challenge and unchallenged white jurors. The prosecutor's explanation for challenging a black juror was that the juror had relatives working in the jail. However, two non-black jurors had potential connections to the jail that, in the Court's opinion, were at least as close, if not closer, than those of the challenged juror.

In Jordan v. Lefevre, 206 F.3d 196 (2d Cir. 2000), the court held that the trial court's ruling that the government's peremptory challenges had been race-neutral was insufficient to satisfy *Batson's* third requirement of an absence of pretext. While the prosecutor had claimed that one of the black jurors challenged had been struck on the grounds that he was young and with no supervisory experience, a white juror of the same age who also had no supervisory experience and had only been in her job for eight months, was not challenged. As the principal difference between the two jurors was their race, the credibility of the prosecutor's explanation was undermined and the Court of Appeals reversed. But compare Stark v. Com., 828 S.W.2d 603 (Ky. 1991) (overruled on other grounds by, Thomas v. Com., 931 S.W.2d 446 (Ky. 1996)) (inconsistent explanations not necessarily fatal); Payton v. State, 830 S.W.2d 722 (Tex. App. Houston 14th Dist. 1992) (challenge of black but not non-black mental health worker justified by passive, apathetic attitude of former).

Conversely, challenges to non-black jurors which are made for the same or similar characteristics which are alleged to justify the peremptory challenge of black jurors are evidence of neutrality. See, e.g., Darby v. State, 601 So. 2d 117 (Ala. Crim. App. 1989). In Ex parte Thomas, 601 So. 2d 56 (Ala. 1992), the court held that where the defendant had unsuccessfully sought the misdemeanor and driving records of veniremembers which the state had used in exercising its peremptory challenges, the trial court could not accept at face value the state's assertion that no white members seated on the jury had worse misdemeanor/driving records than the black veniremembers who had been peremptorily challenged.

In U.S. v. Feemster, 98 F.3d 1089 (8th Cir. 1996) peremptory challenges of two black jurors who had close relationships with persons convicted of serious crimes was held not to be pretextual, the court pointing in part to the fact that the prosecutor had also challenged two white jurors with close relationships with persons charged with felonies. In the same case, however, the court held that there had been no *Batson* violation where a black juror who had taken a course in criminal law and had sat for the LSAT was challenged peremptorily while white jurors with some legal education were not. Here the court saw the distinguishing feature as the fact that none of the white jurors had taken courses in criminal law or sat the LSAT. In Lovejoy v. U.S., 92 F.3d 628, 45 Fed. R. Evid. Serv. 389 (8th Cir. 1996), where the defendant was charged with sexual abuse of his minor daughter, the court upheld the peremptory challenge of the lone black juror, who stated that her nephew had been convicted of molesting a young child and indicated that she did not think that his trial had been fairly conducted. The court took note of the fact that a similarly situated white male juror had also been challenged. In U.S. v. Mathis, 96 F.3d 1577 (11th Cir. 1996), the court found that the peremptory challenge of a Hispanic juror whose son had a criminal conviction did not violate *Batson* despite the fact that a white juror whose son had also been convicted of a criminal offense had not been challenged. The court distinguished the situation of the two jurors by the fact that the white juror's son had not been convicted of a drug-related offense, while the black juror's son had, and the instant prosecution involved drugs.

In U.S. v. Davis, 154 F.3d 772, 49 Fed. R. Evid. Serv. 1487 (8th Cir.

§ 8:7 PEREMPTORY CHALLENGES

1998), the appellants contended that the prosecution's peremptory challenge of the only Native American on the venire violated *Batson*. The government's attorney stated that the juror was struck because she was a guidance counselor and a qualified chemical dependency counselor. The appellants argued that this reason was pretextual and pointed out that the government had not challenged a white juror who was involved with a teen clinic or three white jurors who had law enforcement connections. The government's rejoinder was that the work of these jurors was significantly different from that of a chemical dependency counselor in terms of experience, expertise and perspective. The court agreed, and ruled that there had not been a showing of pretext sufficient to warrant a reversal.

The court in Matthews v. Evatt, 105 F.3d 907 (4th Cir. 1997) made the point in dicta that even the fact that two jurors of different races had given the same answer to the same question, and one was excused while the other was not, did not necessarily establish a violation of *Batson*. Counsel is entitled to make credibility determinations as regards the jurors' responses. While the point about credibility may be well taken, if applied in practice it would virtually defeat most *Batson* claims in situations where the record would otherwise seem strongly to suggest a *Batson* violation.

In Howard v. Moore, 525 U.S. 843, 119 S. Ct. 108, 142 L. Ed. 2d 86 (1998), the prosecutor struck 6/7 prospective black jurors, but only 4/35 white jurors. The court held that this made out a prima facie case of discrimination but that the prosecutor's explanation that the jurors were challenged because of their opposition to the death penalty was race neutral. Although many of the white jurors who had not been challenged had also expressed reservations regarding the death penalty, the prosecutor claimed that the objections voiced by the black jurors had been stronger. The court held that this explanation was sufficient to satisfy the requirements of *Purkett v. Elem*. In a somewhat factually similar case, Kilgore v. Bowersox, 124 F.3d 985 (8th Cir. 1997), the prosecution used 5/9 peremptory challenges to strike all the black jurors on the panel, with the result being that the defendant was tried by an all white jury. The claim that the challenges were in violation of *Batson* was rejected, the court accepting the prosecutor's explanation that the jurors were challenged because of their reservations regarding the death penalty and not because of their race. Although several white jurors with similar reservations were not challenged, the prosecutor explained that their objections to capital punishment were relatively weaker than those of the black jurors. In contrast, in Yancey v. State, 813 So. 2d 1 (Ala. Crim. App. 2001), cert. denied, (July 6, 2001) the court found a *Batson* violation where several black prospective jurors were allegedly struck for their views on capital punishment, but a white prospective juror who held similar views was not challenged. The Court's belief that the challenges were discriminatory was no doubt reinforced by the fact that the prosecution had also struck black prospective jurors who had committed traffic and misdemeanor offenses while not challenging six white prospective jurors who had committed similar offenses.

Add after eleventh paragraph:

The matter, however, is not that simple. For one thing, a prosecutor may not be aware of similarities between jurors of different races in making its challenges. In Lockett v. Anderson, 230 F.3d 695 (5th Cir. 2000), the prosecution explained its challenge of a black juror on the juror's lack of education. However, the prosecution had not challenged five white jurors who lacked a high school education. Nonetheless, the Court of Appeals held that there had been no showing that the prosecutor was aware of the lack of education of the latter.

Another problem is that two prospective jurors are rarely identical in all respects. Jurors may well share some attribute, such as race or sex, but will almost inevitably be distinguishable with respect to others, such as age, educational background, or employment. A court's decision as to whether there has been a violation of *Batson* will often turn on whether the court focuses on the differences between jurors or the similarities. If a party whose use of peremptories is challenged on *Batson* grounds can escape censure by pointing to any differences between two jurors, one of whom has been challenged and the other of whom has not, the value of comparisons is tremendously reduced. Thus, for example, in Hicks v. Johnson, 186 F.3d 634 (5th Cir. 1999) the court held that none of the jurors alleged to be similarly situated to those challenged possessed the same combination of negative qualities as the struck jurors.

In U.S. v. Smith, 324 F.3d 922 (7th Cir. 2003), the strike of a prospective African-American juror was held not to be pretextual when the stated justification was that the juror had made several mistakes on the juror questionnaire which suggested an inability to follow simple instructions. Although several white jurors had also made errors on the questionnaire, their cases were distinguished by the court on the basis of the fact that the black juror had made significantly more errors. Somewhat similarly, the Court of Appeals in U.S. v. Milan, 304 F.3d 273 (3d Cir. 2002), cert. denied, 123 S. Ct. 1956, 155 L. Ed. 2d 869 (U.S. 2003) upheld as race-neutral the peremptory challenge of black female juror whom the prosecutor thought would not "blend" with the other jurors because she had moved from the north New Jersey to south New Jersey only three years previously. The prosecutor had not, however, struck two white jurors who had moved to the south of the State only slightly earlier. The ties to the south Jersey community of both the two jurors who were not struck and the one who was struck, it is submitted, were similarly transient.

In U.S. v. Novaton, 271 F.3d 968, 57 Fed. R. Evid. Serv. 1470 (11th Cir. 2001), cert. denied, 535 U.S. 1120, 122 S. Ct. 2345, 153 L. Ed. 2d 173 (2002) and cert. denied, 537 U.S. 850, 123 S. Ct. 193, 154 L. Ed. 2d 80 (2002) and cert. denied, 537 U.S. 858, 123 S. Ct. 228, 154 L. Ed. 2d 96 (2002) and cert. denied, 537 U.S. 1031, 123 S. Ct. 576, 154 L. Ed. 2d

447 (2002), the Court of Appeals stated that although a white juror who worked for the courts and knew the attorneys in the case had not been challenged, and a Hispanic juror with these traits had been struck, the two situations were distinguishable in that the Hispanic juror had also worked for a judge who had been prosecuted by the federal government, and this additional aspect of the Hispanic juror's background could lead a prosecutor to strike the Hispanic juror but not the white juror. Similarly, the court stated that the fact that three Department of Education employees had not been challenged while a Hispanic social worker had been challenged was not necessarily discriminatory as the positions of the respective jurors may not have been equally "liberal" despite their similar employment. See also U.S. v. Webster, 162 F.3d 308 (5th Cir. 1998). In Moore v. Keller Industries, Inc., 948 F.2d 199 (5th Cir. 1991), the Court of Appeals stated that "because multiple reasons led Keller's counsel to strike both Rackley and Bonner the existence of other jurors with some of their individual characteristics does not demonstrate that the reasons assigned were pretextual." For example, in U.S. v. Steele, 178 F.3d 1230 (11th Cir. 1999), the government peremptorily challenged two female elementary school teachers. The defendant claimed pretext, citing the fact that the government had not challenged a male project engineer at a junior college, a female school systems clerk, and a retired female public school administrator. The Court of Appeals observed that the government could rationally have believed that the accepted jurors' jobs involved different skills and responsibilities than those of an elementary school teacher. Similarly, in U.S. v. Scott, 26 F.3d 1458 (8th Cir. 1994), the prosecutor attempted to justify a peremptory challenge of a black juror on the ground of the juror's previous service in a criminal case. The prosecutor did not, however, strike two white jurors who also had served previously on criminal juries. Despite the established rule in the circuit that the government could not justify peremptory challenges to members of one race unless members of other races with comparable or similar characteristics were also challenged, the court held that no constitutional violation had occurred. It found that the peremptory challenge of the black juror was not comparable because, unlike the white jurors, he had volunteered the verdict on the case on which he had served. The decision seems to reinforce the point made above that there will always be some distinguishing feature between the different race jurors if a court is inclined to look far and hard enough. Arguably the "distinguishing feature" should have to be shown to be material. Whether the mere fact without more that the challenged black juror in *Scott* had volunteered the verdict in the case on which he had served

§ 8:7

while the white jurors had not would meet a materiality test is questionable.

The "dual motivation" analysis of Senkowski seems to be gaining converts. In Wallace v. Morrison, 87 F.3d 1271 (11th Cir. 1996) the court, using a "dual motivation" analysis, held that the district court's finding that the prosecution, although conceding that race entered into its calculations, would have challenged the excluded black jurors in any event and that the district court's finding that the peremptory challenges had not violated the defendant's constitutional rights were not clearly erroneous. Other circuits which have adopted a dual motivation analysis include the Eighth, (U.S. v. Darden, 70 F.3d 1507, 43 Fed. R. Evid. Serv. 321 (8th Cir. 1995)), the Fifth (Lockett v. Anderson, 230 F.3d 695 (5th Cir. 2000)), and the Fourth, (Jones v. Plaster, 57 F.3d 417 (4th Cir. 1995)). See also U.S. v. Taylor, 92 F.3d 1313, 45 Fed. R. Evid. Serv. 442 (2d Cir. 1996). In U.S. v. Tokars, 95 F.3d 1520, 45 Fed. R. Evid. Serv. 967 (11th Cir. 1996) where the government used its first 10 peremptory challenges to remove male jurors (a case of reverse gender discrimination), the court stated that where there was a dual motivation for the challenges, the party who made the challenges bore the burden of establishing that they would have been made even in the absence of the discriminatory motivation. The court in *Tokari* held that the prosecution had carried its burden in this regard. In Weaver v. Bowersox, 241 F.3d 1024 (8th Cir. 2001), the court, adopting a "dual motivation" analysis, held that, discounting the prosecutor's statement that he peremptorily challenged a black juror in part because he did not think that the juror would give the death penalty to a fellow black, there were valid race-neutral reasons for striking the juror. In Guzman v. State, 85 S.W.3d 242 (Tex. Crim. App. 2002) the Texas Court of Criminal Appeals held that where the motivation behind a peremptory challenge may have been both impermissible and permissible in part, if the striking party could show that he would have struck the juror based solely on the neutral grounds, then there was no violation of *Batson*. The court added that its ruling applied only in a criminal context, as the Texas Supreme Court had apparently held that in a civil case a strike motivated in any part by race automatically constituted a violation of equal protection.

In Doss v. Frontenac, 14 F.3d 1313, 63 Fair Empl. Prac. Cas. (BNA) 1274, 63 Empl. Prac. Dec. (CCH) ¶ 42827 (8th Cir. 1994), the defendant-employer being sued for race discrimination challenged black jurors who believed that they had been unfairly discharged from their own jobs but not a white juror whose wife had allegedly been unfairly discharged from her job. The court saw a "sharp" distinction between the vicarious experience of the white juror and the direct experiences of the black jurors, and thus found that there was no violation of the concept of "comparability." Again, the distinction seem less than convincing. Similarly, in U.S. v. Fisher, 22 F.3d 574 (5th Cir. 1994), the Court of Appeals held that the peremptory challenge of a black juror because two members of her family had been arrested for drug offenses was not pretextual despite the fact that the prosecutor did not strike one juror whose son was involved with marijuana and another whose husband had been convicted of bribery; the court said, without explanation, that the black juror's situation was "distinguishable." In Hollingsworth v. Burton, 30 F.3d 109 (11th Cir. 1994), both the challenged black juror and an unchallenged white juror had patronized the grill at which the crime had occurred (one of the declared bases on which the prosecution chose to exercise its peremptory challenges). The court held that the peremptory challenge of the black juror could be justified because, in the Court's words, "white juror Bowman would appear to be slightly preferable as a juror from the perspective of the prosecution to black juror Studmire, regardless of race." Hollingsworth v. Burton, 30 F.3d 109, 113 (11th Cir. 1994). In Luckett v. Kemna, 203 F.3d 1052 (8th Cir. 2000) the defendant alleged that the prosecution's explanation for striking a black juror, that the juror was weak on the death penalty, was pretextual in light of its failure to challenge a white juror who was even weaker on the death penalty. The Court of Appeals found that the defendant had failed to show that the two jurors were in fact similar in all relevant aspects, noting that the white juror was closer in age to the victim while the black juror was closer in age to the defendant.

In Hopp v. City of Pittsburgh, 194 F.3d 434, 81 Fair Empl. Prac. Cas. (BNA) 26 (3d Cir. 1999) the City had decided that, as a general proposition, it would exercise its peremptory challenges against government employees and against individuals who had been involved in discrimination lawsuits. Although most jurors with these characteristics were struck, one was not, and a juror who had neither characteristic but whom counsel "just didn't like" was challenged. The Court of Appeals found no *Batson* violation. It was not impermissible for an attorney who had a general plan of exercising challenges to deviate from the plan to strike an unattractive juror.

Another complicating factor is that often more than one motive lies behind the exercise of a peremptory challenge. Addressing this "dual motivation" situation, the Court of Appeals in Howard v. Senkowski, 986 F.2d 24 (2d Cir. 1993), held that where the trial court finds that race is one of sev-

§ 8:7   JURY SELECTION: LAW, ART & SCIENCE 2D

eral factors in a prosecutor's exercise of peremptory challenges, the prosecutor bears the burden of demonstrating that the challenges would have been exercised for race-neutral reasons even if race had not been a factor. Thus the party against whom improper motivation has been alleged is afforded the affirmative defense of showing that the same action would have been taken even absent the improper motivation. Whether or not the Court's decision complies with the strict letter of *Batson* (it can be argued that what *Batson* requires is a "pure" race-neutral explanation), it arguably contravenes its spirit, which is that race should play no part in jury selection. See also Hill v. State, 827 S.W.2d 860 (Tex. Crim. App. 1992) (race may be factor coexisting with nonracial reasons for peremptory challenge, but may not be the reason for the challenge); King v. Moore, 196 F.3d 1327 (11th Cir. 1999) (where motives for peremptory challenge are both racial and legitimate (in the case, equivocation regarding the death penalty), *Batson* violation occurs only if legitimate reasons are not in themselves sufficient reason for striking juror). However, in Guzman v. State, 85 S.W.3d 242 (Tex. Crim. App. 2002) the Texas Court of Criminal Appeals held that where the motivation behind a peremptory challenge may have been both impermissible and permissible in part, if the striking party could show that he would have struck the juror based solely on the neutral grounds, then there was no violation of Batson. The court added that its ruling applied only in a criminal context, as the Texas Supreme Court had apparently held that in a civil case a strike motivated in any part by race automatically constituted a violation of equal protection.

The above decisions argue in favor of a more activist role for trial judges in critically examining justifications advanced under *Batson* in order to identify those that are pretextual. See Note, *Branding Neutral Explanations Pretextual under* Batson v. Kentucky: *An Examination of the Role of the Trial Judge in Jury Selection,* 48 Hastings L. J. 577 (1997).

In Lewis v. Lewis, 321 F.3d 824 (9th Cir. 2003), the Court of Appeals suggested that it might be helpful to enlist the aid of the respective lawyers on each side in order to evaluate a *Batson* claim. Defense counsel might be able to point to weaknesses in the prosecution's proffered reasons for its peremptory challenges by reference to the transcript of jury selection, and the prosecutor might be able to show support in the record for the proffered reasons for the challenges.

n. 162.
   Add to note 162:
    U.S. v. Wills, 88 F.3d 704, 44 Fed. R. Evid. Serv. 1357 (9th Cir. 1996). In U.S. v. Novaton, 271 F.3d 968, 57 Fed. R. Evid. Serv. 1470 (11th Cir.

PEREMPTORY CHALLENGES § 8:7

2001), cert. denied, 535 U.S. 1120, 122 S. Ct. 2345, 153 L. Ed. 2d 173 (2002) and cert. denied, 537 U.S. 850, 123 S. Ct. 193, 154 L. Ed. 2d 80 (2002) and cert. denied, 537 U.S. 858, 123 S. Ct. 228, 154 L. Ed. 2d 96 (2002) and cert. denied, 537 U.S. 1031, 123 S. Ct. 576, 154 L. Ed. 2d 447 (2002) the Court of Appeals stated that the fact that the government had left several Hispanic jurors unchallenged, and the defendants had exercised peremptory challenges against several Hispanic jurors, supported the government's claim that its challenge of six Hispanic jurors was not racially motivated or a violation of *Batson*.

See also Hayes v. Woodford, 301 F.3d 1054 (9th Cir. 2002) (racial composition of jury is a permissible and relevant factor in assessing the genuineness of alleged race-neutral reasons for peremptory challenges). But compare Davey v. Lockheed Martin Corp., 301 F.3d 1204, 89 Fair Empl. Prac. Cas. (BNA) 1164, 53 Fed. R. Serv. 3d 1263 (10th Cir. 2002) (while composition of jury is a relevant consideration, district court did not clearly err in finding that proffered explanation for peremptory challenge of female juror, that she was at the time unemployed, was pretextual in light of fact juror had past employment, even though four female jurors remained on jury).

n. 163.

Add to note 163:

See also U.S. v. Marin, 7 F.3d 679, 39 Fed. R. Evid. Serv. 1014 (7th Cir. 1993) (race-neutral decision to strike Hispanic juror without high school education supported by acceptance of another Hispanic juror); U.S. v. Munoz, 15 F.3d 395 (5th Cir. 1994) (prosecutor's claim that Hispanic juror was peremptorily challenged because prosecutor did not want arguments on the jury as to the translation of taped conversations between accused and government witness that were partly in Spanish was supported by fact that prosecutor struck non-Hispanic juror who spoke Spanish). See also U.S. v. Atkins, 25 F.3d 1401, 74 A.F.T.R.2d 94-5069 (8th Cir. 1994) (race-neutral explanation for peremptory challenge of black government employee supported by fact that prosecutor had also challenged other jurors with friends or family who worked for the government); U.S. v. Davis, 40 F.3d 1069, 40 Fed. R. Evid. Serv. 1036 (10th Cir. 1994) (government's challenge of black female teacher held justified on the basis that it planned to strike all teachers). U.S. v. Jenkins, 52 F.3d 743 (8th Cir. 1995) (where facial expressions, body language and other signs of disinterest were advanced to justify peremptory challenges of black jurors, evidence that disinterested white jurors were also challenged supported finding that challenges were not pretextual); U.S. v. Campbell, 270 F.3d 702 (8th Cir. 2001), cert. denied, 535 U.S. 946, 122 S. Ct. 1339, 152 L. Ed. 2d 243 (2002) (peremptory challenge of black juror who, as part of his job as a parole officer, argued on behalf of inmates and criminal defendants and ensured that their rights were protected held to be race-neutral where prosecutor had challenged a white male juror on similar grounds).

Add after second sentence in thirteenth paragraph:
See U.S. v. Parra-Ibanez, 951 F.2d 21 (1st Cir. 1991) (questionable explanation for peremptory challenge of one juror will be given reduced weight when explanations for other challenges are of clear good faith). In U.S. v. Darden, 70 F.3d 1507, 43 Fed. R. Evid. Serv. 321 (8th Cir. 1995), the prosecutor advanced several race-neutral reasons for challenging a particular juror but one reason (that young black

§ 8:7   JURY SELECTION: LAW, ART & SCIENCE 2D

women had a tendency to sympathize with drug dealers) that was neither race nor gender neutral. The Court of Appeals upheld the district court's decision to allow the challenge, stating that the decision was the equivalent of a finding that the prosecutor would have struck the juror even absent the impermissible reason.

Add at end of fourteenth paragraph:
In this context, as in others, the objection must be timely. In U.S. v. Elliott, 89 F.3d 1360 (8th Cir. 1996) the defendant claimed for the first time on appeal that the prosecutor had struck several black jurors because of their church-related activities but not white jurors who were actively engaged in church activities. While acknowledging that there might be merit in such a claim, the court of appeal held that the defendant had waived the claim by failing to raise it in a timely fashion.

n. 168.
Add to note 168:
In Ford v. Georgia, 498 U.S. 411, 111 S. Ct. 850, 112 L. Ed. 2d 935 (1991), the Supreme Court, while again declining to impose uniform rules governing the timing of a *Batson* claim, characterized as sensible a state rule which required that such a claim be raised between the time of the selection of the jurors and the administration of their oath. The Court further observed that a state could reasonably adopt a rule that a *Batson* claim would be deemed untimely if raised for the first time on appeal, or after the jury was sworn, or, conversely, before the jury's members were selected.

In U.S. v. Joe, 928 F.2d 99 (4th Cir. 1991), the trial court had permitted the prosecution to make a record of its reasons for challenging black jurors outside the presence of the court, and had deferred consideration of whether there had been a violation of *Batson* until after trial. The Fourth Circuit Court of Appeals was critical of this method of proceeding. The out-of-court explanations deprived the district court of the opportunity to evaluate the credibility of the government's representations, and the deferral of a decision on the merits of the *Batson* claim precluded redress before the jury selection process, not to mention the trial, was completed. The preferable procedure, according to the appeals court, would be first to evaluate the *Batson* claim at the time it was raised to determine whether there was a prima facie case of a violation; second, if a prima facie case was established, to require the prosecution to articulate its reasons for the strikes and to determine at that time if they were race-neutral, providing the defendant the opportunity to show pretext; and third, to thereafter issue a specific ruling supported by facts and reasons in regard to each juror alleged to have been challenged in violation of *Batson*.

Add after fifteenth paragraph:
U.S. v. Alcantar, 897 F.2d 436 (9th Cir. 1990) (court may limit right of defendant to hear and rebut prosecutor's explanations for excluding jurors when prosecutor's reasons would reveal government's case strategy).

n. 170.
Add to note 170:

Whether adversarial hearings are required has been a matter of dispute. Compare U.S. v. Thompson, 827 F.2d 1254 (9th Cir. 1987) (requiring adversary hearings) with U.S. v. Tucker, 836 F.2d 334 (7th Cir. 1988) (recommending but not requiring adversary hearings) with U.S. v. Davis, 809 F.2d 1194, 22 Fed. R. Evid. Serv. 567 (6th Cir. 1987) (adversary hearings not required). See also Williams v. Chrans, 957 F.2d 487 (7th Cir. 1992) ("in most cases adversarial hearing is desirable," but there is no right to present rebuttal evidence in response to prosecution's justifications for peremptory challenges); U.S. v. Jiminez, 983 F.2d 1020 (11th Cir. 1993) (defense counsel not entitled as a matter of right to cross-examine prosecution regarding justifications for peremptory challenges).

In Johnson v. Love, 40 F.3d 658 (3d Cir. 1994), the Court of Appeals stated that when a court is required to apply *Batson* in a post-trial context, it should insist that the state "not only articulate a race-neutral explanation but also come forward with competent evidence of the prosecutor's state of mind when making the challenge." Johnson v. Love, 40 F.3d 658, 667 (3d Cir. 1994). This would seem to put a quite heavy burden on the state. However, the court indicated that its holding was not to be read as saying that the state's burden could never be carried without direct evidence.

Without an adequate record, it is obviously going to prove difficult for an appellate court to review whether or not purposeful discrimination in the exercise of peremptory challenges has occurred. In U.S. v. Hill, 146 F.3d 337 (6th Cir. 1998), the appellate court remanded because of the inadequacy of the record relating to the district court's rulings on *Batson* challenges.

§ 8:8 —Applicability to groups other than blacks

Add after first sentence in fourth full paragraph:
Batson was held inapplicable to fat persons in U.S. v. Santiago-Martinez, 58 F.3d 422 (9th Cir. 1995).

In U.S. v. Cresta, 825 F.2d 538, 23 Fed. R. Evid. Serv. 687 (1st Cir. 1987), the court held that young persons were not a cognizable group for *Batson* purposes. See also U.S. v. Maxwell, 160 F.3d 1071, 1998 FED App. 0338P (6th Cir. 1998); U.S. v. Jackson, 983 F.2d 757 (7th Cir. 1993). At the other end of the age spectrum, the court in Weber v. Strippit, Inc., 186 F.3d 907, 9 A.D. Cas. (BNA) 961 (8th Cir. 1999), an action for discrimination in violation of the Americans with Disability Act (ADA), the defendants challenged all jurors over the age of 50. The Court of Appeals declined to extend *Batson* to peremptory challenges based on age, but held that, even if *Batson* was held applicable, the defendants' explanation was age-neutral. It has also been held that homosexuals are not a cognizable group for *Batson* purposes. See State v. Spitler, 75 Ohio App. 3d 341, 599 N.E.2d 408 (10th Dist. Franklin County 1991). But see People v. Garcia, 77 Cal. App. 4th 1269, 92 Cal. Rptr. 2d 339 (4th Dist. 2000), as modified on denial of reh'g, (Feb. 22, 2000) (holding that, under state constitution, gays and lesbians cannot be excluded from juries). See generally Note,

The Double Bind: Unequal Treatment for Homosexuals within the American legal Framework, 20 B.C. Third World L.J. 145 (2000).

After third sentence in fifth paragraph:
In U.S. v. Villarreal, 963 F.2d 725 (5th Cir. 1992), the defendants argued that the peremptory challenge of jurors whose political belief was opposed to capital punishment violated *Batson*. The court declined to extend *Batson* to political beliefs, pointing out that political beliefs, unlike race, were not an overt and immutable characteristic.

In Morgan v. City of Albuquerque, 25 F.3d 918, 5 A.D.D. 476, 3 A.D. Cas. (BNA) 804 (10th Cir. 1994), a civil rights action, the defendant used two of its peremptory challenges to strike prospective jurors who had associations with persons with physical disabilities. The plaintiff, who was herself physically disabled, claimed that the challenges violated both *Batson* and the Americans with Disabilities Act, 42 U.S.C.A. §§ 12101 et seq. (ADA). The Court of Appeals held that whether or not *Batson* was eventually held to apply to peremptory challenges of jurors with physical disabilities. (On this issue, See Lynch, *The Application of Equal Protection to Prospective Jurors with Disabilities: Will Batson Cover Disability-Based Strikes?*, 57 Alb L Rev 289 (1993); Crehan, *The Disability-Based Peremptory Challenge: Does it Discriminate against Blind Prospective Jurors?*, 25 N. Ky. L. Rev. 531 (1998); Dickhute, *Jury Duty for the Blind in the Time of Reasonable Accommodations: The ADA's Interface with a Litigant's Right to a Fair Trial*, 32 Creighton L. Rev. 849 (1999), it would not in any event apply to jurors who were linked to the disabled only by association. Hart & Cawyer, *Batson and its Progeny Prohibit the Use of Peremptory Challenges based upon Disability and Religion: A Practitioner's Guide for Requesting a Civil Batson Hearing*, 26 Tex Tech L Rev 109 (1995). As to the statutory challenge, the court stated that the purpose of the ADA was to prevent discrimination against the physically disabled and not their associates.

The issue of a disability-based peremptory challenge arose again in U.S. v. Harris, 197 F.3d 870 (7th Cir. 1999). The prosecution struck a black juror, was challenged on *Batson* grounds, and advanced as its race-neutral explanation the fact that the juror suffered from multiple sclerosis. On appeal the defendant argued that a peremptory challenge based on a juror's disability violated due process. The Court of Appeals held that disability was neither a suspect nor quasi-suspect classification, and thus would be not be reviewed under a heightened standard of scrutiny. The court held that, in respect to jury service, a peremptory challenge to a dis-

PEREMPTORY CHALLENGES § 8:8

abled juror might well be rationally related to the state's legitimate interests both in a fair trial and in empanelling an impartial jury. The juror's disability could affect her ability to serve, as she might become drowsy and not be able to pay attention to the evidence.

After "religion" in second sentence in sixth paragraph:
Batson was held not to extend to peremptory challenges based on religious affiliation in State v. Davis, 504 N.W.2d 767, 63 A.L.R.5th 837 (Minn. 1993). In dissenting to the denial of the petition for writ of certiorari in this case, Justices Thomas and Scalia argued that the Court's decision in *J.E.B.* should logically lead to an extension of *Batson* to classifications based on religion (as well as other classifications accorded heightened scrutiny under the Equal protection Clause). Davis v. Minnesota, 511 U.S. 1115, 114 S. Ct. 2120, 128 L. Ed. 2d 679 (1994). The topic has received considerable attention in the literature. See, e.g., Hart & Cawyer, *Batson and its Progeny Prohibit the Use of Peremptory Challenges based upon Disability and Religion: A Practitioner's Guide for Requesting a Civil Batson Hearing,* 26 Tex Tech L Rev 109 (1995); Note, *Extending* Batson v Kentucky *to Religion-Based Peremptory Challenges,* 4 S Cal Interdisc L J 99 (1994); Note, *The Batson Analysis and Religious Discrimination,* 74 Oregon L Rev 721 (1995); Note, *Discrimination Based on Religious Affiliation: Another Nail in the Peremptory Challenge's Coffin,* 29 Ga L Rev 493 (1995); Note, *Religion-Based Peremptory Challenges after* Batson v Kentucky *and* JEB v Alabama*: An Equal Protection and First Amendment Analysis,* 94 Mich L Rev 191 (1995); Note, State v Davis*: Peremptory Strikes and Religion—The Unworkable Peremptory Challenge Jurisprudence,* 9 BYU J Pub L 309 (1995); Note, *Applying the Break: Religion and the Peremptory Challenge,* 70 Ind LJ 569 (1995).

In U.S. v. Somerstein, 959 F. Supp. 592 (E.D. N.Y. 1997), a federal district judge held that *Batson* applies to peremptory challenges based on religion, such as membership in the Jewish faith. Unless the religion of the juror is relevant to the case, such challenges are improper. But what constitutes "relevance" is not always clear, however. In U.S. v. Hill, 249 F.3d 707, 56 Fed. R. Evid. Serv. 1 (8th Cir. 2001), a black juror was challenged, allegedly because of her participation in church activities during her leisure time. The prosecutor explained the challenge by stating that the juror might be overly sympathetic to criminal defendants. Although both race and religion issues were thus implicated, the Court of Appeals found no constitutional violation had occurred. See also Comment, *The Equal Protection Clause, the Free Exercise Clause, and Religion-Based Peremptory Challenges,*

63 U. Chi. L Rev 1639 (arguing peremptory challenges where religion is involved should receive strict scrutiny, and that the challenges should be invalidated if based on religious affiliation, as opposed to a particular relevant belief, which may properly form the basis of a peremptory challenge). In Note, *Will the Religious Freedom Restoration Act be Strike Three against the Peremptory Challenge,* 30 Val U. L Rev 701 (1996) the author argues that the Religious Freedom Restoration Act (RFRA) provides an additional basis for restricting the use of peremptory challenges based on religion.

Religious-based peremptory challenges arguably run afoul of *Batson* when they are based on prejudices about a particular religion, as opposed to some quality peculiar to the juror being challenged which renders the juror unsuitable to serve on the jury. See Comment, *What is a "Religion" in Religious-Based Peremptory Challenges?,* 65 U. Cinc. L. Rev. 1291 (1997). See also Comment, *The Equal Protection Clause, the Free Exercise Clause and Religious-Based Peremptory Challenges,* 63 U. Chicago L. Rev. 1639 (1996) (arguing that religious-based peremptory challenges should be reviewed under a strict scrutiny standard). For an analysis that takes the First Amendment argument even further, See Bader, *Batson Meets the First Amendment: Prohibiting Peremptory Challenges that Violate a Prospective Juror's Speech and Association Rights,* 24 Hofstra L. Rev. 567 (1996).

In U.S. v. Stafford, 136 F.3d 1109 (7th Cir. 1998), decision modified on other grounds, 136 F.3d 1115 (7th Cir. 1998), the Seventh Circuit of Appeals drew a useful distinction between religious affiliation, a religion's general tenets, and a specific religious belief. The court stated that to strike a juror simply for being a member of a particular religion would be improper. However, to strike that same juror on the basis of a religious belief that would prevent the juror from basing his or her verdict on the evidence, or from following the instructions of the court, would be permissible. The in-between and more difficult case, in the Court's opinion, would be one where a juror's religion would make the juror unusually reluctant, or unusually eager, to convict a defendant. The case involved this latter situation, but the court held that a violation of *Batson* had not been made out because no showing had been made that the trial judge had committed plain error.

The prospective juror who was peremptory challenged in U.S. v. Berger, 224 F.3d 107 (2d Cir. 2000) was a rabbi who described himself as an "observant Jew". The reason proffered for the challenge was the juror's expertise and familiarity with Jewish educational institutions rather than his religion per se. The defendants in the case were charged with conspiracy to defraud and various substantive offenses arising from their allegedly illegal efforts to secure government funding for Jewish educational institutions. The prosecutor stated that the juror might be considered an expert by the other jurors and exert undue influence in the deliberation room. The Court of Appeals agreed that the government had provided a nondiscriminatory explanation for its peremptory challenge of the rabbi.

A number of state courts have relied on state constitutions to prohibit peremptory challenges which discriminate on the basis of religion. See, e.g. State v. Hodge, 248 Conn. 207, 726 A.2d 531 (1999); Thorson v. State, 721 So. 2d 590 (Miss. 1998); People v. Langston, 167 Misc. 2d 400, 641 N.Y.S.2d 513 (Sup 1996); Bader v. State, 344 Ark. 241, 40 S.W.3d 738 (2001), cert. denied, 534 U.S. 826, 122 S. Ct. 66, 151 L. Ed. 2d 33 (2001) (questions about a juror's religion may not be asked on voir dire). See generally Annotation, Use of Peremptory Challenges to Exclude Persons from Criminal Jury Based on Religious Affiliation—Post-Batson State Cases, 63 A.L.R. 5th 375. See also Comment, *Thou Shall Not Strike: Religion-Based Peremptory Challenges under Washington State Constitution*, 25 Seattle L. Rev. 451 (2002); Case Note, Bader v. State: *The Arkansas Supreme Court Restricts the Role Religion may play in Jury Selection*, 55 Arkansas L. Rev. 613 (2002).

n. 185.
Add to note 185:
U.S. v. Angiulo, 847 F.2d 956, 26 Fed. R. Evid. Serv. 515 (1st Cir. 1988) (Italian-Americans not cognizable group in absence of showing that they have been or are currently the subject of discriminatory treatment); U.S. v. Marino, 277 F.3d 11, 57 Fed. R. Evid. Serv. 1511 (1st Cir. 2002), cert. denied, 536 U.S. 948, 122 S. Ct. 2639, 153 L. Ed. 2d 819 (2002); Murchu v. U.S., 926 F.2d 50 (1st Cir. 1991) (Irish-Americans not a cognizable group). See also People v. Lopez, 3 Cal. App. 4th Supp. 11, 5 Cal. Rptr. 2d 775 (App. Dep't Super. Ct. 1991) (Chinese jurors). See generally Annotation, Use of peremptory challenges to exclude ethnic and racial groups, other than black Americans, from criminal jury—post-Batson federal cases, 110 A.L.R. Fed. 690; Annotation, Use of peremptory challenges to exclude ethnic and racial groups, other than black Americans, from criminal jury—post-Batson state cases, 20 A.L.R. 5th 398.

Add after third sentence in sixth paragraph:
In one case of role reversal Government of Virgin Islands v. Forte, 865 F.2d 59 (3d Cir. 1989), *Batson* was applied to the peremptory challenge of white jurors. The fact that whites were a minority in the jurisdiction was not as critical as the fact that race was being used as a factor in the exercise of peremptory challenges.

n. 186.
Add to note 186:

§ 8:8   JURY SELECTION: LAW, ART & SCIENCE 2D

The viability of a *Batson* challenge where the challenged jurors are Caucasian is examined in Annotation, Use of peremptory challenges to exclude Caucasian persons, as a racial group, from criminal jury—post-Batson state cases, 47 A.L.R. 5th 259. An example occurred in U.S. v. Spriggs, 102 F.3d 1245, 46 Fed. R. Evid. Serv. 181 (D.C. Cir. 1996), as amended, (Feb. 20, 1997). Likewise, in U.S. v. Parsee, 178 F.3d 374, 52 Fed. R. Evid. Serv. 650 (5th Cir. 1999), the defendants lodged peremptory challenges against 10 jurors, all of whom were Caucasian. The government objected and the court reinstated four of the challenged jurors. However, it then gave the defense three additional challenges, all of which they again used to remove Caucasians. Noting that such rulings inevitably turn on the trial court's assessment of the credibility of counsel's proffered reasons for the challenges, the Court of Appeals found no error.

In U.S. v. Blanding, 250 F.3d 858 (4th Cir. 2001) the defendant, a black former state legislator, had peremptorily challenged a white prospective juror who displayed a confederate flag on the bumper of his automobile. The government's *Batson* objection to the challenge was sustained by the trial court. On appeal, it was held that this was error. Regardless of whether or not an inference of racial bias in respect to the juror was warranted, it was an inference that counsel was entitled to draw in exercising peremptory challenges, especially in light of the fact that the defendant, while a legislator, was known to have publicly and vehemently opposed the flying of the confederate flag over the State House. The Court further found that nothing in the record supported a conclusion that the challenge was pretextual and was based on the fact the juror was white.

See also Comment, Batson v. Kentucky: *Application to Whites and the Effect on the Peremptory Challenge System*, 32 Columbia Journal of Law and Social Problems 307 (1999) (arguing that *Batson* should not be extended to whites if the peremptory challenge is to function effectively as a safeguard of justice).

The case in favor of extending *Batson* to preclude peremptory challenges based on disability is argued in Weiss, *Peremptory Challenges: The Last Barrier to Jury Service for People with Disabilities*, 33 Willamette L. Rev. 1 (1997).

n. 187.

Add to note 187 before "See, e.g.":

In U.S. v. Omoruyi, 7 F.3d 880 (9th Cir. 1993), the court stated that while peremptory challenges based on marital status did not violate *Batson*, in this case the defendant's right to equal protection had been violated when the prosecutor peremptorily challenged two unmarried female jurors. The prosecutor had admitted that the reason for the challenges was a concern that the jurors would be attracted to the male defendant.

Add after note 187:

The constitutionality of gender-based peremptory challenges was addressed by the United States Supreme Court in J.E.B. v. Alabama ex rel. T.B., 511 U.S. 127, 114 S. Ct. 1419, 128 L. Ed. 2d 89, 64 Empl. Prac. Dec. (CCH) ¶ 42967 (1994). Unlike most cases involving such claims, the group allegedly discriminated against consisted of men. The state had used nine of its 10 peremptory challenges to remove male members of the venire. The result was that the case, which involved issues of paternity and child support, was heard by an all-female jury. The jury found that the petitioner was the father of the child in question.

The Supreme Court reversed, holding that a state cannot constitutionally discriminate in jury selection on the basis of gender. The Court stated that it is not permissible to assume that a juror will be biased in favor of one of the parties solely because of the juror's sex. In reaching this conclusion the Court applied the heightened scrutiny test of equal protection which it had developed in other cases involving sex discrimination. Under this test the state would have had to show "an exceedingly persuasive justification" for its disparate treatment of men and women. The Court then proceeded to analyze whether the goal of impaneling a fair and impartial jury provided such a justification. The state argued that men were likely to be more sympathetic to the position of the alleged father in a paternity action while women could be expected to be more receptive to the arguments of the mother. No statistical support was provided for these assertions, however, and the Court rejected them as insufficient. Indeed, the Court pointed out that the state's position rested on stereotypical thinking that was invidious, archaic, and overbroad—and which was condemned by law.

Lest its holding be misinterpreted as signaling the end of peremptory challenges, the majority was quick to add that unacceptable jurors, including those who exhibit characteristics which may be disproportionately associated with a particular sex, would remain subject to peremptory challenge. What one is not allowed to do is to use gender as a proxy for bias. In the future a party will have to put forward a characteristic other than gender to justify a peremptory challenge. Whether general and amorphous characteristics such as inattentiveness, demeanor, and a perception of hostility, all of which have been accepted as race-neutral in cases involving an alleged violation of *Batson* (see note 155, supplement), will suffice remains to be seen. If these are found acceptable, *JEB* may prove as easy to evade as has been the case with *Batson*.

In the course of its opinion the Court observed that a properly conducted voir dire would render reliance on stereotypes unnecessary. The Court's position in this regard, it is submitted, supports the argument in favor of allowing parties a wide leeway on voir dire in terms of both time for questioning and the scope of questioning in order to achieve this objective. Windham v. Merkle, 163 F.3d 1092 (9th Cir. 1998) highlighted a potential tension between *Batson* and *JEB*. In his argument to the Ninth Circuit Court of Appeals, the defendant claimed that the prosecutor had engaged in systematic race and gender discrimination by peremptorily

§ 8:8   JURY SELECTION: LAW, ART & SCIENCE 2D

challenging a number of prospective black women jurors. The prosecutor explained that he had challenged the jurors in order to secure a better gender-balance on the jury. Unfortunately, the defendant failed to raise the gender argument before the trial court and the appellate court refused to entertain it. On the *Batson* issue, the court accepted the prosecutor's explanation that he desired more men on the jury as race neutral, and noted that that 25% of the jury was black.

The decision in *JEB* is important, for it is the first in the *Batson* line of cases which did not involve a claim of racial discrimination. How much further the Court will be prepared to go along this line is not clear. In Davis v. Minnesota, 511 U.S. 1115, 114 S. Ct. 2120, 128 L. Ed. 2d 679 (1994), the Court denied certiorari in a case where a peremptory challenge of a black juror alleged to be in violation of *Batson* was found to be race-neutral following the prosecutor's explanation that the juror was struck not because of his race, but because he was a Jehovah's Witness. The prosecutor stated that it was her experience that members of this religion were reluctant to exercise authority over their fellow human beings in a court of law. This explanation may have disposed of the claim that the peremptory challenge was based on race, but it raised the question whether a peremptory challenge based on a juror's religious affiliation is constitutional. The Minnesota Supreme Court said no, reasoning that *Batson* did not apply beyond the context of race. As indicated, the Supreme Court denied certiorari. In a pointed dissent to the denial of certiorari, Justice Thomas, joined by Justice Scalia, maintained that the case should have been vacated and remanded for further consideration in light of *JEB*, which undercut the Minnesota Supreme Court's rationale that *Batson* was limited to cases of racial discrimination.

JEB v Alabama ex rel TB had been analyzed in a number of law review articles. See, e.g., Carlson, Batson v Kentucky, JEB v Alabama ex rel TB *and Beyond: The Paradoxical Quest for Reasoned Peremptory Strikes in the Jury Selection Process*, 46 Baylor L Rev 947 (1994); Casenote, *Preempting the Peremptory: An Examination of* JEB v Alabama ex rel TB, 3 Geo Mason Indep L Rev 233 (1994); Casenote, JEB v Alabama ex rel TB: *Excellent Ideology, Ineffective Implementation*, 26 St. Mary's LJ 503 (1994); Note, JEB v Alabama ex rel TB *and the Fate of the Peremptory Challenge*, 73 NC L Rev 525 (1995); Note, JEB v Alabama ex rel TB: *The Supreme Court Moves Closer to the Elimination of the Peremptory Challenge*, 54 Md L Rev 261 (1995); Note, *The Numbers Don't Add Up: Challenging the Premise of* JEB v Alabama ex rel TB, 31 Am Crim L Rev 1253 (1994); Comment, *Extending* Batson v Kentucky *to Gender and Beyond:*

The Death Knell for the Peremptory Challenge, 19 S Ill U LJ 381 (1995); Note, Batson v Kentucky *and* JEB v Alabama ex rel TB: *Is the Peremptory Challenge Still Preeminent?,* 36 BC L Rev 161 (1994); Comment, *Constitutional Law: Eliminating Gender-Based Peremptory Strikes: The End of the Peremptory Challenge,* 34 Washburn LJ 193 (1994); Note, *Women's Jury Service: Right of Citizenship or Privilege of Difference?* 46 Stanford L. Rev. 1115 (1994).

In Alverio v. Sam's Warehouse Club, Inc., 253 F.3d 933, 88 Fair Empl. Prac. Cas. (BNA) 233, 80 Empl. Prac. Dec. (CCH) ¶ 40627 (7th Cir. 2001), a sexual harassment case, the venire consisted of three women and 11 men. The defendant peremptorily challenged all three women and the issue was whether this constituted impermissible gender discrimination in violation of *JEB v. Alabama ex rel TB.* The Court of Appeals found that the defendant had identified unique characteristics that pertained only to the three women jurors—unemployment, participation as a plaintiff in a lawsuit, and employment in an insurance company—as well as a general lack of work experience, which satisfied the demands of *Batson* and *JEB.* The fact that an all-male jury heard the case did not, in itself, establish that the peremptory challenges had been discriminatory. The court was not prepared to entertain the contention that sexual harassment juries had necessarily to include female jurors, which it characterized as a sexist idea.

An argument that women approach decisional tasks differently than men—they are less concerned with the strict application of rules and think beyond simple binary, win-loss solutions—is developed in Dooley, *Sounds of Silence on the Civil Jury,* 26 Valparaiso L Rev 405 (1991); Benlevy, *Venus and Mars in the Jury Deliberation Room: Exploring the Differences that Exist among Male and Female Jurors during the Deliberation Process,* 9 S. Cal. Rev. L. & Women's Stud. 445 (2000). Interestingly, Klein and Klastorin discovered little statistical relationship between gender diversity on a jury and whether the jury would reach a verdict. Klein and Klastorin, *Do Diverse Juries Aid or Impede Justice?,* 1999 Wis. L. Rev. 553 (1999).

In Note, *Sex and the Peremptory Strike: An Empirical Analysis of* JEB v. Alabama's First Five Years, 52 Stanford L. Rev. 895 (2000), the author examines what effect the Supreme Court's decision in JEB has had. The answer is probably less than hoped for by its proponents or feared by its opponents. *JEB* has not proven to be a harbinger of greater restrictions on the peremptory challenge, nor has there been a rush to extend the decision into other areas. There have been less than two dozen reversals based on JEB,

§ 8:8   Jury Selection: Law, Art & Science 2d

and about a comparable number of remands. Interestingly, most challenges to sex-based jury discrimination have arisen not in gender-sensitive cases, as was predicted, but in capital cases.

The viability of a *Batson* challenge where the challenged jurors are Caucasian has previously been examined, the relevant cases being collected in Annotation, Use of peremptory challenges to exclude Caucasian persons, as a racial group, from criminal jury—post-Batson state cases, 47 A.L.R. 5th 259. A similar issue is whether the antidiscrimination principle articulated in JEB should be applicable when the group allegedly discriminated against is male. One could argue that males have not historically been discriminated against in the legal system in the same way as females, but a similar argument could be made in respect to white, as opposed to black, jurors. The relevant state cases are collected in Annotation, Examination and challenge of state case jurors on basis of attitudes toward homosexuality, 80 A.L.R. 5th 469.

In U.S. v. Davis, 40 F.3d 1069, 40 Fed. R. Evid. Serv. 1036 (10th Cir. 1994), the government justified its challenge of a black female teacher on the basis that it planned to strike all teachers. The government's explanation was held to be race-neutral. The defendant countered with the argument that the peremptory challenges of all teachers would have a disproportionate impact on women in violation of *JEB v Alabama*. The Court of Appeals rejected the argument on the ground that a showing of disparate impact alone was not a sufficient basis for establishing a *Batson* violation.

In U.S. v. Stedman, 69 F.3d 737 (5th Cir. 1995), the defendants contended that the government had used five of its six peremptory challenges to discriminate on the basis of gender. The Court of Appeals found that the government had provided nondiscriminatory explanations for its challenges: one juror was ambivalent about the concept of aiding and abetting; another lacked strong conviction; a third failed to stay for a conference about conflicts; a fourth had reacted favorably to a defense attorney; and the fifth may have been unable to concentrate on the case because of he concern about a young child. In Johnson v. Campbell, 92 F.3d 951 (9th Cir. 1996), the court declined to extend *Batson* to gay jurors. On the facts of the case, however, the court did not find any evidence of purposeful discrimination, even if sexual orientation were to be protected under *Batson*. In Carey v. Mt. Desert Island Hosp., 156 F.3d 31, 77 Fair Empl. Prac. Cas. (BNA) 861, 50 Fed. R. Evid. Serv. 133 (1st Cir. 1998), Carey's counsel had challenged four prospective female jurors. Counsel indicated that he had relied on a juror rating

PEREMPTORY CHALLENGES § 8:9

system which included such factors as occupation, education, and familiarity with the local region. In light of this explanation, and taking note of the fact that the jury contained five men and five women, the court found that *Batson* had not been violated.

As has been noted in this supplement, there have been numerous post-Batson challenges alleging discrimination against white jurors in jury selection. See generally, Annotation, Use of peremptory challenges to exclude Caucasian persons, as a racial group, from criminal jury—post-Batson state cases, 47 A.L.R. 5th 259. Similarly, post-JEB, the issue has arisen as to whether the Supreme Court's holding applies also to discrimination against male jurors. Relevant state cases are collected in Annotation, Voir Dire Exclusions of Men from State Trial Jury or Jury Panel—Post-J.E.B. v. Alabama ex rel T.B, 511 U.S. 127, Cases, 88 A.L.R. 5th 67.

n. 188.
Add to note 188:
In Pemberthy v. Beyer, 800 F. Supp. 144 (D.N.J. 1992), rev'd on other grounds, 19 F.3d 857 (3d Cir. 1994), the court held that the Latino community was a cognizable racial group for *Batson* purposes, and that a racial group could be defined by a variety of factors including national origin, ethnicity, appearance, habits, and ideas (citing Al-Khazraji v. Saint Francis College, 784 F.2d 505, 30 Ed. Law Rep. 1059, 40 Fair Empl. Prac. Cas. (BNA) 397, 39 Empl. Prac. Dec. (CCH) ¶ 35960 (3d Cir. 1986), judgment aff'd, 481 U.S. 604, 107 S. Ct. 2022, 95 L. Ed. 2d 582, 38 Ed. Law Rep. 1165, 43 Fair Empl. Prac. Cas. (BNA) 1305, 43 Empl. Prac. Dec. (CCH) ¶ 37018 (1987)). Furthermore, the court observed that while surnames and skin color can be misleading, each is evidence of race. Compare U.S. v. Gelb, 881 F.2d 1155 (2d Cir. 1989) ("stereotypical ethnic or religious characterizations of surnames are unreliable and only tenuous indicia of the jury's makeup").

n. 189.
Add to note 189:
In Brown v. Dixon, 891 F.2d 490 (4th Cir. 1989), the court held that *Batson* did not forbid a prosecutor from exercising peremptory challenges against jurors who were opposed to the death penalty but not subject to challenge for cause.

n. 191.
Add to note 191:
See generally, Annotation, Use of peremptory challenges to exclude ethnic and racial groups, other than black Americans, from criminal jury—post-Batson state cases, 20 A.L.R. 5th 398; Slusser, Hrcik, and Eastus, *Batson, J.E.B., and Purkett: A Step-by-Step Guide to Making and Challenging Peremptory Challenges in Federal Court,* 37 S. Texas L. Rev. 127 (1996).

§ 8:9 —Applicability to defense counsel

Add at end of section:
In Georgia v. McCollum, 505 U.S. 42, 112 S. Ct. 2348, 120

L. Ed. 2d 33 (1992), the United States Supreme Court addressed the question of whether *Batson* applied to defense counsel. The defendants, who were white, were charged with assault. The victims of the assault were black. Prior to the start of jury selection, the prosecutor moved to bar the defendants from exercising their peremptory challenges in a racially discriminatory manner. The motion was denied by the trial judge. The Georgia Supreme Court affirmed but the United States Supreme Court reversed, holding that a criminal defendant was constitutionally prohibited from exercising peremptory challenges on a racially discriminatory basis.

In the course of its decision, the Court addressed four issues. The first related to the harm suffered as a result of the challenges. The Court stated that the same injury was sustained by jurors challenged on a racially discriminatory basis, whether the challenges were made by the prosecutor or the defendant. Thus, the rationale of *Batson* applied with equal force to defense counsel. In so reasoning the Court identified, perhaps more clearly than it ever had previously, the true victim in the exercise of racially discriminatory peremptory challenges. It is not the accused, but rather the jurors who are the subject of the discrimination. See also Underwood, *Ending Race Discrimination in Jury Selection: Whose Right Is It Anyway*, 92 Colum L Rev 725 (1992). A secondary victim identified by the Court is the state's judicial system; the community is less likely to have confidence in a system where jurors can be excluded from jury service on the basis of race. The need for such confidence is particularly high in criminal cases with racial overtones.

The Court still had two procedural hurdles to surmount, however. First, it had to find that "state action" as private racial discrimination, no matter how deplorable, is not forbidden by the Constitution. The prosecutor is clearly a state official, but can the same be said of defense counsel? Second, the Court had to find that the state had standing to raise the equal protection issue.

Using a similar analysis to that which it had employed the previous term in Edmonson v. Leesville Concrete Co., Inc., 500 U.S. 614, 111 S. Ct. 2077, 114 L. Ed. 2d 660 (1991) (discussed in §§ 8:6, 8:10), the Court found the requisite state action in the fact that peremptory challenges are the product of governmental creation. Peremptory challenges assist the state in its goal to seek the impaneling of an impartial jury. Further, the jury system itself functions effectively only because of government involvement: the state compiles jury lists, jurors are summoned to court under the authority of the state, and jurors are compensated for their time and efforts by the state. Finally, peremptory challenges occur in state-created courts, a fact which both exacerbates the harmful effects of the discrimination and contributes to its proper characterization as state action. The Court was not persuaded to the contrary by the fact that a defendant's interests in a criminal trial are in fact clearly antagonistic to those of the state.

The question of the prosecutor's standing to challenge the alleged discriminatory exercise of peremptory challenges was aided by the Court's previous decision in Powers v. Ohio, 499 U.S. 400, 111 S. Ct. 1364, 113 L. Ed. 2d 411 (1991) (discussed in §§ 8:6, 8:10, 8:12, and 8:13). In *Powers*, the Court had held that a white defendant had standing to raise the equal protection rights of blacks subjected to discriminatory peremptory challenges. The Court had reasoned that racial discrimination in the selection of jurors "cast[ed] doubt on the integrity of the judicial process," that a litigant had an interest in establishing a relationship with jurors that was significantly impaired by the discrimination and that excluded jurors were not likely to be in a position to discover or challenge the discrimination. The same arguments applied with equal, if not greater, force in the present context and the Court had little problem concluding that the state had the requisite standing.

Finally, the Court addressed the issue of whether a restriction on a defendant's exercise of peremptory challenges would violate the defendant's due process right to a fair trial and Sixth Amendment right to the effective assistance of counsel. The Court, perhaps skewing the issue, stated that the right to a fair trial did not include the right to discriminate on the basis of race. Nor could an unconstitutional course of conduct be carried out under the cloak of the right to counsel. The reasoning behind particular peremptory challenges could, the Court stated, be explained without compromising trial strategy or confidential communications.

The Court's conclusion was that a criminal defendant may not constitutionally discriminate on the basis of race in exercising peremptory challenges. If the state makes out a prima facie case of such discrimination, the defendant will be required to articulate a race-neutral explanation for the challenge.

The implications of *Georgia v McCollum* are explored in a number of articles. See, e.g., Recent Development, *The Beginning of the End of Peremptory Challenges:* Georgia v McCollum, 16 Harv JL & Pub Poly 287 (1993); Note, *Constitutional Law—Fourteenth Amendment Right to Equal Protection—Criminal Defendant's Racially Discriminatory Exercise of Peremptory Challenges. Georgia v McCollum*, 60 Tenn L Rev 229 (1992); Note, *Extending* Batson v Kentucky *to the Crim-*

§ 8:9

inal Defendant's Use of Peremptory Challenges: The Demise of the Challenge Without Cause, 33 BC L Rev 1081 (1992); Case Comment, Georgia v McCollum: *Eliminating the Race-Based Peremptory Challenge Once and for All,* 27 Val U L Rev 257 (1992); Case Comment, *One Step Too Far: The Supreme Court Denies Criminal Defendants the Unfettered Use of the Peremptory Challenge in Georgia v McCollum,* 27 Val U L Rev 287 (1992); Comment, *Saving the Peremptory Challenge: The Case for a Narrow Interpretation of McCollum,* 70 Denv L Rev 313 (1993).

With the Supreme Court having held that *Batson* applies to the defense as well as to the prosecution, the door is open to an appellate court, in evaluating a trial court's rulings on *Batson* strikes by the prosecution or by the defense, to compare how the court ruled on similar challenges by the other side. By such a comparison an appellate court would be able to satisfy itself that the trial court had at least been even-handed in the standards it had applied. But in U.S. v. Kelley, 140 F.3d 596 (5th Cir. 1998), such a comparison was not undertaken. The district court had sustained the government's *Batson*-based objections to various peremptory challenges to white jurors by the defense: one juror was challenged because he had been in the Marine Corps and because his demeanor indicated that he would be pro-prosecution, another was challenged because she seemed to be distracted by a preoccupation with a forthcoming wedding, and a third was challenged because he knew another of the jurors and "did not appear to be fair and impartial." All of these *Batson* challenges to peremptory strikes by the defense were, as indicated, sustained. On the other hand, the court rejected defense *Batson* challenges to four of the government's peremptory strikes of black jurors: one to a juror who allegedly glared at the prosecutors and attempted to read their notes; another to a juror who allegedly suffered from a nervous condition and sat in the back row with her head in her hands; a third to a juror who would suffer a financial burden if she was required to serve; and the last to a young mother who shared the same surname (although spelled differently) as one of the defendants. The appellate court upheld the trial court's rulings, stating that it could see no clear error which would justify reversal. While perhaps looking at each set of challenges in isolation might have warranted such a conclusion, a comparison of the trial court's rulings does seem to suggest that it may have applied a somewhat more indulgent standard when ruling on *Batson* challenges by the prosecution. It is difficult to make such a claim with any degree of assuredness, however, because the appellate court also indicated that the trial judge's evaluation of the credibility of counsel's explanations was entitled to great defer-

§ 8:10

ence on the issue or discriminatory intent. See also Mahaffey v. Page, 151 F.3d 671 (7th Cir. 1998), opinion vacated in part on reh'g, 162 F.3d 481 (7th Cir. 1998) (trial judge may use superior knowledge of prosecutors in determining whether peremptory challenges were motivated by impermissible racial bias).

Given that *Batson* applies in the civil context (*Edmonson*) and it is the rights of the jurors and not the rights of the litigants that *Batson* is primarily designed to protect, there would seem to be no reason why a *Batson* claim could not be raised by a corporate party. But see Dias v. Sky Chefs, Inc., 919 F.2d 1370, 1378–79, 54 Fair Empl. Prac. Cas. (BNA) 852, 6 I.E.R. Cas. (BNA) 1860, 55 Empl. Prac. Dec. (CCH) ¶ 40398 (9th Cir. 1990) (abrogated by, Edmonson v. Leesville Concrete Co., Inc., 500 U.S. 614, 111 S. Ct. 2077, 114 L. Ed. 2d 660 (1991)) and cert. granted, judgment vacated, 501 U.S. 1201, 111 S. Ct. 2791, 115 L. Ed. 2d 965, 55 Fair Empl. Prac. Cas. (BNA) 1544, 6 I.E.R. Cas. (BNA) 1868, 56 Empl. Prac. Dec. (CCH) ¶ 40805 (1991); expressing doubt as to whether a corporation could raise an equal protection claim based on gender exclusion because of fact that corporation was not a member of any class, suspect or otherwise, and was not injured if a juror's rights were violated. This case was vacated and remanded to the Ninth Circuit for further consideration in light of Edmonson v. Leesville Concrete Co., Inc., 500 U.S. 614, 111 S. Ct. 2077, 114 L. Ed. 2d 660 (1991).

In U.S. v. Stewart, 65 F.3d 918 (11th Cir. 1995), the Court of Appeals rejected a suggestion that a stricter standard of appellate review should apply to cases involving race-based peremptory challenges by the defense. The case involved a racially motivated crime against blacks, and the defendants exercised their peremptory challenges against 75% of the black prospective jurors. The trial court disallowed one of the challenges and the Court of Appeals affirmed. The reasons that had been given by the defendant should have logically led to the challenge of similarly situated white jurors, but this did not occur. In U.S. v. Boyd, 86 F.3d 719 (7th Cir. 1996), the court held that the defendant had failed to show that his counsel was ineffective for using a peremptory challenge to remove the only black member of the venire. Defendant himself was black, but apparently his counsel believed that white jurors defer to black jurors or that middle class blacks are "hanging jurors". The court stated that either of these grounds were improper even if factually accurate.

§ 8:10 —Application to civil cases
n. 213.
Add to note 213:

§ 8:10　　　　　　Jury Selection: Law, Art & Science 2d

In Tinner v. United Ins. Co. of America, 308 F.3d 697, 89 Fair Empl. Prac. Cas. (BNA) 1843 (7th Cir. 2002), cert. denied, 123 S. Ct. 1623, 155 L. Ed. 2d 484, 91 Fair Empl. Prac. Cas. (BNA) 608 (U.S. 2003) the attorney for the defendant in a Title VII suit alleging race discrimination asked every member of the panel whether they knew or had heard of anyone who had filed a discrimination claim. The one affirmative response came from the only African-American juror on the panel, who stated that her sister had filed a discrimination lawsuit and that her experience had been an "ordeal." The defendant exercised a peremptory challenge to remove this juror. The plaintiff alleged a violation of *Batson*, claiming that the questions were surrogates for race, and thus constituted purposeful discrimination. The trial court rejected the *Batson* claim, and the Court of Appeals affirmed, finding that the challenge was race-neutral and not pretextual. Both the fact that the juror's sister had filed a discrimination lawsuit and the fact that the juror characterized the experience as an "ordeal" constituted race-neutral reasons for the challenge. Nor did the Court of Appeals accept the argument that because the question might have had a disparate impact (as members of a racial minority were more likely to face discrimination in the workplace and thus more likely to respond affirmatively to the question), it indicated purposeful discrimination.

Add after third paragraph:

In Edmonson v. Leesville Concrete Co., Inc., 500 U.S. 614, 111 S. Ct. 2077, 114 L. Ed. 2d 660 (1991), the United States Supreme Court extended *Batson* and held that a party in a civil case could not exercise its peremptory challenges so as to exclude jurors on account of race. The case arose because the defendant had used two of its three peremptory challenges to strike black prospective jurors. Plaintiff, who was black, moved the court to require the defendant to provide a race-neutral explanation for the challenges. The federal district court denied the motion, ruling that *Batson* did not apply to civil cases. The Supreme Court reversed.

The Court had first to address the "state action" question. The majority conceded that ordinarily conduct of private parties lay beyond the scope of the equal protection clause, which applies only to state and, through the Fifth Amendment's due process clause, federal government entities. Nevertheless, it held that there were sound and sufficient reasons for finding state action. Peremptory challenges have their basis in state or federal statute, rule, or judicial decision. Their sole utility exists within a governmentally created court system, and their function within that system is to assist the court and the government in selecting an impartial jury. In this case, were it not for the federal statute permitting peremptory challenges in federal civil trials, the alleged discrimination could not have occurred.

Continuing with its "state action" analysis, the majority next asked whether it would be fair to deem the private litigant in the case to be a government actor in its use of peremptory challenges (this being the second part of the two-prong test of state action established in Lugar v. Edmondson Oil Co., Inc., 457 U.S. 922, 102 S. Ct. 2744, 73 L. Ed. 2d 482 (1982)). Its answer was affirmative. It was only with the overt, significant assistance of a government official, the trial judge, that the peremptory challenge system could operate. (Indeed it is only with the overt, significant assistance of the government that the federal court system can operate.) In upholding the discriminatory challenges, the trial court becomes a party to the discrimination. Furthermore, the processes involved are those traditionally associated with the government, with none of the attributes of a private actor. In allowing peremptory challenges the government has delegated part of its authority to select the jury to private parties. These private parties must therefore abide by the constitutional requirement of race neutrality by which the government would be bound if it had sole responsibility for jury selection. A final observation made by the Court was that the insult involved in being discriminated against because of one's race is exacerbated by the fact that the discrimination occurs within the courthouse.

Having found state action, the majority went on to consider whether a party to the litigation should be accorded third party (jus tertii) standing to assert the rights of the jurors who were subject to the exercise of discriminatory peremptory challenges. Earlier in the term, the Court had decided that in the criminal context such standing was appropriate (See Powers v. Ohio, 499 U.S. 400, 111 S. Ct. 1364, 113 L. Ed. 2d 411 (1991), § 8:6). The Court found the same reasoning persuasive in the civil context. The civil litigant has suffered an "injury in fact," since discrimination in jury selection casts doubt on the integrity of the judicial process in his case. Furthermore, both the plaintiff in the case and the excluded jurors share a common interest in eliminating racial discrimination from jury selection. A civil party, like a criminal defendant, also has an interest in establishing a relation with a jury chosen in accordance with constitutional standards. Nor is there any reason to doubt that a civil litigant will be an effective advocate for the rights of the excluded jurors, since he stands to gain the reversal of an unfavorable verdict. Finally, the excluded jurors are unlikely to be in a position to assert the violation of their own rights. Although, they can sue on their own behalf, they have little incentive, financial or otherwise, to do so. Accordingly, the Supreme Court concluded that a civil litigant had standing to raise an equal protection claim on behalf of blacks wrongfully excluded from his jury because of an opposing party's exercise of racially inspired peremptory challenges. Of course, this did not resolve the merits of the *Batson* claim, and the Supreme Court remanded the case for determination of these.

§ 8:10   Jury Selection: Law, Art & Science 2d

Justice O'Connor, joined by the Chief Justice and Justice Scalia, dissented. Justice O'Connor was not persuaded that adequate state action had been demonstrated. While conceding that a civil trial and peremptory challenges were creatures of government creation, she did not believe that these facts alone were sufficient to satisfy the demands of state action. The government did not tell parties how to exercise their peremptory challenges, let alone tell them to exercise them on a discriminatory basis. When it came to peremptory challenges, the trial judge was little more than a functionary who informed a challenged juror that he or she was excused. Moreover, whatever motives a party may have for exercising its peremptory challenges, and traditionally peremptory challenges have fallen within the unfettered private choice of the parties, these motives cannot be attributed to the government. Attorneys for private litigants act in behalf of their clients' interests, not in behalf of the interests of the government. Therefore it was incorrect, maintained the dissent, to treat the peremptory challenge as a traditional government function. *Edmonson* and its implications are discussed in Recent Development, Edmonson v Leesville Concrete Co: *Will the Peremptory Challenge Survive Its Battle with the Equal Protection Clause*, 25 John Marshall L Rev 37 (1991).

Note, *Peremptory Challenges in Civil Cases—Does Edmonson Alleviate Racial Discrimination in the Jury Selection Process?*, 13 Miss CL Rev 261 (1992); Note, *A Question of State Action:* Edmonson v Leesville Concrete Co, 75 Marq L Rev 707 (1992); Recent Decision, *Constitutional Law—Race-Based Peremptory Challenge Exclusions No Longer Permitted in Civil Trials*, 62 Miss LJ 209 (1992); Comment, *Constitutional Law: The Challenge to the Challenge—Will Peremptory Challenges Survive the Race-Neutral Rule?* Edmonson v Leesville Concrete Co: *Has Batson Been Stretched Too Far?*, 57 Mo L Rev 569 (1992); Note, *Edmonson v Leesville Concrete Company: Preempting Prejudice*, 25 Akron L Rev 439 (1991); Note, *Peremptory Challenges:* Edmonson v Leesville Concrete Co *and the Batson Motion in Civil Litigation*, 43 SC L Rev 617 (1992).

§ 8:11   —Remedies

Add at end of first paragraph:

In U.S. v. Annigoni, 57 F.3d 739 (9th Cir. 1995), opinion amended and superseded, 68 F.3d 279 (9th Cir. 1995), on reh'g en banc, 96 F.3d 1132 (9th Cir. 1996), the court held that although the defendant's peremptory challenge had been improperly denied, the error was harmless. The court reasoned that there was not the type of "structural error" that required automatic reversal. The decision in Annigoni was reversed by the Ninth Circuit, sitting en banc. *Annigoni* is discussed in Note, *Arbitrary Rationality* 106 Yale L. J. 1959 (1997) (maintaining that the decision is best explained as a protection of the right to an impartial jury), U.S. v. Annigoni, 57 F.3d 739 (9th Cir. 1995), opinion amended and superseded, 68 F.3d 279 (9th Cir. 1995), on reh'g en banc, 96 F.3d 1132 (9th Cir. 1996). The court of appeal held that the trial court's erroneous denial of the defendant's peremptory challenge required an automatic reversal of the defendant's conviction. The court also held that harmless error analysis inapplicable in this context. Ross v. Oklahoma, 487 U.S. 81, 108 S. Ct. 2273, 101 L. Ed. 2d 80 (1988)) (discussed in main text § 8:13) was distinguished because the defendant in Ross, after the court had denied his challenge for cause, used one of his peremptory challenges to excuse the juror in question. Thus the juror whose impartiality was suspect did not sit on the jury which decided the case, and there was no showing that the jury was not impartial. In Annigoni, on the other hand, the juror whose impartiality was suspect did sit on the jury, thus calling into question the impartiality of the jury itself. See also U.S. v. Martinez-Salazar, 146 F.3d 653 (9th Cir. 1998), judgment rev'd, 528 U.S. 304, 120 S. Ct. 774, 145 L. Ed. 2d 792 (2000) (defendant's use of a peremptory strike to remove a juror who should have been excused for cause was not a violation of defendant's constitutional right to an impartial jury). On writ of certiorari to the U.S. Supreme Court, the decision of the Ninth Circuit was reversed. U.S. v. Martinez-Salazar, 528 U.S. 304, 120 S. Ct. 774, 145 L. Ed. 2d 792 (2000). The Supreme Court held that even if the district court erred in refusing to remove a prospective juror for cause, the defendant's constitutional rights were not denied by his having to expend a peremptory challenge to remove the juror in question. For purposes of the Sixth Amendment, the critical issue is whether the jury that tried the defendant was impartial. As long as the jury was impartial, the defendant's Sixth Amendment rights were not violated even though he had to expend a peremptory challenge to achieve the impartial jury. Nor were defendant's due process rights violated, as the defendant was not compelled to use one of his peremptory challenges to remove the juror; he could have allowed the juror to sit and subsequently claimed a denial of his Sixth Amendment right. Needless to say, this is not an attractive choice, but the Court was of the view that "a hard choice is not the same as no choice." The defendant had received the number of peremptory challenges to which he was entitled by law, and he was not forced to exercise a peremptory challenge to cure the trial court's error. The Supreme Court's decision leaves open the pos-

§ 8:11

sibility that a constitutional violation in future cases might be found if an appellant can show that:

(a) the exhausted his full complement of peremptory challenges;
(b) he would have used the peremptory challenge he used to remove the juror in question to strike some other juror;
(c) he made a request for additional peremptory challenges which was denied; and
(d) the jury that heard the case was not impartial.

The Supreme Court's decision resolved a long existing controversy among the federal courts regarding whether automatic reversal should follow the erroneous denial of a challenge for cause (Compare U.S. v. Polichemi, 201 F.3d 858 (7th Cir. 2000), on reh'g, 219 F.3d 698, 54 Fed. R. Evid. Serv. 1407 (7th Cir. 2000), cert. denied, 531 U.S. 1168, 121 S. Ct. 1131, 148 L. Ed. 2d 997 (2001); U.S. v. Hall, 152 F.3d 381, 49 Fed. R. Evid. Serv. 1503 (5th Cir. 1998) (abrogated by, U.S. v. Martinez-Salazar, 528 U.S. 304, 120 S. Ct. 774, 145 L. Ed. 2d 792 (2000)); U.S. v. Cambara, 902 F.2d 144 (1st Cir. 1990) (abrogated by, U.S. v. Martinez-Salazar, 528 U.S. 304, 120 S. Ct. 774, 145 L. Ed. 2d 792 (2000)) (erroneous refusal to remove juror for cause requires automatic reversal) with U.S. v. Brooks, 161 F.3d 1240, 50 Fed. R. Evid. Serv. 899 (10th Cir. 1998); U.S. v. Sithithongtham, 192 F.3d 1119 (8th Cir. 1999); U.S. v. Farmer, 923 F.2d 1557, 33 Fed. R. Evid. Serv. 188 (11th Cir. 1991); U.S. v. Morales, 185 F.3d 74 (2d Cir. 1999) (erroneous denial of challenge for cause constitutes reversible error only if jury which hears case is not impartial), as well as harmonizing the approach in federal courts to erroneous denials of peremptory challenges with that which the Supreme Court had previously articulated in Ross v. Oklahoma, 487 U.S. 81, 108 S. Ct. 2273, 101 L. Ed. 2d 80 (1988), a case involving state law but a comparable constitutional challenge (see main text). A related issue to that considered in *Martinez-Salazar* occurs when a trial court abuses its discretion in striking prospective jurors for cause. In U.S. v. Brooks, 175 F.3d 605 (8th Cir. 1999) the court held that the defendants were not entitled to reversal absent a showing that the jurors who heard the case were not impartial. See also U.S. v. Osigbade, 195 F.3d 900 (7th Cir. 1999) (no showing that defendant was prejudiced by Court's erroneous decision to discharge juror). See also Brecht v. Abrahamson, 507 U.S. 619, 113 S. Ct. 1710, 123 L. Ed. 2d 353 (1993). There had been no showing that the defendant had been denied an impartial jury, as the juror in question would not have been subject for cause. Compare Ford v.

Norris, 67 F.3d 162 (8th Cir. 1995) (constitutional violation involving selection of jurors in a racially discriminatory manner is a "structural defect" which precludes harmless error analysis); Kirk v. Raymark Industries, Inc., 61 F.3d 147, 42 Fed. R. Evid. Serv. 883, 155 A.L.R. Fed. 701 (3d Cir. 1995) (remedy for denial of statutory right to peremptory challenge is per se reversal without requirement of having to prove prejudice). The Supreme Court's decision in Martinez-Salazar is examined in Note and Comment: *The Constitution, Peremptory Challenges, and* United States v. Martinez-Salazar, 22 Whittier L. Rev. 843 (2001). See also Childs, *The Intersection of Peremptory Challenges, Challenges for Cause, and Harmless Error*, 27 Am. J. Crim. L. 49 (1999) (although written prior to the Supreme Court's decision in Martinez-Salazar, the author thoughtfully examines whether lawyers should have to use peremptory challenges to rectify judicial errors in refusing challenges for cause); Pizzi & Hoffman, *Jury Selection Errors on Appeal*, 38 Am. Crim. L. Rev. 1391 (2001) (supporting the approach taken by the Supreme Court in *Martinez-Salazar* and arguing that jury selection errors whose only impact is a net reduction in the number of peremptory challenges available to a party should normally be deemed harmless, as the very purpose of peremptory challenges is to cure erroneous judicial rulings on challenges for cause).

n. 223.

Add to note 223:

It would seem to follow that in the same case some peremptory challenges of minority jurors could be found to be in violation of *Batson* while others were not. See Doss v. Frontenac, 14 F.3d 1313, 63 Fair Empl. Prac. Cas. (BNA) 1274, 63 Empl. Prac. Dec. (CCH) ¶ 42827 (8th Cir. 1994); U.S. v. Baker, 855 F.2d 1353, 26 Fed. R. Evid. Serv. 1069 (8th Cir. 1988).

In Koo v. McBride, 124 F.3d 869 (7th Cir. 1997), the Court of Appeals upheld the trial court's reinstatement of two female jurors as a remedy for their improper challenge on gender discriminatory grounds. Similarly, in U.S. v. Ramirez-Martinez, 273 F.3d 903 (9th Cir. 2001), cert. denied, 537 U.S. 930, 123 S. Ct. 330, 154 L. Ed. 2d 226 (2002), the Court of Appeals found no error in the "remedy" for a *Batson* violation chosen by the trial judge of returning the two improperly struck jurors to the jury venire and returning to the government the two peremptory challenges it had used to excuse the jurors. The defendant argued that the judge should have punished the government by not returning the used challenges but the Court of Appeals disagreed, finding no evidence of egregious bad faith or maliciousness on the part of the government and therefore little reason to punish it.

In Paschal v. Flagstar Bank, 295 F.3d 565, 59 Fed. R. Evid. Serv. 875, 2002 FED App. 0239P (6th Cir. 2002), cert. denied, 123 S. Ct. 1287, 154 L. Ed. 2d 1089 (U.S. 2003), the Court of Appeals held that the district court had not committed reversible error when it recalled an African-American juror who had been removed through the use of a peremptory challenge. The juror in question was the only African-American on the panel and the defendant had attempted to justify the peremptory challenge on the basis that the juror's employment with the state housing development authority might have given her some information about the case. The district court accepted the explanation as race-neutral but, under the third step of the *Batson* analysis, found that the strength of the plaintiff's objection outweighed the credibility of the defendant's asserted justification. The district court's decision was influenced by the fact that the defendant had declined to ask the juror any questions about the nature of her employment. The Court of Appeals, noting that the district court was better placed than it was to assess the credibility of the defendant's attorneys, found no error.

Add after seventh sentence in sixth paragraph:
In U.S. v. Joe, 928 F.2d 99 (4th Cir. 1991), the trial court had permitted the prosecution to make a record of its reasons for challenging black jurors outside the presence of the court, and deferred consideration of whether there had been a violation of *Batson* until after trial. The Fourth Circuit Court of Appeals was critical or this method of proceeding, in part because it precluded redress before the jury selection process, not to mention the trial, was completed. The preferable procedure, according to the appellate court, would be first to evaluate the *Batson* claim at the time it was raised to determine whether there was a prima facie case of a violation; second, it a prima facie case were established, to require the prosecution to articulate its reasons for the strikes and to determine at that time if they were race-neutral, providing the defendant the opportunity to show pretext; and third, to thereafter issue a specific ruling supported by facts and reasons in regard to each juror whose challenge was alleged to be in violation of *Batson*.

Add at end of section:
Another remedy question arises where the trial court has failed to make a finding regarding the prosecutor's credibility, often the critical issue in determining whether the explanation for a peremptory challenge is pretextual. In U.S. v. Thomas, 303 F.3d 138 (2d Cir. 2002) the Court of Appeals, quoting from Barnes v. Anderson, 202 F.3d 150, 156 (2d Cir. 1999) advised that in such circumstances the appropriate course of action usually will be to remand for findings by the trial judge as to the challenged strikes and an ultimate determination on the issue of discriminatory intent based on all the facts and circumstances. If, however, because of the passage of time, the magistrate judge can no longer make the necessary findings, a new trial may be warranted.

A number of claims of ineffective assistance of counsel have involved counsel's failure to object to the prosecution's use of peremptory challenges to exclude minority jurors. Most of these have been unsuccessful. See, e.g., Ruff v. Armontrout, 77 F.3d 265 (8th Cir. 1996) (counsel's failure to raise a *Batson* objection did not amount to ineffective assistance of counsel); Hill v. Jones, 81 F.3d 1015 (11th Cir. 1996) (no ineffective assistance of counsel found in pre-*Batson* case where defense lawyer failed to object to prosecutor's use of peremptory challenges to strike Afro-American jurors). In Duarte v. U.S., 81 F.3d 75 (7th Cir. 1996), the appellant had requested his counsel to include on his jury at least one Spanish juror. According to the appellant, his lawyer responded that the judge and prosecutor would not allow it because they did not like Spanish-speaking people. Without accepting the truth of these allegations, the Court of Appeals stated that if what the appellant had been demanding was the inclusion of a Spanish person on his jury, the claim would be without merit as a defendant has no right to a jury of a particular ethnic composition. If, on the other hand, he had been requesting counsel to make a *Batson* objection to a peremptory challenge, the alleged response was clearly inappropriate.

In Miller v. Francis, 269 F.3d 609, 2001 FED App. 0366P (6th Cir. 2001), cert. denied, 535 U.S. 1011, 122 S. Ct. 1592, 152 L. Ed. 2d 509 (2002) defense counsel had failed to challenge a juror with prior knowledge of the case resulting from the fact that the juror had served as a welfare caseworker for victim's mother. The court stated that in order to make out a claim that counsel had been ineffective in not challenging the juror, the petitioner would have to show that the juror was in fact biased. The trial court had held a separate in camera examination of the juror, at which counsel and the prosecution also participated, following her admission of knowledge of the case and had concluded that the juror's knowledge was neither extensive nor detailed. This feature of the case distinguished it from *U.S. v. Hughes* (see below). Also, unlike in *Hughes*, the juror asserted that she could be fair and impartial and would base her decision on the evidence at trial. Noting that jurors did not have to be totally ignorant of the facts, the Court of Appeals found that counsel had not been ineffective.

In Hale v. Gibson, 227 F.3d 1298 (10th Cir. 2000), cert. denied, 533 U.S. 957, 121 S. Ct. 2608, 150 L. Ed. 2d 764 (2001), the defendant argued that his trial counsel was ineffective in part because he failed to attempt to rehabilitate jurors challenged for cause by the state based on their views on the death penalty. Counsel was also faulted for not having challenged, either for cause or peremptorily, several jurors who the defendant believed had preconceived notions of his guilt. The Court of Appeals found that the for-cause removal of jurors for their views on the death penalty had been appropriate, as all of the challenged jurors had made clear that they could not impose the death penalty in the case regardless of the evidence. The court did not think that the defendant's lawyer had behaved unprofessionally in not attempting to rehabilitate jurors whose answers had suggested that they would have been unable to function properly as jurors in a capital case. As to the defendant's claim of ineffective assistance of counsel based on the failure to challenge six jurors who allegedly had preconceived notions of the defendant's guilt, the court held that there had been no constitutional violation, as all of the jurors held only mild or slight opinions and all stated that they could put aside their opinions and judge the case impartially on the evidence. The court distinguished Johnson v. Armontrout, 961 F.2d 748 (8th Cir. 1992), where the jurors had made unequivocal statements to the effect that they believed the defendant was guilty but had not been challenged by defense counsel. In McMeans v. Brigano, 228 F.3d 674, 2000 FED App. 0353P (6th Cir. 2000), cert. denied, 532 U.S. 958, 121 S. Ct. 1487, 149 L. Ed. 2d 374 (2001), defendant claimed ineffective assistance of counsel based on the failure of his lawyer to exercise unused peremptory challenges against two allegedly biased jurors. The Court of Appeals rejected the argument as there was no support for it in the record. Unfortunately for the defendant, his trial counsel had waived the right to have the voir dire proceedings transcribed.

Hughes v. U.S., 258 F.3d 453, 2001 FED App. 0211P (6th Cir. 2001) was one of the relatively rare cases where a claim of ineffective assistance of counsel based on the failure to challenge a juror succeeded. The facts, however, were fairly blatant. Defendant's counsel had not challenged a juror who stated on voir dire that she did not think that she could be fair. This declaration of bias notwithstanding, the defendant still had to show that the juror was in fact biased. This requirement was satisfied by the fact that the juror had acknowledged a personal relationship with a police officer and police detectives, coupled with the fact that the case involved the theft of a federal marshal's firearm and personal property at gunpoint. That neither the trial judge nor counsel had attempted to rehabilitate the juror distinguished the case from others where jurors had doubted their own ability to be fair but had, after further questioning, concluded that they could in fact be impartial. The Court of Appeals held that the seating of the biased jury required a reversal and ordered a new trial.

In Eagle v. Linahan, 279 F.3d 926 (11th Cir. 2001), the issue was whether appellate counsel's failure to raise a *Batson* claim on appeal rose to the level of a constitutional violation. The Court of Appeals found that the existence of a prima facie case had been implicitly accepted by the trial judge when, in rejecting a *Batson* claim by the defendant, he commented that "both [the defense and the prosecution] were doing what [they] could to get the different races off." Given so obvious a foundation for arguing that there had been error in the trial judge's failure to find a *Batson* violation by the prosecution, and given that (according to the Court of Appeals) the State supreme court would have, in the circumstances, either had to remand the case for an evidentiary hearing into the prosecutor's motive (but given the judge's statement this, again according to the Court of Appeals, would have been unnecessary) or order a new trial, appellate counsel's failure to raise the issue was held to constitute ineffective assistance of counsel. The Court of Appeals also found that the trial court's exclusive reliance on a comparison of the proportion of blacks on the petit jury to the proportion of blacks in the venire in order to determine whether *Batson* had been violated was error.

If the right not to be peremptorily challenged because of one's race is that of the juror, it follows that a juror may seek damages for improper exclusion. This was the theory underlying the plaintiff's suit in Shaw v. Hahn, 56 F.3d 1128 (9th Cir. 1995) (alleging violations of plaintiff's civil rights under 42 U.S.C.A. §§ 1983, 1985, and 1986.) See also Carter v. Jury Commission of Greene County, 396 U.S. 320, 90 S. Ct. 518, 24 L. Ed. 2d 549 (1970) (main text); Underwood, Ending Race Discrimination: Whose Right is it, Anyway?, 92 Colum L Rev 725 (1992). The theory was accepted by the court in *Shaw*, but its effect was neutralized by the Court's decision to give preclusive effect to the ruling by the trial court in the original litigation that the peremptory challenge of the plaintiff was not based on race. This holding is questionable for the juror would have lacked standing to contest her dismissal by virtue of the peremptory challenge. The *Shaw* court did not ignore this point, but stated that there was sufficient identity of interest between the plaintiff in the present action and the party objecting to the peremptory challenge in the former action that they should be held to be in privity.

§ 8:12 Peremptory challenges and the right to a jury drawn from a fair cross section of the community

Add before fifth full paragraph:

The United States Supreme Court directly confronted the claim that the exercise of peremptory challenges by a prosecutor so as to exclude all blacks from a jury violated the fair cross section requirement of the Sixth Amendment in Holland v. Illinois, 493 U.S. 474, 110 S. Ct. 803, 107 L. Ed. 2d 905 (1990). The venire assembled to try the defendant in the case contained two black jurors, both of whom were peremptorily challenged by the prosecutor. On appeal in state court, the defendant contended unsuccessfully that the prosecutor's actions violated both his right to equal protection and his Sixth Amendment right to a jury drawn from a fair cross section of the community. Curiously, by the time the case had reached the United States Supreme Court, the defendant had dropped the equal protection claim.

Perhaps the reason why the defendant preferred to press the Sixth Amendment argument was that he anticipated that the Court would not accord him standing to raise the equal protection claim. After all, the defendant was white and the excluded jurors were black, and in *Batson* the Supreme Court had said that a petitioner had to show both that he was a member of a cognizable racial group and that the prosecution had exercised its peremptory challenges to remove from the venire members of defendant's race. If this was the strategic thinking that underlay defendant's decision to abandon the equal protection claim, however, he was to be proven mistaken. The *Holland* Court not only stated that the defendant had standing to raise a Sixth Amendment claim, but also intimated that he would have had standing to raise an equal protection claim. (The Supreme Court was to make this point about standing explicit in Powers v. Ohio, 499 U.S. 400, 111 S. Ct. 1364, 113 L. Ed. 2d 411 (1991), see § 8:6.).

While the defendant in *Holland* prevailed on the standing issue, he lost in respect to his substantive claim that the exclusion of all blacks from his petit jury was a violation of the Sixth Amendment. A majority of the Supreme Court was not prepared to extend the fair cross section requirement of the Sixth Amendment from the venire context to the petit jury stage. In this respect, the majority distinguished between equal protection and Sixth Amendment rights: The equal protection clause is applicable at both the venire and petit jury stages; the Sixth Amendment right to a jury drawn from a fair cross section of the community is applicable only at the venire stage.

The majority's conclusion was based on its perception of the proper relationship between peremptory challenges, the fair cross section requirement, and the Sixth Amendment right to an impartial jury. The fair cross section requirement is a means of assuring not a representative jury (which the Court had held on numerous occasions was not constitutionally required), but an impartial jury. It did so by preventing the state from skewing the jury pool to eliminate any cognizable group which might be opposed to the state's case. By guarding against such abuse by the state, the fair cross section requirement advanced the goal of impaneling an impartial jury.

It is only after a venire drawn from a fair cross section of the community is tendered to the trial court that the peremptory challenge comes into play. It too is a tool in furtherance of the goal of seating an impartial jury. It does so by allowing each side to eliminate prospective jurors whom it believes might unduly favor the other side. When extremes of partiality have been eliminated, the likelihood of seating an impartial jury is enhanced. That the basis for concluding that the particular jurors will be unduly partial is their race was neither here nor there, according to the majority.

Justice Marshall, joined by Justices Brennan and Blackmun, dissented. Like the majority, Justice Marshall took a functional approach. Where he differed from the majority was in regard to the functions which he saw the cross section requirement as serving. The majority saw the cross section requirement in terms of furthering the goal of impaneling an impartial jury. Justice Marshall identified three distinct purposes behind the requirement: first, to interpose the common sense judgment of the community between the accused and an overzealous or mistaken prosecutor; second, to help preserve public confidence in the fairness of the criminal justice system; and, third, to emphasize that jury service is part of one's civic responsibility.

Starting from these premises, Justice Marshall reasoned to the conclusion that the fair cross section requirement should apply to the petit jury as well as to the venire. A defendant's desire for the common sense judgment of community members is as applicable at the petit jury stage as it is at the venire state; indeed, arguably more so, for it is the petit jury and not the venire which must decide defendant's guilt or innocence. The need to preserve public confidence in the criminal justice system is also important at both stages. Lastly, the implication of incompetence or partiality in the exercise of peremptory challenges against all members of a cognizable group stigmatizes members of that group and denies them their right as citizens to serve on juries.

Nor did Justice Marshall see a decision finding a Sixth Amendment violation as one that would lead the Court down a slippery slope from which there was no escape. The Sixth Amendment only guarantees a fair possibility of a jury which is representative of the community; it does not require proportional representation of all groups in the community. Public confidence would not necessarily be undermined by the exclusion of any particular group, so long as the exclusion was the result of chance rather than discriminatory design. Justice Marshall also was not persuaded that groups such as postmen, clergy, and lawyers would need to be deemed distinctive for fair cross section purposes, as

§ 8:12

hypothesized by the majority. He noted that past successful Sixth Amendment challenges had been limited to women and certain racial minorities.

Justice Stevens filed a separate dissenting opinion. Unlike the majority, he was prepared to address the equal protection aspects of the case (the majority was not prepared to do so because the petitioner had not sought review of his equal protection claim and the grant of certiorari had been limited to the Sixth Amendment question). He noted that a majority of the Court (the four dissenters and Justice Kennedy, concurring) agreed that the equal protection principles enunciated in *Batson* had been violated by the prosecutor's challenge of the only two blacks on the venire. He was also prepared to carry this reasoning one step further and hold that the same showing that would establish a violation of the equal protection clause would establish that the defendant had been deprived of his Sixth Amendment right to a jury drawn from a fair cross section of the community.

Both the majority and the dissenters in *Holland* were at pains to point out that the decision was not to be taken as any reflection on the viability of an equal protection claim under identical circumstances. While such a position is not uncommon for dissenters (for it preserves an option which might allow them to succeed on the merits in the future), it is more surprising coming from those Justices in the majority. If the latter were saying (as apparently they were) that defendant would have succeeded had he couched his claim in equal protection rather than fair cross section terms, it gives fuel to those critics who see the courts as engaged in the play of an elaborate game of their own creation, where adherence to the rules is more important than a just result. Holland lost despite the fact that a constitutional violation had taken place at his trial, and despite the fact that he had correctly identified the nature of the wrong done and the facts giving rise to it. He lost because he had invoked the wrong constitutional language in describing the violation, a matter which the Court could easily have corrected. This approach seems to unduly exalt form over substance, harking back to common law days where a technical error in the niceties of pleading could have fatal consequences for one's substantive claim.

From a point of view of constitutional pragmatism, the *Holland* decision also makes little sense. The Court has seemingly placed constitutional provisions in gratuitous conflict. *Holland* and the Sixth Amendment now permit what *Batson* and the Fourteenth Amendment forbid. Whether or not a clever Justice can reconcile the apparent conflicts, the general appearance of inconsistency will adversely affect the

§ 8:13

Court's stature. *Holland* and its implications are explored in Comment, *The Discriminatory Use of Peremptory Challenges after Holland*, 22 Seton Hall L Rev 58 (1991); Note, *Holland v. Illinois: The Supreme Court Narrows the Scope of Protection against Discriminatory Jury Selection Procedures*, 48 Wash & Lee L Rev 579 (1991); Note, *Holland v. Illinois: A Sixth Amendment Attack on the Use of Discriminatory Peremptory Challenges*, 40 Cath UL Rev 651 (1991)

See also Leipold, *Constitutionalizing Jury Selection in Criminal Cases: A Critical Evaluation,* 86 Georgetown L.S. 945 (1998).

Professor Muller points out a paradox in *Batson*: the proponents of *Batson* would be hardly likely to dispute that jurors who serve will fulfill their constitutional obligation to be impartial. But, if so, then the defendant will never have been disadvantaged, in terms of the verdict, by any *Batson* violation. But if this is so, what is the point of requiring automatic reversal in the case of a *Batson* violation? The way out of the paradox, argues *Muller*, is to recognize that the purpose of requiring automatic reversal is to preserve the democratic composition of the jury and the Sixth Amendment's fair cross section requirement. See Muller, *Solving the Batson Paradox: Harmless Error, Jury Representation and the Sixth Amendment,* 106 Yale LJ 93 (1996). *Muller's* analysis lends further support to the argument that *Holland* was incorrectly decided.

In any event, the lesson of *Holland* (as well as of the Supreme Court's subsequent decision in Powers v. Ohio, 499 U.S. 400, 111 S. Ct. 1364, 113 L. Ed. 2d 411 (1991), See § 8:6), for practicing lawyers is clear: If a prosecutor has used peremptory challenges to systematically exclude members of a cognizable racial group at trial, there has been a violation of the federal Constitution, but it is a violation of the equal protection clause and not of the Sixth Amendment's fair cross section requirement. Of course, if a particular state constitution or statute permits a fair cross section claim (see main text for examples), this claim can and should be raised in state court.

Add after first sentence of last paragraph:
See Note, *Neutralizing the Poison of Juror Racism: The Need for a Sixth Amendment Approach to Jury Selection*, 67 Tul L Rev 2311 (1993).

§ 8:13 Peremptory challenges and the right to an impartial jury

Add after second sentence in fifth paragraph:
Ramirez, *The Mixed Jury and the Ancient Custom of Trial*

by *Jury de Mediatate Linguae: A History and a Proposal for Change,* 74 BU L Rev 777 (1994); Van Ness, Preserving Community Voice: *The Case for Half-and-half Juries in Racially-Charged Criminal Cases,* 28 J Marshall L Rev 1 (1994); Note, *Fulfilling Batson and its Progeny: A Proposed Amendment to Rule 24 of the Federal Rules of Criminal Procedure to Attain a more Race- and Gender-Neutral Jury Selection Process,* 80 Iowa L Rev 1327 (1995); Brand, *The Supreme Court, Equal Protection and Jury Selection: Denying that Race Still Matters,* 1994 Wis L Rev 511; Cammack, *In Search of the Post-Positive Jury,* 70 Ind LJ 405 (1995); See also Sullivan and Amar, *Jury Reform in America—A Return to the Old Country,* 33 Am. Crim. L. Rev. 1141 (1996) (advocating, inter alia, shortened voir dire and the abolition of peremptory challenges). Hoffman, *Peremptory Challenges should be Abolished: A Trial Judge's Perspective,* 64 U. Chicago L. Rev. 809 (1997) makes the point that whatever the benefits of peremptory challenges, they need to be balanced against the cynicism and lowered public confidence in jury trials caused by the widespread perception that peremptory challenges are used by lawyers to manipulate the system and that they undermine the concept of an impartial trial. Whereas Judge Hoffman favors the abolition of peremptory challenges, the prosecutor in the highly publicized Howard Beach case has a different view. Hynes, *Batson should be Applauded: Prosecutor in Howard Beach Case Looks at Peremptory Challenges,* 12 Criminal Justice 24 (1998).

Add after seventh sentence in fifth paragraph:
The view that the Court sees *Batson* and its progeny as a vehicle for addressing racism in society is argued in Herman, *Why the Court Loves Batson: Representation-Reinforcement, Colorblindedness, and the Jury,* 67 Tul L Rev 1807 (1993).

Add to end of fifth paragraph:
Dicta in subsequent Supreme Court cases seem to make clear that the peremptory challenge is in fact designed as a tool for impaneling an impartial jury. In J.E.B. v. Alabama ex rel. T.B., 511 U.S. 127, 114 S. Ct. 1419, 128 L. Ed. 2d 89, 64 Empl. Prac. Dec. (CCH) ¶ 42967 (1994), the Court said that "[t]he only legitimate interest it [the state] could possibly have in the exercise of its peremptory challenges is securing a fair and impartial jury." Likewise in Edmonson v. Leesville Concrete Co., Inc., 500 U.S. 614, 111 S. Ct. 2077, 114 L. Ed. 2d 660 (1991) (discussed in §§ 8:9 and 8:10, supp.) the Court observed that "The sole purpose [of the peremptory challenge] is to permit litigants to assist the government in the selection of an impartial trier of fact."

Add after fifth paragraph:

§ 8:13

The Holland v. Illinois, 493 U.S. 474, 110 S. Ct. 803, 107 L. Ed. 2d 905 (1990), explicitly recognized the link between peremptory challenges and the right to an impartial jury. The Court stated: "One could plausibly argue [although we have said to the contrary, See Stilson v. U S, 250 U.S. 583, 586, 40 S. Ct. 28, 63 L. Ed. 1154 (1919)] that the requirement of an 'impartial jury' impliedly compels peremptory challenges . . .." Holland v. Illinois, 493 U.S. 474, 110 S. Ct. 803, 808, 107 L. Ed. 2d 905 (1990) (emphasis in original). Responding to some of the criticisms of *Batson*, the author of Comment, *Equal Protection: Reconciling the Irreconcilable*, 25 Cap. U. L Rev 425 (1996) argues that the basic goals of equal protection and peremptory challenges are not in conflict, only the processes used to effectuate them; and, in attempting to effect a reconciliation of these conflicting processes, *Batson* strikes an appropriate balance. Professor Fletcher, however, argues that there is an air of unreality to *Batson*, and that it would be better to balance the various biases on the jury than to pretend that cultural differences do not exist. Fletcher, *Political Correctness in Jury Selection*, 29 Suffolk U. L Rev 1 (1995). See also Fahringer, *The Peremptory Challenge: An Endangered Species*, 31 Crim. L Bull 400 (1995); Melilli, *Batson in Practice: What We Have Learned about Batson and Peremptory Challenges*, 71 Notre Dame L Rev 447 (1996). Having accepted this position, the Court also accepted the implications flowing from it and pointed out in the main text; namely, that there was little justification for requiring that the defendant be of the same race as the wrongfully challenged jurors in order to have standing to challenge the wrongful exclusion. Accord Powers v. Ohio, 499 U.S. 400, 111 S. Ct. 1364, 113 L. Ed. 2d 411 (1991).

Add after first sentence in sixth paragraph:
For the view that the peremptory challenge is antithetical to other, more critical, constitutional rights, See Broderick, *Why the Peremptory Challenge Should Be Abolished*, 65 Temple L Rev 369 (1992). See also Colbert, *Challenging the Challenge: Thirteenth Amendment as a Prohibition Against the Racial Use of Peremptory Challenges*, 76 Cornell L Rev 1 (1990); Comment, *Reaching the Final Chapter in the Story of Peremptory Challenges*, 40 UCLA L Rev 517 (1992). An alternative approach is proposed in Note, *Batson's Invidious Legacy: Discriminatory Juror Exclusion and the "Intuitive" Peremptory Challenge*, 78 Cornell L Rev 336 (1993) (arguing that peremptory challenges should only be permitted where there is hard data (objectively verifiable juror information) as opposed to soft data (such as intuition, body language, and tone of voice) to support them.

§ 8:13

An analysis of the peremptory challenge in light of the various functions that the jury is expected to fulfill is provided in Marder, *Beyond Gender: Peremptory Challenges and the Roles of the Jury,* 73 Tex L Rev 1041 (1995).

§ 8:14 Implications for the future

Add after first sentence in first paragraph:

See also Montz & Montz, *The Peremptory Challenge: Should it Still Exist? An Examination of Federal and Florida Law,* 54 U. Miami L. Rev. 451 (2000) (supporting abolition of the peremptory challenge based on its history of discriminatory application, practical unworkability, unamenability to reformation, and general inaccuracy). Whether one supports *Batson* and peremptory challenges generally may depend on the relative weight that one places on wrongful acquittals, wrongful convictions and hung juries. See Neilson & Winter, *Bias and the economics of jury selection,* 20 Int'l Rev. of Law and Economics 223 (2000).

Add after second sentence in first paragraph:

Professor Friedman, accepting half of Justice Marshall's position, argues in favor of eliminating the prosecutor's power to exercise peremptory challenge of prospective jurors while retaining that of the defense. See Friedman, *An Asymmetrical Approach to the Problem of Peremptories,* 28 Crim L Bull 507 (1992). A similar approach is advocated in Ogletree, *Just Say No!: A Proposal to Eliminate Racially Discriminatory Uses of Peremptory Challenges,* 31 Am Crim L Rev 1099 (1994). The case for preserving the prosecutor's peremptory challenge is put forth by three United States attorneys, each with 10 years experience, in Helland, Light, & Richards, *An Asymmetrical Approach to the Problem of Peremptories: A Rebuttal,* 39 Crim L Bull 242 (1994). An economic analysis of the issues is provided in Neilson & Winter, *Bias and the economics of jury selection,* 20 Int'l Rev. of Law and Economics 250 (2000).

The resistance of discriminatory peremptory challenges to judicial control under *Batson* and its progeny had prompted proposals to attack the problem through other means. See, e.g., Altschuler, *Racial Quotas and the Jury,* 44 Duke LJ 704 (1995); Gordon, Beyond Batson v Kentucky: *A Proposed Ethical Rule Prohibiting Racial Discrimination in Jury Selection,* 62 Fordham L Rev 685 (1993); Note, *A New Peremptory Inclusion to Increase Representativeness and Impartiality in Jury Selection,* 45 Case Res L Rev 251 (1994).

A highly innovative proposal that would allow parties both to select desirable jurors and deselect undesirable jurors is advanced by Adams and Lane. Adams and Lane, *Construct-*

ing a Jury that is Both Impartial and Representative: Utilizing Cumulative Voting in Jury Selection, 73 NYU L. Rev. 703 (1998). The authors' proposal is based on a corporate procedure designed to empower minority shareholders. Under a cumulative voting procedure, when vacancies on a board of directors arise, each shareholder is allotted a number of votes equal to the shares controlled by the shareholder multiplied by the number of seats to be filled. The shareholder is then permitted to cast his or her entire bloc of votes for a preferred candidate or divide the votes among a number of different candidates. The authors suggest a similar procedure for jury selection. After all challenges for cause have been ruled on, each side would be allotted a total number of votes to be cast either in favor of seating or removing prospective jurors. A party could opt to cast all of its votes for or against a particular juror, or divide its votes among several jurors. The jurors with the highest vote total (affirmative votes to seat minus negative votes to remove) would comprise the jury. Should such a proposal be adopted, it would raise intriguing strategic decisions for lawyers. Should all of a party's votes be cast in behalf of a juror whom counsel predicts will be particularly favorable and persuasive; or conversely, should all of the party's votes be cast against a juror whom counsel fears will influence the jury in favor of the opposing side? Lawyers who have utilized the scientific techniques discussed in this book will obviously be better placed to make such strategic decisions than those who have not. Where the critical issue is minority representation on the jury, counsel can increase the likelihood of a minority presence by casting a number of bloc votes for minority jurors. The juror would not be able to be removed by a single negative vote of opposing counsel, as now occurs through the exercise of a peremptory challenge. The opposing party might be able to block the seating of minority jurors by casting all its votes against such jurors, but it would pay a heavy price in doing so, for it would lose the opportunity to select preferred jurors.

Add after second sentence in fifth paragraph:

Batson can also pose ethical dilemmas for an attorney. Henning points out that this is virtually the only area where the Supreme Court will allow judicial inquiry into a prosecutor's motive. Henning, *Prosecutorial Misconduct and Judicial Remedies*, 77 Wash. U. L. Q. 713 (1999). This, the author maintain, does more harm than good, at best encouraging disingenuousness and at worst outright lying. In the end it is the integrity of the judicial system that is undermined. Anderson, *Catch Me If You Can: Resolving the Ethical Dilemmas in the Brave New World of Jury Selection,* 32 NE L Rev

§ 8:14 JURY SELECTION: LAW, ART & SCIENCE 2D

343 (1998), agrees, arguing that *Batson* encourages lawyers to manufacture race-neutral reasons for challenging jurors. The solution, according to Anderson, lies in expanding jury pools, reforming voir dire, and allowing a certain number of affirmative juror selections by both parties. A different approach is advocated by the author of Casenote, *Jurors and Litigants Beware—Savvy Attorneys are Prepared to Strike:* Has Purkett v. Elem Signalled *the Demise of the Peremptory Challenge at the Federal and State Levels,* 52 U. of Miami L. Rev. 635 (1998), who proposes quasi-cause challenges which would have to be case-related. Coming at the ethical issues from a different angle, Charlow, *Tolerating Deception and Discrimination after Batson,* 50 Stanford L. Rev. (1997) observes that a judicial finding of a pretextual explanation for a discriminatory peremptory challenge necessarily implicates the ethics of the lawyer making the challenge, thereby exposing that lawyer to possible personal liability. However, the author argues that the costs of liability—possibly unwarranted penalties against the lawyer and a resulting chilling effect on contentious peremptory challenges—militate against sanctions even if that means that a certain level of lawyer disingenuousness may have to be tolerated.

Add after third sentence in fifth paragraph:
King, *The Effects of Race-Conscious Jury Selection on Public Confidence in the Fairness of Jury Proceedings: An Empirical Puzzle,* 31 Am Crim LR 1177 (1994)

Add after first sentence in tenth paragraph:
See also Jones, *Race and American Juries—the Long View,* 30 Creighton L. Rev. 271 (1997) attempting to place cases like that of O.J. Simpson in a context that takes into account the long and not always successful struggle to overcome the exclusion of minorities from jury service.

Part IV

VOIR DIRE

Chapter 9

Voir Dire Generally

> **KeyCite®:** Cases and other legal materials listed in KeyCite Scope can be researched through West's KeyCite service on Westlaw®. Use KeyCite to check citations for form, parallel references, prior and later history, and comprehensive citator information, including citations to other decisions and secondary materials.

§ 9:0 Overview

Add after first sentence:
In Morgan v. Illinois, 504 U.S. 719, 112 S. Ct. 2222, 119 L. Ed. 2d 492 (1992), the United States Supreme Court, speaking in the context of a capital case, stated that "[part] of the guaranty of a defendant's right to an impartial jury is an adequate voir dire to identify unqualified jurors." Morgan v. Illinois, 504 U.S. 719, 112 S. Ct. 2222, 2230, 119 L. Ed. 2d 492 (1992). An alternative constitutional basis for voir dire was identified by the court in Bailey v. State, 838 S.W.2d 919 (Tex. App. Fort Worth 1992), petition for discretionary review refused, (Jan. 13, 1993), which stated that a defendant's state constitutional right to counsel included the right to have counsel question prospective jurors in order to intelligently exercise its peremptory challenges.

§ 9:1 Pre-voir dire questionnaires

Add after fifth sentence in third paragraph:
Some specific questions may, however, threaten to intrude on the jurors' interest in privacy. When that happens, the court has the discretion to monitor or prevent the questioning. See, e.g., State v. Mills, 65 Ohio St. 3d 1447, 601 N.E.2d 42 (1992) (upholding judge's refusal to distribute defense questionnaire which the judge determined unnecessarily infringed upon juror privacy rights).

n. 6.
Add to beginning of note 6:

Bilecki, *A More Efficient Method of Jury Selection for Lengthy Trials*, 73 Judicature 43 (1989); Comment, *Don't Mess with Texas Voir Dire*, 39 Houston L. Rev. 201 (2002) (jury questionnaires provide a thorough and efficient means of discovering partiality). See also Bennett & Hirschhorn, *Voir dire in Criminal Cases: Choosing Jurors to Judge Your Client*, 28 Trial 68 (1992); Fargo, *Jury Questionnaires Can Supplement Voir Dire*, Trial 73 (Oct 1993).

Add after fourth paragraph:

In State v. Bible, 175 Ariz. 549, 858 P.2d 1152 (1993), the court observed that the use of a pretrial questionnaire can address many questions which might normally argue in favor of individualized or in camera voir dire. In Kontakis v. Beyer, 19 F.3d 110 (3d Cir. 1994), the fact that the pre-voir dire questionnaire was completed out of the presence of counsel and the court was argued to deny the accused a fair and impartial jury in violation of the Sixth Amendment. The court found no error. The authority of the holding is limited, however, as the trial court had questioned the jurors orally after they had completed the questionnaire and petitioner's attorney was permitted to submit questions to clear up any misunderstandings resulting from the written answers. Moreover, the petitioner's counsel had failed to exhaust his quota of peremptory challenges.

Add to fifth paragraph:

A trial judge, however, is not required to submit any or all of a counsel's proposed pre-voir dire questions. In U.S. v. Bakker, 925 F.2d 728, 32 Fed. R. Evid. Serv. 303 (4th Cir. 1991), the Court of Appeals held that the trial judge had not abused its discretion in declining to submit to jurors a questionnaire containing questions such as "Do you believe in miracles?" and "Would you be offended by someone blaming the devil?"

Another advantage of pretrial questionnaires is that, unlike in the case of answers given in open court, there is no danger that the impartiality of other jurors will be compromised by virtue of a particular juror's response, made to a voir dire question, which contains prejudicial information. Whether to allow a jury questionnaire lies within the Court's discretion. See, e.g., U.S. v. Schlei, 122 F.3d 944, 48 Fed. R. Evid. Serv. 143 (11th Cir. 1997) (no abuse of discretion in not allowing questionnaire).

Add after sixth paragraph:

One serendipitous advantage of employing pre-voir dire questionnaires is that, effectively used, they can insulate the voir dire from *Batson* challenges. Jurors can be identified by number rather than by name, and questions can be screened so that the answers will not require the jurors to reveal their race, gender, or ethnic background. To complete the picture, the lawyers would be required to make "blind" challenges, without ever physically seeing the jurors. A lawyer would have but little choice to make peremptory challenge decisions based on the answers to the questionnaire and not the jurors' personal characteristics. See Montoya, The Future of the Post-*Batson* Peremptory Challenge: Voir Dire by Questionnaire and the "Blind" Peremptory, 29 U. Mich. J. L Ref. 981 (1996).

A juror who is untruthful in answering a questionnaire is subject to challenge for cause. See Webster v. U.S., 528 U.S. 829, 120 S. Ct. 83, 145 L. Ed. 2d 70 (1999).

Add after seventh paragraph:
Although challenges for cause based on pre-voir dire questionnaire responses are usually nonproblematic, greater caution may need to be exercised in death penalty cases. In U.S. v. Chanthadara, 230 F.3d 1237 (10th Cir. 2000), cert. denied, 534 U.S. 992, 122 S. Ct. 457, 151 L. Ed. 2d 376 (2001) the court, although reserving the issue for another day, flagged the problem of whether a trial court had an obligation to voir dire prospective jurors before removing a juror for cause based on the juror's views of the death penalty. One of the difficulties with excusing jurors based on questionnaire answers is that the trial judge does not have the benefit of observing the juror's demeanor. The opportunity to assess credibility based on demeanor is one of the main justifications for applying an "abuse of discretion" standard of review in respect to juror challenges. Because this opportunity to observe is lacking when the challenge is based on questionnaire responses, the court in *Chanthadara* concluded that the trial judge's decision was not entitled to any particular deference and reviewed de novo whether the questionnaire responses warranted the excusal of the juror in question for cause under the *Witherspoon-Witt* standard.

§ 9:2 Initial conditioning of the panel

Add after first sentence in fifth paragraph:
In U.S. v. Shannon, 21 F.3d 77 (5th Cir. 1994), the court asked whether there was anyone on the panel who could not serve as a fair and impartial juror in the case. One juror responded by stating that he thought that any person who had been brought to trial was guilty of something. The judge then rebuked the juror in front of the other jurors and excused the juror from service. The defendant made no objection at the time, but subsequently claimed that the judge's chastisement of the juror may have had a chilling effect on the candor of the remainder of the panel in responding to

§ 9:2

voir dire questions. The Court of Appeals held that the trial court did not abuse its discretion and that the remarks did not deprive the defendant of a fair and impartial jury. See also U.S. v. Van Chase, 137 F.3d 579, 48 Fed. R. Evid. Serv. 1180 (8th Cir. 1998) (judge's comments designed to alert jurors to possible bias against Native Americans did not constitute plain error). In U.S. v. Rowe, 106 F.3d 1226 (5th Cir. 1997) the trial judge was found to have intimidated two prospective jurors, and, indirectly, the panel One juror, after indicating that she doubted that she could be fair because her brother was an undercover narcotics agent and her father a policeman, was told by the judge that she would be called back "again, and again, and again" until she could figure out how to put aside her personal opinions and do her duty. This exchange was overheard by the entire panel. A second juror who also admitted that she might have difficulty being impartial was subjected to similar threats. The court implied that both jurors were trying to shirk their civil obligation of jury service. When it was suggested by counsel that the judge's conduct might have the effect of inhibiting the remaining jurors' from answering voir dire questions candidly, the court specifically asked if any of the jurors had been intimidated by these exchanges. Not surprisingly, no juror indicated that they had been intimidated, but the appellate court said that it was not prepared to assume that the jurors were fools. It was clearly apparent that any juror who crossed the judge faced, at a minimum, a bawling out and, at worst, an extended tour of jury duty. The Court of Appeals held that the judge's conduct was likely to have inhibited jurors from being honest about their potential biases, thereby rebutting the presumption that jurors give truthful answers to voir dire questions. *Rowe* was distinguished in U.S. v. Vega, 221 F.3d 789, 54 Fed. R. Evid. Serv. 1502 (5th Cir. 2000), cert. denied, 531 U.S. 1155, 121 S. Ct. 1105, 148 L. Ed. 2d 975 (2001) where, in response to a prospective juror's indication that she might not be able to be impartial, the trial judge had stated that it was his impression that the juror did not want to serve and that the court was not impressed with her excuse. The defendant argued that this statement sent a message to the other jurors that honest answers would be met with reprimands or reprisals from the court. The Court of Appeals distinguished Rowe in that there had been no express or implied threat to punish jurors who claimed bias, and no juror in Vega suggested that he or she had been intimidated by the judge's comments. The court concluded that the defendant's right to a fair and impartial jury had not been violated.

Add at end of section:

Indeed, a failure either to explain basic principles, such as the presumption of innocence, or to question jurors about their understanding of such concepts, can constitute reversible error. See, e.g., State v. Lumumba, 253 N.J. Super. 375, 601 A.2d 1178 (App. Div. 1992). On the other hand, one should not presume that explanations given during voir dire will stay in the jurors' minds throughout a long trial, available to be recalled when needed. In Penry v. Johnson, 532 U.S. 782, 121 S. Ct. 1910, 150 L. Ed. 2d 9 (2001), a capital murder case, voir dire had taken place over a month long period. This was followed by a five day trial, deliberations, and then another 5 day trial, this time in regard to penalty. The United States Supreme Court expressed its skepticism that, by the time the penalty stage had been reached, the jurors could be expected to remember explanations given to them during voir dire.

§ 9:3 —Observation by counsel

Add at end of fourth paragraph:

The opportunity to observe jurors during voir dire questioning will be unavailable if the questioning is conducted by means of a pretrial questionnaire (See § 9:1). The fact that the questionnaire is completed out of the presence of counsel and court has, however, been held not to be a constitutional violation. See, e.g., Kontakis v. Beyer, 19 F.3d 110 (3d Cir. 1994).

Whether or not a defendant, as opposed to his attorney, has a right to observe the voir dire, that right may be waived. In Cardinal v. Gorczyk, 81 F.3d 18 (2d Cir. 1996), individual voir dire took place in the bench area. When the attorneys approached the bench for voir dire, the defendant sought to join them. He was instructed by his lawyer, however, to return to his seat. As a consequence he was unable to hear the answers of prospective jurors to the voir dire questions. The Second Circuit Court of Appeals found that the trial judge had not excluded the defendant from the voir dire, and had no reason for believing that the defendant was unable to see or hear the proceedings. The court concluded that by not asserting his right, the defendant had waived it.

In U.S. v. Greer, 285 F.3d 158 (2d Cir. 2002), the court held that the defendant was not entitled to be present during in camera discussions held by the judge with prospective jurors regarding hardship excusals. These discussions were deemed to be routine administrative matters and not part of the formal impaneling process in which the parties and counsel had a right to participate. See also U.S. v. Candelaria-Silva, 166 F.3d 19, 51 Fed. R. Evid. Serv. 210 (1st Cir. 1999); Tankleff v. Senkowski, 135 F.3d 235 (2d Cir.

1998). This characterization of the judge-juror meetings was not altered by the fact that one of the jurors elected to inform the judge during the in camera session that he had reservations about serving on the jury. The judge had told the juror that such concerns should be raised in open court.

§ 9:4 Purposes of voir dire

Add after second sentence in first paragraph:
In Morgan v. Illinois, 504 U.S. 719, 112 S. Ct. 2222, 119 L. Ed. 2d 492 (1992), the United States Supreme Court held that a trial judge must, upon request, ask jurors in a capital case whether they would automatically vote in favor of the death penalty if the defendant were to be convicted. The inquiry was mandated to assure that the defendant could exercise his challenges for cause, with those jurors who would automatically vote in favor of the death penalty being properly subject to challenge for cause. Morgan v. Illinois, 504 U.S. 719, 112 S. Ct. 2222, 119 L. Ed. 2d 492 (1992).

Add after first paragraph:
In Mu'Min v. Virginia, 500 U.S. 415, 111 S. Ct. 1899, 114 L. Ed. 2d 493 (1991) (See § 7:11), the Supreme Court explicitly acknowledged that voir dire serves the dual purposes of "enabling the court to select an impartial jury and assisting counsel in exercising peremptory challenges." Mu'Min v. Virginia, 500 U.S. 415, 111 S. Ct. 1899, 1908, 114 L. Ed. 2d 493 (1991).

Individual states are free, however, to take a more restrictive approach to voir dire. A particularly dogmatic example can be seen in Davis v. State, 93 Md. App. 89, 611 A.2d 1008 (1992), judgment aff'd, 333 Md. 27, 633 A.2d 867 (1993), where the court stated that the sole purpose of voir dire is to identify jurors subject to challenge for cause, and not for the additional and gratuitous service of peremptory challenges, and therefore questions regarding jurors' exposure to pretrial publicity, involvement in similar crimes, acquaintance with parties, lawyers, or witnesses, and relationship to law enforcement may properly be limited to those questions which go directly to establishing disqualifying bias.

§ 9:5 Judge- or counsel-conducted voir dire

n. 8.

Add to note 8:
In Peretz v. U.S., 501 U.S. 923, 111 S. Ct. 2661, 115 L. Ed. 2d 808 (1991) the United States Supreme Court held that a magistrate judge, with a defendant's consent, could conduct jury selection in a felony prosecution. The court distinguished Gomez v. U.S., 490 U.S. 858, 109 S. Ct. 2237, 104 L. Ed. 2d 923 (1989) where it had held that a magistrate

Voir Dire Generally § 9:5

judge lacks the authority to conduct jury selection in a felony case if the defendant objected. A cautionary warning for lawyers is contained in People of the Territory of Guam v. Palomo, 35 F.3d 368 (9th Cir. 1994), as amended, (July 19, 1994). The trial judge in repeated side bar conferences had admonished the attorneys for misbehavior during voir dire. When the offensive conduct persisted, the court curtailed questioning by the lawyers. On appeal this was held to be a permissible exercise of the judge's discretion.

n. 9.
   Add to note 9:
   The court may frame its own questions and use its own words in covering the appropriate areas of concern. U.S. v. Brandon, 17 F.3d 409 (1st Cir. 1994). See also State v. Mills, 65 Ohio St. 3d 1447, 601 N.E.2d 42 (1992) (trial court covered "substance" of necessary areas of inquiry in its questions). U.S. v. Heater, 63 F.3d 311, 76 A.F.T.R.2d 95-5928, 130 A.L.R. Fed. 665 (4th Cir. 1995) (same). And see Nanninga v. Three Rivers Elec. Co-op., 203 F.3d 529 (8th Cir. 2000), reh'g en banc granted, opinion vacated, (Oct. 30, 2000) and on reh'g en banc, 236 F.3d 902 (8th Cir. 2000) (failure to ask specific questions proposed by counsel not error where relevant topics were covered by judge in voir dire); U.S. v. Brooks, 174 F.3d 950, 83 A.F.T.R.2d 99-2202 (8th Cir. 1999) (same); U.S. v. Rahman, 189 F.3d 88, 52 Fed. R. Evid. Serv. 425 (2d Cir. 1999) (Court's comprehensive inquiry into pretrial publicity, and religious and ethnic prejudice, satisfied the demands of the Sixth Amendment, even if specific questions requested by defendants were not asked); U.S. v. Torres, 191 F.3d 799 (7th Cir. 1999) (trial court did not err in not asking specific questions requested by defendants relating to prejudice against illegal Mexican aliens as it did inquire about potential bias arising from defendants' status as noncitizens); U.S. v. Sarkisian, 197 F.3d 966 (9th Cir. 1999) (trial court's questions regarding defendants' ethnicity, use of interpreters, and the jurors' ability to be impartial were sufficient to test for bias and partiality, and justified any failure to ask defendants' requested questions relating to same issues); Gardner v. Barnett, 199 F.3d 915 (7th Cir. 1999) (trial court did not err in not asking specific questions regarding bias against gangs requested by defense when it asked generally about involvement of jurors with street gangs, and admonished jury to follow law, and set aside sympathy and prejudice in reaching its verdict). Compare U.S. v. Tocco, 200 F.3d 401, 53 Fed. R. Evid. Serv. 1116, 2000 FED App. 0002P (6th Cir. 2000) (in high-profile case with unsympathetic press coverage linking defendants to "Mob" and "Detroit Mafia", failure to ask requested questions regarding Mafia and Italian-American prejudice was "mistake", albeit not an error compelling reversal).

n. 10.
   Add to note 10 after "Hamer":
In Medrano v. City of Los Angeles, 973 F.2d 1499, 24 Fed. R. Serv. 3d 108 (9th Cir. 1992), the defendants argued that the court erred in refusing to ask specific questions regarding the jurors' attitudes towards suicide, drug use, firearms, racial prejudice, the proper extent of police authority, police abuse of authority, and the appropriateness of awarding monetary damages for death and injuries. The appellate court found that the district judge had given the jurors an overview of the case and had asked sufficient general questions to justify refusing to ask defendants' requested specific questions. See also Williams v. Collins, 16 F.3d 626 (5th Cir. 1994) (limitation of voir dire questioning on range of punishment did not deprive accused of fundamental fairness).

§ 9:5

In U.S. v. Adams, 305 F.3d 30 (1st Cir. 2002), the Court of Appeals held that jury selection in defendant's case, conducted by consent before a magistrate, was not flawed because of the magistrate's failure to afford defense counsel a final look at the potential alternative jurors before he agreed to the seating of the initial 12 jurors. The court pointed out that defense counsel had already exhausted his peremptory challenges, and had made no attempt to bring the objection to the attention of the district court.

Add after fourth sentence in second paragraph:
In Ratliff v. Schiber Truck Co., Inc., 150 F.3d 949, 49 Fed. R. Evid. Serv. 1450 (8th Cir. 1998), the appellate court held that the district court had not abused its discretion in allowing the lawyers only 20 minutes for voir dire.

n. 11.
Add to note 11:
Failure to re-urge a court to ask a submitted question may constitute a waiver of the party's right to complain about that failure. See U.S. v. LaRouche, 896 F.2d 815, 829 (4th Cir. 1990); Siwek v. Farley, 681 F. Supp. 1034, 1038 (W.D. N.Y. 1988). Waiver has also been found where an overly long list of questions is submitted to the judge, the judge's attention is not drawn to any particular questions as being more essential than the others, and counsel fails to make a timely objection to the judges failure to ask the submitted question. King v. Jones, 824 F.2d 324, 326 (4th Cir. 1987). See also U.S. v. Stevenson, 6 F.3d 1262, 39 Fed. R. Evid. Serv. 832 (7th Cir. 1993) (failure to request inquiry into racial prejudice constituted waiver).

Where the attorneys were provided an unrestricted right to question the jurors, the failure of a judge to ask about the jurors' knowledge of witnesses was held not to be reversible error. U.S. v. Rigsby, 45 F.3d 120, 41 Fed. R. Evid. Serv. 372, 1995 FED App. 0027P (6th Cir. 1995). Cases such as U.S. v. Washington, 819 F.2d 221 (9th Cir. 1987), where the trial court's refusal to ask the jurors about their knowledge of government witnesses was held to be reversible error, were distinguished on the basis that the attorneys in those cases were not allowed to question the jurors.

Add to second paragraph:
A judge has the discretion to reject supplemental questions proposed by counsel if the judge believes the voir dire is otherwise sufficient to expose bias. See U.S. v. Moore, 936 F.2d 1508, 33 Fed. R. Evid. Serv. 1345 (7th Cir. 1991); U.S. v. Powell, 932 F.2d 1337 (9th Cir. 1991); Gacy v. Welborn, 994 F.2d 305 (7th Cir. 1993); U.S. v. Phibbs, 999 F.2d 1053, 38 Fed. R. Evid. Serv. 881 (6th Cir. 1993); U.S. v. Baker, 10 F.3d 1374, 38 Fed. R. Evid. Serv. 638 (9th Cir. 1993), as amended, (Dec. 13, 1993) and (overruled by, U.S. v. Nordby, 225 F.3d 1053 (9th Cir. 2000)); U.S. v. Nielsen, 1 F.3d 855, 93-2 U.S. Tax Cas. (CCH) ¶ 50445, 72 A.F.T.R.2d 93-5580 (9th Cir. 1993). See also U.S. v. Bobo, 994 F.2d 524, 37 Fed. R. Evid. Serv. 1208, 125 A.L.R. Fed. 775 (8th Cir. 1993) (no abuse of discretion in failure of trial court to ask on voir dire whether prospective jurors would be prejudiced by defen-

dant's prior felony convictions, when court gave cautionary instruction at later stage).

Add at end of section:
Although a defendant has a right to be present during voir dire questioning by the judge, the defendant may waive that right. See State v. Bible, 175 Ariz. 549, 858 P.2d 1152 (1993).

§ 9:6 —Arguments for questioning by judge
n. 18.
Add to note 18 after "Ristaino":
See also U.S. v. Brown, 938 F.2d 1482, 33 Fed. R. Evid. Serv. 790 (1st Cir. 1991) (mere fact that defendant was black and all government's witnesses, as well as all jurors, were white did not require judge to conduct voir dire on issue of racial prejudice, even if such questioning might have been advisable).

Add at end of section:
In Scott v. Lawrence, 36 F.3d 871 (9th Cir. 1994), a civil rights action, the trial court revealed sua sponte during voir dire that the plaintiff had previous rape and sexual assault convictions. The Court of Appeals held that this constituted an abuse of discretion. The trial court had not been required to reveal this information, and it had made no determination as to whether the convictions would be introduced into evidence in the case (in actual fact they were not). In addition, the information was clearly prejudicial to the plaintiff.

§ 9:7 —Arguments for questioning by counsel
n. 19.
Add to note 19:
For a generally negative evaluation of the ability of lawyers to select impartial jurors when allowed to conduct voir dire, See Hastie, *Is Attorney-Conducted Voir Dire an Effective Procedure for the Selection of Impartial Jurors*, 40 Am U L Rev 703 (1991). Compare See also Comment, *Don't Mess with Texas Voir Dire*, 39 Houston L. Rev. 201 (2002).

Add after second paragraph:
Support for counsel- rather than judge-conducted voir dire can be indirectly drawn from the Supreme Court's opinion in Morgan v. Illinois, 504 U.S. 719, 112 S. Ct. 2222, 119 L. Ed. 2d 492 (1992). The trial judge, while asking in general terms whether the jurors would follow the law, rejected the defendant's request for a specific question asking if any juror would automatically vote in favor of the death penalty were the defendant to be convicted. The state argued that the Court's general questioning was adequate to protect the defendant's rights, but the United States Supreme Court disagreed. The Court thought that jurors might in their own minds see no inconsistency between responding affirmatively

to questions about fairness or impartiality and thinking that a person convicted of a capital crime should automatically be sentenced to death. Their position might well satisfy their own personal conception of fairness and impartiality. Yet, a juror who believed that death should follow automatically from conviction of a capital offense and who was unwilling to consider mitigating circumstances as required by law and definition would not be following the law. Because the capital defendant was on trial for his life and concerns in this regard could be easily alleviated, the Court was strengthened in its conviction that the defendant should be permitted to probe more closely the jurors' views on this critical issue. It thus found that the general questioning conducted by the trial judge was not sufficient.

The rationale underlying *Morgan* can be generalized. In response to routine questioning by the judge, jurors often will not disclose their true feelings on a topic. Indeed, it may take close questioning to make jurors aware of their true feelings. This process is better conducted by counsel and simply to allow counsel to supplement those questions asked by the court may not be adequate to discover the necessary information. Moreover, as in *Morgan*, a balancing approach which weighs the risks to a defendant against the burden to the court may seem to favor allowing counsel to ask specific questions whenever the charge is serious or the danger of prejudice real. Of course, a trial judge should be able to keep the length and scope of voir dire within reasonable bounds. Counsel should not draw too much succor from these arguments, however, because the Supreme Court in *Morgan* held that the error in the case could have been rectified by the judge asking the defense's requested questions. See also U.S. v. Gillis, 942 F.2d 707 (10th Cir. 1991) (judge's general questioning regarding impartiality was inadequate to determine whether the jurors might be prejudiced as a result of having been subjected to voir dire in a previous trial against the defendant on similar charges).

Add after first sentence in third paragraph:
An example of what the critics are talking about can be found in People v. Taylor, 5 Cal. App. 4th 1299, 7 Cal. Rptr. 2d 676 (2d Dist. 1992). The court preceded its questioning regarding racial prejudice with a reminder to the jury that racial prejudice has no place in the courtroom. This "signaling" was not held to be error, even though the trial involved an interracial murder, and racial prejudice was a critical issue. In most cases, the "signalling" will be more subtle, and may take the form of facial gestures and looks of approval or disapproval.

Add at end of third paragraph:

Sometimes judges are arguably less than even-handed. In U.S. v. Middleton, 246 F.3d 825, 56 Fed. R. Evid. Serv. 1247, 87 A.F.T.R.2d 2001-1783, 2001 FED App. 0122P (6th Cir. 2001), where the defendant was charged with tax evasion, the trial judge refused to ask the defendant's proposed questions regarding bias against tax protestors, but did ask the government's requested questions regarding anti-IRS bias. The Court of Appeals, however, found no abuse of discretion, citing the trial judge's general inquiries regarding the jurors' acceptance of the presumption of innocence, the beyond reasonable doubt standard of proof, and the importance of the verdict being based on the evidence.

At least one empirical study lends support to the lawyers' claim that they are better able than judges to elicit candid responses from jurors. The judge is perceived by jurors as an authority figure, and the jurors in the study apparently attempted to conform their answers to their perception of what the judge wanted to hear. Jones, *Judge-Versus Attorney-Conducted Voir Dire: An Empirical Investigation of Juror Candor*, 11 Law & Hum Behav 131 (1987). See also Comment, *Don't Mess with Texas Voir Dire*, 39 Houston L. Rev. 201 (2002) (arguing against restrictions on leading and "leaning" questions by counsel).

Add after fifth paragraph:
In order to determine whether members of the panel harbor possible hostility toward the client, some lawyers believe that it is useful to have the clients themselves pose voir dire questions directly to the jurors. If effectively done, this process may also help to forge a bond between the client and members of the jury. Most judges, on the other hand, will be wary of permitting an untrained layperson to become involved in a legal process such as jury selection, and counsel may have to convince the judge of the client's competence. Some lawyers have gone so far as to ask that their client be appointed as co-counsel.

§ 9:8 Group, individual, and in camera questioning
n. 24.
Add to note 24:
A trial court is not constitutionally obliged to allow either individual questioning or questioning regarding the content of the pretrial publicity to which the juror has been exposed. See Mu'Min v. Virginia, 500 U.S. 415, 111 S. Ct. 1899, 114 L. Ed. 2d 493 (1991) (upholding the trial court's voir dire of jurors in groups of four). See also U.S. v. Brown, 927 F.2d 406 (8th Cir. 1991) (upholding trial court requirement that counsel address voir dire questions to jurors as a group). U.S. v. ReBrook, 58 F.3d 961, Fed. Sec. L. Rep. (CCH) ¶ 98794 (4th Cir. 1995) (unfavorable publicity in local newspapers did not require individual voir dire, and trial judge did not commit error in questioning of jurors in respect to exposure to

publicity). U.S. v. Bailey, 112 F.3d 758 (4th Cir. 1997) (trial court did not abuse its discretion in refusing individual voir dire in case where the pretrial publicity did not give rise to a presumption of prejudice, and where the judge's questioning was thorough and fair and included all questions requested by the defendant); U.S. v. Schlei, 122 F.3d 944, 48 Fed. R. Evid. Serv. 143 (11th Cir. 1997) (no abuse of discretion in not granting individualized voir dire where no showing that non-impartial jurors had served); Lucero v. Kerby, 133 F.3d 1299 (10th Cir. 1998) (no denial in refusing individual sequestered voir dire, even though one of the jurors, immediately removed when the fact came to light, was the brother of one of the victims in the case).

In U.S. v. Bieganowski, 313 F.3d 264 (5th Cir. 2002), cert. denied, 123 S. Ct. 1956, 155 L. Ed. 2d 851 (U.S. 2003) there had been publicity about the defendant prior to trial which gave rise to a significant possibility of prejudice. During voir dire, one prospective juror had revealed the contents of an inflammatory article in the presence of the panel. After the juror's disclosure, however, the defendant did not request the judge to conduct individual voir dire, although the Court of Appeals stated that this would have been prudent and within the court's discretion. The Court of Appeals also thought that the trial judge would have been better advised to engage in further questioning of the entire venire after the prospective juror had revealed the contents of the article in its presence. In the event, the juror who had revealed the content of the article did not ultimately serve on the jury, the defense having exercised a peremptory challenge to remove him. That, of course, did not resolve the issue of whether the jury had been tainted by the juror's revelations. Without reaching this issue, the Court of Appeals found that the defendant had not suffered such a degree of prejudice to justify a reversal of his conviction. The trial court had instructed the jury not to consider what they had read in the papers, noting that "the papers are not always correct" and, at the conclusion of voir dire, further instructed the jury that "anything you may have seen or heard outside the courtroom is not evidence and must be totally disregarded. You are to decide this case solely on the evidence presented here in court." The fact that the jury had convicted the defendant on only 10 of the 15 counts with which he had been charged indicated to the Court of Appeals that the jury had methodically assessed each of the charges against the defendant. Finally, the Court of Appeals noted that the evidence of guilt was overwhelming.

In Ritchie v. Rogers, 313 F.3d 948, 2002 FED App. 0426P (6th Cir. 2002), extensive pretrial publicity surrounded the defendant's murder trial. The Court of Appeals, after reviewing the Supreme Court's decisions on "presumed prejudice," found that the trial court's denial of a change of venue on this ground was not contrary to, or an unreasonable application of, clearly established law. In the absence of presumed prejudice, the issue became whether the voir dire was sufficiently searching to detect "actual prejudice." The defendant argued that the use of group rather than individual voir dire constituted a denial of due process, but the Court of Appeals found that the trial judge had not committed error, either in allowing the group voir dire or in denying petitioner's motion for a change in venue.

In U.S. v. Allen, 247 F.3d 741, 56 Fed. R. Evid. Serv. 1144 (8th Cir. 2001), cert. granted, judgment vacated on other grounds, 536 U.S. 953, 122 S. Ct. 2653, 153 L. Ed. 2d 830 (2002) and cert. denied, 123 S. Ct. 2273, 156 L. Ed. 2d 132 (U.S. 2003), during defendant's jury selection, the sentencing decision in a related case was returned and engendered a loud emotional outburst which included screams and crying. The outburst was heard by several members of the defendant's venire panel. In response the district court took several remedial steps, including asking general voir dire questions and individual questions on the emotional outbursts, and also gave a cautionary instruction reminding the panel to avoid and disregard anything seen or heard outside the courtroom. The defendant, however, argued that the court had abused its discretion in not striking the entire panel, and, in the alternative, by not striking those jurors who admitted to having heard the outburst. On appeal the court found no abuse of the judge's discretion. As most of the panel had not heard the outburst, and as those who had heard the outburst could not be certain about what it related to, there was no obvious prejudice to the defendant. The district court's individual questioning was held to be sufficient to uncover any prejudice resulting from the incident. Defense counsel had agreed to the judge's questions and had been given the opportunity to ask follow-up questions.

An emotional outburst, but this time from the plaintiff and a witness, was also at issue in Griffin v. City of Opa-Locka, 261 F.3d 1295, 86 Fair Empl. Prac. Cas. (BNA) 1254 (11th Cir. 2001), cert. denied, 535 U.S. 1033, 122 S. Ct. 1789, 152 L. Ed. 2d 648, 88 Fair Empl. Prac. Cas. (BNA) 1599 (2002) and cert. denied, 535 U.S. 1034, 122 S. Ct. 1789, 88 Fair Empl. Prac. Cas. (BNA) 1600 (2002). The first incident in question occurred when, before voir dire, the plaintiff, in an emotional state and crying, had walked through the lobby where the jury panel was waiting and where several of the jurors had observed her. The City moved to strike the entire panel, but the district court denied the motion. The denial was upheld on appeal, the Court of Appeals noting that the trial judge had questioned each of the prospective jurors regarding the incident and how it might affect their impartiality. All the jurors selected had indicated that they could ignore the incident and decide the case on the evidence. The second incident involved a witness who broke down and cried on the witness stand. The judge declined to grant a motion for a mistrial, and the Court of Appeals held that, as the judge was in the best position to assess the possible prejudicial effect of the outburst, the decision lay within his discretion, which had not been abused. The judge had given curative instructions and, indeed, had ultimately struck the testimony of the witness. See also Whitehead v. Cowan, 263 F.3d 708 (7th Cir. 2001), cert. denied, 534 U.S. 1116, 122 S. Ct. 927, 151 L. Ed. 2d 890 (2002) (outburst by victim's mother in presence of jury, while unfortunate, did not require a new trial).

The fact that a defendant is facing a potential death penalty does not in itself mandate individual voir dire. U.S. v. Flores, 63 F.3d 1342, 42 Fed. R. Evid. Serv. 1365 (5th Cir. 1995). The argument that it should is advanced by Acker and Lanier in an article in the Criminal Law Bulletin. Acker & Lanier, Law, Discretion, and the Capital Jury: Death Penalty Statutes and Proposals for Reform, 32 Crim L Bull 134 (1996). Cases which might be profitably cited in support of the trial judge's exercise of discretion to permit such questioning can be found in Justice Marshall's dissenting opinion in *Mu'Min* and include: U.S. v. Addonizio, 451 F.2d 49, 67 (3d Cir. 1971); U.S. v. Davis, 583 F.2d 190, 196 (5th Cir. 1978); Silverthorne v. U.S., 400 F.2d 627, 639 (9th Cir. 1968); State v. Pokini, 55 Haw. 640, 526 P.2d 94, 100–01 (1974); State v. Goodson, 412 So. 2d 1077, 1081 (La. 1982); State v. Claybrook, 736 S.W.2d 95, 99–100 (Tenn. 1987); State v. Herman, 93 Wash. 2d 590, 593–94, 611 P.2d 748, 750 (1980); State v. Finley, 177 W. Va. 554, 355 S.E.2d 47, 50–51 (1987); U.S. v. Colabella, 448 F.2d 1299, 1303 (2d Cir. 1971); U.S. v. Harris, 542 F.2d 1283, 1295 (7th Cir. 1976).

§ 9:8   Jury Selection: Law, Art & Science 2d

In Dougherty v. State, 813 So. 2d 217 (Fla. Dist. Ct. App. 2d Dist. 2002), review denied, 832 So. 2d 105 (Fla. 2002) the court held that the defendant's constitutional right to a fair trial had been violated by the denial of individual voir dire in order to determine if any of the jurors had been tainted by the trial judge's comments at the defendant's previous trial, where the judge had admonished the jury for failing to credit police testimony and for finding the defendant not guilty. The refusal of individual voir dire was held to violate the District Court of Appeal's clear mandate and constituted reversible error.

Add after third sentence in third paragraph:
In State v. Bible, 175 Ariz. 549, 858 P.2d 1152 (1993), the court observed that the pretrial questionnaire used in the case addressed many of the questions which might normally argue in favor of individualized or in camera voir dire, and that therefore there was no error in the trial judge's decision not to allow such voir dire.

Add after third sentence in fourth paragraph:
In U.S. v. Orlando-Figueroa, 229 F.3d 33, 55 Fed. R. Evid. Serv. 1097 (1st Cir. 2000), a case involving substantial but not particularly inflammatory pretrial publicity, the court asked the jurors if any had read or seen anything about the case. The judge then proceeded to individually question each juror who had answered affirmatively as to the circumstances under which the juror had been exposed to publicity and whether, despite the exposure, the juror could decide the case only on the evidence presented. Several jurors were excused by the court. On appeal, this method of proceeding was upheld, the Court of Appeals stating that there was no error in the trial court's decision not to individually voir dire each and every prospective juror.

Add after third sentence in fourth paragraph:
If voir dire is conducted in open court, and a prospective juror answers a question in such a way as to possibly prejudice the other jurors, the court must decide whether to dismiss the entire jury "for cause." This decision rests within the Court's discretion. See U.S. v. Khoury, 901 F.2d 948 (11th Cir. 1990), opinion modified on denial of reh'g, U.S. v. Khoury, 910 F.2d 713 (11th Cir. 1990). In U.S. v. Rojo-Alvarez, 944 F.2d 959 (1st Cir. 1991), a prospective juror who worked for the department of corrections stated on voir dire in the presence of the other jurors that, in her experience, juvenile sex offenders rarely admitted what they had done. The defendants objected to this insinuation that criminal defendants do not tell the truth and requested that the entire venire be dismissed. The judge refused, but offered to give a curative instruction at the defense's request. Such request was never forthcoming. The Court of Appeals found no error, particularly in light of the fact that the juror's state-

ment referred only to juvenile sex offenders, not all criminal defendants, and the judge questioned the jurors as to their impartiality. See also U.S. v. York, 933 F.2d 1343, 33 Fed. R. Evid. Serv. 426 (7th Cir. 1991) (overruled by, Wilson v. Williams, 182 F.3d 562, 51 Fed. R. Evid. Serv. 941 (7th Cir. 1999)). *Rojo-Alvarez* might be compared with Mach v. Stewart, 137 F.3d 630 (9th Cir. 1997), as amended, (Nov. 20, 1997) and as amended, (Feb. 11, 1998), where it was held that the defendant's right to an impartial jury was violated where, in a case involving sexual abuse of a child under 14, the trial judge failed to declare a mistrial after a prospective juror made "expert-like statements", based on her long experience as a social worker, that children did not lie about sexual abuse. The Court of Appeals was prepared to presume that at least one juror's impartiality may have been compromised by these statements, and added that, at a minimum the judge should have conducted further voir dire to see if any juror had in fact been affected. The refusal to dismiss venire which had heard one prospective juror admit to having read a newspaper article which had compromised his impartiality was not error where the trial court polled remaining jurors to determine if they could still be impartial. Similarly, in U.S. v. McKissick, 204 F.3d 1282 (10th Cir. 2000), a juror observed that, based on her seven and a half years of employment as a nurse at the department of corrections, the defendants' body language indicated their guilt. The juror was dismissed for cause, but the defendants' motion for a mistrial based on the juror's remarks was denied. The Court of Appeals found that the trial court had not abused its discretion, noting that the judge had cautioned the remainder of the jury pool to disregard the remarks, stated that the juror was not an expert and indicated that he was unaware of any telltale body language. The Court of Appeals concluded that there had been no showing that the impartiality of the jury as a whole had been compromised. In U.S. v. Knipp, 963 F.2d 839 (6th Cir. 1992), a prospective juror stated that his personal acquaintance with a witness was such that he would believe whatever the witness said. The juror was excused for cause, and the judge gave a curative instruction that the credibility of witnesses was to be based on the evidence. The judge, however, declined to declare a mistrial and the appellate court held that this was not an abuse of discretion. In U.S. v. Garcia-Flores, 246 F.3d 451 (5th Cir. 2001), the defendant was on trial for transporting illegal drugs in his truck. A prospective juror, himself a truck driver, stated that he could not believe that a truck driver would not be aware of the cargo he was carrying. The juror was excused, and the judge explained to the remaining jurors how it might be possible that a driver would not know

§ 9:8   JURY SELECTION: LAW, ART & SCIENCE 2D

the nature of his cargo. The judge then asked the jurors whether they understood that this could happen. On appeal, the court held that the judge's curative efforts were sufficient to safeguard the impartiality of the jury.

The type of problem to be avoided is illustrated by U.S. v. Hernandez, 84 F.3d 931, 44 Fed. R. Evid. Serv. 492 (7th Cir. 1996). During voir dire five members of the venire commented that in their opinion the judicial system was ineffective in apprehending and punishing offenders. The voir dire had not been conducted in camera and the court had accordingly to determine whether these comments compromised the impartiality of the other jurors and required the court to quash the entire venire. The court held that it had not, but the problem would never have arisen if individual voir dire had been conducted in camera. A similar dilemma confronted the trial judge in U.S. v. Lacey, 86 F.3d 956, 44 Fed. R. Evid. Serv. 1158 (10th Cir. 1996) when a prospective juror stated in front of the other jurors that his opinion of the defendant's guilt would be affected if the defendant did not take the stand and proclaim his innocence. The trial judge excused the juror and gave a cautionary instruction, and the appellate court found no abuse of discretion but one cannot know for certain what effect the juror's outburst had. Again, the problem would have been avoided by the use of individual in camera voir dire. And see Neely v. Newton, 149 F.3d 1074 (10th Cir. 1998) where, in response to voir dire questions on the insanity defense, and whether the jurors could return a verdict of NGRI if the facts warranted, one prospective juror referred to the defense as a "cop-out" that "puts people right back out [on the streets] again." Other jurors expressed similar reservations. The jurors in question were excused, and the trial judge told the panel that they should not concern themselves with the consequences of their verdict. On appeal the defendant argued that the court should have done more to correct the jurors' misconceptions or should have explained more fully the consequences of an NGRI verdict. The Court of Appeals found no error, stating that there was no showing that the jury was not impartial or that the defendant had been denied a fair opportunity to uncover juror bias. The technical merits of the holding aside, arguably the better practice would be for a trial judge to inform the jury of the effects of an NGRI verdict, as it can be expected that at least some jurors may be psychologically reluctant to release an "insane" criminal into their community. Again, however, the problem would be avoided by the use of individual in camera voir dire.

In U.S. v. Durman, 30 F.3d 803 (7th Cir. 1994), one of the members of the venire indicated in response to a court question at the beginning of jury selection that he had been previously called as a juror in a case where the defendants had been on trial. The court excused the juror for cause but denied the defense motion that the entire panel be dismissed. The court cautioned the remaining jurors that the fact that the defendants may have been in a courtroom on a previous occasion was no indication of what occurred on that occasion. The Court of Appeals found that this was not error. See also U.S. v. Moutry, 46 F.3d 598 (7th Cir. 1995) (failure of trial judge to strike entire panel after one prospective juror had made a potentially prejudicial remark in front of the other jurors held not to be plain error) U.S. v. Trujillo, 146 F.3d 838, 49 Fed. R. Evid. Serv. 1066 (11th Cir. 1998) (comment by prospective juror, who did not ultimately serve, that he might have seen the defendants in custody in the context of his employment as a corrections officer held not to warrant striking of entire jury panel). In Thompson v. Borg, 74 F.3d 1571 (9th Cir. 1996) a juror disclosed during voir dire that he had read in a newspaper that the defendant had pleaded guilty but had later withdrawn his guilty plea. The court held that this did not amount to prejudicial publicity. The court added that even if the disclosure fell within the category of juror misconduct, the error was harmless.

In U.S. v. Allen, 247 F.3d 741, 56 Fed. R. Evid. Serv. 1144 (8th Cir. 2001), cert. granted, judgment vacated on other grounds, 536 U.S. 953, 122 S. Ct. 2653, 153 L. Ed. 2d 830 (2002) and cert. denied, 123 S. Ct. 2273, 156 L. Ed. 2d 132 (U.S. 2003), a prospective juror, in response to a voir dire question, commented on the inadequacy of life imprisonment as a punishment. Defense counsel moved to dismiss for cause those jurors who had heard the comment but the judge refused. On appeal the court found no abuse of the judge's discretion and that the defendant had not suffered any prejudice.

Add at end of fourth paragraph:
In camera questioning which may be part and parcel of the jury selection process should be distinguished from informal colloquies between a trial judge and a juror ex parte. Nonetheless, in U.S. v. Duke, 255 F.3d 656 (8th Cir. 2001), cert. denied, 534 U.S. 1022, 122 S. Ct. 550, 151 L. Ed. 2d 426 (2001) the Court of Appeals stated that a trial judge has leeway in its management of the trial to question a juror whose qualifications have been called into doubt. In the case there had been not showing that the defendant had been prejudiced by the conversation or that it was in any way inappropriate.

On the other hand, in camera voir dire does have in-built strategic disadvantages. It may inhibit the development of the group "dynamic" that enables jurors to be able to func-

§ 9:8   Jury Selection: Law, Art & Science 2d

tion as an effective unit during deliberations. To achieve this dynamic, it is important that jurors have some sense of each other as persons, and perhaps even be aware of each other's idiosyncrasies and biases. This "sense of the other" is gained in part by listening to the responses of the other jurors to voir dire questions. Through their answers to questions jurors are introducing themselves to each other (as well as to the lawyers) and telling each other background information about themselves. An identification with other jurors will often take place during this phase, part of which comes simply from the awareness that they all are being subjected to the same probing and sometimes embarrassing scrutiny of their private lives and personal views by the lawyers and judge in the case. During breaks in the proceedings jurors often, perforce, will talk to each other. However, when jurors are kept separated and questioned one-by-one in camera, the shared experience of having been subjected to voir dire, which forms a common point for these initial, informal interactions, will be missing. It is in subtle ways such as these that individualized in camera voir dire can frustrate the development of the group dynamic. See generally Treger, *One Jury Indivisible: A Group Dynamics Approach to voir dire,* 68 Chicago-Kent L. Rev. 549 (1992).

Add after first sentence in fifth paragraph:
See, e.g., State v. Kamienski, 254 N.J. Super. 75, 603 A.2d 78 (App. Div. 1992). See also Lynd v. State, 262 Ga. 58, 414 S.E.2d 5 (1992) (denial of sequestered voir dire not abuse of discretion); Castor v. State, 587 N.E.2d 1281 (Ind. 1992) (same).

n. 28.
Add to note 28:
For an evaluation of the continuing viability of *Press-Enterprise Co* in the light of modern social science research, See Jones, *The Latest Empirical Studies on Pretrial Publicity, Jury Bias, and Judicial Remedies—Not Enough to Overcome the First Amendment Right of Access to Pretrial Hearings,* 40 Am U L Rev 841 (1991). See generally Annotation, Exclusion of public and media from voir dire examination of prospective jurors in state criminal case, 16 A.L.R. 5th 152.

Add after third sentence in sixth paragraph:
Although it might be the better practice, it has been held that there is no right to make one's challenges for cause outside the presence of the jury panel. Tuggle v. Thompson, 57 F.3d 1356 (4th Cir. 1995), cert. granted, judgment vacated on other grounds, 516 U.S. 10, 116 S. Ct. 283, 133 L. Ed. 2d 251 (1995).

§ 9:9 Attitudes and demeanor of counsel
n. 29.
Add to note 29:

VOIR DIRE GENERALLY § 9:10

See also Bennett & Hirschhorn, *Voir Dire in Criminal Cases: Choosing Jurors to Judge Your Client*, 28 Trial 68 (1992) (stressing importance of "(1) empathy, which says to the person being interviewed, 'I hear your feelings and thoughts, I hear your world'; (2) respect, which tells people their world will not be judged by the listener; and (3) congruence, which portrays the listener as a genuine person, inwardly and outwardly").

Add to end of first paragraph:
One might have thought that at a minimum a lawyer should be present during voir dire. In Mason v. Mitchell, 320 F.3d 604, 2003 FED App. 0042P (6th Cir. 2003), the defendant argued that lead counsel's absence during parts of jury selection denied him effective assistance of counsel. The Court of Appeals, however, found that the defendant had consented to the absences and that co-counsel had conducted an effective voir dire in counsel's absence.

§ 9:10 Juror's duty of full disclosure

Add after third sentence in first paragraph:
In U.S. v. Coleman, 997 F.2d 1101 (5th Cir. 1993), a juror had failed to mention an encounter with the Bureau of Alcohol, Tobacco, and Firearms when questioned about past troubles with any government agency. The court held that the juror's failure to mention the dispute suggested anti-government bias and justified the trial court's decision to remove the juror.

Add after first paragraph:
The Court of Appeals in U.S. v. Koon, 34 F.3d 1416, 40 Fed. R. Evid. Serv. 1 (9th Cir. 1994), judgment aff'd in part, rev'd in part, 518 U.S. 81, 116 S. Ct. 2035, 135 L. Ed. 2d 392 (1996), advised that when it is brought to the trial judge's attention that a juror may have failed to disclose relevant information during voir dire, the appropriate procedure is for the court to question the juror and excuse him or her if necessary, but not to reopen the whole jury selection process.

n. 33.
Add to note 33 after "Firestone":
But see, Dyer v. Calderon, 151 F.3d 970 (9th Cir. 1998) (state court's finding that juror was impartial was not entitled to presumption of correctness; juror's lies, during voir dire, warranted inference of implied bias; and "implied bias" was not new rule of law). See also Dall v. Coffin, 970 F.2d 964 (1st Cir. 1992) (defendant must show actual prejudice or bias "not as a matter of speculation, but as a demonstrable reality"). In U.S. v. Boney, 977 F.2d 624, 36 Fed. R. Evid. Serv. 1358 (D.C. Cir. 1992), the court held that the trial judge committed error in not holding an evidentiary hearing to determine whether the defendant had been prejudiced by a juror's lying about his felon status. In U.S. v. Walker, 99 F.3d 439 (D.C. Cir. 1996) the court that a juror's failure, in response to a question as to whether any juror had been accused of a crime other than a traffic offense

§ 9:10   JURY SELECTION: LAW, ART & SCIENCE 2D

during the previous 10 years, to disclose that he had been acquitted of a misdemeanor nine years and nine months previous (the actual charge had been filed 10 years and six months previous) was not sufficient to justify a new trial under McDonough.

Add to note 33:

; Annotation, Effect of juror's false or erroneous answer on voir dire regarding previous claims or actions against himself or his family, 66 A.L.R. 4th 509. An argument favoring the relaxation of the present approach by introducing a "possible" rather than an "actual" bias standard is made in Note, *When Jurors Lie: Differing Standards for New Trial,* 22 Am J Crim L 733 (1995)

Add after third paragraph:

See generally Note, *Juror Bias Undiscovered during voir dire: Legal Standards for Reviewing Claims of a Denial of the Constitutional Right to an Impartial Jury,* 39 Drake L Rev 201 (1989/90).

In U.S. v. North, 910 F.2d 843, 30 Fed. R. Evid. Serv. 961 (D.C. Cir. 1990), opinion withdrawn and superseded in part on reh'g, 920 F.2d 940, 122 A.L.R. Fed. 771 (D.C. Cir. 1990), a trial court's refusal to declare a mistrial where a juror had answered untruthfully to a question that might have led either side to challenge the juror for cause was upheld on appeal in large part because no showing had been made that the juror was unfair or partial. In contrast, in U.S. v. Colombo, 869 F.2d 149 (2d Cir. 1989) (failure of jury foreman to disclose that he was a former police officer held reversible error).

In U.S. v. Brown, 26 F.3d 1124 (D.C. Cir. 1994), a youth correction officer reported his law enforcement background on the jury questionnaire but failed to raise his hand when the panel was asked on voir dire about law enforcement background. The oversight was brought to the Court's attention by defense counsel and the court responded by questioning the juror in chambers. The defendant's challenge for cause to the juror on the basis that he had lied in not raising his hand and because the in-chamber questioning may have intimidated the juror was denied. The issue of actual bias of the juror was not directly raised at trial. The Court of Appeals held that there had not been the requisite showing of actual bias amounting to plain error to justify a reversal. See also Fuller v. Bowersox, 202 F.3d 1053 (8th Cir. 2000) (absent showing of bias, defendant's Sixth Amendment rights were not violated by juror's failure to disclose either his own previous employment with a law enforcement agency or the fact that his mother worked at the county jail where the defendant was held pending trial); U.S. v. Williams, 195 F.3d 823, 49 Env't. Rep. Cas. (BNA) 1605 (6th Cir. 1999) (judge's failure to order new trial where juror realized, during deliberations, that she had inadvertently failed to acknowledge that she was familiar with defendant's company, held not an abuse of discretion where both juror and other members of jury indicated that revelation would not affect their impartiality).

In U.S. v. Shaoul, 41 F.3d 811 (2d Cir. 1994), a juror failed to disclose his family relationship with a prosecutor, albeit not the one involved in the case. The Court of Appeals stated that *McDonough* established as a threshold requirement a showing of juror dishonesty. Thus, even though the relationship to the prosecutor might well have been an appropriate grounds for a challenge for cause, the judgment could not be reversed. The court took the opportunity to clarify its previous statement in U.S. v. Langford, 990 F.2d 65, 68, 38 Fed. R. Evid. Serv. 1141 (2d Cir. 1993) to the effect that "[w]e read [*McDonough's*] multipart test as governing not only inadvertent disclosures but also nondisclosures or misstatements that were deliberate." The statement was not to be understood as mandating a new trial whenever a correct disclosure would have sustained a challenge for cause, regardless of the juror's honesty in failing to answer the question correctly.

In U.S. v. Williams, 77 F.3d 1098 (8th Cir. 1996), the defendant, Marcus Williams, had claimed that the crime with which he had been charged had been committed by another person by the same name. During voir dire a juror was asked whether the names of the defendant and a codefendant meant anything to her. Apparently believing that the question related to the two defendants on trial, the juror failed to disclose that she had a grandson by the name of Marcus Williams. Although not a "textbook voir dire" in the eyes of the court (U.S. v. Williams, 77 F.3d 1098, 1101 (8th Cir. 1996)), it declined to order a new trial. Defense counsel, who was aware of the misidentification defense and was in the best position to question the jurors about the "other" Marcus Williams, was in large part responsible for failing to have made clear the nature of the voir dire question.

In Skaggs v. Otis Elevator Co., 528 U.S. 811, 120 S. Ct. 44, 145 L. Ed. 2d 39 (1999), the trial court had asked on voir dire whether any of the jurors had ever participated in a lawsuit either as a party or in some other capacity. None of the panel responded. It subsequently came to light that the foreperson of the jury had been involved in nine separate lawsuits. Skaggs filed a motion for a new trial, arguing that the juror's failure to respond to the Court's question denied her a fair trial. The court then held an evidentiary hearing at which the juror explained that he had failed to respond because he thought that the question related only to lawsuits similar to the one before the court. The judge found that this

§ 9:10

explanation lacked credibility, and that the juror had been intentionally dishonest. Although this finding was sufficient to satisfy the first prong of the *McDonough* test (that a juror has failed to answer honestly a material question on voir dire), the appellate court still had to determine whether a correct response would have provided a basis for a challenge for cause. Skaggs conceded that there were not sufficient grounds for a challenge for cause, and thus her *McDonough* claim had to fail. But this did not end the matter. The appellate court then proceeded to analyze whether the juror lacked impartiality, which would provide an independent ground for a new trial. However, it found no basis for finding either actual or implied bias, and the juror had consistently maintained that he was not biased. Although the court stated that a juror's dishonesty was a factor to be considered, it held that, standing by itself, it could not serve as the basis for a finding of implied bias as a matter of law. Otherwise, the court observed, *McDonough's* two pronged test would effectively be reduced to the single prong of dishonesty. The court speculated that an equally plausible explanation for the juror's silence might have been his embarrassment of having to admit that he had experienced significant financial difficulties in his life which had led to the lawsuits.

In Price v. Kramer, 200 F.3d 1237 (9th Cir. 2000) it was alleged that two jurors had withheld information during voir dire that reflected on their impartiality. One juror, while mentioning that he had had a negative experience with a police officer when a teenager, failed to mention that physical contact had occurred during the incident. The trial court questioned the juror and concluded that this omission was an honest mistake, particularly because with the benefit of hindsight the juror recognized that the officer was only doing his duty. The second incident of alleged misconduct involved a juror who omitted to mention that his half-brother was a police officer and that he himself had participated in a ride-along program approximately 14 years earlier. The trial court again questioned the juror and concluded that it was understandable that he might forget the ride-along program and that the juror had long been estranged from his half-brother. The Court of Appeals found no abuse of the judge's discretion and added that correct answers would not have provided a basis for challenge for causes in any event.

In U.S. v. Greer, 285 F.3d 158 (2d Cir. 2002), one of the jurors had stated in response to a question on the pretrial questionnaire that no relative of his had ever been accused of a crime. In fact, the juror's brother, a drug user (another fact not disclosed by the juror), had been convicted and incarcerated on at least two occasions. The juror also neglected to mention that his brother had been referred to by

Voir Dire Generally § 9:10

one of the government's witnesses at trial and that he (the juror) had received a telephone call during the trial that could have been construed as threatening. In its brief to the Court of Appeals, the defendant elected to focus on the juror's failure to alert the court regarding the telephone contact. The Court of Appeals found that the juror's omissions and less than wholly accurate answers were inadvertent and, furthermore, that accurate answers would not have supported a challenge for cause, as required under the second prong of *McDonough's* two-pronged test. Neither actual, implied, nor inferred bias on the part of the juror had been demonstrated.

In U.S. v. Saya, 247 F.3d 929 (9th Cir. 2001), opinion amended, 2001 WL 476942 (9th Cir. 2001) and cert. denied, 534 U.S. 1009, 122 S. Ct. 493, 151 L. Ed. 2d 404 (2001) a juror, in response to the written questionnaire given to potential jurors, indicated that he had not heard of the case or the defendant, and would be fair and impartial. After the trial was over, however, he admitted that he remembered seeing the defendant's face on television and hearing his name on the news. Subsequently, the juror changed his position, this time declaring that he in fact did not know anything about the defendant at the time the jury was chosen. The trial court found this last declaration to be more credible than the earlier one. In any event, the Court of Appeals found that the misstatements were not material and would not have provided a valid basis for a challenge for cause. Thus, neither prong of McDonough's two pronged test was satisfied.

In Jones v. Cooper, 311 F.3d 306 (4th Cir. 2002), cert. denied, 123 S. Ct. 2613 (U.S. 2003), the defendant had been convicted of murder and sentenced to death. An investigator subsequently employed by the defendant interviewed one of the jurors, who made several statements that indicated that the juror may not have answered certain questions on the jury questionnaire and on voir dire honestly and may in fact have been biased. On the questionnaire, the juror had answered "no" in response to questions asking whether any friends, family or acquaintances had ever been arrested or subjected to a trial. The investigator established that this was false and the Court of Appeals agreed, but stated that under state law it would not have afforded a basis for a challenge for cause. As to the other alleged misstatements, the court was of the opinion that they were more properly characterized as "inconsistencies" than "lies". For example, while the juror stated that she "never went" to the store that was the scene of the crime, she admitted to the investigator that she had. However, on voir dire she had stated that she lived in the area and had noticed that the store was boarded

§ 9:10   JURY SELECTION: LAW, ART & SCIENCE 2D

up after the crime. The court thought that the discrepancy could be attributed to juror's colloquial way of indicating that she rarely patronized the store in question. Two other discrepancies, however, were arguably of greater significance. First, the juror had stated on voir dire that she only had a vague knowledge of case. However, she told the investigator that she was aware of the defendant's previous trial and death sentence. The Court of Appeals explained this away by noting that the questions on voir dire had focused only on the juror's knowledge of the robbery and murder, and not on her knowledge of the defendant's previous trial or death sentence. Secondly, the investigator's affidavit recounted the juror's statement to him "that the Bible mandates imposition of the death penalty in every case of first degree murder" and that she "could not imagine any first degree murder case in which the death penalty would not be appropriate, other than if the defendant grew up in a jungle with no contact with humanity." The Court of Appeals, somewhat incredulously it is submitted, found no inconsistency between these statements regarding the death penalty and the juror's voir dire response where she declared her support for the death penalty "when appropriate" and stated she could fairly balance aggravating and mitigating circumstances. While admitting to being "troubled" by the various misstatements by the juror, the Court of Appeals found that there had not been a violation of McDonough Power Equipment, Inc. v. Greenwood, 464 U.S. 548, 104 S. Ct. 845, 78 L. Ed. 2d 663 (1984), and that the investigator's evidence did not demonstrate that the juror was actually or impliedly biased. See also U.S. v. Arocho, 305 F.3d 627, 59 Fed. R. Evid. Serv. 1556 (7th Cir. 2002) (juror's posttrial statement that he had been in contact with government witness less than five times totaling 30 or 40 minutes was not so inconsistent with his voir dire testimony that he had spoken to the witness only "in passing" as to demonstrate a failure to answer a voir dire question honestly or to require a new trial).

A juror's answers to voir dire questions may not only give rise to a violation of McDonough Power Equipment, Inc. v. Greenwood, 464 U.S. 548, 104 S. Ct. 845, 78 L. Ed. 2d 663 (1984), but also may indicate "implied bias". In Fields v. Woodford, 309 F.3d 1095 (9th Cir. 2002), opinion amended, 315 F.3d 1062 (9th Cir. 2002) a juror disclosed on voir dire that his wife had been the victim of an assault, beating and robbery. What the juror did not reveal, however, was that she had also been kidnapped and raped. Had the juror revealed these features, the parallel between his wife's experience and the facts of the case would have been more evident, as the defendant on trial was charged with kidnapping, robbery, and rape, as well as murder. As no credibility determi-

VOIR DIRE GENERALLY § 9:10

nation to which it owed deference had been made, the Court of Appeals remanded for an evidentiary hearing to consider the question of "implied bias". The Court of Appeals also instructed the district court to determine whether the juror in question had discussed the case with his wife during the trial and, if so, whether it affected his ability to be impartial, as alleged by the defendant.

Add after third paragraph:

In U.S. v. Collins, 972 F.2d 1385 (5th Cir. 1992), the court stated that the *McDonough* framework applied to the concealment of objective material facts, rather than subjective pretrial opinions. In the latter situation, the court said that it would defer to the district court's determination as to whether the defendant had received a fair trial by an impartial jury. Similarly, in U.S. v. Cerrato-Reyes, 176 F.3d 1253 (10th Cir. 1999) the Court of Appeals found that the trial judge had not erred in denying the defendant's motion for a new trial after it came to light for the first time during deliberations that a juror had stated that she lived in a Hispanic neighborhood and was fearful because of prior experiences with non-Hispanic drug dealers. The juror also made strong negative statements about Hispanic neighbors. During voir dire, in response to the court's questions about whether any of the panel were prejudiced against Hispanics or had prior experience with drug dealers, the juror had remained silent. The trial court ruled that the juror had either answered honestly or made a good faith mistake and refused to order a mistrial. The juror denied prejudice throughout the judge's questioning and the appellate court was prepared to defer to the trial judge's evaluation absent clear error, which it did not find.

A more problematic claim of good faith mistake arose in U.S. v. Tucker, 243 F.3d 499 (8th Cir. 2001), cert. denied, 534 U.S. 816, 122 S. Ct. 44, 151 L. Ed. 2d 16 (2001), a prosecution against a former governor of Arkansas. The juror in question had lived with, had a child by, and during trial had married, a man whom the defendant, as governor, had refused clemency. The court upheld the trial judge's ruling that there had been no showing of actual bias on the part of the juror. The court was willing to accept the juror's explanation that she did not think that the question asked of her during voir dire relating to family members applied to the man whom she had lived with and subsequently married, and with whom she had had a child. Nor was the court prepared on the facts to find either implied or presumed bias.

In Dall v. Coffin, 970 F.2d 964 (1st Cir. 1992), the court said that a juror cannot be faulted for failing to disclose information for which he was not specifically asked. It is

© West, a Thomson business, 11/2003

submitted that this technical reading of McDonough is at odds with the arguable duty of a juror to disclose information which might affect his or her ability to be impartial.

In Coughlin v. Tailhook Ass'n, 112 F.3d 1052 (9th Cir. 1997) one of the jurors who heard the case had been convicted of marijuana possession and in theory should have been disqualified from serving under 28 U.S.C.A. § 1865(b)(5). On appeal it was held that there had to be a showing of actual bias on the part of the juror for the court to grant a new trial. Nor did the fact that the juror had been dishonest, and not simply mistaken, in not disclosing this conviction afford an automatic basis for a new trial under *McDonough*. Similarly, in U.S. v. Bishop, 264 F.3d 535, 2001-2 U.S. Tax Cas. (CCH) ¶ 50762, 57 Fed. R. Evid. Serv. 1087, 88 A.F.T.R.2d 2001-5991 (5th Cir. 2001), cert. denied, 535 U.S. 1016, 122 S. Ct. 1605, 152 L. Ed. 2d 620 (2002), where a juror failed to reveal a previous felony conviction, the court began by stating that the fact that a statutorily disqualified felon had served as a juror was not an automatic basis for a new trial. The case having been completed, the defendant had to show that the juror was either biased or fundamentally incompetent, neither of which had been demonstrated. In this case, unlike in *Coughlin*, the juror apparently had not deliberately concealed her conviction, as her lawyer had told her that, because the adjudication of the charge against her had been deferred, she did not have to tell anybody about it.

In U.S. v. Wright, 119 F.3d 630, 47 Fed. R. Evid. Serv. 554 (8th Cir. 1997), a juror, in response to a question regarding his relationship to law enforcement personnel, failed to disclose that he was the nephew of a tribal children's court judge. On appeal, it was held that this answer was not necessarily dishonest and did not deprive the defendant of a fair trial. Similarly in U.S. v. Tucker, 137 F.3d 1016, 48 Fed. R. Evid. Serv. 1145 (8th Cir. 1998), a juror was asked whether any member of her family had ever been charged with a crime. In response to the question, the juror failed to reveal that the man whom she was then living with and with whom she had a child, and to whom she was married during the course of the defendant's trial, had been convicted of serious drugs offenses. The government argued that the juror's answer was accurate because, as she was not married at the time she was asked the question, the person with whom she was living was not a member of her family. The court ruled that the question could have been interpreted as asking about people with whom the juror shared a close familial-like relationship and therefore a *McDonough* hearing was required to determine whether the defendant had been denied his right to an impartial jury. At that hearing the defendant would have to show not only that the juror had deceived the court, but also that she had done so because of partiality, and that if she had given complete and honest answers at voir dire, she would have been subject to challenge for cause. In Von Kahl v. U.S., 242 F.3d 783 (8th Cir. 2001), cert. denied, 534 U.S. 941, 122 S. Ct. 317, 151 L. Ed. 2d 237 (2001) a juror had admitted in voir dire that he had lived in the same small town as the prosecutor, but neglected to state that they had been friends or that they had gone to the same school together. On these facts the Court of Appeals declined to find concealed bias on the juror's part.

In Dyer v. Calderon, 151 F.3d 970 (9th Cir. 1998), a juror was asked in a series of questions whether she or any member of her family had ever been involved with or had been a victim of crime. The juror answered "no", even though her brother had died of a suspicious shotgun wound, the juror herself had once been attacked by a cousin with a knife, her father had been arrested for kidnapping his children, her family home and car had been burglarized on multiple occasions, and her former husband had been arrested for rape. The court, according great deference to the trial judge's firsthand impressions, decided that the juror had not been dishonest or misleading under *McDonough*, and, perhaps more to the point, that there was no reason to believe that the juror would have been excused for cause had she answered more candidly. Dyer v. Calderon, 122 F.3d 720 (9th Cir. 1997), opinion vacated on reh'g en banc, 151 F.3d 970 (9th Cir. 1998).

The Court of Appeals initially affirmed, but, on rehearing en banc, held that the state court's finding that the juror was impartial was not entitled to a presumption of correctness. Moreover, it held that the juror's lies during voir dire warranted an inference of implied bias. Dyer v. Calderon, 151 F.3d 970 (9th Cir. 1998). A similar conclusion was reached in Green v. White, 232 F.3d 671 (9th Cir. 2000) where the court held that a juror's lies concerning his disqualifying criminal history, his inappropriate behavior in making false statements on the jury questionnaire and during voir dire, and his attempts to cover up his behavior in posttrial proceedings, required a finding of actual bias. The juror's pattern of lies had, according to the court, introduced a "destructive uncertainty" into the fact-finding process that entitled the petitioner to relief on the basis of a violation of his right to a fair trial.

Add after second sentence in fifth paragraph:
While an incomplete or not fully accurate answer by a juror to a voir dire question will often be inadvertent, a series of such answers may give rise to an altogether different

§ 9:10

inference. This point seems to have been lost on the court in U.S. v. Patrick, 965 F.2d 1390 (6th Cir. 1992), cert. granted, judgment vacated on other grounds, 507 U.S. 956, 113 S. Ct. 1378, 122 L. Ed. 2d 754 (1993) and adhered to as amended, 993 F.2d 123 (6th Cir. 1993) supra. The juror in question (Cunningham) withheld information or gave misleading answers to several unrelated questions:

1. The venire was asked whether any juror was acquainted with the witness "James Dennis of Clay City." After the witness had testified, Cunningham admitted that he recognized the witness. He states that he had not responded affirmatively to the voir dire question because he knew the witness as "James Ed Dennis.";
2. The venire was asked whether they had any relatives or close friends in law enforcement. Cunningham failed to disclose that his brother was a deputy jailer, subsequently claiming that he was unaware that a deputy jailer was involved in law enforcement. He also failed to disclose his past friendship with a sheriff who by the time of the trial had died;
3. The panel was asked whether they had knowledge of or were familiar with Delmus Gross. Cunningham did not disclose that his brother had bought a truck from Gross's car dealership;
4. The panel was asked whether they had knowledge of or had had dealings with Season Sash. Cunningham did not reveal that his first cousin was employed by Sash. He subsequently claimed that he was not aware of his cousin's employment until after the trial; and
5. Jurors were asked if they had any close relatives or friends who had been a criminal defendant. Cunningham did not acknowledge that his brother had pled guilty to the misdemeanor of possession of gambling records. He first maintained that he thought that the question had only to do with felonies, but after being informed that it was addressed to any crime, said that he did not think that the question applied to a plea bargain.

While any of the juror's misleading answers might not, as the court found, have been deliberate, the cumulative effect certainly seems suspicious. Nonetheless, the court stated that for a new trial to be ordered, the defendants had to show "actual bias," and that the record did not reveal such bias on Cunningham's part.

§ 9:11 Court's duty and discretion

n. 41.

Add to note 41:

Whether to reopen voir dire and, if so, what questions to permit, are matters that lie within a judge's discretion. In U.S. v. Adams, 305 F.3d 30 (1st Cir. 2002), the defendant had requested that voir dire be reopened to determine if any of the jurors had friends or relatives who had suffered in the 9/11 terrorist attack and, if so, whether such jurors could remain impartial. The trial court's refusal to reopen was held not an abuse of its discretion. The defendant was charged with possession of a firearm but not a violent act, and his crime was not alleged to be connected with terrorist activity. The defendant had already confessed in writing to the key facts, so that police credibility, which had already been tested in the original voir dire, was an issue of minimal importance.

In Chavez v. Cockrell, 310 F.3d 805 (5th Cir. 2002), cert. denied, 123 S. Ct. 1501, 155 L. Ed. 2d 241 (U.S. 2003), the defendant had been fitted with a "stun belt", which delivered a 50,000 volt electrical charge if activated. Such a device is used to restrain defendants who are thought to be likely to be unruly during trial. In the case, defendant's stun belt inadvertently was activated, with the effect that defendant first made an outburst, and then collapsed. The issue before the courts was whether the impartiality of the jury was compromised by the incident. The defendant argued that the incident had left an unfavorable impression of the defendant in the jurors' minds. The Court of Appeals rejected the defendant's contention, noting that the judge's extensive inquiry following the incident, as well as the individual questioning of jurors by counsel, had failed to unearth any evidence of partiality on the jurors' part. Both the state appellate court and the state habeas court had determined that the incident had no bearing on the decision to convict, and the Court of Appeals did not believe that this conclusion was manifestly erroneous.

In Kasi v. Angelone, 300 F.3d 487 (4th Cir. 2002), cert. denied, 537 U.S. 1025, 123 S. Ct. 551, 154 L. Ed. 2d 439 (2002), a high profile trial, the jury had convicted the defendant in connection with the murder of several CIA employees. Following its verdict in the guilt phase of the trial, the jurors inquired of the judge whether they should be aware of any activities or information regarding their personal safety and whether there were any precautions or security measures available to them. The defendant then requested individual voir dire of the jurors to determine if there had been discussion or speculation of any such danger and, in the alternative, moved for a mistrial. Both motions were denied. Instead, the judge met with the jurors as a group, and assured them that the same security measures were being taken as would be the case in any capital and high-publicity trial. Two days later, four Americans were murdered in Pakistan, and there was speculation in the media that the murders may have been committed by sympathizers of the defendant as retaliation for his conviction. Defendant brought the news reports to the attention of the court and again requested individual voir dire, this time to determine if any of the jurors had knowledge of the reports. Again, this motion, as well as defendant's alternative motion for a mistrial, was denied. However, the judge did address the jury and, along with his usual inquiry as to whether anyone had been exposed to media accounts of the trial, asked specifically about news reports that had appeared on the front page of various newspapers, TV and radio in relation to the case. There were no positive responses to either query, but the judge subsequently decided to sequester the jury. Shortly after being informed that the jury would be sequestered, one of the jurors sent the judge a private note indicating that she had heard the beginnings of a report about the Pakistan killings on her radio. She stated that had not responded to the judge's inquiry because she had not considered the killings to be related to the trial until the decision to sequester. After consulting with counsel, the judge and counsel proceeded to conduct an individual voir dire of this juror, in which she repeated her assertion that she was not aware (and remained unaware) that the Pakistan killings had anything to do with the trial. She also indicated that she had not discussed the matter with the other jurors and affirmed that she could remain fair and impartial. Defendant moved to conduct an individual voir dire of the other jurors but the motion was denied. Having reviewed these facts and the voir dire, the Court of Appeals held that the trial court's voir dire was sufficient to assure the defendant a fair and impartial jury, and found that the trial court had not abused its discretion in refusing to allow any of the requested instances of individual voir dire.

In Sallahdin v. Gibson, 275 F.3d 1211 (10th Cir. 2002) the Court of Appeals found no abuse of discretion in the trial judge's refusal to reopen voir dire in respect to a juror who had maintained on voir dire that he could be fair and impartial, but later stated that he could not be a fair juror. The decision appears questionable, particularly given that the charge was capital murder, but the court drew support from the failure of the defendant to exercise a peremptory challenge against the juror in question. For the same reason, the court rejected defendant's claim of error in the trial court's refusal to remove another juror for cause. In respect to another juror whom the defendant did challenge peremptorily after the court rejected a challenge for cause, the court held that the peremptory challenge cured any constitutional error.

In U.S. v. Ortiz, 315 F.3d 873, 59 Fed. R. Evid. Serv. 1063 (8th Cir. 2002), cert. denied, 123 S. Ct. 2095, 155 L. Ed. 2d 1078 (U.S. 2003), another capital case, the defendants argued first, that the judge had failed to conduct a sufficiently "searching" voir dire of racial bias to allow them to exercise their peremptory challenges in an intelligent manner; secondly, that the judge had failed to conduct a proper examination of the venire during the death-penalty-qualification phase of the trial; and finally, that the judge had improperly questioned potential jurors regarding their feelings about immunized witnesses during general voir dire. In respect to the first issue, the Court of Appeals stated that, although general questioning on racial bias is sufficient to pass constitutional muster, the better practice is to ask direct probing questions of individual jurors, particularly when the circumstances suggest the possibility of bias. In fact, the judge had individually questioned jurors who had expressed the view on the jury questionnaire that certain races were more violent than other races, and the Court of Appeals found no error in the judge's approach. In respect to the voir dire questioning on death qualification, again the Court of Appeals found no error. Finally, in respect to the alleged improper questioning on the credibility of immunized witnesses, where the defendants alleged that the judge's questions had tended to lend credibility to a government witness who had been granted immunity, the Court of Appeals was of the opinion that the questioning was impartial and fell within the trial court's discretion.

Some issues engender such strong feelings in the community that the possibility of juror bias is high. In such instances, there is a need for specific voir dire questioning. One such issue, identified by the court in U.S. v. Payne, 944 F.2d 1458, 33 Fed. R. Evid. Serv. 1316 (9th Cir. 1991), is child sexual abuse. The trial judge in the case declined to ask defendant's specific questions relating to child sexual abuse, but did engage in general questioning regarding whether any of the jurors or their family members had been victims of crime. These questions elicited information regarding jurors' personal experiences with child molestation cases and led the Court of Appeals to find there had been no abuse of discretion by the judge in declining to ask the more specific questions.

Payne might be profitably contrasted with U.S. v. Miguel, 111 F.3d 666 (9th Cir. 1997), where the Court of Appeals held that the trial court in a sexual abuse case had not abused its discretion in refusing to excuse for cause two jurors who had indicated that they themselves had been the victims of child molestation and two others who were relatives of victims of child molestation. The trial judge had questioned all four jurors individually and had concluded that they could be fair and impartial. The holding is questionable, given that the psychological trauma experienced by child sex abuse victims is often repressed and as a result may not surface in response to voir dire questioning.

In Sasaki v. Class, 92 F.3d 232, 71 Fair Empl. Prac. Cas. (BNA) 709, 69 Empl. Prac. Dec. (CCH) ¶ 44353 (4th Cir. 1996) a sexual harassment case, the refusal of the trial judge to inquire as to whether any jurors, members of their family, or close friends had been the subject of sexual harassment in the workplace was held not to be an abuse of the judge's discretion. The judge apparently had asked general questions likely to have elicited the same information.

In Monroe v. City of Phoenix, Ariz., 248 F.3d 851 (9th Cir. 2001) an arrestee sued the city and a police officer for false arrest and imprisonment, assault, and battery, and for violation of his civil rights. The plaintiff requested the trial judge to inquire about the jurors' attitudes to certain high-profile cases involving police misconduct. The judge declined to do so but asked more general questions relating to police misconduct, as well inquiring about the jurors' views on the Phoenix police department The Court of Appeals found that these questions were sufficient to identify potential bias, and ruled that the trial court had no obligation to ask about the specific cases requested.

See also U.S. v. Lawes, 292 F.3d 123 (2d Cir. 2002) (failure to ask proposed voir dire questions regarding jurors' attitudes toward police was not reversible error).

In U.S. v. Steele, 298 F.3d 906 (9th Cir. 2002), cert. denied, 537 U.S. 1096, 123 S. Ct. 710, 154 L. Ed. 2d 646 (2002) it emerged during voir dire that one of the jurors was an attorney employed as a public defender. The prosecutor then proceeded to ask the juror: "In the course of trying [felony robbery] cases, did you ever make a decision that your client was guilty and you've just got to do whatever you have got to do because that's your job." The juror answered: "I guess so, yeah. You know, it gets—the facts might show one way or the other, and you have to pursue the case if the client wants to or not, it's their decision." Defense counsel objected, arguing that the questioning tainted the jury by creating the erroneous impression that a defense attorney may have to proceed to trial even though the attorney believes the client is guilty. The prosecutor disputed this characterization, but indicated that she would discontinue the voir dire of the juror if the defense would agree to stipulate to excuse the juror for cause. The defense agreed to this stipulation, but also moved for a mistrial, which was denied. In addition, defense counsel refused the offer from the judge for a curative instruction because he believed that such an instruction would only serve to exacerbate the misconceptions already created. On appeal, the Court of Appeals found no abuse of the trial judge's discretion. The Court of Appeals noted that the prosecutor's question did

§ 9:11

not improperly comment on the defendant's counsel or compare defense counsel's experience with that of the juror; that the voir dire of the juror had stopped after the single question and was never referred to again; and that there was no indication that the prosecutor had intentionally sought to create the impression that all defense attorneys would lie or distort the facts to confuse a jury as to their client's guilt. The questioning also was held not to have tainted the jury pool. The juror's answer could not reasonably be viewed as an expert opinion to the effect that all defense lawyers defended obviously guilty clients, and reflected only upon the experience of the particular juror. Further, the fact that the juror was dismissed for cause presumably lessened any potential prejudicial effect on the other jurors. Finally, the Court of Appeals noted that defense counsel had refused a curative instruction that could have obviated any potential prejudice.

Add after second paragraph:

It is often difficult for a court to perceive clearly its own errors. In U.S. v. Iribe-Perez, 129 F.3d 1167 (10th Cir. 1997), the trial judge erroneously informed the jurors that the defendant would be pleading guilty. In fact the defendant did not plead guilty, but the judge permitted jurors who had heard his remark to serve nonetheless. On appeal this was held to be reversible error, the defendant having been denied his right to an impartial jury. The error was not cured by the judge's obtaining a commitment from the jurors to decide the case solely on the evidence. In the circumstances, bias had to be presumed. The decision in Iribe-Perez might be compared with that in Scott v. Mitchell, 209 F.3d 854, 2000 FED App. 0138P (6th Cir. 2000), where the judge, during voir dire, referred to the notoriety of the case and stated "Not only was Mr. Scott—at least from the newspaper reports that I think I had read—was involved in this, there were three other— . . . " At this point the defense objected and the court gave a curative instruction attempting to point out its lack of knowledge of the case beyond the article. The defendant then moved for a mistrial, which the court denied, again stressing its neutrality and the jury's obligation to decide the case solely on the evidence. On these facts the Court of Appeals held that the trial judge had not exceeded his authority in pointing out the existence of the article. It also stated that allegations that a jury had been somehow prejudiced by events that occurred before the jurors took their oath to be impartial had to be viewed with skepticism. Finally, the Court of Appeals was prepared to presume that the two curative instructions that had been given had been effective absent a showing of an "overwhelming probability" that they had been ignored.

n. 43.

 Add to note 43:

Similarly, in U.S. v. Gray, 105 F.3d 956 (5th Cir. 1997), the court found that the trial judge had not abused his discretion in restricting the attorneys on each side to five minutes for additional voir dire and requiring challenges to be made in 10 minutes. See also Ratliff v. Schiber Truck Co., Inc., 150 F.3d 949, 49 Fed. R. Evid. Serv. 1450 (8th Cir. 1998) (district court did not abuse its discretion in allowing counsel 20 minutes for voir dire). Nanninga v. Three Rivers Elec. Co-op., 203 F.3d 529 (8th Cir. 2000), reh'g en banc granted, opinion vacated on other grounds, (Oct. 30, 2000) and on reh'g en banc, 236 F.3d 902 (8th Cir. 2000) (same); U.S. v. Smallwood, 188 F.3d 905 (7th Cir. 1999) (denial of extra time for voir dire beyond 30 minutes allocated by court was not error where counsel neither objected when told time up nor requested additional time; also, doubt was raised in respect to credibility of reason claimed for extra time—that it was needed to probe racial prejudice—by fact that counsel had asked no questions relating to race during initial 30 minutes).

Arbitrarily imposed time limits on voir dire, however, are arguably improper and to be avoided. State v. Jones, 596 So. 2d 1360 (La. Ct. App. 1st Cir. 1992), writ denied, 598 So. 2d 373 (La. 1992); Salazar v. State, 107 Nev. 982, 823 P.2d 273 (1991) (trial court's limitation of defense counsel's voir dire to 30 minutes was arbitrary and unreasonable). See also Woolridge v. State, 827 S.W.2d 900 (Tex. Crim. App. 1992) (trial judge may not impose restrictions on voir dire questions on the mere possibility that questions might lengthen the voir dire process).

In Montiel v. City of Los Angeles, 2 F.3d 335, 37 Fed. R. Evid. Serv. 1008, 26 Fed. R. Serv. 3d 832 (9th Cir. 1993), the court, in reviewing a *Batson* claim, offered a novel reason for a court to exercise its discretion to allow extra time for voir dire under Fed R Crim P 24(a) (criminal cases) and Fed R Civ P 47(a) (civil cases). The court observed that the questioning which occurred during the additional time might shed light on the true reasons for the parties' exercise of peremptory challenges, thereby assisting the appellate court faced with ruling on a claimed *Batson* violation. The United States Supreme Court in J.E.B. v. Alabama ex rel. T.B., 511 U.S. 127, 114 S. Ct. 1419, 128 L. Ed. 2d 89, 64 Empl. Prac. Dec. (CCH) ¶ 42967 (1994) made a similar point. The Court said:

> If conducted properly, voir dire can inform litigants about potential jurors, making reliance upon stereotypical and pejorative notions about a particular gender or race both unnecessary and unwise. voir dire provides a means of discovering actual or implied bias and a firmer basis upon which the parties may exercise their peremptory challenges. See also Comment, *Don't Mess with Texas Voir Dire*, 39 Houston L. Rev. 201 (2002) (arguing against the adoption of rigid time limits on voir dire and for leaving the matter within the discretion of the judge).

While lawyers often complain about the limited time that they are allotted in which to conduct voir dire, it has been pointed out that too often attorneys waste valuable voir dire time lecturing jurors about the law or trying to change long-held attitudes. See Smith, *Challenges of Jury Selection*, 88 ABA Journal 34 (2002). Arguably, lawyers would be better advised, when the time allocated for voir dire is limited, to focus on the most problematic and worrisome aspects of the case at hand. Smith, *Challenges of Jury Selection*, 88 ABA Journal 34 (2002).

Add to fourth paragraph:
In Morgan v. Illinois, 504 U.S. 719, 112 S. Ct. 2222, 119 L. Ed. 2d 492 (1992), the United States Supreme Court held that a trial judge was required, upon a defendant's request, to inquire into the jurors' views on capital punishment. See also Art Press, Ltd. v. Western Printing Machinery Co., 791

§ 9:11 JURY SELECTION: LAW, ART & SCIENCE 2D

F.2d 616 (7th Cir. 1986). The failure to allow questions regarding the level of a juror's education or the juror's attitudes to the general nature or particular facts of the case unduly restricted voir dire.

n. 46.

Add to note 46:

The limitation of voir dire by statute in criminal but not civil cases has been held not to violate the equal protection clause. People v. Leung, 5 Cal. App. 4th 482, 7 Cal. Rptr. 2d 290 (6th Dist. 1992), opinion modified, (Apr. 28, 1992).

Add at end of section:

When potentially prejudicial newspapers articles are published during the trial, the court may have to re-open voir dire in order to determine whether jurors were exposed to the articles and what effect it might have had on them. Of course, to do so will be time-consuming and risks drawing the jurors' attention to articles that they might not have seen. The matter lies within the Court's discretion. But see U.S. v. Zichettello, 208 F.3d 72 (2d Cir. 2000), cert. denied, 531 U.S. 1143, 121 S. Ct. 1077, 148 L. Ed. 2d 954 (2001) ("when a trial court determines that media coverage has the 'potential for unfair prejudice', it is obligated to 'canvass the jury to find out if they have learned of the potentially prejudicial publicity' and, if necessary, voir dire the jury to 'ascertain how much they know of the distracting publicity and what effect, if any, it has had on that juror's ability to decide the case fairly'" citing U.S. v. Gaggi, 811 F.2d 47, 51, 22 Fed. R. Evid. Serv. 586 (2d Cir. 1987)). In U.S. v. Rasco, 123 F.3d 222 (5th Cir. 1997), the articles in question were basically factual, contained little in the way of information that the jurors were not already aware of, and was amenable to a curative instruction (an approach to which defense counsel had not objected to at the time). In these circumstances it was held that the trial court had not abused its discretion in not reopening voir dire. Where a court does choose to re-open voir dire, its decision whether or not to dismiss a juror exposed to the potentially prejudicial article will be upheld absent an abuse of discretion. See U.S. v. Lorefice, 192 F.3d 647 (7th Cir. 1999) (judge was in best position to assess juror's statement that he could be fair despite having seen the article in question).

In U.S. v. Chanthadara, 230 F.3d 1237 (10th Cir. 2000), cert. denied, 534 U.S. 992, 122 S. Ct. 457, 151 L. Ed. 2d 376 (2001) the midtrial publicity was generated by the trial judge, who opined, out of hearing of the jury, that a proffered defense was a "smoke screen." The remark was overheard by a journalist, and subsequently reported in the newspaper. The judge asked the jurors if they had seen or read the article, and six jurors admitted to seeing, but not reading, the article. The judge now gave a curative instruction to the effect that anything that he had said was not evidence and was not to be considered by the jury as reflecting his judgment of the merits of the case or the verdict that they should reach. The court also individually questioned the six jurors who admitted having seen the article to ensure itself that they could remain impartial. All stated that they would not be affected by the article. Nevertheless, the defendant moved for a mistrial. The motion was denied, and the denial was upheld on appeal. The Court of Appeals found that the error was harmless, not because the judge's instructions were able to cure the prejudice but rather because the evidence of defendant's guilt was overwhelming. The court was of the opinion, however, that the judge's remark might have compromised the jury's consideration of the appropriate penalty, and it vacated the sentence of death and remanded for resentencing.

Other midtrial situations can give rise to a need to re-open voir dire. In Soria v. Johnson, 207 F.3d 232 (5th Cir. 2000) the juror in question had stated during voir dire that he did not know of any reason why he could not be fair and impartial. During trial the juror recalled a vague and casual conversation that he had overheard about the killing at issue. The defendant's name had not been mentioned in the conversation, however, and the Court of Appeals found that the trial court had not committed error in declining to re-open voir dire to question the juror about the conversation and its effects on his ability to be impartial. See also Andrews v. Collins, 21 F.3d 612 (5th Cir. 1994).

In State v. Varner, 643 N.W.2d 298 (Minn. 2002) racial bias was improperly introduced during the trial proceedings by a chance remark from one juror to other jurors during a break in a drug and firearm prosecution. The juror had observed that, in his experience, "if you were to walk down that street [in the area of the alleged crime] being a white person and if you were not either beat up or robbed, it was considered a miracle." The Minnesota Supreme Court held that the remark raised serious questions of possible prejudice to the defendant and obligated the trial judge to grant the defendant's request to question all of the jurors about their possible exposure to the comment.

In U.S. v. Reynolds, 189 F.3d 521 (7th Cir. 1999), a juror sent a note to the judge, complaining that the presence in the gallery of Louis Farrakahn, a well known black activist, was distracting. The defendant, when informed of this development, requested that the court voir dire the jury to determine if Farrakhan's presence had prejudiced them in any way. The court declined, observing that the proposed voir dire would call undue attention to the issue and exacerbate any problem that might exist. The judge did, however, inform the jury that spectators had a right to be present in the courtroom and that they had to decide the case based on the evidence. The Court of Appeals held that the trial court did not abuse its discretion in declining to voir dire the jury.

§ 9:12 Example: Racial prejudice questions

n. 53.
   Add to note 53:
   See also U.S. v. Brown, 938 F.2d 1482, 33 Fed. R. Evid. Serv. 790 (1st Cir. 1991) (mere fact that defendant was black and all government's witnesses, as well as all jurors, were white did not require judge to conduct voir dire on issue of racial prejudice, even if such questioning might have been advisable).

Add after first sentence in last paragraph:
   See also U.S. v. Kyles, 40 F.3d 519 (2d Cir. 1994) (trial judge required to inquire into racial bias on voir dire when requested by defendant in a case where there were "substantial indications" that racial or ethnic prejudice could affect jurors). No special circumstances requiring an inquiry into racial bias were found in U.S. v. Okoronkwo, 46 F.3d 426, 75 A.F.T.R.2d 95-1339 (5th Cir. 1995) where the defendants were not charged with a crime of violence. See also U.S. v. Washington, 48 F.3d 73 (2d Cir. 1995) (no racial dimension in respect to crime or evidence that would require specific inquiry into each juror's racial attitudes).

   In U.S. v. Madrigal, 43 F.3d 1367 (10th Cir. 1994), the Court of Appeals held that a trial judge does not necessarily have to use the specific questions preferred by the defendant. Thus the issue of racial bias was held to have been covered by the trial court's questioning of potential jurors regarding their prior associations with the Hispanic community, their knowledge of the Spanish language, and whether they might be prejudiced either for or against the defendant because of his background. See also U.S. v. Okoronkwo, 46 F.3d 426, 75 A.F.T.R.2d 95-1339 (5th Cir. 1995) (although trial judge did not question jurors about possible prejudice to foreigners, he did admonish jury not to take into consideration the defendants' race, nationality, or unusual sounding names).

   In U.S. v. Barber, 80 F.3d 964, 44 Fed. R. Evid. Serv. 281 (4th Cir. 1996) an interracial couple was charged with laundering the proceeds from the sale of marijuana. The trial judge refused to allow voir dire questioning regarding juror racial attitudes and the Court of Appeals affirmed. The latter reasoned that the charge had no racial overtones, and that race was not bound up with the conduct of the trial. It was not prepared to entertain the thesis that there might be some jurors who might be inclined to convict because of a bias against interracial couples. The court stated that to allow questioning on racial attitudes might prove socially divisive and inject race into a trial which had no racial dimensions. A dissenting opinion noted that there had been a 300-year taboo on interracial marriages in the state, that it was not until 1967 that state antimiscegenation laws forbidding such marriages were held unconstitutional [Loving v. Virginia, 388 U.S. 1, 87 S. Ct. 1817, 18 L. Ed. 2d 1010 (1967)], and that public opinion polls indicated that marriages between blacks and whites were still disapproved of by a majority of southerners. In light of this background, and given the fact that the defendants' marriage was undenied and its interracial character obvious, it would have seemed that the better practice, regardless of any legal strictures, would have been to allow questioning on the issue of racial prejudice.

§ 9:13 Scope of examination

n. 56.

  Add to note 56:
  Davis v. State, 830 S.W.2d 206 (Tex. App. Houston 14th Dist. 1992), petition for discretionary review granted, (Sept. 30, 1992) and judgment rev'd on other grounds, 872 S.W.2d 743 (Tex. Crim. App. 1994) (defendant's inquiry into whether jurors held views concerning relationship between being held in jail and presumption of innocence held proper where fact that defendant was being held in jail would be brought out at trial).

n. 57.

  Add to note 57:
  In U.S. v. Fish, 928 F.2d 185 (6th Cir. 1991), the defendant was charged with unlawful possession of a firearm by a felon. On voir dire, the trial court refused to ask questions designed to explore the jurors' experiences with firearms and their opinions regarding the right of an individual to own firearms. The appellate court found no violation of defendant's rights, stating that a judge need only ask those questions the response to which would afford the basis for a challenge for a cause. The trial judge had inquired into general prejudices, biases, and interests, and had permitted counsel to ask further questions, albeit not the ones which were the subject of the appeal. Compare Art Press, Ltd. v. Western Printing Machinery Co., 791 F.2d 616 (7th Cir. 1986) (trial judge erred in not permitting inquiry into the level of a juror's education or the juror's attitudes to the general nature or particular facts of the case). See also U.S. v. Badru, 97 F.3d 1471, 45 Fed. R. Evid. Serv. 1026 (D.C. Cir. 1996) (no right to question jurors about whether any of their friends had ever been charged with a criminal offense).

  Add after second sentence in second paragraph:
  But see Woolridge v. State, 827 S.W.2d 900 (Tex. Crim. App. 1992) (trial judge may not impose restrictions on voir dire

§ 9:13

questions on the mere possibility that questions might lengthen the voir dire process).

Add at end of third paragraph:
State v. Smith, 222 Conn. 1, 608 A.2d 63 (1992) (no error in refusing to allow defense to ask voir dire question about interracial marriage in prosecution for murder).

n. 61.
Add to note 61:
The point is even more compelling when a defendant is charged with a capital offense. In Morgan v. Illinois, 504 U.S. 719, 112 S. Ct. 2222, 119 L. Ed. 2d 492 (1992), the United States Supreme Court held that a trial judge's general questioning in respect to the jurors' fairness and willingness to follow the law was insufficient to detect those members of the panel who would automatically vote for the death penalty if the defendant were to be convicted. Such a belief, that the death penalty should automatically follow from a conviction for a capital offense, was inconsistent with the demands of impartiality. Therefore, it was error for the trial court to fail to accede to the defendant's request for specific questioning on this point. A voir dire question as whether the death penalty was a deterrent was held properly to have been excluded as irrelevant in McQueen v. Scroggy, 99 F.3d 1302, 35 Fed. R. Serv. 3d 1211, 1996 FED App. 0349P (6th Cir. 1996).

n. 63.
Add to note 63:
But compare People v. Campos, 227 Ill. App. 3d 434, 169 Ill. Dec. 598, 592 N.E.2d 85 (1st Dist. 1992) (no error in judge's refusal to ask defendant's proposed questions as to whether jurors believed that fetus was living being, and whether it was a sin to have an abortion, where defendant was charged with intentional homicide of unborn child and not abortion).

§ 9:14 Jurors' privacy rights

Add at beginning of section:
Jurors have many privacy interests, including limiting exposure of sensitive information about themselves, being reassured about their safety, and feeling they are not being unfairly stereotyped. See Rose, *Expectations of privacy? Jurors' views of voir dire questions*, 85 Judicature 10 (2001). The author advocates greater use of questionnaires and the routine use of anonymous juries. Such an approach would, of course, have significant knock-on effects, and would severely impede an attorney's ability to engage in pretrial investigations of prospective jurors. Hamnaford, however, sees the problem more in terms of judges failing to distinguish between information that is relevant to the case and information that is not relevant to the fairness or impartiality of prospective jurors. He advocates destroying or at least sealing information revealed on voir dire after the parties have accepted that a jury verdict is the product of a fair and

VOIR DIRE GENERALLY § 9:14

impartial process. Hamnaford, *Safeguarding Juror Privacy*, 85 Judicature 18 (2001).

Add at end of second paragraph:
See also U.S. v. Taylor, 92 F.3d 1313, 45 Fed. R. Evid. Serv. 442 (2d Cir. 1996) (no violation of Sixth Amendment in judge's refusal to ask open-ended questions).

n. 65.
Add to note 65:
See generally Annotation, Exclusion of public and media from voir dire examination of prospective jurors in state criminal case, 16 A.L.R. 5th 152.

In U.S. v. Darden, 70 F.3d 1507, 43 Fed. R. Evid. Serv. 321 (8th Cir. 1995), the Eighth Circuit Court of Appeals upheld the use of an anonymous jury. The defendants were involved in an extremely violent organized criminal enterprise, the enterprise had a history of intimidating as well as murdering witnesses and many of its members remained at large. The defendants faced possible sentences of life imprisonment, and the case had been highly publicized. There thus was, in the opinion of the court, "ample reason" for impaneling an anonymous jury. The Court of Appeals also approved of the trial court's tactic, used in other jurisdictions, of telling the jurors that they were being identified by number rather than name so that the media would not ask them questions. Accord, U.S. v. Peoples, 250 F.3d 630, 56 Fed. R. Evid. Serv. 331 (8th Cir. 2001). See also U.S. v. DeLuca, 137 F.3d 24 (1st Cir. 1998) (upholding impaneling of anonymous jury and approving judge's explanation that jurors identities were being kept secret to ensure that nonextrajudicial information would be conveyed to them); U.S. v. Collazo-Aponte, 216 F.3d 163, 54 Fed. R. Evid. Serv. 1311 (1st Cir. 2000), cert. granted in part, judgment vacated on other grounds, 532 U.S. 1036, 121 S. Ct. 1996, 149 L. Ed. 2d 1000 (2001).

In U.S. v. Edmond, 52 F.3d 1080, 42 Fed. R. Evid. Serv. 119 (D.C. Cir. 1995), the District of Columbia Court of Appeals held that the district court had not abused its discretion in impaneling an anonymous jury. The defendants were key members of a large-scale drug conspiracy that was known to be willing to resort to violent acts to achieve its goals. They faced penalties that were among the most severe the law could impose, and the father of one of the defendants had reputedly said that he would "take care of witnesses." The trial court minimized the potentially prejudicial impact of an anonymous jury by conducting an extensive voir dire and by explaining to the jurors that the decision to keep their names confidential was not uncommon. The Court of Appeals noted that the defendants' proposed alternative of sequestration, while perhaps sufficient to ensure jury safety during the trial, would not have protected the jurors against subsequent retaliation.

In U.S. v. Krout, 66 F.3d 1420, 43 Fed. R. Evid. Serv. 129 (5th Cir. 1995), the Fifth Circuit Court of Appeals upheld the use of anonymous juries. The defendants in the case were alleged members of the Texas Mexican Mafia. This organization had been linked to numerous murders and admitted a willingness both to interfere with potential witnesses and to corrupt law enforcement authorities. Furthermore, the penalties faced by the defendants were substantial, and the case had been the subject of considerable publicity. See also U.S. v. Riggio, 70 F.3d 336, 43 Fed. R. Evid. Serv. 856 (5th Cir. 1995) (decision to impanel anonymous jury based on defendant's organized crime connections and previous involvement in jury fraud was not abuse of trial court's discretion). U.S. v. Sanchez, 74 F.3d 562, 43 Fed. R. Evid. Serv. 1069 (5th Cir. 1996), also from the Fifth Circuit, is a rare but instructive example of a case where a Court of Appeals found that the trial court had abused its discretion in impaneling an anonymous jury. The defendant, a police officer, had been charged with various civil rights violations. The trial court, fearing that jurors might be afraid of retaliation from rogue officers or might be tampered with during an unavoidable week's delay between jury selection and trial, impaneled an anonymous jury. The Court of Appeals held that this was an abuse of discretion.

Citing *Krout*, the court identified the types of factors that had proved persuasive in other cases cited in this note: the defendant's involvement in organized crime or with a group with the capacity to harm jurors; past evidence of interference with the judicial process or witnesses; the potential that, if convicted, the defendant would incur a substantial penalty; and the danger that extensive publicity could expose jurors to intimidation and harassment. Virtually none of these factors was present in Sanchez's case, however. He was not involved in organized crime nor was he a member of a group that was likely to attempt to harm jurors. There was also no evidence of previous interference with either the judicial process or witnesses, and the case was not of the type that would engender the extensive publicity that might bring about intimidation or harassment of jurors. The court concluded that the defendant's right to be tried before a panel of identified jurors had been violated. Although it was argued that this error was harmless, the Court of Appeals disagreed. It placed significant value in having jurors who could be held responsible for the verdict: "The defendant has a right to a jury of known individuals not just because information such as was redacted here yields valuable clues for purposes of jury selection, but also because the verdict is both personalized and personified when rendered by 12 known fellow citizens." U.S. v. Sanchez, 74 F.3d 562, 565, 43 Fed. R. Evid. Serv. 1069 (5th Cir. 1996). This rhetoric notwithstanding, it is submitted that a court should be solicitous of the not-unreasonable concerns of jurors, who should not have to incur a threat or even a perceived threat to their safety by virtue of performing a public service.

In U.S. v. Mansoori, 304 F.3d 635, 59 Fed. R. Evid. Serv. 1109 (7th Cir. 2002), as amended on denial of reh'g, (Oct. 16, 2002) and cert. denied, 123 S. Ct. 1761, 155 L. Ed. 2d 522 (U.S. 2003), the defendants were charged with a conspiracy that was alleged to have embraced a large-scale, gang-related operation with ready access to firearms and involving elements of organized crime. Although the district court did not make any specific finding that witnesses were at risk of intimidation or that justice was in danger of being obstructed, it ordered an anonymous jury to be empanelled. The Court of Appeals held that, although the defendants had the ability and incentive to threaten jurors, without additional evidence indicating that they were likely to act on that ability and incentive, there was not sufficient evidence to justify the unusual step of juror anonymity. Nonetheless the Court of Appeals held that the decision to empanel an anonymous jury was harmless in light of the judge's careful and conscientious voir dire and the overwhelming evidence of the defendants' guilt. See generally King, *Nameless Justice: The Case for the Routine Use of Anonymous Juries in Criminal Cases*, 49 Vanderbilt L Rev 123 (1996). The case for greater protection of juror privacy is presented in Weinstein, *Protecting a Juror's Right of Privacy: Constitutional Constraints and Policy Options*, 70 Temple L. Rev. 1 (1997). Weinstein argues that jurors deserve protection against invasive, personal questioning and probing investigations into their private life, as well as against threats to their safety. He does not maintain that these juror interests should trump all others, but rather that they should be taken into account and accommodated in ways that do not infringe on a defendant's constitutional right to a fair trial. Possible safeguards include anonymous juries, the elimination of peremptory challenges (as has occurred in England), and the curbing of intrusive pretrial investigations by denying parties access to the jury list prior to trial.

Add at end of section:

Anonymous juries were again at issue in U.S. v. Paccione, 949 F.2d 1183, 34 Fed. R. Evid. Serv. 621 (2d Cir. 1991). The Court of Appeals stated that a trial judge should not order the impaneling of an anonymous jury without:

1. Concluding there was a strong reason to believe the jury needed protection; and
2. Taking reasonable precautions to minimize any prejudice to the defendants.

In its motion, the government had argued that the serious nature of the charges, the potential for long prison sentences, the murder of one of the defendants under suspicious circumstances, the reputed connection of the defendants with organized crime, and the threats already received by a witness made an anonymous jury appropriate. Both the trial court and the appellate court agreed.

The trial court satisfied the second prong of the appellate court's test by instructing the jury at the outset that the special precautions were being taken to protect them from contacts by the media. Thus, the trial court provided a plausible explanation for the anonymity and, thereby, protected the defendants from the prejudice that might have resulted had the true reasons for the precautions been revealed.

In another Second Circuit case, U.S. v. Vario, 943 F.2d 236, 119 Lab. Cas. (CCH) ¶ 10907 (2d Cir. 1991), the Court of Appeals upheld the use of an anonymous jury in a trial for violations of the Racketeer Influenced and Corrupt Organizations Act (RICO) and the Taft-Hartley Act. The government had cited in support of its motion for the anonymous jury the defendant's ties with an organized crime family, grand jury tampering by one of the defendant's coconspirators, and the expected publicity surrounding the case. The Court of Appeals found the latter two reasons persuasive but, curiously, was not swayed by the defendant's alleged connections with organized crime. The court was apparently concerned that the mere mention of the terms mob, Mafia, or organized crime might be sufficient to justify an anonymous jury. The court wanted concrete evidence that jurors would

§ 9:14 Jury Selection: Law, Art & Science 2d

have cause to fear for their safety. The reasoning of the court seems somewhat unrealistic: jurors may have more to fear from a defendant's possible organized-crime connections than from pretrial publicity. Every effort should be made, compatible with safeguarding the defendant's rights, to allay those fears and protect their safety.

Other anonymous jury cases from the same circuit include U.S. v. Aulicino, 44 F.3d 1102 (2d Cir. 1995); U.S. v. Wong, 40 F.3d 1347 (2d Cir. 1994); U.S. v. Amuso, 21 F.3d 1251, 39 Fed. R. Evid. Serv. 569 (2d Cir. 1994); U.S. v. Thai, 29 F.3d 785, 40 Fed. R. Evid. Serv. 1387 (2d Cir. 1994); U.S. v. Tutino, 883 F.2d 1125, 28 Fed. R. Evid. Serv. 466 (2d Cir. 1989); U.S. v. Persico, 832 F.2d 705, 24 Fed. R. Evid. Serv. 137, 89 A.L.R. Fed. 857 (2d Cir. 1987); U.S. v. Thomas, 757 F.2d 1359 (2d Cir. 1985); U.S. v. Gotti, 777 F. Supp. 224 (E.D. N.Y. 1991). Whether an evidentiary hearing on the need for an anonymous jury is required lies in the Court's discretion. U.S. v. Aulicino, 44 F.3d 1102 (2d Cir. 1995).

In U.S. v. Collazo-Aponte, 216 F.3d 163, 54 Fed. R. Evid. Serv. 1311 (1st Cir. 2000), cert. granted in part, judgment vacated on other grounds, 532 U.S. 1036, 121 S. Ct. 1996, 149 L. Ed. 2d 1000 (2001), the defendants were charged with murder and membership in a violent, sprawling drug conspiracy. One defendant was also charged with intimidation and murder of a government witness. The Court of Appeals had no difficulty concluding that an anonymous jury was warranted. The court also approved of the precautionary measures taken by the trial judge in not mentioning the threat to juror safety, but instead justifying the anonymity by concerns relating to publicity.

In U.S. v. Eufrasio, 935 F.2d 553, 32 Fed. R. Evid. Serv. 1262 (3d Cir. 1991), the Third Circuit Court of Appeals held that a trial court may permit an anonymous jury without holding an evidentiary hearing where the court is of the opinion that there is the potential for juror apprehension. There is no inconsistency between a refusal to grant a change in venue and a decision to impanel an anonymous jury. See also U.S. v. Thornton, 1 F.3d 149 (3d Cir. 1993). See, e.g., U.S. v. Childress, 746 F. Supp. 1122 (D.D.C. 1990), aff'd, 58 F.3d 693 (D.C. Cir. 1995). In U.S. v. Crockett, 979 F.2d 1204, 37 Fed. R. Evid. Serv. 217 (7th Cir. 1992), the Seventh Circuit Court of Appeals held that the trial court did not abuse its discretion in impaneling an anonymous jury. See also U.S. v. Pasciuti, 803 F. Supp. 499 (D.N.H. 1992) (upholding anonymous jury in multicount drug prosecution against members of notorious motorcycle gang with reputation for violence and organized criminal activity and history of intimidating witnesses; also some evidence of attempt to intimidate and threaten government witnesses in case at bar). See also U.S. v. Talley, 164 F.3d 989, 51 Fed. R. Evid. Serv. 181, 1999 FED App. 0013P (6th Cir. 1999) (defendant's attempt to kill FBI agent, as well as other attempts to manipulate criminal justice system, justified impaneling of anonymous jury); U.S. v. Dakota, 197 F.3d 821, 1999, 84 A.F.T.R.2d 99-7427, 1999 FED App. 0419A (6th Cir. 1999) (trial court did not abuse its discretion in empanelling partially anonymous jury in order to minimize prejudicial effects of pretrial publicity and an emotional, political atmosphere that created a risk of jury intimidation and improper influence); U.S. v. Boyd, 792 F. Supp. 1083 (N.D. Ill. 1992).

Sometimes specific questions will intrude on the jurors' interest in privacy. When that happens the court has the discretion to monitor or prevent the questioning. See, e.g., State v. Mills, 65 Ohio St. 3d 1447, 601 N.E.2d 42 (1992) (upholding judge's refusal to distribute defense questionnaire which the judge determined unnecessarily intruded on juror privacy rights).

In U.S. v. Ross, 33 F.3d 1507, 41 Fed. R. Evid. Serv. 303 (11th Cir. 1994), the Eleventh Circuit joined those circuits which had previously held that anonymous juries were permissible. The court noted that the impaneling of such a jury was a drastic measure because it might suggest to the jurors that the defendant was a dangerous person from whom the jurors needed to be protected. Such a suggestion had implications for the accused's right to be presumed innocent. The Court of Appeals cited a number of factors which might properly be taken into account:

1. The defendant's involvement in organized crime;
2. The defendant's participation in a group with the capacity to harm jurors;
3. The defendant's past attempts to interfere with the judicial process;
4. The potential that, if convicted, the defendant will suffer a lengthy incarceration and substantial monetary penalties; and
5. Extensive publicity that could enhance the possibility that jurors' names would become public and expose them to intimidation or harassment.

U.S. v. Ross, 33 F.3d 1507, 1520, 41 Fed. R. Evid. Serv. 303 (11th Cir. 1994). The trial judge had found that virtually all of the above factors were present in the case and the Court of Appeals held that this was not an abuse of discretion. The Court of Appeals also approved of the trial judge's neutral explanation to the jurors that it wanted to insulate them from improper communications from either side and that its decision was no reflection on the defense.

Accord, U.S. v. Bowman, 302 F.3d 1228, 59 Fed. R. Evid. Serv. 1018 (11th Cir. 2002), cert. denied, 123 S. Ct. 1923, 155 L. Ed. 2d 829 (U.S. 2003) (district court did not abuse its discretion in sua sponte decision to empanel anonymous jury in murder and racketeering trial of motorcycle club's international president, where club had history of violent conduct and had on previous occasions sought to intimidate witnesses into not testifying, where defendant was accused of kidnapping and murdering club members to punish them for communicating with law enforcement authorities, where president was facing life sentence, and where president's capture and trial had attracted significant publicity; failure to give *Ross* instruction was not error, particularly as defendant had not requested such an instruction).

Accord, U.S. v. Salvatore, 110 F.3d 1131, 46 Fed. R. Evid. Serv. 1407 (5th Cir. 1997) (abrogated by, Cleveland v. U.S., 531 U.S. 12, 121 S. Ct. 365, 148 L. Ed. 2d 221, R.I.C.O. Bus. Disp. Guide (CCH) ¶ 9970 (2000)). U.S. v. Branch, 91 F.3d 699, 45, 45 Fed. R. Evid. Serv. 676 (5th Cir. 1996) is one of the few cases where an anonymous jury was impaneled even though the case did not involve organized crime or violent defendants. The prosecution arose out of a gun battle between the Branch Davidians (the defendants in the case) and federal agents. The jurors' names were withheld but not their occupations, employers, and other information. Thus the jury was only partially or semi-anonymous. The judge's reasoning was that the worldwide attention that had been given the case by the media had created an emotionally charged atmosphere in which the jurors might be subjected to harassment and intimidation. The court of appeal upheld the judge's order and in addition found that the defendants had not suffered any prejudice as a result of the judge's decision. See generally, King, *Nameless Justice: The Case for the Routine Use of Anonymous Juries in Criminal Cases,* 49 Vanderbilt L Rev 123 (1996). State cases that have dealt with the issue of anonymous juries are collected in Annotation, Propriety of using anonymous juries in state criminal cases, 60 A.L.R. 5th 39.

In U.S. v. Edwards, 303 F.3d 606, 59 Fed. R. Evid. Serv. 1042 (5th Cir. 2002), cert. denied, 123 S. Ct. 1272, 154 L. Ed. 2d 1025 (U.S. 2003) and cert. denied, 123 S. Ct. 1294, 154 L. Ed. 2d 1025 (U.S. 2003) and cert. denied, 123 S. Ct. 1286, 154 L. Ed. 2d 1025 (U.S. 2003) and cert. denied, 123 S. Ct. 1369, 155 L. Ed. 2d 209 (U.S. 2003), the defendants in a prosecution for RICO violations, extortion, mail fraud, money laundering and related crimes included a former four-term governor of the State. The trial court empanelled an anonymous jury. While acknowledging that most anonymous jury trial cases involved organized crime, the Court of Appeals, citing U.S. v. Branch, 91 F.3d 699, 45 Fed. R. Evid. Serv. 676 (5th Cir. 1996), stated that an anonymous jury might be appropriate in other cases that attracted unusually intense media interest, evoked highly charged emotional and political fervor, and aroused deep passions in the community. The ex-governor was a polarizing figure in state politics and many of the witnesses were of comparably high profile. The defendants all faced long prison terms if convicted. Examples of attempts to interfere with the judicial process and intimidate witnesses by some of the defendants, as well as by persons who were not parties in the case, were recounted. The trial court was also concerned that jurors might be harassed by members of the media. In these circumstances the Court of Appeals held that the decision to empanel an anonymous jury was warranted. The Court of Appeals pointed out that the degree of anonymity was limited, as the defendants had access to the jurors' zip codes and parishes, as well as extensive information contained in the long jury questionnaires. The defendants had not shown that they were prejudiced by the trial court's decision and the Court of Appeals noted that the possibility of prejudice was minimized by the judge's explanatory instruction that justified the anonymity on the basis of protecting the jurors' privacy from the media and indicated that the jurors had no reason to fear for their safety from the defendants. Accord, U.S. v. Brown, 303 F.3d 582, 59 Fed. R. Evid. Serv. 1032 (5th Cir. 2002), cert. denied, 123 S. Ct. 1003, 154 L. Ed. 2d 915 (U.S. 2003), decided on the same day.

The impaneling of an anonymous jury may have implications for other constitutional interests. In U.S. v. Brown, 250 F.3d 907, 29 Media L. Rep. (BNA) 1779 (5th Cir. 2001), various members of the news media covering a highly publicized trial challenged aspects of a judge's order for an anonymous jury. The Court of Appeals held that precluding members of the news media from interfering with or circumventing the anonymous jury order violated the petitioners' First Amendment rights. The press was entitled to report information about the jury based on facts that it had obtained from sources other than confidential court records, court personnel, or trial participants, but not information that it had illegally gleaned from confidential court files.

§ 9:15 Open- & closed-ended questions

Add at end of second paragraph:
However, a court is not required to ask open-ended questions, even if such questioning would be helpful or desirable. See People v. Taylor, 5 Cal. App. 4th 1299, 7 Cal. Rptr. 2d 676 (2d Dist. 1992). The *Taylor* court reasoned by analogy to

§ 9:15

Mu'Min v. Virginia, 500 U.S. 415, 111 S. Ct. 1899, 114 L. Ed. 2d 493 (1991) (discussed in supplement § 7:11), wherein the United States Supreme Court held that content questioning regarding pretrial publicity was not constitutionally required.

Add after third sentence in second paragraph:
Perhaps the ultimate in open-ended questions, the response to which it is impossible to predict in advance, is that used by Kathleen Zellner, who reportedly asks: "If you were my client, what would you want to know about someone like you on the jury?" quoted in Smith, *Challenges of Jury Selection*, 88 ABA Journal 34 (2002).

§ 9:20 Avoid unfairness

§ 9:21 —Be courteous and sympathetic

Add at end of section:
The importance of a lawyer not appearing to be judgmental of juror responses to voir dire questions is stressed in McElhaney, *Picking a Jury: Who are You Talking to?*, 67 Tenn. L. Rev. 517 (2000).

§ 9:32 —Don't take the first 12 jurors

Add at end of first paragraph:
It is improper, however, for counsel to seek to commit the jurors to counsel's view of the law, and voir dire questions perceived to be designed with this aim in mind may be rejected. See Soria v. Johnson, 207 F.3d 232 (5th Cir. 2000).

See also Bennett & Hirschhorn, *Voir Dire in Criminal Cases: Choosing Jurors to Judge Your Client*, 28 Trial 68 (1992).

§ 9:33 —Have voir dire reported

Add at end of section:
Even if voir dire is not recorded, the record of the proceedings may be reconstructed. In U.S. v. Cashwell, 950 F.2d 699 (11th Cir. 1992), the court reporter did not record voir dire. Cashwell's appellate lawyer, who was not his lawyer at trial, obtained an order from the appellate court remanding the case to the district court for the purpose of reconstructing the voir dire proceedings. The district court held a reconstruction hearing where it received the recollections of defendant's trial lawyer, the court reporter, the judge's courtroom deputy, the government's lawyer, and the judge. The appellate court held that the record as reconstructed was sufficient to accord effective appellate review and enable the appellant to

identify possible errors arising from the voir dire. The record in fact established that defendant's counsel had made no objections during voir dire and, in particular, had not made a timely *Batson* objection to the prosecutor's alleged discriminatory use of peremptory challenges.

Chapter 10
Voir Dire in Civil Cases

> **KeyCite®:** Cases and other legal materials listed in KeyCite Scope can be researched through West's KeyCite service on Westlaw®. Use KeyCite to check citations for form, parallel references, prior and later history, and comprehensive citator information, including citations to other decisions and secondary materials.

§ 10:2 Commitments

Add after first sentence in first paragraph:
The limits of permissible questioning designed to obtain commitments from jurors, with particular emphasis on verdict amount and the weight to be given to evidence, is examined in Bibb, *Voir Dire: What Constitutes an Impermissible Attempt to Commit a Prospective Juror to a Particular Result*, 48 Baylor L. Rev. 857 (1996).

Chapter 11

Voir Dire in Criminal Cases

> **KeyCite®:** Cases and other legal materials listed in KeyCite Scope can be researched through West's KeyCite service on Westlaw®. Use KeyCite to check citations for form, parallel references, prior and later history, and comprehensive citator information, including citations to other decisions and secondary materials.

§ 11:3 Putting jurors at ease

Add after first sentence in first paragraph:
See also Bennett & Hirschhorn, *Voir Dire in Criminal Cases: Choosing Jurors to Judge Your Client*, 28 Trial 68 (1992) (stressing importance of "(1) empathy, which says to the person being interviewed, 'I hear your feelings and thoughts, I hear your world'; (2) respect, which tells people their world will not be judged by the listener; and (3) congruence, which portrays the listener as a genuine person, inwardly and outwardly").

§ 11:7 Areas of voir dire requiring tact and delicacy
§ 11:8 —Religion

Add after first clause of first sentence in first paragraph:
It is not so clear, however, that a lawyer may always inquire about a juror's religion on voir dire. See, e.g., Bader v. State, 344 Ark. 241, 40 S.W.3d 738 (2001), cert. denied, 534 U.S. 826, 122 S. Ct. 66, 151 L. Ed. 2d 33 (2001) (questions about a juror's religion may not be asked on voir dire).

§ 11:14 Specific topics—Reasonable doubt

Add after first sentence in second paragraph:
It has been held, however, that there is no abuse of discretion if a judge does not choose to inquire into the jurors' ability to apply the presumption of innocence. U.S. v. Allah, 130 F.3d 33 (2d Cir. 1997). See also U.S. v. Beckman, 222 F.3d 512, 55 Fed. R. Evid. Serv. 543 (8th Cir. 2000) (while trial court did not, as requested by defendant, specifically ask each juror whether they understood and could apply presumption of innocence, Court's general explanations regard-

§ 11:14　Jury Selection: Law, Art & Science 2d

ing presumption coupled with its question as to whether jurors could apply legal principles as provided to them by court was adequate to satisfy legal duty and defendant's concerns).

Add after second sentence in second paragraph:

Judges too can sometimes become confused in explaining reasonable doubt. In U.S. v. Hernandez, 176 F.3d 719, 51 Fed. R. Evid. Serv. 1478 (3d Cir. 1999), the Court of Appeals held that the trial judge had erred in stating that reasonable doubt was "what you feel inside." The judge's statement seemed to suggest a visceral standard unique to each juror rather than an objective standard. Although less clear-cut, the Court of Appeals in Morris v. Cain, 186 F.3d 581 (5th Cir. 1999) held that a reasonable doubt instruction which used the terms "grave uncertainty", "actual or substantial doubt", and "moral certainty", also violated due process.

In Petrocelli v. Angelone, 248 F.3d 877 (9th Cir. 2001) it was alleged that the trial judge had improperly quantified reasonable doubt by stating that: "Some people say you have got to be convinced, and then others use, sports minded, use a kind of athletic football field, getting to the 97 yard line." The Court of Appeals held that regardless of the propriety of this phrasing of the concept, the judge had given a proper explanation of reasonable doubt in his closing instructions. Accordingly, it could be presumed that the jury had followed the correct instruction.

§ 11:15　—Right not to testify

Add at end of section:

It has been held, however, that the trial judge on voir dire is not required to question jurors regarding the defendant's right not to testify. U.S. v. Aloi, 9 F.3d 438 (6th Cir. 1993); U.S. v. Rodriguez, 993 F.2d 1170 (5th Cir. 1993).

§ 11:16　—Public opinion

Add after second sentence in second paragraph:

The trial court, however, is not constitutionally obliged to allow either individual questioning or questioning regarding the content of the pretrial publicity to which the juror has been exposed. See Mu'Min v. Virginia, 500 U.S. 415, 111 S. Ct. 1899, 114 L. Ed. 2d 493 (1991), Ch 7. Cases which might be profitably cited in support of the trial judge's exercise of discretion to permit such questioning can be found in Justice Marshall's dissenting opinion in *Mu'Min* and include: U.S. v. Addonizio, 451 F.2d 49, 67 (3d Cir. 1971); U.S. v. Davis, 583 F.2d 190, 196 (5th Cir. 1978); Silverthorne v. U.S., 400 F.2d

627, 639 (9th Cir. 1968); State v. Pokini, 55 Haw. 640, 526 P.2d 94, 100–01 (1974); State v. Goodson, 412 So. 2d 1077, 1081 (La. 1982); State v. Claybrook, 736 S.W.2d 95, 99–100 (Tenn. 1987); State v. Herman, 93 Wash. 2d 590, 593–94, 611 P.2d 748, 750 (1980); State v. Finley, 177 W. Va. 554, 355 S.E.2d 47, 50–51 (1987); U.S. v. Colabella, 448 F.2d 1299, 1303 (2d Cir. 1971); U.S. v. Harris, 542 F.2d 1283, 1295 (7th Cir. 1976).

§ 11:18 —Insanity defense

Add after third sentence in second paragraph:

In Neely v. Newton, 149 F.3d 1074 (10th Cir. 1998), the trial court permitted the defendant to address voir dire questions to the jurors on the issue of the insanity defense, and to ask whether they could return a verdict of NGRI if the facts warranted. One prospective juror referred to the insanity defense as a "cop-out" that "puts people right back out [on the streets] again." Others expressed similar reservations. The jurors in question were excused, and the trial judge told the panel that they should not concern themselves with the consequences of their verdict. On appeal the defendant argued that the court should have done more to correct the jurors' misconceptions or should have explained more fully the consequences of an NGRI verdict. The Court of Appeals found no error, stating that there was no showing that the jury was not impartial or that the defendant had been denied a fair opportunity to discover juror bias. The technical merits of the holding aside, arguably the better practice would be for a trial judge to inform the jury of the effects of an NGRI verdict, as it can be expected that at least some jurors may be psychologically reluctant to release an "insane" criminal into their community.

Part V
CHOOSING THE JURY

Chapter 12
Approaches to Jury Selection

> **KeyCite®:** Cases and other legal materials listed in KeyCite Scope can be researched through West's KeyCite service on Westlaw®. Use KeyCite to check citations for form, parallel references, prior and later history, and comprehensive citator information, including citations to other decisions and secondary materials.

§ 12:1 Introduction

Add at end of third paragraph:

An intriguing alternative would be to allow each side to select one half of a jury rather then simply challenging objectionable jurors. See Schwarzer, Reforming Jury Trials, 132 FRD 575, 580–81 (1990). The parties' agreement would of course have to be obtained before such a jury could be selected.

The concept of "affirmative" jury selection, where each side is permitted to make a certain number of affirmative juror selections, is also championed in Anderson, *Catch Me If You Can: Resolving the Ethical Dilemmas in the Brave New World of Jury Selection,* 32 NE L Rev 343 (1998); Fukurai & Davies, *Affirmative Action in Jury Selection: Racially Representative Juries, Racial Quotas, and Affirmative Juries of the Hennepin Model and Jury de Mediatate Linguae,* 4 Va. J. Soc. Pol. & L 645 (1997); Ramirez, *The Mixed Jury and the Ancient Custom of Trial by Jury de Mediatate Linguae: A History and a Proposal for Change,* 74 BU L. Rev. 777 (1994); Ramirez, *Affirmative Jury Selection: A Proposal to Advance Both the Deliberative Ideal and Jury Diversity,* 1998 U. of Chicago Legal Forum 161; Fukurai, *A Quota Jury: Affirmative Action in Jury Selection,* 25 Journal of Criminal Justice 477 (1997) and Note, *What's the Story? An Analysis of Juror Discrimination and a Plea for Affirmative Jury Selection,* 34 Am. Crim. L. Rev. 289. All of the authors seem to envisage affirmative jury selection being used to ensure minority representation on juries, but one cannot help but wonder whether the authors are as sanguine about the fact that affirmative jury selection would open the door to the conscious selection of jurors holding a racial animus and prejudiced jurors generally. In any event, affirmative jury selection seems to be a prescription that in practice will lead to more hung juries, and which may well be inconsistent with the concept of an impartial jury. See J. Abramson, We, The Jury (Basic Books 1994); J. Gobert, Justice, Democracy And The Jury (Dartmouth 1997).

Add at end of fourth paragraph:

A proposal that would allow parties both to select desirable jurors and deselect undesirable jurors is advanced by Adams and Lane. Adams and Lane, *Constructing a Jury that is Both Impartial and Representative: Utilizing Cumulative Voting in Jury Selection,* 73 NYU L. Rev. 703 (1998). The authors' proposal is based on a corporate procedure designed to empower minority shareholders. Under a cumulative voting procedure, when vacancies on a board of directors arise, each shareholder is allotted a number of votes equal to the shares controlled by the shareholder multiplied by the number of seats to be filled. The shareholder is then permitted to cast his or her entire bloc of votes for a preferred candidate or divide the votes among a number of different candidates. The authors suggest a similar procedure for jury selection. After all challenges for cause have been ruled on, each side would be allotted a total number of votes to be cast either in favor of seating or removing prospective jurors. A party could opt to cast all of its votes for or against a particular juror, or divide its votes among several jurors. The jurors with the highest vote total (affirmative votes to seat minus negative votes to remove) would comprise the jury. Should such a proposal be adopted, it would raise intriguing strategic decisions for lawyers. Should all of a party's votes be cast in behalf of a juror whom counsel predicts will be particularly favorable and persuasive; or conversely, should all of the party's votes be cast against a juror whom counsel fears will influence the jury in favor of the opposing side? Lawyers who have utilized the scientific techniques discussed in this book will obviously be better placed to make such strategic decisions than those who have not. While a party might be able to block the seating of a particular juror by casting all its votes against that juror, in doing so it would pay a heavy price, for it would lost the opportunity to select preferred jurors.

Add after first clause of second sentence of seventh paragraph:

Approaches to Jury Selection §12:2

One of the critical bits of information may pertain to the order in which the court intends to seat qualified jurors. In U.S. v. Underwood, 122 F.3d 389 (7th Cir. 1997), the trial judge had indicated that the jury would consist of the first 12 jurors who were not challenged. The judge intended this reference to encompass the first 12 such jurors as they appeared on the jury list, but the defendant thought that the judge meant the first 12 jurors in the order that they had been seated in the jury box. The effect was to cause the defense not to challenge two jurors whom it thought were unlikely to be called because they were relatively low on the seating chart. On appeal it was held that the defendants' Fifth Amendment right to the intelligent exercise of his peremptory challenges had been violated. The trial judge had only himself to blame, however, for after the confusion had come to light, he refused to start over, when this could have been done with minor inconvenience.

§ 12:2 Choosing jurors versus choosing a jury

Add after second paragraph:

In Marder, *Juries, Justice, and Multiculturalism*, 75 S. Cal. L. Rev. 659 (2002), Professor Marder offers two views of the ideal of jury composition. One is based on the idea that each juror is a reasonable person and that the goal is to impanel 12 such reasonable persons; the other is based on the acceptance of the benefits of multiculturalism and argues in favor of culturally diverse juries. Marder presents evidence that the tone and thoroughness of the deliberations and the extent of juror satisfaction is higher on culturally diverse jurors. Her conclusion is that cultural diversity should be valued on juries and that judges should do all they can, short of mandating diversity, to encourage such diverse juries. The argument can also be made that diverse juries bring a greater breadth of perspective to the deliberations and, as a result, are less likely to be sidetracked by prejudice or a narrow view of the facts, and therefore more likely to reach a fair and just verdict. See Gobert, Justice, Democracy and the Jury (Dartmouth 1997).

Add after eleventh paragraph:

It is in part because of considerations such as these that individualized, in camera voir dire needs to be approached with caution. While this format helps to promote candor, ensure that jurors will not be contaminated by responses given by other jurors, or learn what answers are "acceptable" to the court, it may also inhibit the development of the group "dynamic" that may later prove essential in enabling jurors to be able to function as an effective unit. To achieve

§ 12:2

this dynamic, it is important that jurors have some sense of each other as persons, and perhaps even be aware of each other's idiosyncrasies and biases. This "sense of the other" is gained in part by listening to the responses of the other jurors to voir dire questions. Through their answers to questions jurors are introducing themselves to each other (as well as to the lawyers) and telling each other background information about themselves. An identification with other jurors will often take place during this phase, part of which comes simply from the shared experience of being subjected to the same probing and sometimes embarrassing scrutiny of their private lives and personal views by the lawyers and judge in the case. When voir dire is conducted in camera, a lawyer will also lose the opportunity to observe how jurors react to each other's answers to voir dire questions. During breaks in the proceedings jurors often, perforce, will talk to each other. However, when jurors are kept separated and questioned one-by-one in camera, the shared experience of having been subjected to voir dire, which forms a common point for these initial, informal interactions, will be missing. It is in subtle ways such as these that individualized in camera voir dire can frustrate the development of the group dynamic. See generally Treger, *One Jury Indivisible: A Group Dynamics Approach to voir dire,* 68 Chicago-Kent L. Rev. 549 (1992).

§ 12:3 Jury selection where minimal information is available

§ 12:4 —Intuition and personal experience

Add at end of first paragraph:
Recent studies confirm that both prosecutors and defense attorneys seek jurors who emit nonverbal cues indicating that they are receptive to them personally. White, *The Nonverbal Behaviors in Jury Selection,* 31 Crim L Bull 414 (1995).

§ 12:6 —Social science research

Add after first sentence in first paragraph:
The methods and methodologies of practicing attorneys and social scientists are compared in Fulero & Penrod, *The Myths and Realities or Attorney Jury Selection Folklore and Scientific Jury Selection: What Works,* 17 Ohio NUL Rev 229 (1990).

§ 12:7 Identification

Add after fifth paragraph:
The constitutionality of a jury selection strategy which is

dependent on the use of peremptory challenges and which is based on ethnic or racial identification is now very much open to question in light of the decision of the United States Supreme Court in Batson v. Kentucky, 476 U.S. 79, 106 S. Ct. 1712, 90 L. Ed. 2d 69 (1986) (holding modified by, Powers v. Ohio, 499 U.S. 400, 111 S. Ct. 1364, 113 L. Ed. 2d 411 (1991)), See Ch 8. The strategy of seeking jurors who will identify with a key participant is both comparable to and distinguishable from *Batson*. It is distinguishable from *Batson* in the sense that while it involves the challenge of jurors with undesirable traits, the only common denominator among the jurors who are challenged may be their inability to identify with the challenging side, and there may be no discernible racial or ethnic pattern to the challenges. To the extent that the strategy seeks jurors who will identify with a party because of common racial or ethnic characteristics, on the other hand, it may run afoul of *Batson*. The strategy would arguably involve the type of race-conscious decision-making that the Supreme Court seemed to condemn in *Batson*. See generally Kaine, *Race, Trial Strategy and Legal Ethics*, 24 U Rich L Rev 361 (1990).

§ 12:8 Jury selection based primarily on voir dire
§ 12:9 —Verbal and nonverbal responses
n. 22.

Add to note 22:

Some courts have indicated a willingness to consider nonverbal responses in determining a juror's qualifications. See, e.g., Morris v. Spencer, 826 S.W.2d 10 (Mo. Ct. App. W.D. 1992). See also U.S. v. Daly, 974 F.2d 1215, 36 Fed. R. Evid. Serv. 1100 (9th Cir. 1992) (upholding against claimed violation of *Batson* the peremptory challenge of juror judged to be a "loner" because he sat "stone-faced" when everyone else in the room laughed at a humorous situation); Polk v. Dixie Ins. Co., 972 F.2d 83 (5th Cir. 1992) (justification for peremptory challenges of black jurors may be based on evaluation of eye contact); U.S. v. Swinney, 970 F.2d 494 (8th Cir. 1992) (peremptory challenge of black juror because he wore dark glasses and a "big gold watch" and did not make eye contact with prosecutor, although somewhat questionable, was permissible); U.S. v. Todd, 963 F.2d 207 (8th Cir. 1992) (fact that black jurors appeared inattentive, impatient, and hostile to prosecutor constituted race-neutral explanation for peremptory challenges). Both prosecutors and defense attorneys look to nonverbal cues to identify jurors that they believe are receptive to them personally. See White, *The Nonverbal Behaviors in Jury Selection*, 31 Crim L Bull 414 (1995).

§ 12:11 —Facial and body cues

Add after second sentence in first paragraph:

It has been suggested, however, that smiles may not be that self-explanatory and, indeed, may be an indication that a respondent is lying. See Ekman, Friesen, & O'Sullivan, *Smiles When Lying*, 54 J Personality & Soc Psychology 414 (1988).

§ 12:13 —A team approach

Add after fourth sentence of fifth paragraph:
See generally Stolle, Robbennolt & Wiener, *The Perceived Fairness of the Psychologist Trial Consultant: An Empirical Investigation*, 20 Law and Psychology Review 139 (1996).

§ 12:14 Jury selection based on juror profiles and investigations

n. 46.
Add to note 46:
For an assessment of the current state of the art of scientific jury selection, See generally Diamond, *Scientific Jury Selection: What Social Scientists Know and Do Not Know*, 73 Judicature 178 (1990); Fulero & Penrod, *The Myths and Realities or Attorney Jury Selection Folklore and Scientific Jury Selection: What Works*, 17 Ohio NUL Rev 229 (1990). Note, *The Jury Is Still Out: The Role of Jury Science in the Modern Courtroom*, 31 Am Crim L Rev 1225 (1994). Those who argue that scientific jury selection is overrated or ineffective are sometimes misled by unsuccessful examples of the genre where general attitudes of prospective jurors were used as the basis for predicting juror leanings. Research shows that case-specific attitudes are much better predicators of verdicts. See Moran, Cutler & Delisa, *Attitudes Toward Tort Reform, Scientific Jury Selection and Jury Bias: Verdict Inclination in Criminal and Civil Trials*, 18 Law & Psychol Rev 309 (1994).

Although the use of trial consultants and jury selectors has becoming increasingly commonplace, there is little regulation, whether by the state or by the practitioners themselves, of the profession. The issue is examined by Strier and Shestowsky in a thought-provoking article, Strier and Shestowsky, *Profiling the Profilers: A Study of the Trial Consultancy Profession, Its Impact on Trial Justice and What, if Anything, to do about it*, 1999 Wisconsin L. Rev. 441 (1999). The authors make the point that if jury consultancy is as effective as its proponents claim, then it is unfair to any party who cannot afford a consultant's services and perhaps skews the criminal and civil justice systems as well. On the other hand, if the claims for its effectiveness are unfounded, than it is an expensive and time-consuming diversion from the trial. See also, Streir, *Paying the Piper: Proposed Reforms of the Increasingly Bountiful but Controversial Profession of Trial Consultant*, 44 S.D. L. Rev. 699 (2000); Note, *Twelve Carefully Selected Not So Angry Men: Are Jury Consultants Destroying the American Legal System?*, 32 Suffolk U. L. Rev. 463 (1999).

§ 12:15 Authoritarianism ratings

Add after first sentence of third paragraph:
Research demonstrates that overlooking this dimension of authoritarianism is likely to lead to less accurate predictions of juror inclinations. See Moran, Cutler & Delisa, *Attitudes Toward Tort Reform, Scientific Jury Selection and Juror Bias: Verdict Inclination in Criminal and Civil Trials*, 18 Law & Psychol Rev 309 (1994).

§ 12:18 An integrated approach to jury selection

n. 64.

Add to note 64:

The case that nonverbal indices of deception should be sufficient not only to withstand a *Batson* challenge, but also to provide the basis for a challenge for cause is made in Note, *Articulating the Inarticulable: Relying on Nonverbal Behavioral Cues to Strike Jurors during Voir Dire*, 38 Ariz. L. Rev. 739 (1996).

APPENDIX A

Epilogue

Add after second paragraph:

A noted Federal Court of Appeals judge, Nathaniel Jones, argues that the widespread negative reaction to cases such as that of O. J. Simpson needs to be placed in a context that takes account of the historical struggle to overcome the exclusion of minorities from jury service. See Jones, *Race and American Juries—the Long View,* 30 Creighton L. Rev. 271 (1997).

Table of Laws and Rules

UNITED STATES CONSTITUTION, CODES, AND REGULATIONS

United States Code Annotated

16 U.S.C.A. §	Section No.
1910	1:14

18 U.S.C.A. §	Section No.
113(a)(4)	1:6
924(c)(1)(A)(ii)	1:13A
1001	1:5
1014	1:5
3161(h)(8)(A)	4:3A

26 U.S.C.A. §	Section No.
6103(h)(5)	4:3A

28 U.S.C.A. §	Section No.
1333(1)	1:14
1865(b)(5)	6:4, 9:10
1867(d)	6:11
1867(f)	4:5
1875	6:1
2253	8:7

28 U.S.C.A. §	Section No.
2253(c)(2)	8:7
2254(d)(2)	8:7
2254(d)(8)	8:6
2254(e)(1)	8:7

29 U.S.C.A. §	Section No.
794	7:50
2601–1654	1:14

42 U.S.C.A. §	Section No.
1973i(b)	6:8
1981	1:15
1983	1:15, 6:13, 6:18, 7:40, 8:11
1985	8:11
1986	8:11
12101 et seq.	8:8

46 U.S.C.A. §	Section No.
688	1:14

UNITED STATES ACTS

Civil Rights Act of 1964

Act §	Section No.
Title VII	1:15

Civil Rights Act of 1968

Act §	Section No.
Title VIII	1:14

Copyright Act of 1976

Act §	Section No.
504(c)	1:14

Rehabilitation Act

Act §	Section No.
504	1:14

UNITED STATES COURT RULES

Federal Rules of Civil Procedure

Rule	Section No.	Rule	Section No.
6(b)(2)	1:22	47	2:14
7(a)	1:17	47(a)	9:11
23(a)	1:22	48	2:14, 2:18
38(b)(1)	1:22	49(a)	1:22
39(b)	1:17, 1:22	59(a)	1:15
41(b)	1:15	81	1:17
42(b)	1:14		

Federal Rules of Criminal Procedure

Rule	Section No.	Rule	Section No.
11(c)(1)	1:13A, 1:21	24(a)	9:11
23(a)	1:22	24(c)	7:50
23(b)	2:13, 7:5, 7:9, 7:40, 7:50, 7:54	43(a)	8:2
24	8:3		

Table of Cases

A

Adams v. Aiken, 965 F.2d 1306 (4th Cir. 1992)—7:5

Adams v. Cyprus Amax Minerals Co., 149 F.3d 1156, 22 Employee Benefits Cas. (BNA) 1493 (10th Cir. 1998)—1:14

Adams v. Texas, 448 U.S. 38, 100 S. Ct. 2521, 65 L. Ed. 2d 581 (1980)—7:53

Aetna Cas. Sur. Co. v. P & B Autobody, 43 F.3d 1546 (1st Cir. 1994)—1:14

A.F.M., In re Adoption of, 15 P.3d 258, 102 A.L.R.5th 701 (Alaska 2001)—1:8, 1:18

Ag Services of America, Inc. v. Nielsen, 231 F.3d 726 (10th Cir. 2000)—1:15

Air Crash Disaster, In re, 86 F.3d 498, 44 Fed. R. Evid. Serv. 1102, 34 Fed. R. Serv. 3d 1067, 1996 FED App. 0157P (6th Cir. 1996)—8:2

Air Crash Disaster Near Roselawn, Ind. on Oct. 31, 1994, In re, 96 F.3d 932 (7th Cir. 1996)—1:14

Alexander v. Gerhardt Enterprises, Inc., 40 F.3d 187, 68 Fair Empl. Prac. Cas. (BNA) 595, 65 Empl. Prac. Dec. (CCH) ¶ 43389 (7th Cir. 1994)—1:14

Alexander v. U.S., 512 U.S. 1244, 114 S. Ct. 2761, 129 L. Ed. 2d 876 (1994)—7:12

Al-Khazraji v. Saint Francis College, 784 F.2d 505, 30 Ed. Law Rep. 1059, 40 Fair Empl. Prac. Cas. (BNA) 397, 39 Empl. Prac. Dec. (CCH) ¶ 35960 (3d Cir. 1986)—8:8

Allen v. Hardy, 478 U.S. 255, 106 S. Ct. 2878, 92 L. Ed. 2d 199 (1986)—8:5

Allen v. Lee, 319 F.3d 645 (4th Cir. 2003), reh'g—8:5, 8:6

Allison v. Citgo Petroleum Corp., 151 F.3d 402, 81 Fair Empl. Prac. Cas. (BNA) 501, 73 Empl. Prac. Dec. (CCH) ¶ 45426 (5th Cir. 1998)—1:14, 1:15

Allread v. State, 582 N.E.2d 899 (Ind. Ct. App. 2d Dist. 1991)—7:28

Alvarado v. State, 822 S.W.2d 236 (Tex. App. Houston 14th Dist. 1991)—7:5

Alverio v. Sam's Warehouse Club, Inc., 253 F.3d 933, 88 Fair Empl. Prac. Cas. (BNA) 233, 80 Empl. Prac. Dec. (CCH) ¶ 40627 (7th Cir. 2001)—8:7, 8:8

American Heritage Life Ins. Co. v. Orr, 294 F.3d 702 (5th Cir. 2002)—1:14

Amirault v. Fair, 968 F.2d 1404 (1st Cir. 1992)—7:12

Anderson v. Com., 107 S.W.3d 193 (Ky. 2003)—6:4

Anderson v. Cowan, 227 F.3d 893 (7th Cir. 2000)—8:6

Andrews v. Collins, 21 F.3d 612 (5th Cir. 1994)—7:22, 9:11

Andrews v. Deland, 943 F.2d 1162 (10th Cir. 1991)—8:5

Antwine v. Delo, 54 F.3d 1357 (8th Cir. 1995)—7:53

Apprendi v. New Jersey, 530 U.S. 466, 120 S. Ct. 2348, 147 L. Ed. 2d 435 (2000)—1:13A

Arizona v. Fulminante, 499 U.S.

279, 111 S. Ct. 1246, 113 L. Ed. 2d 302 (1991)—8:7

Art Press, Ltd. v. Western Printing Machinery Co., 791 F.2d 616 (7th Cir. 1986)—9:11, 9:13

Austin v. Shalala, 994 F.2d 1170, 41 Soc. Sec. Rep. Serv. 281, Unempl. Ins. Rep. (CCH) ¶ 17452A (5th Cir. 1993)—1:14

Avedon Engineering, Inc. v. Seatex, 126 F.3d 1279, 33 U.C.C. Rep. Serv. 2d 1039 (10th Cir. 1997)—1:14, 1:21

B

Bader v. State, 344 Ark. 241, 40 S.W.3d 738 (2001)—8:8, 11:8

Bailey v. Board of County Com'rs of Alachua County, Fla., 956 F.2d 1112 (11th Cir. 1992)—7:22

Bailey v. State, 838 S.W.2d 919 (Tex. App. Fort Worth 1992)—9:0

Bannister v. Armontrout, 4 F.3d 1434 (8th Cir. 1993)—7:53

Barber v. Ponte, 772 F.2d 982, 19 Fed. R. Evid. Serv. 215 (1st Cir. 1985)—6:16

Barnes v. Anderson, 202 F.3d 150 (2d Cir. 1999)—8:7, 8:11

Barrett v. Peterson, 868 P.2d 96 (Utah Ct. App. 1993)—7:34

Batson v. Kentucky, 476 U.S. 79, 106 S. Ct. 1712, 90 L. Ed. 2d 69 (1986)—2:5, 8:1, 8:7, 12:7

BCCI Holdings (Luxembourg), S.A. v. Khalil, 214 F.3d 168, R.I.C.O. Bus. Disp. Guide (CCH) ¶ 9886 (D.C. Cir. 2000)—1:17

Beacon Theatres, Inc. v. Westover, 359 U.S. 500, 79 S. Ct. 948, 3 L. Ed. 2d 988, 2 Fed. R. Serv. 2d 650 (1959)—1:15

Beck v. State, Dept. of Transp. and Public Facilities, 837 P.2d 105 (Alaska 1992)—7:9

Bershatsky v. Levin, 99 F.3d 555 (2d Cir. 1996)—6:8

Billing v. Ravin, Greenberg & Zackin, P.A., 22 F.3d 1242, 25 Bankr. Ct. Dec. (CRR) 904, 30 Collier Bankr. Cas. 2d (MB) 1844, Bankr. L. Rep. (CCH) ¶ 75822 (3d Cir. 1994)—1:14

Bittinger v. Tecumseh Products Co., 123 F.3d 877, 21 Employee Benefits Cas. (BNA) 1873, 38 Fed. R. Serv. 3d 685, 1997 FED App. 0242P (6th Cir. 1997)—1:14

Blair v. Armontrout, 976 F.2d 1130 (8th Cir. 1992)—8:4

Blyden v. Mancusi, 186 F.3d 252 (2d Cir. 1999)—1:14

Bogosian v. Woloohojian Realty Corp., 323 F.3d 55, 55 Fed. R. Serv. 3d 36 (1st Cir. 2003)—1:14

Bonin v. Vasquez, 794 F. Supp. 957 (C.D. Cal. 1992), aff'd, 59 F.3d 815 (9th Cir. 1995)—7:5, 8:2

Borgh v. Gentry, 953 F.2d 1309, 22 Fed. R. Serv. 3d 114 (11th Cir. 1992)—1:15

Borst v. Chevron Corp., 36 F.3d 1308, 18 Employee Benefits Cas. (BNA) 2217 (5th Cir. 1994)—1:14

Boston v. Bowersox, 202 F.3d 1001 (8th Cir. 1999)—6:7

Bowdry v. United Airlines, Inc., 58 F.3d 1483, 149 L.R.R.M. (BNA) 2714, 130 Lab. Cas. (CCH) ¶ 11356 (10th Cir. 1995)—1:14

Bracy v. Gramley, 81 F.3d 684 (7th Cir. 1996)—7:31

Bradford v. Longmont Mun. Court of City of Longmont, 830 P.2d 1135 (Colo. Ct. App. 1992)—1:8

Brecheen v. Reynolds, 41 F.3d 1343 (10th Cir. 1994)—2:4, 7:10

Brecht v. Abrahamson, 507 U.S. 619, 113 S. Ct. 1710, 123 L. Ed. 2d 353 (1993)—8:11

Brewer v. Marshall, 119 F.3d 993 (1st Cir. 1997)—8:6

Brewer v. Nix, 963 F.2d 1111 (8th Cir. 1992)—6:16

Bright v. Coastal Lumber Co., 962 F.2d 365 (4th Cir. 1992)—7:5

Briley v. Carlin, 172 F.3d 567, 79 Fair Empl. Prac. Cas. (BNA) 1630, 76 Empl. Prac. Dec. (CCH) ¶ 46068 (8th Cir. 1999)—1:21

Britz v. Thieret, 940 F.2d 226 (7th Cir. 1991)—7:11, 7:16

Brooks v. Zahn, 170 Ariz. 545, 826 P.2d 1171 (Ct. App. Div. 1 1991)—7:12

Brouwer v. Metropolitan Dade County, 139 F.3d 817, 4 Wage & Hour Cas. 2d (BNA) 940, 135 Lab. Cas. (CCH) ¶ 33684 (11th Cir. 1998)—6:6

Brown v. Burns, 996 F.2d 219 (9th Cir. 1993)—1:22

Brown v. Dixon, 891 F.2d 490 (4th Cir. 1989)—7:53, 8:8

Brown v. Kelly, 973 F.2d 116 (2d Cir. 1992)—8:7

Brown v. Kinney Shoe Corp., 237 F.3d 556, 84 Fair Empl. Prac. Cas. (BNA) 1510, 80 Empl. Prac. Dec. (CCH) ¶ 40585 (5th Cir. 2001)—8:6, 8:7

Brown v. Sandimo Materials, 250 F.3d 120, 26 Employee Benefits Cas. (BNA) 1391, 167 L.R.R.M. (BNA) 2176 (2d Cir. 2001)—1:14

Bruns v. Amana, 131 F.3d 761, 39 Fed. R. Serv. 3d 772 (8th Cir. 1997)—1:17

Buchanan v. Kentucky, 483 U.S. 402, 107 S. Ct. 2906, 97 L. Ed. 2d 336, 25 Fed. R. Evid. Serv. 120 (1987)—7:53

Buckles v. King County, 191 F.3d 1127 (9th Cir. 1999)—1:15

Buckley v. Barlow, 997 F.2d 494 (8th Cir. 1993)—1:8

Buford v. Group Health Cooperative of Puget Sound, 98 Wash. App. 1063, 2000 WL 44123 (Div. 1 2000)—3:12

Bui v. Haley, 321 F.3d 1304 (11th Cir. 2003)—8:6, 8:7

Bunch v. Thompson, 949 F.2d 1354 (4th Cir. 1991)—7:53

Burden v. Check into Cash of Kentucky, LLC, 267 F.3d 483, R.I.C.O. Bus. Disp. Guide (CCH) ¶ 10181, 2001 FED App. 0349P (6th Cir. 2001)—1:21

Burks v. Borg, 27 F.3d 1424 (9th Cir. 1994)—8:7

Burnham v. State, 821 S.W.2d 1 (Tex. App. Fort Worth 1991)—7:11

Burns v. Lawther, 44 F.3d 960, 31 Fed. R. Serv. 3d 347 (11th Cir. 1995)—1:22

Burns v. Lawther, 53 F.3d 1237 (11th Cir. 1995)—1:17

Burzynski v. Cohen, 264 F.3d 611, 86 Fair Empl. Prac. Cas. (BNA) 1112, 81 Empl. Prac. Dec. (CCH) ¶ 40761, 2001 FED App. 0279P (6th Cir. 2001)—1:14

Butler v. Supreme Judicial Court, 611 A.2d 987 (Me. 1992)—1:18

Byrd v. Blue Ridge Rural Elec. Co-op., Inc., 356 U.S. 525, 78 S. Ct. 893, 2 L. Ed. 2d 953 (1958)—1:18

Byrd v. Collins, 209 F.3d 486, 2000 FED App. 0121P (6th Cir. 2000)—7:53

C

Cabberiza v. Moore, 217 F.3d 1329 (11th Cir. 2000)—2:13, 2:17

Cabral v. Sullivan, 961 F.2d 998 (1st Cir. 1992)—2:13

Caldwell v. Maloney, 159 F.3d 639 (1st Cir. 1998)—8:7

Callins v. Collins, 998 F.2d 269 (5th Cir. 1993)—7:5

Campbell v. Louisiana, 523 U.S. 392, 118 S. Ct. 1419, 140 L. Ed. 2d 551, 172 A.L.R. Fed. 597 (1998)—2:7; 6:1, 6:11, 6:15, 8:6

Cannon v. Gibson, 259 F.3d 1253 (10th Cir. 2001)—7:53

Canty v. State, 597 So. 2d 927 (Fla. Dist. Ct. App. 3d Dist. 1992)—7:28

Capers v. Singletary, 989 F.2d 442 (11th Cir. 1993)—8:5

Cardinal v. Gorczyk, 81 F.3d 18 (2d Cir. 1996)—9:3

Carey v. Mt. Desert Island Hosp., 156 F.3d 31, 77 Fair Empl. Prac. Cas. (BNA) 861, 50 Fed. R. Evid. Serv. 133 (1st Cir. 1998)—8:8

Carter v. Hopkins, 151 F.3d 872 (8th Cir. 1998)—8:6

Carter v. Jury Commission of Greene County, 396 U.S. 320, 90 S. Ct. 518, 24 L. Ed. 2d 549 (1970)—8:11

Carver v. State, 203 Ga. App. 197, 416 S.E.2d 810 (1992)—7:19

Cass County Music Co. v. C.H.L.R., Inc., 88 F.3d 635, 39 U.S.P.Q.2d (BNA) 1429 (8th Cir. 1996)—1:14

Castor v. State, 587 N.E.2d 1281 (Ind. 1992)—9:8

Castro v. Ward, 138 F.3d 810 (10th Cir. 1998)—7:53

Central Alabama Fair Housing Center v. Lowder Realty Co, 236 F.3d 629 (11th Cir. 2000)—8:6

Central Alabama Fair Housing Center v. Lowder Realty Co., 236 F.3d 629 (11th Cir. 2000)—8:6

Chakouian v. Moran, 975 F.2d 931 (1st Cir. 1992)—8:6, 8:7

Chambers v. Johnson, 197 F.3d 732 (5th Cir. 1999)—8:6

Chapman v. State, 593 So. 2d 605 (Fla. Dist. Ct. App. 4th Dist. 1992)—7:13

Chase Commercial Corp. v. Owen, 32 Mass. App. Ct. 248, 588 N.E.2d 705 (1992)—1:21

Chateloin v. Singletary, 89 F.3d 749 (11th Cir. 1996)—1:23, 2:16

Chauffeurs, Teamsters and Helpers, Local No. 391 v. Terry, 494 U.S. 558, 110 S. Ct. 1339, 108 L. Ed. 2d 519, 133 L.R.R.M. (BNA) 2793, 114 Lab. Cas. (CCH) ¶ 11930 (1990)—1:14

Chavez v. Cockrell, 310 F.3d 805 (5th Cir. 2002)—9:11

Cimino v. Raymark Industries, Inc., 151 F.3d 297 (5th Cir. 1998)—1:14

City of Philadelphia Litigation, In re, 158 F.3d 723, 41 Fed. R. Serv. 3d 421 (3d Cir. 1998)—1:22

Clarin Corp. v. Massachusetts General Life Ins. Co., 44 F.3d 471 (7th Cir. 1994)—1:22

Clark v. Runyon, 218 F.3d 915, 84 Fair Empl. Prac. Cas. (BNA) 133, 78 Empl. Prac. Dec. (CCH) ¶ 40176, 48 Fed. R. Serv. 3d 842 (8th Cir. 2000)—1:22

Clark v. State, 601 So. 2d 284

TABLE OF CASES

(Fla. Dist. Ct. App. 3d Dist. 1992)—8:7
Claudio v. Snyder, 68 F.3d 1573 (3d Cir. 1995)—7:50
Clavette v. U.S., 525 U.S. 863, 119 S. Ct. 151, 142 L. Ed. 2d 123 (1998)—1:7
Clay, In re, 35 F.3d 190, 26 Bankr. Ct. Dec. (CRR) 127, 31 Collier Bankr. Cas. 2d (MB) 1732, Bankr. L. Rep. (CCH) ¶ 76122 (5th Cir. 1994)—1:14
Clemmons v. Sowders, 34 F.3d 352, 1994 FED App. 0297P (6th Cir. 1994)—7:51
Cochran v. Herring, 43 F.3d 1404 (11th Cir. 1995)—8:5, 8:6
Codispoti v. Pennsylvania, 418 U.S. 506, 94 S. Ct. 2707, 41 L. Ed. 2d 912 (1974)—1:6
Coleman v. Calderon, 150 F.3d 1105 (9th Cir. 1998)—6:4
Coleman v. General Motors Acceptance Corp., 296 F.3d 443, 53 Fed. R. Serv. 3d 75, 2002 FED App. 0244P (6th Cir. 2002)—1:14
Collier v. Cockrell, 300 F.3d 577 (5th Cir. 2002)—7:53
Columbia Pictures Television, Inc. v. Krypton Broadcasting of Birmingham, Inc., 259 F.3d 1186, 57 Fed. R. Evid. Serv. 559 (9th Cir. 2001)—1:14
Com. v. Chambers, 528 Pa. 558, 599 A.2d 630 (1991)—7:9
Com. v. Gray, 415 Pa. Super. 77, 608 A.2d 534 (1992)—7:42
Com. v. Snodgrass, 831 S.W.2d 176 (Ky. 1992)—8:7
Concordia Co., Inc. v. Panek, 115 F.3d 67, 1997 A.M.C. 2357, 37 Fed. R. Serv. 3d 1079 (1st Cir. 1997)—1:14
Congregation of the Passion, Holy Cross Province v. Touche Ross & Co., 224 Ill. App. 3d 559, 166 Ill. Dec. 642, 586 N.E.2d 600 (1st Dist. 1991)—7:40
Cooper Industries, Inc. v. Leatherman Tool Group, Inc., 532 U.S. 424, 121 S. Ct. 1678, 149 L. Ed. 2d 674, 58 U.S.P.Q.2d (BNA) 1641 (2001)—1:15
Cooperwood v. Cambra, 245 F.3d 1042 (9th Cir. 2001)—8:6
Corwin v. Johnson, 150 F.3d 467 (5th Cir. 1998)—7:53
Coughlin v. Tailhook Ass'n, 112 F.3d 1052 (9th Cir. 1997)—6:4, 9:10
Coulter v. Gilmore, 155 F.3d 912 (7th Cir. 1998)—8:7
Coulter v. Gramley, 93 F.3d 394 (7th Cir. 1996)—8:6
Cox v. Norris, 525 U.S. 834, 119 S. Ct. 89, 142 L. Ed. 2d 70 (1998)—7:10, 7:53
Craig v. Atlantic Richfield Co., 19 F.3d 472, 1994 A.M.C. 1354, 28 Fed. R. Serv. 3d 1044 (9th Cir. 1994)—1:14
Crawford v. Head, 311 F.3d 1288 (11th Cir. 2002)—3:12
Cunningham v. Zant, 928 F.2d 1006 (11th Cir. 1991)—6:8

D

Dairy Queen, Inc. v. Wood, 369 U.S. 469, 82 S. Ct. 894, 8 L. Ed. 2d 44, 133 U.S.P.Q. (BNA) 294, 5 Fed. R. Serv. 2d 632 (1962)—1:15
Dall v. Coffin, 970 F.2d 964 (1st Cir. 1992)—9:10
Darby v. State, 601 So. 2d 117 (Ala. Crim. App. 1989)—8:7
Dardovitch v. Haltzman, 190 F.3d 125 (3d Cir. 1999)—1:14
Davey v. Lockheed Martin Corp., 301 F.3d 1204, 89

Fair Empl. Prac. Cas. (BNA) 1164, 53 Fed. R. Serv. 3d 1263 (10th Cir. 2002)—8:7

Davidson v. Harris, 30 F.3d 963 (8th Cir. 1994)—8:7

Davis v. Baltimore Gas and Elec. Co., 160 F.3d 1023 (4th Cir. 1998)—8:7

Davis v. Executive Director of Dept. of Corrections, 100 F.3d 750 (10th Cir. 1996)—7:39, 7:53

Davis v. Greer, 13 F.3d 1134 (7th Cir. 1994)—8:5

Davis v. Minnesota, 511 U.S. 1115, 114 S. Ct. 2120, 128 L. Ed. 2d 679 (1994)—8:8

Davis v. State, 333 Md. 27, 633 A.2d 867 (1993)—7:52

Davis v. State, 830 S.W.2d 206 (Tex. App. Houston 14th Dist. 1992)—9:13

Davis v. State, 93 Md. App. 89, 611 A.2d 1008 (1992)—9:4

Dawson v. Wal-Mart Stores, Inc., 978 F.2d 205 (5th Cir. 1992)—6:11, 7:5

Deel v. Jago, 967 F.2d 1079 (6th Cir. 1992)—7:11

DeFelice v. American Intern. Life Assur. Co. of New York, 112 F.3d 61, 28 Employee Benefits Cas. (BNA) 1133 (2d Cir. 1997)—1:14

DeLisle v. Rivers, 161 F.3d 370, 1998 FED App. 0350P (6th Cir. 1998)—2:11, 7:10

Del Monte Dunes at Monterey, Ltd. v. City of Monterey, 95 F.3d 1422, 27 Envtl. L. Rep. 20139 (9th Cir. 1996)—1:15

DeLong v. Brumbaugh, 703 F. Supp. 399 (W.D. Pa. 1989)—7:50

Depree v. Thomas, 946 F.2d 784 (11th Cir. 1991)—7:52

Deputy v. Taylor, 19 F.3d 1485 (3d Cir. 1994)—7:53, 8:6

Derden v. McNeel, 938 F.2d 605 (5th Cir. 1991)—7:46

Devier v. Zant, 3 F.3d 1445 (11th Cir. 1993)—2:4, 7:10

Devose v. Norris, 53 F.3d 201 (8th Cir. 1995)—8:6, 8:7

Dias v. Sky Chefs, Inc., 919 F.2d 1370, 54 Fair Empl. Prac. Cas. (BNA) 852, 6 I.E.R. Cas. (BNA) 1860, 55 Empl. Prac. Dec. (CCH) ¶ 40398 (9th Cir. 1990)—8:9

Dill v. City of Edmond, Okl., 155 F.3d 1193, 14 I.E.R. Cas. (BNA) 498 (10th Cir. 1998)—1:17

Dillard v. Merrill Lynch, Pierce, Fenner & Smith, Inc., 961 F.2d 1148, Fed. Sec. L. Rep. (CCH) ¶ 96817 (5th Cir. 1992)—1:21

Dixon v. Hardey, 591 So. 2d 3 (Ala. 1991)—7:23

Doctor's Associates, Inc. v. Distajo, 107 F.3d 126 (2d Cir. 1997)—1:14

Doctor's Associates, Inc. v. Stuart, 85 F.3d 975 (2d Cir. 1996)—1:14

Doe v. Board of County Com'rs, Palm Beach County, Fla., 783 F. Supp. 1379, 58 Fair Empl. Prac. Cas. (BNA) 809, 58 Empl. Prac. Dec. (CCH) ¶ 41471 (S.D. Fla. 1992)—1:15

Doe v. Burnham, 6 F.3d 476 (7th Cir. 1993)—8:6

Doss v. Frontenac, 14 F.3d 1313, 63 Fair Empl. Prac. Cas. (BNA) 1274, 63 Empl. Prac. Dec. (CCH) ¶ 42827 (8th Cir. 1994)—8:7, 8:11

Dougherty v. State, 813 So. 2d 217 (Fla. Dist. Ct. App. 2d Dist. 2002)—9:8

Drew v. Collins, 964 F.2d 411 (5th Cir. 1992)—7:9, 7:53

Duarte v. U.S., 81 F.3d 75 (7th Cir. 1996)—8:11

Table of Cases

Dudley v. Wal-Mart Stores, Inc., 166 F.3d 1317, 79 Fair Empl. Prac. Cas. (BNA) 136, 75 Empl. Prac. Dec. (CCH) ¶ 45753 (11th Cir. 1999)—8:7

Duncan v. Department of Labor, 313 F.3d 445 (8th Cir. 2002)—1:14

Duncan v. State of La., 391 U.S. 145, 88 S. Ct. 1444, 20 L. Ed. 2d 491 (1968)—1:6

Dunham v. Frank's Nursery & Crafts, Inc., 967 F.2d 1121 (7th Cir. 1992)—8:6

Dyer v. Calderon, 122 F.3d 720 (9th Cir. 1997)—9:10

Dyer v. Calderon, 151 F.3d 970 (9th Cir. 1998)—7:4, 9:10

E

Eagle v. Linahan, 279 F.3d 926 (11th Cir. 2001)—8:6, 8:11

Edmonson v. Leesville Concrete Co., Inc., 500 U.S. 614, 111 S. Ct. 2077, 114 L. Ed. 2d 660 (1991)—8:6, 8:9, 8:10, 8:13

Ed Peters Jewelry Co., Inc. v. C & J Jewelry Co., Inc., 215 F.3d 182, 46 Fed. R. Serv. 3d 1130 (1st Cir. 2000)—1:15

E.E.O.C. v. HBE Corp., 135 F.3d 543, 76 Fair Empl. Prac. Cas. (BNA) 495, 72 Empl. Prac. Dec. (CCH) ¶ 45241, 48 Fed. R. Evid. Serv. 866 (8th Cir. 1998)—1:14

Elem v. Purkett, 25 F.3d 679 (8th Cir. 1994)—8:7

Engle v. Mecke, 24 F.3d 133 (10th Cir. 1994)—1:14

Enoch v. Gramley, 70 F.3d 1490 (7th Cir. 1995)—7:23

Enserch Corp. v. Shand Morahan & Co., Inc., 952 F.2d 1485 (5th Cir. 1992)—1:15

Evans v. Smith, 220 F.3d 306 (4th Cir. 2000)—8:7

Exxon Valdez, In re, 270 F.3d 1215, 2002 A.M.C. 1, 32 Envtl. L. Rep. 20320, 154 O.G.R. 1 (9th Cir. 2001)—1:15

F

Fairfield Leasing Corp. v. Techni-Graphics, Inc., 256 N.J. Super. 538, 607 A.2d 703, 18 U.C.C. Rep. Serv. 2d 713 (Law Div. 1992)—1:21

F.D.I.C. v. Marine Midland Realty Credit Corp., 17 F.3d 715 (4th Cir. 1994)—1:15

Federal Deposit Ins. Corp. v. Cafritz, 770 F. Supp. 28 (D.D.C. 1991)—1:17, 1:22

Feltner v. Columbia Pictures Television, Inc., 523 U.S. 340, 118 S. Ct. 1279, 140 L. Ed. 2d 438, 26 Media L. Rep. (BNA) 1513, 46 U.S.P.Q.2d (BNA) 1161, 163 A.L.R. Fed. 721 (1998)—1:14

Fernandez v. Roe, 286 F.3d 1073 (9th Cir. 2002)—8:6

Fields v. Woodford, 281 F.3d 963 (9th Cir. 2002)—7:4, 7:13

Fields v. Woodford, 309 F.3d 1095 (9th Cir. 2002)—7:4, 9:10

Financial Federated Title & Trust, Inc., In re, 309 F.3d 1325, 40 Bankr. Ct. Dec. (CRR) 99, Bankr. L. Rep. (CCH) ¶ 78735 (11th Cir. 2002)—1:22

Fischer Imaging Corp. v. General Elec. Co., 187 F.3d 1165, 39 U.C.C. Rep. Serv. 2d 324 (10th Cir. 1999)—1:15

Fitzgerald v. Greene, 150 F.3d 357 (4th Cir. 1998)—7:4

Fitzgerald v. Withrow, 292 F.3d 500, 2002 FED App. 0198P (6th Cir. 2002)—1:22

F.J. Hanshaw Enterprises v. Emerald River Development, 244 F.3d 1128 (9th Cir. 2001)—1:8

Flamer v. State of Del., 68 F.3d 736 (3d Cir. 1995)—7:10

Flanning v. State, 597 So. 2d 864 (Fla. Dist. Ct. App. 3d Dist. 1992)—2:17

Flemming ex rel. Estate of Flemming v. Air Sunshine, Inc., 311 F.3d 282 (3d Cir. 2002)—1:21

Floyd v. Garrison, 996 F.2d 947 (8th Cir. 1993)—6:8

Ford v. Georgia, 498 U.S. 411, 111 S. Ct. 850, 112 L. Ed. 2d 935 (1991)—8:5, 8:6, 8:7

Ford v. Norris, 67 F.3d 162 (8th Cir. 1995)—8:4, 8:11

Ford v. Seabold, 841 F.2d 677 (6th Cir. 1988)—6:16

Ford v. State, 262 Ga. 558, 423 S.E.2d 245 (1992)—8:7

Fox v. State, 602 So. 2d 484 (Ala. Crim. App. 1992)—7:13

Francone v. Southern Pac. Co., 145 F.2d 732 (C.C.A. 5th Cir. 1944)—7:32

Friedberg, In re, 131 B.R. 6 (S.D. N.Y. 1991)—1:14, 1:15

Frizzell v. Southwest Motor Freight, 154 F.3d 641, 77 Fair Empl. Prac. Cas. (BNA) 1580, 4 Wage & Hour Cas. 2d (BNA) 1505, 74 Empl. Prac. Dec. (CCH) ¶ 45504, 136 Lab. Cas. (CCH) ¶ 33725, 1998 FED App. 0285P (6th Cir. 1998)—1:14

Frost v. Agnos, 152 F.3d 1124, 41 Fed. R. Serv. 3d 538 (9th Cir. 1998)—1:17

Frost v. U.S., 525 U.S. 810, 119 S. Ct. 40, 142 L. Ed. 2d 32 (1998)—7:23

Fuller v. Bowersox, 202 F.3d 1053 (8th Cir. 2000)—9:10

Fuller v. City of Oakland, Cal., 47 F.3d 1522, 67 Fair Empl. Prac. Cas. (BNA) 153, 67 Fair Empl. Prac. Cas. (BNA) 992, 65 Empl. Prac. Dec. (CCH) ¶ 43431, 31 Fed. R. Serv. 3d 617 (9th Cir. 1995)—1:17

Fuller v. Johnson, 114 F.3d 491 (5th Cir. 1997)—7:53

Furman v. Wood, 190 F.3d 1002 (9th Cir. 1999)—7:53

G

Gacy v. Welborn, 994 F.2d 305 (7th Cir. 1993)—9:5

Galarza v. Keane, 252 F.3d 630 (2d Cir. 2001)—8:7

Garcia v. Excel Corp., 102 F.3d 758 (5th Cir. 1997)—8:6

Gardner v. Barnett, 199 F.3d 915 (7th Cir. 1999)—7:44, 9:5

Georgia v. McCollum, 505 U.S. 42, 112 S. Ct. 2348, 120 L. Ed. 2d 33 (1992)—8:9

Getter v. Wal-Mart Stores, Inc., 66 F.3d 1119, 43 Fed. R. Evid. Serv. 94 (10th Cir. 1995)—7:5, 7:32

Ghotra by Ghotra v. Bandila Shipping, Inc., 113 F.3d 1050, 1997 A.M.C. 1936, 37 Fed. R. Serv. 3d 1001 (9th Cir. 1997)—1:14

Gibson v. Bowersox, 78 F.3d 372 (8th Cir. 1996)—8:7

Gilbert v. Moore, 525 U.S. 840, 119 S. Ct. 103, 142 L. Ed. 2d 82 (1998)—7:53

Gilbert v. State, 593 So. 2d 597 (Fla. Dist. Ct. App. 3d Dist. 1992)—7:52

Gillam v. U.S., 528 U.S. 900, 120 S. Ct. 235, 145 L. Ed. 2d 197 (1999)—8:7

Gladhill v. General Motors Corp., 743 F.2d 1049, 16 Fed. R. Evid. Serv. 967 (4th Cir. 1984)—7:32

Table of Cases

Glenn v. Cessna Aircraft Co, 32 F.3d 1462 (10th Cir. 1994)—8:3

Gloria v. Valley Grain Products, Inc., 72 F.3d 497, 69 Fair Empl. Prac. Cas. (BNA) 1163 (5th Cir. 1996)—1:17

Golden v. State, 603 So. 2d 2 (Fla. Dist. Ct. App. 3d Dist. 1992)—7:12

Gomez v. U.S., 490 U.S. 858, 109 S. Ct. 2237, 104 L. Ed. 2d 923 (1989)—9:5

Gonzales v. Thomas, 99 F.3d 978 (10th Cir. 1996)—7:12

Gould v. Aerospatiale Helicopter Corp., 40 F.3d 1033 (9th Cir. 1994)—1:14

Goya Foods, Inc. v. Unanue, 233 F.3d 38 (1st Cir. 2000)—1:22

Granfinanciera, S.A. v. Nordberg, 492 U.S. 33, 109 S. Ct. 2782, 106 L. Ed. 2d 26, 19 Bankr. Ct. Dec. (CRR) 493, 20 Collier Bankr. Cas. 2d (MB) 1216, Bankr. L. Rep. (CCH) ¶ 72855, 18 Fed. R. Serv. 3d 435 (1989)—1:14

Great Plains Equipment, Inc. v. Koch Gathering Systems, Inc., 45 F.3d 962 (5th Cir. 1995)—8:7

Green v. White, 232 F.3d 671 (9th Cir. 2000)—9:10

Green Const. Co. v. Kansas Power & Light Co., 1 F.3d 1005, 26 Fed. R. Serv. 3d 1459 (10th Cir. 1993)—1:16, 1:17, 1:22

Greene v. Georgia, 519 U.S. 145, 117 S. Ct. 578, 136 L. Ed. 2d 507 (1996)—7:53

Greer v. Mitchell, 264 F.3d 663, 2001 FED App. 0304P (6th Cir. 2001)—8:6

Griffin v. City of Opa-Locka, 261 F.3d 1295, 86 Fair Empl. Prac. Cas. (BNA) 1254 (11th Cir. 2001)—7:10, 9:8

Griffith v. Kentucky, 479 U.S. 314, 107 S. Ct. 708, 93 L. Ed. 2d 649 (1987)—8:5

Guilder v. State, 794 S.W.2d 765 (Tex. App. Dallas 1990)—8:7

Guthrie v. State, 598 So. 2d 1013 (Ala. Crim. App. 1991)—8:6

Gutierrez de Martinez v. Drug Enforcement Admin., 111 F.3d 1148 (4th Cir. 1997)—1:14

Guzman v. State, 85 S.W.3d 242 (Tex. Crim. App. 2002)—8:7

H

Hakeem v. Beyer, 774 F. Supp. 276 (D.N.J. 1991), order—2:13

Hale v. Gibson, 227 F.3d 1298 (10th Cir. 2000)—2:11, 7:10, 8:11

Hansen v. State, 592 So. 2d 114 (Miss. 1991)—7:51

Hardin v. City of Gadsden, 837 F. Supp. 1113 (N.D. Ala. 1993)—6:7, 6:12

Harmon v. Marshall, 69 F.3d 963 (9th Cir. 1995)—1:5

Harner v. Dougherty Funeral Home, Inc., 752 F. Supp. 690 (E.D. Pa. 1990)—7:33

Harris v. City of Philadelphia, 47 F.3d 1311, 31 Fed. R. Serv. 3d 497 (3d Cir. 1995)—1:8

Harris v. U.S., 536 U.S. 545, 122 S. Ct. 2406, 153 L. Ed. 2d 524 (2002)—1:13A

Hatch v. State of Okl., 58 F.3d 1447 (10th Cir. 1995)—1:22

Hatco Corp. v. W.R. Grace & Co. Conn., 59 F.3d 400, 41 Env't. Rep. Cas. (BNA) 1338, 25 Envtl. L. Rep. 21238 (3d Cir. 1995)—1:14

Hattaway v. McMillian, 903 F.2d 1440, 16 Fed. R. Serv.

3d 1177 (11th Cir. 1990)—
1:18
Hayes v. Woodford, 301 F.3d
1054 (9th Cir. 2002)—8:7
Haynes v. W.C. Caye & Co.,
Inc., 52 F.3d 928, 67 Fair
Empl. Prac. Cas. (BNA)
1537, 67 Fair Empl. Prac.
Cas. (BNA) 1755, 66 Empl.
Prac. Dec. (CCH) ¶ 43559,
32 Fed. R. Serv. 3d 268
(11th Cir. 1995)—1:20
Henderson v. Walls, 296 F.3d
541 (7th Cir. 2002)—8:6
Heno v. Sprint/United Management Co., 208 F.3d 847, 82
Fair Empl. Prac. Cas.
(BNA) 837 (10th Cir.
2000)—8:7
Hensley v. Crist, 67 F.3d 181
(9th Cir. 1995)—1:22
Herman v. Johnson, 98 F.3d 171
(5th Cir. 1996)—7:53
Herman Miller, Inc. v. Thom
Rock Realty Co., L.P., 46
F.3d 183 (2d Cir. 1995)—
1:21
Hernandez v. New York, 500
U.S. 352, 111 S. Ct. 1859,
114 L. Ed. 2d 395 (1991)—
8:7
Hernandez v. State, 160 Tex.
Crim. 72, 251 S.W.2d 531
(1952)—8:7
Hicks v. Johnson, 186 F.3d 634
(5th Cir. 1999)—8:7
Hidalgo v. Fagen, 206 F.3d 1013
(10th Cir. 2000)—8:3, 8:7
Hill v. Brigano, 199 F.3d 833,
1999 FED App. 0426P (6th
Cir. 1999)—7:10, 7:53
Hill v. Jones, 81 F.3d 1015 (11th
Cir. 1996)—8:6, 8:11
Hill v. State, 827 S.W.2d 860
(Tex. Crim. App. 1992)—8:7
Hill v. Winn-Dixie Stores, Inc.,
934 F.2d 1518, 6 I.E.R. Cas.
(BNA) 1068, 7 I.E.R. Cas.
(BNA) 1671, 119 Lab. Cas.

(CCH) ¶ 10839 (11th Cir.
1991)—6:1
Hobby v. U.S., 468 U.S. 339, 104
S. Ct. 3093, 82 L. Ed. 2d
260 (1984)—2:7, 6:1, 6:11,
6:15, 8:6
Hoffmann v. Alside, Inc., 596
F.2d 822, 19 Fair Empl.
Prac. Cas. (BNA) 825, 19
Empl. Prac. Dec. (CCH)
¶ 9187 (8th Cir. 1979)—1:17
Holder v. Welborn, 60 F.3d 383
(7th Cir. 1995)—8:6, 8:7
Holland v. Illinois, 493 U.S. 474,
110 S. Ct. 803, 107 L. Ed.
2d 905 (1990)—2:11, 6:13,
8:1, 8:6, 8:12, 8:13
Hollingsworth v. Burton, 30
F.3d 109 (11th Cir. 1994)—
8:7
Hopp v. City of Pittsburgh, 194
F.3d 434, 81 Fair Empl.
Prac. Cas. (BNA) 26 (3d Cir.
1999)—8:7
Hopson v. Fredericksen, 961
F.2d 1374 (8th Cir. 1992)—
8:6, 8:7
Horne v. Trickey, 895 F.2d 497
(8th Cir. 1990)—8:4
Horton v. Zant, 941 F.2d 1449
(11th Cir. 1991)—8:5
Houghton v. SIPCO, Inc., 38
F.3d 953, 18 Employee Benefits Cas. (BNA) 2195, 66
Fair Empl. Prac. Cas.
(BNA) 97 (8th Cir. 1994)—
1:14
Houseman v. U.S. Aviation Underwriters, 171 F.3d 1117,
43 Fed. R. Serv. 3d 523 (7th
Cir. 1999)—1:14
Howard v. Moore, 525 U.S. 843,
119 S. Ct. 108, 142 L. Ed.
2d 86 (1998)—7:53, 8:6, 8:7
Howard v. Senkowski, 986 F.2d
24 (2d Cir. 1993)—8:7
Huff v. Dobbins, Fraker, Tennant, Joy & Perlstein, 243
F.3d 1086, 49 Fed. R. Serv.

TABLE OF CASES

3d 228 (7th Cir. 2001)—1:17, 1:22
Hughes v. U.S., 258 F.3d 453, 2001 FED App. 0211P (6th Cir. 2001)—8:11
Hulsey v. West, 966 F.2d 579 (10th Cir. 1992)—1:21
Hurd v. Pittsburg State University, 109 F.3d 1540, 117 Ed. Law Rep. 95, 73 Fair Empl. Prac. Cas. (BNA) 1448, 70 Empl. Prac. Dec. (CCH) ¶ 44615 (10th Cir. 1997)—8:7

I

Ideal Electronic Sec. Co., Inc. v. International Fidelity Ins. Co., 129 F.3d 143, 42 Cont. Cas. Fed. (CCH) ¶ 77224, 39 Fed. R. Serv. 3d 477 (D.C. Cir. 1997)—1:14
Image Technical Services, Inc. v. Eastman Kodak Co., 125 F.3d 1195, 44 U.S.P.Q.2d (BNA) 1065 (9th Cir. 1997)—7:5
Indiana Lumbermens Mut. Ins. Co. v. Timberland Pallet and Lumber Co., Inc., 195 F.3d 368, 45 Fed. R. Serv. 3d 1241 (8th Cir. 1999)—1:14
International Union, United Mine Workers of America v. Bagwell, 512 U.S. 821, 114 S. Ct. 2552, 129 L. Ed. 2d 642, 146 L.R.R.M. (BNA) 2641, 128 Lab. Cas. (CCH) ¶ 11120 (1994)—1:8
Irvin v. Dowd, 366 U.S. 717, 81 S. Ct. 1639, 6 L. Ed. 2d 751, 1 Media L. Rep. (BNA) 1178 (1961)—2:11, 7:11

J

Jackson v. Bailey, 221 Conn. 498, 605 A.2d 1350 (1992)—1:8
Jackson v. City of Little Rock, 26 F.3d 88, 65 Fair Empl. Prac. Cas. (BNA) 1 (8th Cir. 1994)—8:7
J.E.B. v. Alabama ex rel. T.B., 511 U.S. 127, 114 S. Ct. 1419, 128 L. Ed. 2d 89, 64 Empl. Prac. Dec. (CCH) ¶ 42967 (1994)—8:7, 8:8, 8:13, 9:11
Jennings v. McCormick, 154 F.3d 542, 41 Fed. R. Serv. 3d 1474 (5th Cir. 1998)—1:22
Jensen, In re, 946 F.2d 369, 25 Collier Bankr. Cas. 2d (MB) 1351, Bankr. L. Rep. (CCH) ¶ 74339, 21 Fed. R. Serv. 3d 447 (5th Cir. 1991)—1:14
Johnson v. Armontrout, 961 F.2d 748 (8th Cir. 1992)—8:11
Johnson v. Campbell, 92 F.3d 951 (9th Cir. 1996)—8:8
Johnson v. Collins, 964 F.2d 1527 (5th Cir. 1992)—7:53
Johnson v. Love, 40 F.3d 658 (3d Cir. 1994)—8:7
Johnson v. McCaughtry, 92 F.3d 585 (7th Cir. 1996)—6:17
Johnson v. Schmidt, 83 F.3d 37 (2d Cir. 1996)—7:18
Johnson v. State, 600 So. 2d 32 (Fla. Dist. Ct. App. 3d Dist. 1992)—8:7
Johnson v. Vasquez, 3 F.3d 1327 (9th Cir. 1993)—8:6
Jones v. Cooper, 311 F.3d 306 (4th Cir. 2002)—3:12, 9:10
Jones v. Gomez, 66 F.3d 199 (9th Cir. 1995)—8:6
Jones v. Jones, 938 F.2d 838 (8th Cir. 1991)—8:7
Jones v. Plaster, 57 F.3d 417 (4th Cir. 1995)—8:7
Jones v. Ryan, 987 F.2d 960 (3d Cir. 1993)—8:3, 8:6, 8:7
Jones v. Wellham, 104 F.3d 620 (4th Cir. 1997)—2:21
Jordan v. Lefevre, 206 F.3d 196 (2d Cir. 2000)—8:7

Jury Plan of Eastern Dist. of New York, In re, 27 F.3d 9 (2d Cir. Jud. Council 1994)—6:3

Jury Plan of Eastern Dist. of New York, In re, 61 F.3d 119 (2d Cir. Jud. Council 1995)—6:3

K

Kampa v. White Consol. Industries, Inc., 115 F.3d 585, 73 Fair Empl. Prac. Cas. (BNA) 1697, 70 Empl. Prac. Dec. (CCH) ¶ 44757 (8th Cir. 1997)—1:14

Kasi v. Angelone, 300 F.3d 487 (4th Cir. 2002)—9:11

Kavanaugh v. Greenlee Tool Co., 944 F.2d 7, 21 Fed. R. Serv. 3d 616 (1st Cir. 1991)—1:22

Keel v. French, 162 F.3d 263 (4th Cir. 1998)—7:9, 8:6, 8:7

Kilgore v. Bowersox, 124 F.3d 985 (8th Cir. 1997)—7:53, 8:7

Kinder v. Bowersox, 272 F.3d 532 (8th Cir. 2001)—7:44, 7:53

King v. Jones, 824 F.2d 324 (4th Cir. 1987)—9:5

King v. Moore, 196 F.3d 1327 (11th Cir. 1999)—8:7

King v. Shelby Medical Center, 779 F. Supp. 157, 58 Fair Empl. Prac. Cas. (BNA) 435, 58 Empl. Prac. Dec. (CCH) ¶ 41317 (N.D. Ala. 1991)—1:15

Kirk v. Raymark Industries, Inc., 61 F.3d 147, 42 Fed. R. Evid. Serv. 883, 155 A.L.R. Fed. 701 (3d Cir. 1995)—7:9, 7:12, 8:11

Kletzelman v. Capistrano Unified School Dist., 91 F.3d 68, 17 A.D.D. 1417, 35 Fed. R. Serv. 3d 942 (9th Cir. 1996)—1:17

Klinger v. State Farm Mut. Auto. Ins. Co., 115 F.3d 230 (3d Cir. 1997)—1:14

KLK, Inc. v. U.S. Dept. of Interior, 35 F.3d 454, 30 Fed. R. Serv. 3d 789, 129 O.G.R. 441 (9th Cir. 1994)—1:14

Knapp v. Leonardo, 46 F.3d 170 (2d Cir. 1995)—7:10

Knox v. Collins, 928 F.2d 657 (5th Cir. 1991)—8:1

Kobs v. Arrow Service Bureau, Inc., 134 F.3d 893 (7th Cir. 1998)—1:14

Kontakis v. Beyer, 19 F.3d 110 (3d Cir. 1994)—9:1, 9:3

Koo v. McBride, 124 F.3d 869 (7th Cir. 1997)—8:11

Koski v. Standex Intern. Corp., 307 F.3d 672, 89 Fair Empl. Prac. Cas. (BNA) 1865, 84 Empl. Prac. Dec. (CCH) ¶ 41358 (7th Cir. 2002)—1:14

Kotler v. American Tobacco Co., 926 F.2d 1217, Prod. Liab. Rep. (CCH) ¶ 12674 (1st Cir. 1990)—4:5, 7:4, 7:12, 8:3

Krumwiede v. Mercer County Ambulance Service, Inc., 116 F.3d 361, 74 Fair Empl. Prac. Cas. (BNA) 188, 71 Empl. Prac. Dec. (CCH) ¶ 44817, 38 Fed. R. Serv. 3d 142 (8th Cir. 1997)—2:14

L

Lacy v. State, 629 So. 2d 688 (Ala. Crim. App. 1993)—7:5

Lafevers v. State, 1991 OK CR 97, 819 P.2d 1362 (Okla. Crim. App. 1991)—8:2

LaMarca v. Turner, 995 F.2d 1526 (11th Cir. 1993)—1:22

Lancaster v. Adams, 324 F.3d 423 (6th Cir. 2003)—8:6

Landgraf v. USI Film Products, 511 U.S. 244, 114 S. Ct.

Table of Cases

1483, 128 L. Ed. 2d 229 (1994)—1:15
Landscape Properties, Inc. v. Vogel, 46 F.3d 1416, 26 Bankr. Ct. Dec. (CRR) 808, Bankr. L. Rep. (CCH) ¶ 76383 (8th Cir. 1995)—1:14
Langenkamp v. Culp, 498 U.S. 42, 111 S. Ct. 330, 112 L. Ed. 2d 343, 20 Bankr. Ct. Dec. (CRR) 1953, 23 Collier Bankr. Cas. 2d (MB) 973, Bankr. L. Rep. (CCH) ¶ 73668, 18 Fed. R. Serv. 3d 586 (1990)—1:14
LaRette v. Delo, 44 F.3d 681 (8th Cir. 1995)—7:53
LeBlanc-Sternberg v. Fletcher, 67 F.3d 412 (2d Cir. 1995)—1:14
Lee v. Boyle-Midway Household Products, Inc., 785 F. Supp. 533 (W.D. Pa. 1992)—1:17, 1:22
Lehman v. Nakshian, 453 U.S. 156, 101 S. Ct. 2698, 69 L. Ed. 2d 548, 26 Fair Empl. Prac. Cas. (BNA) 65, 26 Empl. Prac. Dec. (CCH) ¶ 31900, 31 Fed. R. Serv. 2d 1373 (1981)—1:14
Leibengood v. State, 866 S.W.2d 732 (Tex. App. Houston 14th Dist. 1993)—6:13, 6:16, 6:18
Leibengood v. State, 866 S.W.2d 732, (Tex. App. Houston 14th Dist. 1993)—6:13, 6:16
Lemley v. State, 599 So. 2d 64 (Ala. Crim. App. 1992)—8:6
Lesko v. Lehman, 925 F.2d 1527 (3d Cir. 1991)—7:53
Lewis v. Lewis, 321 F.3d 824 (9th Cir. 2003)—8:7
Lewis v. U.S., 518 U.S. 322, 116 S. Ct. 2163, 135 L. Ed. 2d 590 (1996)—1:6
Libretti v. U.S., 516 U.S. 29, 116 S. Ct. 356, 133 L. Ed. 2d 271 (1995)—1:8, 1:21
Linton v. Great Lakes Dredge & Dock Co., 964 F.2d 1480, 1992 A.M.C. 2789 (5th Cir. 1992)—1:14
Lockett v. Anderson, 230 F.3d 695 (5th Cir. 2000)—8:7
Lockhart v. McCree, 476 U.S. 162, 106 S. Ct. 1758, 90 L. Ed. 2d 137 (1986)—7:54
Lopez Cantu v. U.S., 528 U.S. 818, 120 S. Ct. 58, 145 L. Ed. 2d 50 (1999)—1:8
Lott v. Coyle, 261 F.3d 594, 2001 FED App. 0274P (6th Cir. 2001)—1:22
Lovejoy v. U.S., 92 F.3d 628, 45 Fed. R. Evid. Serv. 389 (8th Cir. 1996)—8:7
Loving v. Virginia, 388 U.S. 1, 87 S. Ct. 1817, 18 L. Ed. 2d 1010 (1967)—7:42, 9:12
Lucero v. Kerby, 133 F.3d 1299 (10th Cir. 1998)—9:8
Luckett v. Kemna, 203 F.3d 1052 (8th Cir. 2000)—8:6, 8:7
Lugar v. Edmondson Oil Co., Inc., 457 U.S. 922, 102 S. Ct. 2744, 73 L. Ed. 2d 482 (1982)—8:10
Lynd v. State, 262 Ga. 58, 414 S.E.2d 5 (1992)—9:8
Lytle v. Household Mfg., Inc., 494 U.S. 545, 110 S. Ct. 1331, 108 L. Ed. 2d 504, 52 Fair Empl. Prac. Cas. (BNA) 423, 52 Empl. Prac. Dec. (CCH) ¶ 39733, 16 Fed. R. Serv. 3d 1 (1990)—1:15

M

Mach v. Stewart, 137 F.3d 630 (9th Cir. 1997)—9:8
Mackall v. Angelone, 131 F.3d 442 (4th Cir. 1997)—7:53
Mackall v. Murray, 109 F.3d 957 (4th Cir. 1997)—7:53

Madison v. IBP, Inc., 257 F.3d 780, 86 Fair Empl. Prac. Cas. (BNA) 77, 80 Empl. Prac. Dec. (CCH) ¶ 40628 (8th Cir. 2001)—1:15

Mahaffey v. Page, 151 F.3d 671 (7th Cir. 1998)—8:9

Mahaffey v. Page, 162 F.3d 481 (7th Cir. 1998)—8:6, 8:7

Mallett v. Bowersox, 528 U.S. 853, 120 S. Ct. 317, 145 L. Ed. 2d 113 (1999)—2:5

Malone v. Vasquez, 138 F.3d 711 (8th Cir. 1998)—8:7

Mancuso v. Olivarez, 292 F.3d 939, 58 Fed. R. Evid. Serv. 1150 (9th Cir. 2002)—3:12

Mann v. Scott, 41 F.3d 968 (5th Cir. 1994)—7:53

Manning v. U.S., 146 F.3d 808, 40 Fed. R. Serv. 3d 1370, 28 Envtl. L. Rep. 21431 (10th Cir. 1998)—1:14

Marcella v. Brandywine Hosp., 47 F.3d 618, 31 Fed. R. Serv. 3d 557 (3d Cir. 1995)—1:14

Markman v. Westview Instruments, Inc., 517 U.S. 370, 116 S. Ct. 1384, 134 L. Ed. 2d 577, 38 U.S.P.Q.2d (BNA) 1461 (1996)—1:14

Markman v. Westview Instruments, Inc., 52 F.3d 967, 34 U.S.P.Q.2d (BNA) 1321 (Fed. Cir. 1995)—1:14

Marone v. U.S., 10 F.3d 65 (2d Cir. 1993)—1:22

Marseilles Hydro Power, LLC v. Marseilles Land and Water Co., 299 F.3d 643, 53 Fed. R. Serv. 3d 218 (7th Cir. 2002)—1:14

Marshall v. Lonberger, 459 U.S. 422, 103 S. Ct. 843, 74 L. Ed. 2d 646 (1983)—8:6

Marshall v. State, 598 So. 2d 14 (Ala. Crim. App. 1991)—7:22

Marshland Development, Inc., In re, 129 B.R. 626, 21 Bankr. Ct. Dec. (CRR) 1482, 25 Collier Bankr. Cas. 2d (MB) 360, Bankr. L. Rep. (CCH) ¶ 74110 (Bankr. N.D. Cal. 1991)—1:14

Martin v. Telectronics Pacing Systems, Inc., 70 F.3d 39, Prod. Liab. Rep. (CCH) ¶ 14411, 28 U.C.C. Rep. Serv. 2d 531, 1995 FED App. 0335P (6th Cir. 1995)—1:14

Mason v. Mitchell, 320 F.3d 604, 2003 FED App. 0042P (6th Cir. 2003)—9:9

Mata v. Johnson, 99 F.3d 1261 (5th Cir. 1996)—6:15, 7:5

Mathews v. Sears Pension Plan, 144 F.3d 461, 22 Employee Benefits Cas. (BNA) 1193 (7th Cir. 1998)—1:14

Matima v. Celli, 228 F.3d 68, 83 Fair Empl. Prac. Cas. (BNA) 1660, 79 Empl. Prac. Dec. (CCH) ¶ 40306 (2d Cir. 2000), case considered closed by U.S. supreme court, (Mar. 5, 2002)—6:18

Matthews v. Evatt, 105 F.3d 907 (4th Cir. 1997)—8:7

Mauldin, In re, 242 Ga. App. 350, 529 S.E.2d 653, 93 A.L.R.5th 755 (2000)—6:1, 6:8

Maurice, Matter of, 21 F.3d 767, 30 Collier Bankr. Cas. 2d (MB) 1809, Bankr. L. Rep. (CCH) ¶ 75825, 28 Fed. R. Serv. 3d 799 (7th Cir. 1994)—1:14

McAfee v. Martin, 63 F.3d 436, 32 Fed. R. Serv. 3d 1065 (5th Cir. 1995)—1:22

McCain v. Gramley, 96 F.3d 288 (7th Cir. 1996)—8:6

McCall v. Delo, 31 F.3d 750 (8th Cir. 1994)—8:5

McClain v. Prunty, 217 F.3d 1209 (9th Cir. 2000)—8:7

TABLE OF CASES

McCrory v. Henderson, 82 F.3d 1243 (2d Cir. 1996)—8:6, 8:7
McCullough v. Singletary, 967 F.2d 530 (11th Cir. 1992)—1:8
McCurdy v. Montgomery County, Ohio, 240 F.3d 512, 2001 FED App. 0044P (6th Cir. 2001)—8:7
McDonald v. Steward, 132 F.3d 225 (5th Cir. 1998)—1:22
McDonough Power Equipment, Inc. v. Greenwood, 464 U.S. 548, 104 S. Ct. 845, 78 L. Ed. 2d 663 (1984)—3:12, 7:4, 9:10
McElroy by McElroy v. Firestone Tire & Rubber Co., 894 F.2d 1504, Prod. Liab. Rep. (CCH) ¶ 12396 (11th Cir. 1990)—3:14
McFadden v. Johnson, 528 U.S. 947, 120 S. Ct. 369, 145 L. Ed. 2d 287 (1999)—7:53
McGinnis v. Johnson, 181 F.3d 686 (5th Cir. 1999)—6:6
McKeel v. City of Pine Bluff, 73 F.3d 207, 43 Fed. R. Evid. Serv. 734 (8th Cir. 1996)—8:7
McMeans v. Brigano, 228 F.3d 674, 2000 FED App. 0353P (6th Cir. 2000)—8:11
McMillan v. Pennsylvania, 477 U.S. 79, 106 S. Ct. 2411, 91 L. Ed. 2d 67 (1986)—1:8, 1:13A, 1:21
McQueen v. Scroggy, 99 F.3d 1302, 35 Fed. R. Serv. 3d 1211, 1996 FED App. 0349P (6th Cir. 1996)—6:16, 7:5, 7:10, 7:39, 7:52, 7:53, 9:13
Medical Air Technology Corp. v. Marwan Inv., Inc., 303 F.3d 11 (1st Cir. 2002)—1:21
Medrano v. City of Los Angeles, 973 F.2d 1499, 24 Fed. R. Serv. 3d 108 (9th Cir. 1992)—9:5

Mejia v. State, 328 Md. 522, 616 A.2d 356 (1992)—8:6
Members v. Paige, 140 F.3d 699 (7th Cir. 1998)—1:22
Merex A.G. v. Fairchild Weston Systems, Inc., 29 F.3d 821, 29 Fed. R. Serv. 3d 560 (2d Cir. 1994)—1:14
Middle Tennessee News Co., Inc. v. Charnel of Cincinnati, Inc., 250 F.3d 1077, 50 Fed. R. Serv. 3d 200, 186 A.L.R. Fed. 621 (7th Cir. 2001)—1:21
Mile High Industries v. C 222 F.3d 845, 47 Fe Serv. 3d 778 (10th Cir. 2000)—1:15
Miller v. Francis, 269 F.3d 609, 2001 FED App. 0366P (6th Cir. 2001)—7:9, 8:11
Miller v. U.S., 135 F.3d 1254, 48 Fed. R. Evid. Serv. 1089 (8th Cir. 1998)—8:6
Miller-El v. Cockrell, 537 U.S. 322, 123 S. Ct. 1029, 154 L. Ed. 2d 931 (2003)—8:5, 8:7
Mills v. GAF Corp., 20 F.3d 678, 1994 FED App. 0104P (6th Cir. 1994)—8:2
Mitchell v. Rees, 114 F.3d 571, 1997 FED App. 0168P (6th Cir. 1997)—8:6
Monroe v. City of Phoenix, Ariz., 248 F.3d 851 (9th Cir. 2001)—9:11
Monterey, City of v. Del Monte Dunes at Monterey, Ltd., 526 U.S. 687, 119 S. Ct. 1624, 143 L. Ed. 2d 882, 48 Env't. Rep. Cas. (BNA) 1513, 29 Envtl. L. Rep. 21133 (1999)—1:15
Montgomery v. Com., 819 S.W.2d 713 (Ky. 1991)—7:22
Montiel v. City of Los Angeles, 2 F.3d 335, 37 Fed. R. Evid. Serv. 1008, 26 Fed. R. Serv.

3d 832 (9th Cir. 1993)—
9:11
Moody v. Pepsi-Cola Metropolitan Bottling Co., Inc., 915 F.2d 201, 56 Fair Empl. Prac. Cas. (BNA) 1491, 54 Empl. Prac. Dec. (CCH) ¶ 40228, 117 Lab. Cas. (CCH) ¶ 56441, 17 Fed. R. Serv. 3d 1393 (6th Cir. 1990)—1:17, 1:22
Mooney v. State, 817 S.W.2d 693 (Tex. Crim. App. 1991)—7:13
Moore v. Gibson, 195 F.3d 1152 (10th Cir. 1999)—7:53
Moore v. Johnson, 225 F.3d 495 (5th Cir. 2000)—3:16
Moore v. Keller Industries, Inc., 948 F.2d 199 (5th Cir. 1991)—8:7
Morgan v. City of Albuquerque, 25 F.3d 918, 5 A.D.D. 476, 3 A.D. Cas. (BNA) 804 (10th Cir. 1994)—8:8
Morgan v. Illinois, 504 U.S. 719, 112 S. Ct. 2222, 119 L. Ed. 2d 492 (1992)—7:1, 7:9, 7:53, 9:0, 9:4, 9:7, 9:11, 9:13
Morning v. Zapata Protein (USA), Inc., 128 F.3d 213 (4th Cir. 1997)—8:6
Morris v. Cain, 186 F.3d 581 (5th Cir. 1999)—11:14
Morris v. Spencer, 826 S.W.2d 10 (Mo. Ct. App. W.D. 1992)—7:23, 12:9
Morse v. Hanks, 172 F.3d 983 (7th Cir. 1999)—8:7
Moss v. Lockhart, 971 F.2d 77 (8th Cir. 1992)—7:21
Mullen v. Treasure Chest Casino, LLC, 186 F.3d 620, 2000 A.M.C. 1519, 44 Fed. R. Serv. 3d 885 (5th Cir. 1999)—1:14
Mu'Min v. Virginia, 500 U.S. 415, 111 S. Ct. 1899, 114 L. Ed. 2d 493 (1991)—2:11, 7:10, 7:11, 9:4, 9:8, 9:15, 11:16
Murchu v. U.S., 926 F.2d 50 (1st Cir. 1991)—8:8
Murray v. Delo, 34 F.3d 1367 (8th Cir. 1994)—7:53
Murray v. Groose, 106 F.3d 812 (8th Cir. 1997)—7:53
Murray v. Laborers Union Local No. 324, 55 F.3d 1445, 149 L.R.R.M. (BNA) 2457, 149 L.R.R.M. (BNA) 2858, 130 Lab. Cas. (CCH) ¶ 11345, 130 Lab. Cas. (CCH) ¶ 11367, 31 Fed. R. Serv. 3d 1222 (9th Cir. 1995)—2:18, 7:50

N

Nance v. State, 598 So. 2d 30 (Ala. Crim. App. 1992)—8:6
Nanninga v. Three Rivers Elec. Co-op., 203 F.3d 529 (8th Cir. 2000), reh'g—9:5, 9:11
Nathan v. Boeing Co., 116 F.3d 422, 12 I.E.R. Cas. (BNA) 1783, 47 Fed. R. Evid. Serv. 648 (9th Cir. 1997)—7:25
Neely v. Newton, 149 F.3d 1074 (10th Cir. 1998)—9:8, 11:18
Neill v. Gibson, 263 F.3d 1184 (10th Cir. 2001)—7:53
Nelson v. State, 832 S.W.2d 762 (Tex. App. Houston 1st Dist. 1992)—7:9
Newfound Management Corp. v. Lewis, 131 F.3d 108, 39 Fed. R. Serv. 3d 14 (3d Cir. 1997)—1:15
New Port Largo, Inc. v. Monroe County, 95 F.3d 1084, 27 Envtl. L. Rep. 20170 (11th Cir. 1996)—1:15
Nichols v. Thomas, 788 F. Supp. 570 (N.D. Ga. 1992)—7:28
Nickerson v. Lee, 971 F.2d 1125 (4th Cir. 1992)—8:6
Noltie v. Peterson, 9 F.3d 802 (9th Cir. 1993)—7:11

TABLE OF CASES

Northgate Homes, Inc. v. City of Dayton, 126 F.3d 1095 (8th Cir. 1997)—1:14

O

Oken v. Corcoran, 220 F.3d 259 (4th Cir. 2000)—7:53

Okura & Co. (America), Inc. v. Careau Group, 783 F. Supp. 482 (C.D. Cal. 1991)—1:21

Old Chief v. U.S., 519 U.S. 172, 117 S. Ct. 644, 136 L. Ed. 2d 574, 45 Fed. R. Evid. Serv. 835 (1997)—2:20

O'Neal v. Delo, 44 F.3d 655 (8th Cir. 1995)—6:9

Overton v. Newton, 295 F.3d 270 (2d Cir. 2002)—8:6

Owens v. U.S., 528 U.S. 894, 120 S. Ct. 224, 145 L. Ed. 2d 188 (1999)—7:5

P

Pacific Fisheries Corp. v. HIH Cas. & General Ins., Ltd., 239 F.3d 1000, 2001 A.M.C. 952, 49 Fed. R. Serv. 3d 278 (9th Cir. 2001)—1:17

Packer v. Hill, 277 F.3d 1092 (9th Cir. 2002)—7:5

Palace Exploration Co. v. Petroleum Development Co., 316 F.3d 1110, 54 Fed. R. Serv. 3d 924 (10th Cir. 2003)—1:14

Palmer v. Lares, 42 F.3d 975, 41 Fed. R. Evid. Serv. 1209 (5th Cir. 1995)—8:7

Pandazides v. Virginia Bd. of Educ., 13 F.3d 823, 4 A.D.D. 111, 2 A.D. Cas. (BNA) 1711, 88 Ed. Law Rep. 963, 63 Empl. Prac. Dec. (CCH) ¶ 42782 (4th Cir. 1994)—1:14

Paracor Finance, Inc. v. General Elec. Capital Corp., 96 F.3d 1151, Blue Sky L. Rep. (CCH) ¶ 74088, Fed. Sec. L. Rep. (CCH) ¶ 99315 (9th Cir. 1996)—1:21

Parker v. Singletary, 974 F.2d 1562 (11th Cir. 1992)—8:7

Parklane Hosiery Co., Inc. v. Shore, 439 U.S. 322, 99 S. Ct. 645, 58 L. Ed. 2d 552, Fed. Sec. L. Rep. (CCH) ¶ 96713, 26 Fed. R. Serv. 2d 669 (1979)—1:15

Parrish v. Fulcomer, 150 F.3d 326 (3d Cir. 1998)—1:22

Parrott v. Wilson, 707 F.2d 1262, 13 Fed. R. Evid. Serv. 1149 (11th Cir. 1983)—1:17, 1:22

Partee v. Buch, 28 F.3d 636, 65 Fair Empl. Prac. Cas. (BNA) 590, 29 Fed. R. Serv. 3d 421 (7th Cir. 1994)—1:17

Paschal v. Flagstar Bank, 295 F.3d 565, 59 Fed. R. Evid. Serv. 875, 2002 FED App. 0239P (6th Cir. 2002)—8:11

Pasquariello, In re, 16 F.3d 525, 25 Bankr. Ct. Dec. (CRR) 404, 30 Collier Bankr. Cas. 2d (MB) 1006, Bankr. L. Rep. (CCH) ¶ 75723 (3d Cir. 1994)—1:14

Patton v. Yount, 467 U.S. 1025, 104 S. Ct. 2885, 81 L. Ed. 2d 847 (1984)—2:11, 7:11

Payton v. State, 830 S.W.2d 722 (Tex. App. Houston 14th Dist. 1992)—8:7

Peachtree Lane Associates, Ltd., Matter of, 150 F.3d 788, 32 Bankr. Ct. Dec. (CRR) 1235, Bankr. L. Rep. (CCH) ¶ 77747 (7th Cir. 1998)—1:14

Pemberthy v. Beyer, 19 F.3d 857 (3d Cir. 1994)—8:7

Pemberthy v. Beyer, 800 F. Supp. 144 (D.N.J. 1992)—8:8

Penry v. Johnson, 532 U.S. 782,

121 S. Ct. 1910, 150 L. Ed. 2d 9 (2001)—9:2
People v. Bernard, 27 Cal. App. 4th 458, 32 Cal. Rptr. 2d 486 (4th Dist. 1994)—8:6
People v. Bommersbach, 228 Ill. App. 3d 877, 170 Ill. Dec. 894, 593 N.E.2d 783 (1st Dist. 1992)—7:47
People v. Campos, 227 Ill. App. 3d 434, 169 Ill. Dec. 598, 592 N.E.2d 85 (1st Dist. 1992)—9:13
People v. Cannon, 227 Ill. App. 3d 551, 169 Ill. Dec. 681, 592 N.E.2d 168 (1st Dist. 1992)—8:7
People v. Coleman, 223 Ill. App. 3d 975, 166 Ill. Dec. 312, 586 N.E.2d 270 (1st Dist. 1991)—7:50
People v. Danielson, 3 Cal. 4th 691, 13 Cal. Rptr. 2d 1, 838 P.2d 729 (1992)—2:2
People v. Garcia, 77 Cal. App. 4th 1269, 92 Cal. Rptr. 2d 339 (4th Dist. 2000)—8:8
People v. Hill, 3 Cal. 4th 959, 13 Cal. Rptr. 2d 475, 839 P.2d 984 (1992)—2:2
People v. Jimenez, 284 Ill. App. 3d 908, 220 Ill. Dec. 97, 672 N.E.2d 914 (1st Dist. 1996)—7:44
People v. Kirby, 440 Mich. 485, 487 N.W.2d 404 (1992)—1:20
People v. Langston, 167 Misc. 2d 400, 641 N.Y.S.2d 513 (Sup 1996)—8:8
People v. Lanter, 230 Ill. App. 3d 72, 172 Ill. Dec. 147, 595 N.E.2d 210 (4th Dist. 1992)—7:39
People v. Leger, 149 Ill. 2d 355, 173 Ill. Dec. 612, 597 N.E.2d 586 (1992)—7:22
People v. Leung, 5 Cal. App. 4th 482, 7 Cal. Rptr. 2d 290 (6th Dist. 1992)—9:11
People v. Lopez, 3 Cal. App. 4th Supp. 11, 5 Cal. Rptr. 2d 775 (App. Dep't Super. Ct. 1991)—7:5, 8:6, 8:8
People v. Love, 222 Ill. App. 3d 428, 165 Ill. Dec. 10, 584 N.E.2d 189 (1st Dist. 1991)—7:5
People v. Mack, 128 Ill. 2d 231, 131 Ill. Dec. 551, 538 N.E.2d 1107 (1989)—8:7
People v. Manuel, 182 A.D.2d 711, 582 N.Y.S.2d 735 (2d Dep't 1992)—8:7
People v. Merced, 94 Cal. App. 4th 1024, 114 Cal. Rptr. 2d 781 (1st Dist. 2001)—2:21, 7:9, 7:54
People v. Powell, 224 Ill. App. 3d 127, 166 Ill. Dec. 631, 586 N.E.2d 589 (1st Dist. 1991)—7:12
People v. Reaud, 821 P.2d 870 (Colo. Ct. App. 1991)—7:9
People v. Sanchez, 58 Cal. App. 4th 1435, 69 Cal. Rptr. 2d 16 (2d Dist. 1997)—2:20, 7:54
People v. Seuffer, 144 Ill. 2d 482, 163 Ill. Dec. 805, 582 N.E.2d 71 (1991)—7:47
People v. Taylor, 5 Cal. App. 4th 1299, 7 Cal. Rptr. 2d 676 (2d Dist. 1992)—9:7, 9:15
People v. Wadle, 2003 WL 193687 (Colo. Ct. App. 2003)—3:12
People v. Wheeler, 22 Cal. 3d 258, 148 Cal. Rptr. 890, 583 P.2d 748 (1978)—8:6
People v. Zurenko, 833 P.2d 794 (Colo. Ct. App. 1991)—7:47
Peoples Bank of Pratt v. Integral Ins. Co., 251 Kan. 809, 840 P.2d 503 (1992)—7:28
Percell v. International Business Machines, Inc., 785 F. Supp. 1229, 61 Fair Empl. Prac. Cas. (BNA) 1060, 58

Table of Cases

Empl. Prac. Dec. (CCH) ¶ 41323 (E.D. N.C. 1992)—1:15

Peretz v. U.S., 501 U.S. 923, 111 S. Ct. 2661, 115 L. Ed. 2d 808 (1991)—9:5

Perez v. Marshall, 119 F.3d 1422 (9th Cir. 1997)—7:51

Petrocelli v. Angelone, 248 F.3d 877 (9th Cir. 2001)—11:14

Phea v. Benson, 95 F.3d 660 (8th Cir. 1996)—6:18

Pickens v. Lockhart, 4 F.3d 1446 (8th Cir. 1993)—7:53

Pickens v. Soo Line Railroad Co., 264 F.3d 773, 12 A.D. Cas. (BNA) 333 (8th Cir. 2001)—1:18

Pierre v. State, 607 So. 2d 43 (Miss. 1992)—7:5

Pioneer Inv. Services Co. v. Brunswick Associates Ltd. Partnership, 507 U.S. 380, 113 S. Ct. 1489, 123 L. Ed. 2d 74, 24 Bankr. Ct. Dec. (CRR) 63, 28 Collier Bankr. Cas. 2d (MB) 267, Bankr. L. Rep. (CCH) ¶ 75157A, 25 Fed. R. Serv. 3d 401 (1993)—1:22

Pitsonbarger v. Gramley, 103 F.3d 1293 (7th Cir. 1996)—7:53

Pitsonbarger v. Gramley, 141 F.3d 728 (7th Cir. 1998)—7:53

Polk v. Dixie Ins. Co., 972 F.2d 83 (5th Cir. 1992)—12:9

Powers v. Ohio, 499 U.S. 400, 111 S. Ct. 1364, 113 L. Ed. 2d 411 (1991)—2:7, 6:1, 6:11, 6:15, 8:6, 8:9, 8:10, 8:12, 8:13

Powers v. Palacios, 813 S.W.2d 489 (Tex. 1991)—8:6

Preferred Properties, Inc. v. Indian River Estates, Inc., 276 F.3d 790, 2002 FED App. 0006P (6th Cir. 2002)—8:2

Preferred RX, Inc. v. American Prescription Plan, Inc., 46 F.3d 535, 1995 FED App. 0046P (6th Cir. 1995)—1:21, 1:22

Price v. Kramer, 200 F.3d 1237 (9th Cir. 2000)—9:10

Pruett v. Norris, 153 F.3d 579 (8th Cir. 1998)—2:4

Purkett v. Elem, 514 U.S. 765, 115 S. Ct. 1769, 131 L. Ed. 2d 834 (1995)—8:6, 8:7

Q

Quintero v. Bell, 256 F.3d 409, 2001 FED App. 0205P (6th Cir. 2001)—7:19

R

Rachal v. Ingram Corp., 795 F.2d 1210, 5 Fed. R. Serv. 3d 1006 (5th Cir. 1986)—1:14

Rainey v. Conerly, 973 F.2d 321 (4th Cir. 1992)—7:46

Ramseur v. Beyer, 983 F.2d 1215 (3d Cir. 1992)—6:1, 6:17

Randolph v. State, 203 Ga. App. 115, 416 S.E.2d 117 (1992)—8:7

Ratliff v. Schiber Truck Co., Inc., 150 F.3d 949, 49 Fed. R. Evid. Serv. 1450 (8th Cir. 1998)—9:5, 9:11

Ray v. Gream, 860 S.W.2d 325 (Mo. 1993)—7:6

Raymond v. International Business Machines Corp., 148 F.3d 63, 40 Fed. R. Serv. 3d 1177 (2d Cir. 1998)—1:22

Real v. Wal Mart Stores, Inc., 2002 WL 80664 (Cal. App. 2d Dist. 2002), unpublished/noncitable, (Jan. 22, 2002)—3:12

Reynolds v. Benefield, 931 F.2d 506 (8th Cir. 1991)—8:7

Richards v. Procter & Gamble

Mfg. Co., 753 F. Supp. 71, 19 Fed. R. Serv. 3d 185 (E.D. N.Y. 1991)—1:17

Richardson v. Bowersox, 188 F.3d 973 (8th Cir. 1999)—7:9, 7:53

Ricketts v. City of Hartford, 74 F.3d 1397, 43 Fed. R. Evid. Serv. 903 (2d Cir. 1996)—6:13, 6:18

Rideau v. Whitley, 237 F.3d 472 (5th Cir. 2000)—6:17, 6:18

Riley v. Taylor, 277 F.3d 261 (3d Cir. 2001)—8:7

Rine By and Through Rine v. Irisari, 187 W. Va. 550, 420 S.E.2d 541 (1992)—7:25

Ring v. Arizona, 536 U.S. 584, 122 S. Ct. 2428, 153 L. Ed. 2d 556 (2002)—1:13A

Ritchie v. Rogers, 313 F.3d 948, 2002 FED App. 0426P (6th Cir. 2002)—2:4, 9:8

Roberson v. Hayti Police Dept., 241 F.3d 992, 49 Fed. R. Serv. 3d 327 (8th Cir. 2001)—6:18

Rock v. State, 638 So. 2d 933 (Fla. 1994)—8:7

Rodriguez v. Riddell Sports, Inc., 242 F.3d 567, Prod. Liab. Rep. (CCH) ¶ 16004, 56 Fed. R. Evid. Serv. 708 (5th Cir. 2001)—8:2

Rosa v. Peters, 36 F.3d 625 (7th Cir. 1994)—8:6

Ross v. Oklahoma, 487 U.S. 81, 108 S. Ct. 2273, 101 L. Ed. 2d 80 (1988)—7:5, 7:12, 7:53, 8:11

Ruff v. Armontrout, 77 F.3d 265 (8th Cir. 1996)—8:6, 8:11

Rush v. Smith, 45 F.3d 1197 (8th Cir. 1995)—7:50, 8:7

Rush v. Smith, 56 F.3d 918 (8th Cir. 1995)—8:7

Russ v. Standard Ins. Co., 120 F.3d 988, 38 Fed. R. Serv. 3d 211 (9th Cir. 1997)—1:17

S

Salazar v. State, 107 Nev. 982, 823 P.2d 273 (1991)—9:11

Salazar v. State, 795 S.W.2d 187 (Tex. Crim. App. 1990)—8:7

Sallahdin v. Gibson, 275 F.3d 1211 (10th Cir. 2002)—7:5, 7:53, 9:11

Salmon v. Schwarz, 948 F.2d 1131 (10th Cir. 1991)—1:14

Sasaki v. Class, 92 F.3d 232, 71 Fair Empl. Prac. Cas. (BNA) 709, 69 Empl. Prac. Dec. (CCH) ¶ 44353 (4th Cir. 1996)—9:11

Scarpa v. DuBois, 38 F.3d 1 (1st Cir. 1994)—8:6

Scott v. Lawrence, 36 F.3d 871 (9th Cir. 1994)—9:6

Scott v. Mitchell, 209 F.3d 854, 2000 FED App. 0138P (6th Cir. 2000)—9:11

Scott v. State, 599 So. 2d 1222 (Ala. Crim. App. 1992)—8:6

S.E.C. v. Rind, 991 F.2d 1486, Fed. Sec. L. Rep. (CCH) ¶ 97421 (9th Cir. 1993)—1:14

Securities and Exchange Commission v. Commonwealth Chemical Securities, Inc., 574 F.2d 90, Fed. Sec. L. Rep. (CCH) ¶ 96351 (2d Cir. 1978)—1:14

Segrets, Inc. v. Gillman Knitwear Co., Inc., 207 F.3d 56, 54 U.S.P.Q.2d (BNA) 1158 (1st Cir. 2000)—1:14

Sellers v. Ward, 135 F.3d 1333 (10th Cir. 1998)—7:53

Shaw v. Hahn, 56 F.3d 1128 (9th Cir. 1995)—8:11

Shelton v. Consumer Products Safety Com'n, 277 F.3d 998, 58 Fed. R. Evid. Serv. 96, 51 Fed. R. Serv. 3d 1131 (8th Cir. 2002)—1:22

Shurn v. Delo, 177 F.3d 662 (8th Cir. 1999)—8:6

TABLE OF CASES

Silagy v. Peters, 905 F.2d 986, 30 Fed. R. Evid. Serv. 395, 30 Fed. R. Evid. Serv. 399 (7th Cir. 1990)—6:16

Silverthorne v. U.S., 400 F.2d 627 (9th Cir. 1968)—9:8, 11:16

Simmons v. Beyer, 44 F.3d 1160 (3d Cir. 1995)—8:6

Simmons v. Luebbers, 299 F.3d 929 (8th Cir. 2002)—8:7

Simpson v. Office of Thrift Supervision, 29 F.3d 1418 (9th Cir. 1994)—1:14

Singh v. Blue Cross/Blue Shield of Massachusetts, Inc., 308 F.3d 25 (1st Cir. 2002)—1:14

Siripongs v. Calderon, 35 F.3d 1308 (9th Cir. 1994)—7:53

Siwek v. Farley, 681 F. Supp. 1034 (W.D. N.Y. 1988)—9:5

Skaggs v. Otis Elevator Co., 528 U.S. 811, 120 S. Ct. 44, 145 L. Ed. 2d 39 (1999)—9:10

Sledd v. McKune, 71 F.3d 797 (10th Cir. 1995)—8:7

Smith v. Dowden, 47 F.3d 940, 26 Bankr. Ct. Dec. (CRR) 820, Bankr. L. Rep. (CCH) ¶ 76386, 30 Fed. R. Serv. 3d 1184 (8th Cir. 1995)—1:14

Smith v. State, 201 Ga. App. 82, 410 S.E.2d 202 (1991)—7:52

Smith v. Vicorp, Inc., 107 F.3d 816, 37 Fed. R. Serv. 3d 145 (10th Cir. 1997)—7:34

Smyly v. Hyundai Motor America, 762 F. Supp. 428 (D. Mass. 1991)—1:21

SNA Nut Co. v. Haagen-Dazs Company, Inc., 302 F.3d 725 (7th Cir. 2002)—1:14

Society of Separationists, Inc. v. Herman, 939 F.2d 1207 (5th Cir. 1991)—7:40

Solis v. Walker, 799 F. Supp. 23 (S.D. N.Y. 1992)—7:19

Soria v. Johnson, 207 F.3d 232 (5th Cir. 2000)—7:53, 8:6, 9:11, 9:32

South Port Marine, LLC v. Gulf Oil Ltd. Partnership, 234 F.3d 58, 51 Env't. Rep. Cas. (BNA) 1749, 2001 A.M.C. 609, 31 Envtl. L. Rep. 20344 (1st Cir. 2000)—1:14

Spencer v. Murray, 5 F.3d 758 (4th Cir. 1993)—7:11

Spinelli v. Gaughan, 12 F.3d 853, 17 Employee Benefits Cas. (BNA) 2006, 9 I.E.R. Cas. (BNA) 214 (9th Cir. 1993)—1:14

Spivey v. Head, 207 F.3d 1263 (11th Cir. 2000)—2:4, 7:53

Splunge v. Clark, 960 F.2d 705 (7th Cir. 1992)—8:6, 8:7

Spytma v. Howes, 313 F.3d 363, 2002 FED App. 0415P (6th Cir. 2002)—1:22

Stafford v. Saffle, 34 F.3d 1557 (10th Cir. 1994)—2:4, 7:10

Staley v. Bridgestone/Firestone, Inc., 106 F.3d 1504, Prod. Liab. Rep. (CCH) ¶ 14871, 46 Fed. R. Evid. Serv. 526 (10th Cir. 1997)—7:5

Stanford v. Parker, 266 F.3d 442, 2001 FED App. 0334P (6th Cir. 2001)—7:53

Stansbury Poplar Place, Inc., In re, 13 F.3d 122, 25 Bankr. Ct. Dec. (CRR) 95, 30 Collier Bankr. Cas. 2d (MB) 493, Bankr. L. Rep. (CCH) ¶ 75636 (4th Cir. 1993)—1:14

Stark v. Com., 828 S.W.2d 603 (Ky. 1991)—8:7

State v. Atwood, 171 Ariz. 576, 832 P.2d 593 (1992)—6:16

State v. Bible, 175 Ariz. 549, 858 P.2d 1152 (1993)—2:4, 7:5, 7:6, 7:10, 7:16, 9:1, 9:5, 9:8

State v. Bingham, 176 Ariz. 146, 859 P.2d 769 (Ct. App. Div.

1 1993), redesignated as— 7:46

State v. Claybrook, 736 S.W.2d 95 (Tenn. 1987)—9:8, 11:16

State v. Cox, 826 P.2d 656 (Utah Ct. App. 1992)—7:28

State v. Davis, 504 N.W.2d 767, 63 A.L.R.5th 837 (Minn. 1993)—8:8

State v. Echineque, 73 Haw. 100, 828 P.2d 276 (1992)—8:3

State v. Elem, 747 S.W.2d 772 (Mo. Ct. App. E.D. 1988)—8:7

State v. Esposito, 223 Conn. 299, 613 A.2d 242 (1992)—7:22

State v. Finley, 177 W. Va. 554, 355 S.E.2d 47 (1987)—9:8, 11:16

State v. Gary, 822 S.W.2d 448 (Mo. Ct. App. E.D. 1991)—7:52

State v. Gesch, 167 Wis. 2d 660, 482 N.W.2d 99 (1992)—7:23

State v. Gleason, 65 Ohio App. 3d 206, 583 N.E.2d 975 (1st Dist. Hamilton County 1989)—7:39

State v. Goodson, 412 So. 2d 1077 (La. 1982)—9:8, 11:16

State v. Grate, 310 S.C. 240, 423 S.E.2d 119 (1992)—8:7

State v. Hadley, 815 S.W.2d 422 (Mo. 1991)—7:5

State v. Herman, 93 Wash. 2d 590, 611 P.2d 748 (1980)—9:8, 11:16

State v. Hodge, 248 Conn. 207, 726 A.2d 531 (1999)—8:8

State v. Isgitt, 590 So. 2d 763 (La. Ct. App. 3d Cir. 1991)—7:5

State v. Jackson, 629 So. 2d 1374 (La. Ct. App. 2d Cir. 1993)—7:9, 7:51

State v. Jones, 596 So. 2d 1360 (La. Ct. App. 1st Cir. 1992)—9:11

State v. Kamienski, 254 N.J. Super. 75, 603 A.2d 78 (App. Div. 1992)—9:8

State v. Kelly, 823 S.W.2d 95 (Mo. Ct. App. E.D. 1991)—7:46

State v. Long, 590 So. 2d 694 (La. Ct. App. 3d Cir. 1991)—7:11

State v. Lumumba, 253 N.J. Super. 375, 601 A.2d 1178 (App. Div. 1992)—9:2

State v. Mayer, 589 So. 2d 1145 (La. Ct. App. 5th Cir. 1991)—8:2

State v. Mills, 65 Ohio St. 3d 1447, 601 N.E.2d 42 (1992)—9:1, 9:5, 9:14

State v. Nalls, 835 S.W.2d 509 (Mo. Ct. App. E.D. 1992)—7:12, 7:13

State v. Neely, 112 N.M. 702, 819 P.2d 249 (1991)—6:17

State v. O'Brien, 158 Vt. 275, 609 A.2d 981 (1992)—1:7

State v. Pokini, 55 Haw. 640, 526 P.2d 94 (1974)—9:8, 11:16

State v. Ramsey, 864 S.W.2d 320 (Mo. 1993)—7:9, 7:53

State v. Roderick, 828 S.W.2d 729 (Mo. Ct. App. E.D. 1992)—7:52

State v. Ross, 623 So. 2d 643 (La. 1993)—7:53

State v. Shields, 709 S.W.2d 556, 65 A.L.R.4th 739 (Mo. Ct. App. E.D. 1986)—7:12, 7:13

State v. Shurn, 866 S.W.2d 447 (Mo. 1993)—6:17

State v. Smith, 222 Conn. 1, 608 A.2d 63 (1992)—9:13

State v. Smith, 623 So. 2d 682 (La. Ct. App. 4th Cir. 1993)—1:22

State v. Spitler, 75 Ohio App. 3d 341, 599 N.E.2d 408 (10th Dist. Franklin County 1991)—8:8

TABLE OF CASES

State v. Tillman, 220 Conn. 487, 600 A.2d 738 (1991)—6:16

State v. Varner, 643 N.W.2d 298 (Minn. 2002)—7:41, 9:11

State v. Whitfield, 837 S.W.2d 503 (Mo. 1992)—6:18

State v. Wiltshire, 241 Neb. 817, 491 N.W.2d 324 (1992)—1:7

Stilson v. U S, 250 U.S. 583, 40 S. Ct. 28, 63 L. Ed. 1154 (1919)—8:1, 8:13

Stubbs v. Gomez, 189 F.3d 1099 (9th Cir. 1999)—8:7

Sullivan v. Louisiana, 508 U.S. 275, 113 S. Ct. 2078, 124 L. Ed. 2d 182 (1993)—1:5

Swain v. Alabama, 380 U.S. 202, 85 S. Ct. 824, 13 L. Ed. 2d 759 (1965)—8:1, 8:5, 8:7

Sweet v. Delo, 125 F.3d 1144 (8th Cir. 1997)—6:6, 7:53

Sydnor v. Conseco Financial Servicing Corp., 252 F.3d 302 (4th Cir. 2001)—1:21

Szuchon v. Lehman, 273 F.3d 299 (3d Cir. 2001)—7:53

T

Tankleff v. Senkowski, 135 F.3d 235 (2d Cir. 1998)—8:6, 8:7, 9:3

Tegal Corp. v. Tokyo Electron America, Inc., 257 F.3d 1331, 59 U.S.P.Q.2d (BNA) 1385 (Fed. Cir. 2001)—1:14

Texas General Petroleum Corp., Matter of, 52 F.3d 1330, 27 Bankr. Ct. Dec. (CRR) 399, Bankr. L. Rep. (CCH) ¶ 76512 (5th Cir. 1995)—1:14

the Territory of Guam, People of v. Palomo, 35 F.3d 368 (9th Cir. 1994)—9:5

Thomas, Ex parte, 601 So. 2d 56 (Ala. 1992)—8:7

Thomas v. Borg, 159 F.3d 1147 (9th Cir. 1998)—6:17

Thomas v. Com., 864 S.W.2d 252 (Ky. 1993)—7:5, 7:22, 7:30, 7:53, 8:1

Thompson v. Altheimer & Gray, 248 F.3d 621, 85 Fair Empl. Prac. Cas. (BNA) 897, 80 Empl. Prac. Dec. (CCH) ¶ 40636 (7th Cir. 2001)—7:8

Thompson v. Borg, 74 F.3d 1571 (9th Cir. 1996)—7:10, 9:8

Thompson v. Mahre, 110 F.3d 716 (9th Cir. 1997)—1:22

Thorson v. State, 721 So. 2d 590 (Miss. 1998)—8:8

Tidemann v. Nadler Golf Car Sales, Inc., 224 F.3d 719, 47 Fed. R. Serv. 3d 810 (7th Cir. 2000)—7:31, 8:2

Tinner v. United Ins. Co. of America, 308 F.3d 697, 89 Fair Empl. Prac. Cas. (BNA) 1843 (7th Cir. 2002)—8:7, 8:10

Tischmann v. ITT/Sheraton Corp., 145 F.3d 561 (2d Cir. 1998)—1:14

Todd v. Ortho Biotech, Inc., 138 F.3d 733, 76 Fair Empl. Prac. Cas. (BNA) 341, 72 Empl. Prac. Dec. (CCH) ¶ 45239 (8th Cir. 1998)—1:14

Todd v. Schomig, 283 F.3d 842 (7th Cir. 2002)—1:22

Tolbert v. Gomez, 190 F.3d 985 (9th Cir. 1999)—8:5, 8:7

Tolbert v. Page, 182 F.3d 677 (9th Cir. 1999)—8:6

Transmatic, Inc. v. Gulton Industries, Inc., 53 F.3d 1270, 35 U.S.P.Q.2d (BNA) 1035 (Fed. Cir. 1995)—1:21

Trice v. Ward, 196 F.3d 1151 (10th Cir. 1999)—6:17, 6:18

Troupe v. Groose, 72 F.3d 75 (8th Cir. 1995)—8:7

Truesdale v. Moore, 142 F.3d 749 (4th Cir. 1998)—6:8, 7:53

Tuggle v. Thompson, 57 F.3d 1356 (4th Cir. 1995)—9:8

© West, a Thomson business, 11/2003

Tull v. U.S., 481 U.S. 412, 107 S. Ct. 1831, 95 L. Ed. 2d 365, 25 Env't. Rep. Cas. (BNA) 1857, 7 Fed. R. Serv. 3d 673, 17 Envtl. L. Rep. 20667 (1987)—1:14

Turner v. Marshall, 121 F.3d 1248 (9th Cir. 1997)—8:6

Turner v. Marshall, 63 F.3d 807 (9th Cir. 1995)—8:6

Turpin v. Kassulke, 26 F.3d 1392, 1994 FED App. 0224P (6th Cir. 1994)—8:2

Tyus v. Urban Search Management, 102 F.3d 256, 45 Fed. R. Evid. Serv. 1428 (7th Cir. 1996)—7:41

U

Universal Consol. Companies, Inc. v. Bank of China, 35 F.3d 243, 1994 FED App. 0311P (6th Cir. 1994)—1:14

U.S. v. Abbell, 271 F.3d 1286 (11th Cir. 2001)—7:5, 7:54

U.S. v. Abou-Kassem, 78 F.3d 161, 44 Fed. R. Evid. Serv. 499 (5th Cir. 1996)—8:6

U.S. v. Acker, 52 F.3d 509, 42 Fed. R. Evid. Serv. 181 (4th Cir. 1995)—7:50

U.S. v. Adams, 305 F.3d 30 (1st Cir. 2002)—9:5, 9:11

U.S. v. Addonizio, 451 F.2d 49 (3d Cir. 1971)—9:8, 11:16

U.S. v. Aguirre, 108 F.3d 1284 (10th Cir. 1997)—6:17, 6:18

U.S. v. Alanis, 265 F.3d 576 (7th Cir. 2001)—6:18, 8:7

U.S. v. Alarape, 969 F.2d 349 (7th Cir. 1992)—6:17, 7:40

U.S. v. Alcantar, 897 F.2d 436 (9th Cir. 1990)—8:7

U.S. v. Ali, 63 F.3d 710 (8th Cir. 1995)—8:7

U.S. v. Alix, 86 F.3d 429 (5th Cir. 1996)—6:18

U.S. v. Allah, 130 F.3d 33 (2d Cir. 1997)—11:14

U.S. v. Allen, 160 F.3d 1096, 1998 FED App. 0341P (6th Cir. 1998)—6:7, 6:8

U.S. v. Allen, 247 F.3d 741, 56 Fed. R. Evid. Serv. 1144 (8th Cir. 2001)—7:10, 9:8

U.S. v. Allen-Brown, 243 F.3d 1293 (11th Cir. 2001)—8:7

U.S. v. Aloi, 9 F.3d 438 (6th Cir. 1993)—11:15

U.S. v. Alvarado, 923 F.2d 253 (2d Cir. 1991)—8:6

U.S. v. Amerson, 938 F.2d 116 (8th Cir. 1991)—7:46

U.S. v. Amuso, 21 F.3d 1251, 39 Fed. R. Evid. Serv. 569 (2d Cir. 1994)—4:5, 9:14

U.S. v. Anderson, 139 F.3d 291 (1st Cir. 1998)—6:18

U.S. v. Anderson, 303 F.3d 847, 59 Fed. R. Evid. Serv. 1514 (7th Cir. 2002)—7:5

U.S. v. Anderson, 39 F.3d 331 (D.C. Cir. 1994), reh'g in banc granted—8:3

U.S. v. Angiulo, 847 F.2d 956, 26 Fed. R. Evid. Serv. 515 (1st Cir. 1988)—8:8

U.S. v. Annigoni, 57 F.3d 739 (9th Cir. 1995)—8:11

U.S. v. Annigoni, 96 F.3d 1132 (9th Cir. 1996)—8:7

U.S. v. Antar, 38 F.3d 1348, 22 Media L. Rep. (BNA) 2417, Fed. Sec. L. Rep. (CCH) ¶ 98436, 40 Fed. R. Evid. Serv. 1006 (3d Cir. 1994)—3:14, 4:5

U.S. v. Araujo, 62 F.3d 930 (7th Cir. 1995)—7:50

U.S. v. Arce, 997 F.2d 1123, 39 Fed. R. Evid. Serv. 450 (5th Cir. 1993)—6:4

U.S. v. Armendariz-Mata, 949 F.2d 151, 34 Fed. R. Evid. Serv. 399 (5th Cir. 1991)—7:46

U.S. v. Arocho, 305 F.3d 627, 59 Fed. R. Evid. Serv. 1556 (7th Cir. 2002)—9:10

TABLE OF CASES

U.S. v. Ashley, 54 F.3d 311 (7th Cir. 1995)—6:3, 6:17
U.S. v. Atkins, 25 F.3d 1401, 74 A.F.T.R.2d 94-5069 (8th Cir. 1994)—8:7
U.S. v. Aulicino, 44 F.3d 1102 (2d Cir. 1995)—4:5, 9:14
U.S. v. Badru, 97 F.3d 1471, 45 Fed. R. Evid. Serv. 1026 (D.C. Cir. 1996)—7:12, 9:13
U.S. v. Bahna, 68 F.3d 19 (2d Cir. 1995)—6:3
U.S. v. Bailey, 112 F.3d 758 (4th Cir. 1997)—2:4, 7:10, 9:8
U.S. v. Bailey, 76 F.3d 320 (10th Cir. 1996)—6:11
U.S. v. Baker, 10 F.3d 1374, 38 Fed. R. Evid. Serv. 638 (9th Cir. 1993)—7:30, 9:5
U.S. v. Baker, 262 F.3d 124 (2d Cir. 2001)—7:5, 7:54
U.S. v. Baker, 855 F.2d 1353, 26 Fed. R. Evid. Serv. 1069 (8th Cir. 1988)—8:11
U.S. v. Baker, 98 F.3d 330, 45 Fed. R. Evid. Serv. 806 (8th Cir. 1996)—6:13
U.S. v. Bakker, 925 F.2d 728, 32 Fed. R. Evid. Serv. 303 (4th Cir. 1991)—2:4, 7:10, 9:1
U.S. v. Balint, 201 F.3d 928 (7th Cir. 2000)—1:6
U.S. v. Balistrieri, 778 F.2d 1226 (7th Cir. 1985)—6:13
U.S. v. Ballek, 170 F.3d 871 (9th Cir. 1999)—1:6
U.S. v. Barber, 80 F.3d 964, 44 Fed. R. Evid. Serv. 281 (4th Cir. 1996)—7:42, 9:12
U.S. v. Barnette, 211 F.3d 803, 53 Fed. R. Evid. Serv. 1346 (4th Cir. 2000)—7:53, 8:7
U.S. v. Barone, 114 F.3d 1284, 47 Fed. R. Evid. Serv. 211 (1st Cir. 1997)—7:28
U.S. v. Barry, 71 F.3d 1269 (7th Cir. 1995)—6:4
U.S. v. Bartelho, 71 F.3d 436, 43 Fed. R. Evid. Serv. 501 (1st Cir. 1995)—7:19
U.S. v. Bartholomew, 310 F.3d 912, 59 Fed. R. Evid. Serv. 1482, 2002 FED App. 0396P (6th Cir. 2002)—8:7
U.S. v. Bascope-Zurita, 68 F.3d 1057 (8th Cir. 1995)—7:11
U.S. v. Beard, 161 F.3d 1190 (9th Cir. 1998)—7:50, 7:51
U.S. v. Beasley, 48 F.3d 262 (7th Cir. 1995)—7:52
U.S. v. Beckman, 222 F.3d 512, 55 Fed. R. Evid. Serv. 543 (8th Cir. 2000)—11:14
U.S. v. Beckner, 69 F.3d 1290 (5th Cir. 1995)—7:5, 7:10
U.S. v. Benjamin, 252 F.3d 1 (1st Cir. 2001)—6:17
U.S. v. Berger, 224 F.3d 107 (2d Cir. 2000)—8:8
U.S. v. Bergodere, 40 F.3d 512 (1st Cir. 1994)—8:6, 8:7
U.S. v. Bernard, 299 F.3d 467 (5th Cir. 2002)—7:53
U.S. v. Bieganowski, 313 F.3d 264 (5th Cir. 2002)—7:5, 7:10, 9:8
U.S. v. Bishop, 264 F.3d 535, 2001-2 U.S. Tax Cas. (CCH) ¶ 50762, 57 Fed. R. Evid. Serv. 1087, 88 A.F.T.R.2d 2001-5991 (5th Cir. 2001)—6:4, 9:10
U.S. v. Bishop, 291 F.3d 1100, 2002-2 U.S. Tax Cas. (CCH) ¶ 50488, 59 Fed. R. Evid. Serv. 150, 89 A.F.T.R.2d 2002-2745 (9th Cir. 2002)—1:22
U.S. v. Bishop, 959 F.2d 820 (9th Cir. 1992)—8:6, 8:7
U.S. v. Blackman, 66 F.3d 1572, 43 Fed. R. Evid. Serv. 211 (11th Cir. 1995)—8:7
U.S. v. Blanding, 250 F.3d 858 (4th Cir. 2001)—8:8
U.S. v. Blom, 242 F.3d 799 (8th Cir. 2001)—2:4, 7:10

U.S. v. Blotcher, 142 F.3d 728 (4th Cir. 1998)—8:7

U.S. v. Bobo, 994 F.2d 524, 37 Fed. R. Evid. Serv. 1208, 125 A.L.R. Fed. 775 (8th Cir. 1993)—9:5

U.S. v. Boney, 977 F.2d 624, 36 Fed. R. Evid. Serv. 1358 (D.C. Cir. 1992)—6:4, 9:10

U.S. v. Borders, 270 F.3d 1180 (8th Cir. 2001)—7:42

U.S. v. Bornfield, 145 F.3d 1123, 49 Fed. R. Evid. Serv. 601 (10th Cir. 1998)—7:5

U.S. v. Bowman, 302 F.3d 1228, 59 Fed. R. Evid. Serv. 1018 (11th Cir. 2002)—4:5, 9:14

U.S. v. Boyd, 168 F.3d 1077 (8th Cir. 1999)—8:7

U.S. v. Boyd, 792 F. Supp. 1083 (N.D. Ill. 1992)—4:5, 9:14

U.S. v. Boyd, 86 F.3d 719 (7th Cir. 1996)—8:6, 8:9

U.S. v. Bradley, 173 F.3d 225 (3d Cir. 1999)—7:5

U.S. v. Branch, 91 F.3d 699, 45 Fed. R. Evid. Serv. 676 (5th Cir. 1996)—4:5, 9:14

U.S. v. Branch, 989 F.2d 752 (5th Cir. 1993)—8:6

U.S. v. Brandon, 17 F.3d 409 (1st Cir. 1994)—2:4, 9:5

U.S. v. Breen, 243 F.3d 591 (2d Cir. 2001)—7:5

U.S. v. Brewer, 199 F.3d 1283 (11th Cir. 2000)—6:7

U.S. v. Brisk, 171 F.3d 514, 51 Fed. R. Evid. Serv. 932 (7th Cir. 1999)—8:6

U.S. v. Broadus, 7 F.3d 460, 39 Fed. R. Evid. Serv. 765 (6th Cir. 1993)—8:3

U.S. v. Brooks, 161 F.3d 1240, 50 Fed. R. Evid. Serv. 899 (10th Cir. 1998)—7:5, 8:11

U.S. v. Brooks, 174 F.3d 950, 83 A.F.T.R.2d 99-2202 (8th Cir. 1999)—9:5

U.S. v. Brooks, 175 F.3d 605 (8th Cir. 1999)—7:5, 8:11

U.S. v. Brown, 250 F.3d 907, 29 Media L. Rep. (BNA) 1779 (5th Cir. 2001)—3:14, 4:5, 9:14

U.S. v. Brown, 26 F.3d 1124 (D.C. Cir. 1994)—7:52, 9:10

U.S. v. Brown, 289 F.3d 989 (7th Cir. 2002)—8:7

U.S. v. Brown, 299 F.3d 1252, 59 Fed. R. Evid. Serv. 410 (11th Cir. 2002)—8:7

U.S. v. Brown, 303 F.3d 582, 59 Fed. R. Evid. Serv. 1032 (5th Cir. 2002)—4:5, 9:14

U.S. v. Brown, 91 F.3d 1109 (8th Cir. 1996)—6:17

U.S. v. Brown, 927 F.2d 406 (8th Cir. 1991)—9:8

U.S. v. Brown, 938 F.2d 1482, 33 Fed. R. Evid. Serv. 790 (1st Cir. 1991)—7:42, 9:6

U.S. v. Brown, 941 F.2d 656 (8th Cir. 1991)—8:6

U.S. v. Broxton, 926 F.2d 1180 (D.C. Cir. 1991)—8:3

U.S. v. Bryant, 991 F.2d 171 (5th Cir. 1993)—7:52

U.S. v. Bryce, 208 F.3d 346, 54 Fed. R. Evid. Serv. 184 (2d Cir. 1999)—8:7

U.S. v. Buchanan, 213 F.3d 302, 54 Fed. R. Evid. Serv. 265, 2000 FED App. 0060P (6th Cir. 2000)—8:7

U.S. v. Buchanan, 213 F.3d 302, 54 Fed. R. Evid. Serv. 265, 2000 FED App. 0060P (6th Cir. 2000), as—6:18

U.S. v. Burger, 773 F. Supp. 1430 (D. Kan. 1991)—8:2

U.S. v. Burgess, 836 F. Supp. 336 (D.S.C. 1993)—6:8, 6:16

U.S. v. Burrous, 147 F.3d 111 (2d Cir. 1998)—7:40

U.S. v. Bushyhead, 270 F.3d 905 (9th Cir. 2001)—6:3, 6:16

U.S. v. Calabrese, 942 F.2d 218 (3d Cir. 1991)—6:6, 6:11, 7:22

TABLE OF CASES

U.S. v. Calabrese, 942 F.2d 218, (3d Cir. 1991)—6:11

U.S. v. California Mobile Home Park Management Co., 107 F.3d 1374, 20 A.D.D. 658, 36 Fed. R. Serv. 3d 1176 (9th Cir. 1997)—1:22

U.S. v. Cambara, 902 F.2d 144 (1st Cir. 1990)—7:5, 8:11

U.S. v. Campbell, 270 F.3d 702 (8th Cir. 2001)—8:7

U.S. v. Campbell, 317 F.3d 597, 60 Fed. R. Evid. Serv. 1197, 2003 FED App. 0032P (6th Cir. 2003)—8:7

U.S. v. Candelaria-Silva, 166 F.3d 19, 51 Fed. R. Evid. Serv. 210 (1st Cir. 1999)—6:4, 6:6, 6:11, 9:3

U.S. v. Canfield, 879 F.2d 446 (8th Cir. 1989)—6:16

U.S. v. Cannady, 54 F.3d 544 (9th Cir. 1995)—6:3

U.S. v. Cannon, 88 F.3d 1495 (8th Cir. 1996)—2:5

U.S. v. Canoy, 38 F.3d 893 (7th Cir. 1994)—8:7

U.S. v. Cantu, 229 F.3d 544, 2000 FED App. 0365P (6th Cir. 2000)—6:4, 7:5

U.S. v. Carr, 67 F.3d 171, 43 Fed. R. Evid. Serv. 125 (8th Cir. 1995)—8:7

U.S. v. Cashwell, 950 F.2d 699 (11th Cir. 1992)—8:6, 9:33

U.S. v. Casper, 956 F.2d 416 (3d Cir. 1992)—8:6

U.S. v. Castorena-Jaime, 285 F.3d 916 (10th Cir. 2002)—8:7

U.S. v. Causey, 185 F.3d 407 (5th Cir. 1999)—8:7

U.S. v. Cencer, 90 F.3d 1103, 1996 FED App. 0230P (6th Cir. 1996)—7:50

U.S. v. Cerrato-Reyes, 176 F.3d 1253 (10th Cir. 1999)—7:4, 9:10

U.S. v. Chandler, 12 F.3d 1427 (7th Cir. 1994)—8:6

U.S. v. Chandler, 996 F.2d 1073, 39 Fed. R. Evid. Serv. 304 (11th Cir. 1993)—7:6, 7:39, 7:53

U.S. v. Changco, 1 F.3d 837 (9th Cir. 1993)—8:6

U.S. v. Chanthadara, 230 F.3d 1237 (10th Cir. 2000)—6:17, 7:5, 7:53, 9:1, 9:11

U.S. v. Chastain, 198 F.3d 1338, 53 Fed. R. Evid. Serv. 1107 (11th Cir. 1999)—7:5

U.S. v. Chavez, 204 F.3d 1305, 54 Fed. R. Evid. Serv. 426 (11th Cir. 2000)—1:6

U.S. v. Chen, 131 F.3d 375 (4th Cir. 1997)—8:7

U.S. v. Childress, 746 F. Supp. 1122 (D.D.C. 1990), aff'd, 58 F.3d 693 (D.C. Cir. 1995)—4:5, 9:14

U.S. v. Childs, 5 F.3d 1328, 37 Fed. R. Evid. Serv. 1344 (9th Cir. 1993)—8:7

U.S. v. Chinchilla, 874 F.2d 695 (9th Cir. 1989)—8:7

U.S. v. Chorney, 63 F.3d 78 (1st Cir. 1995)—7:50

U.S. v. Christensen, 18 F.3d 822 (9th Cir. 1994)—1:22

U.S. v. Christoffel, 952 F.2d 1086 (9th Cir. 1991)—8:2

U.S. v. Ciurinskas, 148 F.3d 729 (7th Cir. 1998)—1:14

U.S. v. Clark, 184 F.3d 858, 52 Fed. R. Evid. Serv. 126 (D.C. Cir. 1999)—6:7

U.S. v. Clemons, 843 F.2d 741 (3d Cir. 1988)—8:6

U.S. v. Cleveland, 128 F.3d 267, 25 Media L. Rep. (BNA) 2500 (5th Cir. 1997)—3:14

U.S. v. Cobb, 185 F.3d 1193 (11th Cir. 1999)—8:7

U.S. v. Cochran, 955 F.2d 1116, 35 Fed. R. Evid. Serv. 786 (7th Cir. 1992)—8:2

U.S. v. Colabella, 448 F.2d 1299 (2d Cir. 1971)—9:8, 11:16

U.S. v. Coleman, 997 F.2d 1101 (5th Cir. 1993)—9:10

U.S. v. Collazo-Aponte, 216 F.3d 163, 54 Fed. R. Evid. Serv. 1311 (1st Cir. 2000)—4:5, 6:6, 7:19, 8:2, 9:14

U.S. v. Collins, 972 F.2d 1385 (5th Cir. 1992)—3:2, 4:10, 8:6, 8:7, 9:10

U.S. v. Colombo, 869 F.2d 149 (2d Cir. 1989)—9:10

U.S. v. Colt, 126 F.3d 981 (7th Cir. 1997)—1:8

U.S. v. Contreras, 108 F.3d 1255 (10th Cir. 1997)—6:11, 6:17, 6:18

U.S. v. Contreras-Castro, 825 F.2d 185 (9th Cir. 1987)—7:46

U.S. v. Cooke, 110 F.3d 1288 (7th Cir. 1997)—6:17

U.S. v. Copeland, 321 F.3d 582, 61 Fed. R. Evid. Serv. 231, 2003 FED App. 0061A (6th Cir. 2003)—8:7

U.S. v. Coppins, 953 F.2d 86 (4th Cir. 1991)—1:6

U.S. v. Copple, 24 F.3d 535, 94-1 U.S. Tax Cas. (CCH) ¶ 50237, 39 Fed. R. Evid. Serv. 941, 74 A.F.T.R.2d 94-6133 (3d Cir. 1994)—4:3A

U.S. v. Cordoba-Mosquera, 212 F.3d 1194 (11th Cir. 2000)—8:7

U.S. v. Cordova, 157 F.3d 587, 50 Fed. R. Evid. Serv. 263 (8th Cir. 1998)—7:41

U.S. v. Cresta, 825 F.2d 538, 23 Fed. R. Evid. Serv. 687 (1st Cir. 1987)—8:8

U.S. v. Crockett, 979 F.2d 1204, 37 Fed. R. Evid. Serv. 217 (7th Cir. 1992)—4:5, 9:14

U.S. v. Cure, 996 F.2d 1136 (11th Cir. 1993)—8:7

U.S. v. Dakota, 197 F.3d 821, 84 A.F.T.R.2d 99-7427, 1999 FED App. 0419A (6th Cir. 1999)—4:5, 9:14

U.S. v. Daly, 974 F.2d 1215, 36 Fed. R. Evid. Serv. 1100 (9th Cir. 1992)—8:7, 12:9

U.S. v. Darden, 70 F.3d 1507, 43 Fed. R. Evid. Serv. 321 (8th Cir. 1995)—4:5, 8:7, 9:14

U.S. v. Davis, 154 F.3d 772, 49 Fed. R. Evid. Serv. 1487 (8th Cir. 1998)—8:7

U.S. v. Davis, 306 F.3d 398, 2002 FED App. 0329P (6th Cir. 2002)—7:22

U.S. v. Davis, 40 F.3d 1069, 40 Fed. R. Evid. Serv. 1036 (10th Cir. 1994)—8:7, 8:8

U.S. v. Davis, 583 F.2d 190 (5th Cir. 1978)—9:8, 11:16

U.S. v. Davis, 809 F.2d 1194, 22 Fed. R. Evid. Serv. 567 (6th Cir. 1987)—8:7

U.S. v. Dawn, 897 F.2d 1444 (8th Cir. 1990)—8:6

U.S. v. Day, 949 F.2d 973 (8th Cir. 1991)—8:6, 8:7

U.S. v. DeFries, 129 F.3d 1293, 156 L.R.R.M. (BNA) 2999 (D.C. Cir. 1997)—6:6

U.S. v. Delgado-Nunez, 295 F.3d 494 (5th Cir. 2002)—2:3

U.S. v. DeLuca, 137 F.3d 24 (1st Cir. 1998)—4:5, 9:14

U.S. v. Dempsey, 830 F.2d 1084, 24 Fed. R. Evid. Serv. 524 (10th Cir. 1987)—6:4, 7:50

U.S. v. Denman, 100 F.3d 399 (5th Cir. 1996)—8:7

U.S. v. Department of Mental Health, 785 F. Supp. 846, 58 Fair Empl. Prac. Cas. (BNA) 727, 58 Empl. Prac. Dec. (CCH) ¶ 41314, 132 A.L.R. Fed. 671 (E.D. Cal. 1992)—1:15

U.S. v. Diaz, 176 F.3d 52, 52 Fed. R. Evid. Serv. 380 (2d Cir. 1999)—7:5, 8:6, 8:7

U.S. v. Dickerson, 248 F.3d 1036, 56 Fed. R. Evid. Serv. 1216 (11th Cir. 2001)—7:52

TABLE OF CASES

U.S. v. Diggs, 82 F.3d 195, 44 Fed. R. Evid. Serv. 345 (8th Cir. 1996)—8:7
U.S. v. Dischner, 960 F.2d 870, 35 Fed. R. Evid. Serv. 485 (9th Cir. 1992)—2:4, 7:50
U.S. v. Donato, 99 F.3d 426 (D.C. Cir. 1996)—7:50
U.S. v. Douglas, 795 F. Supp. 909 (N.D. Iowa 1991)—6:8
U.S. v. Douglas, 837 F. Supp. 817 (N.D. Tex. 1993)—6:8, 6:11, 6:17, 6:18
U.S. v. Duarte-Higareda, 113 F.3d 1000 (9th Cir. 1997)—1:22
U.S. v. Dubon-Otero, 292 F.3d 1 (1st Cir. 2002)—6:4
U.S. v. Dubose, 146 F.3d 1141 (9th Cir. 1998)—1:14
U.S. v. Duke, 255 F.3d 656 (8th Cir. 2001)—9:8
U.S. v. Duncan, 191 F.3d 569 (5th Cir. 1999)—7:47
U.S. v. Durham, 139 F.3d 1325 (10th Cir. 1998)—2:2
U.S. v. Durman, 30 F.3d 803 (7th Cir. 1994)—9:8
U.S. v. Edmond, 52 F.3d 1080, 42 Fed. R. Evid. Serv. 119 (D.C. Cir. 1995)—4:5, 7:10, 9:14
U.S. v. Edwards, 188 F.3d 230 (4th Cir. 1999)—7:5
U.S. v. Edwards, 303 F.3d 606, 59 Fed. R. Evid. Serv. 1042 (5th Cir. 2002)—4:5, 7:5, 9:14
U.S. v. Edwards, 69 F.3d 419, 43 Fed. R. Evid. Serv. 225 (10th Cir. 1995)—6:18
U.S. v. Einfeldt, 138 F.3d 373, 48 Fed. R. Evid. Serv. 1386 (8th Cir. 1998)—6:8
U.S. v. Elliott, 89 F.3d 1360 (8th Cir. 1996)—8:6, 8:7
U.S. v. Erickson, 75 F.3d 470, 43 Fed. R. Evid. Serv. 944 (9th Cir. 1996)—6:11, 6:18
U.S. v. Escobar-de Jesus, 187 F.3d 148, 52 Fed. R. Evid. Serv. 1039 (1st Cir. 1999)—6:4, 7:42
U.S. v. Esparsen, 930 F.2d 1461 32 Fed. R. Evid. Serv. 1191 (10th Cir. 1991)—8:6
U.S. v. Esparsen, 930 F.2d 1461, 32 Fed. R. Evid. Serv. 1191 (10th Cir. 1991)—6:17, 8:6
U.S. v. Esquivel, 75 F.3d 545 (9th Cir. 1996)—6:13, 6:17, 6:18
U.S. v. Esquivel, 88 F.3d 722, 44 Fed. R. Evid. Serv. 1390 (9th Cir. 1996)—6:17, 6:18
U.S. v. Estrella, 104 F.3d 3 (1st Cir. 1997)—6:4
U.S. v. Etsitty, 130 F.3d 420, 48 Fed. R. Evid. Serv. 265 (9th Cir. 1997)—2:2, 2:5
U.S. v. Eubanks, 68 F.3d 272 (8th Cir. 1995)—8:7
U.S. v. Eufrasio, 935 F.2d 553, 32 Fed. R. Evid. Serv. 1262 (3d Cir. 1991)—4:5, 9:14
U.S. v. Evans, 192 F.3d 698 (7th Cir. 1999)—8:7
U.S. v. Evans, 272 F.3d 1069 (8th Cir. 2001)—7:5
U.S. v. Evans, 917 F.2d 800 (4th Cir. 1990)—7:46
U.S. v. Eyster, 948 F.2d 1196, 34 Fed. R. Evid. Serv. 688 (11th Cir. 1991)—6:7
U.S. v. Farmer, 923 F.2d 1557, 33 Fed. R. Evid. Serv. 188 (11th Cir. 1991)—7:5, 8:11
U.S. v. Feemster, 98 F.3d 1089 (8th Cir. 1996)—8:7
U.S. v. Ferguson, 23 F.3d 135, 1994 FED App. 0136P (6th Cir. 1994)—8:7
U.S. v. Fields, 72 F.3d 1200 (5th Cir. 1996)—8:7
U.S. v. Fike, 82 F.3d 1315, 44 Fed. R. Evid. Serv. 479 (5th Cir. 1996)—6:11, 6:17, 6:18, 8:7

U.S. v. Fish, 928 F.2d 185 (6th Cir. 1991)—9:13

U.S. v. Fisher, 22 F.3d 574 (5th Cir. 1994)—8:7

U.S. v. Fisher, 912 F.2d 728 (4th Cir. 1990)—2:13

U.S. v. Fletcher, 965 F.2d 781 (9th Cir. 1992)—6:16

U.S. v. Flores, 63 F.3d 1342, 42 Fed. R. Evid. Serv. 1365 (5th Cir. 1995)—7:10, 9:8

U.S. v. Flores-Rivera, 56 F.3d 319, 42 Fed. R. Evid. Serv. 499 (1st Cir. 1995)—6:4

U.S. v. Footracer, 189 F.3d 1058 (9th Cir. 1999)—2:2, 6:16, 6:18

U.S. v. Foster, 57 F.3d 727 (9th Cir. 1995)—7:18

U.S. v. 4.0 Acres of Land, 175 F.3d 1133, 51 Fed. R. Evid. Serv. 1586 (9th Cir. 1999)—1:14

U.S. v. Franklyn, 157 F.3d 90 (2d Cir. 1998)—8:6

U.S. v. Frazier, 274 F.3d 1185, 58 Fed. R. Evid. Serv. 138 (8th Cir. 2001)—2:13, 7:5

U.S. v. Fuller, 942 F.2d 454 (8th Cir. 1991)—8:7

U.S. v. Gaggi, 811 F.2d 47, 22 Fed. R. Evid. Serv. 586 (2d Cir. 1987)—9:11

U.S. v. Gaitan-Acevedo, 148 F.3d 577, 49 Fed. R. Evid. Serv. 590, 1998 FED App. 0143P (6th Cir. 1998)—7:4, 7:5

U.S. v. Gallegos, 108 F.3d 1272 (10th Cir. 1997)—6:17, 6:18

U.S. v. Garcia, 936 F.2d 648, 33 Fed. R. Evid. Serv. 206 (2d Cir. 1991)—7:18

U.S. v. Garcia, 991 F.2d 489 (8th Cir. 1993)—6:8, 6:17

U.S. v. Garcia-Flores, 246 F.3d 451 (5th Cir. 2001)—9:8

U.S. v. Garrett, 727 F.2d 1003, 15 Fed. R. Evid. Serv. 262 (11th Cir. 1984)—1:8, 1:22

U.S. v. Gaudin, 515 U.S. 506, 115 S. Ct. 2310, 132 L. Ed. 2d 444 (1995)—1:5

U.S. v. Gault, 141 F.3d 1399 (10th Cir. 1998)—6:17

U.S. v. Geffrard, 87 F.3d 448 (11th Cir. 1996)—7:9, 7:40

U.S. v. Gelb, 881 F.2d 1155 (2d Cir. 1989)—6:16, 6:17, 8:8

U.S. v. Gelb, 881 F.2d 1155, (2d Cir. 1989)—6:17

U.S. v. Gibbs, 182 F.3d 408, 1999 FED App. 0140P (6th Cir. 1999)—8:2, 8:7

U.S. v. Gibson, 135 F.3d 257 (2d Cir. 1998)—7:50

U.S. v. Gillis, 942 F.2d 707 (10th Cir. 1991)—7:5, 7:9, 7:19, 9:7

U.S. v. Gluzman, 154 F.3d 49 (2d Cir. 1998)—2:2

U.S. v. Goland, 959 F.2d 1449 (9th Cir. 1992)—7:45

U.S. v. Gomez-Lepe, 207 F.3d 623 (9th Cir. 2000)—2:17

U.S. v. Gonzalez, 214 F.3d 1109 (9th Cir. 2000)—7:4, 7:13

U.S. v. Gonzalez-Balderas, 11 F.3d 1218 (5th Cir. 1994)—7:39

U.S. v. Gonzalez-Soberal, 109 F.3d 64, 46 Fed. R. Evid. Serv. 868 (1st Cir. 1997)—6:4, 7:50

U.S. v. Gordon, 974 F.2d 97 (8th Cir. 1992)—8:6

U.S. v. Gotti, 777 F. Supp. 224 (E.D. N.Y. 1991)—4:5, 9:14

U.S. v. Grandison, 885 F.2d 143 (4th Cir. 1989)—8:6

U.S. v. Gray, 105 F.3d 956 (5th Cir. 1997)—9:11

U.S. v. Gray, 137 F.3d 765 (4th Cir. 1998)—1:5

U.S. v. Greene, 995 F.2d 793, 37 Fed. R. Evid. Serv. 574 (8th Cir. 1993)—6:4

U.S. v. Greer, 285 F.3d 158 (2d Cir. 2002)—9:3, 9:10

Table of Cases

U.S. v. Griffin, 194 F.3d 808, 52 Fed. R. Evid. Serv. 1593 (7th Cir. 1999)—8:7

U.S. v. Grimmond, 137 F.3d 823, 48 Fed. R. Evid. Serv. 1400 (4th Cir. 1998)—8:7

U.S. v. Grisham, 63 F.3d 1074 (11th Cir. 1995)—6:3

U.S. v. Guerra-Marez, 928 F.2d 665 (5th Cir. 1991)—8:6, 8:7

U.S. v. Hall, 152 F.3d 381, 49 Fed. R. Evid. Serv. 1503 (5th Cir. 1998)—7:5, 7:12, 7:53, 8:7, 8:11

U.S. v. Harbin, 250 F.3d 532 (7th Cir. 2001)—8:3

U.S. v. Hardwell, 80 F.3d 1471, 44 Fed. R. Evid. Serv. 571 (10th Cir. 1996), on reh'g—6:18

U.S. v. Harper, 33 F.3d 1143 (9th Cir. 1994)—8:3

U.S. v. Harrington, 108 F.3d 1460 (D.C. Cir. 1997)—7:50

U.S. v. Harris, 192 F.3d 580, 1999 FED App. 0340P (6th Cir. 1999)—8:5

U.S. v. Harris, 197 F.3d 870 (7th Cir. 1999)—8:8

U.S. v. Harris, 293 F.3d 970, 2002 FED App. 0207P (6th Cir. 2002)—7:22

U.S. v. Harris, 542 F.2d 1283 (7th Cir. 1976)—9:8, 11:16

U.S. v. Hartsfield, 976 F.2d 1349, 36 Fed. R. Evid. Serv. 1237 (10th Cir. 1992)—7:19

U.S. v. Hashimoto, 878 F.2d 1126, 89-2 U.S. Tax Cas. (CCH) ¶ 9432, 66 A.F.T.R.2d 90-5574 (9th Cir. 1989)—4:3A

U.S. v. Heater, 63 F.3d 311, 76 A.F.T.R.2d 95-5928, 130 A.L.R. Fed. 665 (4th Cir. 1995)—9:5

U.S. v. Helms, 897 F.2d 1293 (5th Cir. 1990)—7:50

U.S. v. Hemmingson, 157 F.3d 347 (5th Cir. 1998)—6:6

U.S. v. Hendrieth, 922 F.2d 748, 32 Fed. R. Evid. Serv. 210 (11th Cir. 1991)—8:7

U.S. v. Hernandez, 176 F.3d 719, 51 Fed. R. Evid. Serv. 1478 (3d Cir. 1999)—11:14

U.S. v. Hernandez, 84 F.3d 931, 44 Fed. R. Evid. Serv. 492 (7th Cir. 1996)—9:8

U.S. v. Hernandez-Herrera, 273 F.3d 1213 (9th Cir. 2001)—8:6

U.S. v. Herndon, 156 F.3d 629, 49 Fed. R. Evid. Serv. 1551, 1998 FED App. 0274P (6th Cir. 1998)—7:25

U.S. v. Hill, 146 F.3d 337 (6th Cir. 1998)—6:16, 7:18, 8:7

U.S. v. Hill, 197 F.3d 436 (10th Cir. 1999)—6:17

U.S. v. Hill, 249 F.3d 707, 56 Fed. R. Evid. Serv. 1 (8th Cir. 2001)—8:8

U.S. v. Hines, 943 F.2d 348 (4th Cir. 1991)—7:6

U.S. v. Hinojosa, 958 F.2d 624 (5th Cir. 1992)—6:13

U.S. v. Hinton, 94 F.3d 396 (7th Cir. 1996)—8:7

U.S. v. Hirschberg, 988 F.2d 1509, 38 Fed. R. Evid. Serv. 542 (7th Cir. 1993)—6:16

U.S. v. Hooshmand, 931 F.2d 725, 32 Fed. R. Evid. Serv. 1281 (11th Cir. 1991)—3:14

U.S. v. Horne, 4 F.3d 579 (8th Cir. 1993)—6:17

U.S. v. Howell, 231 F.3d 615, 55 Fed. R. Evid. Serv. 1314 (9th Cir. 2000)—7:5

U.S. v. Huey, 76 F.3d 638 (5th Cir. 1996)—8:6

U.S. v. Hughes, 970 F.2d 227, 36 Fed. R. Evid. Serv. 633 (7th Cir. 1992)—8:5

U.S. v. Huguenin, 950 F.2d 23, 91-2 U.S. Tax Cas. (CCH) ¶ 50571, 68 A.F.T.R.2d 91-5902 (1st Cir. 1991)—4:3A

U.S. v. Humphrey, 287 F.3d 422, 2002 FED App. 0131P (6th Cir. 2002)—8:6, 8:7

U.S. v. Humphrey, 34 F.3d 551 (7th Cir. 1994)—7:23

U.S. v. Huntress, 956 F.2d 1309 (5th Cir. 1992)—7:50

U.S. v. Hurlich, 293 F.3d 1223 (10th Cir. 2002)—1:13A, 1:21

U.S. v. Hursh, 217 F.3d 761, 54 Fed. R. Evid. Serv. 1412 (9th Cir. 2000)—2:17, 7:5

U.S. v. Hutchings, 751 F.2d 230, 17 Fed. R. Evid. Serv. 1274 (8th Cir. 1984)—8:2

U.S. v. Ireland, 62 F.3d 227 (8th Cir. 1995)—6:8

U.S. v. Iribe-Perez, 129 F.3d 1167 (10th Cir. 1997)—9:11

U.S. v. Irurita-Ramirez, 838 F. Supp. 1385 (C.D. Cal. 1993)—6:17

U.S. v. Isom, 88 F.3d 920 (11th Cir. 1996)—7:50

U.S. v. Jackman, 46 F.3d 1240 (2d Cir. 1995)—6:13, 6:18

U.S. v. Jackson, 983 F.2d 757 (7th Cir. 1993)—8:8

U.S. v. James, 113 F.3d 721 (7th Cir. 1997)—8:7

U.S. v. Jenkins, 52 F.3d 743 (8th Cir. 1995)—8:7

U.S. v. Jensen, 41 F.3d 946 (5th Cir. 1994)—7:5

U.S. v. Jiminez, 983 F.2d 1020 (11th Cir. 1993)—8:6, 8:7

U.S. v. Joe, 8 F.3d 1488, 39 Fed. R. Evid. Serv. 920 (10th Cir. 1993)—8:7

U.S. v. Joe, 928 F.2d 99 (4th Cir. 1991)—8:6, 8:7, 8:11

U.S. v. Johnson, 54 F.3d 1150, 41 Fed. R. Evid. Serv. 924 (4th Cir. 1995)—8:7

U.S. v. Johnson, 990 F.2d 1129 (9th Cir. 1993)—2:9, 7:11

U.S. v. Jones, 193 F.3d 948 (8th Cir. 1999)—7:46

U.S. v. Jones, 195 F.3d 379 (8th Cir. 1999)—8:7

U.S. v. Jones, 224 F.3d 621 (7th Cir. 2000)—8:7

U.S. v. Jones, 245 F.3d 990 (8th Cir. 2001)—8:7

U.S. v. Jordan, 223 F.3d 676 (7th Cir. 2000)—8:7

U.S. v. Joseph, 892 F.2d 118 (D.C. Cir. 1989)—7:9, 7:40

U.S. v. Joyner, 201 F.3d 61 (2d Cir. 2000)—6:18

U.S. v. Keller, 142 F.3d 718, 40 Fed. R. Serv. 3d 643, 28 Envtl. L. Rep. 21193, 164 A.L.R. Fed. 759 (4th Cir. 1998)—1:15, 1:17

U.S. v. Kelley, 140 F.3d 596 (5th Cir. 1998)—8:9

U.S. v. Khoury, 901 F.2d 948 (11th Cir. 1990)—9:8

U.S. v. Kim, 111 F.3d 1351, Unempl. Ins. Rep. (CCH) ¶ 15712B, 97-1 U.S. Tax Cas. (CCH) ¶ 50370, 46 Fed. R. Evid. Serv. 1476, 79 A.F.T.R.2d 97-2238 (7th Cir. 1997)—1:22

U.S. v. Knipp, 963 F.2d 839 (6th Cir. 1992)—9:8

U.S. v. Koon, 34 F.3d 1416, 40 Fed. R. Evid. Serv. 1 (9th Cir. 1994)—9:10

U.S. v. Kozel, 908 F.2d 205 (7th Cir. 1990)—1:8

U.S. v. Krout, 66 F.3d 1420, 43 Fed. R. Evid. Serv. 129 (5th Cir. 1995)—4:5, 9:14

U.S. v. Kunzman, 54 F.3d 1522, 42 Fed. R. Evid. Serv. 115 (10th Cir. 1995)—8:6, 8:7

U.S. v. Kyles, 40 F.3d 519 (2d Cir. 1994)—9:12

U.S. v. Lacey, 86 F.3d 956, 44 Fed. R. Evid. Serv. 1158 (10th Cir. 1996)—9:8

U.S. v. Lampkins, 47 F.3d 175 (7th Cir. 1995)—8:7

U.S. v. Lancaster, 96 F.3d 734 (4th Cir. 1996)—7:46

U.S. v. Langford, 990 F.2d 65, 38 Fed. R. Evid. Serv. 1141 (2d Cir. 1993)—9:10

U.S. v. Lanier, 33 F.3d 639, 41 Fed. R. Evid. Serv. 219, 1994 FED App. 0305P (6th Cir. 1994), reh'g—7:10

U.S. v. Lara, 181 F.3d 183, 51 Fed. R. Evid. Serv. 1302 (1st Cir. 1999)—6:8, 6:18, 8:7

U.S. v. LaRouche, 896 F.2d 815 (4th Cir. 1990)—7:52, 9:5

U.S. v. LaValley, 957 F.2d 1309 (6th Cir. 1992)—1:6

U.S. v. Lawes, 292 F.3d 123 (2d Cir. 2002)—7:46, 9:11

U.S. v. Leachman, 309 F.3d 377, 2002 FED App. 0353P (6th Cir. 2002)—1:13A, 1:21

U.S. v. Lehder-Rivas, 669 F. Supp. 1563 (M.D. Fla. 1987)—3:2

U.S. v. Lemmerer, 277 F.3d 579 (1st Cir. 2002)—7:5

U.S. v. Levenite, 277 F.3d 454 (4th Cir. 2002)—2:13, 7:5

U.S. v. Lewis, 40 F.3d 1325, 41 Fed. R. Evid. Serv. 661 (1st Cir. 1994)—8:6

U.S. v. Libretti, 38 F.3d 523 (10th Cir. 1994)—1:8, 1:21

U.S. v. Linney, 134 F.3d 274 (4th Cir. 1998)—1:8

U.S. v. Long, 301 F.3d 1095 (9th Cir. 2002)—7:22

U.S. v. Lopez, 147 F.3d 1 (1st Cir. 1998)—6:17

U.S. v. Lopez, 271 F.3d 472, 58 Fed. R. Evid. Serv. 460 (3d Cir. 2001)—7:5

U.S. v. Lorefice, 192 F.3d 647 (7th Cir. 1999)—9:11

U.S. v. Lowe, 145 F.3d 45, 49 Fed. R. Evid. Serv. 687 (1st Cir. 1998)—7:10, 7:12

U.S. v. Machado, 195 F.3d 454 (9th Cir. 1999)—8:2

U.S. v. Mack, 159 F.3d 208, 50 Fed. R. Evid. Serv. 281, 1998 FED App. 0311P (6th Cir. 1998)—7:50

U.S. v. Madrigal, 43 F.3d 1367 (10th Cir. 1994)—9:12

U.S. v. Magana, 118 F.3d 1173, 47 Fed. R. Evid. Serv. 626 (7th Cir. 1997)—7:9, 8:2

U.S. v. Mahan, 190 F.3d 416, 1999 FED App. 0315P (6th Cir. 1999)—8:7

U.S. v. Mahler, 141 F.3d 811 (8th Cir. 1998)—7:50

U.S. v. Malindez, 962 F.2d 332 (4th Cir. 1992)—8:6

U.S. v. Mansoori, 304 F.3d 635, 59 Fed. R. Evid. Serv. 1109 (7th Cir. 2002)—4:5, 9:14

U.S. v. Marcucci, 299 F.3d 1156 (9th Cir. 2002)—2:20

U.S. v. Marin, 7 F.3d 679, 39 Fed. R. Evid. Serv. 1014 (7th Cir. 1993)—8:7

U.S. v. Marino, 277 F.3d 11, 57 Fed. R. Evid. Serv. 1511 (1st Cir. 2002)—8:8

U.S. v. Marji, 158 F.3d 60, 49 Fed. R. Evid. Serv. 1522 (2d Cir. 1998)—7:12

U.S. v. Marrowbone, 211 F.3d 452, 54 Fed. R. Evid. Serv. 541 (8th Cir. 2000)—8:7

U.S. v. Martinez, 168 F.3d 1043 (8th Cir. 1999)—8:7

U.S. v. Martinez, 981 F.2d 867, 37 Fed. R. Evid. Serv. 748 (6th Cir. 1992)—7:46

U.S. v. Martinez-Salazar, 146 F.3d 653 (9th Cir. 1998)—7:5, 7:6, 8:11

U.S. v. Martinez-Salazar, 528 U.S. 304, 120 S. Ct. 774, 145 L. Ed. 2d 792 (2000)—7:5, 8:11

U.S. v. Maseratti, 1 F.3d 330 (5th Cir. 1993)—7:25, 8:6

U.S. v. Mathis, 96 F.3d 1577 (11th Cir. 1996)—8:7

U.S. v. Maxwell, 160 F.3d 1071,

1998 FED App. 0338P (6th Cir. 1998)—8:7, 8:8

U.S. v. McCarthy, 961 F.2d 972, 35 Fed. R. Evid. Serv. 478 (1st Cir. 1992)—7:28, 7:39

U.S. v. McCoy, 23 F.3d 216 (9th Cir. 1994)—8:7

U.S. v. McFerron, 163 F.3d 952, 1998 FED App. 0380P (6th Cir. 1998)—8:7

U.S. v. McIntyre, 997 F.2d 687, 38 Fed. R. Evid. Serv. 1440 (10th Cir. 1993)—7:52

U.S. v. McKinley, 995 F.2d 1020 (11th Cir. 1993)—6:7

U.S. v. McKinney, 53 F.3d 664 (5th Cir. 1995)—6:12, 6:17, 6:18

U.S. v. McKissick, 204 F.3d 1282 (10th Cir. 2000)—9:8

U.S. v. McLeod, 53 F.3d 322 (11th Cir. 1995)—7:22

U.S. v. McMasters, 90 F.3d 1394 (8th Cir. 1996)—7:50

U.S. v. McMillon, 14 F.3d 948, 38 Fed. R. Evid. Serv. 1334 (4th Cir. 1994)—8:7

U.S. v. McVeigh, 153 F.3d 1166, 50 Fed. R. Evid. Serv. 541 (10th Cir. 1998)—7:11, 7:53

U.S. v. Medina, 161 F.3d 867 (5th Cir. 1998)—7:23

U.S. v. Mendez, 102 F.3d 126 (5th Cir. 1996)—1:22

U.S. v. Mendoza, 157 F.3d 730 (9th Cir. 1998)—7:6

U.S. v. Mendoza-Burciaga, 981 F.2d 192 (5th Cir. 1992)—7:52

U.S. v. Middleton, 246 F.3d 825, 56 Fed. R. Evid. Serv. 1247, 87 A.F.T.R.2d 2001-1783, 2001 FED App. 0122P (6th Cir. 2001)—9:7

U.S. v. Miguel, 111 F.3d 666 (9th Cir. 1997)—7:12, 9:11

U.S. v. Milan, 304 F.3d 273 (3d Cir. 2002)—8:7

U.S. v. Millar, 79 F.3d 338 (2d Cir. 1996)—7:5, 7:40

U.S. v. Miller, 116 F.3d 641, 46 Fed. R. Evid. Serv. 1174 (2d Cir. 1997)—6:8

U.S. v. Miller, 939 F.2d 605 (8th Cir. 1991)—8:7

U.S. v. Miller, 946 F.2d 1344 (8th Cir. 1991)—8:3

U.S. v. Ming, 466 F.2d 1000, 72-1 U.S. Tax Cas. (CCH) ¶ 9449, 29 A.F.T.R.2d 72-1240 (7th Cir. 1972)—8:2

U.S. v. Minore, 292 F.3d 1109 (9th Cir. 2002)—1:13A, 1:21

U.S. v. Montgomery, 210 F.3d 446 (5th Cir. 2000)—8:7

U.S. v. Moore, 149 F.3d 773, 49 Fed. R. Evid. Serv. 995 (8th Cir. 1998)—7:5, 7:53

U.S. v. Moore, 895 F.2d 484 (8th Cir. 1990)—8:6

U.S. v. Moore, 936 F.2d 1508, 33 Fed. R. Evid. Serv. 1345 (7th Cir. 1991)—9:5

U.S. v. Morales, 108 F.3d 1213 (10th Cir. 1997)—6:17, 6:18

U.S. v. Morales, 185 F.3d 74 (2d Cir. 1999)—7:5, 7:46, 8:11

U.S. v. Moreno, 217 F.3d 592 (8th Cir. 2000)—8:6, 8:7

U.S. v. Moreno Morales, 815 F.2d 725, 22 Fed. R. Evid. Serv. 1063 (1st Cir. 1987)—2:5

U.S. v. Morrow, 177 F.3d 272 (5th Cir. 1999)—8:7

U.S. v. Moutry, 46 F.3d 598 (7th Cir. 1995)—7:5, 9:8

U.S. v. Mulder, 273 F.3d 91, 168 L.R.R.M. (BNA) 2681, 58 Fed. R. Evid. Serv. 742 (2d Cir. 2001)—7:5

U.S. v. Muldoon, 931 F.2d 282 (4th Cir. 1991)—7:46

U.S. v. Munoz, 15 F.3d 395 (5th Cir. 1994)—7:52, 8:7

U.S. v. Murillo, 288 F.3d 1126, 59 Fed. R. Evid. Serv. 23 (9th Cir. 2002)—8:7

U.S. v. Murray, 103 F.3d 310,

TABLE OF CASES

46 Fed. R. Evid. Serv. 223 (3d Cir. 1997)—7:10
U.S. v. Nachtigal, 37 F.3d 1421 (9th Cir. 1994)—1:7
U.S. v. Nash, 910 F.2d 749 (11th Cir. 1990)—7:46
U.S. v. Neeley, 189 F.3d 670, 53 Fed. R. Evid. Serv. 35 (7th Cir. 1999)—7:5
U.S. v. Nelson, 102 F.3d 1344 (4th Cir. 1996)—7:50
U.S. v. Nelson, 137 F.3d 1094, 48 Fed. R. Evid. Serv. 1184 (9th Cir. 1998)—6:17
U.S. v. Nelson, 277 F.3d 164 (2d Cir. 2002)—7:4, 7:9, 8:7
U.S. v. Nielsen, 1 F.3d 855, 93-2 U.S. Tax Cas. (CCH) ¶ 50445, 72 A.F.T.R.2d 93-5580 (9th Cir. 1993)—9:5
U.S. v. Norquay, 987 F.2d 475, 38 Fed. R. Evid. Serv. 162 (8th Cir. 1993)—8:3
U.S. v. North, 910 F.2d 843, 30 Fed. R. Evid. Serv. 961 (D.C. Cir. 1990)—9:10
U.S. v. Novaton, 271 F.3d 968, 57 Fed. R. Evid. Serv. 1470 (11th Cir. 2001)—8:6, 8:7
U.S. v. Nururdin, 794 F. Supp. 277 (N.D. Ill. 1992), aff'd, 8 F.3d 1187, 39 Fed. R. Evid. Serv. 1143 (7th Cir. 1993)—6:17
U.S. v. Nururdin, 8 F.3d 1187, 39 Fed. R. Evid. Serv. 1143 (7th Cir. 1993)—2:8, 6:13, 7:52
U.S. v. NYNEX Corp., 781 F. Supp. 19 (D.D.C. 1991)—1:7
U.S. v. Okoronkwo, 46 F.3d 426, 75 A.F.T.R.2d 95-1339 (5th Cir. 1995)—9:12
U.S. v. Olaniyi-Oke, 199 F.3d 767 (5th Cir. 1999)—6:18
U.S. v. Olano, 507 U.S. 725, 113 S. Ct. 1770, 123 L. Ed. 2d 508 (1993)—7:50
U.S. v. Omoruyi, 7 F.3d 880 (9th Cir. 1993)—8:6, 8:8

U.S. v. Orlando-Figueroa, 229 F.3d 33, 55 Fed. R. Evid. Serv. 1097 (1st Cir. 2000)—2:5, 4:5, 6:4, 7:10, 9:8
U.S. v. Ortiz, 315 F.3d 873, 59 Fed. R. Evid. Serv. 1063 (8th Cir. 2002)—7:53, 8:7, 9:11
U.S. v. Osigbade, 195 F.3d 900 (7th Cir. 1999)—7:5, 8:11
U.S. v. Osorio, 801 F. Supp. 966 (D. Conn. 1992)—6:18
U.S. v. Ovalle, 136 F.3d 1092, 1998 FED App. 0060P (6th Cir. 1998)—6:1, 6:7, 6:11, 6:15, 6:18, 8:7
U.S. v. Paccione, 949 F.2d 1183, 34 Fed. R. Evid. Serv. 621 (2d Cir. 1991)—4:5, 9:14
U.S. v. Paradies, 98 F.3d 1266, 46 Fed. R. Evid. Serv. 656 (11th Cir. 1996)—4:5, 6:11, 7:5
U.S. v. Parham, 16 F.3d 844 (8th Cir. 1994)—8:6
U.S. v. Parker, 133 F.3d 322, 48 Fed. R. Evid. Serv. 785 (5th Cir. 1998)—7:6
U.S. v. Parmley, 108 F.3d 922 (8th Cir. 1997)—7:18
U.S. v. Parra-Ibanez, 951 F.2d 21 (1st Cir. 1991)—8:7
U.S. v. Parsee, 178 F.3d 374, 52 Fed. R. Evid. Serv. 650 (5th Cir. 1999)—8:7, 8:8
U.S. v. Pasciuti, 803 F. Supp. 499 (D.N.H. 1992)—4:5, 9:14
U.S. v. Paternostro, 966 F.2d 907, 22 Envtl. L. Rep. 21021 (5th Cir. 1992)—1:6
U.S. v. Patrick, 965 F.2d 1390 (6th Cir. 1992)—9:10
U.S. v. Patterson, 215 F.3d 776 (7th Cir. 2000)—8:3
U.S. v. Patterson, 258 F.3d 788 (8th Cir. 2001)—8:7
U.S. v. Patterson, 26 F.3d 1127 (D.C. Cir. 1994)—7:50

U.S. v. Payne, 944 F.2d 1458, 33 Fed. R. Evid. Serv. 1316 (9th Cir. 1991)—7:11, 7:46, 9:11

U.S. v. Payne, 962 F.2d 1228, 35 Fed. R. Evid. Serv. 686 (6th Cir. 1992)—8:7

U.S. v. Pelensky, 129 F.3d 63 (2d Cir. 1997)—1:8

U.S. v. Pennington, 168 F.3d 1060 (8th Cir. 1999)—7:5

U.S. v. Peoples, 250 F.3d 630, 56 Fed. R. Evid. Serv. 331 (8th Cir. 2001)—4:5, 9:14

U.S. v. Perez, 35 F.3d 632 (1st Cir. 1994)—8:7

U.S. v. Perkins, 105 F.3d 976 (5th Cir. 1997)—8:7

U.S. v. Persico, 832 F.2d 705, 24 Fed. R. Evid. Serv. 137, 89 A.L.R. Fed. 857 (2d Cir. 1987)—4:5, 9:14

U.S. v. Petrie, 302 F.3d 1280, 59 Fed. R. Evid. Serv. 1563 (11th Cir. 2002)—6:6

U.S. v. Phibbs, 999 F.2d 1053, 38 Fed. R. Evid. Serv. 881 (6th Cir. 1993)—9:5

U.S. v. Phillips, 239 F.3d 829 (7th Cir. 2001)—6:18

U.S. v. Pion, 25 F.3d 18 (1st Cir. 1994)—6:17, 6:18

U.S. v. Polichemi, 201 F.3d 858 (7th Cir. 2000), on reh'g, 219 F.3d 698, 54 Fed. R. Evid. Serv. 1407 (7th Cir. 2000)—7:4, 7:5, 7:47, 8:11

U.S. v. Pospisil, 186 F.3d 1023 (8th Cir. 1999)—8:5, 8:7

U.S. v. Pottorf, 769 F. Supp. 1176 (D. Kan. 1991)—4:3A

U.S. v. Powell, 226 F.3d 1181, 55 Fed. R. Evid. Serv. 972 (10th Cir. 2000)—7:13

U.S. v. Powell, 932 F.2d 1337 (9th Cir. 1991)—9:5

U.S. v. Premises Known as RR No. 1 Box 224, Dalton, Scott Tp. and North Abington Tp., Lackawanna County, Pa., 14 F.3d 864 (3d Cir. 1994)—1:8, 1:14

U.S. v. Purdy, 144 F.3d 241 (2d Cir. 1998)—7:5

U.S. v. Quesada-Bonilla, 952 F.2d 597 (1st Cir. 1991)—7:19

U.S. v. Quintero-Barraza, 57 F.3d 836 (9th Cir. 1995)—7:9

U.S. v. Quiroz-Cortez, 960 F.2d 418 (5th Cir. 1992)—7:50

U.S. v. Rahman, 189 F.3d 88, 52 Fed. R. Evid. Serv. 425 (2d Cir. 1999)—9:5

U.S. v. Ramirez-Martinez, 273 F.3d 903 (9th Cir. 2001)—8:11

U.S. v. Ramos, 971 F. Supp. 186 (E.D. Pa. 1997), order aff'd, 151 F.3d 1027 (3d Cir. 1998)—7:10

U.S. v. Rapone, 131 F.3d 188, 72 Empl. Prac. Dec. (CCH) ¶ 45136 (D.C. Cir. 1997)—1:8, 1:17

U.S. v. Rasco, 123 F.3d 222 (5th Cir. 1997)—9:11

U.S. v. Raszkiewicz, 169 F.3d 459 (7th Cir. 1999)—6:3, 6:16

U.S. v. Ray, 238 F.3d 828 (7th Cir. 2001)—7:5

U.S. v. Real Property Known and Numbered as Rural Route 1, Box 137-B, Cutler, Ohio, 24 F.3d 845, 1994 FED App. 0166P (6th Cir. 1994)—7:19

U.S. v. ReBrook, 58 F.3d 961, Fed. Sec. L. Rep. (CCH) ¶ 98794 (4th Cir. 1995)—9:8

U.S. v. Reddix, 106 F.3d 236, 46 Fed. R. Evid. Serv. 508 (8th Cir. 1997)—7:42

U.S. v. Register, 182 F.3d 820 (11th Cir. 1999)—7:5

U.S. v. Reynolds, 189 F.3d 521 (7th Cir. 1999)—9:11

U.S. v. Reynolds, 397 U.S. 14, 90 S. Ct. 803, 25 L. Ed. 2d 12 (1970)—1:15

U.S. v. Rhodes, 177 F.3d 963 (11th Cir. 1999)—7:23

U.S. v. Ricketts, 146 F.3d 492, 49 Fed. R. Evid. Serv. 931 (7th Cir. 1998)—7:46

U.S. v. Riggio, 70 F.3d 336, 43 Fed. R. Evid. Serv. 856 (5th Cir. 1995)—4:5, 9:14

U.S. v. Rigsby, 45 F.3d 120, 41 Fed. R. Evid. Serv. 372, 1995 FED App. 0027P (6th Cir. 1995)—9:5

U.S. v. Rioux, 97 F.3d 648, 45 Fed. R. Evid. Serv. 998 (2d Cir. 1996)—6:4, 6:7, 6:8, 6:17

U.S. v. Roach, 108 F.3d 1477 (D.C. Cir. 1997)—1:8

U.S. v. Roberts, 163 F.3d 998 (7th Cir. 1998)—8:7

U.S. v. Robertson, 45 F.3d 1423 (10th Cir. 1995)—1:22

U.S. v. Robinson, 8 F.3d 418 (7th Cir. 1993)—1:8

U.S. v. Rodriguez, 162 F.3d 135, 50 Fed. R. Evid. Serv. 1030 (1st Cir. 1998)—6:17, 6:18

U.S. v. Rodriguez, 993 F.2d 1170 (5th Cir. 1993)—11:15

U.S. v. Rodriguez-Aguirre, 108 F.3d 1228, 46 Fed. R. Evid. Serv. 813 (10th Cir. 1997)—6:17, 6:18

U.S. v. Rogers, 73 F.3d 774 (8th Cir. 1996)—6:17

U.S. v. Rojo-Alvarez, 944 F.2d 959 (1st Cir. 1991)—9:8

U.S. v. Romero-Reyna, 867 F.2d 834 (5th Cir. 1989)—8:6

U.S. v. Rosa, 946 F.2d 505 (7th Cir. 1991)—1:22

U.S. v. Ross, 33 F.3d 1507, 41 Fed. R. Evid. Serv. 303 (11th Cir. 1994)—4:5, 9:14

U.S. v. Rostoff, 164 F.3d 63 (1st Cir. 1999)—1:14

U.S. v. Rowe, 106 F.3d 1226 (5th Cir. 1997)—5:4, 9:2

U.S. v. Rowe, 144 F.3d 15 (1st Cir. 1998)—7:5

U.S. v. Royal, 100 F.3d 1019 (1st Cir. 1996)—4:5

U.S. v. Royal, 174 F.3d 1 (1st Cir. 1999)—6:11, 6:17

U.S. v. Rudas, 905 F.2d 38 (2d Cir. 1990)—8:7

U.S. v. Ruelas-Arreguin, 219 F.3d 1056 (9th Cir. 2000)—2:3

U.S. v. Russell, 134 F.3d 171 (3d Cir. 1998)—2:17

U.S. v. Rutgard, 108 F.3d 1041 (9th Cir. 1997)—7:10

U.S. v. Rutgard, 116 F.3d 1270 (9th Cir. 1997)—7:10

U.S. v. Saadya, 750 F.2d 1419 (9th Cir. 1985)—1:22

U.S. v. Salameh, 152 F.3d 88, 50 Fed. R. Evid. Serv. 602 (2d Cir. 1998)—7:40

U.S. v. Salvatore, 110 F.3d 1131, 46 Fed. R. Evid. Serv. 1407 (5th Cir. 1997)—9:14

U.S. v. Sanchez, 74 F.3d 562, 43 Fed. R. Evid. Serv. 1069 (5th Cir. 1996)—4:5, 9:14

U.S. v. Sanchez-Lopez, 879 F.2d 541 (9th Cir. 1989)—6:17

U.S. v. Santiago-Martinez, 58 F.3d 422 (9th Cir. 1995)—8:8

U.S. v. Sarkisian, 197 F.3d 966 (9th Cir. 1999)—9:5

U.S. v. Saya, 247 F.3d 929 (9th Cir. 2001)—9:10

U.S. v. Schlei, 122 F.3d 944, 48 Fed. R. Evid. Serv. 143 (11th Cir. 1997)—8:2, 9:1, 9:8

U.S. v. Schneider, 111 F.3d 197, 46 Fed. R. Evid. Serv. 1426 (1st Cir. 1997)—4:5

U.S. v. Scott, 159 F.3d 916 (5th Cir. 1998)—7:9

U.S. v. Scott, 26 F.3d 1458 (8th Cir. 1994)—8:7

U.S. v. Seals, 987 F.2d 1102 (5th Cir. 1993)—8:6

U.S. v. Serino, 163 F.3d 91 (1st Cir. 1998)—8:7

U.S. v. Shannon, 21 F.3d 77 (5th Cir. 1994)—7:5, 9:2

U.S. v. Shaoul, 41 F.3d 811 (2d Cir. 1994)—9:10

U.S. v. Shea, 211 F.3d 658, 53 Fed. R. Evid. Serv. 1353 (1st Cir. 2000)—6:7, 6:16, 7:22

U.S. v. Shenberg, 89 F.3d 1461, 45 Fed. R. Evid. Serv. 58 (11th Cir. 1996)—7:50

U.S. v. Sherwood, 98 F.3d 402 (9th Cir. 1996)—7:10, 8:3

U.S. v. Shinault, 147 F.3d 1266 (10th Cir. 1998)—6:17

U.S. v. Simmons, 961 F.2d 183 (11th Cir. 1992)—7:5

U.S. v. Sinigaglio, 925 F.2d 339, 91-1 U.S. Tax Cas. (CCH) ¶ 50082, 68 A.F.T.R.2d 91-5189 (9th Cir. 1991)—4:3A

U.S. v. Sithithongtham, 192 F.3d 1119 (8th Cir. 1999)—7:5, 8:11

U.S. v. Smallwood, 188 F.3d 905 (7th Cir. 1999)—6:18, 8:7, 9:11

U.S. v. Smith, 223 F.3d 554, 54 Fed. R. Evid. Serv. 970 (7th Cir. 2000)—6:8

U.S. v. Smith, 324 F.3d 922 (7th Cir. 2003)—8:6, 8:7

U.S. v. Sneed, 34 F.3d 1570 (10th Cir. 1994)—8:7

U.S. v. Soderna, 82 F.3d 1370 (7th Cir. 1996)—1:6

U.S. v. Sogomonian, 247 F.3d 348 (2d Cir. 2001)—6:7

U.S. v. Somerstein, 959 F. Supp. 592 (E.D. N.Y. 1997)—8:8

U.S. v. Sotelo, 97 F.3d 782, 45 Fed. R. Evid. Serv. 1054 (5th Cir. 1996)—6:18

U.S. v. Speer, 30 F.3d 605 (5th Cir. 1994)—6:4

U.S. v. Spine, 945 F.2d 143, 91-2 U.S. Tax Cas. (CCH) ¶ 50464, 34 Fed. R. Evid. Serv. 351, 68 A.F.T.R.2d 91-5636 (6th Cir. 1991)—4:3A

U.S. v. Spriggs, 102 F.3d 1245, 46 Fed. R. Evid. Serv. 181 (D.C. Cir. 1996)—6:11, 6:16, 8:7, 8:8

U.S. v. Springfield, 829 F.2d 860 (9th Cir. 1987)—8:2

U.S. v. Stafford, 136 F.3d 1109 (7th Cir. 1998)—8:8

U.S. v. Stedman, 69 F.3d 737 (5th Cir. 1995)—8:8

U.S. v. Steele, 178 F.3d 1230 (11th Cir. 1999)—8:6, 8:7

U.S. v. Steele, 298 F.3d 906 (9th Cir. 2002)—6:5, 7:5, 8:7, 9:11

U.S. v. Steen, 55 F.3d 1022 (5th Cir. 1995)—6:17

U.S. v. Stevenson, 6 F.3d 1262, 39 Fed. R. Evid. Serv. 832 (7th Cir. 1993)—9:5

U.S. v. Stewart, 65 F.3d 918 (11th Cir. 1995)—8:6, 8:7, 8:9

U.S. v. Strissel, 920 F.2d 1162, 30 Fed. R. Evid. Serv. 1079 (4th Cir. 1990)—2:4, 7:11

U.S. v. Swinney, 970 F.2d 494 (8th Cir. 1992)—12:9

U.S. v. Sykes, 292 F.3d 495, 2002 FED App. 0199P (6th Cir. 2002)—1:13A

U.S. v. Symington, 195 F.3d 1080 (9th Cir. 1999)—7:5

U.S. v. Talley, 164 F.3d 989, 51 Fed. R. Evid. Serv. 181, 1999 FED App. 0013P (6th Cir. 1999)—4:5, 9:14

U.S. v. Tapia, 59 F.3d 1137 (11th Cir. 1995)—6:18

U.S. v. Taylor, 92 F.3d 1313, 45 Fed. R. Evid. Serv. 442 (2d Cir. 1996)—8:7, 9:14

Table of Cases

U.S. v. Terry, 60 F.3d 1541 (11th Cir. 1995)—6:5
U.S. v. Thai, 29 F.3d 785, 40 Fed. R. Evid. Serv. 1387 (2d Cir. 1994)—4:5, 9:14
U.S. v. Thomas, 116 F.3d 606 (2d Cir. 1997)—7:5, 7:54
U.S. v. Thomas, 303 F.3d 138 (2d Cir. 2002)—8:6, 8:7, 8:11
U.S. v. Thomas, 320 F.3d 315 (2d Cir. 2003)—8:7
U.S. v. Thomas, 757 F.2d 1359 (2d Cir. 1985)—4:5, 9:14
U.S. v. Thompson, 76 F.3d 442 (2d Cir. 1996)—8:3
U.S. v. Thompson, 827 F.2d 1254 (9th Cir. 1987)—8:7
U.S. v. Thornton, 1 F.3d 149 (3d Cir. 1993)—4:5, 7:5, 9:14
U.S. v. Tibesar, 894 F.2d 317 (8th Cir. 1990)—7:25
U.S. v. Time, 21 F.3d 635, 40 Fed. R. Evid. Serv. 1116 (5th Cir. 1994)—1:8
U.S. v. Tipton, 90 F.3d 861 (4th Cir. 1996)—7:53, 8:6
U.S. v. Tocco, 200 F.3d 401, 53 Fed. R. Evid. Serv. 1116, 2000 FED App. 0002P (6th Cir. 2000)—9:5
U.S. v. Todd, 963 F.2d 207 (8th Cir. 1992)—8:7, 12:9
U.S. v. Tokars, 95 F.3d 1520, 45 Fed. R. Evid. Serv. 967 (11th Cir. 1996)—8:7
U.S. v. Tolliver, 61 F.3d 1189 (5th Cir. 1995)—8:7
U.S. v. Torres, 128 F.3d 38 (2d Cir. 1997)—7:4
U.S. v. Torres, 191 F.3d 799 (7th Cir. 1999)—9:5
U.S. v. Tranakos, 690 F. Supp. 971 (D. Wyo. 1988)—6:8, 6:16
U.S. v. Trujillo, 146 F.3d 838, 49 Fed. R. Evid. Serv. 1066 (11th Cir. 1998)—9:8
U.S. v. Tucker, 137 F.3d 1016, 48 Fed. R. Evid. Serv. 1145 (8th Cir. 1998)—9:10
U.S. v. Tucker, 243 F.3d 499 (8th Cir. 2001)—9:10
U.S. v. Tucker, 836 F.2d 334 (7th Cir. 1988)—8:7
U.S. v. Tutino, 883 F.2d 1125, 28 Fed. R. Evid. Serv. 466 (2d Cir. 1989)—4:5, 9:14
U.S. v. Underwood, 122 F.3d 389 (7th Cir. 1997)—8:7, 12:1
U.S. v. Unterburger, 97 F.3d 1413 (11th Cir. 1996)—1:6
U.S. v. Uwaezhoke, 995 F.2d 388 (3d Cir. 1993)—8:6
U.S. v. Vaccaro, 816 F.2d 443, 22 Fed. R. Evid. Serv. 1570 (9th Cir. 1987)—8:2
U.S. v. Valley, 928 F.2d 130 (5th Cir. 1991)—8:7
U.S. v. Van Chase, 137 F.3d 579, 48 Fed. R. Evid. Serv. 1180 (8th Cir. 1998)—7:41, 9:2
U.S. v. Vario, 943 F.2d 236, 119 Lab. Cas. (CCH) ¶ 10907 (2d Cir. 1991)—4:5, 9:14
U.S. v. Vasquez-Lopez, 22 F.3d 900 (9th Cir. 1994)—8:7
U.S. v. Vega, 221 F.3d 789, 54 Fed. R. Evid. Serv. 1502 (5th Cir. 2000)—5:4, 9:2
U.S. v. Vega, 285 F.3d 256, 58 Fed. R. Evid. Serv. 431 (3d Cir. 2002)—7:5
U.S. v. Vega, 72 F.3d 507 (7th Cir. 1995)—7:5
U.S. v. Victoria-Peguero, 920 F.2d 77, 1993 A.M.C. 1520 (1st Cir. 1990)—7:46
U.S. v. Villarreal, 963 F.2d 725 (5th Cir. 1992)—8:8
U.S. v. Virgen-Moreno, 265 F.3d 276 (5th Cir. 2001)—7:51
U.S. v. Walker, 99 F.3d 439 (D.C. Cir. 1996)—7:12, 9:10
U.S. v. Wallace, 32 F.3d 921 (5th Cir. 1994)—8:7

U.S. v. Walling, 974 F.2d 140 (10th Cir. 1992)—7:19

U.S. v. Walton, 217 F.3d 443, 55 Fed. R. Evid. Serv. 192 (7th Cir. 2000)—8:7

U.S. v. Warren, 16 F.3d 247 (8th Cir. 1994)—6:18

U.S. v. Warren, 25 F.3d 890 (9th Cir. 1994)—8:3

U.S. v. Washington, 48 F.3d 73 (2d Cir. 1995)—9:12

U.S. v. Washington, 819 F.2d 221 (9th Cir. 1987)—9:5

U.S. v. Washington, 836 F. Supp. 192 (D. Vt. 1993), aff'd, 48 F.3d 73 (2d Cir. 1995)—2:4, 7:10, 7:16

U.S. v. Weaver, 267 F.3d 231 (3d Cir. 2001)—6:8, 6:17, 6:18

U.S. v. Webster, 162 F.3d 308 (5th Cir. 1998)—7:5, 8:7

U.S. v. Wells, 63 F.3d 745 (8th Cir. 1995)—1:5

U.S. v. Whitehead, 238 F.3d 949 (8th Cir. 2001)—8:2

U.S. v. Wiggins, 104 F.3d 174 (8th Cir. 1997)—8:7

U.S. v. Williams, 195 F.3d 823, 49 Env't. Rep. Cas. (BNA) 1605 (6th Cir. 1999)—9:10

U.S. v. Williams, 264 F.3d 561, 57 Fed. R. Evid. Serv. 1124 (5th Cir. 2001)—6:18, 8:7

U.S. v. Williams, 272 F.3d 845, 58 Fed. R. Evid. Serv. 822 (7th Cir. 2001)—8:7

U.S. v. Williams, 77 F.3d 1098 (8th Cir. 1996)—9:10

U.S. v. Willie, 941 F.2d 1384, 91-2 U.S. Tax Cas. (CCH) ¶ 50409, 33 Fed. R. Evid. Serv. 1113, 68 A.F.T.R.2d 91-5371 (10th Cir. 1991)—8:6

U.S. v. Wills, 88 F.3d 704, 44 Fed. R. Evid. Serv. 1357 (9th Cir. 1996)—8:7

U.S. v. Wilson, 894 F.2d 1245 (11th Cir. 1990)—7:50

U.S. v. Wittgenstein, 163 F.3d 1164 (10th Cir. 1998)—1:21

U.S. v. Wong, 40 F.3d 1347 (2d Cir. 1994)—4:5, 9:14

U.S. v. Wright, 119 F.3d 630, 47 Fed. R. Evid. Serv. 554 (8th Cir. 1997)—7:52, 9:10

U.S. v. Yang, 281 F.3d 534, 61 U.S.P.Q.2d (BNA) 1789, 2002 FED App. 0062P (6th Cir. 2002)—8:7

U.S. v. York, 933 F.2d 1343, 33 Fed. R. Evid. Serv. 426 (7th Cir. 1991)—9:8

U.S. v. Young, 38 F.3d 338 (7th Cir. 1994)—6:11

U.S. v. Young-Bey, 893 F.2d 178 (8th Cir. 1990)—8:6

U.S. v. Zarnes, 33 F.3d 1454 (7th Cir. 1994)—7:19

U.S. v. Zichettello, 208 F.3d 72 (2d Cir. 2000)—7:25, 9:11

U.S. ex rel. Schumer v. Hughes Aircraft Co., 63 F.3d 1512, 12 I.E.R. Cas. (BNA) 1040, 40 Cont. Cas. Fed. (CCH) ¶ 76828, 136 Lab. Cas. (CCH) ¶ 10308, 33 Fed. R. Serv. 3d 543 (9th Cir. 1995)—1:22

U.S. S.E.C. v. Infinity Group Co., 212 F.3d 180, Fed. Sec. L. Rep. (CCH) ¶ 90966, 55 Fed. R. Evid. Serv. 185, 46 Fed. R. Serv. 3d 625 (3d Cir. 2000)—1:17, 1:22

U.S. Xpress Enterprises, Inc. v. J.B. Hunt Transport, Inc., 320 F.3d 809, 60 Fed. R. Evid. Serv. 772, 55 Fed. R. Serv. 3d 280 (8th Cir. 2003)—8:7

V

Van Meter v. Barr, 778 F. Supp. 83, 57 Fair Empl. Prac. Cas. (BNA) 769, 57 Empl. Prac. Dec. (CCH) ¶ 41209 (D.D.C. 1991)—1:15

TABLE OF CASES

Vansickel v. White, 166 F.3d 953 (9th Cir. 1999)—8:2

Vasey v. Martin Marietta Corp., 29 F.3d 1460, 65 Fair Empl. Prac. Cas. (BNA) 663, 65 Empl. Prac. Dec. (CCH) ¶ 43283, 128 Lab. Cas. (CCH) ¶ 57709, 40 Fed. R. Evid. Serv. 1333 (10th Cir. 1994)—7:32

Vigil v. Zavaras, 298 F.3d 935 (10th Cir. 2002)—3:12

Virgin Islands, Government of v. Forte, 806 F.2d 73 (3d Cir. 1986)—8:6

Virgin Islands, Government of v. Forte, 865 F.2d 59 (3d Cir. 1989)—8:8

Virgin Islands, Government of v. Weatherwax, 77 F.3d 1425 (3d Cir. 1996)—7:10

Von Kahl v. U.S., 242 F.3d 783 (8th Cir. 2001)—9:10

W

Wade v. Oglesby, 74 Ohio App. 3d 560, 599 N.E.2d 748 (6th Dist. Huron County 1991)—1:18

Wade v. Terhune, 202 F.3d 1190 (9th Cir. 2000)—8:6

Wainwright v. Witt, 469 U.S. 412, 105 S. Ct. 844, 83 L. Ed. 2d 841 (1985)—7:53

Waldermeyer v. ITT Consumer Financial Corp., 767 F. Supp. 989, 55 Fair Empl. Prac. Cas. (BNA) 1598, 6 I.E.R. Cas. (BNA) 1241, 57 Empl. Prac. Dec. (CCH) ¶ 40974, 118 Lab. Cas. (CCH) ¶ 35490 (E.D. Mo. 1991)—1:17, 1:22

Waldorf v. Shuta, 3 F.3d 705 (3d Cir. 1993)—7:10

Waldrop v. Southern Co. Services, Inc., 24 F.3d 152, 5 A.D.D. 910, 3 A.D. Cas. (BNA) 595 (11th Cir. 1994)—1:14

Walker v. Goldsmith, 902 F.2d 16 (9th Cir. 1990)—6:7

Wallace v. Morrison, 87 F.3d 1271 (11th Cir. 1996)—8:7

Walls v. Kim, 250 Ga. App. 259, 549 S.E.2d 797 (2001)—7:5, 7:22

Walton v. Arizona, 497 U.S. 639, 110 S. Ct. 3047, 111 L. Ed. 2d 511 (1990)—1:13A

Walzer v. St. Joseph State Hosp., 231 F.3d 1108, 84 Fair Empl. Prac. Cas. (BNA) 527, 80 Empl. Prac. Dec. (CCH) ¶ 40669 (8th Cir. 2000)—7:5

Ward v. Whitley, 21 F.3d 1355 (5th Cir. 1994)—6:18

Washington v. Johnson, 90 F.3d 945 (5th Cir. 1996)—8:7

Watkins v. Kassulke, 90 F.3d 138, 1996 FED App. 0218P (6th Cir. 1996)—7:50

Weaver v. Bowersox, 241 F.3d 1024 (8th Cir. 2001)—8:7

Weber v. Strippit, Inc., 186 F.3d 907, 9 A.D. Cas. (BNA) 961 (8th Cir. 1999)—8:8

Webster v. U.S., 528 U.S. 829, 120 S. Ct. 83, 145 L. Ed. 2d 70 (1999)—7:53, 8:7, 9:1

Weeks v. New York State (Div. of Parole), 273 F.3d 76, 87 Fair Empl. Prac. Cas. (BNA) 161, 81 Empl. Prac. Dec. (CCH) ¶ 40822 (2d Cir. 2001)—8:6

Weems v. State, 262 Ga. 101, 416 S.E.2d 84 (1992)—8:6

Wharton-El v. Nix, 38 F.3d 372 (8th Cir. 1994)—6:18

Wheat v. Johnson, 238 F.3d 357 (5th Cir. 2001)—7:53

White v. McGinnis, 903 F.2d 699, 16 Fed. R. Serv. 3d 369 (9th Cir. 1990)—1:22

Whitehead v. Cowan, 263 F.3d 708 (7th Cir. 2001)—1:22, 2:11, 4:5, 7:10, 9:8

Wilcher v. City of Wilmington, 139 F.3d 366, 13 I.E.R. Cas. (BNA) 1345, 40 Fed. R. Serv. 3d 934 (3d Cir. 1998)—1:21

Wilkins v. Baptist Healthcare System, Inc., 150 F.3d 609, 28 Employee Benefits Cas. (BNA) 1218, 1998 FED App. 0236P (6th Cir. 1998)—1:14

Wilkins v. State, 607 So. 2d 500 (Fla. Dist. Ct. App. 3d Dist. 1992)—7:13

Williams v. Chrans, 945 F.2d 926 (7th Cir. 1991)—8:5

Williams v. Chrans, 957 F.2d 487 (7th Cir. 1992)—2:2, 8:7

Williams v. Collins, 16 F.3d 626 (5th Cir. 1994)—9:5

Williams v. Com., 14 Va. App. 208, 415 S.E.2d 856 (1992)—7:22

Williams v. State, 638 So. 2d 935 (Fla. 1994)—8:7

Williams v. Woodford, 306 F.3d 665 (9th Cir. 2002)—8:6

Willis v. Kemp, 838 F.2d 1510 (11th Cir. 1988)—6:16

Willis v. Zant, 720 F.2d 1212 (11th Cir. 1983)—6:16

Windham v. Merkle, 163 F.3d 1092 (9th Cir. 1998)—8:8

Winter v. Minnesota Mut. Life Ins. Co., 199 F.3d 399 (7th Cir. 1999)—1:17, 1:20

Wolfe v. Brigano, 232 F.3d 499, 2000 FED App. 0394P (6th Cir. 2000)—7:5, 7:9, 7:22, 7:25

Wooddell v. International Broth. of Elec. Workers, Local 71, 502 U.S. 93, 112 S. Ct. 494, 116 L. Ed. 2d 419, 138 L.R.R.M. (BNA) 2881, 120 Lab. Cas. (CCH) ¶ 11010 (1991)—1:14

Woolridge v. State, 827 S.W.2d 900 (Tex. Crim. App. 1992)—9:11, 9:13

Y

Yancey v. State, 813 So. 2d 1 (Ala. Crim. App. 2001)—7:53, 8:6, 8:7

Yeatts v. Angelone, 166 F.3d 255 (4th Cir. 1999)—7:9, 7:53

Young, In re, 869 F.2d 158, 130 L.R.R.M. (BNA) 2908 (2d Cir. 1989)—1:14

Z

Zivkovic v. Southern California Edison Co., 302 F.3d 1080, 13 A.D. Cas. (BNA) 882, 53 Fed. R. Serv. 3d 1179 (9th Cir. 2002)—1:17

Supplement Index

ADMINISTRATIVE LAW
Jury reform, costs to state, § 2:01

ADMIRALTY
Jury trial right, § 1:14

AFFIRMATIVE JURY SELECTION
Generally, § 12:01

ANONYMOUS JURY
Occupations and other pertinent information revealed, semi-anonymous jury, § 4:05, 9:14

ARBITRATION
Jury trial right despite arbitration agreement, § 1:21

AUDITS
Tax cases, inquiry to IRS regarding prospective jurors for, § 4:03A

BENCH TRIAL
Waiver of jury trial by, § 1:21

BURDEN OF PROOF
Jury nullifiers, challenge for cause, § 7:54

BUSINESS DEALINGS OR RELATIONSHIP
Bias or prejudice, juror revealing prior business dealings with party, § 7:25

CHALLENGES FOR CAUSE
Death penalty, § 7:09
Jury nullification, § 7:54
Racially biased organizations, membership in, § 7:44
Smokers, § 7:12

CHANGE OF VENUE
Discriminatory jury pool chosen from completely different racial district, § 2:02, 2:05

CIGARETTES
Smokers, challenges for cause in lung cancer suit, § 7:12

CIVIL CASES
Jury nullification, § 2:18

COSTS
Jury reform, costs to state, § 2:01

DAMAGES
Civil cases, statutory limits, § 2:18

DEATH PENALTY
Challenges for cause, § 7:09

DELIBERATIONS OF JURY
Bias or prejudice where juror reveals prior business dealings with defendant during, § 7:25
Jury nullifiers, challenge for cause, § 7:54

DISABLED PERSONS
Peremptory challenges, disabled persons or persons associated with, § 8:08

DISMISSAL
Jury nullifiers, § 7:54

EMPLOYMENT
Jury Systems Improvement Act, retaliation on return to job after service on jury, § 6:01
Partially anonymous jury, revealing of employment information, § 4:05

FOREIGN SOVEREIGN IMMUNITIES ACT
Jury trial right, § 1:14

GENDER
Peremptory challenges based on, § 8:08

© West, a Thomson business, 11/2003

HUSBAND AND WIFE
Southern bias against interracial couple involved in money laundering scheme, § 9:12

INSANITY DEFENSE
Questions to prospective jurors, § 11:18

INTERNAL REVENUE SERVICE
Availability of IRS information on prospective jurors for tax cases, § 4:03A

INTERRACIAL MARRIAGE
Southern bias against interracial couple involved in money laundering scheme, § 9:12

INTIMIDATION
Judge's intimidation of prospective jurors on voir dire, § 5:04

INVESTIGATION OF VENIRE
IRS information on prospective jurors for tax cases, § 4:03A

JONES ACT
Jury trial right, § 1:14

JUDGES
Intimidation of prospective jurors on voir dire, § 5:04

JURY NULLIFICATION
Challenges for cause, § 7:54
Civil cases, § 2:18
Necessity defense versus, § 2:20

JURY POOL DISCRIMINATION
Unfair advantage acquired where jury pool chosen from completely different racial district, § 2:02, 2:05

JURY PROFILE
Voir dire preparation, § 3:02

JURY REFORM
Ancillary and unintended effects, § 2:01

LIMITATIONS AND RESTRICTIONS
Damages in civil cases, statutory limits on, § 2:18

LUNG CANCER
Smokers, challenges for cause in lung cancer suit, § 7:12

MEMBERSHIP
Racially biased organizations, membership in, § 7:44

NGRI VERDICT
Questions to prospective jurors on voir dire, § 11:18

NOT GUILTY BY REASON OF INSANITY
Questions to prospective jurors on voir dire, § 11:18

OCCUPATIONS
Partially anonymous jury, revealing of employment information, § 4:05, 9:14

PEREMPTORY CHALLENGES
Disabled persons, associations with, § 8:08
Gender based challenges, § 8:08

PROFESSIONAL RELATIONSHIP
Bias or prejudice of juror revealing prior business dealings with party, § 7:25

RACE
Jury nullification on basis of race, § 2:20
Membership in racially biased organizations, § 7:44
Money laundering scheme, Southern bias against interracial couple involved in, § 9:12

RACIAL DISCRIMINATION
Change of venue so jury pool chosen from completely different racial district, § 2:02, 2:05

Index

RACKETEER INFLUENCED AND CORRUPT ORGANIZATIONS ACT
Anonymous jury for violation, § 4:05

RECORDS
Tax cases, inquiry to IRS regarding prospective jurors for, § 4:03A

RELIGIOUS BELIEFS
Capital punishment, challenges for cause, § 7:09

REPRESENTATIVE JURY
Jury reform as affecting representativeness of the jury, § 2:01

RETALIATION
Jury Systems Improvement Act, retaliation on return to job after service on jury, § 6:01

SENTENCE ENHANCEMENT
Right to jury trial, § 1:13A

STATUTORY LIMITS
Damages in civil cases, § 2:18

TAFT-HARTLEY ACT
Anonymous jury for violation, § 4:05

TAXATION
IRS information on prospective jurors for tax cases, § 4:03A

TOBACCO COMPANY
Smokers, challenges for cause in lung cancer suit, § 7:12

VOIR DIRE
Commitments from jurors, § 10:02
Insanity defense, questions as to, § 11:18
Judge's intimidation of prospective jurors, § 5:04
Jury profile, preparation, § 3:02